¡DIME!

UNO

FABIÁN A. SAMANIEGO

University of California, Davis

M. CAROL BROWN

California State University, Sacramento

PATRICIA HAMILTON CARLIN

University of California, Davis

SIDNEY E. GORMAN

Fremont Unified School District
Fremont, California

CAROL L. SPARKS

Mt. Diablo Unified School District
Concord, California

HEATH

D.C. Heath and Company
Lexington, Massachusetts
Toronto, Ontario

Director, Modern Languages
Roger D. Coulombe

Managing Editor
Marilyn Lindgren

Design Manager, Modern Languages
Victor Curran

Teacher's Edition Editor
Kathleen Ossip

Project Editors
Senior Editor: Lawrence Lipson
Susan Cosentino
Meg LeSchack

National Modern Language Coordinator
Teresa Carrera-Hanley

D.C. Heath Consultant
Karen Ralston

Production Coordinator
Patrick Connolly

Teacher's Edition Design
Richard Curran, Sue Gerould,
Marshall Henrichs, David Reiffel

Linguistic Consultant
William H. Klemme

Author Team Manager
J. Thomas Wetterstrom

EXTENDED TEACHER'S EDITION

Introducing ¡DIME!

PURPOSE AND PHILOSOPHY

¡DIME! is designed to develop listening, speaking, reading, and writing competency in Spanish by taking into consideration current second-language acquisition research and the Proficiency Guidelines developed by the American Council on the Teaching of Foreign Languages and the Educational Testing Service.

To develop competency in a foreign language, students must learn to perform a variety of language functions: to list, to ask questions, to describe, to give and follow directions, to narrate, to express opinions and to defend them, to hypothesize, and so forth. Students must learn to perform these functions in a multiplicity of contexts, for example: at home, in school, at work, when traveling, while shopping, while playing. Finally, students must be able to perform these tasks with an appropriate level of accuracy.

If students are to develop competency, they must be provided with ample opportunities to interact in Spanish among themselves and with their teachers. The primary purpose of **¡DIME!** is to provide students with these opportunities. To accomplish this, the principal focus of **¡DIME!** is on the message being communicated rather than on the manipulation of grammatical structures. Thus students will be encouraged and motivated to develop fluency in the language from the beginning, as well as to develop accuracy along a competency continuum that begins with a nongrammatical word phase and leads gradually to a strong sentence phase and, ultimately, to a grammatically correct paragraph phase.

Essential to teaching for communication is the constant use of real-life language in the classroom. This means consciously avoiding teacher talk (i.e., using only "active" vocabulary and structures of Units 1 and 2 and the first lesson of Unit 3, because that is where the class happens to be). Only foreign language teachers speak like that. If students are to learn to communicate in the real world, then they must be exposed to real-world language from the very beginning. In **¡DIME!** great care has been taken to avoid teacher talk and textbook language and to expose students to Spanish as it is spoken by native speakers throughout the Spanish-speaking world. The **_Para empezar_** and **_¿Qué decimos . . . ?_** dialogues/narratives are not limited to the structures and vocabulary previously taught. Rather students are trained from the very beginning to focus on what they understand and to learn to guess at the meaning of unfamiliar words. In the following sections, we offer specific suggestions for making natural language (be it oral or written) comprehensible.

THE EXTENDED TEACHER'S EDITION

This **Extended Teacher's Edition** is designed with margins that wrap around each two-page spread of the Student Text. They include the following information:

- Unit and lesson objectives stated in terms of *Communicative Goals, Culture, Reading* and *Writing Strategies,* and *Structure*
- Purpose and Suggestions for each major section of the Student Text
- Active Vocabulary lists for each lesson
- Suggestions for presenting comprehensible input with or without video
- Specific suggestions for doing the activities and exercises, including variations and expansion
- Answers to the activities and exercises
- Detailed suggestions for teaching Reading and Writing Strategies
- Additional cultural information
- Correlation to ancillary materials at point of use

COMPONENTS OF THE ¡DIME! PROGRAM

¡**DIME!** is a complete three-level program for junior high and senior high school students consisting of the following components:

- **STUDENT TEXT**

- **EXTENDED TEACHER'S EDITION**

- **TEXT-INTEGRATED VIDEO/AUDIO PROGRAM**
  Videocassettes or Videodisc
  Audiocassettes

- **CUADERNO DE ACTIVIDADES**
  ¡A escuchar! / Pronunciación y ortografía
  ¡A escribir!
  ¡A leer!

- **CUADERNO DE ACTIVIDADES, TEACHER'S EDITION**

- **COMPETENCY-BASED TESTING PROGRAM**
  Lesson Quizzes (3 per unit)
  Unit Tests
  Midyear and Final Examinations
  Situation Cards for Oral Evaluation
  Audiocassette with Listening Comprehension Sections

- **TESTING PROGRAM, TEACHER'S GUIDE AND KEY**

- **COPYMASTERS**
  Communicative Pair Activities

- **OVERHEAD TRANSPARENCIES**

- **TEACHER'S RESOURCE PACKAGE**

For a detailed description of the **¡DIME!** ancillaries, see page T23.

SCOPE AND SEQUENCE

LECCIÓN PRELIMINAR

P   **¡AJA! ¡HAY UN LIBRO!**   *Hispanic community, USA*

Unit theme: Students preparing to study Spanish using ¡DIME!

Communicative Goals	• Naming classroom objects and school supplies • Learning to work in cooperative groups
Culture	• Influence of Hispanic cultures in the U.S.
Structure	• Gender of nouns: Introduction • Indefinite and definite articles
Reading Strategy	• Recognizing cognates

UNIDAD 1

¡Hola! ¿Qué tal?   *Montebello, California*

Unit theme: The first week of classes in Montebello High School

	LECCIÓN **1**	LECCIÓN **2**	LECCIÓN **3**
Communicative Goals	• Exchanging greetings • Identifying people • Saying good-bye	• Introducing yourself and others • Responding to introductions • Naming countries and capitals • Giving information about where people are from	• Describing personality traits • Describing physical characteristics • Expressing negative ideas
Culture	• Appropriate form of address • Greetings • Using **tú** and **usted**	• Maps of the Americas • Who is an American? • Countries and nationalities	• How Spanish speakers describe themselves and each other • A Geographical Dictionary in Spanish
Structure and use	• Subject pronouns: Singular forms and use • **Ser:** Singular forms	• **¿De dónde . . . ?** and **ser de**	• Gender of nouns • Gender of adjectives
Reading and Writing Strategies			**Reading Strategy:** Using cognates **Writing Strategy:** Brainstorming

UNIDAD 2

¡Es hora de clase!   *San Juan, Puerto Rico*

Unit theme: Typical school days and after-school activities

	LECCIÓN **1**	LECCIÓN **2**	LECCIÓN **3**
Communicative Goals	• Exchanging information about class schedules • Asking for and telling time • Exchanging phone numbers	• Describing people, places, and things • Giving the location of people and things	• Exchanging information about after-school activities • Talking about future activities • Talking about obligations
Culture	• School schedules • The numerical grading system • Report cards	• **Colegio vs. universidad** • Private schools	• Pen pals from various countries • Favorite pastimes of Spanish speaking young people
Structure	• Numbers: 0–30 • Nouns and definite articles • Telling time • **Tener:** Singular forms	• Adjectives • Subject pronouns: Singular and plural forms • **Estar** • **Ser**	• Infinitives • **Ir** and **ir a** + infinitive • **Tener** and **tener que** . . .
Reading and Writing Strategies			**Reading Strategy:** Scanning **Writing Strategy:** Using clusters

UNIDAD 3

¿Qué hacen ustedes?　México D.F., México

Unit theme: Teenagers' activities in the U.S. and Mexico

	LECCIÓN 1	LECCIÓN 2	LECCIÓN 3
Communicative Goals	• Giving information about destination • Expressing likes and dislikes • Making polite requests	• Discussing weekend activities • Talking about the weather	• Describing everyday activities • Inquiring about everyday activities
Culture	• Shopping in Oaxaca, Mexico • How Mexican teenagers spend their free time	• Popularity of city parks • Chapultepec Park	• Mexican young people and their weekend activities
Structure	• **Ir a** • The indefinite article and **hay** • **Gustar** and **encantar**	• Present tense: Singular forms • Seasons and weather expressions	• Present tense: Plural forms • Indefinite and negative words
Reading and Writing Strategies			**Reading Strategy:** Scanning **Writing Strategy:** Paragraph writing

UNIDAD 4

¡Qué familia!　San Antonio, Texas

Unit theme: Extended family members celebrating birthdays and a wedding

	LECCIÓN 1	LECCIÓN 2	LECCIÓN 3
Communicative Goals	• Identifying family members • Describing your family • Asking about families • Asking about birthdays and age	• Identifying relatives by remarriage • Asking about people you know or want to meet • Expressing what you want to be in the future • Asking people about their professional goals • Asking questions	• Describing how people feel • Describing what is happening at the moment
Culture	• The importance of the extended family • Hispanic first names, last names and nicknames	• Finding telephone numbers • Using a Hispanic telephone directory • Mexico City phone book	• Hispanic population in the U.S. • Hispanic influence in the U.S.
Structure	• Possessive adjectives • Numbers from 30–100 • The months of the year	• Personal **a** • **Conocer** • **Querer** and **venir** • Questions and question words: A summary	• **Estar** with adjectives • Present progressive and -**ndo** verb forms
Reading and Writing Strategies			**Reading Strategy:** Identifying the main idea **Writing Strategy:** Organizing information

UNIDAD 7   ¡Vamos al partido!   Miami, Florida

Unit theme: Enjoying various sports in Miami and coping with sports injuries

	LECCIÓN 1	LECCIÓN 2	LECCIÓN 3
Communicative Goals	• Exchanging information about sports • Pointing out specific people and things	• Giving information about people's physical condition • Giving and following orders • Describing what happened in the past	• Giving and understanding orders • Giving the location of things
Culture	• Popular sports in Latin America • A Hispanic All-Star baseball team	• Understanding dialectical differences • A study on the effect of loud music	• A view of contemporary Miami
Structure	• Demonstratives • Spelling changes in the preterite	• Direct object pronouns • Stem-changing verbs in the preterite: **e → i** and **o → u**	• Affirmative **tú** commands: Irregular forms • Prepositions of location
Reading and Writing Strategies			**Reading Strategy:** Skimming **Writing Strategy:** Retelling an event

UNIDAD 8   En camino a Segovia   Segovia, España

Unit theme: A weekend outing to one of Spain's most picturesque cities

	LECCIÓN 1	LECCIÓN 2	LECCIÓN 3
Communicative Goals	• Describing daily routines • Describing how things are done • Naming foods	• Naming and describing rooms in a house • Expressing extremes • Making comparisons	• Describing what is happening at the moment • Telling what you usually do • Describing something that happened
Culture	• Confusion caused by lexical differences • **El Acueducto de Segovia**: Roman influence in Spain • Variations in names of foods	• Mealtimes in Hispanic countries • **El Alcázar de Segovia** • Cross-cultural variations in the concept of time	• **Gazpacho andaluz / Tortilla española**
Structure	• Reflexive pronouns and verbs • Adverbs	• Preterite of **estar** • Absolute superlatives: **-ísimo** • Comparatives	• Present tense: A summary • Present progressive: Summary • Preterite tense: Summary
Reading and Writing Strategies			**Reading Strategy:** Reading for detailed information **Writing Strategy:** Retelling a story

MATERIAS DE CONSULTA

- Apéndice: El abecedario y pronunciación
- Vocabulario español-inglés
- Índice: Gramática / Funciones / Estrategias

BEGINNING A UNIT

Each unit opens with a two-page photo spread designed to draw students into the unit's location and theme.

Suggestions for beginning a unit

1. Use the locator map to have students identify the location of the unit. Refer to the maps in the **Atlas** (pp. vi–x) to place each location in a broader geographical context and to emphasize the scope of the Spanish-speaking world.

2. Have students study the photo and speculate on the identity of the people, the actions, and the observable cultural elements. Have students make cross-cultural comparisons.

3. Introduce the unit title and ask students to speculate on the likely content or theme of the unit.

4. Play the opening video montage to acquaint students with some of the sights and people of the Spanish-speaking location of the unit. Ask students to give their impressions and opinions about the people and location.

5. As proficiency increases, ask students to contribute explanations or descriptions in Spanish; guide discussions using comprehensible input techniques. (See pages T12-T13.)

6. Provide additional information or offer extra credit to students who investigate each geographical region and share information on climate, lifestyle, population, culture, etc.

UNIDAD 8

¡En camino a Segovia!

Key to icons

In the Extended Teacher's Edition:

Video   Audiocassette

Writing activity   Overhead transparency

Copymaster activity

In the Student Text:

Pair activity

Group activity

TEACHING A LESSON

Instructional Sequence

Each unit in **¡DIME!** consists of three lessons founded on the following competency-based instructional sequence:

> **SETTING THE STAGE**
>
> **COMPREHENSIBLE INPUT**
>
> **GUIDED PRACTICE**
>
> **APPLICATION AND EXTENSION**
>
> **EVALUATION**

This instructional sequence is built into every lesson of **¡DIME!**

ANTICIPEMOS   Setting the Stage

This section opens each lesson with attractive visuals consisting of a combination of photos, realia and art drawings. Here, through the use of critical thinking—conjecture, speculation, prediction, inference and common sense—students are guided to make cross-cultural comparisons as they discover for themselves the lesson theme and new vocabulary. In *Anticipemos* students work with a large variety of authentic materials including class schedules, birthday and wedding invitations, country and city maps, menus, classified ads, etc.

Suggestions for Teaching *ANTICIPEMOS*

1. Have students work individually to study the illustrations and read the questions. Have them discuss the answers to the questions in pairs or small groups. Work together as a full class to recall what everyone has discovered. Offer, and encourage students to offer, additional observations on cultural features or other information.

2. An alternative approach is to have students prepare the *Anticipemos* as a homework assignment before beginning a new lesson. Then have them discuss the answers together in class.

3. In Units 1–4, the *Anticipemos* questions are in English. Beginning with Unit 5, they are in Spanish. Allow students to offer answers in English, but as language proficiency increases, encourage the use of Spanish. When students answer in English, paraphrase their responses in simple Spanish and ask the class to repeat after you.

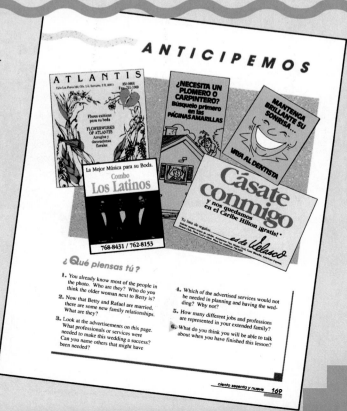

This lively visual presentation of language introduces new vocabulary and structures in meaningful contexts. Through listening, reading, and viewing the video, the receptive skills are emphasized before students are asked to produce any new language.

This Extended Teacher's Edition provides suggestions for combining the use of text, overhead transparencies, and video in ways that allow students to develop a thorough understanding of the language they will need in each lesson and throughout the unit. The margin notes offer detailed information on how to provide effective comprehensible input, including specific suggestions and *Comprehension* or *Early Production Check* questions for each text/video segment. The questions are available on cards in the Teacher's Resource Package.

Suggestions for Teaching *PARA EMPEZAR*

1. Point, demonstrate, act out, contrast, draw quick stick figures on the board or overhead transparencies to communicate meaning. Avoid translating or explaining in English.

2. Ask *Comprehension Check* questions frequently to determine students' real comprehension. Use only yes/no and either/or questions. Have students point out, demonstrate, raise hands, and identify people or actions.

3. Personalize the *Comprehension Checks* by asking students about themselves, their friends and their families.

4. Frequent repetition of the target language is essential to allow students sufficient opportunities to hear and recognize the language being learned. *Para empezar* language is simple and focused. You may break up longer sentences at the outset, but narration should be spoken with natural intonation and speed.

5. Students should not be expected to master, memorize, or reproduce complete utterances at this point. They will begin to use the new language as they become familiar with the vocabulary, concepts, and usage in context.

Vary your presentation techniques, using text, overhead transparencies, and video in different sequences.

A. Using the text alone

Have students focus on the photos/drawings as you narrate, using the techniques suggested below. Break up longer sentences, recombining them after comprehension of the various elements is established.

B. Using the overhead transparencies

The transparencies are provided without written text so that students must rely on listening to your narration and responding to your *Comprehension Check* and *Early Production Check* questions. Have students close their

6. Use the *Para empezar* text for pronunciation practice after comprehension is established.

This highly motivating story board of the video dialogues and action recycles the structures and vocabulary of the *Para empezar* at a slightly higher level. In *¿Qué decimos . . . ?* students learn a variety of language functions: to describe, to exchange information, to express preferences, to extend, accept, or decline an invitation, to describe a series of past events and the like. Students learn to imitate and expand on the functions taught through storylines set in different parts of the Spanish-speaking world, thus allowing for early language production in natural contexts and realistic situations.

books and begin by identifying the people, relationships, and activities. Then narrate as suggested, avoiding the use of English or translation to communicate meaning.

C.   Using the video

Show the video section once without pausing. Then stop and ask students what they think it is about. Replay the video, pausing after each short segment. (Use the digital counter or the bar codes.) Ask the *Comprehension Check* or *Early Production Check* questions. Paraphrase or narrate again to support comprehension. Now play the segment a third time without sound, pausing to ask questions confirming comprehension. (For instructions on using the digital counter and the bar codes, see pages T23—T24.)

5. Play the video without sound and have students narrate the action.

Suggestions for Teaching ¿QUÉ DECIMOS...?

1. This section uses the targeted language in a real-life context with characters and themes that carry through all three lessons of a unit. Encourage students to become familiar with the characters and to recycle previously learned language by asking questions about the people and activities.

2. Ask students to close their books as you narrate the script using the drawings in the text, the overhead transparencies, and the video to clarify meaning without translation. Expect students to begin producing comprehensible language. Ask *Early Production Check* questions requiring one-word or short-phrase answers focused on target vocabulary.

3. Use the *¿Qué decimos . . . ?* dialogues for pronunciation practice, having students read aloud or act out the dialogues, after they fully understand them.

4. As review before the lesson quiz, use the overhead transparencies to have groups of students produce spontaneous dialogues. Rather than insist on memorization, encourage meaningful variation and creativity.

This section combines teacher-directed and student-centered communicative pair and group activities. Students make their first efforts with the new lesson material as they develop productive accuracy and control. Through contextualization and personalization, these activities keep students focused on meaning and content rather than on the manipulation of grammatical structures, and move students from controlled to open-ended responses.

Throughout this section, focused explanations of the structures and vocabulary are presented in margin boxes on a need-to-know basis. These explanations allow you to keep the class focused on communication at this early production/guided practice stage. All structure boxes are correlated at point of use with the reference section *¿Por que se dice así?*, where detailed grammar explanations and additional practice activities can be found.

Suggestions for Using *CHARLEMOS UN POCO*

1. Most activities can be treated as full-class activities followed by individual or pair/small-group practice, or vice versa.

2. Pair and small-group activities should always be brought back to the full class by asking individuals or groups for quick reports or responses.

3. Many activities can be assigned for additional written practice. Activities particularly suited to writing are designated by an icon in the Teacher's Edition.

4. Some pair communication activities are designed to be done using the copymasters. These activities have an icon in the Teacher's Edition.

5. Specific suggestions for adapting or varying activities appear in the margins of the Teacher's Edition.

6. Brief grammar explanations appear in margin boxes at the point where they are needed to complete an activity. Each box is cross-referenced to the grammar section, *¿Por qué se dice así?*, at the back of the book. You may integrate these two sections as appropriate to students' needs and your own teaching style:

a. Assign appropriate *¿Por qué se dice así?* explanations and **Vamos a practicar** exercises as homework in preparation for classroom activities or for additional practice after the corresponding section of *Charlemos un poco* has been completed.

b. Use *¿Por qué se dice así?* in class to provide more detailed explanation and additional practice with particularly difficult structures.

c. Assign the *¿Por qué se dice así?* explanations and activities when the class or individuals need additonal help in accomplishing the tasks in *Charlemos un poco*.

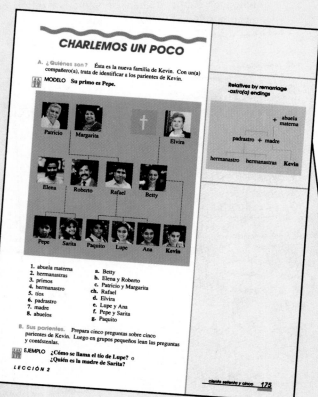

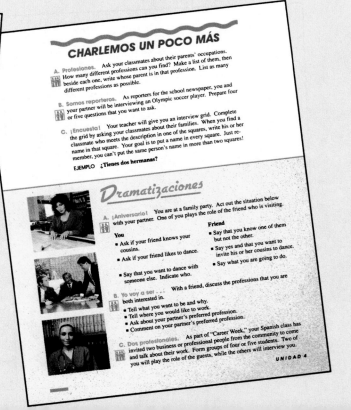

CHARLEMOS UN POCO MÁS Application and Extension

In this section, students have the opportunity to interact with each other in real-life communicative situations. These activities allow students to practice—in more creative settings—the functions just learned. Students are provided here with a wide variety of creative pair and group activities, including cooperative crossword puzzles, look-alike pictures, interview grids, biography cards, bingo searches, and "quiz-show" word games. These are truly interactive activities that encourage students to produce Spanish spontaneously in a variety of contexts. The emphasis is on accomplishing a task under real communication conditions—where the interlocutor's response is unpredictable.

Suggestions for Using CHARLEMOS UN POCO MÁS

1. Because of the interactive and spontaneous nature of these activities, many of them can be done more than once, changing partners or groups.

2. Circulate and listen, keeping the students on task.

3. Monitor time, setting a limit for each activity so that students stay focused on the task.

4. It is best to end an activity before everyone has completed it than to allow so much time that students get off task.

5. Bring the class back together by asking for brief reports from some pairs or groups, or by asking pairs or small groups to reenact their exchanges.

6. Additional specific suggestions for adapting or varying the activities appear in the Teacher's Edition.

7. Pair activities on copymasters are indicated by an icon: these highly motivating activities are carefully integrated into every lesson of the text.

DRAMATIZACIONES Evaluation

This section consists of several role plays designed to have students simulate real-life situations in a variety of contexts. These role plays are cumulative activities that carefully bring together the preceding phases of the instructional sequence and recycle previously learned material. They are open-ended activities that encourage students to use their creativity as they develop fluency in the language.

Suggestions for Using DRAMATIZACIONES

1. Students should not prepare written or memorized scripts, but rather should play out the situation spontaneously.

2. Teachers may wish to grade student performance on some of these activities.

3. Additional specific suggestions for adapting or varying activities appear in the Teacher's Edition.

4. If a video camera is available, have students tape their role plays occasionally. Students can choose some of their productions to show other classes or parents.

IMPACTO CULTURAL   Culture

In Lessons 1 and 2 of each unit, this section contains a short dialogue, **¡No me digas!** or **¡No metas la pata!**, where students are asked to identify the reason for a linguistic *faux pas* or cultural misconception. A short reading follows (***Y ahora, ¡a leer!***), which expands on what caused the misunderstanding. The reading is accompanied by prereading (**Antes de empezar**) and postreading (**Verifiquemos**) activities.

Suggestions for Using *IMPACTO CULTURAL*

1. Students are not expected to comprehend or master all the language of the readings, but rather to seek specific information and to become familiar with specific cultural content.

2. Call on two or three students to read the **¡No me digas!** or **¡No metas la pata!** dialogue aloud. Ask comprehension check questions to verify understanding. Use comprehensible input techniques to clarify meaning.

3. Have students answer the focus question (always the last question) and give reasons for their responses before they refer to the explanations in the back of their books (pages 416–420).

4. Allow time for students to do the **Antes de empezar** prereading activity before they read the ***Y ahora, ¡a leer!*** selection. Go over the answers with the class.

5. Have the class read the selection silently, then have students answer the **Verifiquemos** questions in pairs or in small groups. Go over the answers with the class.

6. Specific suggestions for use of these sections appear in the margins of the Teacher's Edition.

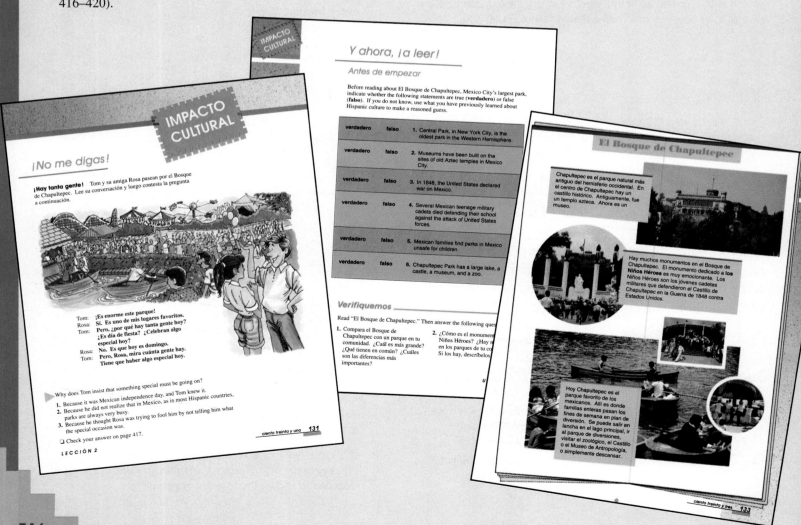

LEAMOS AHORA — Application and Extension

This end-of-unit section contains the principal reading of the unit. The readings come from a variety of sources: letters, newspapers, magazines, and the like. Prereading activities develop reading strategies such as recognizing cognates, scanning to locate specific information, using visual clues, and identifying the main idea. Postreading activities check the students' comprehension.

Suggestions for Using LEAMOS AHORA

1. Have students quickly read and make notes on the **Anticipemos** activity that precedes the reading selection. Then discuss their responses briefly.

2. Discuss the reading strategy targeted in the lesson. Point out that this is probably a strategy they have already learned to apply when reading in their native language. Ask them to give examples of when and how they use this strategy.

3. Ask students to read the selection independently and work through the **Verifiquemos**, making notes of their responses.

4. Have students discuss their responses to the **Verifiquemos** in groups of three or four, then discuss briefly as a class. Have students explain how they arrived at their responses.

5. Have students go back to their predictions in **Anticipemos** to see if they predicted the reading content correctly.

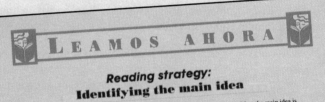

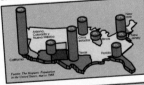

ESCRIBAMOS UN POCO Application and Extension

In this end-of-unit section, students apply language acquired in the unit to a real-life writing task. They are asked to write a short piece such as a letter, a descriptive paragraph, a poem, or a story. Throughout the book, students learn process-writing strategies and techniques such as brainstorming, clustering, organizing information, and making an outline. Students share the first draft with their peers for comments, and suggestions on content and some peer editing, before turning in a final draft for grading.

Suggestions for Using *ESCRIBAMOS UN POCO*

1. Discuss the **Planeando** section with the class. Present the sample writing piece, using techniques of comprehensible input where necessary, or ask students to read aloud. Ask comprehension check questions.

2. Help students to brainstorm lists of ideas or vocabulary they may want to use. Record their suggestions on the board, an overhead transparency, or butcher paper. Or have several students record ideas as class members call them out.

3. Insist that students plan before they write a first draft, using the clustering, charting, or outlining techniques taught.

4. Either allow time in class to prepare a first draft or assign the draft as homework. Emphasize to students that at this stage, getting the ideas on paper is more important than accuracy. They will have opportunities to refine their work later.

5. Try having students do "timed writes" on a topic. On a signal, they begin writing and keep the pencil moving for the full three to five minutes that you allow. After several "timed writes", have students develop one into a finished piece.

6. Allow class time for **Compartiendo**—peer feedback groups. Insist partners begin by noting what they liked or found interesting. Suggestions for improvement should be made tactfully.

7. After revision, a second peer feedback group can focus on accuracy of spelling, grammar, and punctuation. Teach students to edit by focusing on one or two points per composition (i.e., subject/verb agreement, present tense verb endings). Edit a sample composition on a transparency as a model.

8. Consider some form of "publication" for each finished piece—a class book, a newspaper, hanging the papers in a display case or on a classroom wall, an "author's reading."

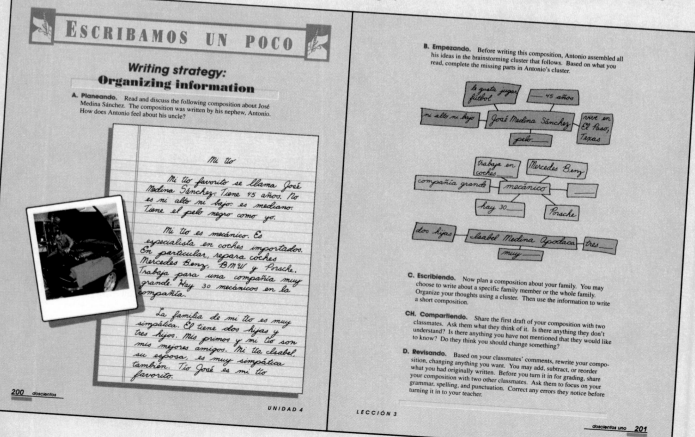

ESCRIBAMOS UN POCO

Writing strategy:
Organizing information

A. Planeando. Read and discuss the following composition about José Medina Sánchez. The composition was written by his nephew, Antonio. How does Antonio feel about his uncle?

Mi tío

Mi tío favorito se llama José Medina Sánchez. Tiene 45 años. No es ni alto ni bajo. Es mediano. Tiene el pelo negro como yo.

Mi tío es mecánico. Es especialista en coches importados. En particular, repara coches Mercedes Benz, BMW y Porsche. Trabaja para una compañía muy grande. Hay 30 mecánicos en la compañía.

La familia de mi tío es muy simpática. Él tiene dos hijas y tres hijos. Mis primos y mi tío son mis mejores amigos. Mi tía Isabel, su esposa, es muy simpática también. Tío José es mi tío favorito.

200 doscientos

UNIDAD 4

B. Empezando. Before writing this composition, Antonio assembled all his ideas in the brainstorming cluster that follows. Based on what you read, complete the missing parts in Antonio's cluster.

le gusta jugar fútbol — 45 años — ni alto ni bajo — José Medina Sánchez — vive en El Paso, Texas — pelo — trabaja en coches — Mercedes Benz — compañía grande — mecánico — hay 30 — Porsche — dos hijas — Isabel Medina Apodaca — tres — muy

C. Escribiendo. Now plan a composition about your family. You may choose to write about a specific family member or the whole family. Organize your thoughts using a cluster. Then use the information to write a short composition.

CH. Compartiendo. Share the first draft of your composition with two classmates. Ask them what they think of it. Is there anything they don't understand? Is there anything you have not mentioned that they would like to know? Do they think you should change something?

D. Revisando. Based on your classmates' comments, rewrite your composition, changing anything you want. You may add, subtract, or reorder what you had originally written. Before you turn it in for grading, share your composition with two other classmates. Ask them to focus on your grammar, spelling, and punctuation. Correct any errors they notice before turning it in to your teacher.

LECCIÓN 3

doscientos uno 201

Detailed grammatical explanations of all major structures appear in this section at the end of the text for greater flexibility in meeting your students' needs. (The pages, bordered in blue, are easy to locate.) All sections of *¿Por qué se dice así?* are cross-referenced to margin boxes in the student text. After each grammar explanation, additional guided practice exercises, called **Vamos a practicar,** are provided. These exercises focus on specific elements of the structures being taught in support of the communicative goals of each lesson.

Suggestions for Using *¿POR QUÉ SE DICE ASÍ?*

The placement of all grammar explanations together at the end of the text allows you to use *¿Por qué se dice así?* as a separate grammar reference manual. As such, you have great flexibility in how much grammar you present and how you present it in class. Some possibilities are listed below. Others will become obvious to you as the needs of individual classes warrant them.

1. Assign appropriate *¿Por qué se dice así?* sections and activities as homework in preparation for classroom activities or for additional practice after the corresponding section of *Charlemos un poco* has been completed.

2. Provide more detailed explanation and additional practice with particularly difficult structures, using *¿Por qué se dice así?* in class.

3. Assign *¿Por qué se dice así?* explanations and activities when class or individuals need additional help in accomplishing tasks in *Charlemos un poco.*

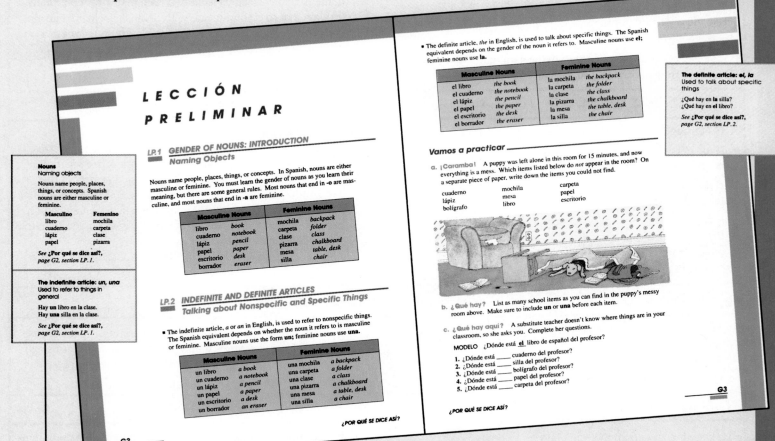

• Margin boxes from the student text, pp. 8 and 9.

WORKING WITH NATIVE SPEAKERS OF SPANISH

Given the approach and the natural language used throughout **¡DIME!**, this program can easily be adapted for use with students who are native speakers of Spanish (NSS) but who do not read or write Spanish. (Native speakers who already read and write Spanish should not enroll in first-year classes. These students should be in courses that focus on the specific needs of NSS: writing, vocabulary expansion through reading, accentuation, grammar review, dialectal variance, and so forth.) The suggestions that follow point out how each section of the five-step instructional sequence in **¡DIME!** can be used with native speakers of Spanish.

ANTICIPEMOS   Setting the Stage for NSS

- Ask all the **¿Qué piensas tú?** questions in Spanish. Expect students to answer in Spanish.

- Expect students to elaborate more when answering questions, drawing from experience within their own community.

- Have students personalize information given whenever appropriate. (e.g., ask about customs within their own family or community relating to parties, weddings. meals, relationships, customs, traditions).

- Avoid passing judgment or allowing other students to pass judgment on any personal information individual students share with the class. All information should be treated as cultural enrichment as the class gets to know more about other Spanish-speaking groups.

PARA EMPEZAR and ¿QUÉ DECIMOS ...?   Comprehensible Input for NSS

- Read the dialogues/narratives or show the video all the way through in each section before asking *Comprehension Check* questions; do not read just one sentence at a time.

- Use the overhead transparencies to have the students recreate the dialogues/narratives in their own words.

- Play the video a second time with the sound turned off and have the students create a script.

- Ask students for variations on any of the new vocabulary. How would they say it? Point out that the way they say it at home is also correct, especially within their own community. Explain that to communicate with Spanish speakers outside their community, it is sometimes necessary to learn other ways of saying the same thing.

CHARLEMOS UN POCO   Guided Practice for NSS

- Go through these activities very quickly.
- If an activity seems too easy, skip it. Do not feel that you have to go over all these activities with native speakers.
- Have students write out answers to a third of these activities in every lesson.
- Frequently have several students do activities on the board so that you can correct their work and teach them to correct each other's work. Native speakers of Spanish often need writing practice more than they need aural/oral practice.

- Make sure students understand the information in the structure/vocabulary margin boxes of *Charlemos un poco.* If necessary, have them turn to *¿Por qué se dice así?* at the back of the book and do the grammar exercises in the **Vamos a practicar** section. Emphasize grammatical nomenclature, since NSS tend to use Spanish correctly without knowing the grammatical rules behind the usage.

CHARLEMOS UN POCO MÁS   Application and Extension for NSS

- Encourage students to use their creativity when doing these activities.
- Always allow time for each pair/group to report back to the class and for the class to comment on what is reported.

- Ask students other ways of saying something when they use vocabulary or structures unique to their community of speakers. Avoid labeling their Hispanic community's expressions as incorrect.

DRAMATIZACIONES   Evaluation for NSS

- Ask students to do all the role plays.
- Have them perform their role plays in front of the class or for each other in groups of six or eight.
- Have students ask comprehension check questions on their role plays to make sure their classmates understood.

- When students perform a role play using their own community's language, accept it fully. Then, to help them focus on some of the distinctive features in their community's speech, ask them to repeat their lines using Spanish as spoken by non-members of their community.

IMPACTO CULTURAL   Culture for NSS

- Ask native speakers to role-play, reading aloud the **¡No me digas!** and **¡No metas la pata!** dialogues.
- Have the class discuss the cultural misunderstanding or *faux pas* built into each dialogue.

- Ask the native speakers if they can give other examples of similar situations they themselves have either experienced or observed.

Y AHORA, ¡A LEER! AND LEAMOS AHORA   Reading for NSS

- Have students read the **Y ahora, ¡a leer!** or **Leamos ahora** silently, or aloud with the class.

- Have students expand on the topic of the reading and provide additional insights or personal reactions they may have.

- Ask students to do more writing with these sections. For example, ask them to write a summary of each paragraph or of the reading itself, to write a list of all vocabulary new to them, and to list the word(s) they would use to answer the **Verifiquemos** questions in writing.

ESCRIBAMOS UN POCO   Writing for NSS

- Always have these students do the writing section.
- Train them to be good editors. Teach them specific skills for editing their classmates' writing.

- Always have them identify vocabulary or verbal expressions particular to their linguistic community, and ask them to provide alternative ways of expressing that information.

¿POR QUÉ SE DICE ASÍ?   Grammar for NSS

- Always have these students read the grammar sections.
- Require that they write out the answers to all the exercises in **Vamos a practicar.**

- Regularly assign specific grammar sections for homework.
- Give frequent but easy pop quizzes on the grammar.

TESTING PROGRAM   Evaluation for NSS

- Be very sensitive and accepting of your students' dialect.
- Do not penalize language use that is valid within the students' linguistic community.
- Offer extra credit to students able to rewrite a dialogue or composition changing all dialectal Spanish (which you

have underlined on their exams) to a more standard variety.
- If you are accepting only standard varieties of Spanish in certain sections of a quiz or exam, be sure the contextualization of those sections warrants nonuse of local dialect. Specify an Argentine family in Spain, or a Mexican teenager in Mexico City, instead of a situation such as "you and your family" or

CLASSROOM MANAGEMENT

In the five-step lesson design of **¡DIME!** the teacher functions variously as producer, director, performer, and audience for the students' production.

At the beginning of the lesson, the teacher is the provider of the language examples, as well as the guide to achieving comprehension and progressing to language production. During the practice phase of each lesson, the teacher is the facilitator; at the end of the lesson, the student is the performer, and the teacher is the evaluator of the quality of the language used to accomplish a task.

Although **¡DIME!** provides for great flexibility in teaching style, teachers should find the following principles useful:

1. Provide clear and consistent guidance as to how the various phases of the lesson are to be accomplished.

2. Give clear, concise directions before students begin pair or group work.

3. Develop a system of rewards and consequences for appropriate behavior in pair/group work—staying focused on the task, using Spanish exclusively, completing the task, etc.

4. Limit time for pair/group work. Students who have too much time will get off task. It is always best to cut an activity off before it is completed than to allow too much time. If a few students always finish before the rest of the class, give them other tasks to keep them focused. Have them write answers on board, prepare comprehension check questions to ask their classmates, do activities orally with another pair, and so forth.

5. Circulate, watch, and listen during pair/group practice.

6. Provide for full-group feedback by asking for a report, a summary of responses, individual or group "reenactments," etc.

7. Establish a means for immediately getting the class to stop talking when you are ready to end an activity: quickly turn the lights on and off, instruct students that when they see you raise your hand they are to immediately stop talking and raise their hands, etc.

8. Evaluate student performance in pair/group work occasionally.

9. Develop a holistic rubric for evaluating/grading oral and written language production.

Holistic grading of written and oral work

If students are to be encouraged to use their new language for communication, we need to evaluate their communication efforts more globally and not just in terms of their mastery of grammar and vocabulary.

A holistic approach to grading can be used to evaluate the overall quality of communicative efforts. In this approach, students are evaluated based on satisfacory completion of the task(s) they are required to perform. It is, therefore, important that students understand the task and the way in which it will be evaluated. There are a number of approaches to holistic grading of activities. The following suggestions may prove helpful.

1. A simple, all-purpose rubric for grading oral and written production:

A	Task was accomplished completely. Language used had very few, minimal errors, none of which interfered with comprehensibility.
B	Task was accomplished. Language had some errors, but only two or three that interfered with comprehensibility.
C	Task was mostly accomplished. Several errors interfered with comprehensibility.
D	Task was not accomplished. Errors rendered language incomprehensible even to teacher and/or classmates.
F	Task was not accomplished. Language was totally incomprehensible. Little or no attempt was made. Majority of task was in English.

2. An even simpler, all-purpose rubric:

+	Performance exceeded expectations.
✔	Performance satisfied expectations.
−	Performance failed to satisfy expectations.

3. A third approach to holistic grading:

■	Specify precisely which elements of a given activity will affect the grade received–for example, pronunciation, number of utterances, variety of sentence types, use of a particular form, inclusion of specific pieces of information.
■	Then develop a description of the performance (written or oral) that defines each grade category.

Maintaining a Student Portfolio

Today many schools and school districts are adopting a system of portfolio assessment. Such a system can serve both as an ongoing measure of a student's progress toward proficiency and as an ongoing gauge of a department's, a school's, or a district's progress toward meeting curriculum goals. ¡DIME! provides teachers with a number of convenient opportunities to assemble a portfolio that would include samples of performance in all skill areas: listening, speaking, reading, writing, and cultural awareness. The portfolio should contain teacher-selected as well as student-selected samples and should follow the student throughout his or her years of Spanish study.

Because the ¡DIME! Testing Program is designed to allow students to demonstrate not only mastery of vocabulary and structure but also of listening comprehension, of spontaneous writing proficiency, and of reading and cultural awareness, inclusion of one or more Lesson Quizzes or Unit Exams each semester is appropriate. Teachers may also choose one finished writing piece each semester and allow students to select a second writing piece for inclusion.

Samples of student speaking proficiency can easily be included through audio taping. Teachers may record student role plays from the *Dramatizaciones* section of each lesson and/or student-student or teacher-student interaction using the Situation Cards. Because it is unnecessary to record every student during every activity, technological requirements need not be oppressive. If each student provides a single audiocassette, and if the teacher provides two small cassette recorders, students may regularly record pair activities on a rotating basis.

Maintaining a video record for each student may prove more of a problem. Yet if teachers have access to the necessary equipment, video samples of student interaction for the whole class are feasible. Again, it is unnecessary to videotape every student for every activity.

A typical student portfolio at the end of the first year of Spanish using ¡DIME! might include:

- **Selected unit exams**
- **Semester exam**
- **Final exam**
- **Student-selected quizzes**
- **Teacher-selected writing piece each semester**
- **Student-selected writing piece each semester**
- **Other student-selected writings or projects**
- **Speaking sample on tape (at least one per semester)**
- **Video sample (at least one per semester)**

Using the ¡DIME! Ancillaries

VIDEO/AUDIO PROGRAM

The **¡DIME!** video offers exciting images from around the Spanish-speaking world. Half of the units were taped in Hispanic communities within the United States (San Antonio, Miami, and Montebello, California) and in Puerto Rico. The other half of the units were taped in Mexico (Mexico City, Guadalajara) and Spain (Madrid, Segovia). There are 50 video segments, 2 in the *Lección preliminar* and 6 per regular unit. Each video unit, which corresponds to visual/textual material in the textbook unit, consists of the following:

• An opening montage of the location

• The *Para empezar* and *¿Qué decimos...?* comprehensible input sections.

In the Teacher's Edition, *Video Notes* on the unit opener page provide additional information about the characters and the salient features of the Spanish spoken in the unit. Specific suggestions for use of the video appear in each lesson.

Each unit in the text is also accompanied by an audiocassette that includes the sound track from the video on one side, and the listening comprehension activities and pronunciation practice (coordinated with the *¡A escuchar!* in the **Cuaderno de actividades**) on the other side.

Using the Video

Videocassette or Videodisc

The **¡DIME!** Video Program is available in two formats: on VHS videocassettes and on videodiscs. Notations in the margins of the Teacher's Edition will allow you to access quickly and easily the segments you want to use.

Using a videodisc player, refer to the bar codes or frame numbers.

Side 1, 7167 to 7799

(See below "Using a Videodisc Player.")

Using a videocassette player, refer to the digital clock counters.

| 03:56 |

The number on each counter corresponds to the number on the counter visible in the lower right corner of the video screen. Press the FAST FORWARD or QUICK button until you reach the counter number, then press PLAY.

Playing a segment

At the beginning of each unit under *Video Notes*, you will see two sets of notations. The first set allows you to play the montage as an introduction to the unit.

The second set allows you to play the entire unit from beginning to end without stopping.

Video Notes

To play the montage, use counter or bar code:

| 03:06 | - | 03:47 |

Side 1, 5655 to 6884

To play the entire unit without stopping:

| 03:06 | - | 08:15 |

Side 1, 6900 to 11601

Most of your video-assisted instruction will take place in the *Para empezar* and *¿Qué decimos . . . ?* sections. At the beginning of these sections, you will find an icon box. The notations beneath the video icon and beneath the box allow you to play the entire *Para empezar* or *¿Qué decimos . . . ?* section without stopping. Example (*Para empezar*, Unit 1, Lesson 1):

Section is available on videocassette or videodisc.

PARA EMPEZAR

Comprehensible Input 1

| TAPE/DISC | | |
03:47–06:23

Side 1, 6900 to 11601

Tape counter numbers show beginning and end of entire section.

Videodisc bar code to play entire section without stopping.

Videodisc frame numbers to play entire section without stopping.

The notations that appear throughout the **Para empezar** and **¿Qué decimos . . . ?** sections allow you to play and to replay various short segments with pauses in order to ask the *Comprehension* or *Early Production Check* questions. A typical segment (Unit 1, Lesson 1) looks like this:

Number identifies segment and ········· corresponds to text and photos / artwork.

Beginning code for videocassette.

2   **04:18** ···

1 ¿Es Beto Chávez?
2 ¿Quién es él?
3 Y ella, ¿es Ana?
4 ¿Es Ana Chávez?
5 ¿Es Ana Montoya?
6 ¿Cómo está Ana? ¿Muy bien?
7 ¿Cómo está Beto? ¿Bien o muy bien?

Point out **Beto** is short for any name ending in **-berto**, such as **Alberto** or **Roberto**.

··· Bar code and frame numbers for videodisc.

Side 1, 7817 to 8601

Using a Videdisc player

The following explanation will show you how to access a video segment using the bar code or the frame number.

If you are using a remote control box:

- Press FRAME.
- Enter the first frame number: 7817.
- Press SEARCH.

Side 1, 7817 to 8601

The player will find frame 7817 and begin playing. It will play to the end of the scene (frame 8601) and freeze.

If you are using a bar code scanner:

- Hold down the READ button. (This button is often blue.)
- Trace the tip of the scanner horizontally across the bar code, from either direction. (You don't need to press hard.)
- When the scanner beeps, the code has been read.

If the scanner is connected by cable to the player, after a few seconds the player will find frame 7817 and begin playing. It will play to the end of the scene (frame 8601) and freeze.

If the scanner is not connected to a cable:

- Press the SEND/REPEAT button. (Usually red).
- Point the flat side (where the SEND/REPEAT button is) at the videodisc player's front control panel until you hear the beep.

Tips for using a bar code scanner:

- Make a full sweep back and forth across the bar code.
- Trace rather quickly across the bar code. (Generally the scanner reads the bar code more easily if the scanning speed is faster.)
- Start and end sweep in the space on either side of the code.

If your first sweep does not achieve a beep, try again:

- Hold the scanner at a different angle.
- If you traced across the top of the bar code, try the middle or bottom.

For specific instructions for operating your school's equipment, ask the Media Specialist for a demonstration.

Spanish Language Variations

Language change and variation are facts of life that need to be recognized and addressed by the language teacher. The people of Chicago speak English with a regional accent different from that of the people in Boston or the people in Atlanta. North Americans speak differently from Britons. Variation, rather than uniformity, seems to be the rule. Spanish is spoken in 20 different countries, plus the United States, and each displays unique variations in pronunciation. So it should be no surprise that Argentines speak differently from Mexicans and that the people of Seville speak differently from the people of Madrid.

Within a given speech community, certain pronunciation patterns often have higher prestige than others. For example, for an English speaker, "dropping" one's *r* during a job interview may have opposite consequences in New York and Boston. In speaking Spanish, you probably have a different pronunciation from that of your colleagues in the department. The problem is, what do you teach your students? Or is it really a problem? Assuming your pronunciation falls within the range of acceptability for any of the Spanish speech comunties throughout the world—be it Madrid, Havana, Mexico City, San Juan, Bogotá, Buenos Aires, or San Antonio, Texas—the best thing you can do is be yourself. Let your Spanish flow naturally so it serves as a good model to your students. You want them to sound like human beings, not like robots.

In the video and audio components of **¡DIME!**, students will hear the Spanish spoken in a variety of locations, by people of different ages. All the Spanish heard on the video is standard Spanish; however, teachers accustomed to various regional accents and students with a good ear will notice some of the differences in pronunciation. The *Video Notes* in the Teacher's Edition point out variations in pronunciation particular to the Spanish-speaking area featured in the unit.

Students will become aware that language variation is a natural phenomenon as they watch the video, listen to recorded materials, and receive instruction from other teachers—and, ultimately, as they interact in genuine communication with real speakers of Spanish.

CUADERNO DE ACTIVIDADES

¡A escuchar!

The listening activities focus specifically on providing practice in, and enhancing, student comprehension of language in context. All listening activities are contextualized to reflect real-life listening. Comprehension is checked by having students fill out schedules, draw pictures, take down phone messages, identify a picture being described, complete appointment books, and the like. These activities are coordinated with the audiocassette program.

Pronunciación y ortografía

This section, which is coordinated with the audiocassette program, addresses elements of pronunciation, spelling, and sound/spelling correlations. Here students learn to distinguish minimal meaningful sound differences in Spanish and practice writing the sound they hear. Extensive practice is provided in recognizing word stress and knowing when written accents are necessary. An effort is made, also, to address differences in Spanish as spoken in various regions of the Spanish-speaking world.

¡A escribir!

This section provides additional guided and extended writing activities for the communicative goals of each lesson. All writing activities are contextualized to keep students focused on the message being communicated. Writing practice ranges from fill-in-the-blank activities to creating short dialogues and paragraphs. In the **Vocabulario personal** sections at the end of the unit, students maintain a list of active vocabulary for each lesson, as well as related vocabulary of personal interest.

¡A leer!

This section of the **Cuaderno** has two theme-related, supplementary readings for each unit. These may be used as additional in-class reading, as homework reading, or as extra reading for students that finish individual or group activities much faster than the rest of the class. These readings are accompanied by both prereading and postreading activities.

THE TESTING PROGRAM

The **¡DIME!** Testing Program consists of 24 lesson quizzes (**Pruebas comunicativas**) and eight unit tests (**Exámenes**). There is also a midyear and a final examination. All tests are available on copymasters, and the listening portions are recorded on audiocassettes. The **Teacher's Guide** contains the *Answer Key* and listening comprehension scripts, as well as additional information on testing and evaluating oral performance.

Pruebas comunicativas

There is a quiz for each lesson in the text. Each quiz consists of four sections: (1) a taped listening comprehension section, (2) a section that requires students to demonstrate their ability to produce language in context and to show mastery of specific elements taught in the lesson, (3) a section that requires students to demonstrate reading comprehension and make appropriate cultural distinctions, and (4) an open-ended section requiring students to demonstrate their proficiency in writing Spanish. The **Pruebas comunicativas** are designed to be administered in 20–25 minutes. Each quiz is worth 50 points.

Exámenes

The unit tests follow the same format as the lesson quizzes: (1) a taped listening comprehension section, (2) a language-in-context section, (3) a reading/cultural comprehension section, and (4) a writing section. The **Exámenes** are designed to be administered in 40–45 minutes. Each exam is worth 100 points. Like the unit exams, the midyear and final exams follow the same format except that there is no writing section. Because of the limited time available to teachers for correcting midyear and final exams, these comprehensive tests have been designed to be effective communicative exams that can be graded quickly.

Interacciones: Situation Cards

These cards feature a series of "situations" or "contexts" designed to generate student-and-student or teacher-and-student interaction using the language taught in the unit and recycling language previously learned. The Situation Cards may also be used in conjunction with the unit exams for teachers who want to evaluate oral language production.

COPYMASTERS

Copymasters are provided for one or two pair/group activities per lesson. These are highly motivating cooperative learning activities that include look-alike pictures, bingo searches, cooperative crossword puzzles, and the like. An icon next to the appropriate activities in the Teacher's Edition signals the use of the copymasters.

OVERHEAD TRANSPARENCIES

To facilitate providing comprehensible input, all the **Para empezar** and **¿Qué decimos . . . ?** illustrations in the text are available as full-color transparencies. The narratives are omitted from the transparencies so that students will depend on listening and understanding when the story lines are being narrated by their teacher.

TEACHER'S RESOURCE PACKAGE

The Teacher's Resource Package contains a variety of useful classroom materials to aid the teacher. These materials include:

- Extended Teacher's Edition
- **Cuaderno de actividades:** Teacher's Edition
- Test Guide and Answer Key
- Comprehension/Early Production Check Cards
- Copymasters: Communicative pair activites
- Ancillary Sampler: Overhead Transparencies, Quizzes and Tests

¡DIME! is designed to be taught in a regular school year to students in grades 7 through 12. The first few lessons may go more quickly than an average 5–7 days per lesson, but a rule of thumb is to plan 20 school days per unit.

Thus, with allowances for the inevitable interruptions (fire drills, assemblies, career days, etc.), teachers should be able to finish the book in a school year of 170–185 days.

Sample Lesson Plan for Unit 4

The following is a model lesson plan for Unit 4. The plan is based on 20 school days with class periods of 50 minutes. Teachers should understand that no model will reflect the specific conditions and needs of any one class, and that considerable flexibility is possible.

It is not necessary to use each and every activity. When students have demonstrated control of a concept or structure, it is time to move on.

DAY 20   **UNIDAD 3**

1. Give Unit 3 Exam. *(40–45 minutes)*
2. Discuss two-page unit opener for Unit 4. *(5-15 minutes)*

Homework: Study Unit 4 Lesson 1 *Anticipemos*, think about answers to ¿**Qué piensas tú?** questions.

DAY 1   **UNIDAD 4**   LECCIÓN

1. Have students pair up to discuss answers to *Anticipemos* questions. *(4 minutes)*
2. Go over *Anticipemos*. *(5 minutes)*
3. Introduce *Para empezar* with book, overheads, and/or video. *(20 minutes)*

4. Have students share first drafts of their Unit 3 paragraphs (Unit 3 *Escribamos un poco*, Activity CH) in peer feedback groups of 3 or 4. *(12 minutes)*
5. Revise paragraph drafts. *(8 minutes)*

Homework: Write "publication" version of paragraph .

DAY 2   **UNIDAD 4**   LECCIÓN

1. Review Lesson 4.1 *Para empezar.* *(5 minutes)*
2. Introduce *¿Qué decimos . . . ?* with book, overheads, and/or video. *(15 minutes)*
3. Do Actividad A, *Charlemos un poco.* *(2 minutes)*
4. Introduce identifying someone's relatives, asking students the names of their relatives, and repeating the information. Point out/discuss boxes next to Activity B. *(5 minutes)*

5. Do Activity B, *Charlemos un poco,* taking turns in pairs, then go over as full class. *(5 minutes)*
6. Introduce exchanging information about one's own relatives. Point out/discuss boxes next to Activities CH, D, and E. *(10 minutes)*
7. Do Activities C and CH, *Charlemos un poco.* *(7 minutes)*

Homework: Study 4.1, *¿Por qué se dice así?* Do selected exercises from A–E.

DAY 3   **UNIDAD 4**   LECCIÓN

1. Check, correct homework. *(10 minutes)*
2. Review *¿Qué decimos . . . ?* *(8 minutes)*
3. Practice identifying and exchanging information about relatives and possessions, Activities D and E in *Charlemos un poco.* *(8 minutes)*
4. Introduce telling ages and dates by reviewing information

about ages and birthdates from *Para empezar* and *¿Qué decimos . . . ?* and telling students about your own family, asking about their families. Point out boxes next to Activities F, G, and H. *(8 minutes)*
5. Practice expressing higher numbers, exchanging information about ages, dates, and activities, Activities F-J, *Charlemos un poco.* *(15 minutes)*

Homework: Study 4.2 and 4.3, *¿Por qué se dice así?*; Do exercises selected from A–CH in each section.

DAY 4 — UNIDAD 4 · LECCIÓN 1

1. Check and correct homework. **(10 minutes)**

2. Practice exchanging information about family members, Activities A-D, *Charlemos un poco más.* Have students change partners for each activity. Go over each activity **(20 minutes)**

3. Introduce cultural content about family relationships with *¡No me digas!* Call on volunteers to read dialogue aloud. Discuss the reason for Mary Ann's surprise. **(5 minutes)**

4. Continue cultural content about Hispanic names with *Y ahora, ¡a leer!* Have students work with a partner to answer **Antes de empezar** questions, then go over quickly. **(4 minutes)**

Read *¿Cómo te llamas?* with students, asking comprehension check questions to confirm understanding. **(5 minutes)**

Have students work in groups of three or four to share answers to **Verifiquemos** questions. **(5 minutes)**

Homework: Assign selected activities in **Cuaderno de actividades,** Unit 4, Lesson 1.

DAY 5 — UNIDAD 4 · LECCIÓN 1

1. Go over *Y ahora, ¡a leer!* with sharing of answers to **Verifiquemos** questions. **(5 minutes)**

2. Check and correct **Cuaderno de actividades** activities. **(10 minutes)**

3. Practice listening comprehension with taped activities. **(15 minutes)**

4. Do **Dramatizaciones.** Have students pair off for Activity A. Go over by asking one pair (or a random pair) to role-play the conversation in front of the class.
Assign Activities B and C to different groups. Have students change groups and role-play the second situation. Go over by having volunteers role play the situation in front of the class. **(19 minutes)**

Homework: Remainder of **Cuaderno de actividades** exercises.

DAY 6 — UNIDAD 4 · LECCIÓN 1

1. Check and correct homework. **(10 minutes)**

2. Warm up for Lesson 1 quiz by asking students for information about their families, relatives' names, ages, birthdays, activities. **(8 minutes)**

3. Administer Lesson 1 quiz. **(20 minutes)**

4. Lesson 2 *Anticipemos* Have students pair off to share responses to *¿Qué piensas tú?* questions, then go over with class discussion of responses. **(12 minutes)**

DAYS 7-12 — UNIDAD 4 · LECCIÓN 2

Lesson 2: Repeat the procedures for Lesson 1, Days 1-6.

DAYS 13-15 — UNIDAD 4 · LECCIÓN 3

For Lesson 3 repeat the procedures for *Anticipemos, ¿Qué decimos...?,* and *Charlemos un poco,* of Lesson 1.

DAY 16 — UNIDAD 4 LECCIÓN 3

1. Check and correct homework. **(10 minutes)**

2. Practice exchanging information about what people are doing, Activities A-CH, **Charlemos un poco más.** Have students change partners or groups for each activity. Go over each activity. **(20 minutes)**

3. Introduce the reading strategy "Identifying the main idea." Read **Anticipemos** with students. Use techniques of comprehensible input to clarify any meanings in the five statements. When you are sure that students understand the statements, take an informal poll to determine who agrees and who disagrees with each one. Briefly discuss **La idea principal.** **(10 minutes)**

4. Read **Verifiquemos** with students. Encourage them to make predictions based on what they know before they read the article. Point out that for each item in **Verifiquemos**, one of the choices will be confirmed by what they read. **(5 minutes)**

5. Have students read the article silently, to confirm their predictions. Emphasize that they do not have to mentally "translate" every word and phrase. Rather they should use all their reading strategies—recognizing cognates, determining meaning from context, scanning for specific information—to confirm or correct their predictions. Students who do not finish the reading in class should complete it as homework. **(5 minutes)**

Homework: Assign selected activities in **Cuaderno de actividades,** Unit 4, Lesson 3. Finish reading.

DAY 17 — UNIDAD 4 LECCIÓN 3

1. Go over reading by sharing of answers to **Verifiquemos** questions. Encourage students to explain where in the article they found the significant information. **(5 minutes)**

2. Check and correct **Cuaderno de actividades** activities. **(10 minutes)**

3. Practice listening comprehension with taped activities. **(15 minutes)**

4. Do **Dramatizaciones.** Have students change partners or groups to role-play at least three of the four situations. Go over by having volunteers role-play the situation in front of the class. **(20 minutes)**

Homework: Remainder of **Cuaderno de actividades** exercises.

DAY 18 — UNIDAD 4 LECCIÓN 3

1. Check and correct homework. **(10 minutes)**

2. Warm up for Lesson 3 quiz by using overhead transparencies of **Para empezar, ¿Qué decimos. . . ?**, and/or **Charlemos un poco**, Activity A, asking students to tell about the people and what they are doing. **(8 minutes)**

3. Administer Lesson 3 quiz. **(20 minutes)**

4. Introduce **Escribamos un poco** with **Planeando.** Ask for volunteers to read José Medina Sánchez's composition about his uncle aloud. Discuss the writing assignment for this unit—a composition about the family (**Escribiendo.)** **(6 minutes)**

5. Brainstorm a list of people and things students might want to include in their compositions. **(6 minutes)**

Homework: Write first draft of composition.

DAY 19 — UNIDAD 4

1. Review for Unit 4 exam.
2. You may want to have students write their composition draft in class.
3. Follow up the composition on Day 1 of Unit 5 with peer feedback groups and revision.

DAY 20 — UNIDAD 4

1. Administer Unit 4 exam. **(5-15 minutes)**
2. Discuss two page opener for Unit 5. **(40-45 minutes)**

Homework: Study Unit 5 Lesson **Anticipemos,** think about answers to **¿Qué piensas tú?** questions

CULTURAL REFERENCES

This chart lists the cultural references in the Student Text and in the Teacher's Edition. Page numbers followed by a P indicate a photo in the Student Text. Page numbers in boldface type refer to cultural information given in the margins of the Teacher's Edition.

¡DIME!
UNO

FABIÁN A. SAMANIEGO
University of California, Davis

M. CAROL BROWN
California State University, Sacramento

PATRICIA HAMILTON CARLIN
University of California, Davis

SIDNEY E. GORMAN
Fremont Unified School District
Fremont, California

CAROL L. SPARKS
Mt. Diablo Unified School District
Concord, California

HEATH

D.C. Heath and Company
Lexington, Massachusetts
Toronto, Ontario

Director, Modern Languages
Roger D. Coulombe

Managing Editor
Marilyn Lindgren

Developmental Editor
Sylvia Madrigal

Design Manager, Modern Languages
Victor Curran

Project Editors
Senior Editor: Lawrence Lipson
Meg LeSchack
Gloria Ryan

National Modern Language Coordinator
Teresa Carrera-Hanley

D.C. Heath Consultant
Karen Ralston

Design and Production
Senior Designer: Angela Sciaraffa
Design Staff: Ann Barnard, Paulette Crowley, Dan
    Derdula, Carolyn Langley, Joan Paley, Martha Podren
Production Coordinator: Patrick Connolly
Photo Supervisor: Carmen Johnson
Photo Coordinator: Connie Komack
Cover Design: Ruby Shoes Studio

Cover Illustration
Clínica de la Raza Mural, East Oakland, California,
© 1990 by Xochitl Nevel Guerrero. Painted by
Xochitl Nevel Guerrero, Zala Nevel, Consuelo Nevel, and
Roberto C. Guerrero. Photos of students by Nancy Sheehan,
© 1993 by D.C. Heath and Company.

Published simultaneously in Canada

Printed in the United States of America

International Standard Book Number: 0-669-23881-3

1 2 3 4 5 6 7 8 9 10 VH 99 98 97 96 95 94 93

FIELD TEST USERS

Dena Bachman
Lafayette High School
St. Joseph, MO

Cathy Boulanger
L. Horton Watkins High School
St. Louis, MO

Janice Costella
Stanley Intermediate School
Lafayette, CA

Karen Davis
Southwest High School
Fort Worth, TX

Beatriz DesLoges
Lexington High School
Lexington, MA

Amelia Donovan
South Gwinnett High School
Snellville, GA

Velda Hughes
Bryan Senior High School
Omaha, NE

Sarah Witmer Lehman
P. K. Yonge Laboratory School
Gainesville, FL

Alita Mantels
Hall High School
Little Rock, AR

Ann Marie Mesquita
Encina High School
Sacramento, CA

Linda Meyer
Roosevelt Junior High School
Appleton, WI

Joseph Moore
Tiffin City Schools
Tiffin, OH

Craig Mudie
Dennis-Yarmouth Regional
  High School
South Yarmouth, MA

Sue Rodríguez
Hopkins Junior High School
Fremont, CA

Janice Stangl
Bryan Senior High School
Omaha, NE

Teresa Hull Tolentino
Seven Hills Upper School
Cincinnati, OH

Grace Tripp
McCall School
Winchester, MA

Carol B. Walsh
Acton-Boxborough Regional
  High School
Acton, MA

Margaret Whitmore
Morton Junior High School
Omaha, NE

LINGUISTIC CONSULTANT

Dr. William H. Klemme
Indiana University
Fort Wayne, IN

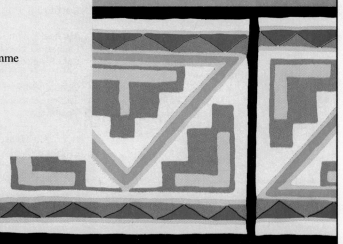

REVIEWERS AND CONSULTANTS

Cathy Abreu
Highland Park High School
Highland Park, IL

Thomas Alsop
Ben Davis High School
Indianapolis, IN

Dr. Robert Ariew
University of Arizona
Tucson, AZ

Dr. Gwendolyn Barnes
St. Olaf College
Northville, MN

Rebecca Block
Newton South High School
Newton, MA

Maria Brock
Miami Norland Senior
 High School
Miami, FL

Carlos Brown
Flagstaff Junior High School
Flagstaff, AZ

Bruce Caldwell
Southwest Secondary School
Minneapolis, MN

Marie Carrera Lambert
Eastchester High School
Eastchester, NY

Joseph Celentano
Syracuse City School District
Syracuse, NY

Cindy Chambers
Provo High School
Provo, UT

Dr. Maria C. Collins
State Department of Education
Topeka, KS

Dr. Ferdinand Contino
South Ocean Middle School
Patchogue, NY

James W. Cooper
Parkway Schools
Manchester, MO

Sharon Cotter
Sagamore Junior High School
Holtsville, NY

Delbys Cruz
Lawrence High School
Lawrence, MA

Robin Fisher
Jericho Middle School
Jericho, NY

Carolyn Frost
Churchill High School
San Antonio, TX

Pamela C. Kaatz
Haltom High School
Fort Worth, TX

Elaine Korb
West Islip High School
West Islip, NY

Herb LeShay
William Floyd School District
Mastic Beach, NY

Dr. Richard Lindley
Austin Community College
Austin, TX

Michael Livingston
Sachem High School
Lake Ronkonkoma, NY

Cenobio Macías
Tacoma Public Schools
Tacoma, WA

Ildefonso Manso
Cambridge, MA

Janet McIntyre
Westfield Academy &
 Central School
Westfield, NY

Millie Park Mellgren
Olson Language Immersion
 School
Golden Valley, MN

Laurie E. Nesrala
Haltom High School
Fort Worth, TX

Janet Obregón
Miami Palmetto High School
Miami, FL

Dr. Terry Peterson
Forest Park High School
Crystal Falls, MI

Mary Ann Price
Newton South High School
Newton, MA

Dr. Linda Pavian Roberts
Waverly Community Schools
Lansing, MI

Robin A. Ruffo
Chaparral High School
Scottsdale, AZ

Paul Sandrock
Appleton High School West
Appleton, WI

Dr. Francoise Santalis
New Rochelle High School
New Rochelle, NY

Carolyn A. Schildgen
Highland Park High School
Highland Park, IL

Debbie Short
Hall High School
Little Rock, AR

Priscilla Sicard
Lowell High School
Lowell, MA

Judith Snyder
Computech Middle School
Fresno, CA

Dr. Emily Spinelli
University of Michigan
Dearborn, MI

Jonita Stepp
P. K. Yonge Laboratory
 School
Gainesville, FL

Stephanie Thomas
Bloomington, IN

Kay Thompson
Green Valley High School
Henderson, NV

Victoria Thompson
Farquhar Middle School
Olney, MD

Dr. Virginia D. Vigil
Northern Arizona University
Flagstaff, AZ

Sharon M. Watts
Omaha Public Schools
Omaha, NE

Nancy J. Wrobel
Anoka Senior High School
Anoka, MN

Dr. Dolly Young
University of Tennessee
Knoxville, TN

Charles Zimmerman
Penfield High School
Penfield, NY

ATLAS

- El mundo

- México, el Caribe y
  Centroamérica

- Sudamérica

- España

EL MUNDO

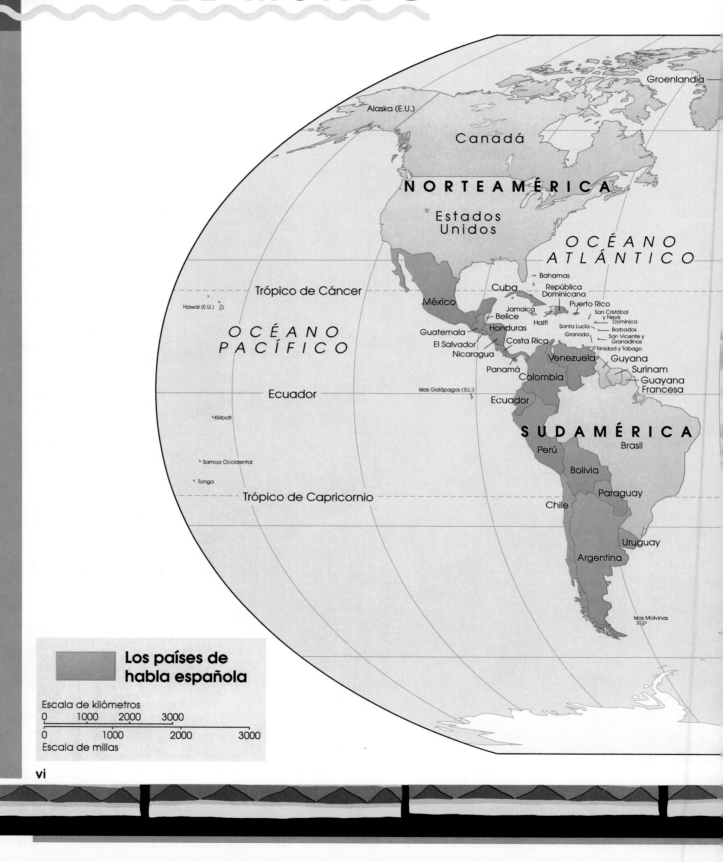

Groenlandia

Alaska (E.U.)

Canadá

NORTEAMÉRICA

Estados
Unidos

OCÉANO
ATLÁNTICO

Trópico de Cáncer

Bahamas

Cuba
República
Dominicana

Hawai (E.U.)

México
Puerto Rico

OCÉANO
PACÍFICO

Jamaica
Belice
San Cristóbal
y Nevis
Dominica

Guatemala
Honduras
Haití
Santa Lucía
Barbados
Granada
San Vicente y
Granadinas

El Salvador
Nicaragua
Costa Rica
Trinidad y Tobago

Islas Galápagos (Ec.)

Panamá
Venezuela
Guyana
Surinam
Guayana
Francesa

Colombia

Ecuador
Ecuador

Kiribati

SUDAMÉRICA

Perú
Brasil

Samoa Occidental

Bolivia

Tonga

Trópico de Capricornio

Paraguay

Chile

Uruguay

Argentina

Islas Malvinas

**Los países de
habla española**

Escala de kilómetros
0   1000   2000   3000

0   1000   2000   3000
Escala de millas

vi

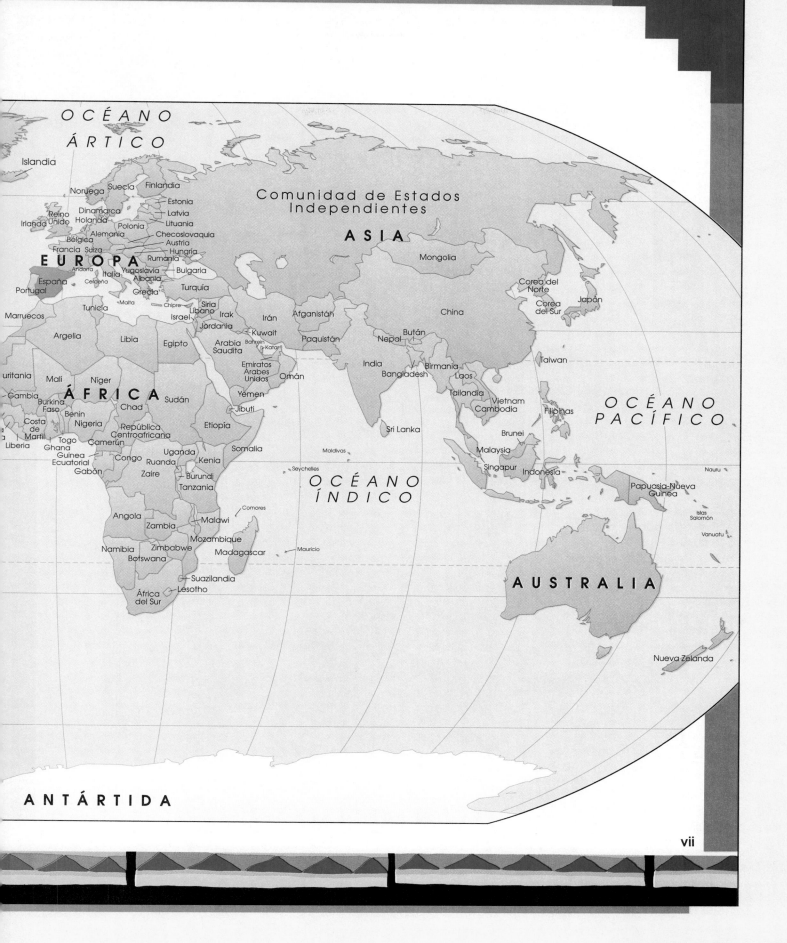

OCÉANO
ÁRTICO

Islandia

OCÉANO
PACÍFICO

Noruega Suecia Finlandia

Reino Dinamarca
Irlanda Unido Holanda
Bélgica
Francia Suiza

EUROPA

España

Portugal

Estonia
Latvia
Lituania
Polonia
Alemania Checoslovaquia
Austria
Hungría
Rumania
Andorra Yugoslavia Bulgaria
Italia Albania
Cerdeña Grecia
Turquía

Comunidad de Estados
Independientes

ASIA

Mongolia

Corea del
Norte

Japón

Corea
del Sur

China

Taiwan

Marruecos

Chipre

Malta Siria
Líbano Irak
Israel Jordania
Kuwait
Bahrein Katar

Irán

Afganistán

Paquistán

Nepal

Butón

Argelia

Tunicia

Libia

Egipto

Arabia
Saudita

Emiratos
Árabes
Unidos Omán

India

Bangladesh

Birmania

Laos

uritania

Mali

Níger

ÁFRICA

Sudán

Yémen

Jibuti

Tailandia
Vietnam
Cambodia

Filipinas

Gambia
Burkina
Faso
Costa Benín
de Nigeria
Marfil Togo
Liberia Ghana
Guinea Camerún
Ecuatorial
Gabón

Chad

República
Centroafricana

Etiopía

Sri Lanka

Brunei

Malaysia

Singapur Indonesia

Nauru

Uganda

Somalia

Maldivas

Congo

Ruanda

Kenia

Seychelles

Zaire

Burundi

Tanzania

Papuasia-Nueva
Guinea

OCÉANO
ÍNDICO

Islas
Salomón

Comores

Vanuatu

Angola

Malawi

Zambia

Mozambique

Mauricio

Namibia

Zimbabwe

Botswana

Madagascar

AUSTRALIA

Suazilandia
Lesotho

África
del Sur

Nueva Zelanda

ANTÁRTIDA

vii

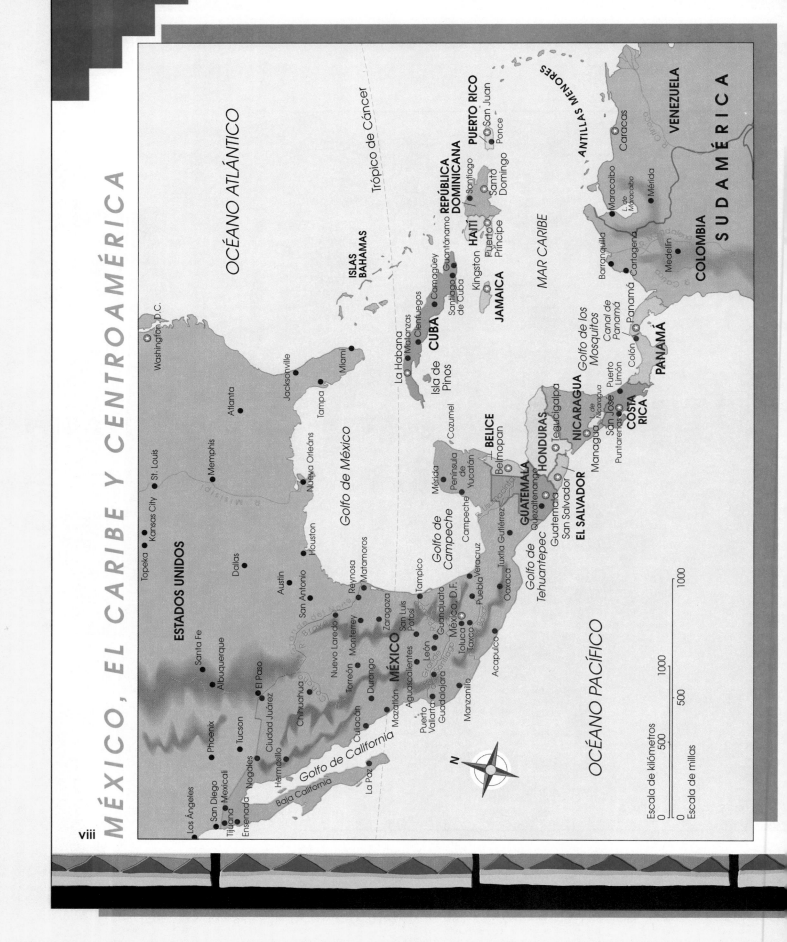

MÉXICO, EL CARIBE Y CENTROAMÉRICA

OCÉANO ATLÁNTICO

Washington, D.C.

Trópico de Cáncer

ISLAS
BAHAMAS

Miami

Jacksonville

Tampa

Atlanta

St. Louis

Memphis

Kansas City

Topeka

ESTADOS UNIDOS

Nueva Orleáns

Golfo de México

La Habana
Matanzas
Cienfuegos

Camagüey

Santiago
de Cuba

CUBA

Isla de
Pinos

Guantánamo

Santiago

**REPÚBLICA
DOMINICANA**

Santo
Domingo

PUERTO RICO

San Juan
Ponce

HAITÍ

Puerto
Príncipe

Kingston

JAMAICA

MAR CARIBE

ANTILLAS MENORES

R. Orinoco

Caracas

VENEZUELA

Maracaibo
L. de
Maracaibo

Mérida

S U D A M É R I C A

Barranquilla

Cartagena

Medellín

COLOMBIA

Panamá

PANAMÁ

Colón

*Canal de
Panamá*

Puerto
Limón

*Golfo de los
Mosquitos*

NICARAGUA

**COSTA
RICA**

San José
Puntarenas

L. de
Nicaragua

Managua

Tegucigalpa

HONDURAS

Belmopán

BELICE

*Península
de
Yucatán*

Mérida

Cozumel

*Golfo de
Campeche*

Campeche

Veracruz

R. Usumacinta

Tuxtla Gutiérrez

Quezaltenango

GUATEMALA

Guatemala

San Salvador

EL SALVADOR

*Golfo de
Tehuantepec*

Oaxaca

Puebla

México, D.F.

Taxco

Toluca

R. Balsas

Acapulco

Manzanillo

Guadalajara

León

Guanajuato

Aguascalientes

San Luis
Potosí

R. Grande de Santiago

Puerto
Vallarta

Durango

MÉXICO

Zaragoza

Tampico

Matamoros

Reynosa

Nuevo Laredo

San Antonio

Austin

Houston

Dallas

Monterrey

Torreón

Culiacán

Mazatlán

R. Bravo del Norte

R. Conchos

Chihuahua

Ciudad Juárez

El Paso

Tucson

Albuquerque

Santa Fe

Phoenix

Nogales

Hermosillo

Mexicali

Tijuana

Ensenada

San Diego

Los Ángeles

La Paz

Baja California

Golfo de California

OCÉANO PACÍFICO

R. Misisipí

Escala de kilómetros
0   500   1000
Escala de millas
0   500   1000

N

SUDAMÉRICA

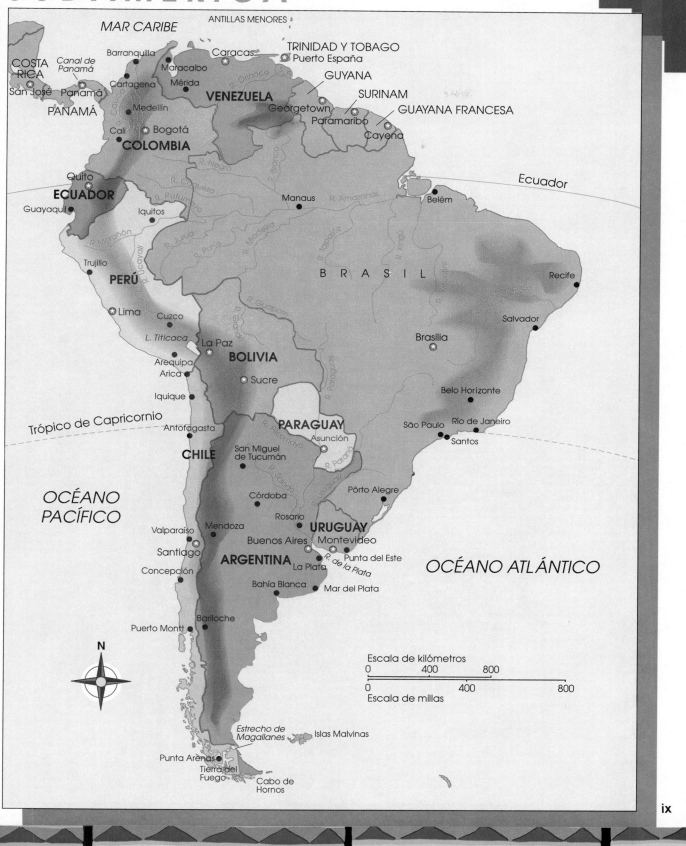

MAR CARIBE

ANTILLAS MENORES

COSTA RICA
Canal de Panamá
Barranquilla
Caracas
TRINIDAD Y TOBAGO
Puerto España
Maracaibo
San José
Panamá
Cartagena
Mérida
VENEZUELA
GUYANA
PANAMÁ
Medellín
Georgetown
SURINAM
Cali
Bogotá
Paramaribo
GUAYANA FRANCESA
COLOMBIA
Cayena
R. Orinoco

Quito
ECUADOR
R. Negro
R. Coquesta
Ecuador
Guayaquil
Iquitos
Manaus
R. Amazonas
Belém
R. Putumayo

R. Marañón
R. Juruá
R. Purus
R. Madeira
R. Tapajós
R. Xingu
Trujillo
PERÚ
B R A S I L
Recife
R. Ucayali
Lima
Cuzco
R. Grande
R. Guaporé
Salvador
L. Titicaca
La Paz
Brasilia
Arequipa
BOLIVIA
Arica
Sucre
R. Paraguay
Iquique
Belo Horizonte
Trópico de Capricornio
PARAGUAY
São Paulo
Río de Janeiro
Antofagasta
Asunción
Santos
R. Pilcomayo
CHILE
San Miguel de Tucumán
R. Salado
OCÉANO PACÍFICO
Córdoba
Pôrto Alegre
R. Paraná
Rosario
Valparaíso
Mendoza
URUGUAY
Santiago
Buenos Aires
Montevideo
Punta del Este
ARGENTINA
La Plata
R. de la Plata
OCÉANO ATLÁNTICO
Concepción
Bahía Blanca
Mar del Plata

Bariloche
Puerto Montt

N

Escala de kilómetros
0   400   800
0   400   800
Escala de millas

Estrecho de Magallanes
Islas Malvinas
Punta Arenas
Tierra del Fuego
Cabo de Hornos

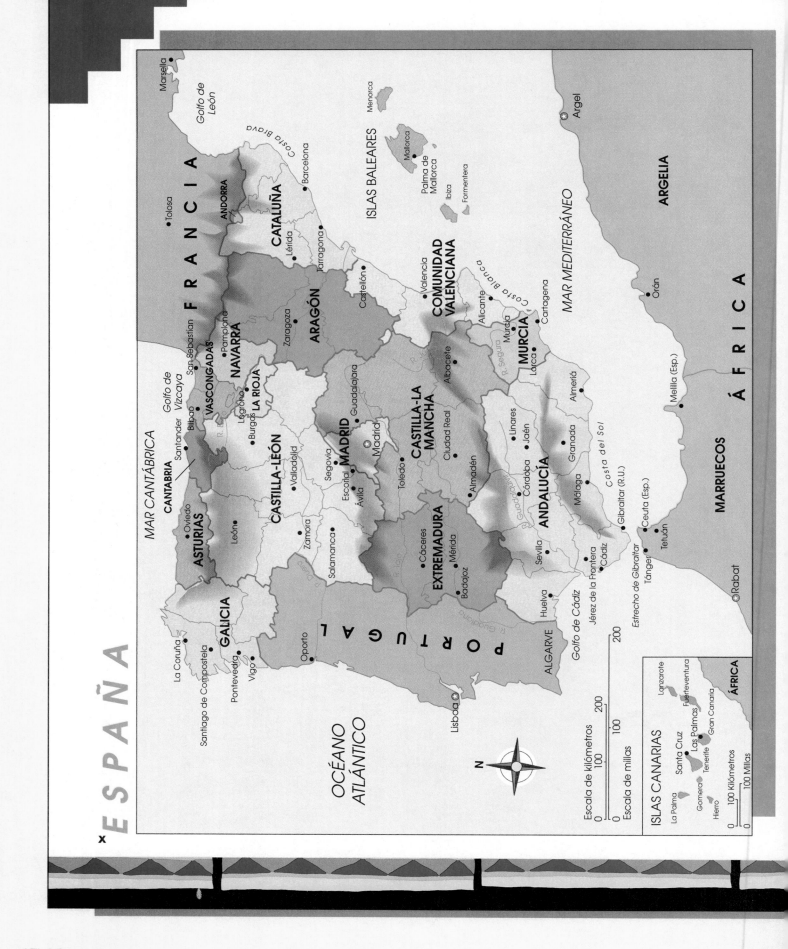

ESPAÑA

OCÉANO ATLÁNTICO

MAR CANTÁBRICO

Golfo de Vizcaya

MAR MEDITERRÁNEO

FRANCIA

Golfo de León

Marsella

Costa Brava

ISLAS BALEARES

Menorca

Mallorca

Palma de Mallorca

Ibiza

Formentera

Argel

ARGELIA

ÁFRICA

ANDORRA

Tolosa

CATALUÑA

Barcelona

Lérida

Tarragona

Castellón

COMUNIDAD VALENCIANA

Valencia

Costa Blanca

Alicante

Murcia

MURCIA

Lorca

Cartagena

Almería

Orán

Melilla (Esp.)

MARRUECOS

San Sebastián

Pamplona

NAVARRA

VASCONGADAS

ARAGÓN

Zaragoza

R. Segura

Albacete

Bilbao

LA RIOJA

Logroño

Burgos

CANTABRIA

Santander

Oviedo

ASTURIAS

León

MADRID

Madrid

Guadalajara

CASTILLA-LA MANCHA

Ciudad Real

Linares

Jaén

Granada

Costa del Sol

Málaga

Gibraltar (R.U.)

Ceuta (Esp.)

Tetuán

Tánger

Rabat

Segovia

Escorial

Ávila

Valladolid

CASTILLA-LEÓN

Zamora

Salamanca

Toledo

Almadén

Córdoba

ANDALUCÍA

Sevilla

Jérez de la Frontera

Cádiz

Estrecho de Gibraltar

Golfo de Cádiz

Cáceres

EXTREMADURA

Mérida

Badajoz

Huelva

R. Guadiana

R. Guadalquivir

GALICIA

La Coruña

Santiago de Compostela

Pontevedra

Vigo

Oporto

PORTUGAL

ALGARVE

Lisboa

R. Tajo

R. Duero

200

N

Escala de kilómetros
0   100   200

Escala de millas
0   100   200

ISLAS CANARIAS

Lanzarote

Fuerteventura

Santa Cruz

Las Palmas

Gran Canaria

La Palma

Gomera

Tenerife

Hierro

ÁFRICA

0   100 Kilómetros
0   100 Millas

¿Cómo te llamas tú?

Here are some of the most frequently used names in Spanish. Find your name in the list or select a name you would like to be called.

Chicos

Alberto (Beto)	Javier
Alejandro (Alex)	Jerónimo
Alfonso	Joaquín
Alfredo	Jorge
Andrés	José (Pepe)
Antonio (Toni, Toño)	Juan (Juancho)
Arturo (Tudi)	Julio
Benjamín	Lorenzo
Bernardo	Lucas
Carlos	Luis
César	Manuel (Manolo)
Clemente (Tito)	Marcos
Cristóbal	Mariano
Daniel (Dani)	Mario
David	Martín
Diego	Mateo
Eduardo (Edi)	Miguel
Emilio	Nicolás (Nico)
Enrique (Quico)	Octavio
Ernesto	Óscar
Esteban	Pablo
Federico (Fede)	Patricio
Felipe	Pedro
Fernando (Nando)	Rafael (Rafa)
Francisco (Cisco,	Ramiro
Paco, Pancho)	Ramón
Gabriel (Gabi)	Raúl
Germán	Ricardo (Riqui)
Gilberto	Roberto (Beto)
Gonzalo	Rodrigo (Rodri)
Gregorio	Rubén
Guillermo (Memo)	Salvador
Gustavo	Samuel
Hernán	Sancho
Homero	Santiago (Santi)
Horacio	Sergio
Hugo	Teodoro
Ignacio (Nacho)	Timoteo
Jacobo	Tomás
Jaime	Víctor

Chicas

Adela	Guadalupe (Lupe)
Adriana	Inés
Alicia	Irene
Amalia	Isabel (Chavela)
Ana	Josefina (Pepita)
Anita	Juana (Juanita)
Ángela	Julia
Antonia (Toni)	Laura
Bárbara	Leonor
Beatriz (Bea)	Leticia (Leti)
Berta	Lilia
Blanca	Lucía
Carla	Luisa
Carlota	Marcela (Chela)
Carmen	Margarita (Rita)
Carolina	María
Catalina	Mariana
Cecilia	Maricarmen
Clara	Marilú
Concepción (Concha,	Marta
Conchita)	Mercedes (Meche)
Cristina (Cris, Tina)	Mónica
Débora	Natalia (Nati)
Diana	Norma
Dolores (Lola)	Patricia (Pati)
Dorotea (Dora)	Pilar
Elena	Ramona
Elisa	Raquel
Eloísa	Rebeca
Elvira	Rosa (Rosita)
Emilia (Emi)	Sara
Estela	Silvia
Ester	Sofía
Eva	Soledad (Sole)
Florencia	Sonia
Francisca (Paca,	Susana (Susanita)
Paquita)	Teresa (Tere)
Gabriela (Gabi)	Verónica (Vero)
Gloria	Victoria (Vicki)
Graciela (Chela)	Yolanda (Yoli)

PASO A PASO CON

¡DIME!

UNIDAD 1

xiii

xiv

U N I D A D 3

¿Qué hacen ustedes?   102
México D.F., México

xv

xvi

U N I D A D 5

xvii

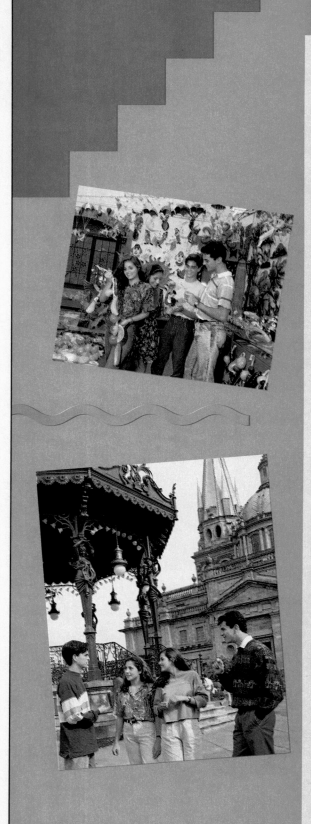

xviii

U N I D A D 7

U N I D A D 8

¡En camino a Segovia!   360
Segovia, España

xx

Paso a paso con ¡DIME!

Purpose This miniunit is specially designed to familiarize students with the organization of **¡DIME!** The **Lección preliminar** leads students through all the steps of a regular lesson (except **Escribamos un poco**) as they learn to talk about their immediate surroundings. Upon completion of **Paso a paso con ¡DIME!** students should have learned the purpose of each section of a lesson by actually having done it.

ANTES DE EMPEZAR

Purpose To get students to examine the format of **¡DIME!** and to help them anticipate how each section works.

ANTICIPEMOS

PARA EMPEZAR

¿QUÉ DECIMOS...?

CHARLEMOS UN POCO

CHARLEMOS UN POCO MÁS

Dramatizaciones

IMPACTO CULTURAL

Y ahora, ¡a leer!

LEAMOS AHORA

ESCRIBAMOS UN POCO

¿POR QUÉ SE DICE ASÍ?

¿Qué piensas tú?

1. You should recognize the book pictured here. What is its title? What do you think the title means?

2. Flip through Unit 1. Now look at Lesson 1. Find each of the titles listed above. Then look at Lessons 2 and 3. Does every lesson have all of the titles? Where do you have to look for the section titled **¿Por qué se dice así?**

3. Although you may not understand all the Spanish in the titles, words such as **anticipemos, cultural,** and **dramatizaciones** probably suggest some meaning to you. What do you think these three words mean? Why can you guess their meanings?

4. Now look carefully at one of the lessons in Unit 1 or Unit 2. Try to decide what each section is for. Write down what you believe is the primary purpose of each section listed. Then, in groups of three or four, compare your list with those of your classmates and try to come to a group consensus on the purpose of each section. Don't try to translate the titles—just observe what each section does or asks you to do.

5. Look at the photos. What class is this? What book are these students using? What is going on in each of the pictures? How do these students and their teacher feel about learning Spanish?

6. In the next couple of class hours, you will work with a model lesson of *¡Dime!* As you do each section, check your group observations, and see if you can figure out what each title means.

7. What do you think the purpose of these two pages is?

Suggestions Ask students to look at the mural on the cover of ¡DIME! and to speculate on its meaning. Then have them flip through the first two units to find each subtitle and figure out what is happening in each section. Finally use the photos to have students focus on cooperative pair and small-group work.

▸ **7 Students should reason that they have examined the format of the textbook in order to help them work with it.**

ANTES DE EMPEZAR

¿Qué piensas tú?

1 Allow students to speculate about the meaning of the textbook title. If they guess it means a ten-cent coin, ask why a Spanish book would be called that. Point out the existence of cognates and the danger of false cognates when learning a foreign language. Mention that **¡Dime!** means *Tell me!* and strongly invites the students to speak.

2 Students should discover that the *Impacto cultural* section (including *Y ahora, ¡a leer!*) occurs only in Lessons 1 and 2, and that the *Leamos ahora* and *Escribamos un poco* sections occur only in Lesson 3. The *¿Por qué se dice así?* section is found at the back of the book.

3 Point out that the words **anticipemos, cultural,** and **dramatizaciones** are cognates— that is, words that look like and have the same meanings as (or meanings similar to) their English equivalents. Tell students that if they learn to recognize cognates, they will be able to expand their vocabulary quickly.

4 Divide students into groups of three and assign each group three of the section titles. It does not matter that several groups will have the same three items. Allow 6–8 min for groups to find their titles and write down what they think the purpose of the section is. Then ask all groups that worked on the same three titles to read what they wrote. If the groups differ, turn to that section of Unit 1, Lesson 1 and help them get to the correct answer. Repeat the process until the purpose of all the sections has been explained.

5 Point out that it is a Spanish class, that students are doing paired/ group work, that the teacher uses video and visuals, and that everyone seems to be having a good time.

6 Have students make reasoned guesses at the meaning of each section title as they complete each section in *Lección preliminar.*

OBJECTIVES

Communicative Goal

• Naming classroom objects and school supplies

Culture and Reading

• *¡No metas la pata!*
  ¡De Nuevo México a Nueva York! Avoiding cross-cultural misunderstandings when talking about food
• *Y ahora, ¡a leer!*
  ¿Inglés o español? Using cognates

Structure

• LP.1 Gender of nouns: Introduction
• LP.2 Indefinite and definite articles

ACTIVE VOCABULARY

This section lists the vocabulary that students are responsible for upon completing each lesson. The list includes all the words and expressions that students are asked to produce in the *Charlemos un poco* and *Charlemos un poco más* sections. A few high-frequency expressions from the *Para empezar* and *¿Qué decimos ... ?* sections are also listed.

¡OJO! There are no active vocabulary lists in the Student Text. Instead, students are asked to generate their own **vocabulario personal** lists at the end of each lesson in the **Cuaderno de práctica.** To guide students to create their own vocabulary lists as complete as the one in the Teacher's Edition, identical section titles **(Materiales escolares, En el colegio, Palabras y expresiones)** and more than adequate space are provided in the **Cuaderno de práctica.**

¡Ajá! ¡Hay un libro!

Materiales escolares

bolígrafo	lista
borrador	mochila
carpeta	papel
cuaderno	hoja de papel
lápiz	regla
libro	tiza

En el colegio

clase	pizarra
escritorio	profesor(a)
español	puerta
estudiante	pupitre
mesa	silla

Palabras y expresiones

en	¡Ajá!
gracias	¡Ay!
hay	¡Caramba!
no	¿Qué?
sí	

Artículos

el	un, una
la	unos, unas

A N T I C I P E M O S

¡Ahorros para el colegio!

Bolígrafos
3/$1.00

Lápices
$1.39

Borradores
$1.69

Cuadernos
$2.50

Papel
$1.69

Calculadoras
$10.95

Tiza
$1.19

Mochilas
$8.99

Carpetas
$.99

Reglas
$1.49

Libros
$5.95

¿Qué piensas tú?

1. What is being sold in this advertisement? When did it appear? Who is expected to read it?

2. Which of the items in the ad do you consider absolutely necessary for school? Does your school require you to have any of these items? Are there any items here you can get along without?

3. Which of the items for sale here do you have with you now?

4. What do you think you will be able to talk about when you have finished this lesson?

Purpose This section gets students to focus on language related to the classroom and encourages them to use critical thinking skills to predict what they will be able to do when they have completed this lesson.

Suggestions Use the photo and the advertisement to introduce the lesson content. The *¿Qué piensas tú?* questions are designed to familiarize students with the lesson vocabulary. Do not expect students to memorize this vocabulary. The goal at this point is simply to raise awareness of and to spark interest in the lesson theme.

¿Qué piensas tú?

These questions are asked and answered in English to get students to focus on the content of the lesson. Whenever students answer in English, repeat key vocabulary in Spanish and have the class repeat after you so that students will start familiarizing themselves with the new lesson vocabulary.

Answers

1 School supplies are being sold: pens, pencils, notebooks, folders, backpacks, erasers, chalk, calculators, books, and rulers. The ad probably appeared at the beginning of the school year. Students and their parents are expected to read it.
2 Answers will vary.
3 Answers will vary.
4 Students will be able to talk about school supplies: what they have, what they need, and what they can buy at the stationery store.

Video Notes

The action of the video in the next two sections, *Para empezar* and *¿Qué decimos ... ?,* takes place in a Spanish-speaking community in the United States. The actors are Puerto Rican.

The pronunciation of the two teenagers, Juan and Armando, falls within the normal range of variations found throughout the Spanish-speaking world. Your students, however, might notice that when Armando says **Juan,** he pronounces the word-final **n** as an English *ng*. They may also think that Juan, when he says **A ver . . .** and "whispers" the word-final **r,** has actually "dropped" it .

For an explanation of the icons used on pages 6–7, including the digital video clock and the videodisc barcodes, see the Teacher's Introduction.

PARA EMPEZAR

Comprehensible Input 1

```
TAPE/
DISC
00:00–
01:56
```

Side 1, 9 to 3500

Comprehension Checks

Use **Comprehension Checks** to determine comprehension without translation. Look for yes/no and one- or two-word answers. If responses are weak or uncertain, clarify in Spanish.

A set of **Comprehension Checks** is on cards in the Teacher's Resource Package.

1   00:08

Suggestions **Puerta:** Point to the door in the photo and in your classroom. **¿Quién sabe?:** Gesture. **Indicios:** Go around the class, pretending to look for clues.
1 ¿Es la puerta de una clase? ¿Qué es? *(Point to door.)*
2 ¿Sabemos qué clase es?
3 ¿Es él detective? ¿Eres tú detective? ¿Eres tú un(a) buen(a) detective? *(Ask several students.)*
4 ¿Busca indicios un buen detective? ¿Qué busca un detective?
5 ¿Quién busca indicios, el detective o el profesor? ¿Busca indicios para resolver el misterio?

Side 1, 250 to 888

2   00:30

Suggestions Point to items on transparency (or in room).
1 ¿Es una clase?
2 ¿Hay pupitres / un escritorio de profesor / una mesa con sillas / un borrador y tiza / una pizarra? ¿Qué hay? *(Point to each again.)*
3 ¿Hay una mochila? ¿Dónde está la mochila, en un pupitre o en el escritorio del profesor?
4 ¿Qué hay en el pupitre, una mochila o un borrador?

Side 1, 906 to 1556

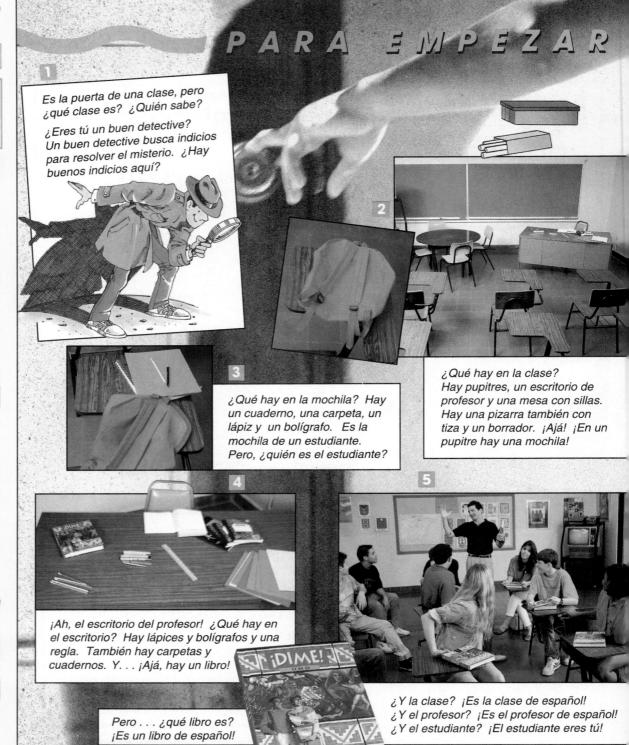

Es la puerta de una clase, pero ¿qué clase es? ¿Quién sabe?

¿Eres tú un buen detective? Un buen detective busca indicios para resolver el misterio. ¿Hay buenos indicios aquí?

¿Qué hay en la clase? Hay pupitres, un escritorio de profesor y una mesa con sillas. Hay una pizarra también con tiza y un borrador. ¡Ajá! ¡En un pupitre hay una mochila!

¿Qué hay en la mochila? Hay un cuaderno, una carpeta, un lápiz y un bolígrafo. Es la mochila de un estudiante. Pero, ¿quién es el estudiante?

¡Ah, el escritorio del profesor! ¿Qué hay en el escritorio? Hay lápices y bolígrafos y una regla. También hay carpetas y cuadernos. Y. . . ¡Ajá, hay un libro!

Pero . . . ¿qué libro es? ¡Es un libro de español!

¿Y la clase? ¡Es la clase de español! ¿Y el profesor? ¡Es el profesor de español! ¿Y el estudiante? ¡El estudiante eres tú!

6   seis

3   00:52

1 ¿Es una mochila? *(Point to back-pack.)*
2 ¿Hay un cuaderno / una carpeta / un lápiz y un bolígrafo?
3 ¿Es la mochila de un profesor o de un estudiante?

Side 1, 1574 to 2205

4   01:14

1 ¿Es un pupitre o un escritorio?
2 ¿Hay lápices / bolígrafos / carpetas y cuadernos en el escritorio? ¿Hay una o dos reglas? *(Gesture.)* ¿Qué hay? *(Point to each item again.)* ¿Hay un libro? ¿Es un libro de español o de matemáticas?

Side 1, 2223 to 3031

5   01:41

1 ¿Es la clase de español o de matemáticas?
2 ¿Es el profesor de español?
3 Y el estudiante, ¿eres tú? *(Ask several students.)*

Side 1, 3049 to 3500

¿QUÉ DECIMOS...?

En la librería

¿Qué más hay en la lista?

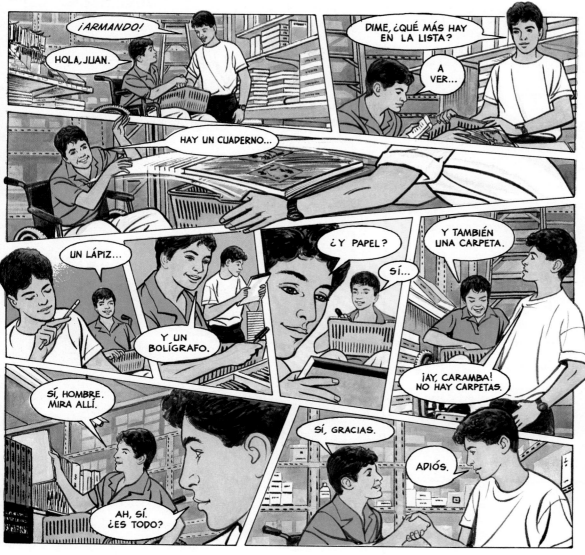

01:57–
03:00

Side 1, 3519 to 5409

Early Production Checks

Use the **Early Production Checks** to verify the students' comprehension and to guide their first productive efforts. These questions are designed to require students to respond using new vocabulary and structures. Students should not be expected to respond in complete sentences every time. Always begin by identifying the characters and by recycling descriptive and/or other appropriate, previously learned material.

A complete set of the **Early Production Checks** is available on cards in the Teacher's Resource Package.

1   **02:01**

¿Qué más hay en la lista?
1 ¿Hay un cuaderno?
2 ¿Hay un lápiz?
3 ¿Hay un bolígrafo?
4 ¿Qué más hay en la lista? ¿una carpeta?
5 ¿Qué hay en la lista?

Side 1, 3639 to 5409

Purpose *Para empezar* and *¿Qué decimos ... ?* are designed to teach the new lesson vocabulary and structures in "real-life" situations. Students should not be overly concerned about understanding every word. The **Comprehension Checks** and **Early Production Checks** will identify the language students will be expected to produce.

Suggestions Have students close books while you narrate each section, using tranparencies to clarify meaning without translation. Then ask the **Comprehension** and **Early Production Checks.** Repeat with each section. You may want to pretend you are the detective and act out the scenario.

Using the video Play one section at a time after narrating it using the transparencies. Freeze the video and ask the questions in the **Comprehension Checks** and **Early Production Checks.** Repeat this process with each section.

CHARLEMOS UN POCO

Guided Practice

A. ¿Qué hay en la lista?
Read the list out of order and ask students to hold up the item mentioned. Then call on individuals to hold up an item and have the class tell what it is.

B. ¿Qué hay en la clase?
Call out the numbers in sequence as you have students identify each item. If students have difficulty with the numbers, simply show them with your fingers. The numbers 0–30 are taught in Unit 2.
1 Hay una pizarra.
2 Hay un escritorio.
3 Hay un bolígrafo.
4 Hay una hoja de papel.
5 Hay una mesa con sillas.
6 Hay un lápiz.
7 Hay una mochila.
8 Hay un libro.
9 Hay un cuaderno.
10 Hay un borrador.

Extension Point to the same items in the class and have the students name them. Then point to other items and have students name them: chalkboard, student's desk, chair, etc.

Using the margin boxes
The margin boxes contain focused grammar explanations and vocabulary that students will need in order to do the corresponding activities. Teachers have the flexibility to limit the grammar explanation to what is in the box, to teach the corresponding structures in the *¿Por qué se dice así?* section at back of the book before or after doing the activities, or simply to assign the grammar as homework and make the students responsible for learning it. Make sure students understand that the structure explanations in the boxes are brief summaries. Detailed explanations appear in the *¿Por qué se dice así?* section and should be referred to as necessary.

To help you do the activities, the side columns in this section contain explanations and vocabulary. If you want more information, use the page references listed for the *¿Por qué se dice así?* section in the back of the book.

Nouns
Naming objects

Nouns name people, places, things, or concepts. Spanish nouns are either masculine or feminine.

Masculino	Femenino
libro	mochila
cuaderno	carpeta
lápiz	clase
papel	pizarra

See **¿Por qué se dice así?**, *page G2, section LP. 1.*

The indefinite article: *un, una*
Used to refer to things in general

Hay **un** libro en la clase.
Hay **una** silla en la clase.

See **¿Por qué se dice así?**, *page G2, section LP. 1.*

The verb *hay*

Hay means both *there is* and *there are.* When used in a question, it means *Is there?* or *Are there?*

¿**Hay** pizarras?
Sí, **hay** una pizarra.

CHARLEMOS UN POCO

A. ¿Qué hay en la lista? Your teacher wants to check that you have the supplies you will need for class. Hold up the items as your teacher reads the list.

> un bolígrafo   un cuaderno
> una carpeta   una regla
> un libro de español   una hoja de papel
> un lápiz

B. ¿Qué hay en la clase? Tell what there is in the classroom below by naming the numbered items you see.

MODELO   número 1
Hay una pizarra.

LECCIÓN PRELIMINAR

C. ¿En la mochila? Ask your partner questions to find out what school supplies are in his or her backpack.

 MODELO Tú: **¿Hay un lápiz?**
Compañero(a): **Sí, hay un lápiz.** o
No, no hay un lápiz.

CH. ¿Mi carpeta? A friend calls to see if he left a folder in your room. Answer your friend's questions.

 MODELO mesa: lápiz / regla
Compañero(a): **¿Qué hay en la mesa?**
Tú: **Hay un lápiz y una regla.**

1. mochila: libro / lápiz
2. mesa: papel / libro
3. cuaderno: bolígrafo / lápiz
4. escritorio: carpeta / cuaderno
5. carpeta: papel / bolígrafo

CHARLEMOS UN POCO MÁS

A. ¡Lo más importante! Make a list of the three things that you think are most important to have for school. Ask three classmates what items are on their lists. If someone has listed the same three items that you have, go to the board and write the items on your lists.

 EJEMPLO Tú: **¿Hay un lápiz en la lista?**
Compañero(a): **Sí, hay un lápiz.** o **No, no hay un lápiz.**

B. ¿En el pupitre? Prepare a list of all the items you can see on one of your classmate's desk but keep the identity of your classmate a secret. Then try to discover the identity of the classmate your partner selected by asking questions. Your partner will then ask you questions as he or she tries to identify the classmate you selected.

EJEMPLO Tú: **¿Hay un bolígrafo en el pupitre?**
Compañero(a): **Sí, hay un bolígrafo.** o
No, no hay un bolígrafo.

LECCIÓN PRELIMINAR

The ***Charlemos un poco más*** activities are designed to allow students to create with language recently learned. Although some activities may appear repetitious of the guided practice in the previous section, they are in fact more open-ended and enable students to be more creative—here, naming school objects.

C. ¿Cuál es la diferencia? Have students sit facing each other and holding their books or pictures up so their partners may not see them. Allow 3–4 min to ask questions and then call on individuals to tell what the differences are.

CH. ¡A escribir! After 2 min are up, have a couple of pairs write their lists on the board. Ask the class if they can add to the list. Correct any spelling errors.

DRAMATIZACIONES

> *Evaluation*

En la librería. Allow 4–5 min to prepare role plays. Ask for volunteers to present their role plays to the class.

Note This role play is not to be written out and memorized but rather presented extemporaneously.

C. ¿Cuál es la diferencia? Without looking at each other's pictures, find four differences in the back-to-school sale advertisement below and the one your teacher gives your partner.

EJEMPLO Tú: **¿Hay una regla?**
Compañero(a): **Sí, hay una regla.** o **No, no hay una regla.**

¡Todo para el estudiante!

Mochilas $10.98

PRECIOS ESPECIALES PARA EL REGRESO A CLASES

Reglas $1.19

Lápices $.49

Libros $6.95

Carpetas $1.09

℗ papelería luna

CH. ¡A escribir! Working in pairs and with books closed, you have exactly two minutes to list as many items as you can see in the classroom.

Dramatizaciones

En la librería. Your best friend broke his leg yesterday. You and another friend have offered to do some shopping for him, since tomorrow is the first day of school. Role-play your shopping trip as you go through the list of school supplies that your best friend needs.

You
- Ask your friend what is on the list.
- Say there are three of the items on the table. Tell which ones.
- Say there are [*the two remaining items*] in [*store in your city*].

Friend
- Name at least five items.
- Say there are no [*the two remaining items*].
- Say thank you.

Purpose The role plays in *Dramatizaciones* are designed to recycle the structures and vocabulary needed to talk about school supplies. Encourage students to work without their textbooks when performing their role plays.

¡No metas la pata!

¡De Nuevo México a Nueva York! Ellen Pierce has just moved from New Mexico to a Puerto Rican section of New York City, where she has become good friends with Yolanda Salas. Read their conversation and then answer the question that follows.

Ellen: **I'm hungry.**
Yolanda: **So am I. Why don't you come to my house for dinner? Mamá will fix you some typical Puerto Rican food.**
Ellen: **I'd love to. I'm starving for some good old frijoles, tacos, or enchiladas. I haven't had them since I left New Mexico.**
Yolanda: **Tacos? Enchiladas? We don't eat them! We're from Puerto Rico!**

Why does Yolanda seem upset with Ellen?

1. Yolanda's mother doesn't know how to prepare tacos and enchiladas.
2. Yolanda doesn't like tacos and enchiladas.
3. Ellen assumes that all Spanish-speaking people eat tacos and enchiladas.

❑ Check your answer on page 416.

LECCIÓN PRELIMINAR

¡No metas la pata!

Purpose The *¡No metas la pata!* section provides additional reading practice in Spanish (this one is in English since it is a model lesson). Here students learn to avoid cross-cultural misunderstandings when talking about food.

Suggestions Have students read the dialogue silently. Then have them select a response to the question that follows. Ask how many selected response 1 and why. Repeat with responses 2 and 3 before having students check their answers on page 416. Ask students if they know the names of foods from other Spanish-speaking countries.

Answers

1 We have no way of knowing if Yolanda's mother knows how to prepare tacos and enchiladas. Reread the conversation and try another answer.
2 This may be correct, but there is no indication of this in the girls' conversation. You should not jump to conclusions. Try again.
③ Ellen doesn't say this, but she implies it. This is the correct answer. New Mexican food is heavily influenced by the foods of Mexico. Puerto Ricans don't eat many corn-based foods. Rather, their diet tends to consist of rice dishes, fried bananas, chicken, and pork.

Y ahora, ¡a leer!

Antes de empezar

The **Antes de empezar** questions are an advance organizer for the **¿Inglés o español?** reading that follows.

Suggestion Use these questions to develop recognition of cognates before doing the reading.

Answers

1 All of them.
Point out Many words, especially those related to New World foods or to ranching and farming, have been borrowed from Spanish for use in English.
2 roast beef, jersey, telephone, pudding, hamburger, sweater, tennis, home run, baseball
Point out Spanish, too, has borrowed many words from English.
3 air, center, professor, conversation, problem, national
Point out The spelling of many Spanish words is only a little different from English words that have the same meaning. The pronunciation, however, may be quite different.

Verifiquemos

Answers

1 All of them are Spanish words. Fourteen are also English words: actor, animal, artificial, color, director, doctor, error, formal, hospital, hotel, ideal, piano, principal, similar
Point out Many words in Spanish and English are spelled alike or almost alike and have the same meaning.
2 Answers will vary.

Y ahora, ¡a leer!

Antes de empezar

Palabras. As you begin to study Spanish, you will be glad to learn that you already know or can guess the meaning of many Spanish words. To prove this to yourself, answer the following questions, working in groups of three or four. Remember that although you may be able to recognize these words in reading them, the Spanish pronunciation may be quite different from English.

1. How many of the following English words have been borrowed from Spanish?

rodeo	chocolate	corral
tomato	ranch	potato
lasso	tobacco	patio

2. The following Spanish words were borrowed from English. What do they mean?

rosbif	pudín	tenis
jersey	hamburguesa	jonrón
teléfono	suéter	béisbol

3. Write the English equivalent of the following Spanish words.

aire	profesor	problema
centro	conversación	nacional

Verifiquemos

Look at the words in the box on the next page. Then answer the following questions.

1. In your opinion, how many of the words in the box are Spanish words? How many are English words?
2. Are there any words you don't understand? Which ones?

Purpose The **Y ahora, ¡a leer!** section is intended to provide additional reading practice. Here students learn about cognates and borrowed words in Spanish and English.

¿Inglés o español?

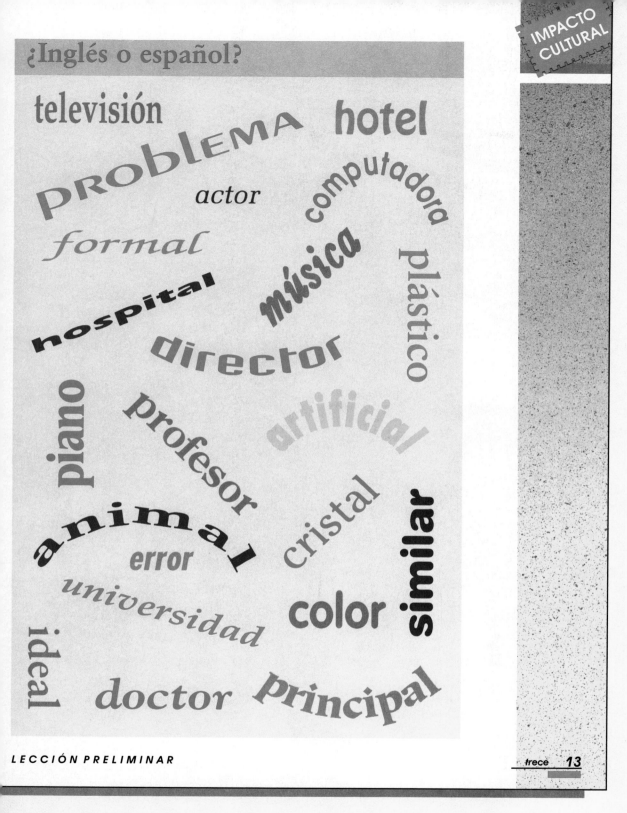

television
PROBLEMA hotel
actor
computadora
formal
música
plástico
hospital
director
piano
profesor
artificial
animal
cristal
similar
error
color
universidad
ideal
doctor
principal

LECCIÓN PRELIMINAR

UNIT OBJECTIVES

Communicative Goals

When students have completed this unit, they will be able to use Spanish . . .
- to exchange greetings
- to say good-bye
- to introduce themselves and others
- to respond to introductions
- to name Hispanic countries and their capitals
- to give information about where people are from
- to describe people's personality traits and physical characteristics
- to express negative ideas

Culture

In this unit, students will discover similarities and differences between the United States and Hispanic countries and communities . . .
- when addressing people
- when referring to "Americans"

Reading and Writing Strategies

- Reading: Using cognates
- Writing: Brainstorming— listing and clustering

Structure

- Subject pronouns: Singular forms and use
- The verb **ser**: Singular forms
- **¿De dónde . . . ?** and **ser de . . .**
- Gender of nouns and adjectives

UNIDAD 1

¡Hola! ¿Qué tal?

UNIT SETTING

Montebello, California, is located nine miles east of the Los Angeles Civic Center. In 1847, it was the site of the Battle of Río San Gabriel, the decisive military encounter that freed California from Mexican rule and led eventually to statehood. Montebello has an estimated population of 58,200, with more than half its residents of Hispanic origin. In this respect, Montebello is representative of many Californian communities. The 1990 census indicates that the Hispanic population of California already exceeds the total population of all but eight states. The Hispanic

Oregón

Océano Pacífico

Sacramento ✪

San Francisco

Nevada

CALIFORNIA

Montebello

Los Ángeles

San Diego

Arizona

| 0 | 200 Kilómetros |
| 0 | 200 Millas |

population of Los Angeles is 1,391,411 out of 3,485,398, an increase of 70.7 percent during the last decade. Predictions are that this trend will continue in the 1990's, leaving California's non-Hispanic white population in the minority by the year 2000.

Video Notes

Each video unit opens with a colorful montage. You may wish to play it as an introduction to the unit.

To play the montage, use counter or bar code:

`03:06` - `03:47`

Side 1, 5655 to 6884

To play the entire unit without stopping:

`03:06` - `08:15`

Side 1, 5655 to 35399

In the American Southwest, there is a Spanish-speaking community dating back to the founding of Santa Fe, NM, in 1610. Features of Southwest Spanish predominate in the video. You will notice **oye** and **ella** pronounced as *óie* and *éia* at times. Also, the Spanish vowel **e** tends to drift toward the English *e* in *pet*. These features are not necessarily attributable to English-language influence, since they are heard elsewhere in the Spanish-speaking world.

In communities such as Montebello, it is also common to hear "Anglos" speak Spanish fluently. For example, Mr. Whitaker, the history teacher, is proud to be able to converse in Spanish with his students and colleagues.

Photo

Montebello High School has a student population of around 2800, drawn from parts of East Los Angeles, Pico Rivera, and Montebello. Approximately 85 percent of the students are Hispanic.

OBJECTIVES

Communicative Goals

- Exchanging greetings
- Identifying people
- Saying good-bye

Culture and Reading

- **¡No metas la pata!**
  ¿Cómo estás? Appropriate form of address
- **Y ahora, ¡a leer!**
  Tú y usted: Informal and formal address
  Saludos y despedidas: General public greetings

Grammar

- 1.1 Subject pronouns: Singular forms
- 1.2 The verb **ser:** Singular forms
- 1.3 Subject pronouns: Use

¡Ojo! There are no active vocabulary lists in the Student Text. Instead, students are asked to generate their own **vocabulario personal** lists at the end of each lesson in the **Cuaderno de práctica.** To guide students to create their own vocabulary lists as complete as the one is the Teacher's Edition, identical section titles **(Materiales escolares, En el colegio, Palabras y expresiones)** and more than adequate space are provided in the **Cuaderno de práctica.**

ACTIVE VOCABULARY

This section lists the vocabulary students are responsible for upon completing each lesson. The list includes all words and expressions that students are asked to produce in the **Charlemos un poco** and **Charlemos un poco más** sections. A few high-frequency expressions from the **Para empezar** and **¿Qué decimos … ?** sections are also listed.

¡Estupendo!

Saludos

Buenos días.
Buenas tardes.
Buenas noches.
¿Cómo está usted?
¿Cómo estás?
¡Hola!
¿Qué tal?
saludo

Respuestas

Bien, gracias.
Bien, ¿y tú?
¡Fatal!
Muy bien, gracias. ¿Y usted?
¡Terrible!

Despedidas

Adiós.
Hasta luego.
Hasta mañana.
despedida

Verbos

ser
  soy
  eres
  es

Personas

amigo(a)
chico(a)
director(a)
él
ella
señor, Sr.
señora, Sra.
señorita, Srta.
tú
usted
yo

Palabras y expresiones

escuela
mi
perro
y

¿Por qué?
¿Quién?

Exclamaciones

¡Ay!
¡Estupendo!
Perdón.
¡Pobrecito(a)!
Por favor.

ANTICIPEMOS

¿ Qué piensas tú ?

1. Who do you think the people are in each of these photos?

2. What do you think the people are saying in each of the photos? Why?

3. Notice what the people are doing in each of the photos. What gestures are they making?

4. What similarities and differences do you observe between what you might do and what these people are doing?

5. What do you think you will learn to say and do in this lesson?

¿Qué piensas tú?

Answers

1 Students should note different relationships: teachers/students, friends (female/female, male/female, male/male).

2 Hello, how are you?, Good-bye, See you later, Glad to see you, This is [name], etc. Behaviors suggest greeting, meeting, taking leave.

3 Kissing, shaking hands, etc.

Point out Spanish-speaking people often shake hands when greeting. Women often kiss on the cheek (one cheek in Latin America, both in Spain), and men shake hands or embrace but do not kiss. Hispanics greet more often than Americans. It is even polite to greet strangers in certain situations, such as when entering a doctor's waiting room. Ask students to greet each other and you, both in and out of class.

4 In the United States, students in a school setting are less likely to kiss, shake hands.

Point out Shaking hands and kissing on the cheek mean good-bye as well as hello.

▶ **5 Students will learn to exchange greetings and say good-bye.**

Purpose To focus on the language used in greeting and saying good-bye, and to develop and use critical thinking skills by encouraging students to observe, analyze, and compare cultural differences without forming judgments.

Suggestions The questions are designed to get students to anticipate what they will learn in the lesson. Although some of the answers may seem obvious, students need to answer them in order to focus on the vocabulary and language functions being taught. Have students explain their answers. Help them discover cross-cultural similarities when greeting and taking leave. The last question always asks students to identify the communicative goals of the lesson.

PARA EMPEZAR

Comprehensible Input 1

 TAPE/DISC 03:47–06:23

Side 1, 6900 to 11601

Comprehension Checks

Ask these questions to determine comprehension without translation. Look for yes/no and one- or two-word answers. If responses are weak or uncertain, provide additional clarification in Spanish. A complete set of the **Comprehension Checks** is available on cards in the Teacher's Resource Package.

1 03:56

Note The video clock at the beginning of each list of questions corresponds to the counter in the lower right corner of the video screen.
1 ¿Es una escuela?
2 ¿Qué escuela es?
3 ¿Es Ana?
4 ¿Es una estudiante? *(Ask about yourself, students.)*

Side 1, 7167 to 7799

2 04:18

1 ¿Es Beto Chávez?
2 ¿Quién es él?
3 Y ella, ¿es Ana?
4 ¿Es Ana Chávez?
5 ¿Es Ana Montoya?
6 ¿Cómo está Ana? ¿Muy bien?
7 ¿Cómo está Beto? ¿Bien o muy bien?

Point out **Beto** is short for any name ending in **-berto**, such as **Alberto** or **Roberto**.

Side 1, 7817 to 8601

3 04:45

1 ¿Quién es?
2 ¿Es profesor?
3 ¿Es el profesor de historia? *(Ask about yourself.)*
4 ¿Dice "Buenos días"? *(Point to morning hours on clock.)*

5 ¿Qué dice?
6 ¿Y los estudiantes dicen "Buenos días, profesor"?
7 ¿Qué dicen los estudiantes?

Side 1, 8619 to 9251

Son profesores y estudiantes de Montebello High School en Montebello, California.

1 Es una escuela. Es Montebello High School.

¿Quién es ella? Es Ana, una estudiante.

2 ¿Quién es el chico? Es Beto. Beto Chávez. ¿Y quién es la chica? Es Ana. Ana Montoya.

Hola, Ana. ¿Qué tal?

Muy bien, gracias.

Muy bien, gracias, Beto. ¿Y tú?

4 ¿Quién es ella? Es la profesora de español, la señorita Montero.

Y ella, ¿quién es? Es la señora León, la profesora de matemáticas.

Buenos días.

Buenos días, profesor.

3 Y él, ¿quién es? Es el señor Whitaker. Es el profesor de historia.

18 dieciocho

Purpose This section is not meant for memorization or mastery; it sets the context for the language used for greeting and saying good-bye and provides comprehensible language without translation. Tell students they are not expected to understand everything at first. They should try to get the gist of what is being said and should not be concerned if they do not understand every word.

4   05:06

1 ¿Es la señorita Montero?
2 Y ella, ¿es la señora León?
3 ¿Quién es? *(Point to both.)*
4 ¿Es profesora? *(Ask about yourself, students.)*
5 ¿Es la profesora de español? ¿de matemáticas? *(Point to both.)*

Side 1, 9270 to 9892

5   05:28

1 ¿Quién es la chica? *(Point to Ana.)*
2 ¿Es por la mañana o por la tarde? *(Point to clock at 1:50.)*
3 ¿Dice "Buenos días" o "Buenas tardes"?
4 ¿Cómo está la señorita Montero?

Side 1, 9910 to 10289

6   05:41

1 ¿Quién es la amiga de Ana?
2 ¿Dice "Mucho gusto" la señorita Montero?
3 ¿Dice "Encantada" Lupe?
4 ¿Qué dice Lupe?
5 ¿Qué dice la señorita Montero?

Side 1, 10322 to 10658

7   05:53

1 ¿Quién es? *(Point to Jaime, Beto, Lupe.)*
2 ¿Quién dice "Adiós"?
3 ¿Es por la mañana o por la tarde?
4 ¿Quién dice "Hasta luego", Beto o Jaime?
5 ¿Quién dice "Hasta mañana", Beto o Lupe?

Side 1, 10676 to 11099

8   06:09

1 ¿Es el director? ¿Quién es?
2 ¿Quién es el director de *[your school]*?
3 ¿Cómo se llama? *(Point to Andrés.)*
4 ¿Es por la tarde o por la noche?
5 ¿Qué dice Andrés?
6 ¿Dice "Buenas noches" por la mañana o por la noche?
7 ¿Hay mucho trabajo? ¿Sí o no?

Side 1, 11132 to 11601

Suggestions Begin by having students close their books while you narrate one section at a time, using the transparencies to clarify meaning without translation. Then ask the questions in the **Comprehension Checks**. Repeat this process after each section. Gesture, demonstrate, or act out various greetings. Use a clock or write various times on the board or on a transparency to clarify morning/afternoon/evening.

Using the video Play one section at a time after narrating it using the transparencies. Freeze the video and ask the questions in the **Comprehension Checks**. Repeat this process with each section.

See the **Video Notes** on page 15.

06:24–
09:21

Side 1, 11610 to 16911

The overhead transparencies may also be used to review, to recreate the text dialogues, and to have students create their own dialogues. Students should not be asked to reproduce dialogues verbatim. They should produce logical, appropriate exchanges prompted by the pictured situations. Language such as **¡Caramba! ¡Ya es hora de clase!** should be treated as supplementary. More able students may incorporate such language.

Early Production Checks

In dialogues 1–5, ask the questions in the **Early Production Checks** to be certain students understand context and characters. Accept one- or two-word answers.

A complete set of the **Early Production Checks** is available on cards in the Teacher's Resource Package.

1   06:31

¡Ay! Perdón.
1 ¿Cómo se llama el chico?
   Se llama Beto Chávez.
2 ¿Cómo se llama la chica?
   Se llama Lupe García.
3 ¿Cómo está Beto?   *Estupendo.*
4 ¿Quién dice "Mucho gusto"?
   Beto.
5 ¿Quién dice "¡Caramba!"?   *Lupe.*
6 ¿Qué dice Lupe para despedirse?
   (Wave good-bye to aid comprehension.)   Hasta luego.
7 ¿Qué dice Beto para despedirse?
   (Wave good-bye to aid comprehension.)   Hasta luego.

Side 1, 11807 to 13329

¿QUÉ DECIMOS..?

Al saludar a amigos y profesores

1 **¡Ay! Perdón.**

UNIDAD 1

Purpose   This section is designed to use the language of greetings and good-byes in real-life situations. Students should not be overly concerned with understanding or translating every word. Comprehension will come with viewing of the video and/or with the teacher's use of the overhead transparencies to help students practice the new language.

2 ¿Qué tal?

3 ¿Quién es?

2   `07:22`

¿Qué tal?

1 ¿Cómo está Lupe?   *Bien.*
2 ¿Cómo está Ana?   *Terrible/Fatal.*
3 ¿Cómo se llama el director de Montebello High School? *Señor Ramos.*
4 ¿Cómo se llama el director o la directora de *[name of your school]*?
5 ¿Quién es el profesor de matemáticas de Montebello High? *El señor Ramos.*
6 ¿Quién es el profesor o la profesora de matemáticas de *[name of your school]*?   …

Side 1, 13343 to 14139

3   `07:49`

¿Quién es?

1 ¿Quién es la señorita Montero? *La profesora de español.*
2 ¿Qué dice la profesora, "Buenos días" o "Buenas tardes"? *Buenos días.*
3 ¿Qué dicen las chicas? *Buenos días, profesora.*
4 ¿Cómo está la Srta. Montero? *Bien.*

Side 1, 14153 to 14927

¡OJO! **Pasen** (page 21) and **siéntese** (page 22) are used for passive comprehension. Students are not expected to produce these structures nor understand the concept of formal commands at this point.

Suggestions   Begin by having students close their books while you narrate one section at a time, using the transparencies to clarify meaning without translation. Then ask the questions in the **Early Production Checks**. Repeat this process with each section.

Using the video   Play one section at a time after narrating it using the transparencies. Freeze the video and ask the questions in the **Early Production Checks**. Repeat this process with each section.

4

08:16

¿Cómo se llama usted?

1 ¿Cómo se llama el profesor?
Samuel Whitaker.

2 ¿Cómo se llama la profesora?
Luisa Montero.

3 ¿Quién es el señor Whitaker, el profesor de inglés o de historia?
Historia.

4 ¿Quién es la señorita Montero, la profesora de español o de historia? *Español.*

5

08:53

Buenas noches.

1 ¿Qué dice Andrés, "Buenas tardes" o "Buenas noches"?
Buenas noches.

2 ¿Dice "Buenas noches" por la mañana, por la tarde o por la noche? *Por la noche.*

3 ¿Quién es el director, el Sr. Ramos o Andrés?
El Sr. Ramos.

4 ¿Quién dice "Adiós, señor", Andrés o el director? *Andrés.*

5 ¿Quién dice "Hasta mañana", Andrés o el director?
El director.

4 ¿Cómo se llama usted?

5 Buenas noches.

CHARLEMOS UN POCO

A. Saludos y despedidas.   It is the first day of school at Montebello High and people are greeting each other or saying good-bye. Tell whether each statement is **un saludo** (*a greeting*) or **una despedida** (*a farewell*).

1. Adiós.
2. Hola, chico.
3. Hasta mañana, señor Ramos.
4. Buenos días, profesor.
5. ¡Señorita Montero! ¿Cómo está usted?
6. Hasta luego, Beto.
7. Buenas tardes, Lupe. ¿Cómo estás?
8. ¿Qué tal, Ana?
9. Buenas noches. Hasta mañana.
10. Buenas noches, señor director. ¿Cómo está usted?

B. ¡Hola!   Select an appropriate response to each greeting or farewell.

a. Buenas tardes. Soy Rebeca Ortiz, la profesora de inglés. Encantada.
b. Buenos días. Soy Silvia. Mucho gusto.
c. Hasta mañana.
ch. Mucho gusto, Carlos.
d. Muy bien, gracias. ¿Cómo está usted?

1.

2.

3.

4.

5.

LECCIÓN 1

Greeting people

In the morning:
Buenos días.

In the afternoon:
Buenas tardes.

In the evening:
Buenas noches.

Anytime:
¡Hola!

Asking how someone is

¿Cómo estás?
¿Cómo está usted?
¿Qué tal?

Responses:
Bien, gracias.
Bien, gracias, ¿y tú?
Muy bien, gracias, ¿y usted?

Saying good-bye

Adiós.
Hasta luego.
Hasta mañana.

Guided Practice

Using the margin boxes
The margin boxes contain focused grammar explanations and vocabulary needed to do the activities. Teachers have the flexibility to limit grammar explanation to what is in the box, to teach the structures in *¿Por qué se dice así?* at the back of the book before or after doing the activities, or simply to assign the grammar as homework and make students responsible for learning it.

Note Additional practice/homework activities are provided in *¿Por qué se dice así?* and in the **Cuaderno**.

Point out **Buenas noches** is said in the evening after dark or after dinner.

Note Students may recall other responses from *¿Qué decimos...?* **Terrible, Fatal, Estupendo.**

Optional vocabulary **Hasta pronto, ¡Chao!** *(informal).*

A. Saludos y despedidas.
Read each item. Have individuals or the full class respond.

1 despedida		**6** despedida
2 saludo		**7** saludo
3 despedida		**8** saludo
4 saludo		**9** despedida
5 saludo		**10** saludo

Extension Have individuals read items out of sequence and call on classmates to respond.

B. ¡Hola! In pairs, one student reads the speech balloon while the other gives the response. Circulate among students. Provide pronunciation help when requested. Resist interrupting the activity. Note common errors and correct them afterwards. Have volunteer pairs act out the situations.
1 b; **2** d; **3** a; **4** c; **5** ch

Purpose The *Charlemos un poco* activities provide guided practice to students beginning to produce new language. As such, the repetition built into the activities is intentional. Students need not do all the activities, once they have demonstrated mastery of the language of greeting, saying good-bye, and identifying people.

Suggestions Demonstrate one or two examples in each activity, using volunteers or calling on more able students to make sure all students understand what is expected. These activities may first be done in pairs and then repeated with the whole class, calling on individuals. This approach works well with large classes.

C. ¿Qué tal? Answers will vary.

CH. ¡Adiós! Allow 2–3 min for students to do in pairs. Then call on pairs of students to stand and act out each exchange. Answers will vary.

Point out Teachers are usually addressed as **señor, señora, señorita,** or **profesor(a).**

Extension Personalize by having students adopt names of persons at your school.

Asking *Who . . . ?*

¿Quién es?	*Who is it?*
¿Quién es él?	*Who is he?*
¿Quién es ella?	*Who is she?*

Note: In writing, questions always begin with an inverted question mark.

D. En la cafetería.
Demonstrate the model. Have students pair off to practice the activity, taking turns asking and answering. Have volunteers act out the exchanges.

1 ¿Quién es ella? Es mi amiga Alicia.
2 ¿Quién es él? Es mi profesor de inglés.
3 ¿Quién es él? Es mi amigo Juan Carlos.
4 ¿Quién es ella? Es mi profesora de historia.
5 ¿Quién es él? Es mi profesor de matemáticas.

Point out The subject pronoun is not usually necessary: **Soy** = *I am,* **Es** = *He is, She is, It is.*

C. ¿Qué tal? Greet five of your classmates and find out how they are doing today. Choose one of the greetings and your own response each time.

 EJEMPLO

You:	**Buenos días.** o **Buenas tardes.**
Partner:	**Hola. ¿Qué tal?** o **Hola. ¿Cómo estás?**
You:	**Bien, gracias, ¿y tú?** o **Terrible, ¿y tú?**
Partner:	**Muy bien, gracias.** o **Fatal.**

CH. ¡Adiós! It's time to go home. Say good-bye to each of the following people. Use several different good-byes.

1. un amigo
2. el director (la directora) de la escuela
3. el profesor (la profesora) de inglés
4. una amiga
5. el profesor (la profesora) de español

D. En la cafetería. You see several new faces in the school cafeteria. Ask a friend who they are.

 MODELO

You:	**¿Quién es él?**
Partner:	**Es mi amigo Ricardo.**

amigo Ricardo 1. amiga Alicia 2. profesor de inglés

3. amigo Juan Carlos 4. profesora de historia 5. profesor de matemáticas

UNIDAD 1

E. ¿Con quién? You overhear various students stop and talk to Mrs. Alicia Ramos, a Spanish teacher, and Tina Chávez, a classmate. Based on what each student says, tell which person is being addressed.

MODELO   Soy Pablo Ortiz, ¿y usted?
la señora Ramos

La señora Ramos   Tina Chávez

1. ¿Qué tal, chica?
2. Buenas tardes, señora.
3. Muy bien, ¿y usted?
4. ¿Cómo está usted?
5. Soy Juan Montero, ¿y tú?
6. Hasta mañana, señora.
7. ¿Cómo estás tú?
8. ¿Eres Tina Castillo?
9. ¿Es usted la profesora de español?
10. Bien, gracias. ¿Y tú?

F. ¿Eres Tomás López? Your teacher will assign everyone in the class a new identity. Keep your new identity a secret until questioned by your classmates.

1. Find Tomás and Eva López by questioning your classmates.

MODELO   You: **¿Eres Tomás López?**
Partner: **No, soy Pablo White.**

2. Now your teacher will give you another identity. Find Mr. and Mrs. Ortega by questioning your classmates.

MODELO   You: **¿Es Ud. la señora Ortega?**
Partner: **No, yo soy la señorita ...**

LECCIÓN 1

Ser

yo	**soy**	*I am*
tú	**eres**	*you are*
usted	**es**	*you are*
él	**es**	*he is*
ella	**es**	*she is*
—	**es**	*it is*

*See ¿**Por qué se dice así?**,
pages G4–G8, sections 1.1, 1.2,
and 1.3.*

Using *tú* and *usted*

Tú is used when addressing family and friends. **Usted** is used to show respect, as when addressing adults, teachers, or people you don't know well.

*See ¿**Por qué se dice así?**,
page G4, section 1.1.*

E. ¿Con quién?
Point out A student addressing a teacher will usually use **usted**, whereas students addressing each other usually use **tú**. Adults addressing each other may use either **tú** or **usted**, depending on the nature of their relationship.
1 Tina
2 la señora Ramos
3 la señora Ramos
4 la señora Ramos
5 Tina
6 la señora Ramos
7 Tina
8 Tina
9 la señora Ramos
10 Tina

F. ¿Eres Tomás López?
Point out The first transparency focuses on informal address, the second on formal address.
1 Distribute identity cards for the **Tomás** and **Eva López** activity and tell students to keep their new identity a secret until questioned by classjmates. After identifying **Tomás** and **Eva**, students should be seated to indicate that they identified the new students.
2 Repeat the activity using the **Señores Ortega** identity cards. You may want to redistribute the identification cards and do both activities several times.

CHARLEMOS UN POCO MÁS

A. Nombres.   Check if your partner remembers everyone's name in the class.

 EJEMPLO   **¿Quién es él (ella)?**   **¿Es** [*wrong name*]**?**
　　　　　　　Es [*name*].　　　o　　**No, es** [*correct name*].

B. ¡Pobre profesor(a)!   Often students help the teacher learn their names on the first days of school. Working in groups of four or five, take turns playing a confused teacher who calls several students by the wrong name.

 EJEMPLO   Teacher: **¿Eres Lupe?**
　　　　　　Student: **No, señor (señora, señorita).**
　　　　　　　　　　　Yo soy [*your name*]. **Ella es Lupe.**

C. Saludos.   You are happy to be back at school. How do you greet the following people on the first day?

1. your best friend on the way to school
2. your principal in the morning
3. your teacher before Spanish class
4. your history teacher after lunch
5. a good friend in the hall after school

Dramatizaciones

A. ¡Hola!   Initiate a conversation with various classmates, especially ones you don't know.

- Greet each other.
- Introduce yourself.
- Say good-bye and introduce yourself to another classmate.

B. ¡Buenas tardes!   Several new Spanish-speaking students are at the Spanish Club's first meeting of the year. Role-play this situation.

- Greet three of the new students.
- Ask how each one is doing.
- End the conversation with an appropriate farewell.

C. Mucho gusto.   A new student has the locker next to yours. Role-play your first conversation. Be creative in acting out how you meet.

- Greet each other appropriately.
- Introduce yourselves.
- Ask each other how you are doing.
- Say good-bye before rushing off to your classes.

26   veintiséis

UNIDAD 1

CHARLEMOS UN POCO MÁS

Application and Extension

Unlike the **Modelo** responses in the exercises of the *Charlemos un poco* section, the **Ejemplo** responses in this section are much more open-ended and often have several possible correct answers.

B. ¡Pobre profesor(a)! Allow 3–4 min. Circulate among students to make sure everyone participates. Monitor the sound level in the room. The sound level should drop as groups complete the task. If it begins to rise again, students are probably off the task. It is always better to stop group activity a little before the task is completed rather than allow too much time. This helps students avoid slipping into English.

C. ¡Saludos! Assign items 1–5 to different pairs of students and allow 3–4 min for preparation. Have several pairs of students present in front of the class. Encourage the use of gestures and expressions such as **terrible, fatal, no muy bien**, etc.

DRAMATIZACIONES

Evaluation

Note These role plays are not to be written out and memorized but rather presented extemporaneously.

A. ¡Hola! Allow 3–4 min. Be sure everyone participates. Circulate among students and introduce yourself to students whose names you do not recall. If class is large, have students do the activity in groups of 6 or 8.

B and C. ¡Buenas tardes!/ Mucho gusto. Assign **B** and **C** to different groups of students at the same time. Allow students 3–4 min for practice. Ask several pairs to present in front of the class. After each presentation, ask comprehension questions. Students may choose new names from the list on page xi.

Purpose The *Charlemos un poco más* activities are designed to allow students to "create" with language recently learned. Although the activities may sometimes appear repetitious of the guided practice in the previous section, they enable students to apply learned language in a variety of possible combinations.

Dramatizaciones is designed to review the lesson structures and functions. Here students are expected to recycle all previously learned structures and vocabulary while performing specific tasks in student-centered role plays. Encourage students to work without their textbooks when performing their role plays.

26 UNIDAD 1   Lección 1

¡No metas la pata!

¿Cómo estás?   Fred, a student from the United States, is studying in Caracas, Venezuela. Read the following dialogue, which takes place on the first day of school. Try to find what goes wrong. Then answer the question that follows.

Tomás:	**Hola, Fred. ¿Cómo estás?**
Fred:	**Bien, gracias. ¿Y tú?**
Tomás:	**Estupendo.**
Fred:	**Oye, Tomás, ¿quién es ese señor?**
Tomás:	**Es el profesor de historia, el señor Peña.**
Sr. Peña:	**Buenos días, jóvenes.**
Tomás:	**Buenos días, señor Peña.**
Fred:	**Hola. ¿Qué tal? ¿Cómo estás?**
Sr. Peña:	**Pues . . . Mmmm . . . Bien, gracias. Adiós.**

Why does Mr. Peña react somewhat coldly to Fred's greeting?

1. Fred should have waited to be formally introduced.
2. Mr. Peña doesn't like having foreign students in his class.
3. Fred's greeting was too familiar.

❏ Check your answer on page 416.

LECCIÓN 1

¡No metas la pata!

Purpose   These short dialogues always include a cultural *faux pas* that students are asked to discover on their own.

Suggestions   Allow 2 min to read the dialogue. *Ask:* How do students in the United States greet a teacher? Would this greeting differ from a student-to-student greeting? How should Fred have greeted Mr. Peña? Finally ask several students to reread the dialogue aloud, correcting Fred's greeting and Mr. Peña's reaction. Students may check responses on page 416.

Answers

Student answers appear on page 416.
1 Since Mr. Peña greeted both of the boys, it was not necessary for Fred to wait to be introduced. Try again.
2 Nothing in the dialogue reveals a negative attitude toward foreign students. Consider another answer.
③ Right! Fred should have used the more formal **usted** form to address a teacher. Can you think of an appropriate greeting?

Y ahora, ¡a leer!

Purpose

Tú y usted provides additional reading practice as students learn more about how to avoid cross-cultural misunderstandings when greeting people.

Antes de empezar

Use these questions as an advance organizer for the readings that follow.

Answers

1 Students use greetings like: *Hi! / Hiya! / How're you doing? / Hey dude.* etc. with each other.

2 They use more formal greetings like: *Hello. / Good morning. / How are you?* and titles like *Mr. / Mrs. / Miss / Dr.* with adults.

3 Students should note that they do talk differently to different groups. They tend to be more informal with each other, more formal when greeting teachers.

Point out The use of **tú** and **usted** is often governed by age difference and degree of familiarity: children frequently address adults as **usted**, students usually address each other as **tú**, two adults (e.g., teachers) may begin addressing each other as **usted,** but as they get to know each other may change to **tú**. Family members usually address each other as **tú**, though this will vary from country to country (in Spain, it is customary to use **tú** with all members of the family, whereas in Colombia, husband and wife usually use **usted** with each other).

¡OjO! Treat **ser/estar** as lexical items at this point. If students are concerned that there seems to be two ways of saying "to be," point out that the **ser** sentences and expressions identify people whereas the **estar** expressions talk about how people are.

Y ahora, ¡a leer!

Antes de empezar

1. What do you and your friends say in English when you greet each other?
2. What do you and your friends say in English when you greet your teacher?
3. How do the greetings you use with teachers and friends differ?

Tú y usted

TÚ

Tú es informal y **usted** es formal. Usamos **tú** con amigos y familia. Usamos **usted** con otras personas.

USTED

Especialmente, usamos **usted** con personas que tienen un título como **señor (Sr.), señora (Sra.), señorita (Srta.), profesor/profesora, (Prof.), doctor (Dr.), doctora (Dra.),** etc.

Verifiquemos

En esta lección observamos el uso de **tú** y **usted** en diferentes expresiones. Identifica las expresiones de **tú** y las expresiones de **usted.**

1. ¿Estás bien?
2. ¿Cómo está, señora?
3. ¿Eres Tomás López?
4. ¿Cómo está?
5. ¿Es el señor López?
6. ¿Es la profesora de matemáticas?
7. Hola. ¿Cómo estás?

Verifiquemos

Answers

1 tú	**5** usted
2 usted	**6** usted
3 tú	**7** tú
4 usted	

Antes de empezar

1. Where are you likely to see a greeting or a good-bye written down? Name several places.
2. Give some examples of written greetings you have seen recently.

Saludos y despedidas. Read these messages, then answer the questions that follow.

Verifiquemos

1. Which messages express a greeting?
2. Which messages express a good-bye?
3. What words are used to express *hello* and *good-bye* in Spanish?
4. Which of these greetings and good-byes are you likely to see in English in your own community? What might they say?

LECCIÓN 1

Purpose Saludos y despedidas provides additional reading practice using materials related to the theme of the lesson—materials like those students might find in a real-life situation.

Antes de empezar

Answers

1 On TV, on greeting cards, on a note or a letter, in an advertisement, in a book or movie title, etc.
2 Responses will probably include specific examples fitting the above categories.

Students should not be expected to understand every word they read. Help students learn to use contextual visual clues to guess at the meaning of unfamiliar words.

Verifiquemos

Answers

1 1, 3, 4, 5
2 2, 6
3 *Hello:* Buenos días, Hola, Buenas tardes. *Good-bye:* Hasta luego, Hasta mañana.
4 Answers will vary.

Communicative Goals

- Introducing yourself and others
- Responding to introductions
- Naming countries and capitals
- Giving information about where people are from

Culture and Reading

- Maps of the Americas
- *¡No metas la pata!* *¡Somos americanos!* Who is an American?
- *Y ahora, ¡a leer!* **Todos somos americanos:** Countries and nationalities

Structure

- 1.4 **¿De dónde . . .?** and **ser de. . .**

ACTIVE VOCABULARY

See note on page 16.

Presentaciones y respuestas

Quiero presentarle a …
Quiero presentarte a …
¿Cómo se llama?
¿Cómo te llamas?
Me llamo…
Mi nombre es…
El gusto es mío.
Encantado(a).
Es un placer.
Igualmente.
Mucho gusto.

Palabras interrogativas

cuál
dónde
  de dónde
  ¿dónde está … ?

Sudamérica

Argentina / Buenos Aires
Brasil / Brasilia
Bolivia / La Paz, Sucre
Chile / Santiago
Colombia / Bogotá
Ecuador / Quito
Paraguay / Asunción
Perú / Lima
Uruguay / Montevideo
Venezuela / Caracas

Palabras y expresiones

americano(a)
capital
de
Estados Unidos
por
pues
ser de

¡Cuidado con … !

LECCIÓN **2**

¿De dónde eres?

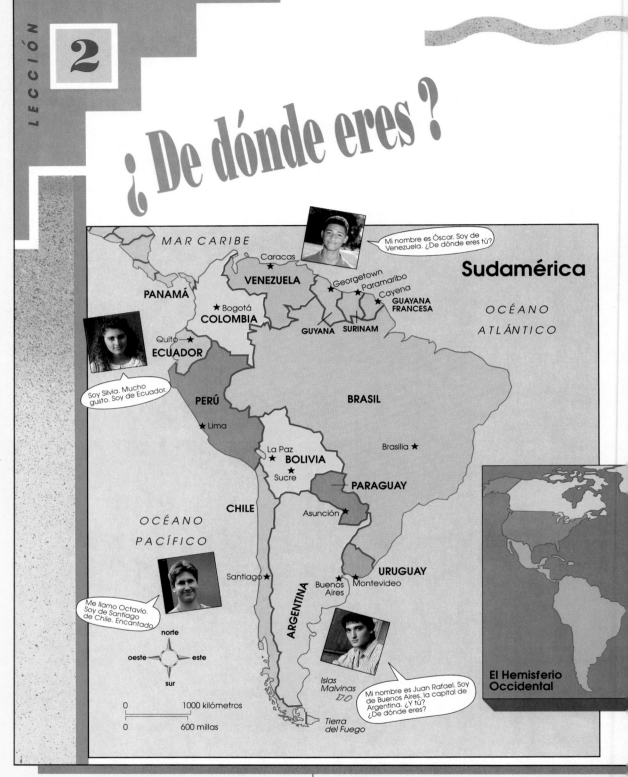

Purpose To acquaint students with Spanish-speaking countries and capitals and with the formulas used to introduce people, to respond to introductions, and to give information about where people are from.

Note Bolivia has its political capital in Sucre and its traditional capital in La Paz.

A N T I C I P E M O S

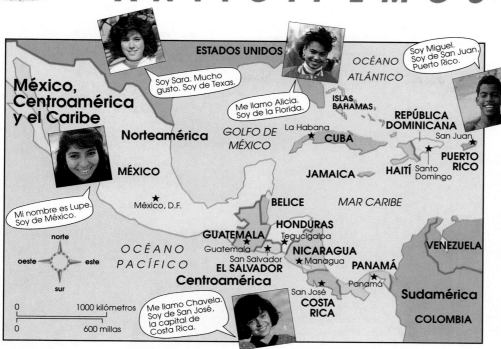

México, Centroamérica y el Caribe

Norteamérica

Soy Sara. Mucho gusto. Soy de Texas.

Me llamo Alicia. Soy de la Florida.

Soy Miguel. Soy de San Juan, Puerto Rico.

ESTADOS UNIDOS

OCÉANO ATLÁNTICO

ISLAS BAHAMAS

GOLFO DE MÉXICO

La Habana ★ CUBA

REPÚBLICA DOMINICANA

San Juan

MÉXICO

Mi nombre es Lupe. Soy de México.

México, D.F. ★

JAMAICA

HAITÍ

Santo Domingo

PUERTO RICO

norte

oeste · este

sur

OCÉANO PACÍFICO

BELICE

MAR CARIBE

GUATEMALA ★
Guatemala

HONDURAS
Tegucigalpa

San Salvador ★ ★ Managua

EL SALVADOR

NICARAGUA

Centroamérica

PANAMÁ

Panamá ★

VENEZUELA

0 ___ 1000 kilómetros

0 ___ 600 millas

Me llamo Chavela. Soy de San José, la capital de Costa Rica.

San José ★

COSTA RICA

Sudamérica

COLOMBIA

¿**Q**ué piensas tú?

1. How do you know if the names on the maps are written in English or in Spanish?

2. Which countries are not Spanish-speaking? What languages are spoken there? Can you explain why several languages are spoken in the Caribbean islands and the countries of Central and South America?

3. Where else in the world is Spanish spoken? Can you explain why Spanish is found in so many parts of the world?

4. What might the people in the pictures be telling you about themselves?

Even though the following questions are in Spanish, you will understand them. Can you answer the questions in English? Can you answer them in Spanish?

5. ¿Está Colombia en el sur o en el norte de Sudamérica? ¿Y Argentina? ¿Y Brasil? ¿Y Perú?

6. ¿Cuál es la capital de Venezuela? ¿De Ecuador? ¿De Colombia?

7. ¿Quién es de San Juan? ¿De México? ¿De Santiago? ¿De San José?

8. ¿De dónde es Octavio? ¿Chavela? ¿Juan Rafael? ¿Silvia?

9. What do you think you will be able to say when you have finished this lesson?

¿Qué piensas tú?

Answers

1 Some unfamiliar spellings and accent marks should tell students the maps are in Spanish.

2 English is spoken in **Belice** and **Guyana**, French in **Haití** and **Guayana Francesa**, Dutch in **Surinam**, and Portuguese in **Brasil**. There was much exploration and empire-building by the various European "mother" countries for political and economic reasons.

3 In Spain and in parts of Africa. Spanish exploration and empire-building for political and economic reasons.

4 What their names are and where they are from. They are also asking where you are from.

5 En el norte; en el sur; en el este; en el oeste.

6 Caracas; Quito; Bogotá.

7 Miguel; Lupe; Octavio; Chavela.

8 De Santiago/de Chile; de San José/de Costa Rica; de Buenos Aires/de Argentina; de Ecuador.

▶**9** **They will be able to introduce themselves and others, to identify countries and capitals, and to talk about where people are from.**

¡OjO! **¡DIME!** follows current usage and journalistic style and does not use the definite article with the names of countries. Because traditional usage is still often heard, however, it is mentioned in the **¿Por qué se dice así?** section 1.4, page G9.

Comprehension Checks

Using the maps or the overhead transparencies, ask **¿Es el Hemisferio Occidental? Es Norteamérica?** *(Remember that Mexico is in North America.)* **¿Es el Caribe? ¿Es Centroamérica? ¿Es Sudamérica? ¿Cuál es la capital de … ? ¿Dónde está … ?**

Suggestions
Use the maps as advance organizer. Accuracy of pronunciation is not vital here. Students should be allowed to discover what they already know, without being distracted by constant correction of pronunciation errors.

Have students learn the names and location of Hispanic countries and capitals. Use copymasters or ask students to trace the map of South America and locate the capitals as homework. As students look at the maps, ask **¿Cuál es la capital de [. . .]? ¿Dónde está?** Model possible answers: **La capital de … es … Está en el norte/sur/este/oeste/centro.**

PARA EMPEZAR

Comprehensible Input 1

09:22–
11:11

Side 1, 16929 to 20218

Comprehension Checks

The questions listed here are examples only. Ask yes/no questions and one- and two-word-answer questions to confirm that students understand key language. A complete set of the **Comprehension Checks** is available on cards in the Teacher's Resource Package.

1   09:29

1 ¿Es Ecuador?
2 ¿Es Quito la capital de Ecuador?
3 ¿Es Silvia López?
4 ¿Es una nueva estudiante?
5 ¿Es una estudiante norteamericana o sudamericana?

Side 1, 17130 to 17995

PARA EMPEZAR

Es el primer día de clases de Silvia, una estudiante sudamericana.

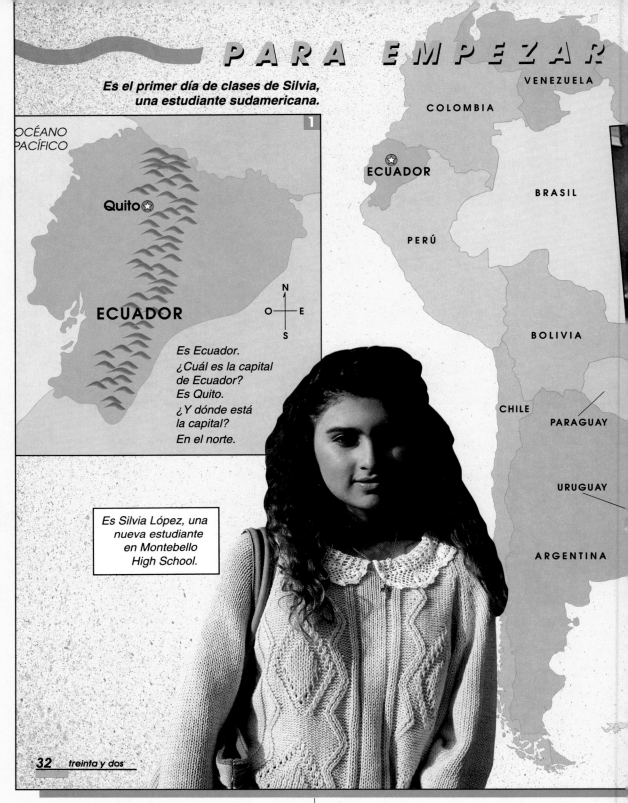

OCÉANO
PACÍFICO

VENEZUELA
COLOMBIA
ECUADOR
BRASIL
PERÚ
Quito
ECUADOR
BOLIVIA
N
O   E
S
CHILE
PARAGUAY
URUGUAY
ARGENTINA

Es Ecuador.
¿Cuál es la capital de Ecuador?
Es Quito.
¿Y dónde está la capital?
En el norte.

Es Silvia López, una nueva estudiante en Montebello High School.

**32** treinta y dos

Purpose This section develops listening comprehension and initial introduction of active vocabulary. Students should not be expected to achieve productive mastery at this point.

 **09:59**

1 ¿Quién es? *(Point to each person.)*
2 ¿Quién dice "Mucho gusto", Silvia o la señorita Montero?
3 ¿Qué dice la señorita Montero?
4 ¿Quién dice "Igualmente", Silvia o la señorita Montero?
5 ¿Qué dice Silvia?

Side 1, 18032 to 18771

 **10:24**

1 ¿Quién es? *(Point to each person.)*
2 ¿Dice "Encantado" Jaime?
3 ¿Está encantada Silvia también?
4 ¿Es Silvia de Ecuador? *(Name other countries.)*
5 ¿Es de Quito? *(Name other cities.)*
6 ¿De dónde es Silvia?

Side 1, 18789 to 19388

 **10:45**

1 ¿Quién es?
2 ¿Cómo se llama la chica? *(Point to each girl.)*
3 ¿Quién dice "Mucho gusto", Silvia o Pilar?

Side 1, 19406 to 19920

 **11:02**

1 ¿Es Silvia?
2 ¿Quién es? *(Point to Silvia, then to Sr. Ramos.)*
3 ¿Quién dice "Mucho gusto"?
4 ¿Quién dice "Bienvenida"?

Side 1, 19938 to 20218

treinta y tres **33**

***S**uggestions* Begin by having students close their books while you narrate one section at a time, using the transparencies to clarify meaning without translation. Then ask the questions in the **Comprehension Checks**. Repeat this process with each section.

Using the video Play one section at a time after narrating it using the transparencies. Freeze the video and ask the questions in the **Comprehension Checks**. Repeat this process with each section.

You may want to act out introductions with students.

TAPE/DISC
11:12–13:52

Side 1, 20226 to 25042

Early Production Checks

A complete set of the **Early Production Checks** is available on cards in the Teacher's Resource Package.

1　　　　11:18

Quiero presentarte …

1 ¿Quién es? *(Point to David/Silvia.)*
  Es David/Silvia.
2 ¿Es de Venezuela Silvia?　*No.*
3 ¿Es de México o de Ecuador?
  Es de Ecuador.
4 ¿Qué dice David? *(Point to speech balloon.)*　*Mucho gusto.*
5 ¿Qué dice Silvia? *(Point to speech balloon.)*　*El gusto es mío.*

Side 1, 20415 to 21058

2　　　　11:40

Encantada.

1 ¿De dónde es Silvia?
  De Ecuador.
2 ¿Qué dice Ana?　*Encantada.*
3 ¿Qué contesta Silvia?
  Igualmente.
4 ¿Quién es una nueva estudiante, Ana o Silvia?　*Silvia.*
5 ¿De qué parte de Ecuador es Silvia?　*De Quito.*
6 ¿Quién es de Quito—Ana, David o Silvia?　*Silvia.*

Side 1, 21079 to 21980

¿ Q U É   D E C I M O S …?

Al presentar a una persona

1 *Quiero presentarte . . .*

2 *Encantada.*

Purpose This section presents the language of introductions in the real-life context of a new high school student. Students should not be asked to memorize dialogues word for word but instead should use the language in the lesson activities that follow.

3 Bienvenida.

4 El gusto es mío.

Bienvenida.

1 ¿Cómo se llama el director?
Señor Ramos.

2 ¿Cómo se llama la nueva estudiante? *Silvia López.*

3 ¿Qué dice el Sr. Ramos?
Buenas tardes. Es un placer. Bienvenida.

4 ¿Qué dice Silvia? *Mucho gusto.*

5 ¿De dónde es Silvia?
De Ecuador.

6 ¿Es de la capital? *Sí.*

7 ¿Cómo se llama la capital de Ecuador? *Quito.*

Side 1, 22009 to 23042

---

4 | 12:46

El gusto es mío.

1 ¿Quién es la nueva amiga de David? *Silvia.*

2 ¿Es Beto amigo de David o de Silvia? *David.*

3 ¿Qué le dice Silvia a Beto?
Mucho gusto.

4 ¿Qué dice Beto? *¡El gusto es mío, preciosa!*

5 ¿Quién es "preciosa", Beto o Silvia? *Silvia.*

Side 1, 23064 to 25042

Note The *¿Qué decimos ... ?* art provided on transparencies can be used in a number of ways. In addition to aiding the presentation/comprehension of material, it can be used again at the end of the lesson. Students can role-play the situations, recalling appropriate phrases as they create new dialogues.

Suggestions Begin by having students close their books while you narrate one section at a time, using the transparencies to clarify meaning without translation. Then ask the questions in the **Early Production Checks.** Repeat this process with each section.

Using the video Play one section at a time after narrating it using the transparencies. Freeze the video and ask the questions in the **Early Production Checks** With the questions, begin developing complete utterances using the language to be learned. Repeat this process with each section.

CHARLEMOS UN POCO

CHARLEMOS UN POCO

Guided Practice

A–CH. Model the exchanges first. Then allow 2–3 min for students to work in pairs. Call on pairs to do introductions for the class. Answers will vary. Check for appropriate use of the **tú/usted** forms.

Note Mi nombre es is a high-frequency locution presented here to forestall production of the incorrect **Me llamo es . . .**

¡OjO! Pronouns are not being taught here. **Me, te, se** are lexical items—parts of formulas that students must use when introducing people. Resist giving too much grammatical information too early.

C. Mi nombre es . . .
Expansion Have students introduce each other in pairs, then introduce new "celebrity" acquaintances to you and classmates.

Optional introductions:
te presento/le presento.

CH. Quiero presentarte a . . .
Remind students that, because the **Ejemplo** responses are always open-ended, they should not simply imitate the models.
  Write "friend" and "adult" on the chalkboard at the top of two columns. Have students brainstorm the ways they have seen for introducing someone. Ask one or two students to write the phrases suggested by their classmates under the appropriate heading. Have students practice pronouncing them before doing this activity.
  Do not allow dependence on the open book. Have students walk around class without textbooks while doing this activity.

Introducing yourself

Me llamo . . .
Mi nombre es . . .
Soy . . .

Y tú, ¿cómo te llamas?
Y usted, ¿cómo se llama?

Introducing someone

To people you address as tú:
Quiero presentar**te** a . . .

To people you address as usted:
Quiero presentar**le** a . . .

Responding to introductions

Mucho gusto.
El gusto es mío.

Encantado(a).
Es un placer.
Igualmente.

A. Me llamo . . .   You are visiting Montebello High. Introduce yourself to the following people.

 MODELO David
    You: **Me llamo [**_your name_**]. Y tú, ¿cómo te llamas?**
    Partner: **Me llamo David.**

    Sr. José Ramos
    You: **Me llamo [**_your name_**]. Y usted, ¿cómo se llama?**
    Partner: **Mi nombre es José Ramos.**

1. Silvia
2. Lisa
3. Srta. Luisa Montero
4. Beto
5. Sr. Samuel Whitaker
6. Lupe
7. Ana
8. Sra. Margarita León

B. ¿Cómo te llamas?   Introduce yourself to four classmates and find out their names.

 MODELO You: **Me llamo . . . Y tú, ¿cómo te llamas?**
    Partner: **Encantado(a). Soy . . .**

C. Mi nombre es . . .   Adopt the name of a celebrity and introduce yourself to four classmates.

 EJEMPLO You: **Me llamo . . . Y usted, ¿cómo se llama?**
    Partner: **Es un placer. Mi nombre es . . .**

CH. Quiero presentarte a . . .   Introduce your partner to four classmates and the teacher.

 EJEMPLO You: **[**_Partner's name_**], quiero presentarte a [**_friend's name_**].**
    Partner: **Mucho gusto.**
    Classmate: **El gusto es mío.**

    You: **Profesor(a), quiero presentarle a mi amigo(a) [**_name_**].**
    Teacher: **Encantado(a).**
    Partner: **Igualmente.**

Purpose These activities provide guided practice to students beginning to produce new language. As such, the repetition built into the activities is intentional. Students need not do all the activities, once they have demonstrated mastery of the structures and vocabulary necessary to talk about Spanish-speaking countries and capitals and to make and respond to introductions.

D. ¿De dónde es? Ask a classmate where the following students are from.

MODELO Lisa Campos
  You: **¿De dónde es Lisa Campos?**
  Partner: **Es de Nevada.**

Estados Unidos

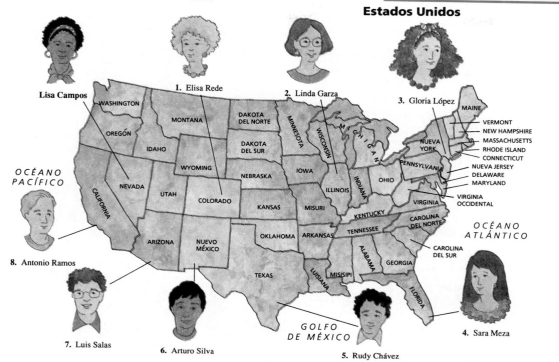

1. Elisa Rede
2. Linda Garza
3. Gloria López
4. Sara Meza
5. Rudy Chávez
6. Arturo Silva
7. Luis Salas
8. Antonio Ramos

Lisa Campos

E. Soy de . . . Tell where you are from and ask four classmates where they are from.

MODELO You: **Soy de . . . Y tú, ¿de dónde eres?**
  Partner: **Soy de . . .**

F. ¿De dónde eres? What would people from these cities say when asked where they are from?

MODELO Perú / Lima
  Partner: **¿De dónde eres?**
  You: **Soy de Perú, de Lima.**

1. Venezuela / Caracas
2. Perú / Lima
3. Bolivia / La Paz
4. Paraguay / Asunción
5. Colombia / Bogotá
6. Chile / Santiago
7. Uruguay / Montevideo
8. Argentina / Buenos Aires
9. Ecuador / Quito
10. Brasil / Brasilia

LECCIÓN 2

Asking or saying where someone is from

Asking where someone is from:

de dónde + ser
ser de

¿De dónde eres?
¿De dónde es usted?
¿De dónde es [*name*]?

Saying where you or someone else is from:

Soy de Chile.
Carlos es de Venezuela.

See **¿Por qué se dice así?**,
page G8, section 1.4.

treinta y siete **37**

A. Presentaciones.
Answers will vary.
Suggested answers for no.1:
Felipe, quiero presentarte a José.
Mucho gusto. Igualmente.
Encourage students to recall a variety of expressions used when introducing someone or when being introduced.

B. Sudamérica. Give each student a map. Have students work in groups of 5 or 6.

Expansion 1 Repeat the activity for the Caribbean area using copymaster.

Expansion 2 Do the activity using both South American and Caribbean copymasters. This would be a good review of countries and capitals before the lesson quiz or unit test.

CHARLEMOS UN POCO MÁS

A. Presentaciones. Complete the conversations in these cartoons with appropriate phrases.

1.

2.

3.

4.

B. Sudamérica. Your teacher will give you and your classmates maps of South America. Find out which country and city your classmates are from according to the country highlighted on their maps.

EJEMPLO   You: **¿De dónde eres?**
           Partner: **Soy de Colombia.**
           You: **¿De Bogotá?**
           Partner: **Sí, de la capital.**

Purpose The *Charlemos un poco más* activities are designed to allow students to create with language recently learned. Although the activities may sometimes appear repetitious of the guided practice in the previous section, they enable students to use—in a variety of combinations—the names of Spanish-speaking countries, introductions, and information about where people are from in new contexts and with greater opportunity for open-ended responses.

C. Recepción internacional. The Spanish Club is hosting a reception for the foreign students and the Spanish teachers at your school. You have been asked to introduce your partner to four new acquaintances.

Help your partner pick a new name and a Spanish-speaking country of origin. Then introduce your partner to several classmates, who in turn will introduce their partners to the two of you. Be sure to mention where the person being introduced is from.

CH. ¡Latinoamericanos! Select a Latin-American country of origin for yourself. Then ask your classmates where they are from and tell them your country. On the blank map your teacher provides, write the names of the students you meet on the country they say they are from. Try to get a classmate's name on every country.

Dramatizaciones

A. Padres e hijos. The Spanish department of your school is having a "Parents Night," and you and a parent are attending. In groups of three, decide who will play the role of the student, the parent, and the teacher.

- The student will introduce the parent and teacher.
- The parent and teacher will greet each other appropriately.

B. Primer día de clases. It is the first day of school, and you have been asked to escort Carlos (Carla) Morales, a student from Ecuador, to classes all day. In groups of five, decide who will play the role of the exchange student, the host student, the principal, a teacher, and another student.

- The host student will introduce the foreign student to the others individually.
- When introduced, each will converse with the foreign student, finding out where he or she is from.
- Each will say good-bye when the host student and the exchange student leave to meet another person.

¡No metas la pata!

Purpose This section is intended to provide additional reading practice as students learn to avoid cross-cultural misunderstandings when they refer to themselves as "Americans."

Suggestions Allow students 1–2 min to read the dialogue. Then ask them to discuss the possible explanations and arrive at a consensus on the correct answer before checking the explanations on page 416.

Answers

1 Nothing is said to indicate that León's knowledge of geography is deficient. In fact, Latin American students are usually very knowledgeable about world geography. Try another answer.

②Actually, North Americans, Central Americans, and South Americans are all Americans. When speaking Spanish, if you are trying to say that you are from the United States, refer to yourself as **norteamericano(a)** to avoid confusion. This is the correct answer.

3 There is no indication that León is trying to fool Jennifer about anything, especially since he just met her. Try another response.

¡No metas la pata!

¡Somos americanos!   Jennifer, a student from the United States, is currently studying in Mexico. Read the dialogue that occurs when a Mexican friend, Tina, introduces Jennifer to her cousin, León. Then answer the question that follows to explain why León responds as he does.

Tina:	**Jennifer, quiero presentarte a mi primo, León.**
Jennifer:	**Mucho gusto, León.**
León:	**El gusto es mío. ¿De dónde eres, Jennifer?**
Jennifer:	**Soy americana.**
León:	**Pero, . . . ¿no somos todos americanos?**

Why did León respond as he did?

1. León doesn't know anything about geography.
2. León thinks Jennifer doesn't realize that he and Tina are Americans also.
3. León is trying to fool Jennifer into thinking that he and Tina are Americans also.

❏ Check your answer on page 416.

Y ahora, ¡a leer!

Antes de empezar

1. If a person from Argentina is a South American, what is a person from Nicaragua? From Peru? From Mexico? From Panama? From the United States?
2. If a person from Chile is a Chilean, what is a person from Guatemala? From Costa Rica? From Ecuador? From Puerto Rico? From Uruguay?

Todos somos americanos :

Sudamericanos, centroamericanos, norteamericanos . . . todos somos americanos. Habitantes de Canadá, Estados Unidos, México, Nicaragua, Perú, Costa Rica, Colombia, Paraguay, Chile . . . todos somos americanos porque todos somos de las Américas.

¿Norteamericanos, centroamericanos, sudamericanos o caribeños?

argentinos	**hondureños**
bolivianos	**mexicanos**
canadienses	**nicaragüenses**
colombianos	**panameños**
costarricenses	**paraguayos**
cubanos	**peruanos**
chilenos	**puertorriqueños**
dominicanos	**salvadoreños**
ecuatorianos	**uruguayos**
estadounidenses	**venezolanos**
guatemaltecos	

Purpose This short reading expands students' knowledge of Hispanic countries and capitals to an awareness of nationalities.

Antes de empezar

Use these questions as an advance organizer for the **Todos somos americanos** reading that follows.

Answers

1 Nicaragua, Panama: Central American. Peru: South American. U.S.: North American.
Point out Mexico is geographically in North America, but Mexicans would not refer to themselves as **norteamericanos.** That term is normally used only for Canadians and U.S. citizens.
2 Guatemalan; Costa Rican; Ecuadoran; Puerto Rican; Uruguayan.

Todos somos americanos

¡OJO! This vocabulary is for recognition only. Students should not be expected to memorize nationalities.

With open books, have students write nationality of each country in appropriate place on map provided. Then, as class repeats each nationality after you for pronunciation practice, ask for corresponding country and continent.

Extra Credit Assign students Latin American countries to research and have them report findings to class.

OBJECTIVES

Communicative Goals

- Describing personality traits
- Describing physical characteristics
- Expressing negative ideas

Reading

- **Leamos ahora**
  Diccionario geográfico
- Reading strategy: Using cognates

Writing

- **Escribamos un poco**
  Writing a short letter
- Writing strategy: Brainstorming

Structure

- 1.5 Gender of nouns
- 1.6 Gender of adjectives

ACTIVE VOCABULARY

See note on page 16.

Descripción de personalidad

cómico(a)	nervioso(a)
desorganizado(a)	organizado(a)
estudioso(a)	popular
exigente	precioso(a)
extrovertido(a)	romántico(a)
generoso(a)	simpático(a)
inteligente	tímido(a)
interesante	tonto(a)
modesto(a)	tranquilo(a)

Descripción física

alto(a)	fuerte
atlético(a)	gordo(a)
bajo(a)	grande
bonito(a)	guapo(a)
delgado(a)	mediano(a)
elegante	moreno(a)
feo(a)	pelirrojo(a)
flaco(a)	rubio(a)

Palabras y expresiones

también	¿no?
al contrario	¿verdad?
ni … ni	

¿Cómo eres?

Purpose To focus students on the language to be learned and to encourage the development and use of critical thinking skills by having students observe and compare physical differences in people without forming judgments.

ANTICIPEMOS

¡Gran oportunidad para ser una estrella!

¿Eres bilingüe?

Necesitamos estudiantes bilingües para preparar el video de Montebello High School:

★ ¡HOLA PUERTO RICO! ★

AUDICIONES CON LA SRTA. MONTERO: EL MARTES A LAS 2:45, EN EL AUDITORIO.

¿Qué piensas tú?

Look at the announcement above. You may not understand every word, but you can probably understand more than you think at first. For example:

1. Who is being invited to participate? What skill should they have?

2. Why are these people needed?

3. What is being prepared? For whom?

Now look at the students in the photo on page 42.

6. Describe the students. What physical characteristics does each of them have?

7. Do you think any of these students are "typical" of students at Montebello High School? Why?

8. Would you be able to describe the "typical" student at your school?

4. What should people who are interested do?

5. What opportunity do the students have here?

9. Do you think there is such a thing as a "typical" student?

10. If you were making this video, what qualities would you be looking for in the people you chose?

11. What do you think you will be able to talk about when you have finished this lesson?

Comprehensible Input 1

13:54–
16:25

Side 1, 25058 to 29644

Comprehension Checks

Comprehension Checks are suggestions only. If responses are hesitant or inaccurate, use gestures and compare students in class to clarify. In the case of visible characteristics such as **pelirrojo(a),** refer to students in class or use pictures cut from magazines or catalogs. For personality traits such as **tímido(a), popular, inteligente,** act out or make reference to famous people known for specific traits. Ask students to point out or name characters in pictures and classmates to further confirm comprehension. Avoid using students to demonstrate traits that might cause discomfort or embarassment.

 1   **13:59**

1 ¿Es Carmen? ¿Ángela? ¿Gloria?
2 ¿Quién es? *(Point to each.)*
3 ¿Cómo se llama ella? *(Point to one, then the other.)*
4 ¿Es morena? ¿Es rubia? *(Ask about students in class.)*
5 ¿Es bonita? ¿Es cómica? *(Ask about students in class.)*

Side 1, 25245 to 26215

 2   **14:32**

1 ¿Es alta? ¿Es baja? *(Point to one, then the other.)*
2 ¿Es mediana?
3 ¿Es delgada?
4 ¿Quién es morena/rubia/ atlética/alta en la clase?

Side 1, 26233 to 26837

1

¿Quiénes son ellas? Son Carmen, Ángela y Gloria.

¿Cómo son? Carmen es morena. Ángela es morena también. Y es muy bonita, ¿no?

Gloria no es morena; al contrario, es rubia. Es muy bonita y cómica.

Carmen

Ángela

Gloria

2

¿Son Carmen, Gloria y Ángela? ¡Sí! Carmen es baja y Ángela es alta. Gloria no es ni alta ni baja. Es mediana. Ángela también es delgada y atlética.

3

Ellas son Ana y Lupe. Ana es la amiga de Lupe. ¿Quién es tímida, Ana o Lupe? ¿Y quién es popular?

44   cuarenta y cuatro

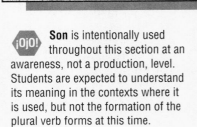 **¡OjO!** **Son** is intentionally used throughout this section at an awareness, not a production, level. Students are expected to understand its meaning in the contexts where it is used, but not the formation of the plural verb forms at this time.

Purpose This section develops comprehension of active vocabulary describing physical and personality traits. Students should not be expected to achieve productive mastery at this point. The goal is not to translate but to read/listen for comprehension.

Jaime es un amigo de Carlos. Es alto y moreno. ¡Es muy elegante! Y es muy guapo, ¿no?

Carlos es muy cómico. No es alto; es bajo. Muy elegante no es . . . pero es muy atlético . . . y muy fuerte, ¿verdad? ¿Es moreno o pelirrojo?

¿Quiénes son? Pues, son Jaime, Carmen y Pirata, el perro. Jaime es alto y Carmen es baja, ¿verdad? Jaime es muy estudioso. Carmen también, y es muy inteligente.

¿Y Pirata? Pues, Pirata es muy bajo y muy gordo. No es inteligente; es tonto. No es bonito; es feo. ¿Es antipático? No, es muy simpático y muy, muy popular.

3 **14:53**

1 ¿Es Ana? ¿Lupe?
2 ¿Quién es? *(Point to each.)*
3 ¿Es morena? ¿rubia? ¿baja? ¿alta? *(Point to both girls.)*
4 ¿Es delgada o gorda? ¿Es mediana?
5 ¿Es bonita? *(Point to each.)*
6 ¿Es tímida? ¿Es popular?

Side 1, 26865 to 27299

4 **15:08**

1 ¿Es Jaime? ¿Es Carlos?
2 ¿Quién es?
3 ¿Es alto/bajo?
4 ¿Es moreno? ¿rubio? ¿pelirrojo?
5 ¿Es elegante Jaime? Y Carlos, ¿es elegante también?
6 ¿Es guapo Jaime?
7 ¿Es muy guapo?
8 ¿Cómo es?
9 ¿Es atlético Carlos?
10 ¿Es fuerte? ¿Es muy fuerte?
11 ¿Es rubio? ¿Es pelirrojo?
12 ¿Cómo es?

Side 1, 27317 to 28295

5 **15:42**

1 ¿Quiénes son? ¿Cómo se llama él/ella? ¿Cómo se llama el perro?
2 ¿Quién es alto? ¿Es alta Carmen? ¿Cómo es Carmen?
3 ¿Son muy diferentes Carmen y Jaime? ¿Son rubios o morenos? ¿Es muy estudioso él? ¿Es muy estudiosa ella? ¿Es inteligente Carmen?

Side 1, 28314 to 28914

6 **16:02**

1 ¿Cómo se llama el perro?
2 ¿Es una persona? ¿Qué es?
3 ¿Es alto o bajo? ¿gordo o flaco?
4 ¿Es inteligente? ¿Es tonto?
5 ¿Es bonito o feo? ¿simpático o antipático?
6 ¿Es popular? [Ask questions 3–6 about students' own dogs.]

Side 1, 28932 to 29635

Suggestions Have students read one section silently. Then read it aloud for them, using overhead transparencies to clarify without translation. Ask **Comprehension Checks**. Yes/no and one- or two-word answers are acceptable. If students volunteer more complete answers, do not correct structure or pronunciation directly. Subtle correction, by repeating student's response accurately, is appropriate.

16:26–
19:38

Side 1, 29647 to 35399

Early Production Checks

1 16:32

Soy alto y moreno.

1 ¿Quién es? *(Point to Jaime, then to Pilar.)* *Es Jaime/Pilar.*
2 ¿Está bien Jaime? *Sí.*
3 ¿Cómo está Pilar? *Bien.*
4 ¿Es alto o bajo Jaime? *Alto.*
5 ¿Es alto(a) *(name students in class)*? …
6 ¿Es rubio o moreno Jaime? *Moreno.*
7 ¿Es moreno(a) *(name students in class)*? …
8 ¿Es gordo o delgado Jaime? *Delgado.* ¿Es muy, muy delgado? ¿Es flaco? *Sí.*
9 ¿Es inteligente y estudioso Jaime? *Sí.*

Side 1, 29828 to 31137

2 17:16

¿Cómo eres tú?

1 ¿Cómo se llama? *(Point to Ana, then to Pilar.)* *Ana/Pilar.*
2 ¿Cómo está Ana, bien o nerviosa? *Nerviosa.*
3 ¿Es tímida Ana? *Sí.*
4 ¿Es bonita o fea Ana? *Bonita.*
5 ¿Es inteligente o tonta? *Inteligente.*
6 ¿Quién es la amiga de Ana? *Lupe.*
7 ¿Es popular Lupe? *Sí.*
8 ¿Es bonita *[name of celebrity]*? … *(Ask for names of other celebrities.)*

Side 1, 31149 to 32321

¿QUÉ DECIMOS...?

Al describir a una persona

1 Soy alto y moreno.

2 ¿Cómo eres tú?

46 cuarenta y seis

UNIDAD 1

Purpose These dialogues are not intended for memorization. They show key language in the context of students describing themselves for a school video. Unfamiliar structures used in these dialogues are intended solely for comprehension, not for mastery or production by students.

3 Pues, . . . soy bonita.

4 ¡Eres muy guapo!

Pues, … soy bonita.

1 ¿Cómo se llama? *(Point to Lupe.)* Lupe.
2 ¿Quién es? *(Point to Pilar.)* Es Pilar.
3 ¿Es Lupe fea o bonita? *Bonita.*
4 ¿Es simpática o antipática? *Simpática.*
5 ¿Es popular o tímida Lupe? *Es popular.*
6 ¿Es modesta? *No.*
7 ¿Cómo es Lupe? *Es bonita / simpática / muy popular. (Ask questions about students in class or about people they know.)*

¡OJO! The use of **les dice** is intended for awareness only. If students ask, say it means *tells you* in this context and that they do not need to be concerned with it at this time.

Side 1, 32337 to 33520

¡Eres muy guapo!

1 ¿Quién es? *(Point to Beto/Pilar.)* Beto/Pilar.
2 ¿Cómo está Beto? *Bien.*
3 ¿Cómo es Beto, grande o pequeño? *Grande.*
4 ¿Es fuerte? *Sí, es fuerte.*
5 ¿Es atlético? *Sí, es atlético.*
6 ¿Es alto o bajo Beto? *Es alto.*
7 ¿Es tonto o inteligente Beto? *Es inteligente.*
8 ¿Es un amigo de Beto? *(Point to Jaime.)* Sí.
9 ¿Dice que Beto es tonto o inteligente? *Tonto.*
10 ¿Cómo es Beto, de verdad? *Es alto/fuerte/guapo/inteligente.*

Side 1, 33539 to 35399

Suggestions Begin by having students close their books while you narrate one section at a time, using the transparencies to clarify meaning without translation. Then ask the **Early Production Checks**. Repeat this process with each section.

Using the video Play one section at a time after narrating it using the transparencies. Freeze the video and ask the **Early Production Checks.** Repeat this process with each section.

Resist overburdening students with unnecessary grammatical explanations. Expressions such as **¿Cómo estás?**, **Dime,** and **Habla con ella** are only bothersome to teachers who immediately think **ser** vs. **estar** or familiar commands. Students simply hear a word or formula, not structures to analyze before they can be understood.

Guided Practice

A. ¡Soy magnífico! Call on individuals to read each description. Have class guess who is being described.

1 Ana
2 Beto
3 Ana, Beto
4 Jaime
5 Jaime
6 Lupe
7 Beto, Jaime

B. Mis nuevos amigos. Allow 1–2 min for students to decide on descriptions of each person listed. Then call on individuals. Answers will vary. Appropriate adjectives include: **Beto:** fuerte, inteligente, alto, guapo; **Lupe:** popular, bonita; **Ana:** bonita, inteligente, simpática; **Jaime:** flaco, alto, estudioso; **Pirata:** tonto, feo, simpático.

C. ¡Mi mejor amigo! Have students complete the sentence **Mi mejor amigo(a) es....** with traits they consider most important. Remind them to use feminine endings with female friends. Have students compare lists in small groups and produce group list of traits all had in common. Ask each group to read their list to class while you write it into a simple paragraph on board or transparency.

Point out Bonito is not usually used to describe men. **Cómico** is used by Hispanics in the U.S. In Spanish-speaking countries, **gracioso** is more common.

Adjectives
Used to describe people or animals

Singular adjectives whose masculine form ends in **-o** have two forms:

masculine	-o	delgado
feminine	-a	delgada

Most other singular adjectives have only one form:

fuer**te**
popula**r**

See **¿Por qué se dice así?**, *pages G10–G14, sections 1.5 and 1.6.*

Y
Used when listing

Use **y** when listing two or more traits.

Ella es modesta, inteligente **y** popular.

The word **y** is spelled **e** when the next word begins with **i** or **hi.**

Ella es bonita **e** inteligente.

See **¿Por qué se dice así?**, *page G12, section 1.6.*

Cognates
Vocabulary expansion

Many adjectives are cognates (words that look like English words). Learning to recognize them can greatly increase your vocabulary.

atlético(a)	modesto(a)
cómico(a)	nervioso(a)
elegante	organizado(a)
estudioso(a)	popular
extrovertido(a)	precioso(a)
generoso(a)	romántico(a)
inteligente	tímido(a)
interesante	tranquilo(a)

CHARLEMOS UN POCO

A. ¡Soy magnífico! The students from Montebello High are describing themselves. Who is talking: Jaime, Ana, Lupe, or Beto?

Jaime

Ana

Lupe

Beto

1. Soy muy tímida.
2. Soy grande, fuerte y guapo.
3. Soy inteligente.
4. Soy estudioso.
5. Soy flaco.
6. Soy bonita y popular.
7. Soy alto y moreno.

B. Mis nuevos amigos. Pilar is writing a letter home describing her new friends at Montebello High. What does she say?

MODELO **Lupe es bonita y morena.**

Lupe	fuerte	alto
Beto	popular	tonto
Ana	bonito	simpático
Jaime	inteligente	guapo
Pirata	flaco	estudioso

C. ¡Mi mejor amigo! From the list below, which traits do you consider most important in a best friend? Do you consider any traits unimportant?

MODELO **Mi mejor amigo(a) es . . .**

delgado	gordo	inteligente
grande	modesto	bonito
fuerte	popular	romántico
simpático	generoso	interesante
guapo	cómico	organizado
atlético	estudioso	tranquilo

Purpose These activities provide guided practice to students beginning to learn how to describe people. As such, the repetition built into the activities is intentional. At this stage, students cannot get too much practice with description.

CH. Persona famosa. Describe your favorite movie star and rock star using the list below.

MODELO **Woody Allen es inteligente, delgado y cómico.**

bajo	bonito	rubio	elegante
tímido	cómico	pelirrojo	interesante
alto	atlético	moreno	inteligente
delgado	romántico	guapo	
tonto	feo	gordo	

D. No es así. You and a friend met a new student named Gloria but are discovering that you did not meet the same person. What do you say?

 MODELO alto
   You: **Es alta, ¿no?**
   Partner: **No, no es alta, es baja.**

1. tímido
2. simpático
3. desorganizado
4. feo
5. moreno
6. gordo
7. tonto
8. tranquilo

LECCIÓN 3

No, ni/ni

Used to express negative ideas

To make a sentence negative, place **no** in front of the verb.

Ella **no** es alta.
Mi profesora **no** es exigente.

Neither/nor is **ni/ni** in Spanish.

No es **ni** alto **ni** bajo.

E. Vecinos. You and your partner have moved into a new neighborhood. Take turns asking questions about your new neighbors. Answer by matching the statements with the appropriate figures in the drawing.

MODELO   You: **¿Cómo es Antonio Romero?**
Partner: **Es delgado y alto.**

Pablo Ledesma

Homero y Hortensia Carrillo

Antonio y Estela Romero

Susana

Cristóbal

Julia

Lobo

a. No es ni alta ni baja. Es rubia.
b. No es delgado. Es gordo.
c. Es muy tímida.
ch. No es ni alto ni bajo. Pero es muy elegante.
d. No es bonito. Es flaco y feo.
e. Es muy fuerte.
f. Es baja y delgada.
g. Es muy elegante y alta.
h. Es delgado y alto.

F. La familia de Pilar. These are pictures of Pilar's family. Describe the people in her family.

1. Papá   **2.** Mamá   **3.** Yolanda

4. Chato   **5.** Reina

G. Descripciones. Describe the following people at your school. The words below may be helpful.

> EJEMPLO   el (la) director(a)
> **La directora es simpática y popular. No es ni alta ni baja.**

nervioso	grande
tímido	bajo
fuerte	romántico
alto	inteligente
exigente	simpático
popular	organizado

1. El (la) director(a)
2. El (la) profesor(a) de matemáticas
3. Mi profesor(a) de historia
4. El señor [*nombre*]
5. La señorita [*nombre*]
6. Mi amigo(a) [*nombre*]

H. ¡Yo soy editor! The editorial staff of your yearbook has asked you to write brief captions for the pictures of three classmates and yourself. Point out two or three positive characteristics in each description.

LECCIÓN 3

 F. La familia de Pilar. Encourage students to use as many descriptors as possible. Answers will vary. Appropriate adjectives include: **Papá:** alto, delgado, guapo; **Mamá:** baja, delgada, morena, bonita; **Yolanda:** pelirroja, baja, delgada; **Chato:** bajo, gordo, feo; **Reina:** bonita, elegante.

Extension Ask students to bring in a picture of their family (or a family out of a magazine) and have them write a short description of each family member. Every day for a week, post 6 pictures (labeled **A–F**) and below them, in arbitrary order, post the six descriptions (labeled **1-6**). Ask students to match each description with the appropriate picture. Useful vocabulary: **papá, mamá, hermano, hermana.**

 G. Descripciones. Extension Have students write a description of one of the persons listed or any other well-known person at the school. Read their descriptions and ask class to identify who is being described. Do not read any with negative characteristics.

 H. ¡Yo soy editor! Collect descriptions and read to class without mentioning names. Ask class to identify person being described. Do not read any with negative characteristics.

Extension Ask students to bring in pictures of three friends labeled with characteristics. Have them share photos in groups or with whole class.

B. El profesor ideal. Have each pair write their sentence on board or on a large sheet of paper to be posted around the room. Students may take turns reading about their ideal teacher.

Extension Describe other teachers at your school and let students guess each one's identity.

C. ¡Mi compañero(a) ideal! Allow 5 min. Then ask five students to write their descriptions of ideal dates on board. The rest of class can write own descriptions at desks. Have students read descriptions on board and suggest famous people who meet "qualifications." Ask questions to confirm celebrity named has all qualities listed.

Extension In 5 min, students survey five classmates to create list of characteristics of ideal companion or date. Then compare their lists.

CH. ¡Misterio!
Extension Have pairs write description of person they believe will be the next victim. In groups of four, have one pair read the description and the other draw a picture of the person being described. Reverse roles and repeat process.

CHARLEMOS UN POCO MÁS

A. Hermanos. Margarita and Francisco are brother and sister. What differences and similarities do you see in them?

B. El profesor ideal. Working in pairs, decide what personality traits are most important in a good teacher. Complete the sentence **El profesor ideal es . . .** or **La profesora ideal es . . .** with as many adjectives as you consider important.

C. ¡Mi compañero(a) ideal! Interview three of your classmates to find out their idea of what the ideal companion or date is like. They will also be interviewing you, so be ready with the characteristics you consider most important.

EJEMPLO **¿Cómo es tu compañero(a) ideal?**
¿Es alto(a)? ¿Es inteligente?

CH. ¡Misterio! You are halfway through a mystery novel and think that you know who the next victim will be. Working in groups of four, decide if the victim will be **1, 2, 3,** or **4.** Then write a description of the person. Read it to the class to see if they can identify the right picture.

Purpose These activities are designed to allow students to create with language recently learned. Although the activities may sometimes appear repetitious of the guided practice in the previous section, they enable students to use description for personal expression and problem solving.

D. ¿Cómo soy yo?   A friend has arranged a blind date for you. You have to describe yourself over the telephone so that your date will recognize you. You will also want to ask your date questions about himself or herself.

E. ¡Volibol!   Your teacher will give you a picture of six volleyball players in the school tournament. You don't know them. Describe each one until your partner can tell you the person's name. On a separate sheet of paper, write the name of each person in the correct order. You could begin by asking **¿Cómo se llama el (la) chico(a) alto(a) y . . . ?**

D. ¿Cómo soy yo? If a screen or divider is available, students could stand on opposite sides while doing this activity.

E. ¡Volibol! Insist students not look at each other's drawings.

Dramatizaciones

A. ¡Socorro!   While shopping, you lost your little brother or sister in a store. Describe the child to the store detective.

- The detective will ask a variety of questions concerning the missing child's name, physical description, and personality traits.
- You will answer all the questions and volunteer any other pertinent information.

B. ¡Socorro (a continuación)!   Play the role of the little brother or sister talking to the store detective.

- The detective will ask a variety of questions concerning your older brother's or sister's name, physical description, and personality traits.
- You will answer all the questions.

C. ¡La cita ideal!   Play "The Ideal Date." You will need at least two contestants, one male and one female. While the contestants prepare questions outside the class, select the candidates—three girls and three boys. Devise a screen so the contestant cannot see the candidates. The teacher will play the role of the host.

CH. Video.   Your Spanish class is going to prepare a video of all class members to send to a sister school. Be prepared to describe yourself in thirty seconds in front of the camera.

DRAMATIZACIONES

Evaluation

Role plays **A** and **B** are designed to be assigned at the same time to different groups of students.

C. ¡La cita ideal! Ask for volunteers. Do not force anyone to play. This may be set up as popular game show, "The Dating Game." Screen may be bed sheet held by two students. Allow each contestant to ask candidates 5 or 6 questions. Have contestant select his/her ideal date. Repeat game as long as there are volunteers.

CH. Video. Borrow video camera and videotape all students. Exchange tapes with another Spanish class in your school or, preferably, in a nearby school.

Purpose In this section, students recycle—in student-centered role plays—all previously learned structures and vocabulary needed to describe people.

Suggestions Encourage students to work without their textbooks when performing their role plays.

A. Anticipemos.
Suggestions Have students discuss questions in groups or pairs, then share responses with class. After reading, have them check accuracy of predictions.

Answers

1 The picture, colors, headlines: **Es práctico. Es completo. ¡Es único!**
2 Answers may include number of pages, illustrations, number of entries, other features, possible uses, etc.

Extension Ask some students to tell what they wrote and to write it on board. After reading advertisement, check to see if students anticipated correctly.

B. Cognados. Select first few cognates for class: **práctico, completo, único, diccionario, geográfico, universal.** Allow 3 min. Ask one pair to read list and have other groups add to it.

Point out Not all words that look alike are true cognates. Some false cognates are: **datos, actualizada.**

Verifiquemos

Answers

1 ch
2 c
3 72
4 More than 500
5 c
6 b

LEAMOS AHORA

Reading strategy: Using cognates

A. Anticipemos. Before we read an advertisement, something usually draws our attention and makes us anticipate the information in it.

1. What draws your attention to the advertisement on the right?
2. What information do you expect to find in this advertisement? Write two things you expect this advertisement to say.

B. Cognados. Cognates are words that look somewhat alike and have similar meanings in two languages. Spanish and English share many cognates, and learning to recognize them will increase your vocabulary very rapidly. Can you recognize these?

americano	protección	clásico	universidad
clase	fotografía	béisbol	

Now, working in pairs, list all the cognates you can find in the text of the advertisement on the right. Write the Spanish words and their English equivalents. You are not expected to understand every word in the advertisement. Simply focus on those words you do understand.

C. Diccionario geográfico. Now read the advertisement on the right, and then answer the questions.

Verifiquemos _____

Now check to see if you understood the reading.

1. This advertisement is for
   a. a universal history book.
   b. a geography textbook.
   c. an atlas.
   ch. a dictionary of geographical facts.

2. According to the ad, this book is ideal for
   a. students.
   b. teachers.
   c. Both of the above.
   ch. Neither of the above.

3. How many color pages are there in this book?

4. How many illustrations are there in this book?

5. This book has maps of
   a. North America.
   b. Spanish-speaking regions.
   c. Both of the above.
   ch. Neither of the above.

6. Which edition of the book is being advertised?
   a. The first.
   b. The second.
   c. The third.
   ch. It does not say.

Purpose This is the principal reading of the unit. Its purpose is to teach students to glean information from a text using limited vocabulary and cognates. Students are not expected to know every word but rather to make intelligent guesses based on words they do understand. This reading strategy should be applied to all subsequent reading selections.

Es práctico.

Es completo.

¡ES ÚNICO!

Este útil diccionario trae más de 22.000 nombres de países, regiones y accidentes geográficos del mundo. Una excelente ayuda para estudiantes, profesores y toda persona que quiera enriquecer sus conocimientos.

72 páginas a color. Más de 500 ilustraciones y recuadros. Tablas estadísticas. Datos sobre lugares históricos, zonas turísticas, centros culturales. Mapas físicos y políticos de continentes, regiones y países.

Adquiera en su puesto de revistas favorito.

El único
DICCIONARIO
GEOGRÁFICO
UNIVERSAL
en español

DICCIONARIO GEOGRÁFICO Universal
72 páginas a color

2da EDICIÓN REVISADA Y ACTUALIZADA

- Único en su clase.
- El primero en español.
- Más de 22.000 nombres de países, regiones y accidentes geográficos del mundo.
- Datos sobre lugares históricos, zonas turísticas, centros culturales.
- Tablas estadísticas.
- Más de 500 ilustraciones y recuadros.
- Mapas físicos y políticos

ESCRIBAMOS UN POCO

A. Planeando.
Suggestions Have students answer questions in English, then talk about their answers. For example:

1 ¿Para quién escribo? Lead students to recognize that new pen pal will be a teenager with similar interests and other similarities and differences. An important difference will be that pen pals may not speak English and are not accustomed to reading Spanish written by non-Spanish speakers. Therefore accuracy will have new importance; pen pal will not "know what you mean" as a Spanish teacher would.

2 ¿Por qué escribo? Students should mention they will be writing to introduce themselves and to respond to questions the pen pal may have asked.

3 ¿De qué escribo? Students should note they will write about themselves in as much detail as possible and will ask questions to find out as much as they can about the pen pal.

B. Empezando. Enrique left out: **delgado, estudioso, inteligente, no tonto, atlético, modesto** and **¿Cómo te llamas?, ¿Cómo es tu familia/escuela?, ¿Cómo son tus profesores?**

Suggestions You may want to have the class brainstorm together, having volunteers list all contributions on board. Remind students that all ideas are acceptable during brainstorming. Individuals will choose appropriate items from the list. Tell them not to be concerned about organizing until the list is complete. The purpose of brainstorming is to generate as many ideas and as much language as possible.

Writing strategy: Brainstorming

Imagine that you have just received the following short letter from Enrique Zapata, your new pen pal in Peru.

> Lima, 10 de septiembre
>
> Querido amigo:
>
> ¡Hola! ¿Cómo estás? ¡Yo... estupendo!
> Me llamo Enrique Zapata. Soy de Perú, de Lima.
> No soy tímido. Soy alto, moreno y guapo.
> También soy romántico y muy popular.
> ¿Cómo eres tú?
>
> Un amigo sudamericano
>
> Enrique

You now need to answer his letter. Your writing will be easier if you follow these steps.

A. Planeando. Before writing, a good writer always plans what she or he is going to write. Good planning includes thinking about these three important questions:

1. **¿Para quién escribo?**   *For whom am I writing?*
2. **¿Por qué escribo?**   *Why am I writing?*
3. **¿De qué escribo?**   *About what am I writing?*

B. Empezando. When you begin to write, try to assemble all of your ideas first. One way to organize your thoughts before writing is to brainstorm a list of everything you might say. Then you can decide what to include, what to leave out, and how to organize what you write.

At the top of the next page is the brainstorming list that Enrique made when he was preparing to write you. Read the letter and study Enrique's brainstorming list. Did Enrique's letter include all the information in his list? If not, what did he leave out?

Purpose In this section, students are asked to apply speaking and writing skills developed in the unit to a real-life writing task. The writing stategy presented should be applied here and in subsequent writing sections. The writing process that students are asked to follow consists of planning, writing a first draft with peer input, and writing a final draft with peer editing.

¡Hola!   estudioso   ¿y tú?
nombre   inteligente   ...¿nombre?
popular   romántico   ...¿Cómo estás?
de Lima   no tonto   ...¿Cómo eres?
de Perú   moreno   ...¿tu familia?
no tímido   delgado
atlético   alto   ...¿tu escuela?
modesto   guapo   ...¿tus profesores?

C. Organizando.   Below is a drawing of the brainstorming cluster that
Enrique Zapata made to organize the information in his brainstorming list.

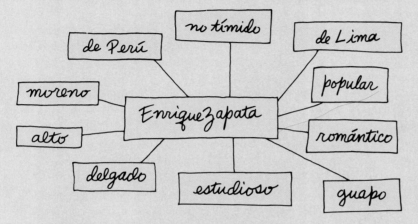

1. What did he decide should be the main theme of his letter?
2. What type of information about himself did he leave out of his letter?
3. What type of information about you did he decide not to request?
4. Is there anything he left out that you wish he had included? What?

CH. Escribiendo.   List all the things you might want to write Enrique in
Spanish. Then study your list and choose one main topic to write about.
From your list select all the information related to your main topic. You
may find it helpful to draw a cluster as Enrique did. Use the information
to write a brief response to Enrique's letter.

D. Compartiendo.   Share a first draft of your letter with a couple of
classmates. Ask them what they think about it. Is there anything they
don't understand? Is there anything they feel should be changed?

E. Revisando.   Rewrite your letter and turn it in to your teacher. Change
anything you want based on your classmates' comments. You may add,
subtract, or reorder what is in the letter.

C. Organizando.

Answers

1 Himself.
2 Too many personality
characteristics.
3 Information about family
and school.
4 Answers will vary.

CH. Escribiendo.
Suggestions Suggest that students who have difficulty follow the model of Enrique's list, cluster, and letter.

D. Compartiendo.
Suggestions In pairs or small groups, allow time for each student to read his or her letter aloud while partner(s) offer(s) help with structure and vocabulary, as well as to comment on content. Students will need to be prepared to deal critically and positively with other's writing. You may wish to prepare a transparency or copies of a letter to model how to critique writing before asking students to do it. Partner(s) should always make at least one positive comment first—I like the way you . . . , It's well-organized, You use a lot of detail, etc.

E. Revisando. Encourage fluency in writing by telling students you will grade letters holistically, focusing on communication rather than on accuracy. You may want to underline grammatical errors, but the grade should be affected only by errors that would confuse a native speaker. See the suggestions for grading writing in the Teacher's Materials for the Testing Program.

Suggestions In this first exploration of the writing process, have students share as much information as possible with classmates. Pair some more able students with weaker ones.

UNIT OBJECTIVES

Communicative Goals

When students have completed this unit, they will be able to use Spanish . . .
- to tell time
- to exchange phone numbers
- to describe their teachers, friends, classes, class schedules, and after-school activities
- to give the location of people and things
- to talk about future activities
- to list and talk about obligations

Culture

In this unit, students will compare and contrast . . .
- school schedules in Hispanic countries with their own
- a report card from Mexico with their own
- the grading system used in Hispanic countries with their own
- types of schools in Hispanic countries with schools in the U.S.
- addresses of Hispanic pen pals with their own

Reading and Writing Strategies

- Reading: Scanning
- Writing: Using clusters

Structure

- Numbers: 0–30
- Nouns and articles
- Telling time
- Adjectives
- Subject pronouns
- Infinitives
- The verbs **tener, ser, estar, ir** and the expressions **tener que** + infinitive and **ir a** + infinitive

¡Es hora de clase!

UNIT SETTING

The Commonwealth of Puerto Rico is a beautiful tropical island about 1,000 miles southeast of Florida. With the Atlantic Ocean to the north and the Caribbean Sea to the south, it measures 100 miles (165 km) long and only 35 miles (58 km) wide. The island's terrain is mountainous, with the Cordillera Central occupying most of its area. The coastline is composed of white sand beaches and coral reefs. Puerto Rico also boasts the only rain forest in the U.S. National Park system—a vast, lushly tropical collection of flora and fauna known as El Yunque.

Archaeologists speculate that the island has been inhabited since the first century A.D. When Columbus arrived in 1493, the **taíno** Indians had already developed an advanced society on **Borinquén,** or "Island of the Brave Lord," as they called it. Today residents still affectionately use the name. The current population of about

Océano Atlántico

San Juan

PUERTO RICO

Mayagüez

• Ponce

25 Kilómetros

25 Millas

Mar Caribe

3,700,000 is made up of descendants of the **taínos,** the Spanish, and Africans brought to the island as slaves in the sixteenth century.

A colony of Spain until the Spanish-American War in 1898, Puerto Rico was then occupied by the United States. Today, as a commonwealth of the U.S., Puerto Rico receives assistance and protection from the federal government but has full authority in all local matters.

Puerto Ricans are U.S. citizens, free to move to the mainland without immigration restrictions. They can vote in all but presidential elections and are exempt from paying federal income taxes. The three major political parties continue to debate whether to maintain the current system, advocate full statehood, or favor complete independence from the U.S.

OBJECTIVES

Communicative Goals

- Exchanging information about class schedules
- Asking for and telling time
- Exchanging phone numbers

Culture and Reading

- *¡No me digas!*
  El horario de Andrea:
  School schedules
- *Y ahora, ¡a leer!*
  ¡Calificaciones!
  The numerical grading system;
  Boleta: Report cards

Structure

- 2.1 Numbers: 0–30
- 2.2 Nouns and articles: Singular and plural forms
- 2.3 Telling time
- 2.4 The verb **tener**: Singular forms

¡Tengo historia ahora!

ACTIVE VOCABULARY

La hora

¿A qué hora es …?	mediodía
a la / las …	menos
¿Qué hora es?	… y cuarto
Es la / Son las …	… menos cuarto
de la mañana	… y media
de la noche	por la mañana
de la tarde	por la noche
medianoche	por la tarde

En el colegio

almuerzo	horario
boleta	mapa
computadora	reloj
diccionario	

Clases

álgebra	gimnasia
arte	historia
ciencias	hora de estudio
… naturales	inglés
computación	literatura
dibujo	matemáticas
educación física	música
español	química
francés	teatro
geografía	

Números 0–30

Días de la semana

semana
lunes
martes
miércoles
jueves
viernes
sábado
domingo

Verbos

tener
  tengo
  tienes
  tiene

Palabras y expresiones

foto	¿Cuándo?
hoy	¡Oye!
las	¡Por fin!
los	¡Uy!
más	
número	
teléfono	
tu	
video	

ANTICIPEMOS

Colegio San Martín

Estudiante: Santarina Flores, Olga Maria   **Año:** Segundo

	LUNES	MARTES	MIÉRCOLES	JUEVES	VIERNES	SÁBADO
9:00	Álgebra 2	Educación física	Álgebra 2	Educación física	Álgebra 2	Folklore de Venezuela
10:00	Inglés 8	Inglés 8	Inglés 8	Inglés 8	Inglés 8	Folklore de Venezuela
11:00	Historia de Venezuela	Historia de Venezuela	Geografía política	Historia de Venezuela	Dibujo	Gimnasia
12:00	Química 1	Química 1	Educación familiar	Computación	Computación	Gimnasia
3:00	Castellano: Literatura	Castellano: Literatura		Castellano: Composición	Castellano: Composición	
4:00	Gimnasia	Álgebra 2		Química 1	Ciencias naturales	
5:00	Música	Álgebra 2		Química 1	Ciencias naturales	
6:00	Francés 3	Francés 3		Francés 3	Francés 3	

¿Qué piensas tú?

1. Whose schedule is this? What school does the student go to?

2. Although the subjects are written in Spanish, you probably have little trouble determining what most of them are. What are they? How do you know? Can you make any guesses about the ones you're not sure of?

3. What information is in the schedule? How often do classes meet? How long is the school day? How long is a class period?

4. In what country do you think the school is located? Why?

5. What similarities are there between your school schedule and this one? What differences?

6. Are there any courses in this schedule that you would like to see your school offer? Why?

7. What differences, do you think, you might find in schedules from other Spanish-speaking areas—for example, Spain, Mexico, or Puerto Rico?

8. What do you think you will be able to talk about when you have finished this lesson?

ANTICIPEMOS

¿Qué piensas tú?

The questions are in English to allow use of higher-level thinking skills beyond students' current skills in Spanish. Encourage answers in Spanish but accept English responses as well.

Answers

1. Olga María Santarina Flores; Colegio San Martín.
2. Most are cognates. Help students determine probable content of unfamiliar subjects. **Castellano: Lit.** = Spanish Literature; **Geografía política** = Political Geography; **Ed. familiar** = Home Economics; **Computación** = Computers; **Castellano: Comp.** = Spanish Composition.
3. School's name, student's name, year in school, times, days, names of classes. Class frequency varies from 1 to 5 times a week. School day is 9 A.M. to 7 P.M. with 2-hr lunch break, except on Wed. and Sat., 9 A.M. to 1 P.M. Most classes are 1 hour; some meet 2 hours.
4. In Venezuela, based on history and folklore classes. A Venezuelan schedule is presented for cross-cultural contrast; Puerto Rican schools have schedules similar to continental U.S.
5. Responses vary.
6. Responses vary.
7. Other countries will study their own history/folklore.
8. **Students will be able to talk about classes they are taking, days, times, and teachers.**

Purpose To focus students on the language necessary to talk about class schedules and to encourage use of critical thinking skills while noting differences and similarities between a Venezuelan class schedule and their own.

Suggestions Describe the schedule in Spanish: **Es el horario de . . . Va al Colegio San Martín. Tiene dieciséis clases.** Students will not understand every word, but they should follow and will hear correct pronunciation as introduction.

Allow students to guess at the difference between **gimnasia** and **educación física.** The two terms are often used interchangeably in Spanish. **Gimnasia artística** is used for gymnastics, as in the Olympic games.

You may wish to point out the student's use of two surnames. Information on Hispanic surnames may be found on page 165.

TAPE/DISC
20:29–22:14

Side 2, 1402 to 4547

Comprehension Checks

A complete set of the **Comprehension Checks** is available on cards in the Teacher's Resource Package.

1   20:37

1. ¿Es Esteban / Raúl / Sara / Mónica? *(Point to each.)*
2. ¿Cómo se llama el chico? ¿la chica? *(Point to each.)*
3. ¿Es estudiante? *(Point to each.)*
4. ¿Eres estudiante?
5. ¿Es Esteban (Sara, Raúl, Mónica) estudiante en la escuela Robinson? *(Point to each.)*
6. ¿Está en San Juan la escuela?
7. ¿Está en San Juan o en *[your city]*?
8. ¿Está San Juan en Puerto Rico o en *[your state]*?

Side 2, 1609 to 2131

2   20:55

Suggestions Draw calendar on board—point to **jueves**. Hold up four fingers. Point to icons.
1. ¿Quién es?
Continue asking point-to, yes/no, either/or, and one- or two-word-answer questions, or use the **Comprehension Checks** in TRP.

Side 2, 2150 to 2624

3   21:11

Suggestions Draw clock showing 9:05. Contrast with clock on overhead. Point to **gimnasia** icon.
1. ¿Son las nueve?
Continue asking Comprehension Check questions, as above.

Side 2, 2643 to 3095

1

Estos chicos son estudiantes en la escuela Robinson, en San Juan, Puerto Rico. Son Sara, Mónica, Raúl y Esteban.

2

Esteban: Hoy es jueves. Tengo cuatro clases por la mañana: computación, gimnasia, química, matemáticas. ¿Qué clases tienes tú?

62 sesenta y dos

4

Sara: Oye, Raúl, ¿a qué hora es la clase de química? ¿Y dónde?
Raúl: Pues, aquí en la sala diecisiete a las diez y media.

3

Esteban: ¿Qué hora es? ¡Uy! ¡Son las nueve . . . y tengo educación física a las nueve y cinco! Adiós.

$2x^2 + 5x = 17$

4   21:27

Suggestions Show 10:30 on board. Identify room numbers of classes/teachers in your school.
Note Ser *(= to take place)* is used when talking about the time or place of an event.
1. ¿Quién es? *(Point to Raúl, then to Sara.)*
Continue asking Comprehension Check questions, as above.

Side 2, 3125 to 3432

Purpose This section is not meant for memorization or mastery; it sets the context for the language needed to talk about school schedules and provides comprehensible language without translation. It also introduces pronunciation and usage of language being learned.

5

Esteban: Sara, es la una . . . Tienes historia ahora, ¿no?

Sara: No, Esteban. Yo tengo historia los lunes, miércoles y viernes.

6

Sara: Oye, Raúl, ¿qué clase tienes a las dos menos cuarto?

Raúl: Español con la Sra. Rodríguez.

Sara: ¡Yo también! Tenemos español juntos.

7

Sara: ¡Ay, por fin son las tres y diez! Oye, Mónica, ¿vamos a estudiar inglés juntas?

Mónica: ¿Cuándo? ¿Por la noche?

Sara: Sí, a las siete, en mi casa.

Mónica: Muy bien, Sara. ¡Hasta luego!

sesenta y tres **63**

$\mathcal{S}$**uggestions** Begin by having students close their books while you narrate one section at a time, using the transparencies to clarify meaning without translation. Then ask the questions in the **Comprehension Checks**. Repeat this process with each section.

Use a clock or write various times on the board or on a transparency to clarify morning/afternoon/evening.

Using the video Play one section at a time after narrating it using the transparencies. Freeze the video and ask the Comprehension Check questions. Repeat this process with each section.

Since numbers are not presented here in the traditional counting sequence, hold up fingers, point to numbers as they are named in the narration/dialogue.

TAPE/DISC
22:15–24:21

Side 2, 4575 to 8351

Early Production Checks

Use the **Early Production Checks** to verify students' comprehension and to guide students' first productive efforts. Students should not be expected to respond in complete sentences every time, since people in real-life discourse rarely do. Ask them to identify people, answer yes/no, either/or, one- and two-word-answer questions. Build to questions requiring more complex responses. Provide for students' "success" at various levels of achievement.

A complete set of the **Early Production Checks** is available on cards in the Teacher's Resource Package.

1   22:21

¡Qué confusión!
Suggestions Recap dialogues in narrative: **Es Carlos Muñoz. Es un nuevo estudiante. Tiene un problema. Su horario es confuso . . .**

 ¡OjO!   **Conmigo** is used for passive comprehension, not for production at this point.

1 ¿Quién es Carlos Muñoz?
  Es un nuevo estudiante.
2 ¿Es su primera semana aquí?
  Sí.
3 ¿Quién es ella?   *Es Sara Torres.*
4 ¿Tiene problemas Sara?
  ¿Carlos? *No. / Sí.*
5 ¿Es confuso el horario de Carlos? *Sí.*
6 ¿Qué clase tiene ahora?
  Geografía.
7 ¿Qué hora es? *Son las diez.*
8 ¿Qué día es? *Lunes.*
9 ¿Dónde es la clase de geografía, en el salón veinte o veintidós?
  En el salón veintidós.
10 ¿A qué hora es la clase de inglés, a las 10:00 o a las 11:15?
  A las 11:15.

¿QUÉ DECIMOS...?
Al hablar de horarios y clases

1   **¡Qué confusión!**

UNIDAD 2

Note In question 9, **ser** is used to describe where an event takes place.

Side 2, 4730 to 6102

Purpose   This section uses the language of class schedules and telling time in real-life situations. Students should not be overly concerned with understanding or translating every word. Comprehension will come with video viewing and/or with teacher's use of the overhead transparencies to help students practice the new language.

2 ¿Qué hora es?

3 ¿Cuál es tu teléfono?

¿Qué hora es?

Accept brief phrases or one- and two-word answers to all **Early Production Checks** as shown in **1** on page 64. It is not necessary for students to answer in complete sentences.

1. ¿Hay clase de computación hoy?
2. ¿Qué día es hoy, lunes o martes?
3. ¿Es la clase de computación los lunes, miércoles y viernes?
4. ¿Cuándo tiene educación física Carlos?
5. ¿Qué clase tiene Carlos los martes y jueves?
6. ¿A qué hora es la clase de educación física?

Side 2, 6127 to 7116

¿Cuál es tu teléfono?

¡Ojo! **Te gusta** is used here for passive comprehension, not for production.

1. ¿Hay clase de computación mañana?
2. ¿Le gusta la clase de computación a Carlos?
3. ¿Es interesante la clase de computación?
4. ¿Quién es exigente?
5. ¿Es muy exigente?
6. ¿Tiene computadora en casa Carlos? ¿Raúl?
7. ¿Van a estudiar juntos Carlos y Raúl?
8. ¿Dónde van a estudiar, en casa de Carlos o en casa de Raúl?
9. ¿Cuándo van a estudiar juntos?
10. ¿Van a estudiar por la tarde o por la noche?
11. ¿Cuál es el número de teléfono de Raúl?
12. ¿Cuál es tu número de teléfono?

Side 2, 7131 to 8351

Suggestions Begin by having students close their books while you narrate one section at a time, using the transparencies to clarify meaning without translation. Then ask the questions in the **Early Production Checks**. Repeat this process after each section.

Using the video Play one section at a time after narrating it using the transparencies. Freeze the video and ask **Early Production Checks**. Repeat this process with each section.

Using the margin boxes
See note on page 23.

Note The numbers 31–100 are presented in Unit 4.

Point out The numbers 16–19 and 21–29 are usually written as one word, but they can also be written as three words: **diez y seis**, **diez y nueve**, **veinte y uno**, etc.

A. Mi nueva escuela.
Read each statement and have class respond, or call on individuals to read each statement and have class respond.

1 sí **2** no **3** sí **4** sí
5 no **6** sí **7** sí **8** no
9 sí **10** no

B. Mi número de teléfono.
Tell students to write down their classmates' phone numbers. Allow 3-4 min. Then verify numbers by asking individual students to read a classmate's number while another student writes it on board.

Extension Collect the numbers that students have written and read several of them in Spanish for dictation. Then ask students to identify their own number, as you read it.

C. ¿Diga?
Point out Numbers beginning with a zero, such as 01 and 05, would be read **cero, uno** and **cero, cinco**.

1 Nueve, diecisiete, veintiséis, veintitrés.
2 Tres, cero, cinco, treinta, trece.
3 Ocho, veintinueve, once, veintisiete.
4 Seis, dieciséis, cero, uno, diez.
5 Cuatro, catorce, veintidós, veintiuno.
6 Siete, veintiocho, dieciocho, quince.
7 Dos, veinticinco, diecinueve, cero, nueve.
8 Cinco, veinticuatro, doce, veinte.
9 Seis, quince, treinta, cero, tres.
10 Nueve, catorce, once, veintiuno.

CH. ¿Qué hay en tu casa?
This activity reenters classroom objects from the preliminary lesson. Check that students do not think **carpeta** is a cognate for *carpet*. Have them answer by telling the number of each item they have in their rooms.

66 UNIDAD 2 Lección 1

Numbers 0–30

0	cero	16	dieciséis
1	uno	17	diecisiete
2	dos	18	dieciocho
3	tres	19	diecinueve
4	cuatro	20	veinte
5	cinco	21	veintiuno
6	seis	22	veintidós
7	siete	23	veintitrés
8	ocho	24	veinticuatro
9	nueve	25	veinticinco
10	diez	26	veintiséis
11	once	27	veintisiete
12	doce	28	veintiocho
13	trece	29	veintinueve
14	catorce	30	treinta
15	quince		

See **¿Por qué se dice así?**, *page G15, section 2.1.*

Plural nouns

Singular	Plural
chic**a**	chic**as**
directo**r**	directo**res**
lápi**z**	lápi**ces**

See **¿Por qué se dice así?**, *page G16, section 2.2.*

66 *sesenta y seis*

A. Mi nueva escuela. Carlos is telling his family about his new school. Would he say each of the following? Answer **sí** or **no** based on what you know about Carlos and his friends.

1. Sara Torres es una nueva amiga.
2. Tengo geografía con Sara.
3. Tengo geografía los lunes.
4. Tengo la clase de inglés con Sara.
5. Tengo computación los martes.
6. Tengo educación física con Raúl.
7. La clase de computación es interesante.
8. La profesora de computación no es exigente.
9. Raúl tiene computadora en casa.
10. Vamos a estudiar juntos esta noche.

B. Mi número de teléfono. Ask four classmates their telephone numbers and give them yours.

EJEMPLO 698-7341
You: **¿Cuál es tu número de teléfono?**
Partner: **Es el seis, nueve, ocho, siete, tres, cuatro, uno.**

C. ¿Diga? In many Spanish-speaking countries, phone numbers are written and said in pairs, starting with the second digit. How would you say these numbers?

MODELO 721 1401 (7-21-14-01)
Siete, veintiuno, catorce, cero, uno.

1. 917 2623	5. 414 2221	8. 524 1220
2. 305 3013	6. 728 1815	9. 615 3003
3. 829 1127	7. 225 1909	10. 914 1121
4. 616 0110		

CH. ¿Qué hay en tu casa? Ask your partner if there are any of the following items in his or her room at home.

MODELO foto
You: **¿Hay fotos?**
Partner: **Sí, hay (seis) fotos.** o
No, no hay fotos.

1. carpeta	5. bolígrafo	9. mesa
2. papel	6. lápiz	10. libro
3. diccionario	7. computadora	11. reloj
4. mochila	8. cuaderno	12. borrador

UNIDAD 2

Point out In negative constructions, **hay** is usually followed by a plural noun, except when referring to one specific item.

Purpose These activities provide guided practice as students begin to produce new language. As such, the repetition built into the activities is intentional. Students need not do all activities, once they have demonstrated mastery of numbers, telling time, and talking about school schedules.

D. ¡Fútbol! Your friend missed the homecoming game and wants to know who was there. What do you say?

MODELO señor Pérez / no
      Partner: **¿Y el señor Pérez?**
      You: **El señor Pérez, no.**

1. director de la escuela / sí   6. doctora García / sí
2. profesores de español / no   7. estudiantes de Colombia / sí
3. chicas de Cuba / sí   8. amigas de Sara / sí
4. señor Medina / no   9. profesor Johnson / no
5. señorita Rivera / sí   10. señora Muñoz / no

E. ¿Qué hora es? Your best friend forgot to wear a watch today and keeps asking you for the time. What do you say?

MODELO **Son las once y cinco.**

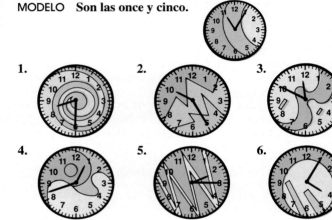

1.   2.   3.

4.   5.   6.

F. ¿A qué hora es? Look at the schedule below as you answer your teacher's questions concerning Lupe's classes.

MODELO ¿A qué hora es la clase de álgebra de Lupe?
        A las ocho y cuarto.

LUNES 28	SEPTIEMBRE
8:15 álgebra	1:00 almuerzo
9:30 historia	3:10 español
10:50 literatura	4:40 música
11:55 geografía	6:00 educación física

H. ¡Ayúdame!

1 Son las cinco y cuarto de la tarde.
2 Son las dos y cuarto de la tarde.
3 Son las tres y cuarto de la tarde.
4 Son las nueve y cuarto de la noche.
5 Son las diez y cuarto de la mañana.
6 Son las dos y cuarto de la tarde.
7 Son las nueve y cuarto de la noche.
8 Son las cuatro y cuarto de la tarde.

I. ¿Por la mañana . . . ?

Have students take notes on partner's answers. Allow 3–4 min, then ask individual students **¿A qué hora es la clase de historia de** *[partner's name]*?

Extension Have students draw a blank schedule, then survey classmates, filling in names and classes. Debrief by asking about different students in the class.

Vocabulario opcional
Orquesta, Banda, Economía doméstica, Curso de manejo, Hora de estudio, Contabilidad, Mecanografía, Ciencias sociales, Biología. Technical courses include **Dibujo técnico, Electrónica, Carpintería, Corte y confección, Cultura de belleza, Mecánica automotriz.**

Note With verbs other than **ser,** some speakers use **en la mañana / tarde / noche** instead of **por** to express general time.

Tener: Singular forms

Tengo español a las ocho.
¿Cuándo **tienes** historia?
Mario no **tiene** álgebra hoy.

*See ¿Por qué se dice así?,
page G20, section 2.4.*

The days of the week and the definite article
Used when saying *on* what day(s) something occurs

The days of the week are **lunes, martes, miércoles, jueves, viernes, sábado,** and **domingo.**

el / los + [*day(s) of week*]

Carlos tiene un examen **el** jueves.
No hay clases **los** sábados.

Time and the preposition *de*

When mentioning a specific time, use

de + {
 la mañana
 la tarde
 la noche
}

Mi clase de química es a las 8:10 **de la mañana.**
Tengo arte a las 2:30 **de la tarde.**

*See ¿Por qué se dice así?,
page G18, section 2.3.*

Time and the preposition *por*

When a specific time is not mentioned, use

por + {
 la mañana
 la tarde
 la noche
}

Tengo inglés **por la mañana.**

*See ¿Por qué se dice así?,
page G18, section 2.3.*

G. ¡Qué confusión! Use the schedule below to answer a confused friend's questions about your schedule.

MODELO gimnasia
Partner: **¿Cuándo tienes gimnasia?**
You: **Tengo gimnasia los martes y jueves.**

Horario de clases

Hora	Materia	Días					Profesor	Sala
9:00	Computación	l		m		v	Srta. Rivera	38
	Gimnasia			m	j		Sr. López	Gim.
10:00	Español	l	m	m	j	v	Sra. Salas	17A
11:00	Inglés	l		m		v	Sr. Wall	21
12:00	Ciencias naturales	l	m	m	j	v	Sra. Guzmán	10B
1:00	Almuerzo							
2:00	Álgebra	l	m	m	j	v	Sra. Estrada	32
3:00	Historia	l		m		v	Sr. Arenas	30

H. ¡Ayúdame! Pat is taking a geography exam. Help her answer these questions regarding time zones: **Cuando son las 12:15 de la tarde en San Francisco, California, ¿qué hora es en . . . ?**

MODELO la Ciudad de México (+2)
Son las dos y cuarto de la tarde.

1. Buenos Aires, Argentina (+5)
2. San Antonio, Texas (+2)
3. Quito, Ecuador (+3)
4. Madrid, España (+9)
5. Anchorage, Alaska (-2)
6. Ciudad Guatemala, Guatemala (+2)
7. París, Francia (+9)
8. Caracas, Venezuela (+4)

I. ¿Por la mañana o por la tarde? Find out when your partner's classes meet.

EJEMPLO You: **¿Tienes biología por la mañana o por la tarde?**
Partner: **Tengo biología a las diez y diez de la mañana. o No tengo biología.**

J. ¿Quién tiene más? Tell who carries more school supplies in his or her backpack or bookbag.

MODELO Pepe 5, libros / Alicia, 3 libros
Pepe tiene dos libros más.

1. Rosa, 8 lápices / Amalia, 5 lápices
2. Beto, 2 cuadernos / yo, 3 cuadernos
3. Yolanda, 1 mochila / yo, 0 mochilas
4. yo, 25 hojas de papel / tú, 10 hojas de papel
5. profesor, 5 bolígrafos / tú, 6 bolígrafos
6. profesora, 15 carpetas / yo, 1 carpeta

J. ¿Quién tiene más?
1 Rosa tiene tres lápices más.
2 Yo tengo un cuaderno más.
3 Yolanda tiene una mochila más.
4 Yo tengo quince hojas de papel más.
5 Tú tienes un bolígafo más.
6 La profesora tiene catorce carpetas más.

CHARLEMOS UN POCO MÁS

A. Mi horario ideal. When would you like to have the following classes? Make a schedule of these classes. Begin at 8:00 A.M. and end at 3:00 P.M. Classes do not have to meet every day. Lunch (**almuerzo**) may be no longer than forty-five minutes.

educación física	ciencia
hora de estudio	música
historia	matemáticas
inglés	español

- Ask several classmates at what time and on which days they are taking each class and tell them about your schedule.
- Find one person who has one or more classes at the same time and on the same days that you do.

B. ¿Cuándo tienes . . . ? You are comparing classes over the phone with a friend. Using the schedules your teacher provides, ask each other about specific classes, times, teachers, room numbers, etc. in order to find out if you and your partner have any classes together.

C. ¡A escribir! Write a brief description of your favorite class this semester by answering each of the following questions.

¿Cuál es tu clase favorita?
¿Cuándo es?
¿Quién es el (la) profesor(a)?
¿Cómo es el (la) profesor(a)?

LECCIÓN 1

CHARLEMOS UN POCO MÁS

A. Mi horario ideal. Allow 4–5 min to make up class schedules. Then allow 5–6 min for students to find classmates with similar schedules. After the activity, ask **¿Quiénes tienen horarios idénticos? ¿Quiénes tienen clases juntos(as)?** Have students with the most classes in common write their schedules on board or on butcher paper.

B. ¿Cuándo tienes . . . ? Allow 2–3 min. Then ask students how many classes they have together, what they are, and at what time they meet. Tell students not to look at each other's schedules.

C. ¡A escribir! Ask students to write a brief description and allow 3–4 min. Encourage them to use adjectives to describe each class. In small groups, ask students to read descriptions to their group. Follow up by asking members of each group questions about other group members' favorite classes.

Purpose The activities in this section are designed to allow students to apply the language of class schedules and telling time to open-ended, personalized situations recently learned. Although they may sometimes appear repetitious of the guided practice in the previous section, these activities enable students to recreate wtih learned language in a variety of combinations. The activities often have several possible correct answers.

A. ¡Qué horario! Allow 3–4 min. Call on individuals to tell what they know about partner's schedule, teachers, etc.

B. La nueva escuela. Allow 4–5 min. Call on different pairs to present in front of class. Ask comprehension questions after each role play to make sure class understood. Allow students playing the "friend" a few minutes to invent the details of the new school schedule while the rest plan and practice the questions they will ask.

Dramatizaciones

A. ¡Qué horario! In a role play with two classmates, compare your class schedules and teachers. Ask for information about your friends' schedules and teachers, and tell them about your schedule and teachers. Some questions you might want to ask are:

¿Qué tienes los lunes a las . . . ?
¿Cómo es el profesor de . . . ?
¿A qué hora es tu clase de . . . ?

B. La nueva escuela. You run into a friend who has moved and is no longer attending your school.

- Greet each other.
- Ask your friend what the new school is like.
- Find out what classes your friend is taking and what his or her teachers are like.
- Tell what your favorite class is and why. Mention when it meets and what the teacher is like.
- Say good-bye.

UNIDAD 2

Purpose These role plays are designed to recycle the structures and vocabulary needed to describe a class, talk about class schedules, and tell time. Encourage students to work without their textbooks when preparing and performing their role plays.

¡No me digas!

El horario de Andrea.   Tom has just received a letter from Andrea, a Venezuelan friend who spent a year at Montebello High. Their friend Carla asks how Andrea is getting along. Read the conversation. Then answer the question that follows to explain Carla's reaction.

Carla:	**Hola, Tom.**
Tom:	**¿Qué tal, Carla? Mira, tengo una carta de Venezuela, de Andrea.**
Carla:	**¿Cómo está Andrea?**
Tom:	**Bien. Pero tiene un horario horrible. ¡Tiene quince clases!**
Carla:	**¿Quince clases? ¡No es posible!**

Why does Carla have trouble believing what Tom tells her about Andrea's schedule?

1. She thinks that only the smartest students are allowed to take so many classes.
2. She doesn't know that Andrea's schedule is typical of school schedules in some Spanish-speaking countries.
3. She thinks that Andrea was exaggerating in her letter.

❑ Check your answer on page 417.

LECCIÓN 1

Purpose This section provides additional reading practice as students learn to avoid cross-cultural misunderstandings when comparing a Venezuelan teenager's class schedule with their own.

Suggestions Allow students 1–2 min to read dialogue. Ask students to discuss possible explanations and arrive at a consensus on correct answer before checking response and explanations on page 417.

Answers

1 There is no real basis in the dialogue for this assumption. Try again.

②Carla is unfamiliar with class schedules in Latin American schools. It is not unusual for Latin American high school students to study twelve to fifteen different subjects a year. Classes do not meet every day, and many schools have late afternoon and Saturday sessions. This is the correct answer.

3 There is nothing in the dialogue that implies that Andrea was exaggerating. If Tom thought that, he would probably have said something like "She must be exaggerating" or "She's got to be kidding." Try another response.

Y ahora, ¡a leer!

Purpose Through use of cognates and context cues, students are asked to glean information from an authentic high school student's report card and a short reading on the grading systems in Hispanic countries.

Antes de empezar

These questions are an advance organizer for the **Calificaciones** and **Boleta** readings that follow. They are designed to get students to think about the grading system used in their school and the information that appears on their own report cards.

Answers

1 Information such as class names, teacher's names, number of "units" or "credits," comments on effort, behavior, weaknesses, etc.

2 Answers will vary.

3 Often no signature. Sometimes teachers, students, or parents may have a place to acknowledge receipt by signing.

Point out This grading scale is used in Mexico. Scales vary in other countries. For example, Venezuela uses a scale of 1–20, with 10 as passing; in Argentina, the following scale is used:

    10 = Sobresaliente
    9 = Distinguido
  7 y 8 = Muy bueno
    6 = Bueno
  4 y 5 = Regular
0, 1, 2 y 3 = Aplazado

Y ahora, ¡a leer!

Antes de empezar

1. Besides your name and grades, what other information always appears on your report cards?
2. What kind of grades does your school give: letter grades *(A-B-C-D-F)* with plus *(+)* and minus *(–)* signs, numerical grades *(1–100),* or another form of grades?
3. Who generally signs your report cards?

Calificaciones

Generalmente los estudiantes en Latinoamérica y en España reciben calificaciones de cero a diez, no calificaciones de A a F. Un diez es la nota más alta; un cero es la más baja. La interpretación de los números normalmente es la siguiente:

10	Excelente
9	Muy bien
8	Bien
7	Regular
6	Suficiente
5 o menor	No suficiente

Verifiquemos

1. What is the name of the student who received this report card? What is the name of the school? Who is the principal of the school?
2. The school is in a neighborhood called **Las Palmas.** In what city is it located? In what country?
3. How many courses did this student take?
4. What grades did the student receive? How are they different from the letter grades in the United States? What are the highest grades the student received? In what courses?

Boleta

This is a first-year high school student's report card. Study it, and then answer the **Verifiquemos** questions across the bottom of the pages.

GOBIERNO DEL ESTADO DE MEXICO | SECRETARIA DE EDUCACION, CULTURA Y BIENESTAR SOCIAL | DIRECCION GENERAL DE EDUCACION | DEPARTAMENTO DE EDUCACION MEDIA BASICA

BOLETA

LA DIRECCION DE LA ESCUELA

NOMBRE
OFIC NO 0307 "DR. ALFONSO GARCIA ROBLES" CLAVE 15EES00590

ESTABLECIDA EN LAS PALMAS

MUNICIPIO DE NEZAHUALCOYOTL

HACE CONSTAR QUE SEGUN REGISTROS QUE OBRAN EN SU ARCHIVO, EN EL CICLO ESCOLAR 1993 - 1994

VERONICA ALCANTAR RAMIREZ

ALUMNO DEL PRIMER AÑO DE SECUNDARIA GRUPO C SE SOMETIO A LAS EVALUACIONES FINALES DE LOS PROGRAMAS CURRICULARES Y OBTUVO LAS CALIFICACIONES QUE A CONTINUACION SE EXPRESAN:

AREAS	CALIFICACION FINAL	RESULTADO
ESPAÑOL	9	ACREDITADA
MATEMATICAS	8	ACREDITADA
CIENCIAS NATURALES	8	ACREDITADA
CIENCIAS SOCIALES	8	ACREDITADA
LENGUA EXTRANJERA	8	ACREDITADA
EDUCACION ARTISTICA	9	ACREDITADA
EDUCACION TECNOLOGICA	7	ACREDITADA
EDUCACION FISICA	8	ACREDITADA

CLAVES

LENGUA EXTRANJERA	EDUC. TECNOLOGICA
1	13

LAS PALMAS X., A 2 DE JULIO DE 19 94

050190
FOLIO

EBC. BEC. OF. ES). BO7
PREMIO NOBEL PAR

EL DIRECTOR DE LA ESCUELA

ENRIQUE MACIAS ROMERO

5. What is the highest grade possible? The lowest? Did the student fail any courses? How do you know?
6. Overall, do you believe this is a good student or a poor student? Why?

7. Do students at this high school take the same number of courses as you do in your freshman year? Are there any differences? If so, what are they?

Verifiquemos

Suggestion Encourage students to answer the questions in Spanish. Nevertheless, you may want to have students answer in English to generate more cross-cultural discussion.

Answers

1 Student: Verónica Alcantar Ramírez. School: Dr. Alfonso García Robles. Principal: Enrique Macías Romero
2 Nezahualcóyotl, México
3 8
4 One 7, five 8's, and two 9's. Numerical grades are used. 9 is highest— in **español** and **educación artística.**
5 10 is probably the highest possible grade, 0 the lowest, based on the **Calificaciones** reading. The student passed all courses, since all are labeled **acreditada.**
6 She is a good student, with high grades.
7 Answers will vary.

OBJECTIVES

Communicative Goals

- Describing people, places, and things
- Giving the location of people and things

Culture and Reading

- **¡No me digas!**
  ¡Qué inteligente!
  "colegio" vs. "universidad"
- **Y ahora, ¡a leer!**
  Colegio americano bilingüe:
  Private schools

Structure

- **2.5** Adjectives: Singular and plural forms
- **2.6** Subject pronouns: Singular and plural forms
- **2.7** The verb **ser**
- **2.8** The verb **estar**

ACTIVE VOCABULARY

En el colegio

colegio	oficina
escuela	pasillo
secundaria	patio
baño	recreo
biblioteca	sala
cafetería	teatro
laboratorio	

Personas

ellas	nosotros
ellos	ustedes
nosotras	

Descripción de clases y profesores

aburrido(a)	fantástico(a)
antipático(a)	fácil
bueno(a)	perfeccionista
difícil	regular
divertido(a)	serio(a)
excelente	

Verbos

estar	somos
estoy	son
estás	
está	
estamos	
están	

Somos fantásticos, ¿no?

Palabras y expresiones

e	¡Claro que sí!
las	
los	

ANTICIPEMOS

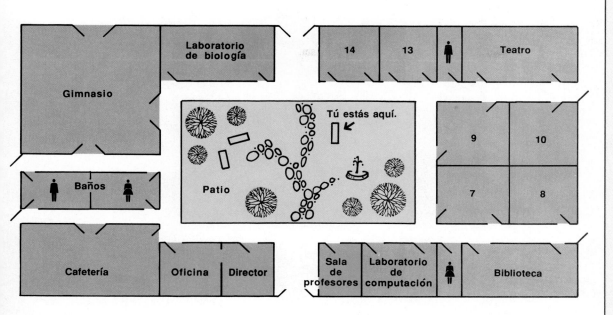

Gimnasio

Laboratorio de biología

14 13 Teatro

Tú estás aquí.

9 10

7 8

Patio

Baños

Cafetería **Oficina** **Director**

Sala de profesores **Laboratorio de computación** **Biblioteca**

¿Qué piensas tú?

This diagram might be given to a new student or a parent visiting school. Although the labels are in Spanish and you have not learned all the words yet, you will probably be able to answer the following questions.

1. What does **Tú estás aquí** probably mean? Why do you think so?

2. Locate these places on the diagram: the cafeteria, the rest rooms, the gym, the office, the library, the computer laboratory, the principal's office, the theater, the teachers' workroom. How did you determine which room was which?

3. What do your school and the school in the diagram have in common? How are they different?

4. Do you think the school on the left is somewhere in the United States or somewhere else in the world? Why?

5. The students at the school on the left are as widely varied as students at your school. You probably know someone who loves math, and you probably know someone who hates it. Each of them would describe math and their math teachers in different terms. What might each of them say? How can you explain such opposing points of view?

6. What similarities and differences would you expect to find between your school and a school in Spain? In Mexico? In Puerto Rico?

7. What do you think you will be able to talk about when you have finished this lesson?

Questions 1–4 ask students to generate some of the language to be learned in this lesson. Question 5 asks them to observe and analyze details in the photo. Question 6 asks them to recognize differences in a school's population without forming judgments.

Answers

1 *You are here.* Many such maps help people locate themselves relative to their surroundings.

2 Point to diagram. Use of cognates and process of elimination help students to identify each location. Avoid translation.

3 Answers will vary. Consider size, type of structure (one- or multiple-story), classes, and courses.

4 This school is in Puerto Rico. Students should observe student population, building style and materials, setting, etc.

5 Math lover: Class is fun, interesting, exciting, easy; teacher is fun, funny, smart, good, interesting. Math hater: Class is boring, difficult; teacher is hard, strict. The two students have different skills, talents, interests. The math hater may not do well in math but may excel at something else.

6 Physical school sites could be quite different—size, structure, equipment. Class schedules are often very different, but courses probably cover similar subject areas. The student body is varied and may have some different expectations. Students may reason that Puerto Rican schools have more in common with U.S. schools than do those in Spain or Mexico.

7 **They will be able to talk about where classes are and to describe classes and teachers.**

Purpose To focus students on vocabulary necessary to talk about where classes are and to describe their teachers and classes. Also to encourage students to use critical thinking skills while comparing and contrasting schools in Spanish-speaking countries with their own school without forming judgments.

Suggestions Use the photo as advance organizer. Students should be allowed to discover the meaning of new vocabulary without translation through use of context clues and cognates. Accuracy of pronunciation is not vital here. Allow students to guess at the meaning without being distracted by constant correction of pronunciation errors.

24:22–26:30

Side 2, 8375 to 12206

Comprehension Checks

These questions are examples only. Ask yes/no and one- and two-word-answer questions to confirm understanding of key language. Expand or omit questions as needed.

The **Comprehension Checks** are available on cards in the TRP.

1   24:31

Suggestions Gesture to show class is included in the "visit." Contrast **No visitamos ahora** with **Vamos a visitar en cinco minutos** to demonstrate use of **ir a** + inf. to express future time.

1 ¿Quién es ella? ¿Cómo se llama el chico?
2 ¿Es la escuela Robinson?
3 ¿Cómo se llama el colegio?
4 ¿Es un colegio fantástico (malo, bueno)?
5 ¿Cómo es la escuela Robinson?
6 ¿Van a visitar unas clases?
7 ¿Qué van a visitar?

Side 2, 8622 to 9221

2   24:51

Point out **Ustedes están en una clase de español también, ¿no?** Name some current actors/comedians who are **divertidos**. Mime having fun **(divertido)** / being bored **(aburrido)**.

1 ¿Es la clase de español? *(other classes)* ¿Qué clase es?
2 ¿Están los estudiantes en la clase de español? *(other classes)*
3 ¿Dónde están los estudiantes? ¿En la clase de historia?
4 ¿Es estupenda la clase?
5 ¿Cómo es la clase? ¿Es aburrida? ¿Es divertida?
6 ¿Es tu clase de español divertida? *(other classes)*

Side 2, 9241 to 9606

76   UNIDAD 2   Lección 2

¡Hola! Soy Carmen.

Y yo soy Raúl.

1

Somos estudiantes aquí en la escuela Robinson. Es un colegio fantástico. Vamos a visitar unas clases.

2

Estos estudiantes están en una clase de español. Es una clase estupenda. El profesor es muy divertido y la clase también es divertida.

3

Aquí tienen una clase de computación. Las computadoras son nuevas y las clases son muy populares.

76   *setenta y seis*

3   25:04

Suggestions Hold up an old, battered book and a new one. Contrast **nuevo/viejo**. The adjective **popular** is a cognate, reentered here in the plural.
1 ¿Es la clase de computación?
Continue asking Comprehension Check questions, as above.

Side 2, 9636 to 9975

Purpose   This section develops listening and reading comprehension of vocabulary needed to describe classes and teachers and to tell where classes meet. Students should not be expected to achieve productive mastery at this point.

5 Estos estudiantes están en el laboratorio de química. ¡Qué serios!, ¿verdad? ¿Por qué? Porque los experimentos son difíciles . . . difíciles pero interesantes.

4 Es el recreo. Aquí estamos mis amigos y yo en el patio. Tengo unos amigos fantásticos. Son simpáticos, inteligentes y divertidos.

6 Ah, aquí están los profesores. Unos son serios; otros son divertidos; otros, exigentes. ¡Pero todos son muy buenos!

7 Bueno. Ésta es la escuela. Es excelente, ¿verdad? Los profesores son muy buenos, las clases son interesantes . . . Y los estudiantes, pues . . . somos fantásticos, ¿no?

setenta y siete **77**

Suggestions Begin by having students close their books while you narrate one section at a time using the transparencies to clarify meaning without translation. Then ask **Comprehension Checks**. Repeat this process after each section.

Using the video Play one section at a time after narrating it using the transparencies. Freeze the video and ask **Comprehension Checks**. Repeat this process with each section.

---

4 25:16

Suggestion Show times of **recreo** in your school.
1 ¿Es el recreo?
2 ¿Están en el patio?
3 ¿Dónde están?
4 ¿Son los amigos de Raúl?
5 ¿Quiénes son los chicos?
6 ¿Son fantásticos (simpáticos, inteligentes, divertidos)?
7 ¿Cómo son los amigos de Raúl?
8 ¿Cómo son tus amigos?

Side 2, 9997 to 10409

5 25:32

Suggestions Contrast **serio/divertido**. Use facial expression or draw faces on board. Contrast **serio/no serio**.
1 ¿Es la clase de química? *(other classes)*
2 ¿Están en el laboratorio (en el gimnasio, etc.)?
3 ¿Dónde están ahora?
4 ¿Son los estudiantes serios?
5 ¿Cómo son los estudiantes?
6 ¿Es la clase de ciencias difícil?
7 ¿Es difícil para ti?
8 ¿Son los experimentos interesantes?
9 ¿Cómo son los experimentos?

Side 2, 10467 to 11094

6 25:54

Suggestion Ask students to guess the meaning of **exigente** from the dialogue context.
1 ¿Son los profesores?
2 ¿Cómo son los profesores? ¿Son serios (divertidos, exigentes, buenos)?
3 ¿Son todos los profesores serios (divertidos, exigentes, buenos)?
4 ¿Cómo son tus profesores?

Side 2, 11121 to 11635

7 26:12

1 ¿Es la escuela de Carmen y Raúl?
2 ¿Cómo es?
3 ¿Cómo son los profesores (las clases, los estudiantes)?
4 ¿Cómo son los profesores (las clases, los estudiantes) aquí en *[your school]*?
5 ¿Son fantásticos ustedes?

Side 2, 11670 to 12206

26:31–
28:33

Side 2, 12240 15885

Early Production Checks

Always begin each set of questions by identifying characters by name and recycling descriptive and/or other appropriate, previously learned material.

A complete set of the **Early Production Checks** is available on cards in the Teacher's Resource Package.

1　　　　　　**26:38**

¿Dónde está?

1 ¿Cómo están Sara y Carmen?
　Bien. / Regular.
2 ¿Está Carlos en el gimnasio?　*No.*
3 ¿Está en la biblioteca?　*No.*
4 ¿Está en el patio?　*No.*
5 ¿Está allí, en el pasillo?
　(Pointing.)　Sí.
6 ¿Quiénes están en el pasillo?
　Carlos, Raúl, Carmen y Sara.
7 ¿Van todos al patio?　*Sí.*
8 ¿Adónde van?　*Al patio.*

Side 2, 12435 to 13084

2　　　　　　**27:00**

Somos muy simpáticos.

Accept brief phrases and one- and two-word answers to all questions in the **Early Production Checks** as shown in **1** above. It is not necessary for students to answer in complete sentences.

1 ¿Cómo son las clases de Carlos?
2 ¿Son fáciles?
3 ¿Cómo son los profesores de Carlos?
4 ¿Le gustan a Carlos?
5 ¿Cómo son los estudiantes?
6 Y Sara, ¿es divertida?

Side 2, 13098 to 13829

¿QUÉ DECIMOS...?

Al hablar de los profesores

1 *¿Dónde está?*

2 *Somos muy simpáticos.*

78 *setenta y ocho*

UNIDAD 2

Purpose This section presents the language of class description and location in real-life contexts. Students should not be asked to memorize the dialogues word for word. Unfamiliar structures are intended solely for comprehension, not for mastery or production.

3 Es muy simpática.

4 ¡Es tan guapo!

Es muy simpática.

1 ¿Qué clase tiene Sara ahora?
2 ¿Cómo se llama la profesora de matemáticas?
3 ¿Es organizada o desorganizada la Sra. Estrada?
4 ¿Es una buena profesora?
5 ¿Es simpática o antipática?
6 ¿Es hora de clase?
7 ¿Qué clase tiene Carlos ahora?
8 ¿Va a llegar tarde o a tiempo?

Side 2, 13848 to 14704

4   `27:54`

¡Es tan guapo!

1 ¿Quiénes son?
2 ¿Ya es hora de clase?
3 ¿Qué clase tiene Carmen ahora?
4 ¿Cómo se llama el profesor de historia?
5 ¿Es organizado o desorganizado el Sr. Arenas?
6 ¿Es un perfeccionista en la opinión de Sara?
7 Para Carmen, ¿es aburrido? ¿guapo?
8 ¿Es alto o bajo? ¿rubio o moreno?
9 ¿Cómo es el profesor, bueno o malo?

Note If students ask, point out that some nouns and adjectives—for example, **perfeccionista**, **optimista**, **pesimista**—end in **-a** in both the masculine and feminine forms.

Side 2, 14719 to 15885

Suggestions Begin by having students close their books while you narrate one section at a time, using the transparencies to clarify meaning without translation. Then ask the **Early Production Checks**. Repeat this process with each section.

Using the video Play one section at a time after narrating it using the transparencies. Freeze the video and ask the **Early Production Checks**. Repeat this process with each section.

CHARLEMOS UN POCO

A. ¿Cómo son? Encourage students to use several adjectives in each description. Answers will vary. Check for agreement in gender and number.

Note Here students do not need to know the finer points about the rules governing the use of **e** and **y**: e.g., **padres _e_ hijos**, but **agua _y_ hielo**.

Plural adjectives
Used to describe several people or things

Mis amigas y yo somos simpátic**as**.
Los buen**os** estudiantes son divertid**os** e inteligent**es**.

Note: The word **y** (_and_) becomes **e** whenever it comes before a word beginning with **i** or **hi**.

See **¿Por qué se dice así?**, _page G22, section 2.5._

The verb _ser:_ Plural forms

nosotros(as)	**somos**
ustedes	**son**
ellos, ellas	**son**

Mis amigos **son** inteligentes y simpáticos.
Sí, y **somos** muy divertidos también.
Pero ustedes no **son** muy modestos.

See **¿Por qué se dice así?**, _pages G24–G26, sections 2.6–2.7._

CHARLEMOS UN POCO

A. ¿Cómo son? Describe a los profesores y estudiantes de la escuela Robinson.

MODELO **El señor Arenas es alto.**

guapo
muy buena
alto
desorganizada
estupendo
simpática
moreno
perfeccionista

Sra. Estrada

Sr. Arenas

MODELO **Los profesores son excelentes.**

simpáticos	excelentes	divertidas
interesantes	fantásticas	

profesores **estudiantes**

clases

Purpose These activities provide guided practice for students beginning to produce new language. As such, the repetition built into the activities is intentional. Students need not do all the activities, once they have demonstrated mastery of the structures and vocabulary necessary to describe teachers and classes and give their location.

B. ¡Somos estupendos! Prepara una lista de las características de los buenos estudiantes.

 MODELO   **Los buenos estudiantes son estudiosos, . . .**

cómico	organizado	estupendo
estudioso	perfeccionista	interesante
exigente	romántico	simpático
generoso	atlético	popular
tímido	divertido	modesto
inteligente	fuerte	¿ . . . ?

C. ¿Y los buenos profesores? En grupos pequeños, preparen una lista de las características de los buenos profesores.

CH. Somos amigos. Most close friends have a lot in common. How are you and your best friend alike?

MODELO   divertido
　　　　　 Somos divertidos(as). o
　　　　　 No somos divertidos(as).

divertido	simpático
organizado	aburrido
cómico	generoso
romántico	atlético
tímido	¿ . . . ?

D. ¡Qué criticones! How do you respond to your friend's criticism of your school?

 MODELO   clases: desorganizado / organizado
　　　　　 Partner: **Las clases son desorganizadas.**
　　　　　 You:　　 **¡No! Las clases son organizadas.**

1. estudiantes: tonto / inteligente
2. director(a): antipático / simpático
3. profesor(a) de . . . : desorganizado / excelente
4. clases: aburrido / interesante
5. tú y yo: feo / guapo
6. profesores: aburrido / divertido
7. colegio: fatal / fantástico
8. exámenes: difícil / fácil

LECCIÓN 2

B. ¡Somos estupendos!
Have students compare their lists in small groups. Then make a combined list of the characteristics given by all in the group. Have one group put its list on board or on butcher paper. Ask the other groups to compare lists with that on board and make combined list for class. Leave new list on board. Answers will vary.

Extension Have students describe their best friend(s).

C. ¿Y los buenos profesores? Have them leave the list from Activity B on the board and add a new list after Activity C. Then as a class they can suggest a third list of traits important for both students and teachers.

CH. Somos amigos.
Point out Adjective endings will have to be feminine if talking about two girls. Answers will vary.

D. ¡Qué criticones! Allow 2–3 min to do in pairs. Then call on individual pairs to repeat each item for class.
1 Los estudiantes son tontos. ¡No! Los estudiantes son inteligentes.
2 El director (La directora) es antipático(a). ¡No! El director (La directora) es simpático(a).
3 El profesor (La profesora) de . . . es desorganizado(a). ¡No! El profesor (La profesora) de . . . es excelente.
4 Las clases son aburridas. ¡No! Las clases son interesantes.
5 Tú y yo somos feos (feas). ¡No! Tú y yo somos guapos (guapas).
6 Los profesores son aburridos. ¡No! Los profesores son divertidos.
7 El colegio es fatal. ¡No! El colegio es fantástico.
8 Los exámenes son difíciles. ¡No! Los exámenes son fáciles.

E. ¿Dónde está . . . ?
Point out Epi is short for **Epicteto.**
Remind students to use the definite
article with titles. Ask where several
teachers in your school are.

1 ¿Dónde están Teresa y Lupe?
   Están en la sala de computación.
2 ¿Dónde están el señor Díaz y
   Mario? Están en la sala de arte.
3 ¿Dónde está la señora Jaén?
   Está en la oficina de la directora.
4 ¿Dónde está el doctor Ruiz?
   Está en la sala de español.
5 ¿Dónde están Toni y José?
   Están en la cafetería.
6 ¿Dónde está Marta?
   Está en la biblioteca.
7 ¿Dónde está el señor Baca?
   Está en el gimnasio.
8 ¿Dónde está Luisa?
   Está en la sala de historia.
9 ¿Dónde están Epi y Eva?
   Están en el teatro.

The verb *estar*
Used to talk about location of
people or things

¿Dónde **estás**?
Estoy en la biblioteca.
Lupe y yo **estamos** aquí.
Julio y María **están** en el patio.

See **¿Por qué se dice así?**,
page G26, section 2.8.

E. ¿Dónde está . . . ?   Ask your partner where you can find the following people.

MODELO   Sra. Torres
   You: **¿Dónde está la señora Torres?**
   Partner: **Está en la sala de matemáticas.**

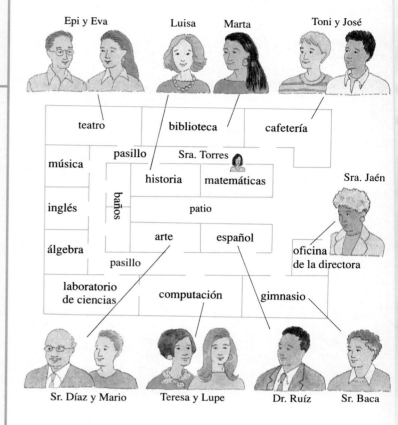

1. Teresa y Lupe
2. Sr. Díaz y Mario
3. Sra. Jaén
4. Dr. Ruíz
5. Toni y José
6. Marta
7. Sr. Baca
8. Luisa
9. Epi y Eva

F. ¿Y a las diez?   Your partner wants to know where you are at certain times of the day. What do you say?

MODELO   8:00 A.M.
   Partner: **¿Dónde estás a las ocho de la mañana?**
   You: **Estoy en casa.**

1. 8:45 A.M.
2. 10:30 A.M.
3. 12:10 P.M.
4. 1:50 P.M.
5. 9:15 A.M.
6. 11:40 A.M.
7. 1:00 P.M.
8. 2:30 P.M.

U N I D A D 2

F. ¿Y a las diez?   Allow 4–5
min. In groups of 3–4, have students poll each other to find other
students who are in the same place
as they at the same time. When finished, each group member should
go to board and write *[name]* **y yo
estamos en** *[place]* **a las** *[time].*

G. Fotos. Carmen is writing captions on the summer camp photos in her album. Where does she say these people are?

MODELO   Sra. Artiga
La Sra. Artiga está en la sala de música.

Sra. Artiga

1. Sr. Zapata

2. Jaime y yo

3. Raúl y Felipe

4. Arturo

5. chicos

G. Fotos.
1 El señor Zapata está en la cafetería.
2 Jaime y yo estamos en el teatro.
3 Raúl y Felipe están en la oficina del director.
4 Arturo está en la biblioteca.
5 Los chicos están en el gimnasio.

CHARLEMOS UN POCO MÁS

A. ¡Ahora mismo!   Tell where the following people are right now.

EJEMPLO   **Mi amigo Tom está en el patio.**

mi amiga(o) . . .
mi amigo(a) . . . y yo
el (la) director(a) . . .
mis amigos(as) . . . y . . .
el profesor . . .
la profesora . . .
yo

clase de . . .
  español
  música
  teatro
  arte
  matemáticas
  inglés
  computación

gimnasio
biblioteca
cafetería
oficina del director
laboratorio de ciencia
patio

LECCIÓN 2

CHARLEMOS UN POCO MÁS

A. ¡Ahora mismo! The ellipses in the first column invite students to personalize the activity using the names of people they know.

Purpose These activities are designed to allow students to create with language recently learned while describing people and giving location in a variety of open-ended contexts.

B. ¿Quiénes somos? Tell students to include physical and personality characteristics in their list and to tell how many people there are in the group that they describe.

C. Visita a la universidad. Have students sit facing each other and insist they not use English. Allow 2–3 min. Then tell students to compare maps to check their work.

CH. ¡A escribir! Have students write in pairs. Ask several pairs to write their paragraphs on board. Allow 2–3 min. Call on pairs to read their paragraphs to class. Go over descriptions on board having class help correct any errors.

DRAMATIZACIONES

A. ¿Hay recados? Model one role play for class, with you playing the assistant principal.

B. ¿Quiénes somos? Assume you are a member of your favorite pop music group. Develop a list of characteristics of your group. Then read your list to your classmates to see if they can guess the name of your group.

C. Visita a la universidad. Your teacher will give you a university map with a list of several people's names. Your partner will get a copy of the same map showing where the people are. Ask your partner where each person is so that you may locate him or her on your map. You may speak only Spanish during this activity and may not look at each other's maps.

CH. ¡A escribir! Write a short description about **Los profesores de** *[your school]* to be included in the Spanish Club newsletter.

Dramatizaciones

A. ¿Hay recados? Your partner works as a student assistant in the school office. Four urgent messages are received for four different students. Role-play the conversation between the assistant principal and the student assistant.

Student Assistant	**Assistant Principal**
■ Ask if there are any messages (**recados**).	■ Say there are four messages and say who they are for.
■ Ask where one student is.	■ Tell what class the student is in (include the subject, teacher's name, and room number).
■ Find out what the student looks like.	■ Describe the student.

Repeat the process for each of the remaining students.

B. ¿Y la nueva escuela? A good friend who moved to another city has returned to visit you six months later. Role-play the situation with a partner.

■ Greet each other appropriately.
■ Exchange information about school, classes, teachers, and students.
■ Ask questions to get detailed information, such as why your friend likes a particular class or teacher.

***P*urpose** Here students recycle all previously learned structures and vocabulary needed to describe people and things and to give location.

***S*uggestions** Do these role plays spontaneously, not from written scripts. Circulate among groups. Limit time allowed so that students do not get off task. Ask several to recreate their exchange for the whole class.

¡No me digas!

¡Qué inteligente! Bill, an exchange student, is being introduced to Sonia's younger brother, José Antonio. Read their conversation. Then answer the question that follows.

Sonia:	**Oye, José Antonio, quiero presentarte a mi amigo Bill.**
José Antonio:	**Mucho gusto.**
Bill:	**El gusto es mío, José Antonio.**
José Antonio:	**Perdona, Sonia. Tengo que estar en el colegio en media hora. Con permiso.**
Bill:	**¡En el colegio! Pero, ¿cuántos años tiene José Antonio? ¿Quince? ¿Dieciséis? ¿Y ya está en la universidad?**
Sonia:	**¡Bill, por favor! José Antonio va al Colegio San José conmigo. ¡Qué ridículo eres!**

Why does Sonia say Bill is being ridiculous?

1. Bill misinterpreted the name of José Antonio's school.
2. Bill thinks José Antonio is too old to be going to college.
3. Bill did not realize that Sonia's younger brother was a whiz kid.

❏ Check your answer on page 417.

LECCIÓN 2

ochenta y cinco **85**

IMPACTO CULTURAL

¡No me digas!

Purpose This is a short dialogue that includes a cross-cultural miscommunication concerning the meaning of the word **colegio**. Students are expected to discover the source of the miscommunication on their own.

Suggestion Before turning to the explanations of answers on page 417, have students themselves try to explain why the wrong answers are wrong.

Answers

1. You have selected the correct answer. **Colegio** refers to a secondary or even a primary school—*not* to a college.
2. That is not at all likely, since José Antonio is Sonia's younger brother. Bill actually says that José Antonio cannot be more than fifteen or sixteen years old. Try again.
3. There is no evidence that José Antonio is a whiz kid. Sonia even says that she and her brother attend the same high school. Try another response.

Purpose This is an authentic advertisement for a private school. Students are expected to glean information from the text without translation, using limited vocabulary and cognates as well as their knowledge of similar advertisements in English.

Antes de empezar

These questions are an advance organizer for the **Colegio Americano Bilingüe** reading that follows.

Answers

1 Answers will vary. If no one in class has attended a private/public school, have students discuss what they think it might be like.
2 Answers will vary widely.
3 Answers will vary. Students may consider quality of education, variety of courses available, discipline, costs, extracurricular activities, uniforms, etc.

Verifiquemos

Answers

1 c
2 c
3 a
4 Nursery school, day care
5 Avenida de Alfonso XIII, 30–34
6 By writing or phoning 413 22 53 or 416 09 52

Y ahora, ¡a leer!

Antes de empezar

1. If you are in a public school, have you ever attended a private school? If you are in a private school, have you ever attended a public school? If so, when, where, and what was it like?
2. How many private schools are there in your community? What are they, and what do they teach?
3. What advantages and/or disadvantages do you think going to a private school might have? Going to a public school?

Verifiquemos

After reading the advertisement on the next page, verify your understanding by completing or answering the following items.

1. This advertisement is for a bilingual
   a. college.
   b. university.
   c. school.
   d. All of the above.

2. The teachers at the **Colegio Americano Bilingüe**
   a. are all from the United States.
   b. are all from Spain.
   c. include both native and bilingual speakers.
   d. None of the above.

3. The classes are from
   a. 9:00 A.M. to 4:30 P.M.
   b. 9:00 A.M. to 5:30 P.M.
   c. 7:45 A.M. to 5:30 P.M.
   d. 7:45 A.M. to 6:30 P.M.

4. What do you think **guardería** means? Why?

5. What is the address of the **Colegio Americano Bilingüe**?

6. How can you get more information?

Colegio Americano Bilingüe

HILL HOUSE MONTESSORI SCHOOL

1 4
años de
experiencia

- Enseñanza reconocida por el Ministerio de Educacíon de España y USA.
- Método abierto e individualizado MONTESSORI.
- Profesorado Licenciado, nativos y bilingües.
- Departamento de Educación Especial y Psicología.
- Horario de Colegio: de 9 a 4.30.
- Horario extendido de guardería: 7.45 a 6.30.
- Informática.

- **Para información y reservas en:**
  Avenida de Alfonso XIII, 30-34.
  Tels. 413 22 53 y 416 09 52

Suggestions Encourage students to make reasoned guesses. They should feel good about how much they do understand rather than frustrated by what they don't understand. Remind students about false cognates. Also remind them that **colegio** can refer to an elementary school, as in this advertisement.

As a prereading activity, have students work in pairs as they list all the cognates they can find in the text of the advertisement. Have one pair read their list and others add to it.

Point out In Spain, **la informática** *(computer science)* is generally used, whereas in Latin America, **la computación** is more common.

3

¿Qué vas a hacer?

OBJECTIVES

Communicative Goals

- Listing and exchanging information about after-school activities
- Talking about future activities
- Listing and talking about obligations

Reading

- **Leamos ahora**
  Amigos por correspondencia:
  Pen pal announcements
- Reading strategy: Scanning

Writing

- **Escribamos un poco**
  Writing a letter to a pen pal
- Writing strategy: Using clusters

Structure

- 2.9 Infinitives
- 2.10 The verb **ir** and **ir a** + infinitive
- 2.11 The verb **tener** and **tener que** . . .

ACTIVE VOCABULARY

Actividades

alquilar	jugar
beber	leer
comer	limpiar
calificar	mirar
correr	participar
escribir	pasear
esperar	practicar
estudiar	preparar
hablar	salir
… por teléfono	trabajar
hacer	ver
… la tarea	

Diversiones

baile	karate
básquetbol	película
bicicleta	piano
carta	refresco
comida	restaurante
fútbol	tele

Verbos

ir	tener
voy	tenemos
vas	tienen
va	tener que
vamos	
van	

Palabras y expresiones

algo	juntos	¡Qué lástima!
autobús	mañana	¡Uf!
casa	para	un poco
con	planes	
cuarto	práctica	
examen	todos	

¿ Qué piensas tú ?

1. What are the people in these photos doing?

2. Which of the activities that you see in these photos do you expect to do after school today?

3. Which of these activities are things you have to do sometimes?

4. What things do American teenagers typically like to do? What things do American teenagers typically have to do?

5. What do you think teenagers in Mexico, Spain, Puerto Rico, or Argentina like to do? What do you suppose they have to do? How do you account for the similarities between their lives and your own? How do you account for the differences?

6. Would you expect to have more in common with teenagers in some of these places than in others? Why?

7. What do you think you will be able to talk about when you have finished this lesson?

ochenta y nueve **89**

¿Qué piensas tú?

These questions are designed to get students to anticipate what they will learn in the lesson by focusing on the lesson vocabulary and language functions being taught. Encourage students to use Spanish in their answers where possible.

Answers

1 Waiting, talking, playing, cleaning, studying, reading, watching TV. Students may not say exact verbs being taught in the lesson. That does not matter here as long as they focus on describing the activities.
2 Answers will vary.
3 Answers will vary.
4 Typically like to do: eat, shop, watch TV, play sports, listen to music. Have to do: help with housework, homework, study, some work.
5 Students should remember differences in school schedules from Lesson 2. Responses may expose cultural misperceptions. Get students to recognize teenagers are much the same everywhere, but cultural expectations might be different. If any cultural misperceptions are expressed, help students discover lack of logic in their thinking.
6 Students will probably have more in common with Puerto Rican teenagers because of relationship between Puerto Rico and United States.
7 **They will be able to talk about what they are going to do and what they have to do.**

Purpose To focus students on activities they do after school and encourage use of critical thinking skills by having students observe and compare their own activities with those of teenagers in Hispanic countries without forming judgments.

Suggestion Before asking the *¿Qué piensas tú?* questions, have class describe the students in the photos in Spanish.

28:34–
30:39

Side 2, 15911 19670

Comprehension Checks

The questions here are guidelines only. Use Total Physical Response (TPR) to ask students to point to characters doing various activities— **¿Dónde está el muchacho que corre? ¿Dónde está la mujer que alquila un video?** Ask students to act out the various activities.

A full set of the **Comprehension Checks** is available on cards in the Teacher's Resource Package.

1   28:41

Suggestions Contrast **después de clases** with **antes de clases** using clock in illustration and one drawn on board.

1 ¿Qué hora es?
2 ¿Van a estudiar Raúl y Sara?
3 ¿Quiénes van a estudiar?
4 ¿Tienen exámenes mañana?
5 ¿Cuántos exámenes tienen mañana, tres o dos?
6 ¿Por qué van a estudiar Raúl y Sara?

Side 2, 16114 to 16628

2   28:58

1 ¿Va a calificar exámenes la Srta. Rivera?
2 ¿Qué va a hacer la profesora?
3 ¿Quién dice "¡Qué lástima!", Esteban o Raúl?

Side 2, 16628 to 17085

3   29:14

1 ¿Va a correr un rato Esteban? ¿Va a calificar exámenes (estudiar, hablar por teléfono, etc.)?
2 ¿Quién va a correr un rato?
3 ¿Qué va a hacer Esteban?
4 ¿Va a hablar por teléfono Carmen?
5 ¿Va a hablar con su profesor de español (una amiga, un amigo)?

90 UNIDAD 2 Lección 3

Es miércoles y Sara, Raúl y Esteban hablan después de clases.

1

Esteban: Hola, Raúl. Hola, Sara.
Raúl: Hola, Esteban.
Sara: Hola.
Esteban: ¿Qué van a hacer esta tarde?
Raúl: Vamos a estudiar.
Sara: Sí, tenemos tres exámenes mañana.
Esteban: ¡Qué lástima!

2

Srta. Rivera: Buenas tardes.
Esteban: Hola.
Sara: Srta. Rivera, ¿qué va a hacer usted mañana?
Srta. Rivera: Tengo que calificar exámenes. Qué lástima, ¿verdad?
Raúl: Sí, ¡qué lástima!

3

Sara: Bueno, ¿y qué van a hacer ustedes esta tarde?
Esteban: Yo voy a correr un rato.
Sara: ¿Y tú, Carmen?
Carmen: Voy a hablar por teléfono . . . con Tomás.

90 noventa

6 ¿Con quién va a hablar Carmen?
7 ¿Qué va a hacer Carmen esta tarde?

Side 2, 17118 to 17639

Purpose This section develops listening and reading comprehension of active vocabulary. Students should not be expected to achieve productive mastery at this point. The goal is not to translate, but to listen for comprehension.

Mónica: Hola, Tomás. ¿Qué van a hacer esta tarde?

Tomás: Carlos y yo vamos a jugar básquetbol. Tenemos práctica a las tres. ¿Y tú, Mónica?

Mónica: ¿Yo? Ahora tengo una clase de baile.

Carlos: Oye, Tomás, ¿qué vas a hacer el sábado por la tarde?

Tomás: Voy a salir con mi amiga Carmen.

Carlos: ¿Y qué van a hacer?

Tomás: Vamos a comer pizza y pasear.

Srta. Rivera: ¿Qué vas a hacer el sábado por la mañana?

Sr. Arenas: Voy a limpiar la casa. Por la tarde, voy a hacer una comida para unos amigos. Y usted, Sra. Estrada, ¿va a limpiar la casa el sábado por la noche?

Sra. Estrada: No. No voy a trabajar. Voy a alquilar una película.

Sara: ¿Qué va a hacer Tomás el domingo por la tarde? ¿Pasear en bicicleta?

Carmen: No, tiene que hacer la tarea.

¿Y tú? ¿Qué vas a hacer este fin de semana? ¿Y qué tienes que hacer para el lunes?

Suggestions To clarify **ir a**, contrast *now* and the *future*: **No corro ahora. Voy a correr esta noche.** To clarify **tener que**, contrast "fun" activities with chores and obligations. Ask **¿Voy a ver la tele? ¿Voy a escuchar música? ¡No! ¿Por qué no? Porque tengo que limpiar la casa. Tengo que calificar exámenes.**

For suggestions on presenting this section with and without the video, see page 77.

7   30:18

1 ¿Quién es? *(Point to both.)*
2 ¿Va a pasear en bicicleta Tomás? *(Substitute other activities.)*
3 ¿Qué tiene que hacer Tomás?
4 ¿Tomás tiene que hacer la tarea el domingo por la tarde o por la noche?

Side 2, 19017 to 19670

4   29:32

1 ¿Van a jugar básquetbol los chicos?
2 ¿Van a jugar básquetbol o van a bailar?
3 ¿Tienen práctica de fútbol?
4 ¿A qué hora tienen práctica, a las dos o a las tres?
5 ¿Va a bailar Mónica?
6 ¿Quién va a bailar?
7 ¿Tiene una clase de baile?

Note In speaking, the common practice is to omit the **a** after the verb **jugar**. For this reason, **jugar** is taught without a relator in this text.

Side 2, 17658 to 18130

5   29:49

Suggestions Help students understand **salir** by saying **Carmen es la amiga de Tomás. Es su novia** (draw a heart on the board). **Tomás y Carmen van a salir juntos. Van a un restaurante. Van a comer.**
1 ¿Va a salir el chico? *(Substitute other activities.)*
2 ¿Va a salir con su amiga (su amigo, su profesor, etc.)?
3 ¿Van a comer? *(Substitute other activities.)*
4 ¿Qué van a comer?
5 ¿Qué más van a hacer?

Side 2, 18165 to 18465

6   30:00

Suggestions Help students understand **trabajar**—mime preparing classes, grading paper, homework. Name a popular rental film. Say **La señora Estrada no va a ver la tele; va a alquilar la película** *[name movie].*
1 ¿El señor Arenas va a limpiar la casa el sábado por la mañana o por la noche?
2 ¿Tiene que trabajar la señora Estrada?
3 ¿Va a alquilar una película la señora Estrada? *(Substitute other activities.)*
4 ¿Va a ver televisión?
5 *(To the class)* ¿Quién va a ver televisión esta noche?

Side 2, 18495 to 19000

30:40–
33:01

Early Production Checks

A complete set of the **Early Production Checks** is available on cards in the Teacher's Resource Package.

1 | **30:46**

¿Qué planes tienes tú?

1 ¿Quiénes son? *Carmen, Sara y Mónica.*

2 ¿Tiene mucha tarea Sara? *Sí.*

3 ¿Tiene que trabajar? *Sí.*

4 ¿Tiene que trabajar por la mañana o por la tarde? *Por la tarde.*

5 Y Anita, ¿va al restaurante o a su clase de baile?
A su clase de baile.

6 ¿Tiene Anita examen mañana?
Sí.

7 ¿En qué clase es su examen?
Matemáticas.

8 ¿Con quién va a salir Carmen hoy? *Con una amiga.*

9 ¿Van a estudiar o van a pasear en bicicleta?
Van a pasear en bicicleta.

2 | **31:13**

¡Uf! Tengo tanto que hacer.

1 ¿Quiénes son? *La Sra. Estrada, el Sr. Arenas y la Srta. Rivera.*

2 ¿Tiene que limpiar la casa o hacer la comida la Srta. Rivera?
Limpiar la casa.

3 ¿Quién tiene que calificar exámenes? *La Srta. Rivera.*

4 ¿Qué va a hacer la Sra. Estrada, ver televisión o limpiar la casa?
Ver televisión.

5 ¿Qué va a hacer el Sr. Arenas esta noche, correr o calificar exámenes? *Correr.*

6 ¿Qué va a alquilar? *Un video.*

Note Some Spanish speakers use *mirar* televisión / un video.

¿QUÉ DECIMOS..?

Al hablar de lo que vamos a hacer

1 **¿Qué planes tienes tú?**

2 **¡Uf! Tengo tanto que hacer.**

Purpose These dialogues are not intended for memorization. They show the language of near-future activities in more natural contexts. Unfamiliar structures in the dialogues contribute to the context and are intended solely for comprehension, not for mastery or production by students.

3 Tenemos práctica de básquetbol.

3   31:55

Tenemos práctica de básquetbol.

1 ¿Qué va a hacer Tomás, practicar básquetbol o estudiar inglés?
Practicar básquetbol.

2 ¿Va a practicar básquetbol por la mañana o por la tarde?
Por la tarde.

3 ¿Qué va a hacer Raúl, practicar básquetbol o estudiar inglés?
Estudiar inglés.

4 ¿Por qué tiene que estudiar?
Tiene examen mañana.

5 ¿Quién va a alquilar una película?
Carlos.

6 ¿Va Raúl a ver la película con Carlos? *No.*

Side 2, 21926 to 22635

4 ¿Vas a esperar el autobús?

4   32:19

¿Vas a esperar el autobús?

1 ¿Quiénes son? *Carlos y Carmen.*

2 ¿Llega tarde el autobús? *Sí.*

3 ¿Qué va a hacer Sara, trabajar o pasear en bicicleta?
Va a trabajar.

4 ¿Dónde trabaja?
En el restaurante de su papá.

5 ¿Va a esperar el autobús Carlos?
No.

6 ¿Qué va a hacer Carlos?
Va a comer algo.

Side 2, 22655 to 23925

LECCIÓN 3

***S**uggestions*   Begin by having students close their books while you narrate one section at a time, using the transparencies to clarify meaning without translation. Then ask the questions in the **Early Production Checks**. Repeat with each section.

Using the video   Play one section at a time after narrating it using the transparencies. Freeze the video and ask the questions in the **Early Production Checks**. Repeat with each section.

CHARLEMOS UN POCO

A. ¿Quién habla? Allow 1–2 min for students to find correct answers in the **¿Qué decimos … ?** section. Then call on individuals or on the whole class.

1 Sara
2 la señorita Rivera
3 Carlos
4 Raúl
5 el señor Arenas
6 la señorita Rivera
7 Carlos
8 Raúl

B. Después de clase. Ask what activities students associate with each sketch before doing.

1 (f) Lisa va a comer pizza.
2 (b) Bárbara va a estudiar.
3 (ch) Ramón va a pasear en bicicleta.
4 (e) Luisa va a hablar por teléfono.
5 (d) Juana va a limpiar la casa.
6 (a) Salvador va a jugar básquetbol.
7 (c) Gustavo va a correr.

Infinitives

The **-ar, -er,** and **-ir** form of the verb is called the infinitive. Infinitives name actions—for example:

habl**ar**   *to talk*
corr**er**   *to run*
escrib**ir**   *to write*

See **¿Por qué se dice así?,** *page G28, section 2.9.*

CHARLEMOS UN POCO

A. ¿Quién habla? Los estudiantes y los profesores de la escuela Robinson hablan de sus planes. ¿Quién habla?

Srta. Rivera   **Sr. Arenas**   **Carlos**   **Raúl**   **Sara**

1. Tengo que trabajar esta tarde.
2. Tengo que limpiar la casa.
3. Voy a comer algo.
4. Voy a estudiar inglés. Tengo examen mañana.
5. Voy a correr.
6. Tengo que calificar exámenes.
7. Todavía no tengo planes.
8. No voy a la práctica de básquetbol.

B. Después de clase. ¿Qué van a hacer estos chicos hoy?

MODELO   alquilar un video
Andrés va a alquilar un video.

Andrés   1. Lisa   2. Bárbara   3. Ramón

4. Luisa   5. Juana   6. Salvador   7. Gustavo

a. jugar básquetbol
b. estudiar
c. correr
ch. pasear en bicicleta
d. limpiar la casa
e. hablar por teléfono
f. comer pizza

Purpose These activities provide guided practice to students beginning to learn how to express obligations and future plans. The repetition built into the activities is intentional.

C. Hoy, por la tarde. ¿Qué planes tienen tú y tus amigos hoy?

EJEMPLO **Mis amigos Hugo y Martín van a estudiar juntos.**

mi amiga . . .
mis amigos . . .
tú
mi amiga . . . y yo
mis amigas . . .
todos ustedes
yo

> estudiar para un examen
> pasear en bicicleta
> jugar fútbol
> leer un libro
> escribir cartas
> hacer la tarea
> trabajar
> ver la tele
> estudiar juntos(as)

CH. ¿Cuándo? Assume you will do the following things tomorrow. Put them in order and tell at what time you will do each one.

EJEMPLO hacer mi tarea
Voy a hacer mi tarea a las 4:00 de la tarde.

1. alquilar una película
2. ir a la escuela
3. hacer una comida
4. beber un refresco
5. hacer mi tarea
6. hablar por teléfono
7. leer un poco
8. ver la tele

D. ¿Qué va a hacer? ¿Qué va a hacer este estudiante la semana del 21 de octubre?

MODELO **El lunes a las cuatro va a estudiar con Carlos.**

OCTUBRE

lunes 21	viernes 25
4:00 estudiar con Carlos	8:00 salir con María y Jaime
6:00 hacer la comida	
martes 22	**sábado 26**
5:30 ir a la clase de piano	am. limpiar la casa
	p.m. pasear en bicicleta
miércoles 23	**domingo 27**
3:00 jugar tenis	5:00 correr con Carlos
jueves 24	**Para hacer**
6:00 ver un video con Ana	

LECCIÓN 3

Ir a + infinitive
Used to talk about future events

yo	**voy**	nosotros(as)	**vamos**
tú	**vas**		
usted	**va**	ustedes	**van**
él, ella	**va**	ellos, ellas	**van**

Voy a escribir una carta.
¿Qué **van a hacer** ustedes?

*See ¿**Por qué se dice así?**,
page G29, section 2.10.*

C. Hoy, por la tarde.
Answers will vary. Encourage students to express their real-life plans if possible.

CH. ¿Cuándo? Answers will vary.

Extension Tell students to check with partner and find out what time he or she is going to do the same activities. Have each report partner's answers to class.

D. ¿Qué va a hacer? Have students create as many sentences as possible.

Expansion Do in pairs.
You: **¿Qué vas a hacer el** *[day]* **a las** *[time]*?
Partner: **Voy a [estudiar con Carlos].**

Suggestion Encourage students to personalize these activities by talking about their actual activities and friends where appropriate.

Tener que + infinitive
Used to talk about obligations

yo	tengo	nosotros(as)	tenemos
tú	tienes		
usted	tiene	ustedes	tienen
él, ella	tiene	ellos, ellas	tienen

¿Tienes que estudiar para el examen?
El martes **tenemos que trabajar** por la noche.

See **¿Por qué se dice así?,** *page G31, section 2.11.*

Responding in the negative

When responding to a yes/no question in the negative, use **no** twice: at the beginning of the sentence and in front of the verb.

¿Tienes que limpiar la casa?
No, no tengo que limpiar la casa.

¿Vas a estudiar esta noche?
No, no voy a estudiar esta noche.

E. Obligaciones. You and some friends are discussing your after-school plans. What do you say?

EJEMPLO **Mi amigo Paul tiene que hacer la tarea.**

mi amigo . . .	practicar karate
yo	limpiar mi cuarto
mis amigas . . .	hacer la tarea
tú	estudiar para un examen
mis amigos . . .	escribir una carta
mi amigo . . . y yo	correr
ustedes	trabajar
mi amiga . . . y yo	salir con unos amigos
	hablar por teléfono
	ir a la clase de piano

F. ¿Qué tienen que hacer? Find out what your partner and his or her brothers and sisters have to do on the weekend.

MODELO limpiar la casa
You: **¿Tienen que limpiar la casa?**
Partner: **Sí, tenemos que limpiar la casa.** o
No, no tenemos que limpiar la casa.

1. hacer la tarea
2. ir a una clase de karate
3. escribir cartas
4. estudiar
5. trabajar
6. practicar el piano
7. alquilar un video
8. leer un libro

CHARLEMOS UN POCO MÁS

A. Y tú, ¿qué vas a hacer hoy? List three things that you are going to do after school today. Then ask several classmates what they have to do. You may ask:

¿Qué tienes que hacer? or
¿Qué vas a hacer?

B. ¿Y tú? Prepare a personal calendar for the coming week. Include all activities you have scheduled for after school and the weekend. Discuss it with your partner.

C. ¿Qué vamos a hacer?   Write down five things that you are going to do on the weekend. Then, in groups of three or four, compare your lists and make a list of the activities of the group.

CH. ¿Estudiamos juntos?   You and a classmate need to arrange a time this weekend when both of you can get together to study for a history exam. Use the schedules provided by your teacher to find a time when both of you are free. You may not look at your partner's schedule.

EJEMPLO   You: **Vamos a estudiar el sábado a las dos. ¿Está bien?**
Partner: **No, porque a las dos tengo que practicar el piano.**

D. Probablemente . . .   In groups, list everything you predict your teacher will be doing in the year 2015. Then ask questions to confirm your predictions.

EJEMPLO   **Va a ser directora de la escuela.**
¿Va a ser usted directora de la escuela?

Dramatizaciones

A. Domingo por la noche.   You are on the phone with a friend. Role-play your conversation.

Compañero(a)

- Ask what your partner is going to do tonight.
- Suggest you rent a video to watch this evening.
- Say "What a shame!" Then say good-bye.

Tú

- Say you have a lot of homework to do.
- Say you have to study for a math exam tomorrow.

B. Nuevos amigos.   You just met a new person in study hall. Talk with him or her.
- Greet the person.
- Introduce yourselves.
- Find out what classes he or she has and say what you are taking.
- Find out what the other person is going to do after school.
- Tell what you are going to do after school.

C. Después de clases.   You and a group of friends are waiting for the school bus after classes. You each tell about two or three things you have planned for the afternoon. Role-play the situation.

LECCIÓN 3

CH. ¿Estudiamos juntos? Have students follow directions on schedules. Insist they not look at partner's schedule and that they speak only Spanish during activity. Compliment pairs who do good job. Invite one or two pairs to reenact their exchange in front of class.

D. Probablemente . . .
Make sure students use **usted** form when addressing you. Encourage as many questions as possible.

Extension Have students predict what some of their classmates are going to be doing in 2005, 2025.

DRAMATIZACIONES

A, B. Assign both **A** and **B** to different pairs at same time. Allow 4–5 min to prepare role plays. Then have students present role plays in front of class. Ask questions to check comprehension.

C. Después de clases.
Have class brainstorm kinds of questions/statements to use in role plays. Allow 4–5 min to prepare role plays. Then have students present role plays in front of class. Ask questions to check comprehension.

In **Dramatizaciones,** this section, students recycle all previously learned structures and vocabulary needed to describe obligations and discuss future plans in student-centered role plays. Encourage students to work without their textbooks when preparing and performing their role plays.

LEAMOS AHORA

A. Anticipemos.

Suggestions Have students answer questions in pairs. Allow 2 min. Call on several pairs to share their answers with class. Ask if others agree. Tell students to come back to their predictions after they have read the selection.

Answers

1 Names, addresses, ages, and pastimes of Hispanic pen pals.

2 Magazines, material from pen pal organization.

Reading strategy: Scanning

A. Anticipemos. Before reading the selection on the next page, glance at the format and answer the following questions.

1. What type of information do you expect to find in this reading?
2. Where would you look for the type of information found in the reading?

B. Empezando. We read for a variety of reasons. For example, we might read the newspaper to find out what an article is about (skimming), to get all the details about a recent disaster (reading for detail), or simply to find out the score of a sports event (scanning).

To scan is to read very quickly to locate a specific piece of information. Scanning is the fastest kind of reading we do. We often combine scanning with reading for detail when we want to find answers to specific questions. We scan to locate the information; then we stop and read for detail.

First, scan to locate information in the selection. Then, when you know where to look, locate the answers to some specific questions.

To scan, take the following steps:

1. Move your eyes as quickly as possible down the page until you find the information you need.
2. Do not read further once you have the information you want.

C. Amigos por correspondencia.

Answers

1 Names are the first entry in each item.

2 Ages are the third entry.

3-4 Countries and cities are found in the **Dirección**—the second entry.

5 Hobbies and interests are the last entry—**Pasatiempos.**

6 The coupon is in the upper left corner of the page.

C. Amigos por correspondencia. Now scan the reading selection to determine where the following pieces of information are located.

1. Names of people
2. Ages of people
3. Countries where people live
4. Cities where people live
5. Pastimes of people
6. A coupon for requesting a pen pal

Verifiquemos

Verifiquemos

Suggestion Students will need to begin by reading the first question and scanning to find its answer. Then the second question, third question, etc.

Use your scanning skills to find the following pieces of specific information.

1. Name the people on the list who are twenty-one or older.
2. How many people are sixteen or younger?
3. Two people on the list are from the Caribbean. Who are they?
4. From what countries are the Central Americans on the list?
5. How many of the South Americans on the list are male? How many are female?

UNIDAD 2

Purpose This is the principal reading of the unit. Its purpose is to teach students to read in Spanish using appropriate strategies. Here they will scan a passage to locate specific information before reading for detailed answers to questions. Students are not expected

Línea directa

¿Quieres ponerte en contacto con amigos de todas partes? Envíanos tus datos utilizando este cupón.

Nombre: _____
Dirección: _____
Edad: _____
Pasatiempos: _____
_____
_____

El cupón dirígelo a:
LINEA DIRECTA REVISTA TU
(Ver dirección en la pág. 3)

Nombre: Silvia Orozco.
Dirección: Heredia, Urb. La Esperanza # 70, COSTA RICA.
Edad: 20 años.
Pasatiempos: Coleccionar todo lo referente al joven cantante Chayanne, tomar fotografías, estudiar, ver televisión y tener amigos de diferentes nacionalidades.

Nombre: Alfonso Mesa.
Dirección: Calle 19 # 4-56, Apto. 2005, Edificio Sabana, Bogotá, COLOMBIA.
Edad: 22 años.
Pasatiempos: Leer, practicar deportes, escuchar música variada, escribir poemas, salir con mis amigas y coleccionar monedas de diferentes países.

Nombre: Carlos L. Pérez.
Dirección: Del Banco de América 1 c. al Este, NICARAGUA.
Edad: 17 años.
Pasatiempos: Ver televisión, tener muchos amigos, ir al cine, leer revistas, escuchar música y escribir versos.

Nombre: Milagro del Carmen Santos.
Dirección: Rdo. Rosendo Llanes, Danlí, El Paraíso, HONDURAS.
Edad: 18 años.
Pasatiempos: Intercambiar correspondencia, estampillas, calcomanías y afiches; escuchar música romántica, leer artículos sobre la cultura de diferentes países y ver televisión.

Nombre: Ilka Murillo.
Dirección: Entrega General Estafeta, El Dorado, PANAMA.
Edad: 14 años.
Pasatiempos: Coleccionar calcomanías, papel para cartas y todo lo referente al grupo Menudo; mantener correspondencia con jóvenes de todo el mundo, ver los videos musicales de mis artistas favoritos y practicar deportes.

Nombre: Josie Aquino.
Dirección: Avenida Franco Bido # 336-A, Nibaje, Santiago, REPUBLICA DOMINICANA.
Edad: 16 años.
Pasatiempos: Escuchar música variada, coleccionar artículos y afiches de George Michael; ir a la playa, a reunirme con mis amistades, bailar, intercambiar correspondencia y ver televisión.

Nombre: Marta Medina.
Dirección: Cra. 15, # 28-02, Apto. 103, Bogotá, COLOMBIA.
Edad: 19 años.
Pasatiempos: Estudiar, escribir, leer libros, coleccionar calcomanías, ver videos musicales de mis artistas favoritos, cuidar las plantas y mantener correspondencia con jóvenes de todas las edades.

Nombre: Angélica Trejo.
Dirección: 2312 Peck Road, El Monte, California, 91732, ESTADOS UNIDOS.
Edad: 21 años.
Pasatiempos: Bailar, ver televisión, leer revistas, escuchar música variada, estudiar con mis amigas, coleccionar versos, practicar deportes e ir a la playa.

Nombre: Isabel Melara.
Dirección: Final 5 Ave. Sur, # 13-A, Urb. La Colina, Sta. Tecla, EL SALVADOR.
Edad: 16 años.
Pasatiempos: Practicar deportes, escuchar música romántica, bailar, salir de compras con mis amigas, coleccionar postales, afiches y calcomanías de mis artistas favoritos.

Nombre: Evelyn Amador.
Dirección: Ave. Guadilla, Buzón 7439, Isabela, 00662, PUERTO RICO.
Edad: 16 años.
Pasatiempos: Escuchar música, ver televisión, leer, escribir poemas, coleccionar calcomanías, salir con mis amistades e intercambiar correspondencia.

Nombre: José C. Pereira.
Dirección: 15886 San Miguel de Sarandón, Santiago de Compostela, La Coruña, ESPAÑA.
Edad: 21 años.
Pasatiempos: Dibujar, leer, escribir, escuchar música variada, planear actividades con mis amistades, practicar deportes e intercambiar correspondencia con chicas y chicos de diferentes países.

Nombre: Eugenia Vila Aguirre.
Dirección: Libertad 1259-1261, Huancayo, PERU.
Edad: 22 años.
Pasatiempos: Practicar deportes, bailar, ver los videos musicales de mis artistas favoritos, salir con mis amigas, mantener correspondencia con jóvenes de todo el mundo y escuchar música.

---

6. Who is the pen pal from the United States? Where does she live?
7. How many people on the list are from Europe? Which country?
8. How many people list "watching TV" as a favorite pastime?
9. How many list "writing poetry"?
10. Do many list "playing sports"? Who are they?
11. Who collects anything and everything having to do with the teen musical group **Menudo**?
12. What is the purpose of the coupon?

LECCIÓN 3

Verifiquemos

Answers

1 Alfonso Mesa, Angélica Trejo, José C. Pereira, Eugenia Vila Aguirre
2 4
3 Josie Aquino, Evelyn Amador
4 Costa Rica, Nicaragua, Honduras, Panama, El Salvador
5 One man, two women
6 Angélica Trejo. El Monte, California
7 One from Spain
8 6
9 3
10 6: Alfonso Mesa, Ilka Murillo, Angélica Trejo, Isabel Melara, José C. Pereira, Eugenia Vila Aguirre, Cinthya Morales
11 Ilka Murillo
12 To publish your own ad with your name, address, and favorite pastime in the magazine *Tú*

Point out Calcomanías are transfers, decals, stickers. **Afiches** are posters.

---

to understand every word. Rather they should focus on looking for the specific pieces of information requested. This strategy should be applied when reading to locate specific information.

ESCRIBAMOS UN POCO

A. Empezando.

Suggestions Remind students that what they write will depend on for whom, why, and about what they are writing. Allow 3–4 min. Ask volunteers to answer the questions. 1. They will write to someone they want to be pen pals with—a native Spanish speaker of about the same age, probably with similar interests, but with different cultural background. 2. They will write to introduce themselves and to ask for information about the pen pal. 3. They will write about themselves—name, age, description—their school and classes, and their interests and pastimes.

B. Planeando.

Suggestions Remind students they learned about brainstorming in Unit 1. You may want to brainstorm as a class activity, having volunteers list words and ideas on the board as they are called out. Have students make brainstorming suggestions in Spanish. Remind them that when brainstorming, all ideas are accepted—they will select those they want to use later.

C. Organizando.

Suggestions Look at the model cluster diagram with class. Point out that this student took a list like theirs and grouped ideas together, with four main ideas in the center bubbles and details surrounding them. Ask what will be added to the cluster diagram before it is finished. To allow for different learning styles, demonstrate how this might have been written as an outline.

Allow 5–6 min for students to make their own clusters or outlines. Ask volunteers to tell what they have included and how they have grouped ideas. Encourage students to add to their cluster as they hear ideas from others.

Writing strategy: Using clusters

A. Empezando.   Choose someone from the reading selection on page 99 with whom you would enjoy corresponding. Before beginning to write, answer the following questions:

1. ¿Para quién escribo?
2. ¿Por qué escribo?
3. ¿De qué escribo?

Remember that a good writer keeps this information in mind, because it helps to determine what to say and how to say it.

B. Planeando.   As you learned in Unit 1, a good way to begin is to brainstorm a list of all the things you might want to include in a letter to a new pen pal. Don't worry that you might not be able to say them all in Spanish. You'll be able to choose which ideas you want to use in your letter.

C. Organizando.   The next step is to cluster the ideas you have brainstormed. In the following example, the writer developed four groups of ideas. Then she added more boxes with details about each idea. She may not write about all of them; but once she has all her ideas in front of her, she can decide what she wants to include in the letter.

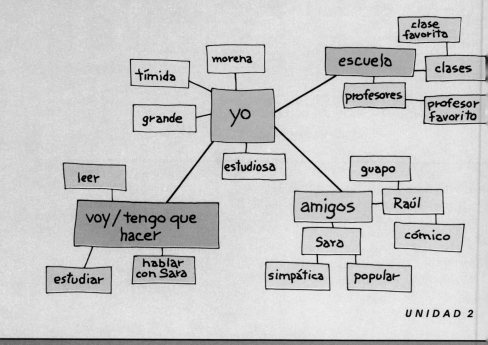

UNIDAD 2

Purpose In this section, students are asked to apply the new writing strategy of writing clusters to a letter-writing task. They will practice these strategies together with strategies they began to develop in Unit 1—prewriting brainstorming, writing a first draft, peer feedback, and revision.

Now to make your own cluster, write the main ideas you will address and draw a box around each one. Draw a line to show how these ideas are connected to each other. Then add more boxes with details about each idea. Each group of ideas can be a paragraph of your letter. Because you now have a lot more to say than you did in Unit 1, your diagram will be more complex. If it will help you get started, use the four main ideas in the model cluster.

CH. Escribiendo. Decide what information in your cluster you will use. Then write a first draft of your letter.

D. Compartiendo. Share the first draft of your letter with a couple of classmates. Ask them what they think about it. Is there anything they don't understand? Is there anything they feel should be changed? Is there anything you haven't said that they feel you should mention?

E. Revisando. Write a final draft of your letter incorporating any suggestions you accepted. You may add, subtract, or reorder anything you had written in the first draft.

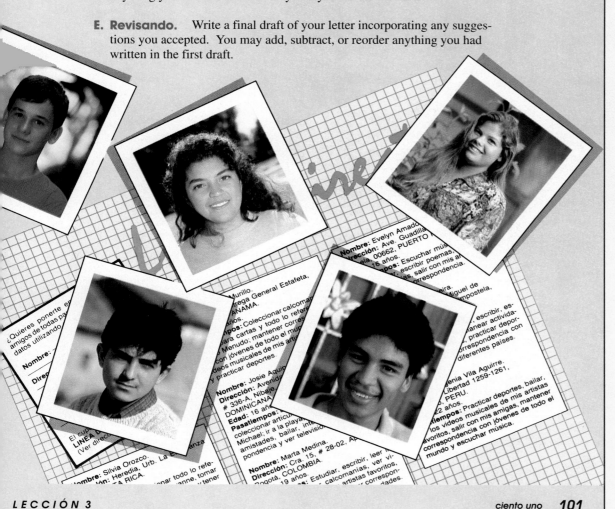

CH. Escribiendo.
Suggestions Allow time to write the first draft. Provide guidance where necessary. You may want to assign the first draft as homework.

D. Compartiendo.
Suggestions Have students gather in "response groups" of two or three. Allow them time to share letters. Encourage them to comment on content, structure, and vocabulary. Remind group members to begin commentary with at least one positive comment and then to make constructive suggestions on content, structure, and vocabulary.

E. Revisando.
Suggestions Tell students you will grade the letter holistically, based on the overall effectiveness of the communication and not on grammatical errors. Underline errors if you wish, but the grade should be affected only by errors that might confuse native speakers accustomed to dealing with foreigners. Later lessons will sug-gest strategies for improving accuracy. At this stage, students should develop a sense that they can already write something a Spanish-speaking pen pal would enjoy reading.

Suggestions You may wish to exchange letters with another class in your school or another school or to provide students with the opportunity to exchange letters with a real pen pal in a Hispanic country. The AATSP (American Association of Teachers of Spanish and Portuguese) or your local foreign language association should be able to provide addresses of international pen pal organizations.

UNIT OBJECTIVES

Communicative Goals

When students have completed this unit, they will be able to use Spanish . . .
- to give information about their community and where they are going
- to express likes and dislikes
- to make polite requests
- to discuss everyday activities

Culture

In this unit, students will discover similarities and differences between the United States and Hispanic countries
- while shopping in Oaxaca, Mexico
- in pop music
- in the activities teenagers prefer
- in the use of public parks

Reading and Writing Strategies

- Reading: Scanning
- Writing: Paragraph writing

Structure

- **Ir a**
- **Vamos a** = Let's
- **a + el → al**
- The indefinite article and **hay**
- The verbs **gustar** and **encantar**
- Polite requests: **gustaría, encantaría**
- Present tense: Singular and plural forms
- The verb **ver**
- The seasons and weather expressions
- Indefinite and negative words

¿Qué hacen ustedes?

UNIT SETTING

Mexico City is an enormous modern metropolis full of skyscrapers, freeways, and people. With a population of over 20 million (1990 census), it is the second-largest city in the world. Built on top of **Tenochtitlán**, the ancient Aztec capital, the city is surrounded by volcanic moun-

tains like the majestic **Popocatépetl** and the beautiful **Iztaccíhuatl.** Modern Mexican architects are famous for their engineering skills, which allow many of the city's skyscrapers to sway gracefully in the area's many earthquakes. The **Zócalo,** in the heart of the city, is Mexico's

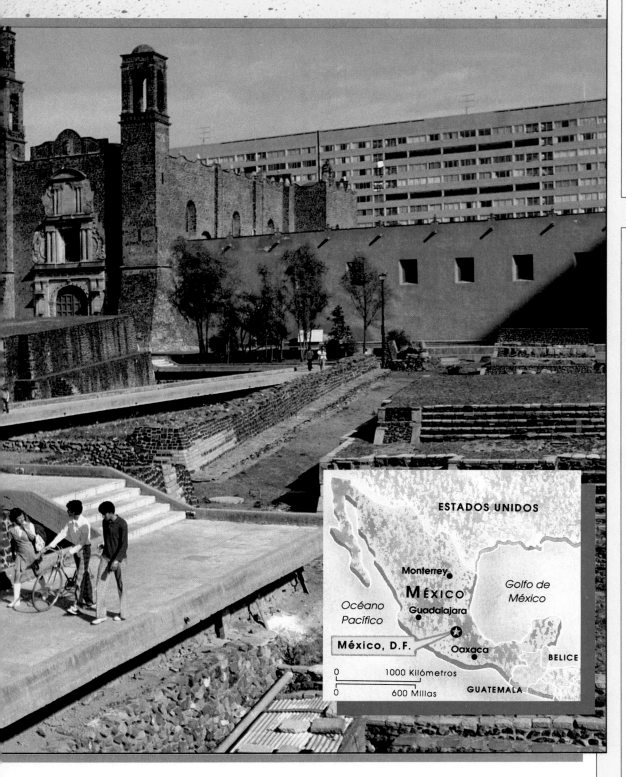

Photo

The **Plaza de las tres culturas** reflects the three cultures that contributed to the development of Mexico. The stonework in the foreground represents pre-Columbian Indian cultures. The bold and striking **Iglesia de San-tiago** represents Spanish colonial culture, and the buildings in the background represent contemporary **mestizo** culture.

Video Notes

To play the montage:

| 00:00 | – | 00:44 |

Side 3, 20 to 1351

To play the entire unit without stopping:

| 00:00 | – | 21:00 |

Side 3, 20 to 37821

In accordance with our policy of using local actors, the actors in this unit are Mexican, except for the actress who plays Kati. She is an American who has spent much of her life in Mexico City.

There is a tendency in Mexico City for word-initial **r** to have a quality somewhat like the *shr* of *shrimp,* especially among female speakers. The tour guide sounds like she is saying **shrestaurantes** for **restaurantes.** (This is also heard in Central America, in the Andes, and in parts of Spain.) In addition, there is a tendency to "whisper" **r** and **d** at the end of a word: **ver y hacer** sounds like *ve y hacé,* and **ciudad** and **universidad** sound like *ciudá* and *universidá.* Another Mexico City tendency is, in certain contexts, for **b** to sound more like [v] than the more standard [ɓ]: **el bosque** sounds like *el vosque.*

Constitution Square. In pre-Columbian times, it was the main Aztec ceremonial center. Current excavations have yielded treasures from the **Templo mayor**, the main pyramid of the ancient city of **Tenochtitlán.** The **Zócalo** now houses the **Palacio nacional**, the official seat of the presidency, and the **Catedral de México**, the largest religious building in North America.

¡Vamos de compras !

ACTIVE VOCABULARY

En el centro

café	museo
centro	parque
…comercial	tienda
cine	…de discos
monumento	

Gustos

encantar	gustar
me encanta(n)	me gusta(n)
te encanta(n)	te gusta(n)
le encanta(n)	le gusta(n)
(me, te, le)	(me, te, le)
encantaría	gustaría

Verbos

bailar	tomar
escuchar	vamos
hay	

Pronombres y complementos

a mí	me
a ti	te
a usted	le
a él	
a ella	

En un centro comercial

de compras
disco
en oferta
novela
oferta

Palabras y expresiones

a	¿Adónde?
al	al aire libre
aquí	¿De veras?
mucho	fin de semana
un / uno, una	ir de compras
unos, unas	¿Qué pasa?
	¿Quiénes?

A N T I C I P E M O S

¿Qué piensas tú?

Answers

1 Tickets are for bullfights, soccer game, ballet, the observation floor at the top of the Latin American Tower, the amusement park in Chapultepec Park, museums and archaeological sites, and the American Circus. All events are taking place in Mexico City. Students may not guess location if they are not familiar with sites such as the **Palacio de Bellas Artes**, the **Torre Latinoamericana**, and the **Bosque de Chapultepec**.

2 Answers will vary. People will choose to do things and go places according to their age and interests.

3 Answers will vary.

4 Students should recognize that different backgrounds, tastes, talents, and ages lead to different interests.

5 They are in a shopping center. Students may guess downtown or shopping. Various merchandise is available—clothes, books, records, sports equipment, toys, gifts, furniture, etc.

6 Spanish-speaking teenagers will have the same range of interests, likes, and dislikes as American teenagers, but there may be some things they like to do that are not typical of Americans—going to the park with the family, for instance. There may be differences in what is available and/or what is considered appropriate for teenagers.

7 **They will be able to talk about what there is to do, where to go, likes and dislikes.**

¿ Qué piensas tú ?

1. What are these tickets for? Where are these events taking place? How do you know?

2. If you were choosing what to do this weekend, which of these activities would appeal to you? Why? Which would appeal to other members of your family? Why?

3. What kinds of things do you like to do on weekends? What do your parents like to do on weekends? Your brothers and sisters?

4. If something seems really good, fun, or interesting to you, why don't some people like it?

5. Where are the teenagers that you see in the photo? What kinds of merchandise are probably available there?

6. You know that in Spanish-speaking countries, teenagers' lives are like yours in some ways and different in other ways. What kinds of things do you think they like to do? What kinds of things do you think they probably don't like to do? Why?

7. What do you think you will be able to talk about when you have finished this lesson?

ciento cinco **105**

Purpose This section focuses students on language related to weekend activities they like or dislike and encourages students to develop and use critical thinking skills as they observe differences and similarities in how Mexican teenagers spend their weekends.

Suggestions Use the illustrations as an advance organizer. Students should not try to translate the information on the tickets but should rely on cognates and visual clues to determine what the tickets are for. Detailed information is less important than the perception that the tickets represent a variety of weekend activities. Have students explain their answers. Help them discover cross-cultural differences and similarities in weekend activites.

TAPE/DISC		
00: 45– 05:07		

Side 3, 1369 to 9214

Comprehension Checks

Ask these questions to determine comprehension without translation. Look for yes/no and one- or two-word answers. If responses are weak or uncertain, provide additional clarification in Spanish.

A complete set of the **Comprehension Checks** is available on cards in the TRP.

1   **00:54**

1. ¿Es la Ciudad de México? *(Substitute other cities.)*
2. ¿Van a visitar el Bosque de Chapultepec?
3. ¿Van a ir de compras a un centro comercial?
4. ¿Adónde van de compras?
5. ¿Cómo se llama el centro comercial, Plaza Universidad o Plaza Chapultepec?
6. ¿Es uno de los mejores centros comerciales de la capital?

Side 3, 1650 to 2572

2   **01:26**

1. ¿Van por el Paseo de la Reforma primero?
2. ¿Qué es el Paseo de la Reforma, un parque o una avenida?
3. ¿Es una avenida muy importante?
4. ¿Hay monumentos?
5. ¿Son hermosos o feos?
6. ¿Es el Ángel de la Independencia un hermoso monumento?

Side 3, 2595 to 3600

3 – 5   **02:00**

1. ¿Es el Zócalo una plaza o un parque?
2. ¿Es la plaza principal?

¿Qué te gusta hacer?

☺ ¡Me gusta!   ☹ ¡No me gusta!

☺	☹	1.	ir a restaurantes
☺	☹	2.	ir a fiestas
☺	☹	3.	ir al cine
☺	☹	4.	ir a cafés
☺	☹	5.	ir a parques
☺	☹	6.	ir a centros comerciales
☺	☹	7.	jugar fútbol
☺	☹	8.	leer
☺	☹	9.	ver la tele
☺	☹	10.	pasear en bicicleta

Amigos, bienvenidos a la Ciudad de México. Hoy vamos a hacer un tour por toda la ciudad. Luego vamos a visitar el Bosque de Chapultepec. Y finalmente, vamos de compras a Plaza Universidad, uno de los mejores centros comerciales de la capital.

Primero vamos por el Paseo de la Reforma, la avenida más importante de la ciudad. Aquí en la capital hay hermosos monumentos, como el Ángel, el monumento de la Independencia.

Guía: Bueno, ¿y ahora qué van a hacer ustedes dos?
Kati: A mí me gustaría ir de compras. Me encanta ir de compras. ¿Vamos?
Teresa: ¿De compras? ¿Ahora? Bueno, pero primero me gustaría tomar un refresco. ¿Por qué no vamos a ese café?

106   *ciento seis*

Guía: *Nuestro tour termina aquí, en la Zona Rosa, una zona comercial con las tiendas más elegantes de toda la ciudad. También hay excelentes restaurantes y cafés al aire libre.*

3. ¿Van a visitar la Catedral en la plaza?
4. ¿Qué van a visitar en la plaza?
5. ¿Hay parques y teatros en la Ciudad de México?
6. ¿Es un teatro?
7. ¿Es un teatro muy importante?
8. ¿Qué es?

Side 3, 3620 to 5482

Purpose   This section sets the context for the language needed to talk about weekend activities and provides comprehensible language without translation.

Ahora estamos en el Zócalo, la plaza principal. Aquí vamos a visitar la Catedral.

Hay magníficos parques y teatros.

El Bosque de Chapultepec es el parque más grande de la capital. Los fines de semana hay mucha gente aquí. Hay mucho que ver y hacer.

El Palacio de Bellas Artes es un teatro muy importante.

Guía: *Aquí estamos en el centro comercial Plaza Universidad.*
Turista: *¿Hay buenas ofertas aquí?*
Guía: *Hay estupendas ofertas . . . y mucho más. Hay tiendas de toda clase. Hay cines con películas en español, en inglés, en alemán, en francés. ¡A mí me encanta este centro comercial!*

Hay varios museos en el Bosque y vamos a visitar el Museo de Antropología.

ciento siete **107**

---

6 - 7 `03:03`

Suggestion Locate Chapultepec on a map of Mexico City.
1 ¿Es el Bosque de Chapultepec?
2 ¿Es un parque?
3 ¿Es un parque en la Ciudad de México?
4 ¿Es grande o pequeño el parque?
5 ¿Les gusta a los mexicanos ir al parque los fines de semana?
6 ¿Cuándo les gusta ir al parque?
7 ¿Hay mucho que ver y hacer en el parque?
8 ¿Hay varios museos en Chapultepec?
9 ¿Es un museo? ¿Cómo se llama?
10 ¿Van a visitar el Museo de Antropología?

Side 3, 5500 to 6715

8 `03:44`

Suggestions Name local shopping centers students will know. Gesture and/or use facial expression to clarify **me encanta**.
1 ¿Es Plaza Universidad un centro comercial?
2 ¿Cómo se llama un centro comercial en *[your town]*?
3 ¿Hay buenas ofertas en Plaza Universidad?
4 ¿Hay buenas ofertas en el centro comercial *[name of shopping center in your town]*?
5 ¿A la guía le gusta o le encanta Plaza Universidad?
6 ¿A ti te encanta *[your shopping center]*?
7 ¿Son las ofertas en Plaza Universidad buenas, excelentes o estupendas?
8 ¿Hay cines en Plaza Universidad?
9 ¿Hay un cine en *[your town]*? ¿Cómo se llama?
10 ¿Hay películas en español (inglés, francés, alemán) en *[movie theater in your town]*?

Side 3, 6733 to 7500

9 `04:10`

Suggestion Point out the **Zona Rosa** on the map of Mexico City.
1 ¿Termina el tour en la Zona Rosa?
2 ¿Qué es la Zona Rosa, un centro comercial o una zona comercial?
3 ¿Hay tiendas en la Zona Rosa?
4 ¿Cómo son las tiendas?
5 ¿Hay cafés en la Zona Rosa?
6 ¿Hay cafés al aire libre?

Side 3, 7522 to 8315

Suggestions Have students raise their hands if they like or dislike the activities listed in **¿Qué te gusta hacer?** Narrate one section at a time, using the transparencies to clarify meaning without translation. Ask **Comprehension Checks**. Repeat this process with each section.

Using the video Play one section at a time after narrating it using the transparencies. Freeze the video and ask the **Comprehension Checks.** Repeat this process with each section.

10 `04:37`

1 ¿A quién le gustaría ir de compras, a Kati o a la guía?
2 ¿A quién le gustaría tomar un refresco?

Side 3, 8338 to 9214

05:08–
08:14

Side 3, 9243 to 14816

Early Production Checks

Always begin each set of questions by identifying the characters and by recycling descriptive and/or other appropriate, previously learned material.

A complete set of the **Early Production Checks** is available on cards in the Teacher's Resource Package.

1   `05:13`

¡Vamos de compras!

1 ¿Quién es ella? *(Point to Alicia, then to Kati.)*

2 ¿Cómo está Kati?   *Bien.*

3 ¿Tiene Alicia planes para el fin de semana?   *Sí.*

4 ¿Adónde va la familia de Alicia?   *Al parque.*

5 ¿Qué recomienda Kati, ir al parque o ir de compras?   *Ir de compras.*

6 ¿Adónde va Kati mañana, al parque o a Plaza Universidad?   *A Plaza Universidad.*

7 ¿Qué va a comprar, discos o pizza?   *Discos.*

8 ¿Le encantaría ir de compras a Alicia?   *Sí.*

9 ¿Qué le encantaría a Alicia?   *Ir a Plaza Universidad.*

10 ¿Con quién necesita hablar Alicia?   *Con su mamá.*

11 ¿Cuándo van a hablar por teléfono otra vez?   *En quince minutos.*

Side 3, 9399 to 10936

¡OjO!   The use of object pronouns here is for listening comprehension only. Students should not be asked to produce these structures nor to understand the grammatical concept at this point.

¿ Q U É   D E C I M O S . . . ?

Al hacer planes para el fin de semana

1 *¡Vamos de compras!*

UNIDAD 3

Purpose This section uses the language of making weekend plans in natural contexts. Students should not be overly concerned with understanding or translating every word of the dialogues. Comprehension will come with use of overhead transparencies and/or video viewing to help students practice the new language.

2 Necesito hablar con papá.

3 ¡Vamos!

Point out In Hispanic families, teenagers are not likely to make plans to go out without first checking with their parents. It would be considered disrespectful not to ask for permission.

2   06:05

Necesito hablar con papá.

Note Accept brief phrases or one- and two-word answers to all **Early Production Checks** as shown in **1** on page 108. It is not necessary for students to answer in complete sentences.

1 ¿Quiénes van al parque mañana?
2 ¿A Alicia le gustaría ir al parque?
3 ¿Adónde le gustaría ir?
4 ¿Con quién le gustaría ir de compras?
5 ¿Le permite la madre ir a Alicia?
6 ¿Con quién tiene que hablar Alicia?
7 ¿Dónde está el papá de Alicia?
8 ¿Con quién está el papá de Alicia?
9 ¿Es Riqui? *(Point to all three.)*
10 ¿Qué le gustaría hacer a Alicia?
11 ¿Qué dice el padre de Alicia, sí o no?

Side 3, 10954 to 12842

3   07:09

¡Vamos!

1 ¿Quién es?
2 ¿Con quién habla Daniel?
3 ¿Alicia va al parque o va de compras?
4 ¿Con quién va de compras?
5 ¿De dónde es Kati, de Norteamérica o de Sudamérica?
6 ¿Adónde van Daniel, Alicia y Kati?
7 ¿Van a ver una película en inglés o en español?

Side 3, 12878 to 14816

Suggestions Begin by having students close their books while you narrate one section at a time, using the transparencies to clarify meaning without translation. Then ask the **Early Production Checks.** Repeat this process with each section.

Using the video Play one section at a time after narrating it using the transparencies. Freeze the video and ask the **Early Production Checks.** Repeat this process with each section.

A. ¿Quiénes van?
Call on individuals to answer based on the dialogues. Encourage them to name more than one person in response to the plural question **¿Quiénes?**

1 Alicia y Kati
2 Mamá, papá y Daniel
3 Alicia y Kati
4 Alicia, Kati y Daniel
5 Mamá y papá
6 Alicia y Kati
7 Alicia y Kati
8 Alicia, Kati y Daniel

B. ¿Vas al museo?
Allow 2–3 min. Then ask ¿**Va** *[name]* **a** *[place]* **los fines de semana?** Remind students that when answering in the negative in Spanish, **No, no . . .** is used.

1 ¿Vas al parque? Sí, voy al parque. *o* No, no voy al parque.
2 ¿Vas a la biblioteca? Sí, voy a la biblioteca. *o* No, no voy a la biblioteca.
3 ¿Vas al gimnasio? Sí, voy al gimnasio. *o* No, no voy al gimnasio.
4 ¿Vas a la clase de baile? Sí, voy a la clase de baile. *o* No, no voy a la clase de baile.
5 ¿Vas al centro comercial? Sí, voy al centro comercial. *o* No, no voy al centro comercial.
6 ¿Vas al colegio (a la escuela)? Sí, voy al colegio (a la escuela). *o* No, no voy al colegio (a la escuela).
7 ¿Vas al cine? Sí, voy al cine. *o* No, no voy al cine.
8 ¿Vas a la tienda de discos? Sí, voy a la tienda de discos. *o* No, no voy a la tienda de discos.

Ir a + [place]
Used to tell where someone is going

Voy a la tienda.
Los chicos **van al** parque.

See **¿Por qué se dice así?**,
page G33, section 3.1.

---

a + el → al

The word **a** followed by **el** becomes **al.**

Vamos **al** centro comercial.
¿Van **al** cine o a la biblioteca?

See **¿Por qué se dice así?**,
page G33, section 3.1.

CHARLEMOS UN POCO

A. ¿Quiénes van?   ¿Quiénes van o no van a estos lugares?

Alicia y Kati

Daniel

Mamá y papá

MODELO   ¿Quiénes van al parque?
Mamá, papá y Daniel.

1. ¿Quiénes van al centro comercial?
2. ¿Quiénes van al parque?
3. ¿Quiénes no van al parque?
4. ¿Quiénes van al cine?
5. ¿Quiénes no van al cine?
6. ¿Quiénes van de compras a Plaza Universidad?
7. ¿Quiénes van a la tienda de discos?
8. ¿Quiénes van a ver una película?

B. ¿Vas al museo?   Find out if your partner usually goes to the following places on weekends.

MODELO   You: **¿Vas al museo?**
         Partner: **Sí, voy al museo.** o
                   No, no voy al museo.

1.

2.

3.

4.

5.

6.

7.

8.

U N I D A D 3

Purpose These activities provide guided practice to students as they begin to produce the language needed to discuss weekend plans.

C. ¿Adónde van?   Hoy es sábado. ¿Adónde van todos?

MODELO   **Papá va a la biblioteca.**

nosotros	{ centro comercial
mis amigos	laboratorio
yo	restaurante
dos amigas	oficina
tú	tiendas
mi mamá y yo	patio
papá	clase de música
ustedes	biblioteca
mi amiga . . .	gimnasio
	parque

CH. ¿Adónde?   Ask your partner where these people are going.

MODELO   Cecilia / clase de español
You: **¿Adónde va Cecilia?**
Partner: **Va a la clase de español.**

1. el profesor García / clase de música
2. tú / gimnasio
3. Susana y Chavela / clase de computación
4. ustedes / oficina del director
5. Paco / clase de álgebra
6. yo / laboratorio
7. Beto / biblioteca
8. los profesores / patio

D. ¿Qué hay en tu mochila?   Your friend's backpack is too full. Ask what is in it.

MODELO   You: **¿Hay bolígrafos?**
Partner: **Sí, hay seis bolígrafos.**

   1.

   2.

3.

4.

5.

6. ¿...?

LECCIÓN 1

CH. ¿Adónde? Allow 2–3 min. Then call on different pairs to act out each exchange.
1 ¿Adónde va el profesor García? Va a la clase de música.
2 ¿Adónde vas tú? Voy al gimnasio.
3 ¿Adónde van Susana y Chavela? Van a la clase de computación.
4 ¿Adónde van ustedes? Vamos a la oficina del director.
5 ¿Adónde va Paco? Va a la clase de álgebra.
6 ¿Adónde voy yo? Vas al laboratorio.
7 ¿Adónde va Beto? Va a la biblioteca.
8 ¿Adónde van los profesores? Van al patio.

The verb form *hay*

Spanish uses **hay** to express:
    there is / there are
    Is there? / Are there?

¿Hay un centro comercial por aquí?
¿Hay discos en oferta?
Sí, pero no **hay** discos de Luis Miguel.

See **¿Por qué se dice así?,** *page G34, section 3.2.*

D. ¿Qué hay en tu mochila? Allow 2–3 min. Then call on different pairs to act out each exchange.
1 ¿Hay libros? Sí, hay cinco libros.
2 ¿Hay carpetas? Sí, hay tres carpetas.
3 ¿Hay lápices? Sí, hay dos lápices.
4 ¿Hay cuadernos? Sí, hay cuatro cuadernos.
5 ¿Hay diccionarios? Sí, hay un diccionario.
6 . . .

Suggestion Demonstrate each **modelo** using volunteers so all students will know what is expected.

E. ¿Qué hay aquí? Answers will vary.

Expansion Tell students to answer honestly with reference to your community. Allow 2–3 min. Then ask **¿Hay teatros (etc.) en** *[community]*? **¿Cuántos? ¿Cuáles son?**

F. Encuesta. Allow 2–3 min. Call on individuals to confirm what their friends said by asking **¿Le gusta la tarea a** *[name]*? etc. Answers will vary.

Point out **Encantar** should not be used in the negative. One never says **No me encanta,** but rather **No me gusta.**

Gustar
Expressing likes

I like	me gust**a**
you like	te gust**a**
	le gust**a**
he, she likes	le gust**a**

See ¿Por qué se dice así?, page G36, section 3.3.

Gustar and encantar
Expressing likes and dislikes

When talking about one thing:

(no) me gust**a**	me encant**a**
(no) te gust**a**	te encant**a**
(no) le gust**a**	le encant**a**

When talking about more than one thing:

(no) me gust**an**	me encant**an**
(no) te gust**an**	te encant**an**
(no) le gust**an**	le encant**an**

See ¿Por qué se dice así?, page G36, section 3.3.

G. ¡Me encantan! Have one student poll group members about the first item, then another about the second item, and so forth. Allow 2–3 min. Then ask each group **¿A cuántas personas en tu grupo les gusta . . . ?** Have one student at the board doing tally of each item.

Extension Have students ask you if you like these things. Be sure they use the **usted** form.

E. ¿Qué hay aquí? An out-of-town friend is visiting you for the weekend and wants some information about your community. Answer your friend's questions.

MODELO cine
Partner: **¿Hay cines aquí?**
You: **Sí, hay un cine.** o
Sí, hay cines. o
No, no hay cine.

1. museos
2. restaurantes
3. gimnasios
4. colegios
5. cines
6. teatros
7. cafés
8. parques
9. tiendas de video
10. centros comerciales
11. bibliotecas
12. ¿ . . . ?

F. Encuesta. Pregúntale a un(a) amigo(a) si le gustan estas cosas. Después, contesta las preguntas de tu amigo(a).

MODELO parque
Tú: **¿Te gusta el parque?**
Compañero(a): **Sí, ¡me encanta!** o
No, no me gusta.

1. fútbol
2. hacer la tarea
3. educación física
4. cafetería del colegio
5. trabajar
6. ir de compras
7. bailar
8. química
9. hablar por teléfono
10. estudiar

No me gusta	Me gusta	Me encanta
●	●	●

G. ¡Me encantan! Pregúntale a cada persona de tu grupo si le gustan estas cosas.

MODELO Tú: **¿Te gustan los videos?**
Compañero(a): **No, no me gustan.** o
Sí, me encantan.

1. exámenes
2. videos
3. computadoras
4. películas románticas
5. ciencias
6. sábados
7. clases de baile
8. tiendas de discos

H. ¿Y a tu profesor(a)? En tu opinión, ¿qué le gusta a tu profesor(a)?

MODELO fútbol
No le gusta el fútbol. o
Le gusta mucho el fútbol. o
Le encanta el fútbol.

1. videos
2. cafetería del colegio
3. exámenes
4. computadoras
5. sábados
6. tiendas de discos
7. bailar
8. biblioteca
9. béisbol
10. conciertos

I. No me gusta. You have a friend who never wants to do anything. What happens when you invite your friend to do the following?

MODELO escuchar discos
You: **¡Vamos a escuchar discos!**
Partner: **No, no me gusta escuchar discos.** o
No, no me gustan los discos.

1. bailar
2. ver televisión
3. alquilar unos videos
4. salir
5. jugar tenis
6. comer pizza
7. ir al parque
8. correr
9. ver una película
10. escuchar discos

J. ¿Te gustaría? Ask your partner if he or she would like to do the following things with you.

MODELO ir al cine
You: **¿Qué te gustaría hacer esta tarde?**
¿Ir al cine?
Partner: **Sí, me encantaría.** o
No, no me gustaría.

1. ver la tele
2. estudiar
3. ir al parque
4. comer
5. ir de compras
6. jugar tenis
7. pasear en bicicleta
8. jugar fútbol
9. correr
10. ir a un café
11. hablar español
12. ver un video

LECCIÓN 1

Vamos a + [infinitive or place]
Used to suggest doing something with someone

Vamos a is used to invite someone to do something. It is equivalent to *let's* in English.

Vamos a correr esta tarde.
Vamos al cine.

See ¿Por qué se dice así?,
page G33, section 3.1.

Gustaría and encantaría
Used when making polite requests

The **-ía** ending on the verbs **gustar** and **encantar** is used to say what you would like or to soften requests.

¿Te gustaría ir? *Would you like to go?*
¡Me encantaría! *I would love to!*

See ¿Por qué se dice así?,
page G36, section 3.3.

H. ¿Y a tu profesor(a)?
Allow 2–3 min. Then ask **En tu opinión, ¿me gusta el fútbol?** etc.

Extension Have students work in groups of 3 or 4. Ask each group to agree whether you really like, like, or dislike the items.

I. No me gusta.

Point out The definite article is generally used when **gustar** is followed by a noun.

1 ¡Vamos a bailar!
No, no me gusta bailar.
2 ¡Vamos a ver televisión!
No, no me gusta ver televisión.
o No, no me gusta televisión.
3 ¡Vamos a alquilar unos videos!
No, no me gusta alquilar los videos. *o* No, no me gustan los videos.
4 ¡Vamos a salir!
No, no me gusta salir.
5 ¡Vamos a jugar tenis!
No, no me gusta jugar tenis.
o No, no me gusta el tenis.
6 ¡Vamos a comer pizza!
No, no me gusta comer pizza.
o No, no me gusta la pizza.
7 ¡Vamos a ir al parque!
No, no me gusta ir al parque.
o No, no me gusta el parque.
8 ¡Vamos a correr!
No, no me gusta correr.
9 ¡Vamos a ver una película!
No, no me gusta ver películas. *o* No, no me gustan las películas.
10 ¡Vamos a escuchar discos!
No, no me gusta escuchar discos. *o* No, no me gustan los discos.

¡OjO! **Gustaría** and **encantaría** should be treated simply as lexical variations of **gustar** and **encantar** used to express softened requests. Students should not be expected to understand the conditional nor to produce all conjugations of these verbs at this point.

CHARLEMOS UN POCO MÁS

CHARLEMOS UN POCO MÁS

A. ¿Adónde vamos?
Insist students not look at each other's schedules until the task is completed. Then have them use schedules to correct each other's writing.

B. Gustos. Allow 3-4 min for this activity. After task is completed, ask questions such as **¿A quién le gusta limpiar la casa?** and **¿Qué le gusta hacer a** *[student's name]*?

Expansion Ask classmates if teachers like to do these things. Keep a tally.

C. ¡Bienvenidos! Allow 5–6 min. Then ask each group to put its itinerary on board. Compare and reach consensus, asking: **¿Qué van a hacer a las 9:00,** ir a *[name]* or visitar *[name]*?

CH. ¡A escribir!
This activity is designed to challenge students' reading skills as well as to give them the opportunity to write a descriptive paragraph. Allow 8–10 min to write. Guide students to avoid trying to express more than they know how at this point. If students want to express their likes or dislikes in the plural, you may wish to give them **nos gusta(n)**. Have students who finish first write their paragraphs on board. Correct the board work, pointing out differences between grammar errors and noncommunicative errors.

 A. ¿Adónde vamos? You need to meet with a friend but are having difficulty finding a convenient time. Using the schedules your teacher provides, write down your friend's schedule for the day as your partner reads it to you. Then read your schedule for the day so that your partner may write it down. Compare your schedules and decide when you can meet.

MODELO You hear: **A las nueve voy a la biblioteca.**
You write: **9:00   biblioteca**

B. Gustos. Ask several classmates if they like to do the activities pictured below. Keep a list of those who like to do these activities and those who don't.

C. ¡Bienvenidos! A group of teenagers from Mexico is visiting your school next Saturday, and your Spanish class will be hosting them. In small groups, discuss what there is to do, visit, and see in the community and decide on a 9:00 A.M. to 9:00 P.M. itinerary. **¡En español!**

CH. ¡A escribir! Below are four teenagers who are looking for pen pals. In pairs, discuss who would be the most suitable pen pal for the two of you. Then write a short description of yourselves to send to the person whom you selected.

You may begin by writing **Somos** *[nombre]* **y** *[nombre]* . . .

 ¡Hola, amigos! Me llamo Carmen Andrade. Soy de Puerto Rico. Me encanta escuchar música rock y ver videos musicales norteamericanos. También me gusta estudiar y leer novelas.

Jorge Antonio Miranda. Soy de Panamá, de la capital. Me gusta practicar deportes, ir al cine, correr, pasear en bicicleta. No me gusta ver televisión.

114 *ciento catorce*

UNIDAD 3

Purpose The *Charlemos un poco más* activities in this section are designed to allow students to "create" with language recently learned and in a variety of open-ended contexts. The activities often have several possible correct answers.

Mi nombre es Caridad Espinosa. Soy española. Me encantan las fiestas, dibujar, intercambiar correspondencia, tener muchos amigos, ir al cine y coleccionar todo lo relacionado a José José. Pueden escribirme en inglés o en español.

Soy David Barrio. Soy de Venezuela. Me gusta mucho escuchar música romántica, ver videos musicales de los años 50, escribir poemas, ir al cine y ver películas de los años 50 y 60.

Dramatizaciones

A. Sábado. It is Saturday morning, and you call a friend to make plans for the day.

- Invite your friend to go shopping.
- Suggest that you go to your favorite shopping center.
- Your friend doesn't like to go shopping and suggests another activity.
- Accept your friend's suggestion.
- Ask at what time.
- Decide on a time.

B. ¡El fin de semana! You are spending the weekend at a friend's house because your parents are out of town.

- Ask your friend what you are going to do on Saturday morning.
- After he or she suggests a couple of things, mention two or three things that you like to do or places where you like to go.
- Decide where you are going and agree on a time.

C. ¡Mi ideal! You just saw your best friend with a person whom you have been wanting to meet for quite some time. Find out from your partner who the person is. Ask your partner what the person likes to do, where he or she likes to go, and other questions to get as much information as you can.

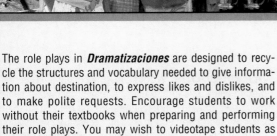

The role plays in **Dramatizaciones** are designed to recycle the structures and vocabulary needed to give information about destination, to express likes and dislikes, and to make polite requests. Encourage students to work without their textbooks when preparing and performing their role plays. You may wish to videotape students as they do some of the activities.

DRAMATIZACIONES

A, B, C. Assign **A, B**, and **C** at same time. Allow 5–6 min to prepare. Call on pairs to present to class. Ask comprehension questions after each presentation.

C. ¡Mi ideal! Have students brainstorm the information they would like to know before they prepare their role plays.

¡No me digas!

Purpose This section provides additional reading practice as students discover interesting cross-cultural information about shopping in Oaxaca, Mexico.

Suggestions Allow 1–2 min to read the dialogue. Ask students to discuss possible explanations and arrive at consensus on correct answer before checking response and explanations on page 417.

Point out In most larger cities, businesses no longer close for **siesta** because traffic makes it difficult for most employees to go home for lunch. In smaller cities, like Oaxaca, most businesses do close for two to three hours in the afternoon.

Answers

1 There is no evidence in this dialogue that people don't work in the afternoon. Try another response.

② In Spain, Mexico, and most Latin American countries, the principal meal of the day is lunch. Many businesses close between 2:00 and 4:00 so that employees may go home for their main meal. Currently, however, in the larger cities, major department stores and international businesses remain open throughout the afternoon. Most stores do close later in the evening to allow additional shopping time. This is the correct answer.

3 Shops in Mexico, as in most cities of the Western world, do close down on certain religious holidays, but no indication was given that Tom was shopping on a religious holiday. Try another response.

IMPACTO CULTURAL

¡No me digas!

De compras. Tom Winters está de visita en Oaxaca, México. Llama por teléfono a Rosa, su amiga mexicana.

	Rin, rin.
Rosa:	**¿Bueno?**
Tom:	**Hola, Rosa. Habla Tomás.**
Rosa:	**Hola, Tomás. ¿Cómo estás?**
Tom:	**Pues, no muy bien, Rosa. ¿Qué pasa aquí? Es imposible ir de compras en esta ciudad.**
Rosa:	**¡Hombre! ¿Por qué dices eso?**
Tom:	**Mira, en este momento estoy en el centro y casi todas las tiendas están cerradas.**
Rosa:	**¿Cerradas?**
Tom:	**Sí, cerradas.** *Closed! Closed!*
Rosa:	**Pero, Tomás, ¡son las tres y media! No es hora de ir de compras.**

Why does Rosa say that 3:30 is no time to go shopping?

1. Shops in Oaxaca are open only in the morning. No one works in the afternoon.
2. Most shops close from 2:00 to 4:00, then open again in the evening.
3. On religious holidays, all shops close at 3:00 P.M. so that shop clerks can go to church services in the early evening.

❏ Check your answer on page 417.

Y ahora, ¡a leer!

Antes de empezar

Prepare a chart comparing the activities of teenagers in the United States and Mexico. First list American teenagers' most popular activities (**Actividades más populares**), their favorite summer activities (**Actividades de verano**), and their favorite group activities (**Actividades en grupo**). Then draw up a similar list for Mexican teenagers. If you don't know, make a reasoned guess.

116 ciento dieciséis

Antes de empezar

This activity is an advance organizer for the **Pasatiempos en la capital** reading that follows. It will help students establish what they know/don't know about a topic and to predict what they may learn/read about. Anticipating the content of a text is a key strategy used by good readers.

Suggestions Working in small groups, students fill out the chart. Encourage them to make reasoned guesses if they don't know. Then have them do the reading and come back to their charts and make any necessary changes. Students should realize how similar teenagers in other countries are to themselves.

Pasatiempos en la capital

A los jóvenes de la capital de México les gusta hacer una gran variedad de cosas los fines de semana. Una de las actividades más populares es ir a pasar varias horas en un centro comercial. Hay muchos centros por toda la ciudad pero los más populares son la Plaza Satélite, la Plaza Perisur, la Plaza Coyoacán, la Plaza Relox y la Plaza Inn.

En verano hay actividades para todos los jóvenes. Para los aventureros hay campamentos, para los estudiosos hay escuelas de verano, para los músicos hay clases particulares de piano o de guitarra, para los artistas hay clubes de teatro, de baile o de pintura. También hay clubes para agricultores, para aficionados a la música rock y para los coleccionadores. Y sí, claro, para los deportistas hay fútbol, fútbol americano, béisbol, baloncesto, tenis, natación y mucho más.

Por lo general los jóvenes salen en grupo hasta tener unos 16 o 17 años. A los 16 o 17 comienzan a salir en pareja y generalmente dos o tres parejas salen juntas. Van a los cafés o cafeterías a comer, van al cine, van a caminar a las alamedas centrales o van a fiestas en casa de amigos. También les gusta salir a comer comida chatarra y beberse un refresco en lugares como McDonald's, Kentucky Fried Chicken y Denny's.

Verifiquemos

1. ¿Qué hacen los jóvenes mexicanos los fines de semana?
2. Compara tus actividades con las actividades de los jóvenes mexicanos. ¿Cuáles son similares? ¿Cuáles son distintas?
3. ¿Qué diferencias hay entre México y Estados Unidos cuando un chico sale con una chica?

LECCIÓN 1

Purpose This section is intended to expand students' reading ability without translation as they learn how teenagers in Mexico City like to spend their weekends.

Note The phrase **comida chatarra** is Mexican slang for *fast food*. Students should be able to understand its meaning from the context.

Verifiquemos

Answers

Have students refer to the charts they wrote in **Antes de empezar**. Record student contributions on the board in two columns headed **Semejanzas** and **Diferencias**. Encourage students to express their answers without reading complete lines from the text. This may require that they simplify the language to the subject/verb kind of sentences they control most comfortably. Students should conclude there are not that many differences except, perhaps, for dating customs.

OBJECTIVES

Communicative Goals

- Discussing weekend activities

Culture and Reading

- *¡No me digas!*
  ¡Hay tanta gente!
  Popularity of city parks
- *Y ahora, ¡a leer!*
  El Bosque de Chapultepec:
  Mexico's largest park

Structure

- 3.4 Present tense: Singular forms
- 3.5 The seasons and weather expressions

¡Me encanta el parque!

ACTIVE VOCABULARY

El tiempo

tiempo	sol
hace buen ...	hace ...
hace mal ...	viento
calor	hace ...
hace ...	está lloviendo
fresco	está nevando
hace ...	llueve
frío	nieva
hace ...	

Las estaciones

estaciones	primavera
invierno	verano
otoño	

En el parque

autobús	parque de
bosque	diversiones
helado	carros chocones
lago	carusel
lancha	juegos infantiles
	montaña rusa
	zoológico

Verbos

calificar	estudiar
caminar	hablar
comer	leer
comprar	mirar
correr	preparar
descansar	subir
escribir	tomar
escuchar	ver
esperar	visitar

Palabras y expresiones

cuando	¡Dígame!
entrevista	¡Qué bien!
gente	
niña, niño	
periódico	
radio	
tarde	

ANTICIPEMOS

¿Qué piensas tú?

1. What are the people in the large photo doing? What information do they expect to find? What do you think they might be able to do here?

2. Are there parks in your town? What kinds of activities are available there? Who uses your parks most?

3. Where are the people in the other photos? What are they doing? What day of the week do you think it is? Why?

4. Which of the activities in the photos might you do on a weekend? With whom do you spend your free time?

5. How much of your weekend time do you spend doing things with your family? What things does your family do together? What things influence how much time you spend with your family?

6. How do you think the way you spend your weekends compares with the way teenagers in Mexico City spend theirs?

7. What do you think you will be able to talk about when you have finished this lesson?

¿Qué piensas tú?

Answers

1 They are looking at a map. Map locates different museums in Chapultepec Park in Mexico City. Visitors can go to museums, go to amusement rides/games, rent boats on lake, stroll, picnic, play, sleep, rest, read, relax, watch people. Students will name obvious things prompted by the photos but may need to be guided to express others.

2 Answers will vary. Except in larger cities, park facilities may be quite limited. Students will name many of the same things as in **1**. They may feel younger children and/or older people use the park most.

3 Places: café, shop, museum or public building, amusement park. Activities: eating, drinking, shopping, looking at mural, going out with friends or family, going on rides. It is probably a weekend day since all seem to have free time.

4 Answers will vary.

5 Answers will vary. Work, social, and sports obligations of both parents and children affect family time together, as do age, tastes, interests, and the types of activities available.

6 Students may speculate that Hispanic families are more likely to spend time together but may not be clear as to why they have this impression.

7 **They will be able to talk about weekend activities.**

Purpose The purpose of this section is to focus students on the language necessary to talk about weekend activities. It also encourages students to develop and use critical thinking skills while observing cultural differences and similarities in the amount of time spent with family in the U.S. and in Hispanic countries.

TAPE/DISC	🎞	▱
08:15–11:36		

Side 3, 14839 to 20883

Comprehension Checks

The questions listed here are examples only. Ask yes/no questions, one- and two-word-answer questions to confirm that students understand key language.

A full set of the **Comprehension Checks** is available on cards in the TRP.

1 `08:22`

Suggestions Point out the temperature on a thermometer. Indicate warm temperatures to illustrate **hace calor**. Point out the sun. Mime listening, running, reading, resting.

1 ¿Es el Bosque de Chapultepec?
2 ¿Es un parque? ¿Cómo se llama?
3 ¿Es primavera?
4 ¿Hace buen / mal tiempo?
5 ¿Hace sol?
6 ¿Pasa la familia Chávez el sábado en el parque?
7 ¿Qué hace Alicia, escucha la radio o ve televisión?
8 ¿Quién corre, Daniel o Riqui?
9 ¿Qué hace Riqui, mira a la gente o toma un refresco?
10 ¿Quién lee un libro, su mamá o su papá? ¿Qué hace su mamá?
11 ¿Quién descansa, su mamá o su papá? ¿Qué hace su papá?

Side 3, 15083 to 16915

2 `09:26`

Suggestions Act out buying, drinking, eating. Name U.S. brands of **refrescos** and **helados**. Point out the boat and gesture/act out **subir a la lancha**. Draw several people = **la gente**.

1 ¿Es primavera? ¿verano?
Continue asking Comprehension Check questions, as above, or use the **Comprehension Checks** in the TRP.

Side 3, 16973 to 18155

LAS CUATRO ESTACIONES EN EL BOSQUE DE CHAPULTEPEC

El clima de México es muy agradable. Por eso, durante todo el año la gente visita el Bosque de Chapultepec.

 junio julio agosto

 marzo abril mayo

1

2

En verano hace calor. Por eso, a much[...] gente le gusta ir al Lago de Chapultepe[...]

Y aquí están los Chávez otra vez. Ante[...] de subir a la lancha, la señora compra [...] un refresco y dos helados. El helado de [...] chocolate es para el papá. Es su sabor [...] favorito.

En primavera hace sol pero no hace calor. Hace buen tiempo. La familia Chávez pasa el sábado en el Bosque de Chapultepec.

Daniel corre. Alicia escucha la radio y mira a la gente. ¿Y Riqui? Ah, Riqui toma un refresco. Mientras tanto, su mamá lee un libro y su papá simplemente descansa.

120 ciento veinte

3

En verano llueve casi todos los días e[...] la Ciudad de México. Pero no llueve t[...] el día—sólo dos o tres horas por la tar[...]

3 `10:06`

1 ¿Llueve mucho en la Ciudad de México? ¿En [your town]?
Continue asking Comprehension Check questions.

Side 3, 18176 to 18523

Purpose This section develops listening and reading comprehension of active vocabulary. Students should not be expected to achieve productive mastery at this point.

septiembre
octubre
noviembre

4 **10:18**

Suggestions Name a local or well-known zoo. Mime **mirar los animales.** Name several animals one would see in a zoo. Mime **caminar.**
1 ¿Es otoño? ¿verano/primavera?
2 ¿Qué tiempo hace en el otoño?
3 ¿Visitan Eloísa Miramontes y su hijo el jardín zoológico?
4 ¿Mira Jorge los animales?
5 ¿Camina su madre?
6 ¿Le gusta a su madre caminar por el parque?
7 ¿Le gusta a Jorge mirar los animales? ¿Le encanta?

Side 3, 18541 to 19330

diciembre
enero
febrero

En otoño generalmente hace buen tiempo.

Eloísa Miramontes y su hijo visitan el jardín zoológico. A Jorge le encanta mirar los animales y a su madre le gusta caminar por el parque.

5

5 **10:45**

Suggestions Name a local amusement park. Point to the roller coaster and the bumper cars to introduce the terms **la montaña rusa** and **los carros chocones.**
1 ¿Pasa la tarde Daniel en el parque de diversiones?
2 ¿Quién pasa la tarde en el parque de diversiones?
3 ¿Riqui también pasa la tarde en el parque de diversiones?
4 ¿Quién sube a la montaña rusa, Riqui o Daniel?
5 ¿Quién sube a los carros chocones, Riqui o Daniel? ¿Quién sube al carusel?

Side 3, 19350 to 20165

Hoy Daniel pasa la tarde en el parque de diversiones con su hermano Riqui. Daniel sube a la montaña rusa. Riqui no. Él sube a los carros chocones o al carusel.

En invierno durante el día es agradable, pero por la mañana hace fresco y por la noche hace frío.

Los domingos mucha gente visita uno de los seis museos del parque. Entre los más famosos están el Museo de Antropología y el Castillo de Chapultepec.

6 **11:13**

Point out Sunday is a popular day to visit museums because admission is free.
1 ¿Es verano? ¿Es primavera/otoño/invierno?
2 ¿Hace frío o hace fresco de día en invierno?
3 ¿Hace frío o hace fresco de noche?
4 ¿Qué tiempo hace en invierno en la capital?
5 Y en *[your town]*, ¿qué tiempo hace en el invierno?
6 ¿Visita mucha gente el Castillo de Chapultepec en el invierno?
7 ¿Cuándo visita mucha gente el Castillo?
8 ¿Visita mucha gente los museos?
9 ¿Cuántos museos hay en el Bosque de Chapultepec?

Side 3, 20197 to 20883

ciento veintiuno **121**

*S*uggestions Begin by having students close their books while you narrate one section at a time, using the transparencies to clarify meaning without translation. Then ask the **Comprehension Checks.** Repeat this process with each section.

Using the video Play one section at a time after narrating it using the transparencies. Freeze the video and ask the **Comprehension Checks.** Repeat this process with each section.

Point out Mexico City has a mild climate. Winter night temperatures rarely drop below 40°F (5°C), which residents consider **frío.** Summer is distinguished by its heavy rainfall, with higher temperatures around 75°F (24°C).

¿QUÉ DECIMOS...?

11:37–14:45

Side 3, 20907 to 26554

Early Production Checks

Use the **Early Production Checks** to begin developing complete utterances about weekend activities.

A full set of the **Early Production Checks** is available on cards in the Teacher's Resource Package.

1   **11:44**

¡Bienvenidos a Chapultepec!

1 ¿Quién es? *(Point to Pedro.)* *Pedro Solís.*
2 ¿Es Pedro Solís?   *Sí.*
3 ¿Cómo se llama?   *Pedro Solís.*
4 ¿Es el programa por la mañana o por la tarde?   *Es por la tarde.*
5 ¿Dónde está Pedro Solís? *En el Bosque de Chapultepec.*
6 ¿Cómo es el parque, hermoso o feo?   *Hermoso.*
7 ¿Es Eloísa Miramontes? *(Point to Eloísa.)*   *Sí.*
8 ¿Cómo se llama ella? *Eloísa Miramontes.*
9 ¿Le gusta el parque a Eloísa? *(¿Te gusta a ti?)*   *Sí.*
10 ¿Camina Eloísa en el parque? *Sí.*
11 ¿Qué escucha?   *La radio.*
12 ¿Bebe café o refrescos? *Refrescos.*
13 ¿Mira la tele o a la gente? *A la gente.*
14 ¿Hay museos en el parque?   *Sí.*
15 ¿Visita los museos Eloísa?   *Sí. (Pero es difícil.)*
16 ¿Le gusta o le encanta el Museo de Antropología a Eloísa? *Le encanta.*

Side 3, 21120 to 22930

¿QUÉ DECIMOS...?
Al hablar de los pasatiempos

1 ¡Bienvenidos a Chapultepec!

UNIDAD 3

Purpose This section uses language needed for discussing pastimes in real-life contexts. Students should not be asked to memorize dialogues word for word.

2 ¡Uy! Perdón.

2 `12:46`

¡Uy! Perdón.
Accept brief phrases or one- and two-word answers to all **Early Production Checks,** as in **1** on page 122. It is not necessary for students to answer in complete sentences.

1 ¿Quién es? *(Point to Pedro, then to boy.)*
2 ¿Dónde están?
3 ¿Quién dice "¡Uy! Perdón"?
4 ¿Qué va a comprar el muchacho, un helado o un refresco?
5 ¿Pasa Riqui mucho tiempo en el parque?
6 ¿Qué hace la mamá de Riqui en el parque, descansa o lee? ¿Escribe cartas?
7 ¿Qué hace el papá de Riqui en el parque?
8 ¿Visita Riqui el zoológico?
9 ¿Sube a las lanchas Riqui?
10 ¿Le gusta a Riqui el zoológico? (¿Te gusta a ti?)
11 ¿Le gusta el parque de diversiones? (¿Y a ti?)

Side 3, 22959 to 25065

LECCIÓN 2

ciento veintitrés **123**

Suggestions Begin by having students close their books while you narrate one section at a time, using the transparencies to clarify meaning without translation. Then ask the **Early Production Checks.** Repeat this process with each section.

Using the video Play one section at a time after narrating it using the transparencies. Freeze the video and ask the **Early Production Checks.** Repeat this process with each section.

¡Es fantástica!

1 ¿Quién es? *(Point to each boy.)*
2 ¿Van a subir a la montaña rusa Daniel y Martín?
3 ¿Quiénes van a subir a la montaña rusa?
4 ¿Sube Riqui a la montaña rusa? ¿Sube al carusel? ¿a los carros chocones?
5 ¿Va Riqui con Daniel y Martín?
6 ¿Va a tomar un helado Riqui?
7 ¿Qué va a tomar Riqui?

Side 3, 25088 to 26554

3 ¡Es fantástica!

CHARLEMOS UN POCO

A. ¿Quién habla? Can you tell who might say this—**Eloísa, Riqui,** or **Pedro Solís**?

Eloísa   **Riqui**   **Pedro Solís**

1. Escucho la radio.
2. Tomo muchos helados.
3. Esta tarde vamos a pasear por el Bosque de Chapultepec.
4. Voy al parque de diversiones.
5. ¿Qué hacen tus papás aquí?
6. En invierno no, porque hace frío.
7. Miro a la gente.
8. Es ideal para pasear con el niño.
9. ¿Visita los museos del parque?
10. Mi mamá escribe cartas en el parque.

B. Después de las clases. Find out which of the following activities your partner does after school.

MODELO   practicar el piano
          You: **¿Practicas el piano?**
          Partner: **No, no practico el piano.**

hablar por teléfono
comprar helados
escuchar la radio
correr
escribir cartas
limpiar la casa
preparar la comida
estudiar español
ver televisión
subir a las lanchas
leer el periódico
pasear en bicicleta
descansar
esperar el autobús

C. ¿Y tu profesor(a)? Find out what your teacher usually does after school. Ask as many questions as possible.

LECCIÓN 2

Present tense: Singular forms

-ar escuchar	**-er** leer	**-ir** escribir
escucho	leo	escribo
escuchas escucha	lees lee	escribes escribe
escucha	lee	escribe

Escucho discos todos los días.
¿**Lees** el periódico por la noche?
Eloísa **escribe** cartas.

See **¿Por qué se dice así?**, *page G38, section 3.4.*

CHARLEMOS UN POCO

A. ¿Quién habla? Call on individuals to read each description. Have class guess who is being described, referring to dialogues if necessary.
1 Eloísa
2 Riqui
3 Pedro Solís
4 Riqui
5 Pedro Solís
6 Riqui
7 Eloísa
8 Eloísa
9 Pedro Solís
10 Riqui

B. Después de las clases. Allow 3–4 min for pair work. Then ask individual students what their partners do: **¿Qué hace** *[partner's name]*? Answers will vary. Check for correct verb forms.

Expansion Ask students to go to board and write two things that their partners do.

C. ¿Y tu profesor(a)? Tell students to refer to the list in **B** for ideas on what to ask. Remind students to use the **usted** form.

Purpose These activities provide guided practice to students beginning to produce the structures and vocabulary necessary to describe weekend activities.

Suggestion Be sure to provide success for all students by matching appropriate tasks to students of various levels of ability.

Ver

veo
ves
ve
ve

Notice that the **yo** form does not drop the **-e** before the ending is added.

CH. ¿Qué ven? What do these people see during their visit to Chapultepec Park?

MODELO Santiago
Santiago ve el Lago de Chapultepec.

D. Pasatiempos. Tell what the following people do in their free time.

 EJEMPLO **Mi amigo Jaime camina en el parque.**

mi profesor	escuchar	jardín zoológico
usted	limpiar	exámenes
mi profesora	caminar	en el parque
tú	leer	cartas
yo	calificar	televisión
mi amigo	visitar	libros
mi amiga	escribir	la casa
mi papá	ver	la radio
mi mamá	correr	en un café
¿ . . . ?	pasear	¿ . . . ?
	estudiar	
	comer	
	¿ . . . ?	

UNIDAD 3

E. Horarios diferentes. Estas personas tienen horarios diferentes. Describe sus horarios.

MODELO   Pablo/Sra. Vidal
A las diez de la mañana Pablo practica karate y la Sra. Vidal califica exámenes.

1. Juan/Marta

2. Toño/Sr. Pérez

3. Albertina/Srta. López

4. Sr. Morales/Susana

5. Lisa/Miguel

6. Sr. Silva/Arturo

7. Virginia/Patricio

8. Sr. Rivera/Kati

LECCIÓN 2

E. Horarios diferentes.
1 Al mediodía Juan come y Marta corre.
2 A las dos y media de la tarde Toño toma (bebe) un refresco y el señor Pérez lee el periódico.
3 A las cuatro y cuarto de la tarde Albertina pasea en bicicleta y la señorita López limpia la casa.
4 A las seis de la tarde el señor Morales prepara (la) comida y Susana alquila un video.
5 A las nueve y media de la noche Lisa estudia y Miguel ve televisión.
6 A las tres menos cuarto de la tarde el señor Silva habla por teléfono y Arturo escucha la radio.
7 A las nueve y media de la mañana Virginia espera el autobús y Patricio escribe una carta.
8 A las siete de la noche el señor Rivera descansa y Kati lee un libro.

Weather expressions
Used to talk about the weather

With hacer:

¿Qué tiempo **hace**?
Hace . . .

buen tiempo. mal tiempo.

calor. fresco.

frío. sol.

viento.

With other verbs:

Está lloviendo. or **Llueve.**

Está nevando. or **Nieva.**

See **¿Por qué se dice así?**, *page G40, section 3.5.*

F. ¿Qué tiempo hace?   What does this world traveler say when you ask about the weather in each place he plans to visit?

EJEMPLO Santo Domingo
You: **¿Qué tiempo hace en Santo Domingo?**
Partner: **Hace buen tiempo. Hace mucho sol.**

1. Tegucigalpa **2.** La Paz **3.** Madrid

4. México **5.** Buenos Aires **6.** La Habana

7. Santiago **8.** Montevideo **9.** Puerto Rico

UNIDAD 3

G. ¿Qué haces? Find out what your friend does in different types of weather.

EJEMPLO   frío
You: **¿Qué haces cuando hace frío?**
Partner: **Cuando hace frío, hablo por teléfono
           o voy de compras.**

1. sol
2. viento
3. mucho calor
4. nieva
5. buen tiempo

6. mucho frío
7. llueve
8. mal tiempo
9. fresco

H. ¡Las cuatro estaciones! Describe the weather in your community during the various seasons.

EJEMPLO   invierno
           **En invierno hace mal tiempo. Hace mucho frío,
           llueve y nieva.**

1. verano
2. otoño

3. invierno
4. primavera

Las cuatro estaciones

el verano   el otoño

el invierno   la primavera

*See ¿Por qué se dice así?,
page G40, section 3.5.*

CHARLEMOS UN POCO MÁS

A. Cuando nieva . . . List three things you do on weekends when it's raining and three things you do when it's snowing. Then tell several classmates and listen to what they say they do.

EJEMPLO   **Cuando llueve yo limpio la casa y . . .**

B. ¿Tú también haces eso? Working in groups of four, talk about what you do on a typical Saturday in the summer, fall, winter, and spring. For each season, find one thing that each member of your group does that no one else in the group does. Be prepared to report on these activities to the whole class.

C. ¿Juntos o no? Your teacher will give you and your partner copies of Clarita's and Professor Morales' schedules. Compare your schedule with your partner's to find what activities Professor Morales and his daughter Clarita do together during the day.

EJEMPLO   **A las seis de la mañana el profesor Morales corre.
           Clarita también corre. o Clarita no corre.**

LECCIÓN 2

CHARLEMOS UN POCO MÁS

A. Cuando nieva . . . Allow 3–4 min. Then ask students to write the most interesting comment they heard on board. If they find a class-mate that listed the same things, have them go to board and write their names and what they do.

**Vocabulario opcional
esquiar** *(to ski)*, **patinar (sobre hielo)** *(to ice-skate)*, **andar en trineo** *(to go sledding)*, **hacer un monigote de nieve** *(to make a snowman)*, **tirar pelotas de nieve** *(to throw snowballs)*

Extension Repeat having students list the three things they most like to do on windy days or when it's very hot.

B. ¿Tú también haces eso? Insist students speak only Spanish. Allow 5-8 min. Ask someone from each group to report what one member does that no one else does.

 C. ¿Juntos o no? In pairs, allow 2–3 min for students to take turns saying what each person does at each time.

Purpose These activities are designed to allow students to create with language recently learned. Although they may sometimes appear repetitious of the guided practice in the previous section, these activities enable students to use description of weekend activities in a variety of possible combinations.

CH. En el parque.
Give one partner a picture.
The other uses the textbook.
Neither partner should see the other's picture.

CH. En el parque. There are six differences between the drawing below and the one your teacher will give your partner. Describe your drawings in detail until you find the six differences. You may not look at each other's drawing.

EJEMPLO You: **Una chica corre.**
Partner: **Un chico corre.**

DRAMATIZACIONES

A. ¡Un nuevo amigo! Allow 3–4 min to prepare. Have students present to class. Ask comprehension questions after each presentation or have presentors themselves ask the questions.

B. Te presento a . . . This activity is a sequel to **A** and should be done the same day. You may want to have students take notes when they do **A** so that they can refer to them in **B**.

C. ¡Somos profesores! Students may choose to use either **tú** or **usted** when doing this activity. The important thing is that they be consistent once the choice is made.

Dramatizaciones

A. ¡Un nuevo amigo! You have just met a new friend. You want to find out more about each other.

- Greet each other.
- Find out what each of you studies and which classes each of you likes and dislikes.
- Find out what you each do after school and on the weekends.
- Find out each other's favorite winter and summer activities and what you like to do when the weather is bad.
- Say good-bye.

B. Te presento a . . . Now that you have made a new friend, introduce him or her to your classmates. Be sure to mention your friend's . . .

- name.
- classes.
- favorite after-school and weekend activities.
- favorite winter and summer activities.
- favorite pastimes when it is raining or windy.

C. ¡Somos profesores! You and your partner are teachers, enjoying a free period in the teachers' lounge. Role-play the conversation you would have. You may talk about your students and what you must do after school, or about the weather, or about your usual weekend activities and what you are going to do this weekend.

130 *ciento treinta*

UNIDAD 3

Purpose This section has students recycle, in student-centered role plays, all previously learned structures and vocabulary needed to describe weekend activities.

Suggestions Do the role plays spontaneously, not from written scripts. Circulate among groups. Limit time allowed so that students do not get off task. Ask one or two pairs to recreate their exchange for the whole class.

¡No me digas!

¡Hay tanta gente! Tom y su amiga Rosa pasean por el Bosque de Chapultepec. Lee su conversación y luego contesta la pregunta a continuación.

Tom: **¡Es enorme este parque!**
Rosa: **Sí. Es uno de mis lugares favoritos.**
Tom: **Pero, ¿por qué hay tanta gente hoy? ¿Es día de fiesta? ¿Celebran algo especial hoy?**
Rosa: **No. Es que hoy es domingo.**
Tom: **Pero, Rosa, mira cuánta gente hay. Tiene que haber algo especial hoy.**

Why does Tom insist that something special must be going on?

1. Because it was Mexican independence day, and Tom knew it.
2. Because he did not realize that in Mexico, as in most Hispanic countries, parks are always very busy.
3. Because he thought Rosa was trying to fool him by not telling him what the special occasion was.

❑ Check your answer on page 417.

LECCIÓN 2

Purpose This section provides additional reading practice as students learn to avoid cross-cultural misunderstandings about the use of public parks in Hispanic countries.

Suggestions First have pairs read and answer questions. Then ask for show of hands to see how many selected each answer. Discuss possible answers as a class before checking responses on page 417.

Answers

1 There is no indication that Tom knew what day it was. In fact, he kept asking Rosa what the special occasion might be. Try another response.

2 It is not unusual to see whole families—including aunts, uncles, and grandparents—enjoying themselves in the parks on any Saturday or Sunday. The parks are generally well-kept and provide very inexpensive entertainment for the whole family. This is the correct answer.

3 There is no indication that Tom believed Rosa was trying to fool him. He was simply surprised to see so many people in the park.

Y ahora, ¡a leer!

Purpose This section is intended to expand students' reading ability without translation as they learn about Chapultepec Park in Mexico City.

Antes de empezar

This activity is an advance organizer for the reading that follows.

Suggestions Allow students to decide on answers individually or in pairs. They are expected to draw from previous knowledge of history and geography as well as to use common sense in answering these questions. If they are not sure of correct answers, tell them to make intelligent guesses. Then have them read passage and come back to their answers to see if they wish to change any of them.

Answers

1 falso
2 verdadero
3 verdadero
4 verdadero
5 falso
6 verdadero

Verifiquemos

Suggestions Question 1 should be answered in Spanish. Encourage students to avoid reading full sentences from the textbook to answer questions. You may want to model how to break information down into units that students are comfortable with.

Students may need to use English to describe any monuments in their hometown parks. Answers to both questions will vary.

IMPACTO CULTURAL

Y ahora, ¡a leer!

Antes de empezar

Before reading about El Bosque de Chapultepec, Mexico City's largest park, indicate whether the following statements are true (**verdadero**) or false (**falso**). If you do not know, use what you have previously learned about Hispanic culture to make a reasoned guess.

verdadero	falso	1. Central Park, in New York City, is the oldest park in the Western Hemisphere.
verdadero	falso	2. Museums have been built on the sites of old Aztec temples in Mexico City.
verdadero	falso	3. In 1848, the United States declared war on Mexico.
verdadero	falso	4. Several Mexican teenage military cadets died defending their school against the attack of United States forces.
verdadero	falso	5. Mexican families find parks in Mexico unsafe for children.
verdadero	falso	6. Chapultepec Park has a large lake, a castle, a museum, and a zoo.

Verifiquemos

Read "El Bosque de Chapultepec." Then answer the following questions.

1. Compara el Bosque de Chapultepec con un parque en tu comunidad. ¿Cuál es más grande? ¿Qué tienen en común? ¿Cuáles son las diferencias más importantes?

2. ¿Cómo es el monumento a los Niños Héroes? ¿Hay monumentos en los parques de tu comunidad? Si los hay, descríbelos.

Chapultepec es el parque natural más antiguo del hemisferio occidental. En el centro de Chapultepec hay un castillo histórico. Antiguamente, fue un templo azteca. Ahora es un museo.

Hay muchos monumentos en el Bosque de Chapultepec. El monumento dedicado a **los Niños Héroes** es muy emocionante. Los Niños Héroes son los jóvenes cadetes militares que defendieron el Castillo de Chapultepec en la Guerra de 1848 contra Estados Unidos.

Hoy Chapultepec es el parque favorito de los mexicanos. Allí es donde familias enteras pasan los fines de semana en plan de diversión. Se puede salir en lancha en el lago principal, ir al parque de diversiones, visitar el zoológico, el Castillo o el Museo de Antropología, o simplemente descansar.

Suggestions Have students work in groups of four or five. Assign one picture to each group. Tell each group to read the caption and prepare to describe the picture in their own words to rest of class. They should avoid using vocabulary students will not understand.

Encourage students to make reasoned guesses about the meaning of unfamiliar vocabulary. They should feel good about how much they do understand rather than frustrated by what they do not.

Students should be encouraged to develop stagies for dealing with unknown words in a reading selection. Research shows that even in their native language, good readers apply several strategies when dealing with unknown words encountered in a text. In one frequently used strategy, readers mentally "shelve" the word, reading to the end of the sentence or section. If they understand the sentence without the shelved word, they "throw it out."; if the word's meaning becomes clear from the context, they continue reading. In another strategy, readers also consider whether any words they already know might be related to the unknown word. If so, they reread to see if the new word makes sense once the context is understood. Students should be encouraged to develop similar strategies in Spanish.

Point out Chapultepec Park is situated in the largest wooded area in Mexico City, thus **el bosque** *(forest, woods).*

The Spanish viceroy, Matías de Gálvez, built a summer home at the current site of **El Castillo**, using the stones of an Aztec palace. This home later served as Mexico's military academy and as a palace for Maximilian and Carlota. Today it is a museum.

During the Mexican War of 1848, the invading Americans attacked the military academy, known as **El Castillo**. Several teenage cadets died defending the school in what was the final battle before the Americans captured Mexico City.

The **Museo de Antropología** is one of the great museums of the world—the *London Times* calls it the greatest. You may want to give extra credit for special reports on museum-related topics such as **el calendario azteca, Tenochtitlán, los aztecas,** or **Maximiliano y Carlota.**

¿Qué hacen por aquí?

OBJECTIVES

Communicative Goals

- Describing everyday activities
- Inquiring about everyday activities

Reading

- **_Leamos ahora_**
  Películas de la semana: TV guide
- Reading strategy: Scanning

Writing

- **_Escribamos un poco_**
  Answering a letter
- Writing strategy: Paragraph writing

Structure

- 3.6 Present tense: Plural forms
- 3.7 Indefinite and negative

ACTIVE VOCABULARY

Diversiones

concierto de rock	jardín zoológico
deporte	juego
discoteca	

Frecuencia

a veces	nunca
frecuentemente	raras veces
los fines de	siempre
semana	todos los días

Palabras negativas e indefinidas

algo	nada
alguien	nadie

Palabras y expresiones

en	a pie
especial	en coche
pasar	hacer la comida

ANTICIPEMOS

¿Qué piensas tú?

These questions are designed to get students to anticipate what they will learn in the lesson.

Answers

1 Singing, talking, laughing, playing instruments, smiling, eating, walking, watching, looking, etc.
2 Answers will vary.
3 Some activities may not be available to them—cafés, discos. They may not be allowed in similar places unaccompanied.
4 Allow students to express their own opinions about dating in the U.S.
5 They probably don't know much about Hispanic dating practices.

Point out In Hispanic countries, teenagers tend not to go out on dates until the age of 16 or 17. Before that, they will go out in groups of four to ten friends. Even at 16 and 17, young people tend to double-date rather than go out alone.

▶ 6 **They will be able to expand their ability to talk about what people do.**

¿Qué piensas tú?

1. Look at the photos on these two pages. How many different activities can you identify?

2. Which of these activities are things you and your friends sometimes do?

3. Are any of these activities things you and your friends probably wouldn't do? Why?

4. At what age do American teenagers begin to date? Where do they go on their dates?

5. What do you know about dating in Hispanic cultures? In Spanish-speaking countries, how old do you think kids have to be before they're allowed to date?

6. What do you think you will be able to talk about when you have finished this lesson?

ciento treinta y cinco **135**

Purpose To focus students on activities people do and to encourage students to develop and use critical thinking skills as they learn to compare dating customs in the U.S. with those in Hispanic countries without forming judgments.

Suggestion Ask students to use the Spanish they already know to describe in Spanish the people in the photos and some of the activities shown.

TAPE/DISC
14:46–17:50

Side 3, 26576 to 32104

Comprehension Checks

The **Comprehension Checks** are available on cards in the Teacher's Resource Package.

1 14:53

Suggestions List the days of the week. Point out **viernes, sábado,** and **domingo** as **el fin de semana.**

1 ¿Quién es?
2 ¿Es el fin de semana?
3 ¿Cuántos días hay en un fin de semana? ¿Cuáles son?

Side 3, 26787 to 27249

2 15:09

Suggestions Show that **tomar** = **comer** or **beber** by alternating **comer/tomar** and **beber/tomar** in identical contexts. Mime eating. Indicate *yourself alone* = **tomo** and *yourself and others* = **tomamos.**

1 ¿Qué día es?
2 ¿Son las cuatro? *(other times)*
3 ¿Qué hora es?
4 ¿Están las jóvenes en el colegio o en un café?
5 ¿Dónde están las jóvenes?
6 ¿Toman algo?
7 ¿Charlan mientras comen?
8 ¿Qué hacen en el café?
9 ¿Salen a caminar después de tomar algo?
10 ¿Miran a la gente?
11 ¿Es interesante mirar a la gente?

Side 3, 27267 to 28040

3 15:35

Suggestions Mime the activities. Emphasize that *oneself + others* = **-amos.**

1 ¿Son las cinco y media? *(other times)*
2 ¿Qué hora es?

3 ¿Van las jóvenes a casa o al teatro?
4 ¿Dónde están las jóvenes?
5 ¿Escuchan discos (casetes, discos compactos)?
6 ¿Ven televisión? *(other activities)*
7 ¿Hablan mucho?
8 ¿Qué hacen las jóvenes en casa?
9 ¿Qué haces tú en casa los viernes por la noche?

Side 3, 28058 to 28708

Hola. Soy Alicia Chávez.
¿Qué hacemos mis amigos y yo un fin de semana típico?
Pues, a ver . . .

viernes

Los sábados mis amigas y yo vamos de compras. Kati y Teresa siempre compran algo. Yo nunca compro nada.

Mis amigas y yo charlamos mientras tomamos algo en un café. Después salimos a caminar. Mirar a la gente es muy interesante, ¿no?

A las cinco y media vamos a casa. Escuchamos discos y casetes o vemos televisión. También hablamos mucho.

Purpose This section develops listening and reading comprehension of active vocabulary. Students should not be expected to achieve productive mastery at this point. The goal is not to translate but to read/listen for comprehension.

sábado 5

Por la tarde comemos — si es posible en un restaurante al aire libre. El muchacho que trabaja en el restaurante es muy guapo.

domingo 7

11:00

Los domingos siempre salimos de casa un poco antes de las once y vamos a la iglesia. Después paseamos y comemos juntos.

8 DISCOTECA

6:00

Por la tarde, mi amigo Martín me lleva a una discoteca. ¡Cuánta gente hay!
Me encanta esta música. El guitarrista toca y canta muy bien.

A veces hay una fiesta en casa de un amigo. Kati y Daniel bailan muy bien, ¿no?

Y ustedes, ¿qué hacen un fin de semana típico?

ciento treinta y siete **137**

17:51–21:00

Early Production Checks

A complete set of the **Early Production Checks** is available on cards in the Teacher's Resource Package.

1   **17:56**

Nadie canta como ellos.

1 ¿Quiénes son? *(Point to each.)*
   Alicia y Kati.
2 ¿Miran un casete o un disco compacto?
   Un disco compacto.
3 ¿Es un casete de Madonna? ¿de Prince? ¿de Menudo?
   No. / No. / Sí.
4 ¿Son guapos o feos los cantantes de Menudo?
   Guapos.
5 ¿Cantan en inglés también?   *Sí.*
6 Y el grupo americano, ¿es popular en EE.UU.?   *Sí.*
7 ¿Adónde necesitan ir Kati y Alicia?   *Al cine.*
8 ¿Quién va al cine también? *Daniel.*
9 ¿Dónde están, en un café o en el cine?   *En el cine.*
10 ¿Hay mucha o poca gente en el cine?   *Mucha.*
11 ¿Van a entrar todos?   *No.*
12 ¿Miran los jóvenes la película? *No.*
13 ¿Adónde van, a un restaurante o a una tienda?   *A un restaurante.*
14 ¿Dónde está el restaurante? *En la Zona Rosa.*
15 ¿Cómo es la pizza allí, mala o rica?   *Rica.*

¿QUÉ DECIMOS...?
Al hablar del fin de semana

1   *Nadie canta como ellos.*

138   ciento treinta y ocho   **UNIDAD 3**

Purpose   These dialogues show how to describe weekend activities in more natural contexts. Unfamiliar structures are intended solely for comprehension, not for mastery or production by students.

2 ¿Qué hacen por aquí?

3 Bailas muy bien.

LECCIÓN 3

ciento treinta y nueve **139**

2 `19:07`

¿Qué hacen por aquí?
Accept brief phrases or one- and two-word answers to all **Early Production Checks**, as in **1** on page 138. It is not necessary for students to answer in complete sentences.

1 ¿Quienes son? *(Point to David, Martín, and Daniel.)*
2 ¿Dónde están David y Martín, en una tienda o en un restaurante?
3 ¿Qué hacen David y Martín, comen o leen?
4 ¿Qué comen los chicos?
5 ¿Comen Daniel, Alicia y Kati con los muchachos?
6 ¿Qué comen las chicas y David?
7 ¿Adónde van David y Martín por la noche, a un restaurante o a una fiesta?
8 ¿Van Kati y Alicia a la fiesta también?

Side 3, 34400 to 35870

3 `19:57`

Bailas muy bien.
1 ¿Cómo baila Kati, bien o mal?
2 ¿Le gusta bailar a Kati?
3 Y a ti, ¿te gusta bailar? *(Ask several students.)*
4 ¿Dónde bailan más, en EE.UU. o en México?
5 ¿En EE.UU., van al cine?
6 ¿En EE.UU., miran mucha o poca televisión?
7 ¿Hablan por teléfono mucho o poco en EE.UU.?
8 ¿Con quién hablan por teléfono?
9 ¿Salen a pasear en EE.UU.?
10 ¿Los amigos de Kati salen a pie? ¿en coche?
11 ¿Sales tú en coche siempre? *(Ask several students.)*

Point out Because cars are very expensive in all Hispanic countries, teenagers do not usually have their own. Instead they walk or use public transportation.

Side 3, 35903 to 37821

***S*uggestions** Begin by having students close their books while you narrate one section at a time, using the transparencies to clarify meaning without translation. Then ask the **Early Production Checks**. Repeat this process with each section.

***U*sing the video** Play one section at a time after narrating it using the transparencies. Freeze the video and ask the **Early Production Checks**. Repeat this process with each section.

CHARLEMOS UN POCO

A. ¿Qué hacen? Allow students to look for the answers in the *¿Qué decimos ... ?* dialogue if they need to.

1	sí	7	no
2	no	8	sí
3	sí	9	no
4	no	10	no
5	no	11	sí
6	no	12	sí

Extension One student reads the questions and class responds.

B. ¡Es sábado!

1 Daniel y Kati bailan en una fiesta.
2 David y Alicia toman (beben) refrescos en una fiesta.
3 Alicia y Kati escuchan discos compactos.
4 Daniel y Kati comen (toman) helados.
5 Alicia y Kati corren.
6 Alicia y Martín hablan por teléfono.
7 Daniel, David y Martín van de compras.
8 Daniel y Alicia ven televisión.

Present tense: Plural forms

-ar	-er	-ir
mir**ar**	le**er**	sal**ir**
mir**amos**	le**emos**	sal**imos**
mir**an**	le**en**	sal**en**
mir**an**	le**en**	sal**en**

Le**emos** novelas románticas.
Ustedes siempre sal**en** en coche, ¿no?
Los buenos atletas corr**en** todos los días.

See **¿Por qué se dice así?,** *page G42, section 3.6.*

A. ¿Qué hacen?   Según el diálogo, ¿qué hacen Alicia y Kati durante el fin de semana?

1. ¿Bailan en una fiesta?
2. ¿Ven una película?
3. ¿Comen al aire libre?
4. ¿Van a una discoteca?
5. ¿Leen libros?
6. ¿Pasean por el parque?
7. ¿Practican deportes?
8. ¿Van a un restaurante?
9. ¿Preparan comida?
10. ¿Suben a las lanchas?
11. ¿Comen pizza?
12. ¿Van de compras?

B. ¡Es sábado!   ¿Qué hacen estos chicos los sábados?

MODELO   **David y Martín comen en un café al aire libre.**

David y Martín

1. Daniel y Kati

2. David y Alicia

3. Alicia y Kati

4. Daniel y Kati

UNIDAD 3

Purpose These activities provide guided practice to students beginning to learn how to describe things people do. The repetition built into the activities is intentional.

5. Alicia y Kati

6. Alicia y Martín

7. Daniel, David y Martín

8. Daniel y Alicia

C. Los jóvenes mexicanos. Generalmente, ¿qué hacen los jóvenes en la Ciudad de México los fines de semana?

MODELO   pasear por el parque
Pasean por el parque.

1. bailar
2. mirar a la gente en el parque
3. ir a fiestas
4. tomar refrescos en un café
5. practicar deportes
6. ir al cine
7. salir con amigos
8. ir de compras
9. comer en un restaurante
10. subir a los juegos

LECCIÓN 3

C. Los jóvenes mexicanos.
Do this activity as a class. Personalize it by asking individuals **¿Vas tú de compras los fines de semana? ¿Bailas en una discoteca?** etc.
1 Bailan.
2 Miran a la gente en el parque.
3 Van a fiestas.
4 Toman refrescos en un café.
5 Practican deportes.
6 Van al cine.
7 Salen con amigos.
8 Van de compras.
9 Comen en un restaurante.
10 Suben a los juegos.

Allow 2–3 min. Call on individuals to tell what they are doing in each drawing.

1 ¿Van de compras?
Sí, vamos de compras.

2 ¿Escuchan discos compactos?
Sí, escuchamos discos compactos.

3 ¿Bailan?
Sí, bailamos.

4 ¿Hablan por teléfono?
Sí, hablamos por teléfono.

5 ¿Corren?
Sí, corremos.

6 ¿Compran discos?
Sí, compramos discos.

7 ¿Toman refrescos?
Sí, tomamos refrescos.

8 ¿Alquilan videos?
Sí, alquilamos videos.

CH. ¿Y en Estados Unidos? ¿Cómo pasan ustedes los fines de semana en Estados Unidos? Contesta las preguntas de tu nuevo(a) amigo(a) mexicano(a).

 MODELO Compañero(a): **¿Ven la tele?**
Tú: **Sí, vemos la tele.**

1.  **2.**

3.  **4.**

5.  **6.**

7.  **8.**

D. ¿Qué hacen ustedes? ¿Qué hacen ustedes en estos lugares?

MODELO en la biblioteca
En la biblioteca estudiamos, leemos y escribimos.

1. en un centro comercial
2. en el parque
3. en un café
4. en una fiesta
5. en la clase de español
6. en un concierto de rock
7. en la escuela
8. en casa

E. ¿Y ustedes? ¿Qué hacen los profesores los fines de semana? Preparen preguntas para su profesor(a).

MODELO escuchar música
¿Escuchan música ustedes?

1. escribir cartas
2. comer en un restaurante
3. ir de compras
4. practicar deportes
5. salir con amigos
6. ver un video
7. comer pizza
8. pasear en bicicleta
9. correr
10. ¿ . . . ?

F. A veces. ¿Con qué frecuencia hacen tú y tus amigos estas actividades?

EJEMPLO caminar en el parque
Nunca caminamos en el parque.

nunca	raras veces	a veces	frecuentemente	siempre
•	•	•	•	•

1. visitar un jardín zoológico
2. ir a museos
3. comer pizza
4. practicar karate
5. calificar exámenes
6. leer el periódico
7. trabajar
8. subir a las lanchas
9. escribir cartas
10. estudiar español

JARDÍN ZOOLÓGICO

Call on individuals. Encourage students to come up with as many activities as possible for each site. Answers will vary. Check for appropriateness.

Extension Divide class into groups of four and allow students exactly 2 min to write as many activities as they can for **en un centro comercial**. Call on one group to read answers. Have other groups add to list. Repeat for each item.

E. ¿Y ustedes? Allow 2–3 min to prepare questions. Then have individuals ask you what teachers do. Encourage students to expand the activity by coming up with original questions.

1 ¿Escriben cartas ustedes?
2 ¿Comen ustedes en un restaurante?
3 ¿Van de compras ustedes?
4 ¿Practican deportes ustedes?
5 ¿Salen ustedes con amigos?
6 ¿Ven ustedes un video?
7 ¿Comen ustedes pizza?
8 ¿Pasean ustedes en bicicleta?
9 ¿Corren ustedes?

Expressions of frequency

The following words express varying degrees of frequency from *never* to *always*.

nunca
raras veces
a veces
todos los días
frecuentemente
siempre

Ellos **nunca** escriben cartas.
Nosotras **a veces** hablamos en español.
Yo **siempre** estudio en casa.

See **¿Por qué se dice así?,** *page G44, section 3.7.*

G. ¿Quién?

1 ¿Alguien escucha música?
No, nadie escucha música.
2 ¿Alguien habla por teléfono?
Sí, Beto habla por teléfono.
3 ¿Alguien lee un libro?
No, nadie lee un libro.
4 ¿Alguien ve la tele?
No, nadie ve la tele.
5 ¿Alguien escribe cartas?
Sí, Marta escribe cartas.
6 ¿Alguien pasea en bicicleta?
Sí, Carlota y Eva pasean en bicicleta.
7 ¿Alguien corre en el parque?
Sí, Susana y Pepe corren en el parque.
8 ¿Alguien toma un helado?
No, nadie toma un helado.
9 ¿Alguien alquila un video?
Sí, Manuel alquila un video.
10 ¿Alguien come pizza?
Sí, David y Marcos comen pizza.

H. ¿Qué pregunta?

1 ¿Vas a comprar algo?
2 ¿Alguien va al centro hoy?
3 ¿Vas a preparar algo especial para comer?
4 ¿Alguien va a alquilar un video?
5 ¿Alguien va a limpiar la casa?
6 ¿Vas a beber algo?
7 ¿Vas a escuchar algo?
8 ¿Alguien va a escribir cartas?

Negative and indefinite words

Indefinite	Negative
algo	**nada**
alguien	**nadie**

¿**Alguien** aquí habla francés?
No, **nadie** habla francés.
¿Hay **algo** bueno en la tele?
No, no hay **nada** bueno esta noche.

See **¿Por qué se dice así?**, *page G44, section 3.7.*

G. ¿Quién?   Ask your partner if anyone is doing the following activities.

Carlota y Eva   **Manuel**   **David y Marcos**

Marta   **Beto**   **Susana y Pepe**

 MODELO   comer pizza
Tú: **¿Alguien come pizza?**
Compañero(a):   **Sí, David y Marcos comen pizza.**

tomar un refresco
Compañero(a):   **¿Alguien toma un refresco?**
Tú: **No, nadie toma un refresco.**

1. escuchar música
2. hablar por teléfono
3. leer un libro
4. ver la tele
5. escribir cartas
6. pasear en bicicleta
7. correr en el parque
8. tomar un helado
9. alquilar un video
10. comer pizza

H. ¿Qué pregunta?   You overhear your mother's telephone conversation. What did her neighbor ask her?

MODELO   ¿ . . . ?   No, nadie va a ver televisión.
¿Alguien va a ver televisión?

¿ . . . ?   No, no voy a leer nada.
¿Vas a leer algo?

1. ¿ . . . ?   No, no voy a comprar nada.
2. ¿ . . . ?   No, nadie va al centro hoy.
3. ¿ . . . ?   No, no voy a preparar nada especial para comer.
4. ¿ . . . ?   No, nadie va a alquilar un video.
5. ¿ . . . ?   No, nadie va a limpiar la casa.
6. ¿ . . . ?   No, no voy a beber nada.
7. ¿ . . . ?   No, no voy a escuchar nada.
8. ¿ . . . ?   No, nadie va a escribir cartas.

CHARLEMOS UN POCO MÁS

A. ¿Cuándo?   Find out when your partner usually does the following activities. Then, in groups of four, tally the group's responses and report the results to the class.

 EJEMPLO   **¿Cuándo escribes cartas?**
Nunca escribo cartas.

todos los días	los fines de semana	nunca
por la mañana/noche	a veces	¿ . . . ?

subir a las lanchas   ir a un parque de diversiones
hacer la comida   ver la tele
trabajar en un café   bailar
salir con amigos   alquilar un video
hablar por teléfono   leer el periódico
escribir cartas   limpiar la casa
pasear en bicicleta   estudiar
correr   esperar el autobús

B. Tú y tu familia.   Your teacher will give you a bingo grid with a different activity indicated in each square. Ask your classmates if they do a specific activity with their family on the weekend. If they say they do, have them sign the appropriate square to verify it. Let your instructor know when you have completed a vertical, horizontal, or diagonal line on your card.

 MODELO   Tú: **¿Corren en el parque?**
Compañero(a):   **Sí, corremos en el parque.**

C. ¿Sólo $60?   A three-day weekend is coming up, and you and a couple of friends will be spending it together. You each have $20 to spend. In groups of three, prepare a list indicating what you will do on Saturday, Sunday, and Monday and report to the class. You may not spend more than $60 in all. The following are visual suggestions of activities you may consider.

CHARLEMOS UN POCO MÁS

A. ¿Cuándo? Write days of the week on board and identify **todos los días** by saying "**lunes sí, martes sí, miércoles sí**" etc. Identify **nunca** by listing all the days and saying **no** for each one. Identify **el fin de semana** by pointing to specific days. Identify **a veces** by contrasting with **todos los días, nunca**, and specific days. Write 6:00 A.M., 12:00 noon, and 6:00 P.M. on board. Review **por la mañana** (etc.) by pointing to appropriate ranges of time. Allow 5–6 min for students to do activity. Then call on individuals to tell who does which activity at a specific time.

Note The plural forms of **salir** have been presented. Give students the singular form **salgo** for this activity.

B. Tú y tu familia. Allow students to move around class talking to each other in Spanish. Limit the number of squares one person may sign. When one student has bingo, verify by asking individuals who signed card if they do what is indicated. Allow activity to continue to see who can get two bingos on same card, then three, etc.

C. ¿Sólo $60? Allow 4–5 min. Tell students they must indicate cost of each activity. Insist they speak Spanish. Afterwards have each group tell what they will do. Ask class if estimated costs are realistic.

Purpose These activities are designed to allow students to create with language recently learned in the context of open-ended and personalized situations. Although they may sometimes appear repetitious of the guided practice in the previous section, these activities enable students to use the structures and vocabulary necessary to describe things people do in a variety of possible combinations.

CH. Siempre. Nunca. A veces. Your class is taking a survey to find out how teenagers spend the weekend. Your assignment is to survey at least five classmates. Record their answers as **Siempre, Nunca,** or **A veces** on the grid your teacher provides. Then, in groups of four or five, tally the responses. You may begin by asking: **¿Escuchas la radio los fines de semana?**

D. ¡Identifícalos! Write a list of as many different actions as you can identify in this drawing. Then, in groups of three or four, compare your lists and come up with a group list.

EJEMPLO **Un chico corre en el parque.
Dos señoras van de compras.**

Dramatizaciones

A. El viernes por la noche. You can't decide what to do Friday evening. Your parents make some suggestions. With a partner, role-play this situation.

Teenager

- Say you are not going to do anything tonight.

- Say nobody ever does that.

- Say you sometimes like to do the first activity mentioned but not all the time. Then say you are going to do something else.

- Say where you are going to do the activity and with whom. Ask what your parent is going to do.

Parent

- Suggest something for your teenager to do.

- Suggest another couple of activities.

- Ask where your teenager is going to do the activity.

- Say what you are doing this evening.

B. ¡De compras! You are out shopping with two friends. You enter a music store. Role-play the following conversation.

- Talk about your favorite rock stars.
- Tell what they look like and why you like them.
- Decide what tapes or CDs to buy.
- Decide what to do after you leave the music store.

C. Y ahora, ¿qué? You and two friends are at your favorite hangout having a soft drink. Role-play a conversation that includes comments about the following topics.

- Your favorite teachers
- Your favorite classes
- A new student at school
- Where you are going and what you plan to do after you finish your drinks

Purpose In this section, students recycle all previously learned structures and vocabulary needed to describe what people do. The format is student-centered role plays. Encourage students to work without their textbooks when preparing and performing their role plays.

DRAMATIZACIONES

A, B, C. Assign **A, B,** and **C** at the same time to different groups. Allow students 5–6 min to prepare role plays and then have each group present theirs to class. Ask each group to prepare three or four comprehension check questions to ask class about their own role play.

A. Anticipemos.
Suggestions Have students work in pairs and allow 2 min to answer these questions. Call on several pairs to share their answers with class. Ask if others agree. Tell students to come back to predictions after they have read selection.

Answers

1 Movie titles, day and date, channels, times, actors' and directors' names

2 A television listing

Películas de la semana
Suggestions Review "Scanning" from Unit 2, page 98. Tell students to read the first question, then to scan the selection for answer. Repeat this procedure for each question. You may wish to point out that in order to understand this reading, students will need to draw on their background knowledge about movies, actors, etc.

Questions 2 and 3 require knowledge of the 24-hour clock, presented in Unit 2. See if students recall the concept. If not, explain before asking students to scan for these answers.

Verifiquemos

Answers

1 **Oda a la juventud** is Chinese. The others are American. Names of directors and actors indicate nationality.

2 At night

3 No. Both begin after 10:00.

4 **La misteriosa dama de negro** is a comedy.

5 The oldest is **El misterioso Mr. Wong y Asesinato por televisión** (1935). The most recent is **Oda a la juventud** (1985).

6 No. The channel is indicated as either TVE-1 or TVE-2.

7 **Oda a la juventud** and **Pero … ¿quién mató a Harry?** are in color.

8 Answers will vary. Students may recognize Jack Lemmon, Fred Astaire, Shirley MacLaine, and other American actors.

L E A M O S   A H O R A

Reading strategy: Scanning

A. Anticipemos. Before reading this selection, glance at the format and answer the following questions.

   1. What type of information do you expect to find in this reading?
   2. Where would you look for this type of information?

B. Buscando información. In **Unidad 2,** you learned to scan—that is, to read quickly in order to locate specific information. We usually scan when we know exactly what information is needed and where to look to find it.

C. Películas. First read the questions, then scan the selection to find the specific information.

Películas de la semana

LUNES 5

La misteriosa dama de negro
TVE-2. 22.35h.   Cine-club.
★★★ *Comedia (1962). B/N. 119 min.*
Dir.: Richard Quine. Int.: Jack Lemmon, Kim Novak (foto), Fred Astaire, Lionel Jeffries.
Mezcla de comedia y misterio en un argumento que sirvió para que Kim Novak fuera reconocida en el cine. Buena réplica la de Lemmon intentando averiguar si ella es la asesina de su esposo.

Oda a la juventud
TVE-1. 01.00h.   **Cine-club madrugada.**
★★ *Drama (1985). Color. 92 min.*
Dir.: Zhang Nuanxin. Int.: Li Fengxu (foto), Feng Yuanzhenog, Guo Jianguo.
La revolución cultural en China cambia el modo de vida de los jóvenes. Una chica es obligada a trasladarse a una granja en el campo y cuando acepta el cambio, tiene que volver a la Universidad.

MARTES 6

Pero… ¿quién mató a Harry?
TVE-1. 22.30 h.   *Sesión de noche.*
★★★ *Intriga (1955). Color. 97 min.*
Dir.: Alfred Hitchcock. Int.: Shirley McLaine (foto), John Forsythe, Mildred Natwick.
Gran derroche del particular humor de Hitchcock en esta película, con muerto incluido, alrededor del cual gira el argumento. Los vecinos de la comunidad se interrogan acerca del porqué de este asesinato.

El misterioso Mr. Wong y Asesinato por televisión
TVE-1. 01.00h.   **Filmoteca del martes.**
★★ *Intriga (1935). B/N. Subt. 59 y 57min.*
Dirs.: W. Nigh/C. Staniford. Int.: Bela Lugosi, Boris Karloff (foto), Arlene Judge.
La leyenda de Confucio que entregó unas monedas mágicas a sus amigos.
Durante los primeros experimentos con la TV, un hombre muere misteriosamente.

Verifiquemos

1. Tell where you think each movie was filmed. What makes you think that?
2. Are these movies being shown at night or during the day?
3. If on Monday you were allowed to watch TV in the evening only until 10:00, could you see one of these movies? Why or why not?
4. Are any of these movies comedies? If so, which ones?

5. What is the oldest movie being shown on these two days? The most recent one?
6. Are all of these movies being shown on the same channel? How do you know?
7. Are any of these movies being shown in color? If so, which ones?
8. Do you recognize any of the actors? If so, who are they?

Purpose This is the principal reading of the unit. Its purpose is to allow students to practice scanning a passage to locate specific information before reading for detailed answers to questions. Students are not expected to understand every word or to translate the passage. Rather they should focus on looking for the specific pieces of information requested. This strategy should be applied when reading to locate specific information.

ESCRIBAMOS UN POCO

Writing strategy:
Paragraph writing

A. Pensando.   In the last letter you received from Mexico, your pen pal asked how you spend your weekends. Prepare to answer your pen pal's letter by addressing the following questions.

1. **¿Para quién escribo?**
2. **¿Por qué escribo?**
3. **¿De qué escribo?**

B. Empezando.   In place of a cluster, make a list of things you do every weekend, depending on the weather. Indicate the approximate time of day when you do these things.

C. Escribiendo.   Decide which information in your list you will use and write a first draft of a one- or two-paragraph letter explaining how you spend your weekends. Remember to always begin a paragraph by making a general comment about what you will be writing. For example, in writing about your weekends, you might say something like:

> **Mis fines de semana son muy aburridos.** o
> **Me encantan los fines de semana.** o
> **Hay mucho que hacer en [**_your town_**] durante los fines de semana.**

CH. Compartiendo.   Share a first draft of your letter with a couple of classmates. Ask them what they think of it. Is there anything they don't understand? Is there anything they feel should be changed? Is there anything you haven't said that they feel you should mention?

D. Revisando.   Write a final draft of your letter, incorporating any of your classmates' suggestions that you accepted. You may add, subtract, or reorder anything you had written in the first draft.

LECCIÓN 3   _ciento cuarenta y nueve_ **149**

A. Pensando. Allow 3–4 min for students to decide whom to write to and to answer the three questions.
1 They are writing for a Hispanic pen pal of about their own age.
2 They are writing in response to a question from the pen pal.
3 They are writing about their weekend activities.
Ask individuals to share answers to questions with class. Make sure students realize they will not be writing just a schedule of their activities but will need to describe their favorite pastimes.

B. Empezando.
Suggestions Explain that students should simply list the times in one column and what they do in the other: **9:00—correr**, etc.

C. Escribiendo.
Suggestions Allow students time to write first draft. Read what they are writing and provide guidance where necessary. You may want to assign the draft as homework.

CH. Compartiendo.
Suggestions Have students gather in "response groups" of two or three. Allow them time to share letters. Remind group members to begin commentary with at least one positive comment and then to make constructive suggestions on content, structure, and vocabulary.

D. Revisando.
Suggestions Tell students you will grade the letter holistically—that is, on the overall effectiveness of the communication. Underline grammatical errors if you wish, but the grade should be affected only by errors that would confuse a native speaker accustomed to dealing with foreigners. Later lessons will suggest strategies for improving accuracy.

Purpose In this section, students are asked to apply speaking and writing skills developed in the unit to a real-life writing task. They will use strategies they began to develop in Unit 1—prewriting, brainstorming, and clustering; writing a first draft; peer feedback; and revision.

Suggestions You may wish to exchange letters with another class in your school or another school or to provide students with the opportunity to exchange letters with a real pen pal in a Hispanic country.

¡Qué familia!

UNIT OBJECTIVES

Communicative Goals

When students have completed this unit, they will be able to use Spanish . . .

- to identify family members and relatives by remarriage
- to describe their family, how people feel, and what is happening at the moment
- to ask for information about families, birthdays and age, professional goals, and people they know or want to meet
- to ask questions

Culture

In this unit, students will study and compare . . .

- first and last names and nicknames
- use of the phone directory
- Hispanics in the United States

Reading and Writing Strategies

- Reading: Identifying the main idea
- Writing: Organizing information

Structure

- Possessive adjectives
- Numbers: 30–100
- The months of the year
- **Tener años**
- The verbs **conocer, querer,** and **venir**
- **Estar** with adjectives
- Personal **a**
- Questions and question words: A summary
- The present progressive and **-ndo** verb forms

UNIT SETTING

San Antonio, Texas, is the ninth-largest city in the United States. Although founded in 1691, permanent settlement did not begin until 1718 with the establishment of the Mission of San Antonio de Valero, later called the Alamo, site of an 1836 battle between the Mexicans and Texans.

Spanish and Mexican cultures have played a major role throughout the approximately 300-year history of this city. Today over 53 percent of San Antonio's population is Spanish-speaking and/or has a Hispanic surname. Probably the most popular tourist destination in Texas,

Photo

The San Antonio River is a gentle, jade-green waterway that winds its way through the city of San Antonio, linking museums, parks, and skyscrapers. The River Walk, or **Paseo del Río**, is the downtown section of the San Antonio River. During the day when shops and galleries are open, tourists and San Antonians come to stroll and to eat or enjoy a cool drink in one of the many sidewalk cafés. At night, the **Paseo del Río** is lighted, and music from the many night spots along the waterway can be heard by strollers and river taxi riders.

Video Notes

To play the montage:

Side 4, 9 to 1350

To play the unit without stopping:

Side 4, 9 to 32110

The Spanish spoken in San Antonio is representative of the Spanish spoken throughout the American Southwest. The **e** tends to have the more open sound of the *e* in *pet*. At times, the **i** drifts in the direction of the **e,** making **visita** sound like **vesita,** and **hoy** and **soy** sound like **hóe** and **sóe.** The **y** and the **ll** are pronounced more like the *i* in the words **yo** and **ella,** which sound more like **ió** and **éia.** Some San Antonians also consistently use [v] where other Spanish speakers would use [b̸], **la boda** being pronounced as *la voda.*

San Antonio welcomes an estimated 10 million visitors a year who enjoy such sites as the Alamo, the River Walk, the cobblestone paths of **La Villita,** the Mexican market in Market Square, the Spanish Governor's Palace (dating back to 1749), the Navarro House (home of an early San Antonio mayor), and much more. Many influential Hispanics currently hold political office and determine the policy and laws of the city and nearby communities.

OBJECTIVES

Communicative Goals

- Identifying family members
- Describing your family
- Asking about families
- Asking about birthdays and age

Culture and Reading

- *¡No me digas!*
  ¡Toda la familia!
  The nuclear family
- *Y ahora, ¡a leer!*
  ¿Cómo te llamas?
  Hispanic names

Structure

- **4.1** Possessive adjectives
- **4.2** Numbers: 30–100
- **4.3** The months of the year

¿Cuántos años cumples?

ACTIVE VOCABULARY

La familia

familia	hijos
abuela	hermana
abuelo	hermano
abuelos	hermanos
maternos	tía
paternos	tío
madre	tíos
mamá	prima
padre	primo
papá	primos
padres	sobrina
esposa	sobrino
esposo	sobrinos
esposos	nieta
hija	nieto
hijo	nietos

Nombres

apellido	sobrenombre
nombre	

Los meses

mes	julio
enero	agosto
febrero	septiembre
marzo	octubre
abril	noviembre
mayo	diciembre
junio	

Posesión

mi(s)
tu(s)
su(s)
nuestro(s),
  nuestra(s)

Cumpleaños

año	edad
celebrar	fecha
¿cuántos?	piñata
cumpleaños	romper
cumplir __ años	tener __ años

Palabras y expresiones

novia	¡Felicidades!
pequeño(a)	¡Por supuesto!
	¿Qué fecha es
¡Bravo!	hoy?
¿Cuál es la fecha	¡Qué raro!
de hoy?	

Números

30–100

ANTICIPEMOS

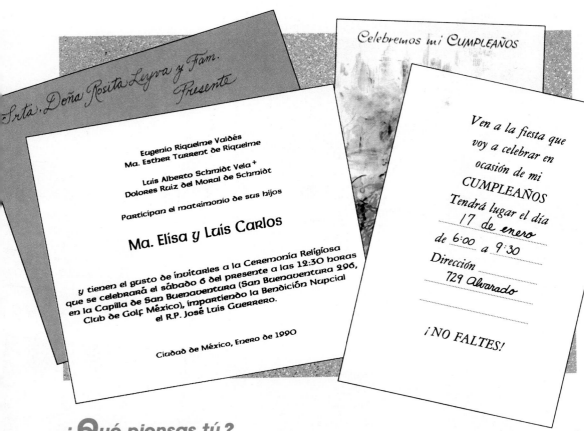

Srta. Doña Rosita Leyva y Fam.
Presente

Eugenio Riquelme Valdés
Ma. Esther Turrent de Riquelme

Luis Alberto Schmidt Vela +
Dolores Ruiz del Moral de Schmidt

Participan el matrimonio de sus hijos

Ma. Elisa y Luis Carlos

y tienen el gusto de invitarles a la Ceremonia Religiosa
que se celebrará el sábado 6 del presente a las 12:30 horas
en la Capilla de San Buenaventura (San Buenaventura 296,
Club de Golf México), impartiendo la Bendición Nupcial
el R.P. José Luis Guerrero.

Ciudad de México, Enero de 1990

Celebremos mi CUMPLEAÑOS

Ven a la fiesta que
voy a celebrar en
ocasión de mi
CUMPLEAÑOS
Tendrá lugar el día
17 de enero
de 6:00 a 9:30
Dirección
729 Alvarado

¡NO FALTES!

¿Qué piensas tú?

1. What do you think the people on the left are celebrating? Why do you think so?

2. Who do you think the people are? Are they related to each other? What makes you think so? How do you think they are related?

3. What events do the above invitations refer to? How do you know?

4. What information is included on both invitations? What information appears on only one of the invitations?

5. How do you celebrate birthdays? How did you celebrate when you were younger? Who do you invite to your birthday celebrations?

6. Who do people normally invite to weddings?

7. Would you expect the celebration of birthdays and weddings in Hispanic communities to be similar to or different from such celebrations here? How? Why?

8. What do you think you will be able to talk about when you have finished this lesson?

¿Qué piensas tú?

Point out **Presente** (or **Pte.**) on the envelope of an invitation means that it was hand delivered, a common formality in Hispanic countries. For more formal occasions, **E.S.M.** (for **En sus manos**) is used to mark a hand-delivered invitation.

Answers

1 The occasion might be a birthday, baptism, confirmation, holiday, or the like. Students may reason that it is a birthday or a wedding because of invitations. They should look at the people present, how they are dressed, etc.

2 The guests include family and friends. Have students speculate on relationships.

3 Wedding; birthday party. Format, information included should provide clues.

4 Both invitations include date, time, location. Only wedding invitation includes names of parents and officiating priest.

5 Students will indicate a variety of customs, depending on their own cultural differences and ages. They will probably mention inclusion of family and friends. Encourage them to be specific about family members included.

6 Answers will vary. Students may indicate that members of the extended family are more often included in weddings than in birthdays, and that the guest list includes friends and business associates of the parents.

7 Students will expect differences but will probably not be sure of what kinds. Hispanic students in class might mention the presence of the extended family, lots of food, dancing, **piñatas**, etc.

8 **They will be able to talk about celebrations, dates, ages, family members. If some of these things are not obvious, help students identify them by focusing on the information in questions 1–4.**

Purpose To focus students on language related to celebrations, dates, ages, and family members, and to use critical thinking skills by encouraging students to observe differences and similarities between Hispanic birthday and wedding celebrations and their own without forming judgments.

Suggestions Use the illustrations as an advance organizer. Have students explain their answers. Help them discover cross-cultural similarities in birthdays and weddings.

21:52–
23:58

Side 4, 1373 to 5183

Comprehension Checks

The **Comprehension Checks** are available on cards in the TRP.

1   21:59

1 ¿Es Ana? ¿Quién es?
2 ¿Es la familia de Ana?
3 ¿Es el padre de Ana? ¿Son sus hermanos? ¿sus abuelos?

Side 4, 1615 to 1850

2   22:08

1 ¿Quién es? *(Point to each.)*
2 ¿Cómo se llama el padre de Ana?
3 ¿Tiene 44 años? *(other ages)*
4 ¿Es el hermano (la hermana) de Ana? ¿Cómo se llama?
5 ¿Tienes hermanos (hermanas)? ¿Cómo se llama(n)?
6 ¿Tiene Paquito 9 años? *(other ages)*
7 ¿Tiene Lupe 13 años? *(other ages)*
8 ¿Tiene Ana 16 años? *(other ages)*

Side 4, 1871 to 2340

3   22:25

1 ¿Es el abuelo de Ana? ¿la abuela? ¿Quién es?
2 ¿Cómo se llama el abuelo? ¿la abuela?
3 ¿Tiene 78 años el abuelo?
4 ¿Cuántos años tiene el abuelo?
5 ¿Es Patricio el padre del padre de Ana?
6 ¿Son los abuelos paternos o los abuelos maternos de Ana?

Side 4, 2360 to 2739

4   22:38

1 ¿Es el tío de Ana (Paquito, Lupe)? ¿Quién es? ¿Cómo se llama?
2 ¿Es el hermano del papá de Ana?
3 ¿Es la tía? ¿Cómo se llama?
4 ¿Quién es el niño? ¿la niña?
5 ¿Tiene Pepe seis años? ¿Tiene Sarita ocho años?

¡Hola, amigos! Soy Ana. Y quiero presentarles a mi familia—Papá, mis hermanos y mis abuelos.

Mi padre se llama Rafael. Tiene cuarenta y cuatro años. Mi hermano Paquito tiene nueve años y mi hermana Lupe tiene trece años. ¿Y yo? Pues, tengo dieciséis.

Éste es mi abuelo Patricio. Tie... sesenta y ocho años. Mi abue... se llama Margarita. Son los padres de mi papá. Son mis abuelos paternos.

Mi tío Roberto es el hermano de mi papá. Su esposa, mi tía Elena, es muy bonita, ¿verdad? Pepe y Sarita son mis primos. Pepe tiene seis años y Sarita tiene ocho. Ay, ¡qué niños!

¿Ella? No, no es mi madre. Es Betty, la novia de mi padre. El hijo de Betty se llama Kevin. Tiene diecisiete años.

6 ¿Cuántos años tiene Pepe? ¿Sarita?
7 ¿Es Pepe (Sarita) el primo (la prima) de Ana? ¿hermano(a)? *(other relationships)*
8 ¿Quién es la prima (el primo) de Pepe? ¿de Sarita?
9 ¿Son Pepe y Sarita pequeños?
10 ¿Tienes primos (primas, tíos, tías)? ¿Cómo se llaman?

Side 4, 2757 to 3290

Purpose This section is not meant for memorization or mastery; it sets the context for the language needed to talk about celebrations, dates, ages, and family members and provides comprehensible language without translation.

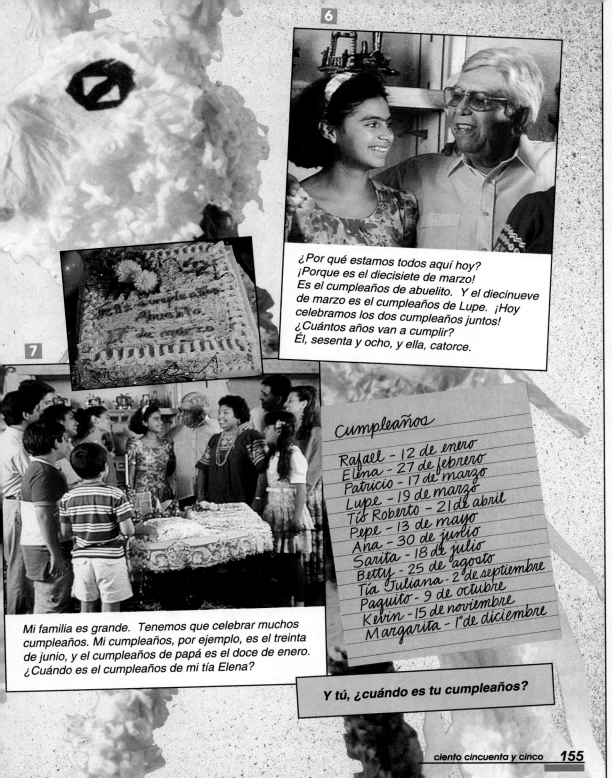

6

¿Por qué estamos todos aquí hoy?
¡Porque es el diecisiete de marzo!
Es el cumpleaños de abuelito. Y el diecinueve
de marzo es el cumpleaños de Lupe. ¡Hoy
celebramos los dos cumpleaños juntos!
¿Cuántos años van a cumplir?
Él, sesenta y ocho, y ella, catorce.

7

Cumpleaños

Rafael – 12 de enero
Elena – 27 de febrero
Patricio – 17 de marzo
Lupe – 19 de marzo
Tío Roberto – 21 de abril
Pepe – 13 de mayo
Ana – 30 de junio
Sarita – 18 de julio
Betty – 25 de agosto
Tía Juliana – 2 de septiembre
Paquito – 9 de octubre
Kevin – 15 de noviembre
Margarita – 1° de diciembre

Mi familia es grande. Tenemos que celebrar muchos
cumpleaños. Mi cumpleaños, por ejemplo, es el treinta
de junio, y el cumpleaños de papá es el doce de enero.
¿Cuándo es el cumpleaños de mi tía Elena?

Y tú, ¿cuándo es tu cumpleaños?

ciento cincuenta y cinco **155**

5 `22:56`

Suggestions Draw a stick figure of Betty with a large engagement ring on her left hand to show **novia**. Point out that **novia** here means "engaged." Point out that Betty is a non-Hispanic Spanish teacher. Ask students to give reasons why her son Kevin, who was also born in the U.S., speaks Spanish so well.

1 ¿Es la madre de Ana?
2 ¿Cómo se llama?
3 ¿Es la novia de Rafael?
4 ¿Cómo se llama el chico?
5 ¿Es el hijo de Betty?
6 ¿Es Ana la hija de Betty? *(other names)*
7 ¿Tiene Kevin diecisiete años? *(other ages)*

Note Vocabulary of family relations by remarriage will be presented in Lesson 2.

Side 4, 3309 to 3746

6 `23:11`

Suggestion Review names of days. **Point out "Las mañanitas"** is the traditional birthday song. Although there are Spanish lyrics to "Happy Birthday," it is not traditionally sung.

1 ¿Qué día es?
2 ¿Es el diecisiete de marzo? *(other dates)*
3 ¿Es el cumpleaños de Patricio? *(other family members)*
4 ¿Es el diecinueve de marzo el cumpleaños de Lupe? *(other dates)*
5 ¿Quién tiene cumpleaños el diecinueve de marzo? ¿el diecisiete?
6 ¿Tiene Lupe trece años ahora?
7 ¿Va a cumplir catorce el diecinueve de marzo?
8 ¿Cuántos años va a cumplir Lupe el diecinueve de marzo?

Side 4, 3764 to 4520

7 `23:37`

Suggestion Identify months and dates.

1 ¿Es grande la familia de Ana?
2 ¿Tienen muchas fechas que celebrar?
3 ¿Es el cumpleaños de Ana el 30 de junio? *(other dates)*
4 ¿Es el cumpleaños de Elena el 27 de febrero? *(other dates)*

Suggestions Begin by having students close their books while you narrate one section at a time, using the transparencies to clarify meaning without translation. Then ask the **Comprehension Checks**. Repeat this process with each section.

Using the video Play one section at a time after narrating it using the transparencies. Freeze the video and ask the **Comprehension Checks**. Repeat this process with each section.

5 ¿Cuándo es el cumpleaños de . . . ? *(Ask about all listed birthdays.)*
6 ¿Es grande tu familia?
7 ¿Tienes que celebrar muchas fechas?

Side 4, 4542 to 5183

TAPE/
DISC

23:59–
28:16

Side 4, 5193 to 12904

Early Production Checks

A complete set of the **Early Production Checks** is available on cards in the Teacher's Resource Package.

1   24:07

¡Feliz cumpleaños!

Suggestion Use a family tree to clarify meaning of **hijos** and **nietos**. **Point out** **Tía Juliana** is really Ana's **tía abuela** (great-aunt), but everyone refers to her as **tía Juliana**.

1. ¿Qué día es hoy, el dieciséis o el diecisiete de marzo? *Es el diecisiete de marzo.*
2. ¿Qué mes es? *Marzo.*
3. ¿Qué celebran hoy, el cumpleaños del abuelo o del tío? *Del abuelo.*
4. ¿Cuántos años cumple el abuelo, sesenta y ocho o setenta y ocho? *Sesenta y ocho.*
5. En la opinión del abuelo, ¿es joven o viejo? *Joven.*
6. ¿Es fuerte? *Sí.*
7. ¿Quién es Juliana, la hermana o la tía del abuelo? *La hermana.*
8. ¿Quién quiere conocer a Juliana, los nietos o los sobrinos de Patricio y Margarita? *Los nietos.*

Side 4, 5420 to 6992

2   25:00

¿Cuántos años tienes?

Accept brief phrases or one- and two-word answers to all **Early Production Checks**, as above. It is not necessary for students to answer in complete sentences.

Suggestions Use a family tree to clarify meaning of **sobrinos**. Act out action of **romper la piñata**. Also help with meaning of **gigantes**.

1. ¿Quién es? *(Point to Elena, then Roberto, Rafael.)*
2. ¿Es Elena la esposa de Roberto o de Rafael?
3. ¿Es el papá de Elena o de Ana? *(Point to Rafael.)*

156   UNIDAD 4   Lección 1

¿QUÉ DECIMOS...?

Al hablar de nuestra familia

1   ¡Feliz cumpleaños!

2   ¿Cuántos años tienes?

4. ¿Saludan todos a la tía Juliana?
5. ¿A quién saludan?
6. ¿Son Sarita y Pepe los hijos de Elena o Ana?
7. ¿Cuántos años tiene Sarita, seis u ocho? ¿Y Pepe?
8. ¿Son Paquito y Lupe sobrinos o hijos de Elena?
9. ¿Cuántos años tiene Paquito? ¿Y Lupe?
10. ¿Cuándo es el cumpleaños de Lupe, hoy o en dos días?
11. ¿Celebran el cumpleaños de Lupe o de abuelito hoy?

Side 4, 7008 to 8666

Purpose This section uses the language of dates and family relationships in real-life situations. Students should not be overly concerned with understanding or translating every word. The **Early Production Checks** will help to identify the language that students will be expected to produce.

3 ¡Dale, dale, dale!

4 ¡Todos están invitados!

¡Dale, dale, dale!
Suggestion Point out that **Dale, dale . . .** is a well-known children's rhyme used at parties whenever there is a **piñata**. A rough translation would be: *Hit it, hit it, hit it. / Don't miss your aim. / Measure the distance / And make your claim.*

1 ¿Saluda Paquito a su tía Juliana?
2 ¿Qué mira Paquito, la piñata?
3 ¿Quién va a romper la piñata?
4 ¿Qué está ya?
5 ¿Quién va primero, Paquito o sus primos?
6 ¿Quién es? *(Point to Pepe.)*
7 ¿Rompe Pepe la piñata?
8 ¿Quién va después de Pepe, Paquito o Sarita?
9 ¿Quién rompe la piñata?

Side 4, 8686 to 11345

¡Todos están invitados!
Suggestion To explain meaning of **conocen**, use two students or draw two people on board. Say **No se conocen.** Then introduce them: **Bob, quiero presentarte a Nancy.** Have them greet each other and shake hands. Tell class **Ahora sí se conocen.**

To explain **boda** and **nos casamos**, draw stick figures of Betty and Rafael. Emphasize Betty's engagement ring. Write **el 24 de junio** on board. Say **Betty y Rafael se casan el 24 de junio. La boda es el 24 de junio.** Show pictures of weddings cut from magazines. Also review **novia.** Say **Es una boda. Ellos se casan pronto.**

To explain **iglesia,** name several churches in your community.

1 ¿Quién es? *(Point to Roberto, then to Rafael.)*
2 ¿Quién tiene un anuncio importante?
3 ¿Es Betty la novia de Roberto o de Rafael?
4 ¿Es Kevin el hijo de Rafael o de Betty?
5 ¿Quiénes van a casarse?
6 ¿Cuándo van a casarse, el 24 o el 25 de junio?
7 ¿Va a ser la boda en la iglesia de San Antonio de Padua?
8 ¿Están todos invitados a la boda?
9 ¿Quién dice "¡Bravo! ¡Felicidades!"?
10 ¿Qué dicen todos?

Side 4, 11372 to 12904

Suggestions Begin by having students close their books while you narrate one section at a time, using the transparencies to clarify meaning without translation. Then ask the **Early Production Checks.** Repeat this process with each section.

Using the video Play one section at a time after narrating it using the transparencies. Freeze the video and ask the **Early Production Checks.** Repeat this process with each section.

CHARLEMOS UN POCO

A. ¿Quién lo dice?

1 Paquito
2 Rafael
3 Patricio
4 Rafael
5 Rafael
6 Patricio
7 Paquito
8 Paquito

B. La familia de Paquito.

Allow 1–2 min for students to figure out relationships on their own. Call on individuals for correct answers.

Point out The cross on the family tree means the person (in this case, Paquito's mother) has died.

1 Roberto es su tío.
2 Margarita es su abuela.
3 Elena y Roberto son sus tíos.
4 Sarita es su prima.
5 Rafael es su padre.
6 Lupe y Ana son sus hermanas.
7 Pepe es su primo.
8 Margarita y Patricio son sus abuelos.

Extension Ask **¿Cuál es la relación entre** *[name]* **y** *[name]***?** Have class figure out that **Pepe y Sarita son los sobrinos de Rafael** and **Lupe es la nieta de Patricio y Margarita.**

Possessive adjectives: *su, sus*

	Singular	Plural
her/his	**su**	**sus**

Manuel es **su** hermano.
Elisa y Ramón son **sus** padres.

See **¿Por qué se dice así?,** *page G46, section 4.1.*

Male and female relatives

The masculine plural is used to refer to two or more relatives when the group includes both males and females.

abuelos	=	abuelo y abuela
padres	=	papá y mamá
hermanos	=	hermano(s) y hermana(s)
tíos	=	tío(s) y tía(s)
primos	=	primo(s) y prima(s)
sobrinos	=	sobrino(s) y sobrina(s)
nietos	=	nieto(s) y nieta(s)

CHARLEMOS UN POCO

A. ¿Quién lo dice?   ¿Quién dice esto en el video de Ana?

Patricio

Paquito

Rafael

1. Voy yo, voy yo.
2. ¡Su atención, por favor!
3. Hola, hermana. ¿Cómo estás?
4. ¡Espera, hijo! Primero tus primos.
5. Nos casamos el veinticuatro de junio.
6. Sesenta y ocho, niña, y todavía joven y fuerte.
7. Mira la piñata.
8. ¡Voy a romperla yo!

B. La familia de Paquito.   Identifica a los miembros de la familia de Paquito.

MODELO   **Elena es su tía.**

1. Roberto
2. Margarita
3. Elena y Roberto
4. Sarita
5. Rafael
6. Lupe y Ana
7. Pepe
8. Margarita y Patricio

Purpose These activites provide guided practice as students begin to produce new language needed to describe the family and talk about age and birthdates.

C. ¿Cómo se llaman? Nombra a tus parientes.

MODELO   hermano
> **Mi hermano se llama Scott Palmer.** o
> **No tengo hermanos.**

1. abuelo materno
2. tíos
3. padre
4. primos
5. hermanos
6. abuela paterna
7. hermanas
8. madre

CH. ¿Y tu familia? Pregúntale a tu compañero(a) sobre su familia.

MODELO   Tú: **¿Cómo se llaman tus padres?**
Compañero(a): **Mi papá se llama _____ y mi mamá se llama _____.** o
Mis padres se llaman _____ y _____.

D. ¿Y su árbol genealógico? Pregúntale a tu profesor(a) sobre sus parientes. Intenta construir su árbol genealógico.

EJEMPLO   **¿Tiene usted tíos?**
¿Cómo se llaman sus tíos?
¿Dónde viven?

abuelos maternos	tíos
abuelos paternos	primos
hermanos	sobrinos
hijos	nietos
padres	esposo(a)

E. ¿Qué pasó? During vacation, your classroom was painted and many items are now missing. As your partner plays the role of the teacher, ask where the missing items are.

MODELO   libros / biblioteca
Tú: **¿Dónde están nuestros libros?**
Compañero(a): **Sus libros están en la biblioteca.**

1. cuadernos / oficina
2. carpetas / mesa grande
3. computadora / biblioteca
4. diccionarios / sala 37
5. mesas pequeñas / cafetería
6. papel / escritorio
7. videos / teatro
8. libros / sala 22

LECCIÓN 1

Possessive adjectives: *mi, mis, tu, tus, su, sus*

	Singular	Plural
my	**mi**	**mis**
your	**tu**	**tus**
	su	**sus**

¿Cómo se llama **tu** tío?
Mi tío se llama Arturo.

¿Dónde están **tus** primos?
Mis primos están en México.

Sus padres viven en Guadalajara y **su** abuela en la capital, ¿no?

*See **¿Por qué se dice así?**, page G46, section 4.1.*

Possessive adjectives: *nuestro(a), nuestros(as)*

	Singular	Plural
our	**nuestro**	**nuestros**
	nuestra	**nuestras**

Nuestro colegio está en la Calle Ocho.
Nuestras mochilas están en la sala 21.

*See **¿Por qué se dice así?**, page G46, section 4.1.*

C. ¿Cómo se llaman? Call on individuals. Also ask **¿Cuántos hermanos (tíos, primos) tienes?** Tell students to answer **Un hermano se llama . . . , otro se llama . . .** Or have students use the model **Mis hermanos se llaman . . .**

Note Use family tree on page 158 to point out the difference between **parientes** and **padres**.

CH. ¿Y tu familia? Allow 2–3 min. Then ask **¿Cómo se llaman los padres de [partner]? ¿Cuántos hermanos (primos, tíos) tiene? ¿Cómo se llaman?**

D. ¿Y su árbol genealógico? Students should get accustomed to using **usted** to address you and **tú** to address each other. Encourage students to ask many questions. Help them by saying **Pregúntenme si tengo . . .** (You may also want to have them ask your relatives' ages.) When finished, ask several students to draw your family tree on board. Then ask **¿Cuántos primos tengo? ¿Cómo se llaman? ¿Cuántos años tiene . . . ? ¿Dónde vive?**

E. ¿Qué pasó? Demonstrate model taking the role of teacher. Allow 2–3 min to do in pairs. Then call on individuals to give correct responses.

1 ¿Dónde están nuestros cuadernos? Sus cuadernos están en la oficina.
2 ¿Dónde están nuestras carpetas? Sus carpetas están en la mesa grande.
3 ¿Dónde está nuestra computadora? Su computadora está en la biblioteca.
4 ¿Dónde están nuestros diccionarios? Sus diccionarios están en la sala 37.
5 ¿Dónde están nuestras mesas pequeñas? Sus mesas pequeñas están en la cafetería.
6 ¿Dónde está nuestro papel? Su papel está en el escritorio.
7 ¿Dónde están nuestros videos? Sus videos están en el teatro.
8 ¿Dónde están nuestros libros? Sus libros están en la sala 22.

Suggestions Demonstrate examples using volunteers to assure all students know what is expected.
    These activities may first be done in pairs and then repeated with the whole class, calling on individuals. This approach works well with large classes.

F. ¡Vamos a México!

1 Clara ya tiene treinta y cuatro dólares.
2 Ramón ya tiene noventa y siete dólares.
3 Rafael ya tiene sesenta y un dólares.
4 Inés ya tiene cincuenta y seis dólares.
5 Nicolás ya tiene cuarenta y nueve dólares.
6 Raquel ya tiene setenta y cinco dólares.
7 Víctor ya tiene cien dólares.
8 Cecilia ya tiene ochenta y tres dólares.

G. ¿Y el bebé?

Also ask **Y tú, ¿cuántos años tienes? ¿Cuántos años tienen tus hermanos?**

Vocabulario opcional
el (la) hijo(a) mayor,
el (la) hijo(a) menor

Julio tiene setenta y un años.
Herlinda tiene sesenta y cinco años.
Javier tiene cuarenta años.
Cecilia tiene treinta y cinco años.
Arturo tiene dieciocho años.
Ernesto tiene nueve años.
Isabel tiene dieciséis años.
Gilberto tiene trece años.

H. ¿Cuándo es tu cumpleaños?

Point out **Cumpleaños** is both singular and plural. Allow 2–3 min. Ask **¿Quiénes cumplen años en [mes]? ¿Cuándo es su cumpleaños?**

Extension Construct a birthday calendar for the entire class on butcher paper or on poster board. Ask students to supply information about their classmates until everyone's birthday is listed. Then keep it posted on bulletin board throughout the year.

Counting: 30–100

30	treinta
31	treinta y uno
40	cuarenta
42	cuarenta y dos
50	cincuenta
53	cincuenta y tres
60	sesenta
64	sesenta y cuatro
70	setenta
75	setenta y cinco
80	ochenta
86	ochenta y seis
90	noventa
97	noventa y siete
100	cien

See ¿Por qué se dice así?, page G48, section 4.2.

Tener años
Talking and asking about age

¿Cuántos años tienes?
Tengo catorce años.

¿Cuántos años tiene tu tío?
Tiene veintinueve.

¿Qué edad tiene usted?
Sesenta y ocho.

Es el [día] de [mes]

Giving dates:

Mi cumpleaños **es el 5 de julio.**
Hoy **es el primero de enero.**
Nuestro aniversario **es el 26 de octubre.**

Writing dates:

6-9-91: **el seis de septiembre**

See ¿Por qué se dice así?, page G50, section 4.3.

F. ¡Vamos a México! The Spanish Club is selling candy to raise money for a trip to Mexico. How much money have the students already collected?

MODELO   Gloria / $52
   Gloria ya tiene cincuenta y dos dólares.

1. Clara / $34
2. Ramón / $97
3. Rafael / $61
4. Inés / $56
5. Nicolás / $49
6. Raquel / $75
7. Víctor / $100
8. Cecilia / $83

G. ¿Y el bebé? Ésta es la familia Chacón. ¿Cuántos años tiene cada persona?

MODELO   **Ernesto tiene nueve años.**
   Gilberto tiene . . .

Julio y Herlinda - edad 71, 65   Javier y Cecilia - edad 40, 35
Arturo - edad 18   Ernesto - edad 9   Isabel - edad 16   Gilberto - edad 13

H. ¿Cuándo es tu cumpleaños? Pregúntales a varios compañeros cuántos años tienen y cuándo es su cumpleaños. ¿Quién cumple años el mismo mes que tú?

MODELO   Tú: **¿Cuántos años tienes?**
   Compañero(a):   **Tengo _____ años.**
   Tú: **¿Cuándo es tu cumpleaños?**
   Compañero(a):   **Es el _____ de _____.**

I. Edad y fecha de nacimiento. Carlos is helping his boss look up the following employees' ages and birth dates in the office files. What does he find?

MODELO   Norma Vargas 5-7-69
                 Norma Vargas tiene _____ años.
                 Su cumpleaños es el cinco de julio.

Javier Barrios	18-6-71
Elena Valdez	29-10-42
Mario Flores	15-2-59
José Alvarado	30-8-75
Lisa Rodríguez	10-11-53
Eduardo Chávez	8-4-74
María Lemos	13-1-63
Sara Blanco	4-3-40

J. Los sábados. Pregúntale a un(a) compañero(a) si algunos miembros de su familia hacen estas actividades los sábados.

MODELO   Tú: **¿Trabaja tu padre?**
        Compañero(a): **Sí, mi padre trabaja.** o
                       No, mi padre no trabaja.

descansar	estudiar
leer el periódico	visitar a amigos
pasear en bicicleta	ir de compras
limpiar la casa	escribir cartas
ver televisión	trabajar
escuchar música	tocar un instrumento
practicar deportes	musical

CHARLEMOS UN POCO MÁS

CHARLEMOS UN POCO MÁS

A. Nuestras familias. Allow 4–5 min. Do not allow students to look at each other's drawings until they have finished describing.

B. La familia ideal. Students may be asked to bring in a picture of each imaginary family member as a homework assignment. If done in class, ask students to bring old newspapers and magazines of favorite movie or pop personalities.

C. Crucigrama. Student A has all the vertical clues on his/her puzzle. Student B has all the horizontal clues.

```
HERMANA  PADRES
I     A    R    O
J     D    I    B  M
A     R    M    R  A
  HERMANOS    NIETOS
     B  S     N  E
     U        O  R
     E        R  N
     L     PRIMO
     O           S
   TIOS
     I
PRIMA
```

CH. Todos somos parientes. Distribute one set of cards among every five students. Tell students they may not look at anyone's card.

A. Nuestras familias. As you describe your family, your partner will draw your family tree. Then reverse roles and you draw while your partner describes his or her family.

 EJEMPLO   **Mi abuelo materno se llama Andrés.**

B. La familia ideal. You and your partner are siblings. Make up a family tree of famous people the two of you would like to have as your grandparents, parents, brothers and sisters. Don't forget to include yourselves! Describe your family tree to the class.

 EJEMPLO   **Nuestros padres son Tom Cruise y . . .**
Nuestros abuelos son . . .

C. Crucigrama. Your teacher will give you and your partner a cooperative crossword puzzle. One of you will have only the vertical clues, and the other one will have only the horizontal clues. First, complete your part of the crossword puzzle, then ask your partner for his or her clues and fill in the remaining part of your puzzle. By exchanging clues, you should be able to solve the entire puzzle. Don't look at each other's puzzles!

 EJEMPLO   Tú: **¿Cuál es el número cinco horizontal?**
Compañero(a): **Mis primos son los _____ de mis tíos.**
Answer: **hijos**

CH. Todos somos parientes. Work in groups of five. Your teacher will give each of you a biography card. Assume the identity on your card and try to find out how everyone in your group is related. Ask each other questions and answer each question honestly according to the information on your card. As you gain information about the other members of your group, draw a family tree to show how all of you are related.

 EJEMPLO   **¿Cómo te llamas?**
¿Cuántos años tienes?
¿Dónde vives?

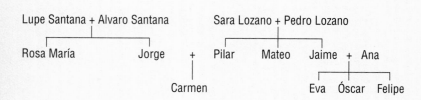

Purpose The *Charlemos un poco más* activities are designed to allow students to create with learned language in a variety of possible combinations. Responses are much more open-ended and often have several possible correct answers.

D. Las cuatro estaciones.   Your teacher will label each corner of the room with a different season.

- Go stand in the corner that represents the season during which your birthday falls.
- Find out the birth dates of each person in your corner and arrange yourselves in chronological order.
- Find out what everyone in your corner likes to do to celebrate his or her birthday.

Dramatizaciones

A. ¡Fiestas!   You are talking about parties in the United States with an exchange student from Colombia. What does the student ask, and what do you say?

Exchange Student	**You**
■ Ask what parties are like in the United States.	■ Describe a typical party in detail.
■ Ask if parties are held on the weekend or during the week.	■ Tell when parties are usually held.
■ Find out where parties are held.	■ Say where you usually go to parties.
■ Ask if there is going to be a party in [*this month*].	■ Respond. Also mention that you are going to have a party on your birthday. Give the date.

B. ¿Sábado, 23?   You and two friends are trying to find a three-hour period when you can get together to plan a surprise birthday party for your best friend. Role-play the situation. Each of you should suggest a couple of dates, times, and places before you can come to an agreement.

C. ¡Feliz cumpleaños!   You and a friend are at your grandmother's sixtieth birthday celebration. Two cousins from out of town are also there. In groups of four, role-play the situation. Your partners will decide who will play the roles of your friend and your cousins. Be sure to greet your cousins and introduce them to your friend. Find out whether your cousins are enjoying the party and why, and how your friend's family celebrates birthdays.

LECCIÓN 1

ciento sesenta y tres **163**

D. Las cuatro estaciones.
Insist that students speak only Spanish. Model the questions they will need to ask: **¿Cuándo es tu cumpleaños? ¿Qué te gusta hacer para tu cumpleaños?** After students have arranged themselves, ask several to tell you the birthdates and favorite activities of students in their group.

Extension While students are still standing, ask those who would prefer to have been born in a different month to go to the appropriate corner. Then have students in each corner ask each other why they like the specific month and season: **¿Por qué te gustan abril y la primavera?** Call on several to tell you what their group members said.

DRAMATIZACIONES

A, B, C. You may want to assign **A, B**, and **C** at same time. Allow students 8–10 min to prepare role plays. Have each group present role play to the class. Ask questions after each presentation to check comprehension.

IMPACTO CULTURAL

¡No me digas!

Purpose This section provides additional reading practice through interesting cross-cultural information about the extended family. It should be used to discourage students from forming stereotypes and to show them how to look deeper into their preconceived ideas about Hispanic culture.

Suggestions Allow students 1–2 min to read dialogue. Ask class to discuss possible explanations and arrive at consensus on correct answer before checking responses and explanations on page 418.

Answers

①Mary Ann did not know that most Hispanics include not only parents and children in their family, but also aunts, uncles, and grandparents, and sometimes even cousins. This is the correct answer.

2 Nothing in the dialogue indicates that Mary Ann thought about this. This is not the correct answer.

3 This is a possible answer. However, Mary Ann did not mention anything about the grandmother living alone. Try another response.

Point out The concept of a retirement home is not common in Hispanic society, precisely because the extended family usually cares for elders.

Y ahora, ¡a leer!

Purpose This section is intended to provide additional reading practice as students learn why Hispanics often have several last names and the origin of Hispanic first names and nicknames.

Antes de empezar

Use these questions as an advance organizer for the readings that follow.

¡No me digas!

¡Toda la familia! Mary Ann is visiting a Hispanic friend, Teresa, in San Antonio, Texas. Read their conversation. Then answer the question that follows to explain Mary Ann's reaction.

Mary Ann:	**Tu familia es muy simpática, Teresa. Y me gusta tu hermano. ¡Es muy guapo! Pero, ¿quién es la señora rubia?**
Teresa:	**Es mi tía Francisca. Ella vive aquí con nosotros.**
Mary Ann:	**¿Ah, sí? Pero, ¿no vive tu abuela con ustedes?**
Teresa:	**Sí. Abuelita está con nosotros también. Ella ya tiene setenta y cuatro años.**
Mary Ann:	**¡Caramba! Hay muchas personas en esta casa — ¡tus padres, tu abuela, tu tía, tus tres hermanos y tú! ¡Qué raro!**

▶ Why does Mary Ann think that Teresa's family is unusual?

1. Mary Ann isn't used to households that include so many relatives.
2. Mary Ann doesn't think that Teresa's aunt looks like the rest of the family.
3. Mary Ann doesn't understand why the grandmother is not living in her own house or in a retirement home.   ❑ Check your answer on page 418.

Y ahora, ¡a leer!

Antes de empezar

1. List all the cognates you can find in the paragraph titled **Nombres.** Give their English equivalent.
2. How many of your friends have nicknames? Do you know where their nicknames came from?
3. List all the first names you can find in the paragraph titled **Apellidos.** Then list all the last names you can find in the same paragraph.

Answers

1 Cognates: César *(Caesar)*, Augusto *(Augustus)*, Maximiliano *(Maximilian)*, corresponden *(correspond)*, famosos *(famous)*, históricos *(historical)*, comunes*(common)*, Jesús *(Jesus)*, Ester *(Esther)*, santos *(saints)*, origen *(origin)*, bíblico *(Biblical)*, calendario *(calendar)*, hispano *(Hispanic)*, diferente *(different)*, importante *(important)*, recibir *(receive)*.

2 Answers will vary. Students should recognize, however, that some nicknames are derived from first names whereas others may refer to physical or personality traits.

3 *First names:* Rosa, Ignacio, Beatriz. *Last names:* Leyva, Rocha, Torres, Velázquez, Gutiérrez, López.

¿Cómo te llamas?

Nombres

Unos nombres— César, Augusto, Carlota, Maximiliano—corresponden a famosos personajes históricos. Otros nombres comunes— Jesús, Pedro, Benjamín, Rita, Ester, Miriam— son nombres de santos o nombres de origen bíblico.

En el calendario hispano, hay un santo diferente para cada día del año. Para los hispanos, el día de su santo es una fecha muy importante. Es común recibir tarjetas y también regalitos en el día del santo.

Sobrenombres

Los sobrenombres son nombres informales que usamos con amigos y parientes. Casi siempre son derivados del nombre de pila de la persona: Toño (Antonio), Lupe (Guadalupe), Juanita (Juana), Juancho (Juan), Maribel (María Isabel). Pero no todos los sobrenombres son derivados del nombre de pila: Paco o Pancho (Francisco), Pepa (Josefa), Pepe (José). En general, los sobrenombres son muy populares entre los hispanos.

Apellidos

Rosa Leyva Rocha, Ignacio Torres Velázquez, Beatriz Gutiérrez López. Generalmente, en los países de habla española, las personas tienen dos apellidos: Leyva Rocha, Torres Velázquez, Gutiérrez López . . . El primero es el apellido del padre; el segundo es el apellido de la madre.

Suggestion If students have difficulty understanding the meaning of **sobrenombres**, use the names of students in the class to illustrate its meaning: *Susie-Susan, Gil-Gilbert, Bobby-Robert, Pat-Patrick.*

Point out
• **Nombres** are also referred to as **nombres de pila** (names received at the baptisimal font). **Sobrenombres** are also referred to as **apodos.**
• **Regalitos** are small, inexpensive gifts.

Point out Christian calendars typically list several saints for one day. Space limitations allow only one name to appear on each date of the calendar.

IMPACTO CULTURAL

*e*nero

1 San Justino
2 San Macario
3 San Daniel
4 San Prisciliano
5 Sta. Amelia
6 Los Stos. Reyes
7 San Luciano
8 San Apolinar
9 San Julián
10 San Gregorio
11 San Higinio
12 San Alfredo
13 San Hilario
14 Sta. Macrina
15 San Mauro
16 Sta. Priscila
17 San Antonio
18 Sta. Margarita
19 San Mario
20 Sta. Cristina
21 Sta. Inés
22 San Vicente
23 San Ildefonso
24 San Francisco
25 Sta. Elvira
26 Sta. Paula
27 Sta. Ángela
28 Sto. Tomás de Aquino
29 San Sulpicio
30 Sta. Martina
31 Sta. Marcela

*m*arzo

1 San Albino
2 San Carlos
3 San Emeterio
4 San Casimiro
5 San Cristóbal
6 Sta. Coleta
7 Sta. Teresa
8 San Juan
9 Sta. Francisca
10 San Pablo
11 San Ramiro
12 Sta. Josefina
13 Sta. Patricia
14 Sta. Matilde
15 San Clemente
16 San Abraham
17 San Patricio
18 San Eduardo
19 San José
20 Sta. Eufemia
21 San Roberto
22 San Zacarías
23 San Fidel
24 San Rómulo
25 San Humberto
26 San Manuel
27 Sta. Lidia
28 San Castor
29 San Victorino
30 San Fernando III
31 San Benjamín

*m*ayo

1 San José Obrero
2 San Germán
3 Sta. Violeta
4 San Silvano
5 San Ireneo
6 Sta. Floriana
7 San Reynaldo
8 San Benedicto
9 San Nicolás
10 Sta. Leonor
11 San Máximo
12 San Aquileo
13 Sta. Imelda
14 Sta. Justina
15 San Cecilio
16 San Honorato
17 San Pascual
18 Sta. Claudia
19 San Pedro Celestino
20 San Bernardino
21 Sta. Virginia
22 San Emilio
23 San Miguel
24 Sta. Susana
25 Sta. Sofía
26 San Felipe
27 Sta. Carolina
28 San Luciano
29 San Esteban
30 San Félix
31 Sta. Petronila

*j*ulio

1 San Aaron
2 San Martiniano
3 Sta. Bertha
4 Sta. Isabel
5 Sta. Filomena
6 San Isaías
7 Sta. Claudia
8 San Adrián
9 Sta. Blanca
10 Sta. Amalia
11 San Abundio
12 San Hilario
13 San Joel
14 San Camilo
15 San Donaldo
16 Ntra. Sra. del Carmen
17 Sta. Generosa
18 San Federico
19 San Arsenio
20 Sta. Margarita
21 San Daniel
22 Sta. María Magdalena
23 Sta. Brígida
24 Sta. Cristina
25 Santiago Apóstol
26 Sta. Ana
27 Sta. Natalia
28 San Víctor
29 Sta. Lucila
30 San Abel
31 San Ignacio de Loyola

*s*eptiembre

1 San Augusto
2 San Antolín
3 Sta. Basilisa
4 Sta. Rosalia
5 San Bertín
6 San Donacio
7 Sta. Regina
8 Sta. Adela
9 San Gorgonio
10 San Teodardo
11 San Jacinto
12 San Tobías
13 San Amado
14 Sta. Salustía
15 Ntra. Sra. de los Dolores
16 San Cornelio
17 Sta. Ariadna
18 San Eustorgio
19 Sta. Constanza
20 Sta. Fausta
21 San Mateo Apóstol
22 San Mauricio
23 San Liberio
24 San Gerardo
25 Sta. Aurelia
26 San Cosme y Damián
27 Sta. Judith
28 San Wenceslao
29 San Miguel, Gabriel, Rafael
30 San Jerónimo

*n*oviembre

1 Sta. Cirenia
2 San Justo
3 San Martín de Porres
4 San Carlos Borromeo
5 San Teotimo
6 San Francisco Gil
7 San Ernesto
8 San Victorino
9 Sta. Eustolia
10 San León
11 Sta. Ernestina
12 San Josafat
13 San Diego
14 San Laurencio
15 San Eugenio
16 San Edmundo
17 Sta. Victoria
18 San Teodulfo
19 Sta. Inés
20 San Octavio
21 San Demetrio
22 Sta. Cecilia
23 San Clemente
24 Sta. Flora
25 San Moisés
26 San Conrado
27 San Virgilio
28 San Rufo
29 Beato Federico
30 San Andrés

*f*ebrero

1 Sta. Brígida
2 Sta. Caterina
3 San Blas
4 San Gilberto
5 San Isidoro
6 Sta. Dorotea
7 San Ricardo
8 San Esteban
9 Sta. Apolonia
10 San Guillermo
11 Ntra. Sra. de Lourdes
12 San Benito
13 Sta. Beatriz
14 San Valentín
15 Sta. Jovita
16 San Simón
17 San Teodulo
18 San Simeón
19 Sta. Lucía
20 San Silvano
21 Sta. Irene
22 Sta. Margarita
23 Sta. Romana
24 San Alberto
25 San Sebastián
26 San Néstor
27 Sta. Honorina
28 San Román
29 San Rufino

*a*bril

1 Sta. Jaquelina
2 Sta. Ofelia
3 San Sixto
4 San Isidoro
5 Sta. Emilia
6 San Timoteo
7 San Juan Bautista
8 San Alberto
9 Sto. Tomás
10 San Ezequiel
11 Ntra. Sra. de la Piedad
12 San Andrés
13 San Martín
14 San Lamberto
15 Sta. Anastasia
16 Sta. Julia
17 San Rodolfo
18 San Perfecto
19 San Crescencio
20 San Cesareo
21 San Anselmo
22 San Bartolomé
23 Sta. Elena
24 San Alejandro
25 Sta. Antonieta
26 San Marcelino
27 Sta. Zita
28 San Vidal
29 San Severo
30 San Jaime

*j*unio

1 San Segundo
2 San Erasmo
3 Sta. Olivia
4 San Rutilo
5 Sta. Eloisa
6 San Norberto
7 San Pablo Obispo
8 San Maximino
9 San Feliciano
10 San Getulio
11 Sta. Rosalina
12 San Nazario
13 San Antonio de Padua
14 San Rufino
15 San Vito
16 Sta. Alicia
17 San Isauro
18 San Teodulo
19 Sta. Juliana
20 San Silverio
21 San Luis Gonzaga
22 San Paulino
23 San Pelayo
24 San Fermín
25 San Salomón
26 San David
27 Ntra. Sra. del Socorro
28 San Plutarco
29 San Pedro y San Pablo
30 Sta. Luciana

*a*gosto

1 San Alfonso
2 Ntra. Sra. de los Ángeles
3 San Nicodemus
4 San Aristarco
5 San Osvaldo
6 San Esteban
7 San Cayetano
8 Sto. Domingo de Guzmán
9 San Román
10 San Lorenzo
11 San Clara
12 San Fortino
13 San Hipolito
14 San Calixto
15 La Asunción de María Santísima
16 Sta. Serena
17 San Jacinto
18 San Lauro
19 San Luis Obispo
20 San Samuel
21 San Camerino
22 San Sinforiano
23 San Claudio
24 Sta. Micaela
25 San Luis Rey
26 San Alejandro
27 Sta. Mónica
28 San Agustín
29 Sta. Cándida
30 Sta. Rosa de Lima
31 San Ramón

*o*ctubre

1 Sta. Teresita del niño Jesús
2 San Gerino
3 Sta. Ma. Josefa
4 San Francisco de Asis
5 San Plácido
6 San Bruno
7 San Marcos
8 San Demetrio
9 Sta. Sara
10 San León
11 Sta. Clemencia
12 Ntra. Sra. del Pilar
13 San Fausto
14 San Rolando
15 Sta. Teresa
16 San Florentino
17 San Salomón
18 San Lucas
19 San Noel
20 San Artemio
21 Sta. Celina
22 Sta. María Salomé
23 Sta. Agustina
24 Sta. María Cloret
25 Sta. Daría
26 San Luciano
27 Sta. Antonieta
28 San Judas Tadeo
29 San Teodoro
30 San Cenobio
31 San Quintín

*d*iciembre

1 San Eloy
2 Sta. Eva
3 San Lucio
4 Sta. Bárbara
5 San Cirano
6 San Emiliano
7 San Ambrosio
8 La Inmaculada Concepción
9 Sta. Delfina
10 Sta. Eulalia
11 San Damaso
12 Ntra. Sra. de Guadalupe
13 San Bartolo
14 San Juan de la Cruz
15 Sta. Cristina
16 Sta. Adelaida
17 Sta. Yolanda
18 San Salvador
19 San Adán
20 San Julio
21 San Severiano Obispo
22 San Demetrio
23 Sta. María Luisa
24 Sta. Irma
25 La Natividad del Sr.
26 San Dionisio
27 San Teodoro
28 Stos. Inocentes
29 San Saturnino
30 San Bonifacio
31 Sta. Paulina

Verifiquemos

1. Busca tu nombre o el nombre de tus amigos en el calendario. ¿Cuál es la fecha de tu santo? ¿Del santo de algunos de tus amigos?
2. ¿Cuáles son algunos sobrenombres de personas hispanas que tú conoces?
3. Combina estos nombres con sus sobrenombres.

Chicos		**Chicas**	
Alejandro	Manolo	Teresa	Marilú
Rafael	Beto	Cristina	Lola
Guillermo	Nacho	María Luisa	Meche
Ignacio	Rafa	Isabel	Tere
Manuel	Quico	Dolores	Chavela
Enrique	Alex	Mercedes	Pepa
Roberto	Memo	Josefa	Tina

4. ¿Cuál es el apellido del padre de César Vargas García? ¿De su madre? ¿Cuál es el apellido del padre de Alicia Chávez Moreno? ¿De su madre?

César Vargas García + Alicia Chávez Moreno

Juan Ramón Vargas Chávez

5. Completa los nombres de Susana y Alfonso.

Alfredo García Blanco + Lorenza Mendoza Velasco

Susana ___ ? ___ ? ___

Mario Saldívar Rojas + Sofía Torres Chávez

Alfonso ___ ? ___ ? ___

6. ¿Cuál es el apellido de los abuelos maternos de Susana y Alfonso? ¿De sus abuelos paternos?

LECCIÓN 1

OBJECTIVES

Communicative Goals

- Identifying relatives by remarriage
- Asking about people you know or want to meet
- Expressing what you want to be in the future
- Asking people about their professional goals
- Asking questions

Culture and Reading

- *¡No me digas!*
  ¡No está en la guía!
  Finding telephone numbers
- *Y ahora, ¡a leer!*
  Datos personales:
  Using a Hispanic telephone directory

Structure

- **4.4** Personal **a**
- **4.5** The verb **conocer**
- **4.6** The verbs **querer** and **venir**
- **4.7** Questions and question words: A summary

ACTIVE VOCABULARY

Palabras interrogativas

¿Cómo?	¿Dónde?
¿Cuál(es)	¿Adónde?
¿Cuándo?	¿De dónde?
¿Cuánto(a)?	¿Por qué?
¿Cuántos(as)?	¿Qué?
	¿Quién(es)?

Profesiones

The professions listed here are used in the lesson exercises. Students should learn 8–10 professions that apply to their relatives or that they themselves are interested in pursuing.

actor	escritor(a)
actriz	fotógrafo(a)
agricultor	futbolista
artista	maestro(a)
autor	médico(a)
camarero(a)	músico(a)
cantante	político(a)
cocinero(a)	reportero(a)
doctor(a)	secretario(a)
enfermero(a)	

¿Quieres conocer a mi nueva familia?

Parientes

hermanastra
hermanastro
madrastra
padrastro
pariente

Bodas

boda
casado(a)
divorciado(a)
novia
novio
soltero(a)

Verbos

conocer
querer
sacar
… fotos
venir

Palabras y expresiones

guía telefónica
muchacha
muchacho
muy
nuevo(a)

con permiso
¡Qué lástima!

¿Qué piensas tú?

Answers

1 Rafael, his parents Patricio and Margarita, and his children Ana, Lupe, and Paquito, Betty and her son Kevin. Next to Betty is her mother, who was not introduced before.

2 Stepmother/father, stepbrother/ sister, mother/father-in-law.

3 Florist, musicians, travel agent. Other possibilities: baker, priest, caterer, chauffeur, bartender, janitor, organist, photographer, hairdresser, manicurist, tuxedo rental, bridal shop.

4 Plumber, carpenter, dentist. Reasons should be fairly obvious.

5 Answers will vary. Encourage students to name the real jobs and professions of their family members and friends.

6 **Students will be able to talk about relatives by remarriage and about professions.**

¿Qué piensas tú?

1. You already know most of the people in the photo. Who are they? Who do you think the older woman next to Betty is?

2. Now that Betty and Rafael are married, there are some new family relationships. What are they?

3. Look at the advertisements on this page. What professionals or services were needed to make this wedding a success? Can you name others that might have been needed?

4. Which of the advertised services would not be needed in planning and having the wedding? Why not?

5. How many different jobs and professions are represented in your extended family?

6. What do you think you will be able to talk about when you have finished this lesson?

Purpose To focus students on the language necessary to talk about family members by remarriage and about professions, and to encourage the development and use of critical thinking skills.

Suggestions Use the photo to review identifying, describing, and expressing ages.

TAPE/
DISC

28:17–
30:12

Side 4, 12911 to 16390

Comprehension Checks

The **Comprehension Checks** are available on cards in the TRP.

1　　　　28:25

Suggestions Ask questions to identify the people in the family photo in the album. Draw or refer to a family tree to clarify new family members. Indicate all are **parientes.**
1　¿Es Ana? ¿Quién es?
2　¿Es el álbum de Ana?
3　¿Son fotos de los nuevos parientes de Ana?
4　¿Qué hay en el álbum?

Side 4, 13165 to 13423

2　　　　28:34

Suggestions Draw couples, labeling each **Sr. y Sra.** *[surname].* Identify husbands as **esposos**, wives as **esposas.** Also, draw a gravestone. Indicate that Elvira's husband is **muerto**, so Elvira is **viuda.** Say that Rafael is **viudo** too.
Point out Doña is a title of respect used with an older woman's first name.
1　¿Quién es? ¿Es Betty la nueva esposa del padre de Ana?
2　¿Quién es la nueva esposa del padre de Ana?
3　¿Es la madrastra de Ana?
4　¿Quién es la madrastra de Ana? ¿de Paquito? ¿de Lupe?
5　¿Es profesora de español Betty?
6　¿Es Doña Elvira la madre de Betty? ¿de Rafael?
7　¿Es la madre o la suegra de Rafael?
8　¿Quién es la suegra de Rafael?
9　¿Es viuda Elvira?
10　¿Vive su esposo o está muerto?

Side 4, 13442 to 13955

3　　　　28:52

Suggestions Name several actors. Explain Kevin is a young

Éstas son las fotos de la boda de mi padre. ¿Quieres conocer a mis nuevos parientes?

*Patricio, Margarita, Paquito
Rafael, Betty, Elvira, Kevin
Ana, Lupe*

2

La nueva esposa de mi padre se llama Betty. Betty es mi madrastra. Ella es profesora de español. Es muy inteligente y . . . muy bonita, ¿no? Doña Elvira, la madre de Betty, es viuda. Su esposo está muerto.

170 ciento setenta

3

¿Conoces a Kevin? Kevin es mi hermanastro. Es muy guapo, ¿no? Él quiere ser actor de cine. Mi papá es el nuevo padrastro de Kevin . . . y Lupe y yo somos sus hermanastras.

student, but **quiere ser actor** when he is older. Contrast **Ahora es estudiante** with **Quiere ser actor.**
1　¿Quién es?
2　¿Es Kevin el hermano o el hermanastro de Ana?
Continue asking Comprehension Check questions, as above, or use the **Comprehension Checks** in the TRP.

Side 4, 13974 to 14480

Purpose This section develops listening and reading comprehension of vocabulary needed to talk about weddings and relatives by remarriage.

¿Quién es este muchacho? ¿Es un pariente nuevo? ¡Ah, no! Es Diego, el fotógrafo de la boda. Es muy buen fotógrafo. Siempre saca excelentes fotos.

Tía Juliana, la secretaria, Pepe, Diego, Lola, Mario

¡Qué bonita!, ¿verdad? Es nuestra prima Lola. Lola es una cantante muy buena. Es divorciada, pero tiene un novio muy guapo. Yo también quiero ser cantante. ¿Qué quieres ser tú?

Esta señora es mi tía Juliana. Es una escritora muy famosa. Tiene sesenta y nueve años y vive en México. No es casada; es soltera. La otra señora es su secretaria.

Éste es Mario, el novio de Lola. Mario es futbolista. ¿Conoces a mi primo Pepe? ¡Pepe también quiere ser futbolista!

ciento setenta y uno **171**

4 `29:10`
Suggestion Mime **sacar fotos**.
1 ¿Es pariente el muchacho en la foto?
2 ¿Quién es?
3 ¿Es fotógrafo Diego?
4 ¿Qué es Diego?
5 ¿Saca buenas fotos?
6 ¿Conoces a un fotógrafo? (¿Cómo se llama?)

Side 4, 14512 to 14945

5 `29:25`
Suggestion Name some **cantantes**.
Point out Novio means *boyfriend*.
1 ¿Es la prima de Ana?
2 ¿Cómo se llama?
3 ¿Es cantante?
4 ¿Quién es cantante?
5 ¿Quién es una famosa cantante americana? ¿un famoso cantante americano?
6 ¿Es divorciada Lola?
7 ¿Tiene novio?
8 ¿Quiere ser cantante Ana?
9 ¿Quieres ser cantante? *(other professions)* ¿Qué quieres ser?

Side 4, 14971 to 15390

6 `29:40`
Suggestions Name several football players. Remind students that American football and **fútbol** are different games.
1 ¿Es el novio de Lola?
2 ¿Es futbolista (fotógrafo, cantante)?
3 ¿Quién es futbolista?
4 ¿Quiere Pepe ser futbolista (fotógrafo, cantante)?
5 ¿Qué quiere ser Pepe?
6 ¿Quieres tú ser futbolista?

Side 4, 15409 to 15895

7 `29:57`
Suggestions Name some **escritoras** students would know. Point out couples who are **casados**. Explain **soltera: Juliana no tiene esposo. No es casada. Es soltera.**
1 ¿Quién es? ¿Es casada o soltera?
2 ¿Tiene 69 años?
3 ¿Cuántos años tiene?
4 ¿Eres soltera(o)?
5 ¿Dónde vive tía Juliana?

Suggestions Begin by having students close their books while you narrate one section at a time, using the transparencies to clarify meaning without translation. Then ask **Comprehension Checks**. Repeat this process with each section.

Using the video Play one section at a time after narrating it using the transparencies. Freeze the video and ask **Comprehension Checks.** Repeat this process with each section.

6 (Pointing to secretary.) ¿Es secretaria? (other professions)
7 ¿Quién en la clase quiere ser secretaria? (other professions)

Side 4, 15916 to 16390

30:13–33:46

Side 4, 16396 to 22799

Early Production Checks

A full set of the **Early Production Checks** is available on cards in the Teacher's Resource Package.

1   30:19

¿Conoces a mi hermanastro?

1 ¿Quién es? *(Point to Kevin, then to Julio.)*   Kevin / Julio.
2 ¿Conoce Kevin a todas las personas?   No.
3 ¿Conoce Kevin a algunas de las personas?   Sí.
4 ¿Son muchas personas parientes de la madre de Kevin o de su padrastro?   De su padrastro.
5 ¿De quién son parientes muchas de las personas?   De su padrastro.
6 ¿Quién es? *(Point to Paquito.)*   Paquito.
7 ¿Conoce Kevin a Paquito?   Sí.
8 ¿Es Paquito el nuevo hermanastro de Kevin o de Julio?   De Kevin.
9 ¿Qué relación hay entre Paquito y Kevin?   Son hermanastros.
10 ¿Cómo está Paquito?   Aburrido.
11 ¿Le gustan las bodas a Paquito?   No.
12 ¿Te gustan las bodas a ti? *(Ask several students.)*   . . .

Side 4, 16585 to 17502

2   30:51

¿Ya están todos listos?

Accept brief phrases or one- and two-word answers to all **Early Production Checks,** as above. It is not necessary for students to answer in complete sentences.

1 ¿Es el fotógrafo?
2 ¿Quién es? *(Point to photographer, Julio, Kevin.)*
3 ¿Es hora de sacar fotos?
4 ¿Qué va(n) a hacer ahora?

5 ¿Quiénes van primero, los novios o los padres de la novia?
6 ¿Es viuda la abuela de Kevin?
7 ¿Quién es viuda?
8 ¿Quiere el fotógrafo a los niños en la primera fila?
9 ¿Dónde quiere a los niños?
10 ¿Le gustan las bodas (los fotógrafos) a Paquito?
11 ¿Cómo está Paquito?

Side 4, 17519 to 18995

172   UNIDAD 4   Lección 2

¿QUÉ DECIMOS...?

Al hablar de la nueva familia

1   ¿Conoces a mi hermanastro?

2   ¿Ya están todos listos?

Purpose This section presents the language of family members and professions in real-life contexts. The language used here is an authentic sampling of Spanish as spoken by the Hispanic community of San Antonio, Texas. For example, Kevin—like the young actor who plays him—has one Spanish-speaking and one English-speaking parent. Like many such children, he speaks both languages with a slight accent.

¿Qué quieres ser?

1 ¿Quién es? *(Point to Paquito, Juliana, Kevin.)*
2 ¿Es escritora o profesora Juliana?
3 ¿Qué es Juliana?
4 ¿Es muy famosa?
5 ¿Quiere Kevin conocer a tía Juliana?
6 ¿Quién presenta a Kevin?
7 ¿Quién dice "Bienvenido", Kevin o tía Juliana?
8 ¿Cuántos años tiene Kevin?
9 ¿Qué quiere ser Kevin, médico o reportero?

Note We also know from the *Para empezar* that Kevin is interested in acting.

10 ¿Y Paquito, qué quiere ser, médico o reportero?
11 ¿Es reportero el padre de Paquito?
12 ¿Qué es el padre de Paquito?
13 ¿Está solo Julio?
14 ¿Quién es el hermanastro de Paquito?
15 ¿Qué es Kevin?
16 ¿Van a ser buenos amigos Paquito y Kevin?

Side 4, 19013 to 20925

Suggestions Begin by having students close their books while you narrate one section at a time, using the transparencies to clarify meaning without translation. Then ask **Early Production Checks.** Repeat this process with each section.

Using the video Play one section at a time after narrating it using the transparencies. Freeze the video and ask **Early Production Checks.** Repeat this process with each section.

¡Ojo! The double object pronouns used here (e.g., **te las presento**) are for recognition only. Students should not be expected to understand or produce this structure at this point.

1 ¿Conoce Kevin a todos?
2 ¿Hay mucha gente que no conoce Kevin?
3 ¿Quién es? *(Point to singer.)*
4 ¿Es una cantante?
5 ¿Es viuda, casada o divorciada?
6 ¿Quién es, el hijo o el novio de la cantante?
7 ¿Es futbolista?
8 ¿Quiénes son las dos chicas?
9 ¿Son hermanastras o primas de Kevin?
10 ¿Cuándo va a conocerlas Julio, ahora o luego?

Side 4, 20946 to 22799

CHARLEMOS UN POCO

A. ¿Quiénes son? Ésta es la nueva familia de Kevin. Con un(a) compañero(a), trata de identificar a los parientes de Kevin.

MODELO **Su primo es Pepe.**

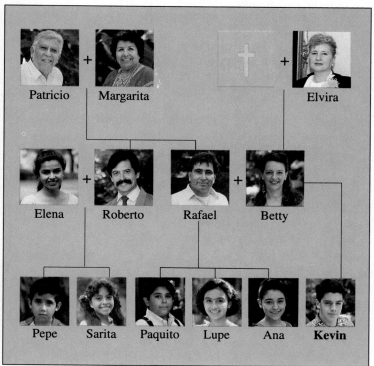

1. abuela materna
2. hermanastras
3. primos
4. hermanastro
5. tíos
6. padrastro
7. madre
8. abuelos

a. Betty
b. Elena y Roberto
c. Patricio y Margarita
ch. Rafael
d. Elvira
e. Lupe y Ana
f. Pepe y Sarita
g. Paquito

B. Sus parientes. Prepara cinco preguntas sobre cinco parientes de Kevin. Luego en grupos pequeños lean las preguntas y contéstenlas.

EJEMPLO **¿Cómo se llama el tío de Lupe?** o
¿Quién es la madre de Sarita?

LECCIÓN 2

Relatives by remarriage
-astro(a) endings

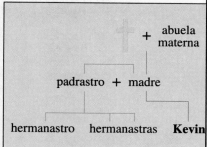

ciento setenta y cinco **175**

CHARLEMOS UN POCO

A. ¿Quiénes son? Allow 3–4 min to do exercise in pairs. Then review answers with entire class.

¡OJO! The **-astro(a)** endings are presented here as active vocabulary because of the changing structure of the nuclear family in the U.S. Students who have experienced remarriage of a parent should be able to describe their family accurately. It should be pointed out, however, that in Hispanic society, the **-astro** endings are generally avoided or used only to talk about someone in the third person. One simply speaks in more general terms, such as **la esposa de mi padre** o **el hijo del esposo de mi madre.**

You may want to point out that Patricio and Margarita are actually Kevin's **abuelastros,** though **abuelos** is normally used.

1 Su abuela materna es Elvira.
2 Sus hermanastras son Lupe y Ana.
3 Sus primos son Pepe y Sarita.
4 Su hermanastro es Paquito.
5 Sus tíos son Elena y Roberto.
6 Su padrastro es Rafael.
7 Su madre es Betty.
8 Sus abuelos son Patricio y Margarita.

B. Sus parientes. Allow 2–3 min to prepare questions individually. Then in groups of 4 or 5, have them ask each other their questions.

Purpose These activities provide guided practice to students beginning to produce new language necessary to describe family members by remarriage and to ask and answer questions about what they and their friends want to be in the future.

C. ¿Qué hacen?

1 ¿Qué hacen los músicos?
Los músicos tocan música.

2 ¿Qué hacen los cocineros?
Los cocineros preparan comida.

3 ¿Qué hacen los escritores?
Los escritores escriben libros.

4 ¿Qué hacen los secretarios?
Los secretarios escriben cartas.

5 ¿Qué hacen los estudiantes?
Los estudiantes hacen la tarea.

6 ¿Qué hacen los doctores?
Los doctores trabajan en hospitales.

7 ¿Qué hacen los camareros?
Los camareros trabajan en restaurantes.

8 ¿Qué hacen los agricultores?
Los agricultores cultivan la tierra.

9 ¿Qué hacen los artistas?
Los artistas hacen dibujos.

Extension 1 Have the students work in pairs listing as many things as they can that each profession does.

Extension 2 Have students name a famous person or a well-known personality (TV or movies). Class has to give person's profession. Example: **Florence Nightingale—enfermera, Los Beatles—músicos,** etc.

CH. Tú debes ser . . . Allow

3–4 min. Call on several pairs to tell what profession they selected for the first individual, then the second, third, etc. Answers may vary.

1 En mi opinión, Joaquín debe ser maestro (profesor).

2 En mi opinión, Laura debe ser ingeniera.

3 En mi opinión, Roberto debe ser agricultor.

4 En mi opinión, Sara debe ser cocinera.

5 En mi opinión, Manuel debe ser político.

6 En mi opinión, Patricia debe ser música (cantante).

7 En mi opinión, Rafael debe ser bombero.

8 En mi opinión, María debe ser secretaria (escritora).

9 En mi opinión, Elodia debe ser mecánica.

D. ¿A quiénes conoces?

Allow 2–3 min. Then ask **¿Conoce al director** [partner's name]**?**
¿al secretario? ¿al enfermero? etc.
Answers will vary.

Profesiones

abogado(a)   hombre/mujer de negocios

agricultor   ingeniero(a)

artista   maestro(a)

bombero    mecánico(a)

camarero(a) 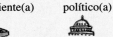   médico(a)

cocinero(a)   músico(a)

dependiente(a)   político(a)

enfermero(a)   reportero(a)

escritor(a)   secretario(a)

Conocer (a)
Used when talking about knowing people

conozco	conocemos
conoces	
conoce	conocen
conoce	conocen

¿Conoces a mi hermana?
No, pero **conozco a** tu hermano.

¿Conocen ustedes **al** profesor?
Sí, y **conocemos a** su esposa.

Note: You must use **a** when **conocer** is followed by a person.

See **¿Por qué se dice así?,**
pages G51–G52, sections 4.4 and 4.5.

176 *ciento setenta y seis*

C. ¿Qué hacen?   Pregúntale a tu compañero(a) qué hacen estas personas.

MODELO   Tú: **¿Qué hacen los médicos?**
Compañero(a): **Los médicos trabajan en hospitales.**

1. músicos	escribir cartas
2. cocineros	hacer la tarea
3. escritores	hacer dibujos
4. secretarios	trabajar en hospitales
5. estudiantes	cultivar la tierra
6. doctores	tocar música
7. camareros	preparar comida
8. agricultores	trabajar en restaurantes
9. artistas	escribir libros

CH. Tú debes ser . . .   Con un(a) compañero(a), selecciona una profesión para estos estudiantes.

MODELO   Lisa estudia química y biología. Le gusta visitar hospitales.
En mi opinión, Lisa debe ser médica.

1. A Joaquín le gusta trabajar con los niños. Él es muy paciente y siempre explica todo muy bien.

2. Laura es buena en matemáticas y en arte.

3. A Roberto le gusta trabajar al aire libre y cultivar plantas. También le gustan los animales.

4. A Sara le gusta mucho la comida. Prepara unos platos especiales.

5. Manuel es muy simpático y le gusta la gente. Él es el presidente estudiantil de su colegio.

6. A Patricia le gusta ir a las fiestas y bailar. También canta.

7. A Rafael le gusta hacer gimnasia. Él es grande y muy fuerte.

8. María escribe a máquina muy rápido. Ella es muy buena en sus clases de inglés.

9. A Elodia le gustan mucho los coches. Cuando sus amigos tienen problemas con sus coches, siempre hablan con Elodia.

D. ¿A quiénes conoces?   Tienes que presentar a un estudiante nuevo. Pregúntale si ya conoce a estas personas.

MODELO   profesor de inglés
Tú: **¿Conoces al profesor de inglés?**
Compañero(a): **Sí, conozco al profesor de inglés.
Se llama ____. o
No, no conozco al profesor de inglés.**

1. director(a) de la escuela	**5.** enfermero(a) de la escuela
2. profesores(as) de español	**6.** maestro(a) de música
3. maestro(a) de arte	**7.** profesores(as) de historia
4. secretario(a) de la escuela	**8.** cocinero(a)

UNIDAD 4

¡Ojo! The list of professions is not intended as active vocabulary. Students should learn 8–10 professions that apply to their relatives or that they themselves are interested in pursuing.

Point out
• The feminine of **bombero** is **mujer bombero**. The tendency in spoken Spanish is also to say **la mujer médico** and **la mujer músico** rather than to use the feminine forms.

• **Artista** is both masculine and feminine and is also used to mean "entertainer."

• **Dependiente** is both masculine and feminine, though the feminine form **dependienta** is also used.

E. ¿Quiénes son? ¿Conocen ustedes a estas personas?

MODELO Beto
Sí, conocemos a Beto. o

Lilia
No, no conocemos a Lilia.

1. Kevin	**2.** Mónica	**3.** Sr. Ramos	**4.** Lupe

5. Óscar	**6.** Riqui	**7.** Kati	**8.** Sra. Castellano

F. ¡Feliz cumpleaños! ¿Qué quieren estas personas para su cumpleaños?

MODELO **Mi papá quiere un libro.**

1. mi amigo	**6.** nosotros(as)
2. mis amigas	**7.** mi papá
3. yo	**8.** mis abuelos
4. tú	**9.** mi mamá
5. mi hermano(a)	**10.** ¿ . . . ?

LECCIÓN 2

E. ¿Quiénes son? Ask ¿Conocen a [Beto]?

Point out The photos are of characters students have already met in their book or will meet in future units.

1 Sí, conocemos a Kevin.
2 No, no conocemos a Mónica.
3 Sí, conocemos al señor Ramos.
4 Sí, conocemos a Lupe.
5 No, no conocemos a Óscar.
6 Sí, conocemos a Riqui.
7 Sí, conocemos a Kati.
8 No, no conocemos a la señora Castellano.

Extension Ask about people at your school or in your community.

Querer

quiero	queremos
quieres	
quiere	quieren
quiere	quieren

See **¿Por qué se dice así?,** *page G54, section 4.6.*

G. Planes profesionales.

Allow students to move around class asking several classmates what they want to be. When they find someone with the same future plans, tell them to stop asking and go to board and write *[Name]* **y** *[name]* **quieren ser** *[profession]*. Allow 4–5 min, then go over what they wrote on the board with class.

H. ¡Hay reunión!

1 vienen
2 vienes
3 vengo
4 viene
5 venimos
6 vienen
7 viene
8 vienen

I. ¿A qué hora?

1 ¿A qué hora viene el profesor García? Viene a las doce y media.
2 ¿A qué hora vienen Susana y Fernando? Vienen a las tres menos cuarto.
3 ¿A qué hora viene Luis? Viene a las tres.
4 ¿A qué hora vienen tus primos? Vienen a las cuatro y cuarto.
5 ¿A qué hora vienen la directora y su familia? Vienen a la una.
6 ¿A qué hora viene la banda? Viene a las dos y cuarto.
7 ¿A qué hora vienes tú? Vengo a las tres y media.
8 ¿A qué hora vienen tus hermanos? Vienen a las cuatro menos cuarto.

Querer ser

Used when talking about what you want to be

Y tú, ¿qué **quieres ser**?
¡Quiero ser presidente!

See **¿Por qué se dice así?,** *page G54, section 4.6.*

Venir

vengo	venimos
vienes	
viene	vienen
viene	vienen

Note that **venir** is irregular in the **yo** form. Also note that its stem vowel changes from **e → ie.**

See **¿Por qué se dice así?,** *page G54, section 4.6.*

de + el → del

The word **de** followed by **el** becomes **del.**

¿Vienen **del** gimnasio?
Yo vengo **del** laboratorio y Tere viene de la biblioteca.

G. Planes profesionales. Pregúntales a varios amigos qué quieren ser.

 MODELO Tú: **¿Qué quieres ser tú?**
Compañero(a): **Yo quiero ser mecánico(a).**

H. ¡Hay reunión! Hay una reunión del club de español después del colegio. ¿De dónde vienen todos?

MODELO Carlitos _viene_ del gimnasio.

1. Mis hermanos _____ de la biblioteca.
2. Tú _____ de la clase de música.
3. Yo _____ de la oficina.
4. Elena _____ del teatro.
5. Nosotros _____ del laboratorio de química.
6. Inés y Roberto _____ de la cafetería.
7. Martín _____ de la sala de computación.
8. Ustedes _____ de la clase de inglés.

I. ¿A qué hora? Hay una fiesta en el parque. Pregúntale a tu compañero(a) a qué hora vienen los otros invitados.

 MODELO Juan

Tú: **¿A qué hora viene Juan?**
Compañero(a): **Viene a las tres y media.**

1. el profesor García

5. la directora y su familia

2. Susana y Fernando

6. la banda

3. Luis

7. tú

4. tus primos

8. tus hermanos

UNIDAD 4

J. El reportero. Working with a partner, figure out what questions a reporter asked in order to get the following information from these four professionals.

Me llamo Carmen González. Soy maestra de escuela primaria. Trabajo en la escuela Cabrillo. Enseño los grados 3 y 4. Me gusta mucho trabajar con los niños.

Soy Elena Cabrera Hidalgo. Soy dependienta en una tienda grande. Trabajo en el departamento de música. Trabajo ocho horas al día, desde las 2:00 de la tarde hasta las 10:00 de la noche. Escucho música toda la tarde. Me encantan las canciones de José José.

Question words

¿Quién?
¿Quiénes?

¿Qué?

¿Cuál?
¿Cuáles?

¿Dónde?
¿Adónde?
¿De dónde?

¿Cuánto?
¿Cuántos?

¿Cuándo?
¿Cómo?
¿Por qué?

Note that all question words require a written accent.

See ¿**Por qué se dice así?**, *page G56, section 4.7.*

J. El reportero.
1 Cómo, Cuál, Dónde, Qué, Qué
2 Cómo, Dónde, qué, Cuántas, Qué, Quién
3 Cómo, Cuál, Dónde, Qué, quién
4 Cómo, Qué, Dónde, Dónde

1. ¿ _____ se llama usted?
   ¿ _____ es su profesión?
   ¿ _____ trabaja?
   ¿ _____ le enseña?
   ¿ _____ le gusta?

2. ¿ _____ se llama usted?
   ¿ _____ trabaja?
   ¿ En _____ departamento trabaja?
   ¿ _____ horas al día trabaja?
   ¿ _____ hace por la tarde?
   ¿ _____ es su artista favorito?

Soy Fernando Lobato. Soy secretario en una compañía muy grande. Escribo cartas y hablo por teléfono con muchas personas. Siempre hay mucho trabajo.

Soy Felipe Herrera. Soy ingeniero civil. A veces estoy todo el día en una oficina, pero generalmente trabajo al aire libre. Prefiero trabajar al aire libre.

3. ¿ _____ se llama usted?
   ¿ _____ es su profesión?
   ¿ _____ trabaja?
   ¿ _____ hace?
   ¿Con _____ habla?

4. ¿ _____ se llama usted?
   ¿ _____ hace usted?
   ¿ _____ trabaja?
   ¿ _____ prefiere trabajar, en una oficina o al aire libre?

LECCIÓN 2

CHARLEMOS UN POCO MÁS

A. Profesiones. Ask your classmates about their parents' occupations. How many different professions can you find? Make a list of them, then beside each one, write whose parent is in that profession. List as many different professions as possible.

B. Somos reporteros. As reporters for the school newspaper, you and your partner will be interviewing an Olympic soccer player. Prepare four or five questions that you want to ask.

C. ¡Encuesta! Your teacher will give you an interview grid. Complete the grid by asking your classmates about their families. When you find a classmate who meets the description in one of the squares, write his or her name in that square. Your goal is to put a name in every square. Just remember, you can't put the same person's name in more than two squares!

EJEMPLO ¿**Tienes dos hermanas?**

Purpose
Purpose These activities are designed to allow students to create with language recently learned as they talk about professions and new family relationships in a variety of open-ended and personalized contexts.

A. Profesiones. Allow students 5–8 min to collect information. Then ask three students to write their lists (professions only, not names of individuals) on board. Have class add professions to lists if any have been omitted.

B. Somos reporteros. Allow 3–4 min. Then you role-play the soccer player at a press conference. Call on different "reporters" to ask their questions.

Extension 1 Have one student in class be the soccer player.

Extension 2 Repeat activity for other professions: a rock star, a model, a baseball player, etc.

C. ¡Encuesta! Have students move around class talking with several classmates. Allow 2–3 min. Ask who completed all the squares (or all but one, all but two, etc.). Check by asking students whose names appear on the form if the information is true.

Dramatizaciones

A. ¡Aniversario! You are at a family party. Act out the situation below with your partner. One of you plays the role of the friend who is visiting.

You
- Ask if your friend knows your cousins.
- Ask if your friend likes to dance.
- Say that you want to dance with someone else. Indicate who.

Friend
- Say that you know one of them but not the other.
- Say yes and that you want to invite his or her cousins to dance.
- Say what you are going to do.

B. Yo voy a ser . . . With a friend, discuss the professions that you are both interested in.
- Tell what you want to be and why.
- Tell where you would like to work.
- Ask about your partner's preferred profession.
- Comment on your partner's preferred profession.

C. Dos profesionales. As part of "Career Week," your Spanish class has invited two business or professional people from the community to come and talk about their work. Form groups of four or five students. Two of you will play the role of the guests, while the others will interview you.

180 ciento ochenta

DRAMATIZACIONES

Purpose This section has students recycle, in student-centered role plays, all previously learned structures and vocabulary needed to describe family members by remarriage and to talk about future professional plans.

Suggestions Do these role plays spontaneously, not from written scripts. Circulate among groups. Limit time allowed so that students do not get off task. Ask students to recreate their exchange for the whole class.

A, B, C. Assign **A, B,** and **C** at the same time. Allow students 4–5 min to prepare role plays. Then have them present role plays to class. Ask comprehension check questions after each presentation.

¡No me digas!

¡No está en la guía!   In a café in Mexico, Claudio meets his American friend, Larry, who appears to be very upset. Read their conversation. Then answer the question that follows.

Claudio:	**Hola, Larry. Pero, hombre, ¿qué te pasa?**
Larry:	**Ay, perdona, Claudio. Necesito hablar con Jorge urgentemente y no puedo encontrar su número de teléfono.**
Claudio:	**Pero . . . si está en la guía telefónica. Estoy seguro.**
Larry:	**¡Qué va! ¡No está! No hay un Jorge Salinas Chacón. Hay un Héctor Chacón y un Julio Chacón y una . . .**
Claudio:	**¿Chacón? ¡Pero, Larry, . . . por favor!**

What was Larry's mistake?

1. He was not spelling **Chacón** correctly.
2. He did not know that Jorge had an unlisted number.
3. He does not know how to use a Hispanic telephone directory.

❏ Check your answer on page 418.

LECCIÓN 2

ciento ochenta y uno   **181**

Purpose   This section provides additional reading practice as students learn to avoid cross-cultural misunderstandings when using a Hispanic telephone directory.

Suggestions   Read the dialogue aloud for students so they may hear the proper intonation. Then have them read it. Check comprehension with appropriate questions. Before turning to explanations of answers on page 418, have students themselves try to explain why the wrong answers are wrong.

Answers

1 There is no evidence that Larry didn't spell **Chacón** correctly. Try again.
2 Larry says that the number is not listed, but Claudio says that he is certain it is. There must be another reason.
③ Larry is looking for the number of Jorge Salinas Chacón under **Chacón** and not under **Salinas**. He has forgotten that names are alphabetized by the father's last name, not the mother's maiden name. This is the correct answer.

Y ahora, ¡a leer!

Purpose This section provides additional reading practice as students learn how to use telephone directories in Hispanic countries.

Antes de empezar

This chart serves as an advance organizer for the **Datos personales** reading that follows. Do not be concerned if students do not have correct answers initially. After students do the reading, have them go back to their charts and change any of their answers, if they wish. Then go over the correct answers with class.

Answers

1 In U.S.: first and last name and address. In Mexico: students should assume this much appears in Mexican directories as well. In the reading, they will learn that, in addition, Hispanic directories give both parents' last names, whether women are married, single, or widowed, and postal zone or ZIP code.

2 In U.S.: usually one week. In Mexico: one to five years.

3 In U.S.
Ricardo López Cabrera
Lupe Llanos Carrión
Enrique Chávez Castro
Manuel Cruz Cernuda
María Luisa Carrillo Corella
Marta León Cuadrado

In Mexico
María Luisa Carrillo Corella
Manuel Cruz Cernuda
Enrique Chávez Castro
Marta León Cuadrado
Ricardo López Cabrera
Lupe Llanos Carrión

IMPACTO CULTURAL

Y ahora, ¡a leer!

Antes de empezar

Prepare a chart similar to the one below and fill in the information requested about phone companies and telephone books in the United States and Mexico. If you don't know the answers, make reasoned guesses.

La guía telefónica	En EE.UU.	En México
1. Besides the phone number, what other information about subscribers appears in the telephone book?	1. ____ 2. ____ 3. ____	1. ____ 2. ____ 3. ____
2. After you call, how long do you think you have to wait for the phone company to install a phone in your home?	(day, week, month, year, longer)	(day, week, month, year, longer)
3. List the following names alphabetically as you would expect them to appear in a phone book. María Luisa Carrillo Corella Lupe Llanos Carrión Manuel Cruz Cernuda Ricardo López Cabrera Enrique Chávez Castro Marta León Cuadrado	1. ____ 2. ____ 3. ____ 4. ____ 5. ____ 6. ____	1. ____ 2. ____ 3. ____ 4. ____ 5. ____ 6. ____

Verifiquemos

Answer the questions that follow by scanning this information taken from a Mexico City phone book.

CASTRILLÓN LEONOR VALDEZ DE
   HOMERO 1837-D-701 ZP 10 395-0684
CASTRILLÓN LUZ AGUILAR DE
   E PALLARES PORTILLO 65-2 ZP 21 544-1587
CASTRILLÓN MA TERESA LEÓN DE
   TEHUANTEPEC 144-12 ZP 06 564-5062
	CASTRILLÓN MA TERESA V VDA DE
	   HERSCHELL 10 ZP 5 545-950
	CASTRILLÓN Y LUNA VÍCTOR M
	   COLORINES 49-401 CP 04380 574-119
	CASTRILLÓN YOLANDA FERNÁNDEZ VDA DE
	   EL GRECO 39-202-B CP 03910 598-193

1. Hay sólo un hombre en esta lista. ¿Cómo se llama? ¿Cuál es su dirección? ¿Su número de teléfono?
2. Una de las María Teresas es viuda. ¿Cuál es su número de teléfono?
3. ¿Cuál es el apellido del esposo de la otra María Teresa?
4. ¿Hay otras viudas? ¿Quiénes son?
5. ¿Es casada o soltera Luz Aguilar? Explica tu respuesta.

182 ciento ochenta y dos

UNIDAD 4

Verifiquemos

Answers

1 Víctor M. Castrillón y Luna. Dirección: Colorines 49-401 Casilla Postal 04380. 574-1194.

2 545-9507.

3 Apellido del esposo de la otra es Castrillón.

4 Yolanda Fernández Castrillón es viuda.

5 Es casada. El apellido de su esposo es Castrillón. El apellido de su padre es Aguilar.

Datos personales

Un soltero acaba de conocer a una mujer muy interesante en una fiesta. Ahora él quiere invitarla a salir pero, antes de llamar, decide informarse un poco sobre ella. ¿Es divorciada o viuda? ¿Dónde vive? ¿Cuál es el apellido de sus padres? ¿El de su ex-esposo, si fue casada? ¿Cuál es su número de teléfono? ¿Su zona postal?

Toda esta información está a mano, para cualquier persona que tenga un teléfono instalado en su casa bajo su propio nombre. ¿Dónde? ¡En la guía telefónica, por supuesto!

La guía telefónica en países hispanos incluye muchos más datos personales que la guía telefónica en Estados Unidos, especialmente sobre las mujeres. Y también hay otras diferencias. Por ejemplo, los nombres de individuos están bajo el primer apellido, no el segundo.

Probablemente, usted ahora está pensando que es muy fácil conseguir información personal en un país hispano . . . pero hay un pequeño problema. En Estados Unidos todo el mundo tiene teléfono pero en los países hispanos, ¡no! En muchos países hispanos es difícil y caro conseguir una línea telefónica. A veces hay que esperar dos o tres años, y aún más, antes de que le puedan instalar un teléfono en casa. Por eso, mucha gente ni tiene teléfono en casa ni está incluida en la guía telefónica.

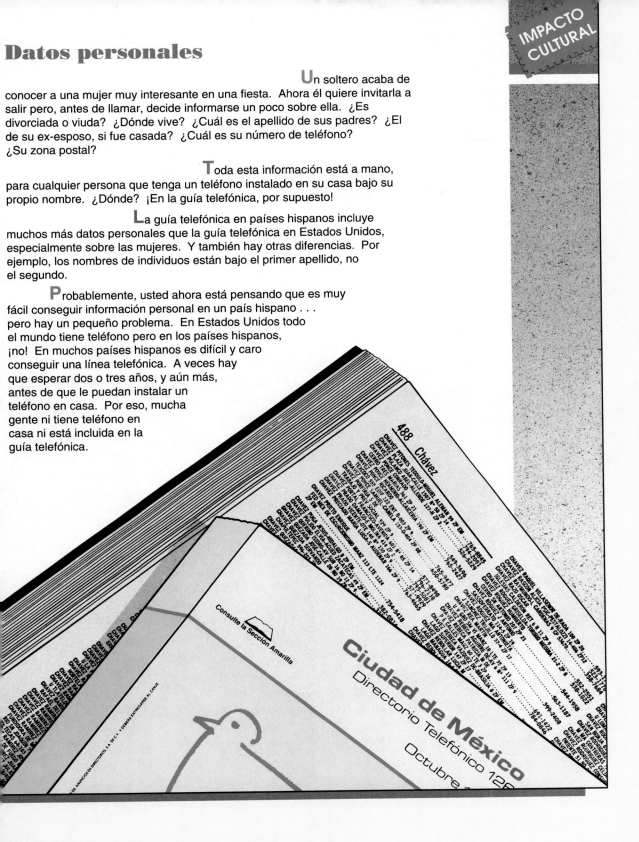

OBJECTIVES

Communicative Goals

- Describing how people feel
- Describing what is happening at the moment

Reading

- *Leamos ahora*
  Los hispanos en Estados Unidos: Presente y futuro
- Reading strategy:
  Identifying the main idea

Writing

- *Escribamos un poco*
  Writing a short composition
- Writing strategy:
  Organizing information

Structure

- **4.8 Estar** with adjectives
- **4.9** The present progressive and **-ndo** verb forms

ACTIVE VOCABULARY

Estados de ánimo

cansado(a)
contento(a)
emocionado(a)
furioso(a)
listo(a)
ocupado(a)
preocupado(a)
triste

Verbos

cortar
charlar
hacer dibujos
hacer ejercicio
tocar un instrumento

Palabras y expresiones

animal
artículo
delicioso(a)
hispano(a)
pastel

¡Por fin!
¡Qué mala suerte!
¡Qué ridículo!

¡Los novios están bailando !

ANTICIPEMOS

¿Qué piensas tú?

1. Look carefully at the photo on the left and at the drawing above. How many different activities can you find people doing? Name as many as you can.

2. Can you find the boy standing on his head in the drawing? Describe where he is to someone in the class who can't find him.

3. Look again at the people in the photo and the drawing. How do you think these people feel? What words come to mind when you try to describe how they feel?

4. Where do you think the photo on the left was taken? Could it be in any city in the United States? Why or why not?

5. Which cities in the United States have strong Hispanic influences? Which Spanish-speaking countries do you think have influenced these cities? Why?

6. What do you think you will be able to talk about when you have finished this lesson?

¿Qué piensas tú?

Answers

1 Dancing, standing, looking, crying, thinking, smiling, eating, drinking, talking, playing, singing, sitting, walking, cutting, serving, sleeping, hiding, toasting, etc.

2 He is in front of a woman wearing a blue dress who is dancing with a man in a gray suit. He is behind a woman in a yellow dress introducing two men. The men are shaking hands.

3 Happy, sad, bored, etc. Encourage students to describe one of the figures in the drawing and tell how he/she feels: "The boy sleeping is tired and bored."

4 San Antonio, Texas. This may be obvious since this unit is set in San Antonio. Students should observe architecture, climate, dress, obvious Mexican influence. They should recognize that it could be any city in the Southwest but not in other parts of the country.

5 Major cities in southwestern states such as Albuquerque and Santa Fe, New Mexico, Phoenix and Tucson, Arizona, San Diego and Los Angeles, California (Mexican influence); New York (Puerto Rican influence); Miami, Florida (Cuban influence).

▶**6** **What people are doing right at the moment; how people feel. Students may have difficulty expressing the first concept here. Help them focus by pointing out that all these things are going on at the same time. Have them notice how they phrase their answers—with *-ing* verbs (present participles).**

Purpose To focus students on vocabulary that expresses emotions and that generates narration of events taking place right at the moment. Also to encourage students to develop and use critical thinking skills as they learn to recognize and appreciate cultural influences on several major American cities.

Suggestion Have students describe the illustrations using previously learned vocabulary and structures before asking the *¿Qué piensas tú?* questions.

TAPE/
DISC

33:47–
36:05

Side 4, 22806 to 26952

Comprehension Checks

A full set of the **Comprehension Checks** is available on cards in the Teacher's Resource Package.

1   33:54

Suggestions Identify characters and relationships. Act out **nerviosa, contenta**.
1 ¿Quién es?
2 ¿Son sus dibujos?
3 ¿Son dibujos de la boda de su papá?
4 ¿Quién es? *(Betty, Ana, Lupe)*
5 ¿Está Betty muy nerviosa?
6 ¿Quién está nerviosa?
7 ¿Están Ana y Lupe nerviosas?
8 ¿Están contentas?
9 ¿Les gustan las bodas?

Side 4, 23025 to 23705

2   34:18

Suggestions Act out **triste**. Contrast **triste** and **emocionado** by showing contrasting situations: broken heart = **triste**, beautiful music = **emocionado**; dog died = **triste**, sweethearts embracing = **emociona-do**. Act out or draw **llorando**. Continue asking questions, as above.

Side 4, 23728 to 24185

3   34:34

Suggestions Give the names of some **canciones de amor**. Act out **bailando**. Point out Papá and Betty. Continue asking questions, as above.

Side 4, 24205 to 24755

4   34:53

Suggestions Identify characters and relationship. Act out **furioso, comer, no permite**.
1 ¿Quién es? *(Point to Pepe, abuela.)*
Continue asking questions, as above, or use the **Comprehension Checks** in the TRP.

Side 4, 24785 to 25080

Hola. Éstos son mis dibujos de la boda de papá.

1 Betty está lista para entrar en la iglesia. Está muy nerviosa. Ana y Lupe no están nerviosas. Están contentas porque les gustan las bodas.

2 Mi abuela y la madre de Betty están llorando. Pero no están tristes; están emocionadas. ¡Qué ridículas son las bodas!

3 ¡Qué ridícula es la recepción! La banda está tocando música romántica y la cantante está cantando canciones de amor. ¡Pero nadie está bailando, . . . sólo Papá y Betty!

4 Pepe está furioso. Quiere comer pastel pero abuela no le permite comer nada.

186 ciento ochenta y seis

Purpose This section develops listening and reading comprehension of active vocabulary. Students should not be expected to achieve productive mastery at this point. The goal is not to translate but to read/listen for comprehension.

5

Suggestions Identify Paquito. Act out **cansado**.
1 ¿Quién es?
2 ¿Está cansado Paquito?
3 ¿Está aburrido Paquito?
4 ¿Cómo está Paquito, divertido o aburrido?

Side 4, 25100 to 25410

6

Suggestions Act out cutting the cake. Use body language to clarify **¡Por fin!**
1 ¿Quiénes son?
2 ¿Están cortando el pastel?
3 ¿Quiénes están cortando el pastel?
4 ¿Qué están cortando?

Side 4, 25430 to 25660

7

Suggestions Identify characters and relationships—Pamela and Leslie are Kevin's cousins. Mime **bailar, comiendo, bebiendo.**
1 ¿Quiénes son?
2 ¿Quiere bailar Pamela? ¿Leslie?
3 ¿Quiénes quieren bailar con Julio?
4 ¿Con quién quieren bailar?
5 ¿Está comiendo pastel Julio? *(others)*
6 ¿Está bebiendo ponche Julio? *(others)*
7 ¿Quién está comiendo pastel (bebiendo ponche)?
8 ¿Qué está haciendo Julio?
9 ¿En tu opinión, son ridículas las chicas?

Side 4, 25678 to 26165

8

Suggestions Identify characters doing various activities. Contrast with Pepe and Paquito, who aren't doing anything.
1 ¿Quién es? *(Point to Pepe, Paquito.)*
2 ¿Qué están haciendo los chicos?
3 ¿Quiénes no están haciendo nada?
4 ¿Qué hay que hacer para los adultos?
5 ¿Qué hay que hacer para los niños?
6 ¿Son aburridas las bodas para los niños?

Side 4, 26188 to 26952

Suggestions Begin by having students close their books while you narrate one section at a time, using the transparencies to clarify meaning without translation. Then ask **Comprehension Checks**. Repeat this process with each section.

Using the video Play one section at a time after narrating it using the transparencies. Freeze the video and ask **Comprehension Checks**. Repeat this process with each section.

Point out Pamela and Leslie are typical of Hispanic teenagers in the U.S. who continue to use Spanish at home but speak mostly English at school and with friends. Pamela, the older sister, speaks better Spanish, as is often the case. Leslie speaks Spanish with a noticeable accent. The girls need to make an effort to maintain their Hispanic language and culture, or they may lose them.

36:06–
38:57

Side 4, 26960 to 32110

Early Production Checks

A full set of the **Early Production Checks** is available on cards in the Teacher's Resource Package.

1   **36:11**

¡Ay! Es tan guapo.

1 ¿Quién es? *(Point to Pamela, then to Leslie.)*   *Pamela / Leslie.*

2 ¿Le gustan las bodas a Pamela? ¿Y a Leslie?   *Sí / Sí.*

3 ¿Está comiendo Pamela? ¿Leslie?   *Sí / No.*

4 ¿Está rica la comida?   *Sí.*

5 ¿Cómo está la comida?   *Rica.*

6 ¿Por qué no está comiendo Leslie, está triste o está pensando en Julio?   *Está pensando en Julio.*

7 ¿En quién está pensando, en Kevin o en Julio?   *En Julio.*

8 ¿Está Kevin al lado de tía Betty? ¿Y Julio?   *Sí / Sí.*

9 ¿Dónde están Kevin y Julio?   *Al lado de tía Betty.*

10 ¿Le gusta Julio a Leslie?   *Sí.*

11 ¿Cómo es Julio, guapo o feo?   *Guapo.*

12 ¿Está comiendo y bebiendo Julio?   *Sí.*

13 ¿Qué está haciendo Julio?   *Está comiendo y bebiendo.*

14 ¿Están hablando Kevin y Julio?   *Sí.*

15 ¿Qué están haciendo Kevin y Julio?   *Están hablando.*

16 ¿Quiere Leslie hablar con Julio?   *Sí.*

Side 4, 27152 to 28680

¿QUÉ DECIMOS...?

Al hablar de lo que está pasando

1   ¡Ay! Es tan guapo.

188   ciento ochenta y ocho

UNIDAD 4

Purpose   These dialogues show the language of emotions and activities of the moment in more natural contexts. Unfamiliar structures are intended solely for comprehension, not for mastery or production by the students.

2 ¡Y ahora están bailando!

3 ¿De veras?

¡Y ahora están bailando!

Accept brief phrases or one- and two-word answers to all **Early Production Checks,** as shown in **1** on page 188. It is not necessary for students to answer in complete sentences.

1 ¿Quién es? *(Point to Leslie, then to Pamela.)*
2 ¿Están bailando los novios?
3 ¿Están bailando Pamela y Leslie?
4 ¿Está bailando Kevin?
5 ¿Qué está haciendo Kevin?
6 ¿Con quién está bailando Kevin?
7 ¿Está bailando o conversando Julio?
8 ¿Con quién está conversando?
9 Y ahora, ¿qué están haciendo Julio y Ana?
10 ¿Tiene buena o mala suerte Leslie?
11 ¿Por qué tiene mala suerte?

Side 4, 28705 to 29785

¿De veras?

¡OJO! **Vea** is intended for recognition only. Students should not be expected to produce this form nor understand its use at this point.

1 ¿Quiénes son?
2 ¿Están hablando Pamela y Leslie?
3 ¿De qué están hablando?
4 ¿Está mirando Pamela a Julio?
5 ¿Está mirando Leslie a Julio?
6 ¿Son hermanas Pamela y Leslie?
7 ¿En la opinión de su hermana, es tonta Leslie?
8 ¿Todavía está bailando Julio con Ana?
9 ¿Qué hacen los chicos, vienen hacia las chicas?
10 ¿Cómo está Leslie ahora?
11 ¿Por qué está nerviosa Leslie?

Side 4, 29805 to 30901

Suggestions Begin by having students close their books while you narrate one section at a time, using the transparencies to clarify meaning without translation. Then ask **Early Production Checks.** Repeat this process with each section.

Using the video Play one section at a time after narrating it using the transparencies. Freeze the video and ask **Early Production Checks.** Repeat this process with each section.

Pero, ¿por qué ahora?

1 ¿Quién es? *(Point to each one.)*
2 ¿Son Pamela y Leslie primas o hermanas de Kevin?
3 ¿Cómo están Pamela y Leslie?
4 ¿Le gusta la música a Julio?
5 ¿Invita Julio a Pamela o a Leslie a bailar?
6 ¿Acepta la invitación Pamela?
7 En tu opinión, ¿está cansada Pamela?
8 ¿Invita Julio a Leslie a bailar?
9 ¿Acepta Leslie?
10 ¿No está cansada Leslie?
11 ¿Qué van a hacer los novios, cortar el pastel?
12 ¿Hay música cuando cortan el pastel?
13 ¿Bailan Julio y Leslie?
14 ¿Está contenta o triste Leslie?

Side 4, 30926 to 32110

CHARLEMOS UN POCO

A. ¿Quién está hablando? ¿Quién dice esto, Pamela, Leslie, Kevin o Julio?

 Pamela   **Leslie**   **Kevin**   **Julio**

1. ¿Por qué no estás comiendo?
2. ¡Kevin, nuestro primo nuevo!
3. ¡Qué tonta eres!
4. ¿Hacia nosotras? ¿De veras?
5. ¡Estoy tan nerviosa!
6. Hola, primas. ¿Cómo están?
7. Gracias, pero estoy cansada.
8. Leslie, ¿quieres?

B. ¡Una boda! Mañana es la boda de tu primo. ¿Cómo está la familia del novio?

 EJEMPLO **La novia está muy nerviosa pero muy contenta.**

1. yo
2. su mamá
3. sus abuelos
4. su padrastro
5. sus hermanastros
6. la novia
7. el novio

- cansado
- contento
- aburrido
- nervioso
- listo
- emocionado
- furioso
- triste
- ocupado

C. ¿Qué emoción? Imagínate que tú y estas personas están en estos lugares o situaciones. ¿Cómo se sienten?

 EJEMPLO tú: en la clase de español
Estoy un poco nervioso(a), pero no estoy aburrido(a).

1. tú y un(a) amigo(a): en una fiesta
2. tú: en un examen final
3. tú: en la oficina del director
4. tu familia: en una boda
5. tú y tu novio(a): en una discoteca
6. tu padre: en el trabajo
7. tus amigos: en el recreo
8. tú: en el gimnasio

LECCIÓN 3

Estar + adjective
Saying how you feel

Estoy furioso con los niños.
Mamá **está** muy **emocionada**.
Estamos contentos pero **cansados**.

See ¿Por qué se dice así?, page G59, section 4.8.

CHARLEMOS UN POCO

A. ¿Quién está hablando?
Read each statement and have class identify who is speaking.
1 Pamela
2 Leslie
3 Pamela
4 Leslie
5 Leslie
6 Kevin
7 Pamela
8 Julio

Extension Call on individual students to read the statements.

B. ¡Una boda! Do in pairs. Allow 3–4 min. Then redo as class activity. Answers will vary. Check for adjective agreement.

C. ¿Qué emoción? Do in groups of three to four. Allow 1 min for each group to list possibilities for **en una fiesta**. Ask one group to read their list and other groups to add to it. Repeat process with other items.

Suggestion Encourage students to personalize responses to **B** and **C**.

Purpose These activities provide guided practice to students learning to describe what is happening at the moment and how people are feeling. The repetition built into the activities is intentional.

1 ¿Estás leyendo el periódico?
   No, estoy estudiando español.
2 ¿Estás descansando? No, estoy aprendiendo un baile nuevo.
3 ¿Estás haciendo la tarea?
   No, estoy viendo la tele.
4 ¿Estás descansando?
   No, estoy escuchando la radio.
5 ¿Estás practicando el piano?
   No, estoy leyendo un libro.
6 ¿Estás preparando la comida?
   No, estoy estudiando.
7 ¿Estás comiendo? No, estoy escribiendo una carta.
8 ¿Estás viendo un programa en la tele? No, estoy leyendo un libro.
9 ¿Estás practicando el piano?
   No, estoy descansando.
10 ¿Estás escuchando discos?
   No, estoy preparando la comida.

Extension Use this transparency (first seen in Unit 3) to have students tell what the people you point to are doing, using the present progressive.

The present progressive
Used to describe an action in progress

> **estar + -ndo** verb form

-ar verbs: **-ando**
> ¿Están estudi**ando**?
> No, estamos descans**ando**.

-er/-ir verbs: **-iendo**
> ¿Qué estás hac**iendo**?
> Estoy v**iendo** la tele y
> le**yendo*** el periódico.

*In **-er/-ir** verbs, **-iendo** changes to **-yendo** if the verb stem ends in a vowel.

See ¿Por qué se dice así?,
page G62, section 4.9.

CH. Rin, rin . . .   Un(a) amigo(a) te habla por teléfono y quiere saber qué estás haciendo. ¿Qué le dices?

MODELO   descansar / comer
> Compañero(a): **¿Estás descansando?**
> Tú: **No, estoy comiendo.**

1. leer el periódico / estudiar español
2. descansar / aprender un baile nuevo
3. hacer la tarea / ver la tele
4. descansar / escuchar la radio
5. practicar el piano / leer un libro
6. preparar la comida / estudiar
7. comer / escribir una carta
8. ver un programa en la tele / leer un libro
9. practicar el piano / descansar
10. escuchar discos / preparar la comida

D. ¡Todos están ocupados!   ¿Qué están haciendo estas personas?

MODELO   Natalia y Alicia
Natalia y Alicia están estudiando.

1.   2.

Jorge   Samuel y Marcos

3.

Susana

4.

Alfredo y Marta

5.

Mari Carmen

6.

Paco y Beatriz

7.

Arturo

8.

Teresa y Anita

LECCIÓN 3

D. ¡Todos están ocupados!
1 Jorge está escuchando la radio.
2 Samuel y Marcos están leyendo el periódico.
3 Susana está corriendo (en el parque).
4 Alfredo y Marta están bailando.
5 Mari Carmen está limpiando (la casa).
6 Paco y Beatriz están comiendo pastel.
7 Arturo está jugando fútbol.
8 Teresa y Anita están paseando en bicicleta.

E. ¡Qué trabajo!

Los reporteros están escribiendo un artículo.
Los maestros están calificando exámenes.
Los secretarios están hablando por teléfono.
Los artistas están haciendo dibujos.
Los músicos están tocando instrumentos musicales.
Los cocineros están preparando comida.
Los políticos están hablando con la gente.
Los enfermeros están trabajando en los hospitales.
Los escritores están escribiendo libros (leyendo libros).
Los futbolistas están jugando fútbol (haciendo ejercicio).

F. ¿Sus parientes?

Have students first do activity in pairs Then do with whole class.

1 ¿Qué está haciendo el padre de la novia? Está sacando fotos.
2 ¿Qué están haciendo los tíos de la novia? Están tomando refrescos.
3 ¿Qué está haciendo la hermana de la novia? Está bailando con su novio.
4 ¿Qué está haciendo la madrastra de la novia? Está saludando a los invitados.
5 ¿Qué están haciendo los abuelos de la novia? Están hablando con los novios.
6 ¿Qué están haciendo los hermanos de la novia? Están comiendo pastel.
7 ¿Qué está haciendo el sobrino de la novia? Está tocando el piano.
8 ¿Qué está haciendo la tía de la novia? Está charlando con amigos.

E. ¡Qué trabajo! Son las diez de la mañana. ¿Qué están haciendo estas personas?

MODELO **Los políticos están hablando con la gente.**

reporteros	preparar comida
maestros	jugar fútbol
secretarios	hacer ejercicio
artistas	hablar con la gente
músicos	leer libros
cocineros	trabajar en los hospitales
políticos	calificar exámenes
enfermeros	escribir libros
escritores	hacer dibujos
futbolistas	hablar por teléfono
	escribir un artículo
	tocar instrumentos musicales

F. ¿Sus parientes? Estás en una recepción de bodas. ¿Qué están haciendo los parientes de la novia? Pregúntale a un(a) amigo(a).

MODELO prima / cortar el pastel
Tú: **¿Qué está haciendo la prima de la novia?**
Compañero(a): **Está cortando el pastel.**

1. padre / sacar fotos
2. tíos / tomar refrescos
3. hermana / bailar con su novio
4. madrastra / saludar a los invitados
5. abuelos / hablar con los novios
6. hermanos / comer pastel
7. sobrino / tocar el piano
8. tía / charlar con amigos

CHARLEMOS UN POCO MÁS

A. ¿Qué están haciendo? Es el fin de semana y estás en el parque. ¿Qué están haciendo estas personas?

CHARLEMOS UN POCO MÁS

A. ¿Qué están haciendo?
Call on individuals to describe as many different actions taking place as possible.

Extension Divide class into three groups. Have each group write possible answers on separate slips of paper for one of these questions: **¿Quién? ¿Qué? ¿Dónde?** Put the slips into three bags labeled to correspond to the three questions. Have students form original (and perhaps humorous) sentences by drawing a slip from each bag. Example: **El presidente / está jugando tenis / en la oficina.**

Purpose These activities are designed to allow students to create with language recently learned as they describe what is happening at the moment in a variety of open-ended contexts.

B. ¡Qué divertido! Have students work in groups of three to four. Allow 3–4 min. Insist that everyone participates.

Extension Repeat the activity having everyone write five things they do on the weekend, after school, at the mall, at a football game.

C. ¡Video! Have groups read their descriptions and have class guess where they are. Tell students they may select places not on list.

CH. ¿Cuál es? Allow 3–4 min. Students should find five differences.

Extension Use the Unit 3, Lesson 2, *Charlemos un poco más,* Activity **CH** copymaster to have students tell what is happening in the park using the present progressive.

B. ¡Qué divertido!   Write down five things that you might do at a party. Then, in small groups, take turns acting out the activities on your list, while your classmates identify them.

 EJEMPLO   Compañero(a):   **¿Estás tocando el piano?**
Tú: **Sí, estoy tocando el piano.** o
No, no estoy tocando el piano.

C. ¡Video!   You and your partner made a video to send to a friend in another state. Prepare the narration that will be added to the video. Tell what you and your friends are doing and feeling in each shot. Be as creative as possible.

 EJEMPLO   tú y dos amigos: en un jardín zoológico
Aquí estamos caminando y mirando los animales. Hay muchas personas aquí hoy. David y Roberto están comiendo pizza. Estamos muy contentos.

1. un amigo: en la cafetería
2. tu familia: en una boda
3. tú: en un baile
4. tú y varios amigos: en el parque
5. dos amigas: en un centro comercial
6. tú y . . . : en . . .

CH. ¿Cuál es la diferencia?   Your teacher will give you a drawing almost identical to the one below. Describe it to your partner. Your partner, in turn, will describe the drawing in the text to you. Without looking at each others' drawings, find five differences between them.

 EJEMPLO   Tú: **La novia está bailando. Está bailando con su abuelo.**
Compañero(a):   **Sí, la novia está bailando con su abuelo.** o
No, la novia no está bailando con su abuelo.

UNIDAD 4

Dramatizaciones

DRAMATIZACIONES

A. ¡Estoy solo! Tell students playing relatives that they must decide between themselves who says what.

A, B, C. Assign **A, B,** and **C** at the same time. Allow students 5–6 min to prepare role plays. Call on various groups to present their role plays to class. Be sure to ask comprehension check questions after each presentation.

A. ¡Estoy solo! You are at home alone and two relatives drop by for a visit. What do you do?

You
- Greet them.
- Say where they are and what each person is doing.
- Respond.

Relatives
- Ask where various members of the family are.
- Ask at what time the parents will return (**regresar**).
- Say the two of you will return at that time also.

B. ¡Una fiesta! A friend of yours is ill and is missing a great party. Call him or her from the party. Be sure to do the following:
- Greet your friend and identify yourself.
- Find out how your friend is feeling.
- Explain where you are and describe what is happening.
- Answer your friend's questions about who is at the party and what they are doing.
- Say how you are feeling at the moment.
- End the conversation politely.

C. ¡Preséntame! You are at a party talking to a friend when you see someone you just have to meet. Your friend, it turns out, knows that person very well. Role-play the situation. Find out as much as you can about the person you are interested in: name, family, school, interests, etc.

CH. ¿Quién está hablando? You are with your friend having a soft drink at a favorite after-school hangout. However, you are in a corner booth with your back toward everyone else. Role-play the situation as you ask your friend who is there and what they are doing.

Purpose In this section, students recycle, in student-centered role plays, all previously learned structures and vocabulary needed to describe what is happening at the moment. Encourage students to work without their books when preparing and performing their role plays.

LEAMOS AHORA

A. Anticipemos.
Suggestions Have students answer these questions in small groups. After students have read the selection, have them come back to their predictions and see how accurate they were.

1 Estoy de acuerdo.
2 Estoy de acuerdo.
3 No estoy de acuerdo.
4 No estoy de acuerdo.
5 No estoy de acuerdo.

B. La idea principal.
Point out Sometimes it is necessary to read the first two sentences of a paragraph to get a clear indication of the paragraph's content.

1 Paragraph 2
2 Paragraph 4
3 Paragraph 1
4 Paragraph 3

LEAMOS AHORA

Reading strategy:
Identifying the main idea

A. Anticipemos. Before you read the following selection, record your impressions of Hispanics in the United States by indicating if you agree (**Estoy de acuerdo**) or disagree (**No estoy de acuerdo**) with the statements that follow. After you read the selection, come back and change any of your answers, if necessary.

1. Muchos estados, ríos, montañas, ciudades, calles y vecindades en Estados Unidos tienen nombres hispanos.
2. El inglés tiene muchas palabras de origen español.
3. Todos los hispanos en Estados Unidos viven en California, Texas y la Florida.
4. Todos los hispanos en Estados Unidos vienen de México.
5. Estados Unidos ya no acepta a inmigrantes latinos.

B. La idea principal. When reading, it is important to identify the main ideas expressed by the author. Usually each paragraph expresses one or two main ideas. Often the main idea is stated in the first sentences of a paragraph.

Before you begin to read, look at the main ideas listed below. Then scan the first sentence of each of the four paragraphs to find the main ideas. Match the main ideas listed below with the appropriate paragraphs. Work *very quickly*. Do not read every word at this point.

1. Hay hispanos en muchas regiones de Estados Unidos.
2. La población hispana es de gran importancia ahora y va a ser de gran importancia en el futuro de Estados Unidos.
3. En Estados Unidos hay mucha influencia hispana.
4. Hay hispanos de muchos países en Estados Unidos.

C. EE.UU. hispano. Now read the article and then answer the questions.

Verifiquemos

1. Name as many rivers, mountains, states, and cities in the United States as you can with Spanish names.

2. **Los hispanos en Estados Unidos: Presente y futuro** is about
   a. the history of Hispanics in the United States.
   b. the influence of Hispanics in United States culture.
   c. the influence of the United States in Hispanic culture.
   ch. None of the above.

3. The influence of the Spanish language on American English
   a. is apparent in the names of foods and architectural styles.
   b. can only be heard in the southwestern United States.
   c. is limited to the names of foods.
   ch. All of the above.

198 *ciento noventa y ocho*

UNIDAD 4

Purpose Here students will learn to identify the main ideas of a passage as they read. Students are not expected to understand every word. Rather, they should focus on looking for the main idea of each paragraph.

Los hispanos en Estados Unidos: Presente y futuro

Hoy día es imposible visitar Estados Unidos y no ver, por todas partes, la influencia hispana. Ríos, montañas, siete estados y un gran número de ciudades, calles y vecindades llevan nombres hispanos. Ni la lengua del país ha escapado la influencia hispana. En el oeste, hablamos de **rodeo, lasso, corral** y **bronco;** en la construcción, de **adobe** y **patio;** en la cocina, de **tomate, chocolate, chile** y recientemente de **tapas, nachos** y **fajitas.**

La mayoría de los hispanos en Estados Unidos viven en el suroeste del país. Pero esto está cambiando. En los últimos años, nuevos grupos de hispanos se han establecido en otras partes del país, en particular en la Florida y en Nueva York.

La mayor parte de hispanos en Estados Unidos vienen de México. Pero también hay números impresionantes de puertorriqueños, cubanos, salva-

> **Hoy día es imposible visitar Estados Unidos y no ver, por todas partes, la influencia hispana.**

doreños, nicaragüenses y otros. El crecimiento de la población hispana influye en la realidad política del país. Esto es verdad, en particular, en estados como California, Texas, la Florida e Illinois.

Sin duda, la población latina ya es una fuerza vital en Estados Unidos. Pero, ¿cuál va a ser su importancia en el futuro de este país? Las proyecciones de la Oficina del Censo indican que esta comunidad va a tener una extraordinaria importancia política y social.

Distribución geográfica de EE.UU. hispano

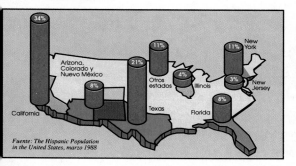

Fuente: The Hispanic Population in the United States, marzo 1988

Origen de la población hispana de EE.UU.

Crecimiento de la población hispana

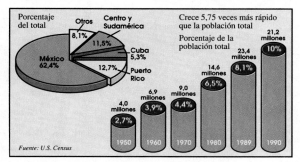

Fuente: U.S. Census

4. The majority of Hispanics in the United States live in the
   a. east.   **c.** southwest.
   b. south.   **ch.** northeast.

5. Over 50% of the Hispanics living in the United States come from
   a. South America.   **c.** Cuba.
   b. Central America.   **ch.** Mexico.

6. The Hispanic population has already been politically influential in
   a. California and Texas.
   b. Illinois.
   c. Florida.
   ch. All of the above.

Verifiquemos

Answers

1 Some possibilities are:
  Rivers: Rio Grande, Rio Colorado, Rio Sacramento
  Mountains: Sierra Nevada, Sangre de Cristo
  States: California, Colorado, Florida, Nevada, New Mexico, Texas, Montana
  Cities: Albuquerque, Amarillo, El Paso, Las Vegas, Los Angeles, San Antonio, San Francisco, Santa Barbara, Santa Fe, Buena Vista, Valparaiso, Boca Raton . . .

2 b
3 a
4 c
5 ch
6 ch

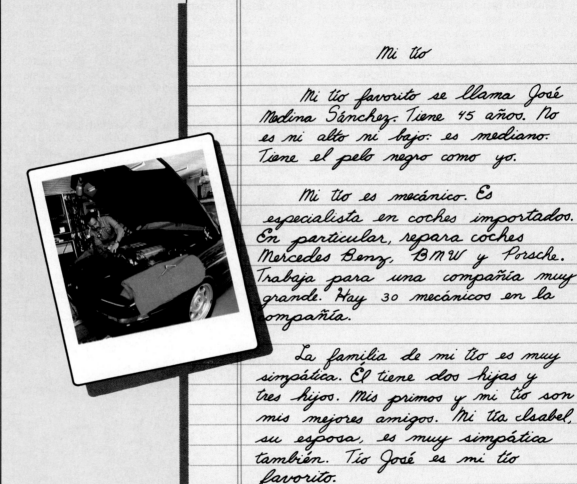

ESCRIBAMOS UN POCO

A. Planeando. Students should recognize that Antonio likes and admires his uncle. He says that José is his favorite uncle and describes what José does with a sense of pride.

Writing strategy:
Organizing information

A. Planeando. Read and discuss the following composition about José Medina Sánchez. The composition was written by his nephew, Antonio. How does Antonio feel about his uncle?

Mi tío

Mi tío favorito se llama José Medina Sánchez. Tiene 45 años. No es ni alto ni bajo: es mediano. Tiene el pelo negro como yo.

Mi tío es mecánico. Es especialista en coches importados. En particular, repara coches Mercedes Benz, BMW y Porsche. Trabaja para una compañía muy grande. Hay 30 mecánicos en la compañía.

La familia de mi tío es muy simpática. Él tiene dos hijas y tres hijos. Mis primos y mi tío son mis mejores amigos. Mi tía Isabel, su esposa, es muy simpática también. Tío José es mi tío favorito.

UNIDAD 4

Purpose In this section, students are asked to apply speaking and writing skills developed in the unit to a real-life writing task. They will use strategies they began to develop in Unit 1: prewriting, brainstorming and clustering, writing a first draft, peer feedback, and revision.

B. Empezando. Before writing this composition, Antonio assembled all his ideas in the brainstorming cluster that follows. Based on what you read, complete the missing parts in Antonio's cluster.

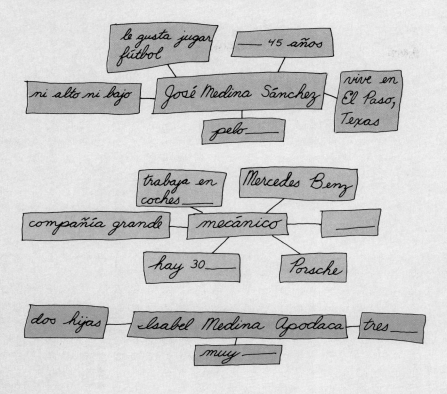

C. Escribiendo. Now plan a composition about your family. You may choose to write about a specific family member or the whole family. Organize your thoughts using a cluster. Then use the information to write a short composition.

CH. Compartiendo. Share the first draft of your composition with two classmates. Ask them what they think of it. Is there anything they don't understand? Is there anything you have not mentioned that they would like to know? Do they think you should change something?

D. Revisando. Based on your classmates' comments, rewrite your composition, changing anything you want. You may add, subtract, or reorder what you had originally written. Before you turn it in for grading, share your composition with two other classmates. Ask them to focus on your grammar, spelling, and punctuation. Correct any errors they notice before turning it in to your teacher.

Suggestion Briefly review the strategies practiced in earlier units: brainstorming and clustering.

B. Empezando. Allow 5–6 min for students to make their own clusters or outlines. Ask volunteers to tell what they have included and how they have grouped ideas. Encourage students to add to theirs as they hear ideas from others.

Suggestions Remind students that they learned about brainstorming in Unit 1. You may want to brainstorm as a class activity, having volunteers list words and ideas on board as they are called out. Have students make brainstorming suggestions in Spanish. Remind them that when brainstorming, all ideas are accepted—they will select those they want to use later.

Look at Antonio's cluster diagram with class. Point out that he took a list like theirs and grouped ideas together, with the main ideas in the center bubbles and details surrounding each main idea. Check to see that students found the missing information in Antonio's cluster.

tiene 45 años
pelo **negro**
trabaja en coches **importados**
BMW
hay 30 **mecánicos**
tres **hijos**
muy **simpática**

C. Escribiendo. Allow students time to write the first draft. Provide guidance where necessary. You may want to assign the first draft as homework.

CH. Compartiendo. Ask students to gather in "response groups" of two or three. Allow them time to share compositions. Remind group members to begin commentary with at least one positive comment and then to make constructive suggestions on content, structure, and vocabulary.

D. Revisando. Tell students you will grade the composition holistically based on overall effectiveness of communication. Underline grammatical errors if you wish, but the grade should be affected only by errors that would confuse a native speaker accustomed to the writing of a nonnative. Later lessons will suggest strategies for improving accuracy. At this stage, students should develop a sense they can already write something a Spanish speaker would find interesting.

UNIT OBJECTIVES

Communicative Goals

When students have completed this unit, they will be able to use Spanish . . .

- to describe location and clothing
- to ask for and give directions
- to order people to do something
- to exchange money
- to express preferences and make a purchase
- to name snack foods, order a snack, and take an order at a café

Culture

In this unit, students will study and compare . . .

- the custom of **el paseo** in Madrid
- the numbering of floors in a department store
- a department store directory

Reading and Writing Strategies

- Reading: Reading aloud
- Writing: Making an outline

Structure

- Affirmative **tú** commands: Regular forms
- Prepositional phrases: Location
- Numbers: 100-1,000,000
- The verbs **saber, salir,** and **dar**
- Stem-changing verbs: **e → ie, o → ue, e → i**
- The verbs **gustar** and **encantar:** A summary
- Ordinal numbers
- **Tener** idioms
- Indirect object pronouns

¡Bienvenidos a Madrid!

UNIT SETTING

Madrid, the capital of Spain, is the seat of the government and a residence for the king of Spain and his family. It is also home to a large number of world-renowned attractions such as the **Museo del Prado,** the **Parque del Retiro,** the **Ciudad Universitaria,** the **Real Academia,** and the **Palacio Real.** Madrid had its beginnings as a little Moorish town and fortress called *Majrit.* It began to take on political importance as early as 1239 when the first Cortes were summoned to meet in Madrid. Its status as capital city, however, was not

Video Notes

To play the montage:

| 00:00 | – | 00:40 |

Side 5, 10 to 1214

To play the entire unit:

| 00:00 | – | 19:58 |

Side 5, 10 to 35909

In this unit, you will hear Argentine as well as Madrid Spanish.

About Argentine Spanish:
The **s** in syllable-final position is pronounced like English aspirated *h*, as it is in 13 of the 20 Spanish-speaking capitals. In the Río de la Plata region, as well as in Medellín, Colombia, and Oaxaca, Mexico, the **ll** and the **y** are combined into one sound, the *zh* in *measure:* **calle** and **mayo** are pronounced *cazhe* and *mazho*. The Argentine teenagers in the video, like the younger generation in Buenos Aires, take this sound one step further, making it similar to the English *sh* in *sheep:* **calle** and **mayo** are pronounced *cashe* and *masho*.

About the Spanish of Madrid:
The **z** and the soft **c** are given the theta [θ] sound in *thin:* **zapato** and **cinco** are pronounced *thapato* and *thinco.* The **ll** and the **y** are combined into one sound, the *dg* of *edge,* so that **calle** and **ayer** are pronounced with an English *j* sound. The **s** tends toward *sh,* but not quite. Notice how **sándwich mixto** is pronounced by the female customer in **Para empezar,** Lesson 3.

Photo

The **Plaza Mayor,** with its remarkable architectural unity, dates back to 1619. It has been used for ceremonial purposes, tourna-ments, horse races, and bullfights. In the center stands a statue of Felipe III on horseback. The buildings on all four sides are currently occupied by municipal offices, shops, and cafés on the lower floors and by family dwellings on the upper floors. In the southwest corner of the Plaza is the picturesque **Arco de los Cuchilleros** *(Arch of the Knifemakers),* which leads into a crowded section of old Madrid.

established until 156l when Felipe II moved the court from Toledo to Madrid. Today Madrid is a city of approximately four and a half million people.

OBJECTIVES

Communicative Goals

- Describing location
- Asking for and giving directions
- Ordering people to do something
- Exchanging money

Culture and Reading

- *¡No me digas!*
  Madrid de noche:
  An evening in Madrid
- *Y ahora, ¡a leer!*
  El paseo:
  The evening walk

Structure

- **5.1** Affirmative **tú** commands: Regular forms
- **5.2** Numbers: 100–1,000,000
- **5.3** The verbs **saber, salir,** and **dar**

ACTIVE VOCABULARY

Al dar direcciones

bajar	a la derecha
cruzar	a la izquierda
al …	al lado de
deber	cerca de
doblar	entre
pasar	lejos
quedar	… de
tomar	media

En la ciudad

almacén	esquina
banco	estación
calle	fuente
correos	hotel
oficina de …	iglesia
sellos	plaza
cuadra	

Casa de cambio

cheque	dinero
… de	dólar
viajero	peseta
cambiar	

Números
100–1.000.000

Verbos

dar	recibir
hacer	saber
poner	salir

Palabras

composición	paseo
guitarra	recepción
hasta	regalo
novio	puerta

¡Toma el metro !

Purpose To focus students on the language related to tourism and sightseeing and to encourage students to observe and compare differences and similarities between Hispanic cities and their own.

A N T I C I P E M O S

¿Qué piensas tú?

Beginning in this lesson, these questions are in Spanish. Students should be allowed to answer in either Spanish or English. Whenever they answer in English, repeat their answer in Spanish and have class repeat after you to familiarize themselves with the new vocabulary.

Answers

1 Un banco. Porque necesitan cambiar dólares a pesetas.

2 50 dólares = 5.750 pesetas. 200 francos franceses = 3.600 pesetas. 100 marcos alemanes = 6.100 pesetas. 300 libras esterlinas = 54.000 pesetas.

Point out Exchange rates change daily. The ones shown were valid at publication. Students may want to research current rates.

3 Banco, correo, hoteles, cafés, restaurantes, museos, parques, monumentos, tiendas, etc. Porque van a necesitar comer, encontrar un lugar donde quedarse, divertirse y comunicarse con sus familiares o amigos.

4 Nuevo vocabulario: *Can you tell me where there is a bank near here? How do I get there? There is one about four blocks from here. Go down this street for two blocks. Then turn left, etc.* Al contestar en inglés, deles usted el español y pídales que lo repitan.

5 Nuevo vocabulario: *Where is the . . . ; How do I get to the . . . ; etc. Right, left, straight ahead, nearby, far away, # blocks, turn, walk, cross (street), pass, etc.* Al contestar en inglés, deles usted el español y pídales que lo repitan.

6 Semejanzas: tipos de negocios, población, tráfico, sistema de transportación **Diferencias:** Estilo y tamaño de edificios, anchura de las calles, letreros neón, etc.

7 Número de personas, diversidad de razas, estado económico, recursos naturales, industria, cultura, etc. La mayoría de las

¿Qué piensas tú?

1. ¿Qué buscan las personas en las fotos? ¿Por qué dices eso?

2. Si un turista norteamericano cambia 50 dólares a pesetas en el banco, ¿cuántas pesetas le dan? ¿Si un turista francés cambia 200 francos? ¿Si un turista alemán cambia 100 marcos? ¿Si un turista inglés cambia 300 libras?

3. En tu opinión, ¿qué lugares de la ciudad van a interesarles a los turistas? ¿Por qué crees eso?

4. En tu opinión, ¿qué le preguntan los jóvenes al policía? ¿Qué contesta el policía?

5. ¿Qué preguntas cuando necesitas direcciones para llegar a un lugar? ¿Qué expresiones usas para dar direcciones?

6. ¿Es tu ciudad similar a esta ciudad o diferente? Explica las semejanzas y diferencias.

7. En tu opinión, ¿qué factores determinan la apariencia física de una ciudad? ¿Por qué crees que las ciudades españolas se ven diferentes de las ciudades norteamericanas?

8. ¿De qué vas a poder hablar al final de la lección?

Suggestions Use illustrations as an advance organizer. Help students discover cross-cultural similarities between Madrid and U.S. cities.

ciudades españolas son mucho más antiguas que las de EE.UU.; por lo tanto, las calles son más estrechas y el plan de la ciudad no fue diseñado para el tráfico actual.

8 Pedir y dar direcciones, hablar de dónde están las cosas y usar números más grandes—de cien a un millón.

Side 5, 2149 to 5305

Comprehension Checks

The **Comprehension Checks** are available on cards in the TRP.

1   `00:49`

Suggestions Name local department stores and shops. Identify each as **almacén** or **tienda.** Point out gift boxes = **regalo.** Gesture, demonstrate, act out prepositions of location, directions (right, left), and actions (turn, cross, pass). Talk about where students are seated in the classroom—John is next to/behind/in front of Sue.

1 ¿Es Carla?
2 ¿Quién es?
3 ¿Quiere ir al almacén (al parque, a la escuela)?
4 ¿Quiere comprar un regalo para su novio (su hermano, su madre, etc.)?
5 ¿Queda lejos o cerca el almacén?
6 ¿Debe Carla doblar a la derecha (a la izquierda)?
7 ¿Debe caminar una cuadra (dos cuadras)?
8 ¿Está el almacén a la derecha (a la izquierda)?
9 ¿Hay una tienda (un café, una escuela) enfrente del almacén?

Side 5, 1470 to 2351

2   `01:19`

Suggestions Show that Enrique **sale del hotel / Necesita regresar al hotel.** Demonstrate by leaving and returning to the classroom. Trace Enrique's route on the transparency.

1 ¿Quién es?
2 ¿Necesita salir del o regresar al hotel?
3 ¿Está lejos del hotel o cerca del hotel?
4 ¿Tiene que tomar el autobús? ¿Tiene que caminar?
5 ¿Tiene que tomar el autobús número 6 o número 7?

206 UNIDAD 5 Lección 1

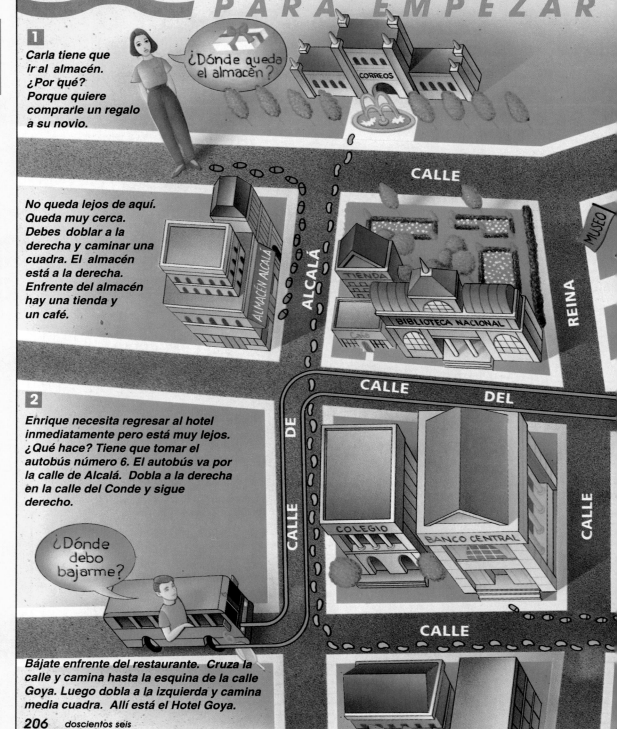

1

Carla tiene que ir al almacén. ¿Por qué? Porque quiere comprarle un regalo a su novio.

¿Dónde queda el almacén?

No queda lejos de aquí. Queda muy cerca. Debes doblar a la derecha y caminar una cuadra. El almacén está a la derecha. Enfrente del almacén hay una tienda y un café.

2

Enrique necesita regresar al hotel inmediatamente pero está muy lejos. ¿Qué hace? Tiene que tomar el autobús número 6. El autobús va por la calle de Alcalá. Dobla a la derecha en la calle del Conde y sigue derecho.

¿Dónde debo bajarme?

Bájate enfrente del restaurante. Cruza la calle y camina hasta la esquina de la calle Goya. Luego dobla a la izquierda y camina media cuadra. Allí está el Hotel Goya.

206 doscientos seis

6 ¿Va el autobús por la calle de Alcalá?
7 ¿Dobla el autobús en la calle del Conde?
8 ¿Dobla a la derecha o a la izquierda?
9 ¿Sigue todo derecho?
Continue asking Comprehension Check questions, as above.

Side 5, 2370 to 3616

Purpose This section sets the context for the language needed to ask for and give directions and provides comprehensible language without translation.

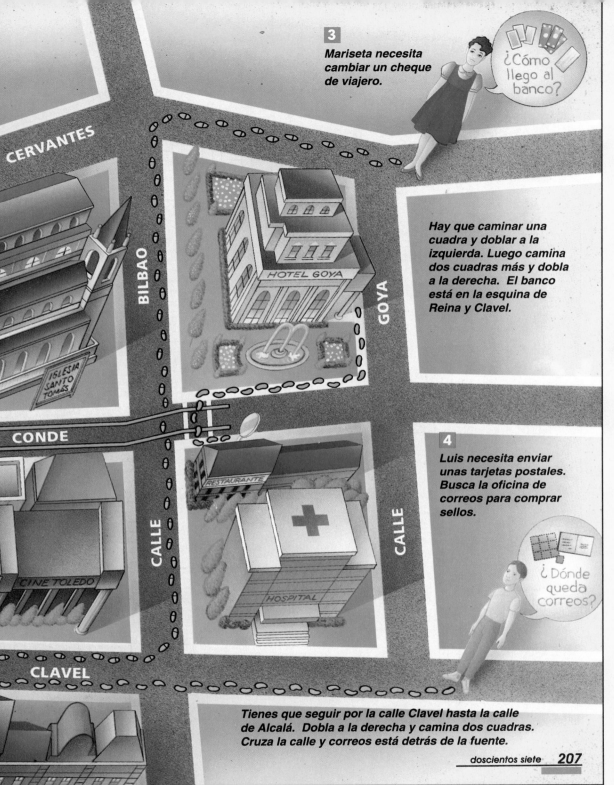

3

Mariseta necesita cambiar un cheque de viajero.

¿Cómo llego al banco?

Hay que caminar una cuadra y doblar a la izquierda. Luego camina dos cuadras más y dobla a la derecha. El banco está en la esquina de Reina y Clavel.

CERVANTES

BILBAO

HOTEL GOYA

GOYA

ISLESIA SANTO TOMÁS

CONDE

RESTAURANTE

CALLE

4

Luis necesita enviar unas tarjetas postales. Busca la oficina de correos para comprar sellos.

CALLE

CINE TOLEDO

HOSPITAL

¿Dónde queda correos?

CLAVEL

Tienes que seguir por la calle Clavel hasta la calle de Alcalá. Dobla a la derecha y camina dos cuadras. Cruza la calle y correos está detrás de la fuente.

doscientos siete **207**

3   02:01

Suggestion Trace Mariseta's route.
1 ¿Quién es?
2 ¿Necesita cambiar un cheque de viajero? ¿comprar un regalo? ¿regresar al hotel?
3 ¿Tiene que ir al banco (al almacén, al hotel)? *(other places)*
4 ¿Hay que caminar (tomar el autobús)?
5 ¿Hay que caminar una cuadra (dos cuadras, media cuadra)?
6 ¿Hay que doblar a la derecha o a la izquierda?
7 ¿Luego camina dos o tres cuadras más?
8 ¿Dobla ahora a la izquierda o a la derecha?
9 ¿Está el banco en la esquina?
10 ¿Está en la esquina de Reina y Clavel (Reina y Alcalá)?

Side 5, 3635 to 4390

4   02:27

Suggestions Show envelopes, postcards, stamps. Trace Luis's route.
1 ¿Quién es?
2 ¿Necesita enviar unas tarjetas postales (cambiar un cheque de viajero)?
3 ¿Busca la oficina de correos (el hotel, el banco, el almacén)?
4 ¿Tiene que comprar sellos (un regalo)?
5 ¿Tiene que seguir por la calle Clavel (la calle de Alcalá)?
6 ¿Dobla en la calle de Alcalá (la calle del Conde)?
7 ¿Dobla a la derecha o a la izquierda?
8 ¿Camina dos cuadras (una cuadra, media cuadra)?
9 ¿Cruza la calle?
10 ¿Camina todo derecho o cruza la calle?
11 ¿Está correos detrás de la fuente (del banco, de la tienda)?
12 ¿Está correos enfrente de la fuente?

Expansion activity In small groups, have students choose other destinations and points of departure and describe how to get there. For example, **¿Cómo llego al . . . si estoy en . . . ?**

Side 5, 4409 to 5305

Suggestions Begin by having students close their books while you narrate one section at a time, using the transparencies to clarify meaning without translation. Then ask **Comprehension Checks**. Repeat this process with each section.

Using the video Play one section at a time after narrating it using the transparencies. Freeze the video and ask **Comprehension Checks**. Repeat with each section.

TAPE/DISC

02:57–
06:31

Side 5, 5318 to 11720

Early Production Checks

The **Early Production Checks** are available on cards in the TRP.

| 1 | 03:03 |

¿Tengo que llevar a Víctor?

1 ¿Es Manolo o Víctor? *(Point to Víctor first, then Manolo.)* *Víctor / Manolo.*

2 ¿Es Mamá o Papá? *(Point to Mamá first, then Papá.)* *Mamá / Papá.*

3 ¿Quién es? *(Point to Víctor, Manolo, Mamá, and Papá.)* *Víctor / Manolo / Mamá / Papá.*

4 ¿Tiene que ir Manolo con Víctor? *Sí.*

5 ¿Quiere ir Manolo con Víctor? *No.*

6 ¿Tienen que ir a la oficina de correos? *Sí.*

7 ¿Adónde tienen que ir? *A la oficina de correos.*

8 ¿Tienen que comprar sellos? *Sí.*

9 ¿Tienen que enviar unas tarjetas postales? *Sí.*

10 ¿Qué tienen que comprar, sellos o tarjetas postales? *Sellos.*

11 ¿Qué tienen que enviar, sellos o tarjetas postales? *Tarjetas postales.*

12 ¿Saben dónde queda la oficina de correos? *No.*

13 ¿Baja Manolo a preguntar en la recepción? *Sí.*

14 ¿Adónde baja Manolo? *A la recepción.*

15 ¿Baja a preguntar o a comprar sellos? *A preguntar.*

16 ¿Deben regresar Víctor y Manolo antes de las cinco? *Sí.*

17 ¿A qué hora deben regresar? *Antes de las cinco.*

18 ¿Qué deben hacer Víctor y Manolo antes de las cinco? *Deben regresar.*

Side 5, 5478 to 6711

¿QUÉ DECIMOS...?

Al pedir direcciones

1 *¿Tengo que llevar a Víctor?*

UNA FAMILIA ARGENTINA ESTÁ DE VISITA EN MADRID.

Hotel Casón del Torme

¡PERO, MAMÁ! ¿TENGO QUE LLEVAR A VÍCTOR?

MANOLO, ESCUCHA. PRIMERO, DEBEN IR A LA OFICINA DE CORREOS A COMPRAR SELLOS Y ENVIAR ESTAS TARJETAS POSTALES.

¿SABEN CÓMO LLEGAR A CORREOS?

YO TAMPOCO SÉ, HIJO. BAJA A LA RECEPCIÓN Y PREGUNTA CÓMO SE LLEGA.

SÍ. ¡Y YA!

NO, NO SÉ. ¿DÓNDE QUEDA?

BUENO, PAPÁ.

Y VÍCTOR, NO OLVIDEN. DEBEN ESTAR EN EL RESTAURANTE DEL HOTEL ANTES DE LAS CINCO, ¿EH?

BUENO, HASTA LUEGO.

¡MANOLO, ESPÉRAME!

208 doscientos ocho

***P*urpose** This section uses real language needed to give and understand directions in real-life contexts. Students should not be asked to memorize dialogues word for word but rather to understand the new language in context.

2 ¿Cómo llego a correos?

Accept brief phrases or one- and two-word answers to all **Early Production Checks**, as shown in **1** on page 208. It is not necessary for students to answer in complete sentences.

1 ¿Quién es? *(Point to Manolo, then receptionist.)*
2 ¿Queda lejos o cerca la oficina de correos?
3 ¿Hay que tomar el metro o el autobús?
4 ¿Hay una estación de metro a unas cuatro manzanas?
5 ¿Dónde está la estación de metro?
6 ¿Al salir del hotel dobla a la derecha o a la izquierda?
7 ¿Sigue una manzana o dos manzanas?
8 ¿Camina una manzana más o dos manzanas más?
9 ¿Cuánto camina?
10 ¿Está la entrada del metro enfrente o detrás de un cine?
11 ¿Toma el metro para Ventas?
12 ¿Qué toma para Ventas, el metro o el bus?
13 ¿Baja en la estación Banco de España?
14 ¿En qué estación baja?

Side 5, 6732 to 8984

LECCIÓN 1

doscientos nueve **209**

Suggestions Begin by having students close their books while you narrate one section at a time, using the transparencies to clarify meaning without translation. Then ask **Early Production Checks**. Repeat with each section.

Using the video Play one section at a time after narrating it using the transparencies. Freeze the video and ask **Early Production Checks**. Repeat with each section.

Tenemos que cambiar un cheque.

Accept brief phrases or one- and two-word answers to all **Early Production Checks**, as in **1**. It is not necessary for students to answer in complete sentences.

1 ¿Quién es? *(Point to Víctor, Manolo, then the policeman.)*
2 ¿Dónde queda correos, cerca o lejos?
3 ¿Queda detrás o enfrente de la fuente?
4 ¿Sabe Manolo cuánto dinero tiene Víctor?
5 ¿Necesita comprar un regalo?
6 ¿Qué necesita comprar?
7 ¿Es el regalo para su papá o para su novia?
8 ¿Tienen mil doscientas pesetas?
9 ¿Tienen que cambiar un cheque de viajero?
10 ¿Qué tienen que cambiar?
11 ¿Van a un banco?
12 ¿Adónde van?
13 ¿Tienen un billete de mil pesetas? ¿de cinco mil? ¿de diez mil?
14 ¿Tienen dos monedas de quinientas pesetas?
15 ¿Tienen tres monedas de quinientas pesetas?
16 ¿Tienen cuatro monedas de cien? ¿tres? ¿dos?
17 ¿Tienen mil doscientas pesetas en total?
18 ¿Tienen cinco mil doscientas pesetas en total?
19 ¿Cuánto dinero tienen en total?

Side 5, 9004 to 11720

3   *Tenemos que cambiar un cheque.*

210   doscientos diez

CHARLEMOS UN POCO

A. ¿Quién habla?   Identifica a la persona que habla.

Recepcionista

Papá

Manolo

Víctor

1. Primero, deben ir a la oficina de correos.
2. ¿Salgo por esa puerta?
3. Tengo que comprarle un regalo a mi novia.
4. Bájate en la estación Banco de España.
5. Tenemos que cambiar un cheque de viajero.
6. Manolo, baja a la recepción y pregunta cómo se llega.
7. Camina dos manzanas más.
8. ¡Vamos de compras!
9. Toma el metro para Ventas.
10. ¿Cómo llego a correos?

B. ¿Dónde están?   Contesta las preguntas.

MODELO   ¿Dónde está Javier?
Está detrás de su padre.

1. ¿Dónde está Anita?
   ¿Dónde está la madre de Anita?

2. ¿Dónde están Javier y Anita?
   ¿Dónde está su madre?

3. ¿Dónde está Javier?
   ¿Dónde está Anita?

4. ¿Dónde está el padre?
   ¿Dónde están Javier y Anita?

LECCIÓN 1

Prepositional phrases
Used to show location

¿Dónde están los niños?

Está **enfrente de**
sus padres.

Está **detrás de**
sus padres.

Están **al lado de**
su madre.

Está **entre** sus
padres.

Están **a la
izquierda de**
su madre.

Está **a la
derecha de**
su madre.

Está **cerca de**
su padre.

Está **lejos de**
su padre.

CHARLEMOS UN POCO

A. ¿Quién habla?
1 Papá
2 Manolo
3 Manolo
4 Recepcionista
5 Manolo
6 Papá
7 Recepcionista
8 Manolo
9 Recepcionista
10 Manolo

B. ¿Dónde están?
1 Anita está enfrente de su madre.
  La madre está detrás de Anita.
2 Javier y Anita están a la derecha
  de su madre. Su madre está a la
  izquierda de Javier y Anita.
3 Javier está lejos de su madre.
  Anita está cerca de su madre.
4 El padre está entre Javier y Anita.
  Javier y Anita están al lado de su
  padre.

Purpose   These activities provide guided
practice as students begin to produce new language
necessary to give location and to use directions,
commands, and numbers 100–1,000,000.

C. ¿Dónde queda? Have students work in pairs. Ask one student to read the descriptions and another to find the place being described. Then call on individuals to check their answers.

1 Está enfrente del hospital. (f)
2 Está lejos de mi casa, al lado de la tienda. (ch)
3 Está entre el hotel y el colegio. (e)
4 Está al lado del hospital, enfrente del café. (h)
5 Está entre mi casa y el parque. (g)
6 Está enfrente de mi casa. (d)
7 Está al lado del hotel, en la esquina. (b)
8 Está enfrente de la iglesia. (c)
9 Está al lado del almacén, cerca de la plaza. (a)

C. ¿Dónde queda? Según Alicia, ¿dónde están los lugares mencionados abajo?

 MODELO   almacén
Está entre el café y la tienda.

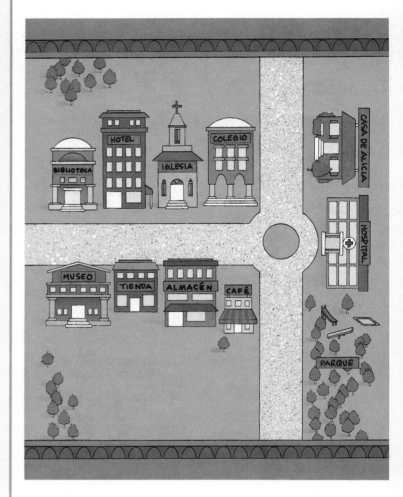

1. plaza	**a.** Está al lado del almacén, cerca de la plaza.
2. museo	**b.** Está al lado del hotel, en la esquina.
3. iglesia	**c.** Está enfrente de la iglesia.
4. parque	**ch.** Está lejos de mi casa, al lado de la tienda.
5. hospital	**d.** Está enfrente de mi casa.
6. colegio	**e.** Está entre el hotel y el colegio.
7. biblioteca	**f.** Está enfrente del hospital.
8. almacén	**g.** Está entre mi casa y el parque.
9. café	**h.** Está al lado del hospital, enfrente del café.

CH. Van a . . . Varios jóvenes reciben estas instrucciones del policía en la **Plaza Constitución.** ¿Adónde van?

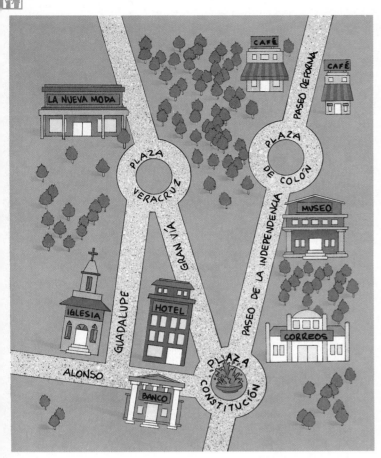

1. Camina por todo el Paseo de la Independencia. Está a la derecha, antes de llegar a la primera plaza.
2. Está cerca. Sigue derecho por la calle Alonso. Cruza la calle Guadalupe. Está a la derecha, en la esquina.
3. Está allí mismo, detrás de la fuente.
4. Sigue media manzana por Alonso. Queda a la izquierda, enfrente del hotel.
5. Toma el autobús que va por el Paseo de la Independencia. Al cruzar la Plaza de Colón, la calle se llama Paseo Reforma. Hay dos en esa calle.
6. Está un poco lejos. Toma el autobús por Gran Vía hasta llegar a la Plaza Veracruz. Pasa por la plaza y el almacén está a la izquierda.

LECCIÓN 1

Commands used when giving directions

Dobla a la derecha (izquierda).
Sigue derecho.
Camina media (una, dos, . . .) cuadra(s).
Toma el autobús (metro, tren).
Pasa por el parque.
Cruza la calle.

See ¿**Por qué se dice así?**, *page G65, section 5.1.*

CH. Van a . . . Have students figure out where each set of instructions leads by working in pairs. Then call on individuals to verify that they reached correct destinations.
1 Van al museo.
2 Van a la iglesia.
3 Van a correos.
4 Van al banco.
5 Van al café.
6 Van a la Nueva Moda.

D. ¡Primero a correos!
Answers may vary.

1 Para ir a correos, dobla a la derecha en la calle A y camina dos cuadras y media.
2 Para ir al almacén, dobla a la izquierda en la avenida F y camina hasta la calle B. Dobla a la derecha y camina media cuadra.
3 Para ir a la tienda, sigue derecho en la calle B hasta la Avenida I.
4 Para ir a la iglesia, dobla a la izquierda en la Avenida I y camina dos cuadras.
5 Para ir al restaurante, dobla a la derecha en la Avenida I y camina una cuadra hasta la calle C. Dobla a la izquierda.
6 Para ir al parque, sigue la calle C hasta la Avenida G. Dobla a la izquierda en la avenida G y camina una cuadra. Dobla a la derecha y camina una cuadra.
7 Para ir al café, dobla a la izquierda en la avenida F y camina una cuadra hasta la calle B. Dobla a la derecha en la calle B y camina dos cuadras.
8 Para ir a la casa, dobla a la derecha en la calle B y camina media cuadra hasta la Avenida H. Camina una cuadra hasta la calle A. Dobla a la izquierda.

Extension Have students give these directions in reverse.

E. ¡Pobre Federico!
1 Estudia para la clase de español.
2 Escribe tu composición.
3 Busca un regalo para tu tía.
4 Corre al banco.
5 Llama a tu abuela.
6 Limpia la casa.
7 Practica el piano.
8 Lee tu libro de historia.
9 Cambia un cheque de viajero.
10 Toma el autobús.

Follow-up variation It's a typical weekend and your mother (father) is telling you various things you have to do. What does she (he) say?

F. ¿Cuánto tengo? Check
current exchange rate in local newspaper or bank and point out to students. If you have Spanish money, bring to class to show to students. Ask: What differences do you observe with U.S. money (color, size, amounts, pictures, etc.)?

1 Mil ciento pesetas.
2 Siete mil trescientas pesetas.
3 Quinientas pesetas.
4 Mil setecientas pesetas.
5 Cinco mil novecientas pesetas.
6 Mil pesetas.
7 Seis mil quinientas pesetas.
8 Cuatro mil seiscientas pesetas.

Tú commands
Used when telling people what to do

Infinitive	-ar	-er, -ir
Ending	-a	-e

Estudia más.
Lee el capítulo para mañana.
Escribe esto en la pizarra.

*See **¿Por qué se dice así?**, page G65, section 5.1.*

Números: 100–1.000.000

100	cien
210	doscientos diez
320	trescientos veinte
430	cuatrocientos treinta
540	quinientos cuarenta
650	seiscientos cincuenta
760	setecientos sesenta
870	ochocientos setenta
980	novecientos ochenta
1.090	mil noventa
2.200	dos mil doscientos
3.400	tres mil cuatrocientos
4.600	cuatro mil seiscientos
5.800	cinco mil ochocientos
10.900	diez mil novecientos
51.000	cincuenta y un mil
100.000	cien mil
1.000.000	un millón

Necesito trescient**as** peset**as**.
Tienen dos mil seiscient**os** pes**os**.

*See **¿Por qué se dice así?**, page G66, section 5.2.*

D. ¡Primero a correos!   José tiene que ir a muchos lugares hoy. ¿Qué instrucciones le da su mamá?

MODELO   casa de José → correos
Para ir a correos, dobla a la derecha en la calle A y camina dos cuadras y media.

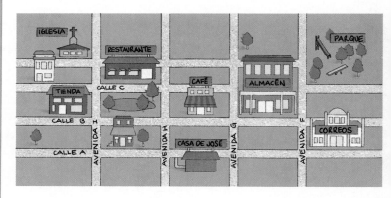

1. casa de José → correos
2. correos → almacén
3. almacén → tienda
4. tienda → iglesia
5. iglesia → restaurante
6. restaurante → parque
7. parque → café
8. café → casa de José

E. ¡Pobre Federico!   Todo el mundo le da órdenes a Federico. ¿Qué le dicen?

MODELO   comprar sellos.
Compra sellos.

1. estudiar para la clase de español
2. escribir tu composición
3. buscar un regalo para tu tía
4. correr al banco
5. llamar a tu abuela
6. limpiar la casa
7. practicar el piano
8. leer tu libro de historia
9. cambiar un cheque de viajero
10. tomar el autobús

F. ¿Cuánto tengo?   Tienes que cambiar dólares a pesetas. ¿Cuántas pesetas te dan?

MODELO   1.000
Mil pesetas.

1. 1.100	**3.** 500	**5.** 5.900	**7.** 6.500
2. 7.300	**4.** 1.700	**8.** 4.600	**6.** 1.000

G. ¿Adónde van?   ¿Adónde van estos vuelos?

MODELO   Tú: **¿Adónde va el vuelo setecientos sesenta y siete?**
Compañero(a):   **El vuelo setecientos sesenta y siete de Iberia va a Perú.**

SALIDAS		
LÍNEA AÉREA	**VUELO**	**DESTINO**
Iberia	767	Lima
TWA	150	Buenos Aires
Lan Chile	2500	Bogotá
Avianca	950	Caracas
Iberia	575	Miami
Aeroméxico	1165	Managua
Avianca	700	Quito
Lan Chile	1500	Santiago
Aeroméxico	6336	San José

H. Caja de cambio.   ¿Cuántos dólares le dan estas personas al cajero y cuántas pesetas reciben en cambio?

MODELO   Sr. Jones: $10 / 1.150 ptas.
El Sr. Jones le da diez dólares y recibe mil ciento cincuenta pesetas.

1. yo: $20 / 2.300 ptas.
2. Adán y Gregorio: $45 / 5.175 ptas.
3. Sra. Carrera: $60 / 6.900 ptas.
4. tú: $35 / 4.025 ptas.
5. mi hermana y yo: $50 / 5.750 ptas.

I. Reunión familiar.   ¿A qué hora salen tú y tus parientes de la reunión familiar?

MODELO   tus tíos / 22:00
Compañero(a):   **¿A qué hora salen tus tíos?**
Tú: **Salen a las diez de la noche.**

1. tus padres / 19:30
2. tu tía Isabel / 20:00
3. tú y tu hermana / 18:00
4. el esposo de tu prima / 11:45
5. los abuelos de tu primo / 14:00
6. tú / 20:30

LECCIÓN 1

Dar

doy	damos
das	
da	dan
da	dan

Notice the irregular **yo** form.

See **¿Por qué se dice así?**, *page G68, section 5.3.*

Salir

salgo	salimos
sales	
sale	salen
sale	salen

Notice the irregular **yo** form.

See **¿Por qué se dice así?**, *page G68, section 5.3.*

---

doscientos quince **215**

4 ¿A qué hora sale el esposo de tu prima? Sale a las doce menos cuarto de la mañana.
5 ¿A qué hora salen los abuelos de tu primo? Salen a las dos de la tarde.
6 ¿A qué hora sales tú? Salgo a las ocho y media de la noche.

G.   ¿Adónde van?
1 ¿Adónde va el vuelo ciento cincuenta? El vuelo ciento cincuenta de TWA va a Argentina.
2 ¿Adónde va el vuelo dos mil quinientos? El vuelo dos mil quinientos de Lan Chile va a Colombia.
3 ¿Adónde va el vuelo novecientos cincuenta? El vuelo novecientos cincuenta de Avianca va a Venezuela.
4 ¿Adónde va el vuelo quinientos setenta y cinco? El vuelo quinientos setenta y cinco de Iberia va a Estados Unidos.
5 ¿Adónde va el vuelo mil ciento sesenta y cinco? El vuelo mil ciento sesenta y cinco de Aeroméxico va a Nicaragua.
6 ¿Adónde va el vuelo setecientos? El vuelo setecientos de Avianca va a Ecuador.
7 ¿Adónde va el vuelo mil quinientos? El vuelo mil quinientos de Lan Chile va a Chile.
8 ¿Adónde va el vuelo seis mil trescientos treinta y seis? El vuelo seis mil trescientos treinta y seis de Aeroméxico va a Costa Rica.

H.   Caja de cambio.
This activity is based on an exchange rate of 125 pesetas to the dollar. Have students do in pairs first. Then check on individual responses. You may want to redo with current exchange rate.
1 Yo le doy veinte dólares y recibo dos mil trescientas pesetas.
2 Adán y Gregorio le dan cuarenta y cinco dólares y reciben cinco mil ciento setenta y cinco pesetas.
3 La señora Carrera le da sesenta dólares y recibe seis mil novecientas pesetas.
4 Tú le das treinta y cinco dólares y recibes cuatro mil veinticinco pesetas.
5 Mi hermana y yo le damos cincuenta dólares y recibimos cinco mil setecientas cincuenta pesetas.

I.   Reunión familiar.
1 ¿A qué hora salen tus padres? Salen a las siete y media de la noche.
2 ¿A qué hora sale tu tía Isabel? Sale a las ocho de la noche.
3 ¿A qué hora salen tú y tu hermana? Salimos a las seis de la tarde.

CHARLEMOS UN POCO MÁS

Saber

sé	sabemos
sabes	
sabe	saben
sabe	saben

Notice the irregular **yo** form.

See **¿Por qué se dice así?**, *page G68, section 5.3.*

J. Madrid. ¿Cuánto saben ustedes de Madrid?

EJEMPLO yo / saber que Madrid / ser / capital / España
Yo sé que Madrid es la capital de España.

1. yo / saber que Madrid / estar / centro / país
2. Silvia y Samuel / saber que Madrid / tener / metro excelente
3. tú y Carlos / saber que Madrid / ser / ciudad más grande de España
4. él y ella / saber que el Rey Juan Carlos no / vivir / Palacio Real
5. Alicia / saber que / Museo del Prado / ser uno de los mejores del mundo
6. usted y yo / saber que la Plaza Mayor / tener cafés al aire libre, tiendas y oficinas

CHARLEMOS UN POCO MÁS

A. ¡Mucho talento! The Spanish Club is planning to have a talent show. With a partner, prepare a list of students in your class and what they know how to do.

 EJEMPLO **Gloria sabe bailar el tango.**
Yo sé contar a un millón en español.

B. ¡Donaciones! The business community in your town has decided to help your school by donating specific items. In groups, decide what each group of professionals gives the school. Some groups were very generous, so use large amounts.

EJEMPLO **La Asociación de Secretarias le da diez mil lápices al colegio.**

Los cocineros de [tu ciudad]	computadoras
La Asociación de Músicos	lápices
El Partido Demócrata	guitarras
El Partido Republicano	libros
La Asociación de Mujeres de Negocio	teléfonos
La Asociación de Profesores	pizzas
Unos abogados muy ricos	$$$

C. Reunión familiar. All of your relatives are coming to a family reunion at your house on Sunday. Tell from where and at what time they leave in order to arrive by noon.

EJEMPLO **Mis tíos Roberto y Rita salen de Reno a las ocho.**

CH. Plano de Madrid. Use the **Metro** map below to tell your partner how to get from one stop to another.

 EJEMPLO de Ventas a Cuatro Caminos
Toma el número 5 a Diego de León. Cambia en Diego de León al número 6 hasta Cuatro Caminos.

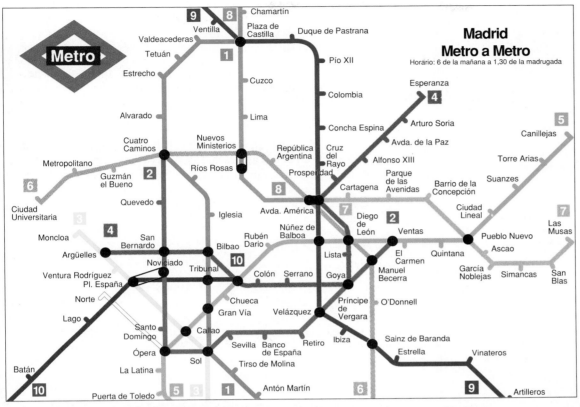

1. de Ópera a Avda. de América
2. de Gran Vía a Plaza de Castilla
3. de Ópera a Ciudad Universitaria
4. de Cuatro Caminos a Pueblo Nuevo
5. de Argüelles a Ciudad Universitaria
6. de Cuatro Caminos a Goya

D. ¡Mi perro perdido! You and your partner are trying to find your lost dog, Bombón. Your teacher will give each of you a town map. One of the maps shows where Bombón has gone. The partner with that map describes how to follow Bombón's tracks, while the other draws the route on the unmarked map. When you find Bombón, compare the two maps.

E. ¡Necesito ir a . . . ! Use the map your teacher gives you to tell your partner how to get from the train station to the places specified on the map your teacher gives him or her. Then ask your partner how to get to the following places: **hotel, correo, tienda, hospital, restaurante, teatro.**

LECCIÓN 1

CH. Plano de Madrid.
Point out If you wish, tell students that **cambiar** may mean *to change* or *to exchange*.

D. ¡Mi perro perdido! Tell students they may not look at each other's maps. Allow 3–4 min. Then have students compare maps to check their ability to give and follow directions.

E. ¡Necesito ir a . . . ! Tell students they may not look at each other's maps. Allow 3–4 min. Then call on individuals to tell you how to get to several places mentioned on both maps.

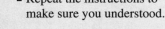

DRAMATIZACIONES

A. Nuevos amigos. Have students work in pairs. Allow 6–8 min to prepare. Also have each pair prepare 2–3 comprehension questions to ask class to check that everyone understood their presentation. Remind students to answer the phone with **Aló, Hola, Diga, Bueno,** etc. and to say *good-bye* at the end of the conversation. (It may be helpful if students draw a map showing where friend lives before beginning this activity.)

Dramatizaciones

A. Nuevos amigos. A new friend calls you from the center of town and needs directions to your house. Role-play the phone call.

Amigo(a)
- Ask if the house is far.
- Ask how to get to the house.

- Repeat the instructions to make sure you understood.

Tú
- Say it is [near/far].
- Be specific in your answer. Mention any landmarks.

B. ¿Dónde queda? You agreed to meet your parents for lunch at a new restaurant but have lost the address. You ask a police officer for directions. Role-play the situation with a partner.

Tú
- Ask where the restaurant is located.
- Ask for directions to that address.
- Find out if you should walk or take the bus, taxi, or metro.
- If you must use public transportation, ask how much it is.

Policía
- Give address of the restaurant.
- Give directions.
- Suggest the most appropriate form of transportation.
- Indicate the fare.

C. ¿Son hermanos? You and a friend are discussing two new students at your school.

Tú
- Ask if your friend knows the names of the new students.
- Ask if your friend knows where they live.
- Ask for their phone numbers.
- Ask at what time the new students leave school.
- Say good-bye to your friend until tomorrow morning.

Amigo(a)
- Tell their names.
- Answer that you don't but that you know their phone numbers.
- Give their phone numbers.
- Tell when they leave.
- Respond appropriately.

CH. Perdón, necesito ayuda. A newcomer to the city asks you for directions to a place you know well. Give directions and answer the newcomer's questions about how to get there. If appropriate, include information about what bus or metro line to take and at which stops to get on or off. Mention landmarks and how close or far this place is.

218 doscientos dieciocho

UNIDAD 5

Purpose These role plays are designed to recycle the structures and vocabulary needed to express locations and give directions. Encourage students to work without their books when preparing and performing their role plays.

218 UNIDAD 5 Lección 1

IMPACTO CULTURAL

¡No me digas!

Madrid de noche.   Tom is taking an evening stroll with his friend
Martín in Madrid. Read their conversation. Then answer the question
that follows.

Tom: ¡Qué noche más formidable! Dime, Martín, ¿qué
            hora es?
Martín: Creo que son las nueve y media.
Tom: ¿Las nueve y media de la noche? ¡Imposible!
            Mira cuánta gente hay en la calle . . . y cuántos niños
            también. (*Pasa un niño corriendo.*)
Martín: Pues, Tom, te digo que son las nueve y media de la
            noche. (*Mirando el reloj*)
Tom: Entonces, no entiendo. ¿Qué pasa hoy? ¿Es un día
            festivo o qué?
Martín: Pues no, no pasa nada . . . ¿No te gusta la gente?

Why is Tom surprised?

1. He is amazed to see the streets crowded at that late hour.
2. He does not realize that large families live in that part of town.
3. He doesn't think it's safe for children to be on the streets after dark.

❏ Check your answer on page 418.

LECCIÓN 1

Purpose This short dialogue
includes interesting cross-cultural
information about Hispanic cities
that students are asked to discover
on their own.

Suggestions Allow students
to discuss possible explanations and
try to arrive at consensus on correct
answer before they check the explanations on page 418.

Answers

① Tom doesn't realize that an
   evening stroll (**un paseo**) is
   customary in many Hispanic cities.
   Entire families can be seen on the
   streets, even late into the evening.
   This is the correct answer.
2 Nothing in the dialogue indicates
   that Tom is unaware that large
   families live in that part of town.
   Consider another answer.
3 Tom may consider the streets
   unsafe, but the dialogue gives
   no indication that this is why
   he is surprised. Try again.

IMPACTO CULTURAL

Y ahora, ¡a leer!

Antes de empezar

Suggestions Use these questions as an advance organizer for the reading that follows. Have students write their answers to question 1 working in pairs. Tell them to guess if they don't know. After they have read **El paseo,** have them come back to their answers and change any of them, if they wish to do so. For question 2, divide class in thirds. Ask one-third to list cognates in first paragraph, another third the second paragraph, and the third group the last paragraph.

Answers

1 Answers for the U.S. will vary. Answers for Spain, according to the reading, are:

1 sí   3 sí   5 sí   7 sí
2 sí   4 no   6 no

2 tradición, hispanas, familia, conversan, observan, adultos, simplemente, comentan, café, general, grupo, común, manera, planes

Verifiquemos

Answers will vary. Students should mention "weekend cruising" in their cars or "going to the mall" as similar ways teenagers meet other teens in the U.S. Accept some answers in English if students lack appropriate vocabulary.

Y ahora, ¡a leer!

Antes de empezar

1. En tu opinión, ¿cuáles de estas actividades hacen diariamente los jóvenes norteamericanos y cuáles hacen los jóvenes españoles?

Actividades diarias	Estados Unidos	España
1. Salir a pasear con la familia por la tarde.	sí / no	sí / no
2. Ir de compras por la tarde con un pariente.	sí / no	sí / no
3. Conversar y observar a la gente con un pariente mientras caminan por la calle.	sí / no	sí / no
4. Salir en auto con un(a) amigo(a) a tomar un refresco.	sí / no	sí / no
5. Tomar un helado o un refresco con tu familia caminando por la calle o en un parque cerca de tu casa.	sí / no	sí / no
6. Pasear en auto con un grupo de amigos una o dos horas por la tarde.	sí / no	sí / no
7. Salir a caminar con un grupo de amigos.	sí / no	sí / no

2. Prepara una lista de los cognados en la lectura.

Verifiquemos

Primero lee la lectura sobre *El paseo* en la siguiente página. Luego, contesta las preguntas a continuación.

1. ¿Existe el paseo o algo similar en tu ciudad? Explica.
2. ¿Sale tu familia a caminar? ¿Adónde van ustedes?
3. ¿Dónde y cuándo se juntan tus padres con otros adultos para conversar o comentar las últimas noticias?
4. ¿Qué hacen tú y tus amigos para conocer a otros jóvenes? ¿Adónde van? ¿Cómo comienzan una conversación?
5. ¿Creen que el paseo es una buena manera de conocer a otras personas? ¿Por qué sí o por qué no?

EL PASEO

Dar un paseo antes o después de cenar es una tradición en muchas ciudades hispanas. Los domingos por la noche, familias, novios y amigos salen a dar un paseo: caminan y conversan mientras observan a los otros caminantes.

Familias enteras salen a pasear. Los adultos conversan sobre las últimas noticias o simplemente comentan los precios en los escaparates de las tiendas. Los niños corren por todos lados jugando con sus hermanos, primos o amigos. A veces, después de caminar un rato, los niños (y los adultos también) toman un helado en la calle o entran en un café a tomar algo.

Los jóvenes también salen de paseo. A veces salen con sus familias, pero, por lo general, a ellos les gusta pasear en grupo con sus amigos. Es común ver grupos de chicos o chicas paseándose. A veces los grupos se juntan a conversar. De esta manera se conocen y hacen planes para el paseo siguiente.

LECCIÓN 1

doscientos veintiuno **221**

¿Qué quieres comprar?

OBJECTIVES

Communicative Goals

- Expressing preferences
- Making a purchase
- Describing clothing

Culture and Reading

- *¡No me digas!*
  La planta baja:
  The ground floor
- *Y ahora, ¡a leer!*
  Guía de departamentos:
  Shopping in a department store

Structure

- 5.4 The verbs **gustar** and **encantar**: A summary
- 5.5 Stem-changing verbs: **e → ie** and **o → ue**
- 5.6 Ordinal numbers

ACTIVE VOCABULARY

En un almacén

caro(a)	dependiente
departamentos	piso
de caballeros	planta
de deportes	… baja
de electrónica	
del hogar	
joyería	
perfumería	
zapatería	

Ropa

ropa	pantalones
blusa	sombrero
botas	sudadera
calcetines	suéter
par de …	traje
camisa	vestido
camiseta	zapatos
chaqueta	… deportivos
falda	talla
jeans	

Colores

amarillo(a)	morado(a)
anaranjado(a)	negro(a)
azul	rojo(a)
blanco(a)	rosado(a)
gris	verde
marrón	

Números ordinales

primero(a), primer	quinto(a)
segundo(a)	sexto(a)
tercero(a), tercer	séptimo(a)
cuarto(a)	octavo(a)
	noveno(a)

Complementos indirectos

Verbos o→ue, e→ie

contar (ue)	jugar (ue)
costar (ue)	pensar (ie)
encontrar (ue)	poder (ue)
entender (ie)	preferir (ie)

Verbos regulares

encantar
gustar
llamar
llevar
pagar

Palabras y expresiones

invitación
joven
sándwich
largo(a)
por ejemplo

ANTICIPEMOS

Promoción válida del 25 de enero al 15 de febrero

CHICOS CHICAS 12 - 15

1 JERSEY ....
2 CHAQUETA 2.975
BLUSA 6.900
BERMUDAS 3.200
3 CAZADORA 3.700
4 CHAQUETA 7.675
5 JERSEY 9.500
 .... 2.975

El Corte Inglés

¿ Qué piensas tú ?

1. ¿Dónde están los dos jóvenes? ¿Qué están haciendo?

2. ¿Qué tipo de información hay en el directorio? ¿En qué planta hay ropa para jóvenes? ¿Libros y discos? ¿Algo para comer? ¿Ropa para hombres?

3. Mira el anuncio en esta página. ¿Cómo se llama el almacén? ¿Es una promoción especial? ¿Cuáles son las fechas de la promoción? ¿Qué cosas están en oferta? ¿Para personas de qué edad son estas cosas?

4. ¿En qué departamento de El Corte Inglés están las cosas anunciadas? ¿En qué planta?

5. En tu opinión, ¿son similares los almacenes de España a los almacenes de Estados Unidos? ¿Cuáles son algunas diferencias? Explica tu respuesta.

6. ¿Qué tipo de ropa te gusta llevar? ¿Cuáles son tus colores favoritos? ¿Por qué?

7. En tu opinión, ¿se visten los jóvenes españoles más formalmente que los jóvenes norteamericanos? Explica tu respuesta.

8. ¿De qué vas a poder hablar al final de la lección?

¿Qué piensas tú?

Allow students to answer in either Spanish or English. Whenever they answer in English, repeat their answer in Spanish and have class repeat after you so that they will start familiarizing themselves with the new vocabulary.

Encourage students to guess meanings of **zapatería**, **confección** (ready-to-wear clothing), **electrodomésticos** (small appliances), and **juguetes** (toys). They may need help to deduce the meaning of **juventud** from **joven**.

Answers

1 En un almacén. Están buscando ropa.

2 Nombres de departamentos del almacén e información sobre aparcamiento. Jóvenes—planta 5; discos y libros—semi-sótano; comida—planta 6; ropa para hombres—planta 2.

Extension Ask about items found on other floors: zapatos, ropa para niños, etc.

3 El Corte Inglés. Es una promoción especial del 25 de enero al 15 de febrero. En oferta hay jerseys, chaquetas, blusas, bermudas y cazadoras. Son para jóvenes de 12 a 15 años.

4 Están en la planta 5: Juventud.

5 Hay muchas semejanzas pero hay diferencias también. Por ejemplo, tienen más dependientes y el sistema de pagar es diferente.

6 Vocabulario nuevo: *Answers will vary. Weather, fashion, cost will influence choices.*

7 *Students may assume that Spanish teenagers will be more formal. Show ads from current Spanish magazines to demonstrate that all teenagers have much in common.*

8 **De ir de compras en un almacén y de preferencias en ropa.**

Purpose To focus on language related to shopping for clothing and to encourage students to use critical thinking skills to observe, analyze, and compare cultural differences and similarities in shopping.

Suggestions Use illustrations as advance organizer. Students should be allowed to discover meaning of new vocabulary without translation, through the use of context clues and cognates.

Point out In the department store directory from Spain, notice the Spanish spelling **vídeo** (with written accent). Elsewhere in this text, the Latin American spelling **video** (without written accent) is used.

06:32–
09:16

Side 5, 11757 to 16676

Comprehension Checks

The **Comprehension Checks** are available on cards in the TRP.

1 06:39

Suggestions Clarify **llevan** by pointing out what you and various students are wearing. Here and throughout *Para empezar*, point out articles of clothing and colors as they are identified on yourself and on students.

1 ¿Son espías?
2 ¿Es una mujer? ¿un hombre?
3 ¿Llevan impermeables?
4 ¿Son los impermeables beige?
5 ¿Llevan sombreros?
6 ¿Son los sombreros negros?
7 ¿De qué color son los impermeables ¿los sombreros?
8 ¿Llevas tú un impermeable? ¿un sombrero?
9 ¿Es él el espía? ¿Es ella la espía? *(Students don't know yet, so they should say* **No sé.***)*

Side 5, 11953 to 12708

2 07:05

Suggestion Show magazine pictures for **de moda.**

1 ¿Van los espías de compras?
2 ¿Quiénes van de compras?
3 ¿Hay mucha ropa de moda en el almacén?
4 ¿Dónde hay mucha ropa de moda?
5 ¿Es elegante la ropa? ¿Es caro?
6 ¿Es elegante (caro) el vestido?
7 ¿Es elegante el traje?
8 ¿Le gusta el traje al espía?
9 ¿Qué le gusta al espía?

Side 5, 12729 to 13479

1

Hay dos espías aquí— una mujer y un hombre. ¿Quiénes son? ¿Qué llevan? Llevan impermeables beige y sombreros negros. ¡Pero todos llevan los mismos impermeables y sombreros! Entonces, ¿cuáles son los dos espías?

2

Los espías van de compras. Hay mucha ropa de moda en este almacén. ¡Pero es muy cara! Por ejemplo, ese vestido es muy elegante, ¿no? Pero, ¡qué caro! Y ese traje le gusta mucho al espía.

3

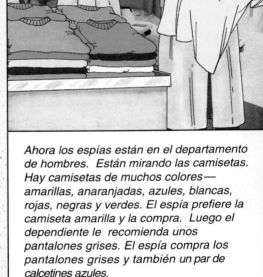

Ahora los espías están en el departamento de hombres. Están mirando las camisetas. Hay camisetas de muchos colores— amarillas, anaranjadas, azules, blancas, rojas, negras y verdes. El espía prefiere la camiseta amarilla y la compra. Luego el dependiente le recomienda unos pantalones grises. El espía compra los pantalones grises y también un par de calcetines azules.

3 07:30

1 ¿Están los espías en el departamento de hombres?
2 ¿En qué departamento están los espías?
Continue asking Comprehension Check questions, as above.

Side 5, 13499 to 14570

Purpose This section develops listening and reading comprehension of language needed to describe what people are wearing.

Ahora los espías están en la segunda planta, en el departamento de mujeres. El espía encuentra una falda rosada y una blusa roja para la espía. Pero la blusa roja no combina muy bien con la falda. Además, la espía prefiere ropa deportiva. Entonces se prueba unos jeans y una sudadera gris. La talla es perfecta. Ella decide comprarlos.

En el departamento de deportes la espía se prueba unos zapatos deportivos. ¿Cuánto cuestan los zapatos deportivos? ¿Son caros? No, no cuestan mucho. Hoy están en oferta. Ella decide comprar los zapatos. El espía paga en la caja.

Esta noche hay una fiesta y mucha gente está aquí. ¿Puedes encontrar a los dos espías? ¿Qué llevan?

---

4 ⬛ 08:07

Point out Both **planta** and **piso** refer to the floor of a building and are used interchangeably in this text. Jeans have various names in different countries: **vaqueros** (Spain), **mahones** (Puerto Rico), **pantalones mecánicos, jeans, bluyines,** etc.

1 ¿Están los espías en la segunda planta? ¿en la primera? ¿en la tercera?
2 ¿En qué piso están los espías?
3 ¿Están en el departamento de mujeres? ¿de hombres?
4 ¿En qué departamento están?
5 ¿Encuentra el espía una falda rosada? ¿una blusa roja? *(other colors, other articles of clothing)*
6 ¿Para quién encuentra el espía la falda y la blusa?
7 ¿Combina bien la blusa con la falda?
8 ¿Prefiere la espía ropa deportiva? ¿ropa elegante?
9 ¿Qué tipo de ropa prefiere la espía?
10 ¿Se prueba unos jeans? ¿una sudadera? *(other articles)*
11 ¿Es la talla perfecta?
12 ¿Compra la espía los jeans? ¿la sudadera? *(other articles)*
13 ¿Qué compra la espía?
14 ¿Prefieres tú la ropa deportiva o la ropa elegante?

Side 5, 14588 to 15492

5 ⬛ 08:38

1 ¿Están los espías en el departamento de deportes? *(other departments)*
2 ¿Se prueban unos zapatos deportivos? *(other articles of clothing)*
3 ¿Están los zapatos en oferta?
4 ¿Cuestan mucho los zapatos?
5 ¿Compran los espías los zapatos?
6 ¿Qué compran los espías?
7 ¿Pagan en la caja?
8 ¿Dónde pagan?

Side 5, 15512 to 16310

6 ⬛ 09:05

Suggestions Ask questions about what each of the characters in the illustration is wearing. Identify the spies by eliminating those who are wearing the wrong clothes.

1 ¿Hay una fiesta esta noche?
2 ¿Qué hay esta noche?
3 ¿Hay mucha gente en la fiesta?

Suggestions Begin by having students close their books while you narrate one section at a time, using the transparencies to clarify meaning without translation. Then ask **Comprehension Checks.** Repeat the process with each section.

Using the video Play one section at a time after narrating it using the transparencies. Freeze the video and ask **Comprehension Checks.** Repeat with each section.

4 ¿Lleva este hombre pantalones grises? *(other articles the male spy bought)*
5 ¿Qué lleva este hombre?
6 ¿Lleva esta mujer unos jeans? *(other articles the female spy bought)*
7 ¿Qué lleva esta mujer?
8 ¿Es el espía? ¿Es la espía?
9 ¿Quién es el espía? ¿la espía?

Side 5, 16328 to 16676

09:17–
12:39

Side 5, 16710 to 22750

Early Production Checks

The **Early Production Checks** are available on cards in the TRP.

1   09:23

¿Qué le piensas comprar?
1 ¿Quién es? *(Point to each.)*
   Manolo / Víctor / La dependiente.
2 ¿Dónde están, en una iglesia o en un almacén? *En un almacén.*
3 ¿Qué quiere comprar Manolo, una camiseta? *Sí.*
4 ¿Para quién quiere comprar la camiseta, para Víctor o para su novia? *Para su novia.*
5 ¿Dónde pueden encontrar las camisetas, en la sección de deportes? *Sí.*
6 ¿Qué pueden encontrar en la sección de deportes?
   Una camiseta.
7 ¿Dónde está la sección de deportes, en la tercera o en la cuarta planta?
   En la cuarta planta.
8 ¿Toman el ascensor o las escaleras? *Las escaleras.*

Side 5, 16867 to 17835

2   09:56

¿Cuánto cuesta?
Point out In Spain, the use of **tú** rather than **usted** is widespread. Waiters, taxi drivers, and store clerks readily use **tú** with their customers.

Note Accept brief phrases or one– and two–word answers to all **Early Production Checks,** as in **1** above. It is not necessary for students to answer in complete sentences.

1 ¿Quién es? *(Point to each.)*
2 ¿Es la mañana, la tarde o la noche?
3 ¿Busca Manolo un regalo?
4 ¿Qué busca Manolo?
5 ¿Para quién es el regalo?
6 ¿Qué recomienda el dependiente, una camiseta?
7 ¿Cuesta mucho?

¿QUÉ DECIMOS..?

Al ir de compras

1 ¿Qué le piensas comprar?

2 ¿Cuánto cuesta?

226   *doscientos veintiséis*   *UNIDAD 5*

8 ¿Cuesta dos mil setecientas pesetas?
9 ¿Cuánto cuesta?
10 ¿Es parte del dinero de Víctor?
11 ¿Recuerda Manolo que parte del dinero es de Víctor?
12 ¿Compran la camiseta azul?
13 ¿Siguen buscando?
14 ¿Adónde quiere ir Víctor, a la sección de zapatos o a la sección de deportes?

Side 5, 17855 to 19650

Purpose This section presents language needed to describe what people are wearing in real-life contexts. Students should not be asked to memorize dialogues word for word.

3 ¿Cuál es tu talla?

4 ¿Cómo que no tenemos dinero?

¿Cuál es tu talla?

1 ¿Quién es? *(Point to Manolo, then salesclerk.)*
2 ¿Le gustan las camisas a Manolo?
3 ¿Están de moda las camisas?
4 ¿Están muy de moda?
5 ¿Sabe Manolo su talla? ¿Qué talla llevas tú? *(Ask student.)*
6 ¿Son diferentes las tallas en España?
7 ¿Se prueba una camisa Manolo?
8 ¿Qué se prueba Manolo?
9 ¿Es su talla?
10 ¿Le gusta o le encanta?
11 ¿Paga en la caja?
12 ¿Dónde paga?

Side 5, 19720 to 21381

¿Cómo que no tenemos dinero?

1 ¿Quién es? *(Point to Víctor, Manolo, and cashier.)*
2 ¿Cuesta cuatro mil novecientas pesetas la camisa?
3 ¿Cuánto cuesta la camisa?
4 ¿Compra algo más Manolo?
5 ¿Hay zapatos fabulosos?
6 ¿Quiere comprar los zapatos Víctor?
7 ¿Puede comprar los zapatos Víctor?
8 ¿Por qué no puede comprar los zapatos?

Side 5, 21404 to 22750

Suggestions Begin by having students close their books while you narrate one section at a time, using the transparencies to clarify meaning without translation. Then ask **Early Production Checks.** Repeat the process with each section.

Using the video Play one section at a time after narrating it using the transparencies. Freeze the video and ask **Early Production Checks.** Repeat with each section.

CHARLEMOS UN POCO

Vocabulario opcional

pantalones cortos, traje de baño, sandalias, abrigo, guantes, bufanda, botas.

A. ¡De compras!
Call on individuals. These statements/questions are generic. They do not refer to the *¿Qué decimos ... ?* in this lesson.

1 dependiente
2 cliente
3 dependiente
4 dependiente
5 cliente
6 dependiente
7 cliente
8 cliente
9 cliente
10 dependiente

B. ¡Gustos diferentes!

1 ¿Te gustan las sudaderas rosadas? Sí, pero me gustan más las sudaderas moradas.

2 ¿Te gustan las faldas azules? Sí, pero me gustan más las faldas grises.

3 ¿Te gustan las blusas amarillas? Sí, pero me gustan más las blusas marrones.

4 ¿Te gustan los suéteres anaranjados? Sí, pero me gustan más los suéteres blancos.

5 ¿Te gustan los vestidos rojos? Sí, pero me gustan más los vestidos verdes.

6 ¿Te gustan los zapatos negros? Sí, pero me gustan más los zapatos blancos.

7 ¿Te gustan los sombreros anaranjados? Sí, pero me gustan más los sombreros morados.

8 ¿Te gustan los trajes grises? Sí, pero me gustan más los trajes azules.

9 ¿Te gustan las chaquetas grises? Sí, pero me gustan más las chaquetas verdes.

Expansion Your parent is shopping for you. How does he/she respond to the clerk's questions?
Dependiente: **¿Le gustan los zapatos marrones?**
Mamá o Papá: **No, prefiere los negros.**

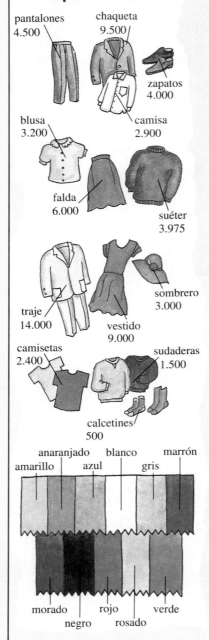

¡En oferta!
Ropa de invierno

pantalones 4.500
chaqueta 9.500
zapatos 4.000
blusa 3.200
camisa 2.900
falda 6.000
suéter 3.975
traje 14.000
vestido 9.000
sombrero 3.000
camisetas 2.400
sudaderas 1.500
calcetines 500

anaranjado   blanco   marrón
amarillo   azul   gris
morado   rojo   verde
negro   rosado

CHARLEMOS UN POCO

A. ¡De compras!
Estás en el almacén. ¿Quién está hablando, un **cliente** o un **dependiente**?

1. Estas camisetas son muy populares.
2. Perdón. No puedo encontrar los suéteres.
3. ¿Qué color prefiere usted?
4. ¿Cuál es tu talla?
5. Busco un regalo para mi novia. ¿Qué me recomienda?
6. ¿Puedo ayudarte?
7. ¿Dónde pago?
8. ¿Cuánto cuesta esa chaqueta?
9. Prefiero los pantalones negros.
10. El rojo cuesta 2.700 pesetas.

B. ¡Gustos diferentes!
Tú y un(a) amigo(a) están mirando un catálogo. ¿Qué dicen?

MODELO Tú: **¿Te gustan las camisetas verdes?**
Amigo(a): **Sí, pero me gustan más las camisetas negras.**

1. 2. 3.
4. 5. 6.
7. 8. 9.

Purpose These activities provide guided practice to students beginning to produce new language necessary to make a purchase, express preferences, and describe clothing.

C. Los jóvenes norteamericanos.   Un(a) dependiente hispana quiere saber qué les gusta a los jóvenes norteamericanos. Contesta sus preguntas.

 MODELO   Compañero(a): ¿Les gustan los jeans?
　　　　　　 Tú: **Sí, nos gustan los jeans.** o
　　　　　　　　　 Nos encantan. o
　　　　　　　　　 No, no nos gustan los jeans.

1.　　　　　2.　　　　　3.　　　　　4.

5.　　　　　6.　　　　　7.　　　　　8.

CH. Ropa favorita.   ¿Cuál es la ropa favorita de los miembros de tu familia?

EJEMPLO   **A mamá le gustan los sombreros blancos.**

a mi tía	sombreros blancos
a mi abuelo	faldas largas
a mis primos	ropa elegante
a papá	pantalones azules
a mí	ropa cara
a mi hermana	camisetas feas
a mi mamá y a mí	vestidos bonitos
	jeans
	ropa informal
	blusas azules
	¿ . . . ?

LECCIÓN 2

D. ¡Feliz cumpleaños!

1 Mi amigo . . . piensa comprarle un sombrero rojo.
2 Mi amiga . . . y yo pensamos comprarle una falda blanca.
3 Mis amigos . . . y . . . piensan comprarle una sudadera rosada.
4 Mis amigas . . . y . . . piensan comprarle una blusa negra.
5 Tú piensas comprarle un suéter morado, ¿verdad?
6 Su mamá piensa comprarle un vestido verde.
7 Su hermana piensa comprarle un libro interesante.
8 Yo pienso comprarle un bolígrafo caro.
9 Su papá piensa comprarle unos zapatos negros.
10 Su primo piensa comprarle una mochila roja.

Follow-up variation In groups of 3–4, decide what each person in the group prefers to buy if it were your birthday (or the birthday of school principal or another teacher in school).

E. Otro fin de semana.
Answers will vary. Encourage students to personalize by using their own friends' names.

F. ¡Hay fiesta! Allow 2–3 min
for students to do in pairs. Then call on students to repeat activity for class. When students have finished, personalize the activity by asking students what they can do to help a friend give a party.

1 ¿Quién puede preparar los sándwiches? Paco puede preparar los sándwiches.
2 ¿Quiénes pueden enviar las invitaciones? Gloria y Fito pueden enviar las invitaciones.
3 ¿Quiénes pueden llamar a los amigos? Tú y Silvia pueden llamar a los amigos.
4 ¿Quién puede buscar la música? Beto puede buscar la música.
5 ¿Quiénes pueden tocar la guitarra? Ana y Susana pueden tocar la guitarra.
6 ¿Quiénes pueden cantar para los invitados? Tú y yo podemos cantar para los invitados.
7 ¿Quién puede comprar los refrescos? Yo puedo comprar los refrescos.
8 ¿Quién puede hacer el pastel? Tú puedes hacer el pastel.

Pensar: e → ie

pienso	pensamos
piensas	
piensa	piensan
piensa	piensan

Querer and **preferir** follow the same **e → ie** pattern.

See **¿Por qué se dice así?,** *page G71, section 5.5.*

Poder: o → ue

puedo	podemos
puedes	
puede	pueden
puede	pueden

Encontrar follows the same **o → ue** pattern.

See **¿Por qué se dice así?,** *page G71, section 5.5.*

D. ¡Feliz cumpleaños! Es el cumpleaños de una amiga. ¿Qué le van a comprar todos?

MODELO   mi amiga . . . / camiseta / amarillo
Mi amiga Lupe piensa comprarle una camiseta amarilla.

1. mi amigo . . . / sombrero / rojo
2. mi amiga . . . y yo / falda / blanco
3. mis amigos . . . y . . . / sudadera / rosado
4. mis amigas . . . y . . . / blusa / negro
5. tú / suéter / morado / ¿verdad?
6. su mamá / vestido / verde
7. su hermano / libro / interesante
8. yo / bolígrafo / caro
9. su papá / zapatos / negro
10. su primo / mochila / rojo

E. Otro fin de semana. Tú y tus amigos están hablando de lo que prefieren hacer este fin de semana. ¿Qué dicen?

EJEMPLO   **Esteban prefiere leer novelas.**

yo mis amigos tú mi amigo . . . mi amiga y yo mi amiga . . .	querer preferir pensar	ver la tele pasear en bicicleta alquilar un video ir a bailar comer pizza ir de compras leer novelas hablar por teléfono escuchar música salir con unos amigos ¿ . . . ?

F. ¡Hay fiesta! Tú vas a dar una fiesta. Pregúntale a un(a) amigo quién puede ayudarte.

MODELO   Laura: limpiar la casa
Tú: **¿Quién puede limpiar la casa?**
Compañero(a): **Laura puede limpiar la casa.**

1. Paco: preparar los sándwiches
2. Gloria y Fito: enviar las invitaciones
3. tú y Silvia: llamar a los amigos
4. Beto: buscar la música
5. Ana y Susana: tocar la guitarra
6. tú y yo: cantar para los invitados
7. yo: comprar los refrescos
8. tú: hacer el pastel

G. ¿Dónde está?

G. ¿Dónde está? Tú y tus amigos están en el almacén Alarcón, pero no encuentran lo que buscan. ¿Qué le preguntan al dependiente?

 MODELO   mi amiga y yo
          Tú: **Perdón, señor, pero mi amiga y yo no encontramos las blusas.**
          Compañero(a): **Están en el departamento de señoras.**

1. mi amiga   **2.** mis amigas   **3.** mis amigos

4. yo   **5.** mi amigo y yo   **6.** mi amiga y yo

H. La nueva dependiente.

H. La nueva dependiente. El director del almacén Alarcón está hablando con una nueva dependiente. ¿Qué le dice?

MODELO   departamento de niños
          El departamento de niños está en el tercer piso.

1. departamento de electrónica
2. departamento de señoras
3. departamento de jóvenes
4. joyería
5. cafetería
6. departamento de caballeros
7. perfumería
8. departamento de deportes
9. zapatería
10. departamento de niños

LECCIÓN 2

**Almacén Alarcón
Departamentos**

Planta / Piso
10 Departamento de electrónica
 9 Departamento del hogar
 8 Cafetería
 7 Departamento de caballeros
 6 Departamento de señoras
 5 Departamento de jóvenes
 4 Departamento de deportes
 3 Departamento de niños
 2 Zapatería
 1 Perfumería
PB Joyería

Ordinal numbers
Used to establish order

*primero	sexto
segundo	séptimo
*tercero	octavo
cuarto	noveno
quinto	décimo

***Primero** and **tercero** change to **primer** and **tercer** before a masculine singular noun.

*See ¿**Por qué se dice así?**, page G74, section 5.6.*

PB refers to **planta baja**, the ground floor of Spanish buildings.

G. ¿Dónde está? Have students refer to **Almacén Alarcón** chart as they do this activity. Allow 2–3 min for students to do in pairs. Then call on different pairs to role-play each item.

1 Perdón, señor, pero mi amiga no encuentra las camisetas. Están en el departamento de jóvenes.
2 Perdón, señor, pero mis amigas no encuentran las faldas. Están en el departamento de señoras.
3 Perdón, señor, pero mis amigos no encuentran las sudaderas. Están en el departamento de caballeros (jóvenes, deportes).
4 Perdón, señor, pero yo no encuentro el perfume. Está en la perfumería.
5 Perdón, señor, pero mi amigo y yo no encontramos las camisas. Están en el departamento de caballeros (jóvenes).
6 Perdón, señor, pero mi amiga y yo no encontramos los zapatos deportivos. Están en el departamento de deportes (la zapatería).

H. La nueva dependiente. Have students refer to **Almacén Alarcón** chart as they do this activity.

1 El departamento de electrónica está en el décimo piso.
2 El departamento de señoras está en el sexto piso.
3 El departamento de jóvenes está en el quinto piso.
4 La joyería está en la planta baja.
5 La cafetería está en el octavo piso.
6 El departamento de caballeros está en el séptimo piso.
7 La perfumería está en el primer piso.
8 El departamento de deportes está en el cuarto piso.
9 La zapatería está en el segundo piso.
10 El departamento de niños está en el tercer piso.

Costar

Costar is an **o → ue** stem-changing verb used mostly in the third person singular and plural.

La falda **cuesta** quinientas mil pesetas. ¿Cuánto **cuestan** las blusas?

*See **¿Por qué se dice así?**, page G71, section 5.5.*

I. En el almacén. Varias personas van de compras. ¿Qué hacen allí?

EJEMPLO **Mamá encuentra una blusa roja en el departamento de señoras.**

		suéter
		jeans
papá		falda
yo	querer comprar	vestido
Paquito	encontrar	camisa
mamá y yo	buscar	zapatos
mis tíos	preferir comprar	sudadera
tú		blusa
		camiseta
		pantalones

J. ¿Yo millonario(a)? You have just inherited a large sum of money and are on a shopping spree in a large department store. Buy *everything* in the store window.

15.800 ptas · 11.500 ptas · 1.500 ptas · 1.900 ptas · 3.100 ptas · 56.000 ptas · 5.600 ptas · 3.100 ptas · 14.999 ptas · 5.100 ptas · 1.010 ptas · 9.399 ptas · 3.700 ptas

MODELO pantalones
Tú: **Quiero comprar los pantalones grises. ¿Cuánto cuestan?**
Compañero(a): **¿Los pantalones grises? Cuestan catorce mil novecientas noventa y nueve pesetas.**

1. zapatos	**4.** falda	**7.** suéter	**10.** blusa
2. vestido	**5.** camiseta	**8.** trajes	**11.** jeans
3. camisa	**6.** chaqueta	**9.** botas	**12.** sudadera

CHARLEMOS UN POCO MÁS

A. Vamos de compras. You won a **1.000.000 peseta** shopping spree! Using this advertisement, make a list of the items you want to buy for each member of your family. Next to each item, write the color and the price. Compare your list with your partner's. Recommend other items or colors or comment on whether you also want to buy those items.

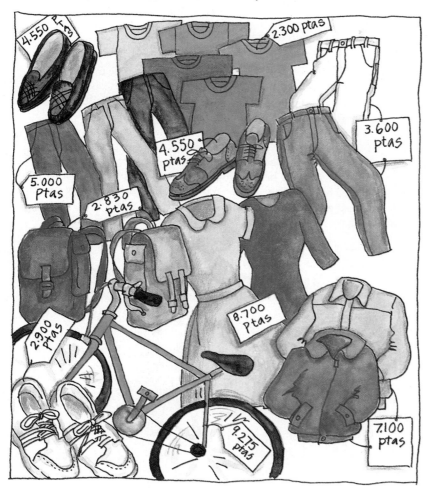

B. ¿Quién es el detective? A member of your class is an undercover detective, but only your teacher knows the person's identity. Find out who it is by asking yes / no questions about the person's clothing.

 EJEMPLO You: **¿Lleva pantalones azules?**
Teacher: **Sí, lleva pantalones azules.**

LECCIÓN 2

A. Vamos de compras.
Allow 4–5 min. Then call on individuals and ask **¿Qué quieres comprar para tu** *[relative]*? **¿Cuánto cuesta?**

B. ¿Quién es el detective?
Do first as class activity, then in small groups. Write name of student on piece of paper. A "yes" answer allows same student to ask another question or to guess identity of mystery student. First person to identify "detective" takes teacher's place and game continues as students try to identify new "detective."

Purpose These activities are designed to allow students to create with the language of making purchases and describing clothing.

C. Desfile de modas.

Announce the day before that there will be a fashion show. Tell students they may want to dress especially for the occasion. Students may bring appropriate background music for their presentation.

Variation Have students do a four-seasons fashion show: they bring in seasonal clothing or describe what is worn different seasons.

CH. ¡Mi talento especial!

Allow 2–3 min. Encourage students to write at least two things. Help shy students focus on strengths. Then in groups of 5 or 6, ask students to tell others in their groups what they can do. If two students mention same thing, have them go to board and write *[name]* **y** *[name]* **pueden** *[what they can do]*. Verify by asking individuals if it is true and having them answer **Sí, nosotros podemos . . .**

D. ¡Nos encanta! Students

should write either **A** *[name]* **y a mí nos gusta / encanta . . .** or **A** *[name]* **y a** *[name]* **les gusta / encanta . . .**

E. ¿Son los mismos?

Tell students they may not look at each other's drawings as they describe the people and decide if any are the same persons.

F. En orden, por favor.

Allow 2–3 min to prepare lists. Then, in small groups, ask students to read their lists to other members of their groups to find the person in the group that has the closest schedule to their own.

C. Desfile de modas. In groups of five or six, prepare a fashion show commentary for each member of your group. Take turns modeling the clothing you have worn to school today while a group member describes your outfit to the class. Alternate roles so that everyone in the group has an opportunity to both model and describe.

CH. ¡Mi talento especial! Everyone has special talents. What special talents do you have? Write two or three things that you can do that make you particularly proud.

EJEMPLO **Yo puedo tocar la guitarra.** o
Yo puedo hacer un pastel de chocolate.

D. ¡Nos encanta! Write down two things that you like to do and two things that you love to do. In groups of four, read your lists to each other. Identify the person whose list is most similar to yours. Go to the board and write what the two of you have listed in both categories.

E. ¿Son los mismos? You and your partner are at a party, where your partner has met four interesting people. (Your teacher will provide your partner with a drawing of these four people.) You have met the four people pictured below, whose names you can't remember. Are they the same four people your partner met? Describe them and then decide whether or not you have met the same four people.

F. En orden, por favor. List ten things that you do on school days in the order in which you do them. Include the classes you attend during the day.

EJEMPLO **Primero, voy al colegio. Segundo, voy a mi clase de historia. Tercero, . . .**

Dramatizaciones

A. ¡Es mi favorita! Take notes as you interview four or five classmates to find out . . .

- what their favorite outfit is.
- what color or colors it is.
- when they wear it.
- if it is old or new.

B. ¡Qué elegante! You and your mother (or father) are shopping for a new jacket for you. Role-play the situation with a partner.

Tu mamá (papá)	**Tú**
■ Recommend a jacket.	■ Say you prefer a different color than the one he or she recommends.
■ Ask what he or she thinks about another jacket.	■ Respond.
■ Ask if he or she likes it.	■ Respond and comment on the style.
■ Ask how much it costs.	■ Respond.
■ Indicate if you think it is expensive or inexpensive.	■ Say that you like it and that you want to buy it.

C. En la tienda. You are shopping for a complete new outfit. You know what you want and in what colors, but you don't want to spend a great deal of money. Role-play your conversation with a clerk.

- Tell the clerk what you are looking for.
- Ask the prices of various items.
- Find out what colors are available.
- Decide what to buy and ask the clerk for the total price.

CH. Vamos de compras. It is a rainy Saturday afternoon, and you want to go shopping. Call your friend and make plans.

Tú	**Amigo(a)**
■ Invite your friend to go shopping.	■ Indicate that you do want to go but you have to do something first.
■ Say where you want to shop and what you want to buy.	■ Tell what you need to buy.
■ Indicate four stores at which you want to shop, naming them in the order in which you will go to them.	■ Ask directions to the first store where you will meet.
■ Explain the best way to get there. Be specific.	■ Ask questions to be sure you understand the directions.

A. ¡Es mi favorita! Allow 4–5 min. Then call on individuals to report to class on the most interesting information they gathered.

Expansion Ask a friend to recommend an outfit for you to wear on various occasions—to school, on a date, to a dance or party.

B. ¡Qué elegante! Work in pairs as half the class prepares **B** and half **C**. Allow 6–8 min. Ask comprehension questions after each pair presents their role play.

Purpose Here students recycle all previously learned structures and vocabulary needed to make purchases and describe clothing.

Suggestions Do these role plays spontaneously, not from written scripts. Circulate among groups. Limit time allowed so that students do not get off task. Ask one or two pairs to recreate their exchange for the whole class.

IMPACTO CULTURAL

¡No me digas!

Purpose This short dialogue includes some interesting cross-cultural miscommunication in the use of floor numbers. Students are expected to discover the problem on their own.

Suggestion Before you turn to explanations of the answers on page 418, have students themselves try to explain why the wrong answers are wrong.

Answers

1 Rick may well think that Betty is trying to distract him, since he is confused about what floor he is on. Actually, Betty knows that they are on the wrong floor. Try another answer.

②In Spain, as in all Spanish-speaking countries, the ground floor of multistory buildings is the **planta baja.** On elevators, the button for the ground floor is marked **PB. La primera planta** is the first floor above the ground floor. This is why Betty suggests they have to go up one floor.

3 The shoes are on sale according to the advertisement in the window. This is not the cause for the confusion.

Y ahora, ¡a leer!

Antes de empezar

Suggestions Have students work in pairs. Assign question 1 to half the pairs and question 2 to the other half. Allow 4–5 min. Then call on individual pairs to read their answers and ask class to comment.

 ¡Ojo! **Aparcamiento** *(parking)* in other countries is referred to as **estacionamiento, parqueo,** and **parqueadero.**

Answers

1 Las respuestas varían. Este almacén tiene ocho pisos—siete plantas más la planta baja.
2 Las respuestas varían.

¡No me digas!

La planta baja. Rick and Betty are American tourists shopping in Madrid. Read their conversation. Then answer the question that follows.

Rick:	**Mira, Betty, hay zapatos deportivos en oferta. Vamos a verlos.** *(Entran en el almacén.)* **Perdón, señor. ¿En qué planta está el departamento de deportes?**
Señor:	**En la primera planta.**

Después de un rato . . .

Rick:	**¡Qué raro! Deben estar por aquí pero no los encuentro.**
Betty:	**¿Los zapatos? ¡Hombre! Están en la primera planta.**
Rick:	**Sí, ya sé.**
Betty:	**Bueno. Vamos a subir.**
Rick:	**¿Subir? ¿Para qué? Sube tú si quieres. ¡Yo no voy a subir hasta encontrar el departamento de deportes!**

▶ Why does Rick refuse to go up one floor?

1. He thinks Betty is trying to distract him so she can do her own shopping.
2. He doesn't understand how the floors are numbered.
3. The tennis shoes are not really on sale. The sign on the window was meant only to get the shoppers' attention.   ❏ Check your answer on page 418.

Y ahora, ¡a leer!

Antes de empezar

1. ¿Cuántos pisos tiene el almacén más grande de tu ciudad? ¿Cuántos pisos tiene este almacén?
2. ¿Hay aparcamiento en los almacenes de tu ciudad? ¿Es aparcamiento subterráneo? ¿Sabes cuántos pisos de aparcamiento hay?

236 *doscientos treinta y seis*

UNIDAD 5

Guía de departamentos

P-4	Servicios: Aparcamiento.		
P-3	Servicios: Aparcamiento.		
P-2	Servicios: Aparcamiento.		
P-1	Servicios: Aparcamiento. Caja de Aparcamiento. Taller de Montaje de Accesorios del Automóvil. Carta de Compras. Objetos Perdidos. Consigna del Supermercado. Foto-Matón. **SALIDA:** Aparcamientos P-2, P-3 y P4.		

SEMI-SOTANO

Departamentos: **Hogar Menaje.** Artesanía. Cerámica. Cristalería. Cubertería. Accesorios del Automóvil. Loza. Orfebrería. Porcelana (Lladró-Capodimonte). Platería. Regalos de hogar. Vajillas. Saneamientos. Exposición de baños. Electrodomésticos (grandes y pequeños). Muebles de cocina. Plásticos. Artículos de limpieza. Ferretería. Menaje de acero inoxidable. Baterías de cocina. **Imagen y Sonido.** Discos. T.V. Vídeo. Hi-Fi. Micro-Informática. Instrumentos musicales. Radioaficionados. **Plantas y flores. Animales.** Accesorios. Animales. Peces y tortugas.

PLANTA BAJA

Departamentos: **Complementos de moda.** Perfumería. Cosmética. Joyería. Bisutería. Relojería. Fumador (Cartier, Dupont). Librería. Papelería. Rincón del pintor. Bolsos. Cinturones. Marroquinería. Pañuelos. Medias. Sombreros. Paraguas. Abanicos. Turismo. Juegos de mesa. Fotografía. Golosinas. Pastelería. Bombonería.

 1.ª PLANTA

Departamentos: **Hogar Textil.** Mantelerías. Toallas. Tapicería. Visillos y cortinas. Alfombras y moquetas. Colchones y cojines. Ropa de cama y mesa. Edredones y mantas. Patrones moda. Lanas y sedas. Boutique de tejidos. Papeles pintados. Persianas. **Zapatería** (Señoras, Caballeros, Jóvenes y Niños).

 2.ª PLANTA

Departamentos: **Caballeros.** Boutiques internacionales (Guy Laroche, Christian Dior, Pierre Balmain, Paul & Shark, Golf and Green, Canova's Club, Burberrys). Pantalones. Americanas. Trajes. Camisería. Coordinados sport. Prendas de abrigo. Punto. Ropa interior. Piel. Baño. Complementos moda. Tallas especiales. Sastrería a medida. Artículos de viaje. Zapatería caballero.

 3.ª PLANTA

Departamentos: **Infantil: Niños/as (4 a 10 años).** Pantalones. Camisería. Ropa interior. Punto. Complementos. Tiendas Tizza's y Bus Stop. Colegios. Zapatería. **Bebés.** Confección. Punto. Ropa interior. Zapatería bebé. Caprichos. Carrocerías. Tiendas Dulces y Baby-Bus. **Chicos/as (11 a 14 años).** Punto. Camisería. Pantalones. Confección. Ropa interior. Tiendas Aguaviva, C2C y Brotes. **Juguetería.** Modelismo. Juegos. Bicicletas. Maquetas y accesorios. Radio control.

 4.ª PLANTA

Departamentos: **Señoras.** Boutiques internacionales (Pierre Balmain, Guy Laroche, Balenciaga, George Rech, Roberto Verinno, Francisco Delgado, Paco Casado, Geiger, Lasserre, Burberrys, Golf and Green, Olivier Strelli). Boutique alta peletería. Ante y napa. Faldas y blusas. Pantalones. Pronovias. Punto. Sport. Vestidos. Chaquetas. Abrigos. Tallas especiales. Priscille. Lencería y corsetería. Futura mamá. Uniformes de Servicio. Tienda del baño sras. Zapatería sra. y complementos.

 5.ª PLANTA

Departamentos: **Moda Joven Ella.** Tiendas jóvenes (Drach, Ziva, Joly, Carla, Tintoretto, Arco Iris, Mexx. Internacionales). Punto. Sport. Faldas y blusas. Pantalones. Vestidos. Bañadores. Lencería y Corsetería. Prendas de abrigo. **Moda Joven El.** Tienda Peter Lord. Tienda Pietro Peretti. Tienda Miguel Beruel. Prendas de abrigo. Camisería. Bañadores. Ropa interior. Pantalones. Punto. Trajes y americanas. Sport. Tiendas internacionales. Piel. Tienda vaquera (él y ella). **Zapatería joven** (Camper y Rover). **Discos.** Complementos moda.

6.ª PLANTA

Departamentos: **Deportes.** Zapatería deportiva. Tenis. Esquí. Hípica. Golf. Montaña. Caza y pesca. Gimnasia y atletismo. Ciclismo y moto. Armería. Boutique Surf. Tiempo libre. Tienda Lacoste. **Supermercado.**

7.ª PLANTA

Departamentos: **Oportunidades.** Tienda de Regalos (Cosas). Promociones especiales.

 El Corte Inglés

MADRID · PRINCESA

1. Indica a qué planta de El Corte Inglés Princesa debes ir para comprar los cosas que buscas.
   a. Mañana tu prima va a cumplir seis años y le buscas un regalo.
   b. Este año tú piensas regalarle una chaqueta a tu padre el Día del Padre. Sabes que en El Corte Inglés tienen chaquetas muy bonitas.
   c. La próxima semana tú vas a una discoteca por primera vez. Quieres ropa nueva para la ocasión.
   ch. Tu madre es tu mejor amiga y quieres comprarle un regalito.
   d. Tu tía se va a casar y tú necesitas comprarle un regalo de bodas.
2. ¿En qué planta encuentras las siguientes cosas?

libros	zapatos deportivos	ropa interior	trajes de baño
perfume	zapatos de mujer	comida	bicicletas

UNIDAD 5 Lección 2 **237**

Guía de departamentos

Suggestions Encourage students to make reasoned guesses about unknown words. They should feel good about how much they *do* understand rather than frustrated by what they don't understand. Remind students about false cognates.

Verifiquemos

Point out The word **Princesa** refers to the street where one branch of the store is located.

Answers

1 a. Planta 3: Niños, Juguetería
   b. Planta 2: Caballeros
   c. Planta 5: Moda joven
   ch. Planta 4: Señoras o Planta baja: Complementos de moda
   d. Planta 1: Hogar textil o Semi-sótano: Hogar menaje
2 Libros: Planta baja
   Perfume: Planta baja
   Zapatos deportivos: Planta 6
   Zapatos de mujer: Plantas 1 y 4
   Ropa interior: Plantas 2, 3, 4, 5
   Comida: Planta 6
   Trajes de baño: Plantas 2, 4, 5
   Bicicletas: Planta 6

Y ahora, ¡a leer!

Purpose This is an authentic department store directory. Students are expected to glean information from it without translation, using limited vocabulary and cognates.

OBJECTIVES

Communicative Goals

- Naming snack foods
- Ordering a snack
- Taking an order at a café

Reading

- **Leamos ahora**
  La sopa castellana:
  Readers' Theater
- Reading strategy:
  Reading aloud

Writing

- **Escribamos un poco**
  Short descriptive composition
- Writing strategy:
  Making an outline

Structure

- 5.7 Stem-changing verbs:
  e → i
- 5.8 **Tener** idioms
- 5.9 Indirect object pronouns

¿ Qué pedimos ?

ACTIVE VOCABULARY

En un café

almuerzo	cuenta
carta	propina
cuchara	rico

Bebidas

agua	leche
… mineral	limonada
café	

Comidas

bizcocho	pollo
hamburguesa	… frito
jamón	queso
manzana	sándwich mixto
melón	sopa
naranja	
papas / patatas	
… fritas	

Modismos con *tener*

tener hambre	tener prisa
tener sed	tener razón
tener calor	
tener frío	

Verbos e → i

conseguir (i)	servir (i)
decir (i)	repetir (i)
seguir (i)	vestir (i)
pedir (i)	

Otros verbos

almorzar (ue)	traer
buscar	fuimos
desear	hicieron
explicar	

Palabras y expresiones

caliente	con énfasis
fiesta	lo siento
libre	sí, claro
otro	
para	
universidad	
vale	

ANTICIPEMOS

CAFÉ BILBAO

Bocadillos variados

Jamón serrano 250 Ptas.	**Jamón york** 250 Ptas.
Queso 225 Ptas.	**Hamburguesa** 300 Ptas.
Sándwich 225 Ptas.	**Sándwich mixto** 250 Ptas.

Patatas fritas 200 Ptas.

Bebidas

Refrescos variados	115 Ptas.
Limonada	115 Ptas.
Zumo de naranja	150 Ptas.
Agua mineral	125 Ptas.
Leche	100 Ptas.
Café con leche	110 Ptas.
Té	100 Ptas.

Postres

Fruta	85 Ptas.
Helado	200 Ptas.
Flan	175 Ptas.
Bizcocho	150 Ptas.

¿Qué piensas tú?

1. Estudia el menú. ¿Crees que este menú es para una comida principal? ¿Por qué crees que sí o que no?

2. ¿Es como los menús en Estados Unidos? ¿Cuáles son las semejanzas y las diferencias?

3. ¿Crees que es la hora de la comida principal del día? ¿Qué están comiendo las personas en la foto? Explica tu respuesta.

4. ¿Cuánto crees que va a costar la comida en dólares? ¿Cuánto deben dejar de propina para el camarero?

5. En tu opinión, ¿cuál es la diferencia entre un café y un restaurante?

6. ¿Qué tipo de restaurante en Estados Unidos es más similar a un café español?

7. ¿De qué vas a poder hablar al final de la lección?

Purpose To focus students on the language needed to order a snack in a café. Also to encourage students to observe and compare U.S. restaurants with cafés in Hispanic countries without forming judgments.

¿Qué piensas tú?

Point out Spaniards use **zumo** for *juice* whereas Latin Americans use **jugo**.

Answers

1 No. Es un menú de bocadillos. Un menú de comidas principales es más grande y ofrece una variedad de platos.

2 Es semejante a los menús de lugares como Burger King o McDonald's. No es como los menús de restaurantes que sirven una cena completa.

3 No en España ni en países hispanos. Los estudiantes pueden creer que es la comida principal porque es probable que ellos mismos coman entre las 5:00 y las 6:00 de la noche. Después de expresar ellos sus ideas, vale explicar que en los países hispanos la cena es normalmente a las nueve de la noche. Aquí sólo están tomando la merienda— unos bocadillos a eso de las 5:00 o 6:00 de la tarde.

4 Hágales recordar el valor del dólar en pesetas al contestar la primera pregunta. Si saben algo de propinas, es probable que los estudiantes asuman que el quince por ciento es la propina apropiada. Vale mencionar que en España y en muchos países hispanos, la propina se incluye en la cuenta.

5 Las respuestas van a variar. Es probable que mencionen que un restaurante tiene un menú más variado y ofrece varios cursos: entremés, ensaladas, sopas, carnes, pescados, etc. Un café usualmente ofrece sándwiches y unos cuantos platos.

6 Las respuestas van a variar pero es probable que mencionen restaurantes como McDonald's, Burger King, Denny's, etc.

7 **Van a aprender el nombre de varias comidas. También van a aprender a pedir la merienda en un café. Finalmente aprenderán a decir que tienen hambre, sed, prisa, etc.**

TAPE/
DISC
12:40–
17:01

Side 5, 22778 to 30600

Comprehension Checks

The **Comprehension Checks** are available on cards in the TRP.

1   **12:46**

1 ¿Quién es? ¿Cómo se llama?
2 ¿Es camarero?
3 ¿Qué es Antonio?
4 ¿Es fácil la vida de un camarero?
5 ¿Es la vida de un camarero fácil o difícil?

Side 5, 22961 to 23455

2   **13:03**

Suggestions Point at menu = **carta**. Glance at watch or clock, look impatient = **tengo prisa.** Fan yourself = **tengo calor.** Contrast **tener calor / frío.** Pant = **tengo sed.** Rub stomach = **tengo hambre.** Point at drinks as they are named. Gesture towards self = **traerme.** Draw a bill on board = **cuenta.**

1 ¿Es la carta?
2 ¿Quiere el hombre ver la carta?
3 ¿Tiene prisa el hombre?
4 ¿Tiene mucho tiempo el hombre?
5 ¿Quiere beber (comer) algo?
6 ¿Sirven café? ¿café con leche?
7 ¿Tiene calor (frío, sed) el hombre?
8 ¿Quiere beber algo caliente o frío?
9 ¿Quiere café? ¿café con leche?
10 ¿Hay refrescos? ¿agua mineral?
11 ¿Pide agua mineral con o sin gas?
12 ¿Tiene hambre el hombre?
13 ¿Quiere algo para comer?
14 ¿Quiere la cuenta?
15 ¿Qué le trae el camarero?

Side 5, 23470 to 24333

Hola. Buenas tardes, amigos. Soy Antonio, camarero de aquí de El Rincón. Hoy van a ver que la vida de un camarero no es fácil.

2

Camarero: ¿La carta, señor?
Cliente: No. Tengo mucha prisa. ¿Qué hay de beber?
Camarero: Café, café con leche o . . .
Cliente: ¡No, no! Tengo calor. No quiero tomar nada caliente. Prefiero algo frío.
Camarero: Sí, señor. Hay refrescos, agua mineral . . .
Cliente: Vale. Agua mineral, sin gas.
Camarero: ¿Nada más, señor? ¿Algo para comer?
Cliente: ¡No, no! No tengo hambre. Tengo sed—y mucha prisa. Puede traerme la cuenta también.
Camarero: Sí, señor.

Hay personas que siempre tienen prisa.

Ahora, los turistas.

3

Camarero: ¿Están listos para pedir?
Señor: Creo que sí. ¿Tiene jamón serrano?
Camarero: Sí, señor, claro.
Señor: Un bocadillo de jamón serrano y un café. ¡No! Una limonada. ¡No! Café. Sí, sí. Quiero un café con leche.
Camarero: Un bocadillo de jamón serrano y un café con leche. Gracias, señor. ¿Y para la señora?
Señora: ¿Tienen fruta?
Camarero: Sí. Manzanas, naranjas y melón.
Señora: ¿Nada más?
Camarero: Lo siento, señora. El bizcocho es la especialidad de la casa.
Señora: Muy bien, un bizcocho . . . y melón. Y me trae una cuchara para comer el melón, por favor.
Camarero: Gracias. Perfecto.

Otras personas no saben lo que quieren.

240 doscientos cuarenta

3   **13:13**

Suggestions Point out foods as they are named. Look regretful = **Lo siento.** Draw/show a spoon.
1 ¿Son turistas?
2 ¿Quién es? *(Point to man, woman.)*
Continue asking Comprehension Check questions, as above.

Side 5, 24375 to 26786

Purpose This section develops listening and reading comprehension of structures and vocabulary needed to order a snack and take an order at a café.

Camarero: ¿Están listos para pedir?

Mamá: Sí. ¿Ya sabes lo que quieres, Luisito?

Luisito: Sí. Un perrito y un refresco.

Mamá: Pero, Luisito, siempre pides un perrito y un refresco. ¿No quieres algo diferente hoy?

Luisito: ¡No, no y no! ¡Quiero un perrito y un refresco!

Camarero: ¿Y para usted, señora?

Mamá: Sí, una hamburguesa, por favor, y una limonada.

Camarero: Está bien. Gracias.

Hay gente que sabe exactamente lo que quiere.

¡Los turistas nunca saben cuánto dejar!

¿Jamón o queso? ¡Jamón y queso! Es la solución perfecta.

Camarero: Hola. Buenas tardes, señorita. ¿Qué le puedo traer?

Señorita: Un sándwich de . . . ¡Ay, no sé! Me gusta mucho el queso. Pero también me gusta el jamón.

Camarero: Entonces, ¿un sándwich mixto?

Señorita: Sí, claro. Un sándwich mixto.

Camarero: Muy bien. Gracias.

Señor: ¿Cuánto debemos? Aquí está el total—son dos mil trescientas cincuenta pesetas.

Señora: Dejamos propina, ¿no?

Señor: No, no creo. Aquí dice que el servicio va incluido.

Señora: Tienes razón, mi amor.

No, señor, no tiene razón. ¡Siempre hay que dejar algo para el camarero! ¡La vida de un camarero no es nada fácil!

doscientos cuarenta y uno **241**

4   14:55

1 ¿Sabe Luisito lo que quiere?
2 ¿Quiere un perrito y un refresco?
3 ¿Siempre pide Luisito un perrito y un refresco?
4 ¿Quiere Luisito algo diferente hoy?
5 ¿Quiere la señora una hamburguesa?
6 ¿Quiere una limonada para beber?

Side 5, 26829 to 27832

5   15:30

1 ¿Sabe la señorita exactamente lo que quiere?
2 ¿Le gusta mucho el queso a la señorita? ¿el jamón?
3 ¿Recomienda un sándwich mixto el camarero?
4 ¿Quiere un perrito y un refresco?
5 ¿Qué es un sándwich mixto?
6 ¿Pide un sándwich mixto la señorita?

Side 5, 27861 to 28864

6   16:04

Suggestions Mime paying. Explain (in Spanish) that **propina** is **dinero para el camarero por el servicio**.

1 ¿Saben los turistas cuánto dejar?
2 ¿Deben los señores pagar dos mil trescientas cincuenta pesetas?
3 ¿Cuánto deben pagar?
4 ¿Deben dejar propina?
5 ¿Va el servicio incluido?
6 ¿Va el servicio incluido en Estados Unidos?
7 ¿Dónde va el servicio incluido?

Side 5, 28898 to 30098

7   16:45

1 ¿Tiene razón el señor?
2 ¿Tiene razón el camarero?
3 ¿Es fácil la vida de un camarero?
4 ¿Quieres ser camarero?

Side 5, 30117 to 30600

Suggestions Begin by having students close their books while you narrate one section at a time, using the transparencies to clarify meaning without translation. Then ask **Comprehension Checks.** Repeat the process with each section.

Using the video Play one section at a time after narrating it using the transparencies. Freeze the video and ask **Comprehension Checks.** Repeat with each section.

TAPE/
DISC

17:02–
19:58

Early Production Checks

The **Early Production Checks** are available on cards in the TRP.

1	**17:08**

¡Tengo mucha hambre!

1 ¿Quién es? *(Point to Manolo, Víctor, Mamá, Papá.)* Manolo / Víctor / Mamá / Papá.
2 ¿Tiene mucha hambre Víctor? *Sí.*
3 ¿Qué tiene Víctor? *Tiene mucha hambre.*
4 ¿Llegan tarde Víctor y Manolo? *Sí.*
5 ¿No hicieron nada en particular? *Sí.*
6 ¿Qué hicieron, fueron al Corte Inglés? *Sí.*
7 ¿Hay una mesa libre? *Sí.*
8 ¿Qué hay? *Una mesa libre.*

2	**17:27**

¡Siempre pides lo mismo!
Accept brief phrases or one- and two-word answers to all **Early Production Checks,** as shown in **1** above. It is not necessary for students to answer in complete sentences.

1 ¿Quién es? *(Point to Papá, Mamá, Víctor, Manolo, waiter.)*
2 ¿Es la carta?
3 ¿Quieren ver la carta?
4 ¿Qué quieren ver?
5 ¿Piden la comida?
6 ¿Qué quiere Víctor, una hamburguesa y papas fritas?
7 ¿Siempre pide lo mismo Víctor?
8 ¿Van a merendar o a cenar?
9 ¿Qué van a hacer?
10 ¿Van a cenar más tarde?
11 ¿Cuándo van a cenar?
12 ¿Qué va a pedir Manolo, una limonada o leche?
13 ¿Quiere una limonada grande o pequeña?

¿QUÉ DECIMOS...?

Al tomar algo en un restaurante

1 *¡Tengo mucha hambre!*

2 *¡Siempre pides lo mismo!*

Purpose These dialogues are not intended for memorization. They show language in more natural contexts. Unfamiliar structures are solely intended for comprehension, not for mastery or production by students.

3 ¿Qué les puedo traer?

doscientos cuarenta y tres **243**

¿Qué les puedo traer?
Point out Spaniards say **patatas**,
Latin Americans say **papas**.

1 ¿Quién es? *(Point to waiter.)*
2 ¿Están listos para pedir?
3 ¿Para qué están listos?
4 ¿Está lista la mamá?
5 ¿Pide café con leche?
6 ¿También pide un bizcocho?
7 ¿Qué pide la mamá?
8 ¿Sabe el papá qué es
   el sándwich mixto?
9 ¿Lleva jamón y queso
   el sándwich mixto?
10 ¿Qué lleva un sándwich mixto?
11 ¿Pide un sándwich mixto
    el papá?
12 ¿Pide café o agua mineral para
    beber?
13 ¿Qué pide para beber?
14 ¿Pide fruta Manolo?
15 ¿Pide una manzana, una naranja
    o melón?
16 ¿Qué quiere comer Víctor?
17 ¿Quiere una limonada?

Side 5, 32494 to 33897

Suggestions Begin by having students close
their books while you narrate one section at a time, using
the transparencies to clarify meaning without translation.
Then ask **Early Production Checks.** Repeat the process with
each section.

Using the video Play one section at a time after
narrating it using the transparencies. Freeze the video and
ask **Early Production Checks.** Repeat with each section.

UNIDAD 5 Lección 3 **243**

¿Qué dinero? ¿Qué zapatos?

1. ¿Están buenas las papas?
2. ¿Quién quiere probarlas?
3. ¿Pide permiso para probarlas?
4. ¿Juega Víctor con la cuchara?
5. ¿Piensa la mamá que Víctor juega con la cuchara?
6. ¿Come muy rápido Víctor?
7. ¿Piensa la mamá que Víctor come muy rápido?
8. ¿Tienen prisa?
9. ¿Está furioso Víctor con Manolo?
10. ¿Gastó Manolo el dinero de Víctor?
11. ¿Quién dice "Chist", Víctor o Manolo?
12. ¿Está confundida la madre?

Side 5, 33918 to 34783

La cuenta, por favor.

1. ¿Desean algo más?
2. ¿Desean la cuenta?
3. ¿Qué desean?
4. ¿Sabe cuánto debe dejar de propina el papá?
5. ¿Tiene que dejar propina?
6. ¿Va incluido el servicio?
7. ¿Por qué no debe dejar propina?
8. ¿Deben dejar algo?
9. ¿Tiene razón el padre?
10. ¿Le dejan una buena propina al camarero?
11. ¿Fue amable el camarero?
12. ¿Quién fue muy amable?

Side 5, 34802 to 35909

4 ¿Qué dinero? ¿Qué zapatos?

5 La cuenta, por favor.

CHARLEMOS UN POCO

A. ¡En el restaurante! ¿Qué pasa cuando Víctor y Manolo van con sus padres a un restaurante? Para contarlo, pon estas oraciones en orden cronológico.

La familia sale del restaurante.
El camarero les sirve la comida.
La familia llega al restaurante.
El camarero les presenta la carta.
Todos deciden qué quieren pedir.

La familia come.
Papá encuentra una mesa libre.
Papá pide la cuenta.
La familia pide la comida.

B. ¿Qué desean? Eres camarero(a) en un café. ¿En qué orden haces estas preguntas?

¿Y para beber?
¿Les traigo sándwiches mixtos?
¿Una limonada grande o pequeña?

¿Quieren algo más?
¿Están listos para pedir?
¿Desean ver la carta?

C. ¡Vamos a comer! José y Rosa están almorzando en una cafetería. Completa la conversación entre el camarero, José y Rosa con las siguientes frases.

No, sólo la cuenta.
Muy ricos.
Sí, queremos dos
   sándwiches mixtos.

¿Tienen bizcocho?
Gracias.
Agua mineral.
Dos, por favor.

CHARLEMOS UN POCO

A. ¡En el restaurante! Allow 2–3 min to do in pairs. Then call on individual students.
La familia llega al restaurante.
Papá encuentra una mesa libre.
Papá pide la cuenta.
El camarero les presenta la carta.
Todos deciden qué quieren pedir.
La familia pide la comida.
El camarero les sirve la comida.
La familia come.
Papá pide la cuenta.

B. ¿Qué desean?
¿Desean ver la carta?
¿Están listos para pedir?
¿Les traigo sándwiches mixtos?
¿Y para beber?
¿Una limonada grande o pequeña?
¿Quieren algo más?

Extension In pairs, have students prepare a dialogue between a client and a waiter at restaurant. Have the waiter use these questions.

C. ¡Vamos a comer! Allow 2–3 min to do in pairs. Then call on one pair to read first half of dialogue, another pair to read second half.
Gracias.
Sí, queremos dos sándwiches mixtos.
Agua mineral.
Muy ricos.
¿Tienen bizcocho?
Dos, por favor.
No, sólo la cuenta.

Purpose This section guides students through their first productive efforts with the structures and vocabulary needed to talk about food and order a meal.

CH. ¿Qué van a pedir?

1 Alicia pide melón.
2 Julio y Jorge piden patatas fritas.
3 Yo pido una hamburguesa.
4 Maricarmen pide un sándwich de jamón.
5 Todos nosotros pedimos la cuenta.
6 Ustedes piden café con leche.
7 Tú pides agua mineral.
8 Tú y yo pedimos la cuenta.

D. Comida vegetariana.
Allow 2–3 min to do in pairs. Then call on individuals.

1 ¿Sirven sándwiches de queso?
No, señor(ita). No servimos sándwiches de queso.
2 ¿Sirven sándwiches mixtos?
No, señor(ita). No servimos sándwiches mixtos.
3 ¿Sirven sándwiches de jamón?
No, señor(ita). No servimos sándwiches de jamón.
4 ¿Sirven refresco de naranja?
Sí, señor(ita). Servimos refresco de naranja.
5 ¿Sirven limonada? Sí, señor(ita). Servimos limonada.
6 ¿Sirven papas fritas?
Sí, señor(ita). Servimos papas fritas.
7 ¿Sirven melón? Sí, señor(ita). Servimos melón.
8 ¿Sirven manzanas?
Sí, señor(ita). Servimos manzanas.
9 ¿Sirven bizcocho? Sí, señor(ita). Servimos bizcocho.
10 ¿Sirven naranja? Sí, señor(ita). Servimos naranja.

E. ¿Otro pastel?

1 Maricarmen trae unos discos.
2 Yo traigo mucha limonada.
3 Lorenzo trae dos pizzas.
4 Tú traes un pastel de chocolate.
5 Víctor y Josefa traen los refrescos.
6 Nosotros traemos las papas fritas.
7 Ustedes traen las hamburguesas.
8 Eduardo trae su guitarra.

F. La familia. Answers will vary.

Pedir
Used to ask for something

pido	pedimos
pides	
pide	piden
pide	piden

See **¿Por qué se dice así?,** *page G75, section 5.7.*

Servir

sirvo	servimos
sirves	
sirve	sirven
sirve	sirven

See **¿Por qué se dice así?,** *page G75, section 5.7.*

Traer

traigo	traemos
traes	
trae	traen
trae	traen

CH. ¿Qué van a pedir? Tú y unos amigos van a un café después de clase. ¿Qué pide cada uno?

MODELO   Tina / refresco
Tina pide un refresco.

1. Alicia / melón
2. Julio y Jorge / patatas fritas
3. yo / hamburguesa
4. Maricarmen / sándwich de jamón
5. todos nosotros / la cuenta
6. ustedes / café con leche
7. tú / agua mineral
8. tú y yo / la cuenta

D. Comida vegetariana. Estás en un restaurante vegetariano por primera vez. Pregúntale al camarero si sirven estas comidas.

MODELO   hamburguesas
Tú: **¿Sirven hamburguesas?**
Camarero: **No, señor(ita). No servimos hamburguesas.**

1. sándwiches de queso
2. sándwiches mixtos
3. sándwiches de jamón
4. refresco de naranja
5. limonada
6. papas fritas
7. melón
8. manzanas
9. bizcocho
10. naranja

E. ¿Otro pastel? Mario va a dar una fiesta y todos deciden traer algo. ¿Qué traen?

MODELO   Rosamaría: el pastel
Rosamaría trae el pastel.

1. Maricarmen: unos discos
2. yo: mucha limonada
3. Lorenzo: dos pizzas
4. tú: un pastel de chocolate
5. Víctor y Josefa: los refrescos
6. nosotros: las papas fritas
7. ustedes: las hamburguesas
8. Eduardo: su guitarra

F. La familia. Tú y tu familia van a su restaurante favorito. Describe lo que ocurre ahí.

EJEMPLO **Mamá pide agua mineral.**

mi hermano		hamburguesa
yo		bizcocho
mamá	pedir	papas fritas
tú	recomendar	helados
niños	servir	manzana
nosotros	preferir	agua mineral
papá	querer	melón
camarero	traer	naranja
mis hermanas	¿ . . . ?	jamón
camarera		leche
¿ . . . ?		¿ . . . ?

G. ¿Qué pasa?

Describe la situación de las personas en los dibujos.

MODELO **No tiene razón.**

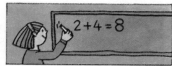

 1.
 2.
 3.
 4.

 5.
 6.
 7.
 8.

 9.
 10.

H. ¿Por qué?

Lee lo que dice cada persona. Luego describe su situación según su comentario.

EJEMPLO   Mamá: No todos los hispanos en Estados Unidos son de México.
Mamá tiene razón.

1. Antonio: ¡Camarero! Tráeme algo para beber, por favor.
2. Panchito: Mamáaaa, ¿qué hay para comer?
3. Rubén y Lalo: $20 - 13 + 7 \times 2 = 27$
4. Gloria: ¡Huy! Mi clase de biología es a las 10:00 y ya son las 10:05.
5. Ramón y yo: Debemos ir al lago hoy. La temperatura va a subir a más de 105 grados Fahrenheit.
6. Papá: No hay hispanos en Nueva York.
7. yo: ¡Caramba! Está nevando y la temperatura está bajo cero.
8. Juanita: $5 \times 3 - 7 + 2 = 10$

LECCIÓN 3

Tener idioms

Tener calor   **Tener frío**

Tener hambre   **Tener sed**

Tener razón   **No tener razón**

Tener prisa

¿Tienes hambre?
No, pero **tengo sed.**

See **¿Por qué se dice así?,**
page G78, section 5.8.

G. ¿Qué pasa?

1 Tiene hambre.
2 Tiene sed.
3 Tienen prisa.
4 Tiene razón.
5 Tiene frío.
6 Tiene prisa.
7 No tiene hambre.
8 No tiene prisa.
9 No tiene razón.
10 Tiene calor.

Expansion Personalize by asking **¿Qué comes tú cuando tienes hambre? ¿Siempre tengo razón? ¿Qué tomas cuando tienes sed? ¿Adónde vas cuando tienes prisa?**

H. ¿Por qué?

Have one student read each item, another tell why.

1 Antonio tiene sed.
2 Panchito tiene hambre.
3 Rubén y Lalo no tienen razón.
4 Gloria tiene prisa.
5 Ramón y yo tenemos calor.
6 Papá no tiene razón.
7 Yo tengo frío.
8 Juanita tiene razón.

I. ¡Pobrecita!

1 Su hermano le sirve un refresco.
2 Su hermana le lee un libro.
3 El perro le trae el periódico.
4 Sus tíos le traen flores.
5 Su abuela y su mamá le preparan la comida.

J. ¡Qué negativo!

Remind students that, when used alone, **¿Cómo?** may express surprise. Allow 2–3 min to do in pairs. Then call on individual pairs.

1 Nunca me traes helado.
  ¿Cómo? Siempre te traigo helado.
2 Nunca me das dinero.
  ¿Cómo? Siempre te doy dinero.
3 Nunca me sirves hamburguesas.
  ¿Cómo? Siempre te sirvo hamburguesas.
4 Nunca me preparas limonada.
  ¿Cómo? Siempre te preparo limonada.
5 Nunca me compras ropa nueva.
  ¿Cómo? Siempre te compro ropa nueva.
6 Nunca me alquilas videos.
  ¿Cómo? Siempre te alquilo videos.
7 Nunca me das fiestas.
  ¿Cómo? Siempre te doy fiestas.
8 Nunca me llevas al cine.
  ¿Cómo? Siempre te llevo al cine.

K. ¡Le encanta!

1 Debes servirle pizza.
2 Debes servirles hamburguesas.
3 Debes servirnos melón.
4 Debes servirnos bizcocho.
5 Debes servirle tacos.
6 Debes servirme papas fritas.
7 Debes servirle limonada.
8 Debes servirles helado.

Indirect object pronouns

me	nos
te	
le	les
le	les

See **¿Por qué se dice así?**, *page G79, section 5.9.*

Indirect object pronouns
Placement

Indirect object pronouns precede a conjugated verb.

Yo **le** escribo todos los días.
Ella siempre **nos** da el dinero.

See **¿Por qué se dice así?**, *page G79, section 5.9.*

Indirect object pronouns
Placement

Indirect object pronouns may follow and be attached to an infinitive or an **-ndo** form.

Quieren dar**nos** el dinero hoy.
Estoy escribiéndo**le** a mamá.

See **¿Por qué se dice así?**, *page G79, section 5.9.*

---

248 *doscientos cuarenta y ocho*

I. ¡Pobrecita! Juanita está muy enferma. ¿Qué hacen todos para ella?

MODELO   su papá
   Su papá le trae unos libros.

1. su hermano	**3.** el perro	**5.** su abuela y
2. su hermana	**4.** sus tíos	su mamá

J. ¡Qué negativo! Paquito está muy negativo hoy. ¿Qué le dice a su padre? ¿Cómo le contesta su padre?

MODELO   comprar regalos
   Paquito: **Nunca me compras regalos.**
   Padre: **¿Cómo? Siempre te compro regalos.**

1. traer helado
2. dar dinero
3. servir hamburguesas
4. preparar limonada
5. comprar ropa nueva
6. alquilar videos
7. dar fiestas
8. llevar al cine

K. ¡Le encanta! ¿Qué le dice un camarero al otro sobre los gustos de los empleados y algunos clientes?

MODELO   Al señor Gamboa le encanta la fruta.
   Debes servirle fruta.

1. A Mariela le gusta la pizza.
2. A los señores López les gustan las hamburguesas.
3. A Rafael y a mí nos gusta el melón.
4. A Miguel y a mí nos encanta el bizcocho.
5. Al profesor de español le encantan los tacos.
6. A mí me gustan las papas fritas.
7. A Nicolás le gusta la limonada.
8. A Sara y a Lucía les gusta el helado.

L. En un café. Tú y una amiga, Silvia, están en su café favorito. ¿Qué les dices a tu amiga y al camarero?

MODELO   pedir una pizza (a Silvia)
Silvia, ¿puedes pedirme una pizza?

traer un refresco (al camarero)
Camarero, ¿puede traernos un refresco?

1. buscar una mesa (al camarero)
2. servir helado (al camarero)
3. pedir un refresco (a Silvia)
4. explicar la carta (a Silvia)
5. dar la cuchara (a Silvia)
6. traer otra cuchara (al camarero)
7. pasar la pizza (a Silvia)
8. servir otro refresco (al camarero)

M. ¡Ya estamos listos! Tú estás en tu restaurante favorito con un grupo de amigos. Ya están listos para pedir. ¿Qué le dices al camarero?

MODELO   dos refrescos para Clara y Julio
Les puede traer dos refrescos a Clara y Julio.

1. limonada para Eva
2. café con leche para Víctor
3. refresco de naranja para ti
4. agua para todos
5. papas fritas para todos
6. hamburguesas para Víctor y Julio
7. sándwich mixto para Clara
8. sándwich de jamón para ti

N. ¿Tú y tu familia? Tu amigo(a) quiere saber qué hicieron tú y tu familia durante la semana de vacaciones. ¿Qué le dices?

MODELO   lunes por la tarde: cine
Amigo(a): **¿Qué hicieron el lunes por la tarde?**
Tú: **Fuimos al cine.**

1. sábado por la mañana: universidad
2. sábado por la noche: teatro
3. domingo por la tarde: un museo
4. lunes por la noche: concierto
5. martes por la mañana: centro comercial
6. miércoles por la tarde: parque
7. jueves por la noche: cine
8. viernes por la tarde: un club deportivo

LECCIÓN 3

Hicieron / Fuimos

These two past tense verb forms are very useful when talking about what you did and where you went.

¿Qué **hicieron** tú y Toni?
Fuimos al cine.
Después **fuimos** a un café.

L. En un café.
1 Camarero, ¿puede buscarnos una mesa?
2 Camarero, ¿puede servirnos helado?
3 Silvia, ¿puedes pedirme un refresco?
4 Silvia, ¿puedes explicarme la carta?
5 Silvia, ¿puedes darme la cuchara?
6 Camarero, ¿puede traernos otra cuchara?
7 Silvia, ¿puedes pasarme la pizza?
8 Camarero, ¿puede servirnos otro refresco?

M. ¡Ya estamos listos!
1 Le puede traer una limonada a Eva.
2 Le puede traer un café con leche a Víctor.
3 Me puede traer un refresco de naranja a mí.
4 Nos puede traer agua a todos.
5 Nos puede traer papas fritas a todos.
6 Les puede traer hamburguesas a Víctor y Julio.
7 Le puede traer un sándwich mixto a Clara.
8 Me puede traer un sándwich de jamón a mí.

N. ¿Tú y tu familia?
Note The past-tense forms **hicieron** and **fuimos**, both high-frequency vocabulary, appeared in the *¿Qué decimos ... ?* section of this lesson. Allow 2–3 min to do in pairs. Then ask individuals what they did.
1 ¿Qué hicieron el sábado por la mañana? Fuimos a la universidad.
2 ¿Qué hicieron el sábado por la noche? Fuimos al teatro.
3 ¿Qué hicieron el domingo por la tarde? Fuimos a un museo.
4 ¿Qué hicieron el lunes por la noche? Fuimos a un concierto.
5 ¿Qué hicieron el martes por la mañana? Fuimos al centro comercial.
6 ¿Qué hicieron el miércoles por la tarde? Fuimos al parque.
7 ¿Qué hicieron el jueves por la noche? Fuimos al cine.
8 ¿Qué hicieron el viernes por la tarde? Fuimos a un club deportivo.

Expansion Ask students ¿**Qué hicieron tú y tu familia durante el fin de semana?** Susan, ¿qué hicieron tú y Karen el sábado por la tarde?

CHARLEMOS UN POCO MÁS

A. Lo siento, pero . . . Allow 2–3 min to do in pairs. Then call on different pairs to do each one for class.

Extension Have students order for two, three, or four people, and have waiter indicate that they are out of more than one item.

A. Lo siento, pero . . . You and your friend are at a café. As you order, the waiter tells you that your choice is not available and asks you to select something else. Use the drawings below as a guide.

MODELO Tú: **Quiero las papas fritas, por favor.**
Camarero: **Lo siento, señor. Hoy no tenemos papas fritas. ¿Le traigo otra cosa?**
Tú: **Sí. ¿Puede traerme un sándwich de jamón?**
Camarero: **Muy bien, señor.**

B. ¿Qué dicen? Allow 3–4 min. Then call on several pairs to read their dialogues to class.

B. ¿Qué dicen? With a partner, write a dialogue for this cartoon strip. Then read your dialogue to the class.

C. Fuimos a . . . Call on different students to ask someone in class. Encourage students to give different answers.

C. Fuimos a . . . Ask your classmates what they did on the weekend. Respond using any of the cues in the drawing your teacher gives you.

EJEMPLO Tú: **¿Qué hicieron tú y [Marty] este fin de semana?**
Amigo(a): **[Marty] y yo fuimos al zoológico.**

Purpose The *Charlemos un poco más* activities are designed to allow students to create with language while talking about food in a variety of open-ended situations.

CH. ¿Qué van a pedir? You are at a café where your partner is the waiter or waitress. Study the menu that your teacher gives you and note what you would like to order in the following situations. Check the cost of each item when you order. Your partner will consult the menu to answer your questions and to say what is available. Be prepared to choose again if something is unavailable or too expensive. Write down your final order, the cost of each item, and the total cost of the meal.

1. Order a snack and something to drink for you and your friend. Your friend hates chicken but you love it. You only have 890 pesetas and you are treating.

2. You invited your mother out to lunch. Since today is her birthday, you insist on treating. You want to order a combination plate for both of you, but you only have 850 pesetas.

D. Encuesta. Your teacher will give you a grid. Ask your classmates questions to find out if they fit any description in the grid. If they do, have them sign the appropriate square to verify it. Let your teacher know when you have completed a vertical, horizontal, or diagonal line on your grid.

EJEMPLO   Tú: **¿Tienes hambre ahora?**
         Compañero(a):   **No, no tengo hambre.** o
                              Sí, tengo mucha hambre.

Dramatizaciones

A. Entrevista. Interview six classmates about where they go and what they buy when they are hungry or thirsty. Also ask how much they spend. Write down their responses and report to the class the most popular places, foods, and drinks as well as the average amount your friends spend in one day on snack food.

B. Camareros por un día. Be the waiter or waitress as two classmates come to your restaurant.

- Greet the guests.
- Ask if they want to see the menu.
- Ask for their order.
- Suggest that you bring them dessert.
- Ask if they want anything more.
- Give them the bill and thank them.

C. El Café Madrileño. With three classmates, decide who will play the roles described below. Create a skit for the four characters.

- The waiter who gives outstanding service to earn a big tip
- The diner who cannot make up his or her mind
- The diner who doesn't have much money
- The diner who is very hungry

LECCIÓN 3

CH. ¿Qué van a pedir? Allow 3–4 min for each situation. Then check the costs of several pairs to make sure they did not overspend.

D. Encuesta. Allow students to move around class talking to each other in Spanish. Limit the number of squares one person may sign so that they will have to talk to several classmates. When one student has bingo, verify by asking individuals who signed the grid if they do what is indicted. Allow activity to continue in order to see who can get two bingos on same card, then three, etc.

DRAMATIZACIONES

A. Entrevista. Allow 4–5 min. Then call on several students to report their findings. Try to identify the most popular place, snack, and amount spent by the whole class.

B and C. Have class form groups of 3 or 4. Ask trios to prepare role play **B,** and groups of 4 to do role play **C.** Allow 5–8 min, then have several groups present to class. Ask comprehension questions after each presentation.

In **Dramatizaciones,** students recycle all previously learned structures and vocabulary needed to talk about food and to order a meal in a restaurant in student-centered role plays. Encourage students to work without their books when preparing and performing their role plays.

A. Anticipemos.

Suggestions Have students work in pairs and allow 2 min to answer these questions. Call on several pairs to share their answers with the class. Ask if others agree. For question 7, read the first phrase— **Gira a la derecha**—and have students repeat after you. Then, sitting on a chair, mime a half turn to the right on your chair. Ask class to tell you what **Gira a la derecha** means. Repeat action if necessary. Repeat the process with each stage direction. Practice following stage directions correctly using Total Physical Response (TPR). Have 2–4 students follow the stage directions in front of the class as you call them out. Ask class if each direction was correctly interpreted. Then have the whole class follow the stage directions as you give them.

Answers

1. Dramatic reading/play/readers' theater. It is written as a play with stage instructions.
2. Usually done on stage for an audience
3. Answers will vary.
4. **La sopa castellana**
5. Lope de Cervantes y Unamuno
6. Four
7. Rotate right.   Pretends to
   Rotate left.   put the soup
   Rotate a half   on the table.
      turn.   Pretends to
   Facing the   put his or her
      audience.   finger into
   With emphasis.   the soup and
   Back to the   taste it.
      audience.   Shrugging his
   Stomping his   or her
      or her feet.   shoulders.
   Complaining.   Enfuriated.
   Pretends to   With an
      bring bread   exasperated
      and water.   voice.
   Pretends to eat
      bread.

LEAMOS AHORA

Reading strategy: Reading aloud

A. Anticipemos. Before reading this selection, glance at the format of this reading and answer the following questions.

1. What type of reading is this? How do you know?
2. Is this type of reading usually done alone at home, in the classroom, or elsewhere? Explain your answer.
3. How do you expect the reading to be handled in your class? Why?
4. What is the title of the work?
5. Who is the author of the work?
6. How many performers are required to put on this work?
7. As your teacher mimes the following stage directions, tell what you think they mean.

Gira a la derecha.	Finge acción con pan y agua.
Gira a la izquierda.	Finge comer pan.
Gira media vuelta.	Finge poner sopa en la mesa.
Cara al público.	Finge meter un dedo en la
Con énfasis.	sopa para probarla.
Espalda al público.	Se encoge de hombros.
Pisando violentamente.	Enfadada.
Quejándose.	Con voz exasperada.

B. Lectura dramatizada. Readers' Theater is an approach to reading that results in performance. In Readers' Theater you are not required to act but will learn some simple acting procedures and stage directions. When the class prepares this play for presentation, you will not be required to memorize your parts, but repeated reading during rehearsals may result in memorization.

C. Un cuento español. Now listen as your teacher reads the play. Then answer your teacher's questions. Later you will be asked to participate in Readers' Theater.

Purpose This is the principal reading of the unit. Its purpose is to teach students to read using appropriate strategies. Here they will read aloud. Students are expected to read with good pronunciation and intonation. Class is encouraged to prepare a dramatic reading for other classes, teachers, or administrators.

La sopa castellana

Reparto: NARRADOR 1   NARRADOR 2   COMENTADOR   LA MUJER

Al empezar, la mujer está sentada, cara al público. El comentador está sentado, espalda al público. Los narradores están de pie, Narrador 1 a la derecha de la Mujer, Narrador 2 a la izquierda del Comentador.

NARRADOR 1:	La sopa castellana,
NARRADOR 2:	un cuento español
LA MUJER:	escrito por
COMENTADOR:	*(Gira media vuelta a la derecha. Cara al público.)* Lope de Cervantes y Unamuno.
NARRADOR 1:	Una mujer entra en un restaurante muy elegante.
NARRADOR 2:	El camarero la lleva a una mesa. *(Comentador gira a la derecha. Cara al público.)*
NARRADOR 1:	Ella lee la carta y pide la cena.
LA MUJER:	La sopa castellana, por favor, con pan. Y para beber, agua mineral. *(Comentador gira a la izquierda. Espalda al público.)*
NARRADOR 1:	Pone la servilleta en las rodillas. *(La mujer finge acción con la servilleta.)*
NARRADOR 2:	El camarero trae el pan y el agua mineral. *(Comentador gira a la derecha. Cara al público. Finge acción con pan y agua. Gira a la izquierda. Espalda al público.)*
NARRADOR 1:	La mujer prueba el pan. *(La mujer finge comer pan.)*
NARRADOR 2:	El camarero trae la sopa castellana. *(Comentador gira a la derecha. Cara al público. Finge poner sopa en la mesa.)*
NARRADOR 1:	La mujer no hace nada. Después de un momento, dice:
LA MUJER:	No puedo tomar la sopa.
COMENTADOR:	¿Por qué no?

NARRADOR 2:	El camarero prueba la sopa y dice:
COMENTADOR:	*(Finge meter un dedo en la sopa para probarla.)* No está demasiado caliente.
LA MUJER:	*(Quejándose.)* No puedo tomar la sopa.
NARRADOR 2:	El camarero llama al cocinero.
COMENTADOR:	La señora no puede tomar la sopa. *(Se encoge de hombros y gira a la izquierda. Da la espalda al público.)*
LA MUJER:	*(Enfadada.)* ¡No puedo tomar la sopa!
COMENTADOR:	*(Gira a la derecha pisando violentamente. Cara al público.)* ¿Por qué no?
NARRADOR 2:	El cocinero prueba la sopa.
COMENTADOR:	*(Finge meter un dedo en la sopa para probarla.)* No está demasiado salada.
NARRADOR 2:	El cocinero llama al dueño del restaurante.
COMENTADOR:	La señora no puede tomar la sopa.
LA MUJER:	¡No—puedo—tomar—la—sopa! *(Con énfasis.)*
NARRADOR 1:	*(Finge ser el dueño.)* ¿Por qué no?
NARRADOR 2:	El dueño prueba la sopa.
NARRADOR 1:	*(Finge meter un dedo en la sopa para probarla.)* Mmm. ¡Qué rica!
LA MUJER:	¡No—puedo—tomar—la—sopa! *(Con énfasis.)*
NARRADORES Y COMENTADOR:	¿Por qué no puede usted tomar la sopa?
LA MUJER:	*(Con voz exasperada.)* Porque no tengo cuchara. *(La mujer se para.)*
TODOS:	Porque no tiene cuchara. *(Todos hacen una reverencia y salen.)*

Suggestions Begin by readng the play to class for comprehension. As you read, act out each part to help students comprehend without translation. Ask comprehension questions and use TPR to teach stage direction vocabulary.

Once students understand the play, divide class into groups of four; pass out copies of corresponding copymaster to every student, and go over directions on copymaster. Tell students that each group will have to prepare the play and present it to the class.

You may want to invite other classes, teachers, and administrators to watch the presentations. You may also have students select the best presentation for open house or for school visitations.

The author's name, **Lope de Cervantes y Unamuno,** is made up of names of famous Spanish men of letters: **Lope de Vega (1562–1635) escribió 24 volúmenes de versos y entre 700 y 800 comedias en tres actos; Miguel de Cervantes Saavedra (1547–1616) escribió versos, comedias y novelas.** *Don Quijote de la Mancha* **es su obra más conocida; Miguel de Unamuno (1864–1936), principalmente ensayista y pensador, también escribió cuentos y novelas.**

ESCRIBAMOS UN POCO

A. Empezando. Have class read the Madrid composition silently. Ask one-quarter of class to prepare two or three comprehension questions about the first paragraph. Do the same with paragraphs 2, 3, and 4. Call on individuals from each group to ask their questions and have class respond. Discuss answers to the two questions in the direction lines.

Writing strategy:
Making an outline

A. Empezando. Read and discuss the following composition about Madrid. The composition was written by Marisol in her Spanish class after visiting Madrid. How does she describe Madrid? Does she give enough information about the city?

> Madrid
>
> Madrid es la capital de España. Es una ciudad muy grande y muy hermosa. Está en el centro de España.
>
> Hay muchos lugares que visitar en Madrid, por ejemplo, la Plaza Mayor, la Puerta del Sol, la Plaza de España, el Parque del Retiro, el Palacio Real y el museo del Prado. También hay un parque de diversiones y un zoológico.
>
> A los madrileños les gusta mucho caminar por la ciudad. Por eso hay muchos parques y lindas avenidas. Por la noche, generalmente entre las 8 y las 10, la gente sale a dar un paseo. Padres e hijos, abuelos y jóvenes: todos salen a caminar por la ciudad.
>
> A los madrileños les encanta su ciudad y a los turistas también.

Purpose In this section, students are asked to apply speaking and writing skills developed in the unit to a real-life writing task. They will use strategies they began to develop in Unit 1 to write a short composition about their hometown or a large city recently visited.

B. Planeando. Now plan a composition about your hometown or a large city you have visited. Think about what there is to see and do and what your favorite places are. Organize your thoughts using a cluster.

C. Organizando. Organize the information in your cluster into an outline using the categories below. You may want to eliminate some categories or add others.

I. Name of the city and one or two unique features
II. Geographical location
III. Things to see and do
IV. What residents think about their city or town

CH. Escribiendo. Use the information in your outline to write a short composition.

D. Compartiendo. Share a draft of your composition with two classmates. Ask them what they think of it. Is there anything they don't understand? Is there anything you have not mentioned that they would like to know? Do they think you should change something?

E. Revisando. Based on your classmates' comments, rewrite your composition, changing anything you want. You may add, subtract, or reorder what you had originally written. Before you turn it in for grading, share your composition with two other classmates. Ask them to focus on your grammar, spelling, and punctuation. Correct any errors they notice before you give it to your teacher.

B. Planeando. Remind students that what they write will depend on for whom, why, and about what they are writing. Allow 3–4 min. Ask volunteers to answer the questions.

C. Organizando. Have several students read their outlines to class or write them on board. Discuss the completeness of each outline presented.

CH. Escribiendo. Allow students time to write their first draft. Provide guidance where necessary. You may want to assign the first draft as homework.

D. Compartiendo. Have students gather in "response groups" of two or three. Allow them time to share compositions. Encourage them to comment on content, structure, and vocabulary. Remind group members to begin commentary with at least one positive comment and then to make suggestions on content, structure, and vocabulary.

E. Revisando. Tell students you will grade composition holistically. Underline grammatical errors if you wish, but the grade should be affected only by errors that would confuse a native speaker accustomed to dealing with foreigners. At this stage, students should develop a sense they can already write something a Spanish-speaking pen pal would enjoy reading.

UNIT OBJECTIVES

Communicative Goals

When students have completed this unit, they will be able to use Spanish . . .
- to describe what they and others did
- to extend an invitation
- to accept or decline an invitation
- to describe a series of events in the past

Culture

In this unit, students will study and compare . . .
- classical and folk ballet
- **el Ballet Folklórico de México**
- shopping in traditional Mexican markets
- bargaining in a Mexican market
- **mariachi** music
- the origins of Mexico City

Reading and Writing Strategies

- Reading: Identifying the main idea
- Writing: Writing a free-form poem

Structure

- Preterite tense: Regular verbs
- Preterite of **ir, hacer, ser, dar, ver, poder, tener, venir, decir**

¡Me encantó Guadalajara!

UNIT SETTING

Guadalajara, Mexico, is a sophisticated city about three hundred miles northwest of Mexico City. With a population of 3.2 million, it is Mexico's second-largest city. Because it is located in a productive green valley at an altitude of more than five thousand feet, Guadalajara claims to have the best climate in North America. The weather is usually clear, dry, and mild, with temperatures in the 70's or 80's all year round. Guadalajara is a city of parks and gardens full of tropical flowers, lovely old plazas, and gracious old buildings. It includes urban

districts with art galleries, bookstores, gourmet restaurants, and luxury hotels. In addition, Guadalajara boasts some of the best-known murals of Jalisco's foremost modern painter, José Clemente Orozco.

Video Notes

To play the montage:

20:08 – 20:46

Side 6, 11 to 1170

To play the entire unit without stopping:

20:08 – 43:46

Side 6, 11 to 42213

The 14-year-old actress who plays Mónica has a Mexican mother and an American father. She was raised in the United States and moved to Mexico a year ago to attend high school in Guadalajara. It is interesting to contrast Mónica's Southwest United States Spanish with that of her hosts in Guadalajara. Note in particular that in Guadalajara Spanish, the **ll** and the **y** are merged into one sound and are pronounced like the *dg* in *edge*—as they are in Madrid. Guadalajara Spanish generally follows the phonological patterns typical of Latin American Spanish.

Photo

The teenagers are visiting the **Palacio del Gobernador,** which houses the office of the Governor of the State of Jalisco. Built in 1643, the palace is Jalisco's most historic structure. In 1810, Father Miguel Hidalgo, leader of the Mexican war of independence, decreed an end to slavery there. The building contains some of Orozco's most famous murals, depicting Hidalgo's role in the struggle for freedom.

Note Point out where Guadalajara is in relation to Mexico City. Remind students that **D.F.** stands for **Distrito Federal.**

OBJECTIVES

Communicative Goal

- Describing what you and others did

Culture and Reading

- *¡No metas la pata!*
  Te invito al ballet:
  Classical vs. folk ballet
- *Y ahora, ¡a leer!*
  ¡Viva el mariachi!
  Mexico's musical heritage

Structure

- 6.1 Preterite tense:
  Regular verbs
- 6.2 Preterite of **ir**

¡Qué linda es la ciudad!

ACTIVE VOCABULARY

Al visitar una ciudad mexicana

artesanía	exhibición
ballet folklórico	mariachi
canción	mercado
comedia	mural
excursión	programa

Al estar impresionado

enorme	impresionante
fabuloso(a)	¡Qué sorpresa!
hermoso(a)	

Al hablar del pasado

anoche	esta mañana
ayer	la semana pasada

Verbos

ayudar	ir *(pret.)*
decidir	resistir

Palabras y expresiones

kilo	hacer un informe
pronto	una docena de
taco	rosas
tenis	
vuelo	

ANTICIPEMOS

¿Qué piensas tú?

1. Mira las tarjetas de embarque. ¿Quién es la chica que acaba de llegar? ¿De dónde viene? ¿Adónde va?

2. ¿Qué crees que va a hacer allá? ¿Por qué crees eso?

3. Si ella les manda estas tarjetas postales a sus padres, ¿qué crees que les va a decir?

4. Mira las fotos. Imagina que tú eres un(a) turista. ¿A cuáles de estos lugares te gustaría ir? ¿Por qué?

5. Después de un tour por esta ciudad, ¿qué diría un turista en una carta a sus amigos o familiares?

6. En tu opinión, ¿por qué quiere una chica de Chicago viajar a México?

7. ¿De qué vas a poder hablar al final de la lección?

¿Qué piensas tú?

Answers

1 Es Mónica Levine. Viene de Chicago. Va a Guadalajara.

2 Probablemente viene a visitar a la familia.

3 **Nuevo vocabulario:** Encourage students to "quote" her probable words: I've arrived. The flight was fine. The ___'s met me at the airport. They gave me flowers. etc.

4 Las respuestas varían. Cada estudiante nombrará lugares que le interesen.

5 **Nuevo vocabulario:** I went to . . . , I saw, I visited, I bought, I ate, I drank, etc.

Point out The tourist will report in the past tense.

6 Hay muchas atracciones en México para una turista norteamericana: influencia de culturas indias, comidas regionales (tacos, enchiladas, mole, etc.), música regional como la música de los mariachis y muchas artesanías típicas de México.

▶**7** **Van a aprender a hablar de lo que hicieron durante el día y de lo que unos turistas hicieron durante un tour.**

Purpose To focus students on language needed to talk about what they did during the day or while on a tour.

Suggestions Use the illustrations as an advance organizer. Have students explain their answers. Help them discover cross-cultural similarities in what one writes home about when traveling and things one does when in a foreign country.

PARA EMPEZAR

TAPE/ DISC
20:47–25:51

Side 6, 1189 to 10312

Comprehension Checks

A full set of the **Comprehension Checks** is available on cards in the Teacher's Resource Package.

1   `20:55`

Suggestion Act out **descubre** and "calling" Óscar.

Point out The metric system of measurement is used in Mexico. One kilo(gram) = 2.2 pounds.
1 ¿Quién es?
2 ¿Empieza la señora Estrada a preparar la comida?
3 ¿Qué empieza a preparar?
4 ¿Tiene papas?
5 ¿Llama a su hijo (su hija)?
6 ¿Cómo se llama su hijo?
7 ¿Tiene Óscar que comprar papas?
8 ¿Tiene que comprar medio kilo (un kilo, dos kilos)?
9 ¿Qué tiene que comprar?

Side 6, 1395 to 2421

2   `21:29`

Suggestion Use slips of paper as bills of various denominations and act out "giving" them to students.
1 ¿Cuánto tiempo pasó?
Continue asking **Comprehension Checks,** as in **1** above.

Side 6, 2441 to 3413

3   `22:02`

Suggestions Emphasize here and throughout that all of this happened before Óscar got home. Act out leaving the house, meeting a friend.
1 ¿Salió Óscar de la casa?
Continue asking **Comprehension Checks.**

Side 6, 3432 to 3666

4   `22.11`

1 ¿Fueron al centro? *(other places)*
Continue asking **Comprehension Checks.**

Side 6, 3695 to 4407

La señora Domínguez empieza a preparar la comida cuando descubre que no hay papas. Llama a su hijo y le dice:
Madre: ¡Óscar! Óscar, hijo. ¿Puedes ir a comprarme unas papas?
Óscar: Sí, mamá.
Madre: Dos kilos, ¿eh?

Cinco horas más tarde . . .
Madre: ¡Cinco horas! ¿Qué te pasó? Y las papas, ¿dónde están?
Óscar: ¡Ay, qué tonto soy! ¡Las papas! Perdona, mamá . . .
Madre: ¿Y el dinero? Te di un billete de cincuenta mil.
Óscar: ¿El dinero? Ah, sí, el dinero. No vas a creerme, mamá, pero . . .

. . . cuando salí de la casa, me encontré con Javier.

Fuimos al centro, donde vimos a Lilia y a su amiga, Mónica. Ellas nos invitaron a pasear por la ciudad.

Visitamos el Teatro Degollado.

También vimos el mural en el Palacio de Gobierno. ¡Le encantó a Mónica!

260 doscientos sesenta

Purpose This section sets the context for the language needed to talk about what one did during the day and provides comprehensible language without translation.

Luego fuimos al mercado. Las chicas pasaron mucho tiempo mirando las artesanías. Finalmente, no compraron nada.

Luego, fuimos a la Plaza de los Mariachis. Pedimos unos refrescos y . . . como buen caballero, yo pagué las bebidas.

Cuando llegaron los mariachis, les pedí unas canciones para las chicas.

Fue tan emocionante, mamá. Tocaron y cantaron tan bien que Mónica empezó a llorar. Claro . . . Javier y yo pagamos la música.

Por fin, acompañamos a las chicas a su casa en taxi. Y por supuesto, el taxi lo pagué yo.

¿El dinero? ¿Es posible, mamá? Empecé con más de cien mil pesos, y ahora sólo tengo . . . a ver, ¡cinco, diez, quince mil pesos!

doscientos sesenta y uno **261**

22:35

5

Suggestions Point out the **Teatro Degollado** and the **Palacio del Gobernador** on the map (page 267). Tell students that the Teatro Degollado is home to Guadalajara's symphony orchestra and a center of the city's cultural life. Events held there include operas, ballets, and concerts. Its beautiful interior has been compared with that of La Scala in Milan.
1 ¿Visitaron los chicos y las chicas el Teatro Degollado? *(other places)*
Continue **Comprehension Checks**.

Side 6, 4426 to 5348

6   **23:07**

Suggestion Point out and name the **artesanías** in the photo.
1 ¿Fueron al mercado? *(other places)*
Continue **Comprehension Checks**.

Side 6, 5366 to 6481

7   **23:45**

Suggestion Contrast behavior of **un buen caballero** and someone with less gallantry.
1 ¿Fueron a la Plaza de los Mariachis?
Continue **Comprehension Checks**.

Side 6, 6500 to 7069

8   **24:04**

Suggestion Act out crying.
1 ¿Llegaron los mariachis?
Continue **Comprehension Checks**.

Side 6, 7088 to 8560

9   **24:54**

1 ¿Acompañaron los chicos a las chicas a casa?
Continue **Comprehension Checks**.

Side 6, 8579 to 9720

10   **25:32**

Suggestions Act out counting the money. Account for the missing money—so much for the drinks, so much to the mariachis, so much for the taxi.

Suggestions Begin by having students close their books while you narrate one section at a time, using the transparencies to clarify meaning without translation. Then ask **Comprehension Checks**. Repeat this process with each section.

Using the video Play one section at a time after narrating it using the transparencies. Freeze the video and ask **Comprehension Checks** Repeat this process with each section.

1 ¿Empezó Óscar con más de cien mil pesos?
Continue **Comprehension Checks**.

Side 6, 9738 to 10312

UNIDAD 6   Lección 1   **261**

¿QUÉ DECIMOS …?

TAPE/
DISC

25:52–
31:19

Side 6, 10336 to 20140

Early Production Checks

A complete set of the **Early Production Checks** is available on cards in the Teacher's Resource Package.

Note Accept brief phrases or one- and two-word answers to all **Early Production Checks,** as shown in **1**. It is not necessary for students to answer in complete sentences.

1　　　　　**25:58**

¡Saludos de México!
1　¿Quién es? *Mónica.*
2　¿De dónde es? *De Chicago.*
3　¿Dónde está pasando el verano, en México o en Venezuela? *En México.*
4　¿A quiénes les escribe Mónica? *A sus papás.*
5　¿Extraña Mónica a sus padres? *Sí.*
Continue asking questions, as above.

Side 6, 10505 to 11822

2　　　　　**26:42**

Me recibieron con rosas.
Point out The typical Mexican meal in the video includes pipián verde (carne de puerco en una salsa de mole verde), arroz a la mexicana, frijoles, tortillas, chiles jalapeños y agua de Jamaica *(nonalcoholic drink made from a red flower boiled in water, sweetened, and served cold).*
1　¿Dónde está Mónica?
2　¿Quiénes recibieron a Mónica con rosas?
Continue asking questions, as above.

Side 6, 11837 to 13293

3　　　　　**27:32**

Paseamos en una calandria.
1　¿Le gusta Guadalajara a Mónica?
2　¿Cuánto le gusta?
3　¿Cómo es la ciudad, hermosa o fea?
Continue asking questions, as above.

Side 6, 13310 to 15746

¿QUÉ DECIMOS…?
Al hablar de lo que hiciste

1 **¡Saludos de México!**

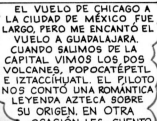

MÓNICA, UNA CHICA MEXICANO-AMERICANA PASA EL VERANO EN MÉXICO.

EL VUELO DE CHICAGO A LA CIUDAD DE MÉXICO FUE LARGO, PERO ME ENCANTÓ EL VUELO A GUADALAJARA. CUANDO SALIMOS DE LA CAPITAL VIMOS LOS DOS VOLCANES, POPOCATÉPETL E IZTACCÍHUATL. EL PILOTO NOS CONTÓ UNA ROMÁNTICA LEYENDA AZTECA SOBRE SU ORIGEN. EN OTRA OCASIÓN LES CUENTO LA LEYENDA.

QUERIDOS PAPÁS, ¡SALUDOS DE MÉXICO! ¿CÓMO ESTÁN TODOS? LOS EXTRAÑO MUCHO.

2 **Me recibieron con rosas.**

EL PRIMER DÍA LILIA Y SU MAMÁ ME RECIBIERON CON UNA DOCENA DE ROSAS. ¡IMAGÍNENSE, ROSAS! ESA NOCHE CENAMOS EN CASA. LA COMIDA MEXICANA ES RIQUÍSIMA.

ESTOY MUY CONTENTA AQUÍ CON LA FAMILIA DE LILIA. TODOS SON MUY SIMPÁTICOS.

3 **Paseamos en una calandria.**

¡Y ME ENCANTA GUADALAJARA! LA CIUDAD ES MUY LINDA Y HAY TANTO QUE HACER. AYER LILIA Y YO DECIDIMOS HACER UN PEQUEÑO TOUR POR LA CIUDAD. POR LA MAÑANA ELLA ME LLEVÓ AL CENTRO.

PRIMERO, PASEAMOS EN UNA CALANDRIA. (ASÍ LLAMAN A LOS COCHES DE CABALLO.) ¡QUÉ DIVERTIDO!

DESPUÉS NOS ENCONTRAMOS CON ÓSCAR Y JAVIER, LOS PRIMOS DE LILIA. ELLOS DECIDIERON ACOMPAÑARNOS AL TEATRO DEGOLLADO…

…Y AL PALACIO DE GOBIERNO, DONDE HAY UN MURAL MUY IMPRESIONANTE DE OROZCO.

Purpose This section uses real language to describe what an American teenager did during her first days in Guadalajara.

4 ¡Caminamos hasta no poder más!

POR LA TARDE FUIMOS AL MERCADO LIBERTAD. ¡ES ENORME! HAY DE TODO.

CAMINAMOS Y CAMINAMOS HASTA NO PODER MÁS. VIMOS MUCHAS ARTESANÍAS MUY BONITAS, PERO ME RESISTÍ Y NO COMPRÉ NADA

AL SALIR DEL MERCADO VI A UN VENDEDOR CON UNAS BLUSAS TÍPICAS. YA NO RESISTÍ MÁS. ME COMPRÉ UNA BLUSA HERMOSÍSIMA.

5 ¡Cantaron para nosotras!

DESPUÉS DE TANTO CAMINAR, FUIMOS A LA PLAZA DE LOS MARIACHIS. TOMAMOS UN REFRESCO Y ESCUCHAMOS LA MÚSICA.

DE REPENTE, UN MARIACHI EMPEZÓ A TOCAR Y CANTAR EN NUESTRA MESA ¡QUÉ SORPRESA!

LOS PRIMOS DE LILIA PAGARON LA MÚSICA. ¡QUÉ SIMPÁTICOS! ¡Y ÓSCAR ES MUY GUAPO! ESPERO VERLO OTRO VEZ.

PRONTO LES ESCRIBO MÁS. UN ABRAZO PARA TODOS DE MÓNICA.

LECCIÓN 1

doscientos sesenta y tres **263**

Suggestions Begin by having students close their books while you narrate one section at a time, using the transparencies to clarify meaning without translation. Then ask the **Early Production Check**s. Repeat this process with each section.

Using the video Play one section at a time after narrating it using the transparencies. Freeze the video and ask the **Early Production Checks.** Repeat this process with each section.

12 ¿Son simpáticos los primos de Lilia?
13 ¿Cómo es Óscar?
14 ¿Espera Mónica ver a Óscar otra vez?
15 ¿A quién espera ver otra vez?

Side 6, 17535 to 20140

---

4 [28:54]

¡Caminamos hasta no poder más!
Point out Mercado Libertad is supposedly the largest public market in the Western Hemisphere. Unlike most stores, where prices are fixed, this is the place to bargain *(regatear)*.

1 ¿Quiénes son?
2 ¿Fueron al Mercado Libertad por la tarde?
3 ¿Adónde fueron por la tarde?
4 ¿Es enorme el mercado?
5 ¿Cómo es el Mercado Libertad?
6 ¿Hay de todo allí?
7 ¿Qué hay en el Mercado Libertad?
8 ¿Caminaron mucho?
9 ¿Vieron muchas artesanías en el Mercado Libertad?
10 ¿Qué vieron en el Mercado Libertad?
11 ¿Le gustaron las artesanías a Mónica?
12 ¿Compró Mónica muchas cosas o resistió?
13 ¿Al salir del mercado, compró una blusa Mónica?
14 ¿Qué compró Mónica?

Side 6, 15766 to 17511

5 [29:53]

¡Cantaron para nosotras!
Point out
• Mariachis are Mexican "troubadours." For more information, see the reading on page 271.
• The Plaza de los Mariachis was once the most popular place to hear mariachi music. Now the nearby town of Tlaquepaque is the favorite spot.

1 ¿Fueron a la Plaza de los Mariachis?
2 ¿Qué hicieron en la Plaza de los Mariachis, tomaron un refresco y escucharon música?
3 ¿Qué tomaron?
4 ¿Qué escucharon?
5 ¿Empezó a tocar y cantar un mariachi?
6 ¿Qué hizo un mariachi de repente?
7 ¿Tocó y cantó el mariachi para las chicas?
8 ¿Fue una sorpresa?
9 ¿Pagaron los primos de Lilia la música?
10 ¿Quiénes pagaron la música?
11 ¿Qué hicieron los primos de Lilia?

CHARLEMOS UN POCO

CHARLEMOS UN POCO

A. ¿Dónde? Allow 2–3 min for students to decide on correct answers individually. Then call on individual students. Have class confirm their answers.

1 el centro
2 la Plaza de los Mariachis
3 el Mercado Libertad
4 la Plaza de los Mariachis
5 el Mercado Libertad
6 la Plaza de los Mariachis
7 el centro
8 la Plaza de los Mariachis
9 el Mercado Libertad

B. Ayer. Allow 2–3 min for students to ask questions working in pairs. Then call on individuals, asking **¿Quién habló por teléfono ayer?**

1 ¿Hablaste por teléfono?
Sí, hablé por teléfono. *o*
No, no hablé por teléfono.
2 ¿Comiste un sándwich?
Sí, comí un sándwich. *o*
No, no comí un sándwich.
3 ¿Estudiaste español?
Sí, estudié español. *o*
No, no estudié español.
4 ¿Paseaste en bicicleta?
Sí, paseé en bicicleta. *o*
No, no paseé en bicicleta.
5 ¿Escuchaste música?
Sí, escuché música. *o*
No, no escuché música.
6 ¿Escribiste una composición?
Sí, escribí una composición. *o*
No, no escribí una composición.
7 ¿Descansaste?
Sí, descansé. *o*
No, no descansé.
8 ¿Tomaste un refresco?
Sí, tomé un refresco. *o*
No, no tomé un refresco.
9 ¿Saliste con un(a) amigo(a)?
Sí, salí con un(a) amigo(a). *o*
No, no salí con un(a) amigo(a).
10 ¿Compraste algo nuevo?
Sí, compré algo nuevo. *o*
No, no compré nada nuevo.

Preterite tense

Singular verb endings

-ar	-er, -ir
-é	-í
-aste	-iste
-ó	-ió

¿Qué **compraste**?
No **encontré** nada.
¿Dónde **comió** Antonia?
No **salí** del trabajo hasta las 7:30.

See **¿Por qué se dice así?**,
page G83, section 6.1.

C. ¡Qué ocupada! Call on individuals by asking random times: **¿Qué hizo a las 10:00? ¿a las 8:30?**
A las diez menos cuarto, habló con Nico Muñoz.
A las diez, escribió una carta a los padres de los estudiantes.
A las once y media, comió con la profesora Gómez.

A las doce y media, llaman al Sr. Blanco.
A la una y media, preparó un informe para los profesores.
A las dos y media, visitó la clase de español.
A las tres, alquiló un video para la clase de biología.
A las cuatro y media, salió para casa.
A las seis, jugó tenis.

A. ¿Dónde? Según Mónica, ¿dónde pasaron estas cosas: en **el Mercado Libertad,** en **el centro** o en **la Plaza de los Mariachis?**

1. Visitamos el Teatro Degollado.
2. Escuchamos a los mariachis.
3. Vimos muchas artesanías bonitas.
4. Los primos de Lilia pagaron la música.
5. Caminamos hasta no poder más.
6. Un mariachi cantó y tocó en nuestra mesa.
7. Paseamos en una calandria.
8. Tomamos un refresco.
9. Compré una blusa.

B. Ayer. Eres una persona muy curiosa. Pregúntale a tu compañero(a) qué hizo ayer.

 MODELO tomar helado
Tú: **¿Tomaste helado?**
Compañero(a): **Sí, tomé helado.** o
No, no tomé helado.

1. hablar por teléfono
2. comer un sándwich
3. estudiar español
4. pasear en bicicleta
5. escuchar música
6. escribir una composición
7. descansar
8. tomar un refresco
9. salir con un(a) amigo(a)
10. comprar algo nuevo

C. ¡Qué ocupada! La directora de la escuela es una persona muy ocupada. ¿Qué hizo ayer?

MODELO **A las ocho, recibió a los nuevos estudiantes.**

23 de marzo		martes	
8:00 / 8:30	recibir a los nuevos estudiantes	1:00 / 1:30	Preparar un informe para los profesores
9:00 / 9:30	9:45 hablar con Nico Muñoz	2:00 / 2:30	visitar la clase de español
10:00 / 10:00	escribir una carta a los padres de los estudiantes	3:00 / 3:00	alquilar un video para la clase de biología
11:00 / 1:30	comer con la Prof. Gómez	4:00 / 4:30	salir para casa
12:00 / 12:30	llamar al Sr. Blanco	5:00 / 5:30	6:00 jugar tenis

Purpose These activities provide guided practice to students beginning to produce new language necessary to talk about what they did during the day.

CH. Una familia muy ocupada. Pregúntale a tu compañero(a) acerca de las actividades de su familia el fin de semana pasado.

MODELO ver una película
  Tú: **¿Vieron una película?**
  Compañero(a): **Sí, vimos una película.** o
  No, no vimos una película.

1. comer en un restaurante
2. salir de la ciudad
3. correr juntos
4. pasear en el parque
5. caminar por el centro
6. hablar con los abuelos
7. comprar algo (nada)
8. preparar tacos
9. limpiar la casa
10. alquilar un video

D. Rin, rin. Suena el teléfono. Es abuelita. Quiere saber qué hicieron todos anoche. ¿Qué le dice su nieta?

MODELO hermana: salir con unos amigos
  Mi hermana salió con unos amigos.

1. papá y yo: preparar la comida
2. mamá: ayudar a Rosita
3. Beto y Memo: jugar fútbol
4. mamá y yo: decidir descansar
5. yo: estudiar para un examen
6. tía Elena: salir de compras
7. mi hermanita: llorar mucho
8. Natalia: comer pizza

E. En la plaza. Muchas personas fueron a la plaza el domingo pasado. ¿Qué hicieron?

MODELO **el Sr. Muñoz**
  El Sr. Muñoz descansó.

1. Arturo y Rubén
2. Inés
3. la Srta. Ramos

4. Sofía y Gilberto
5. el Sr. Gamboa
6. Susana y Carolina

LECCIÓN 1

Preterite tense
Plural verb endings

-ar	-er, -ir
-amos	-imos
-aron	-ieron

Salieron esta mañana a las 6:00.
¿Estudiaron en la biblioteca?
No **bebimos** nada.

*See **¿Por qué se dice así?**,
page G83, section 6.1.*

CH. Una familia muy ocupada. Have students repeat the activity—one student asks partner all questions, then vice versa. Then have one person from each pair go to board and write the things both families did: **Las familias de Brad y Carol comieron en un restaurante, corrieron juntos y . . .** Allow 3–4 min.

1 ¿Comieron en un restaurante?
  Sí, comimos en un restaurante. *o*
  No, no comimos en un restaurante.
2 ¿Salieron de la ciudad?
  Sí, salimos de la ciudad. *o*
  No, no salimos de la ciudad.
3 ¿Corrieron juntos?
  Sí, corrimos juntos. *o*
  No, no corrimos juntos.
4 ¿Pasearon en el parque?
  Sí, paseamos en el parque. *o*
  No, no paseamos en el parque.
5 ¿Caminaron por el centro?
  Sí, caminamos por el centro. *o*
  No, no caminamos por el centro.
6 ¿Hablaron con los abuelos?
  Sí, hablamos con los abuelos. *o*
  No, no hablamos con los abuelos.
7 ¿Compraron algo?
  Sí, compramos algo. *o*
  No, no compramos nada.
8 ¿Prepararon tacos?
  Sí, preparamos tacos. *o*
  No, no preparamos tacos.
9 ¿Limpiaron la casa?
  Sí, limpiamos la casa. *o*
  No, no limpiamos la casa.
10 ¿Alquilaron un video?
  Sí, alquilamos un video. *o*
  No, no alquilamos un video.

D. Rin, rin.
Point out All -ar and -er stem-changing verbs are regular in the preterite.
1 Papá y yo preparamos la comida.
2 Mamá ayudó a Rosita.
3 Beto y Memo jugaron fútbol.
4 Mamá y yo decidimos descansar.
5 Yo estudié para un examen.
6 Tía Elena salió de compras.
7 Mi hermanita lloró mucho.
8 Natalia comió pizza.

E. En la plaza.
1 Arturo y Rubén corrieron.
2 Inés tocó la guitarra.
3 La señorita Ramos tomó un refresco.
4 Sofía y Gilberto bailaron.
5 El señor Gamboa escribió una carta.
6 Susana y Carolina escucharon música.

F. Encuesta. Pregúntale a un(a) amigo(a) si le gustaron ciertas cosas.

No me gustó. No me gustaron.	Me gustó. Me gustaron.	Me encantó. Me encantaron.
•	•	•

MODELO Tú: **¿Te gustó el concierto en el parque?**
Compañero(a): **Sí, ¡me encantó!** o
No, no me gustó. o
Sí, me gustó.

1. las clases de baile
2. la fiesta de [tu amiga(o) . . .]
3. el programa de música
4. las películas [título] y [título]
5. la exhibición de arte
6. el concierto de [grupo]
7. el baile
8. los videos de [artista]
9. la comedia del club de teatro
10. la excursión a [lugar]

G. ¿Adónde fuiste? Pregúntale a tu compañero(a) si fue a varios lugares durante la semana.

MODELO un concierto de rock
Tú: **¿Fuiste a un concierto de rock anoche?**
Compañero(a): **Sí, fui a un concierto de rock anoche.** o
No, no fui a un concierto de rock anoche.

VOCABULARIO ÚTIL:

anoche	la semana pasada
esta mañana	el sábado pasado
ayer	el fin de semana

1. el cine
2. la biblioteca
3. un baile
4. el colegio
5. el parque
6. una clase de música
7. el gimnasio
8. una fiesta

Ir

fui	fuimos
fuiste	
fue	fueron
fue	fueron

See **¿Por qué se dice así?**, *page G86, section 6.2.*

Talking about the past

The preterite tense is often used with expressions such as:

esta mañana	*this morning*
ayer	*yesterday*
anoche	*last night*
la semana pasada	*last week*
el fin de semana	*the weekend*

UNIDAD 6

H. Un día interesante. Ayer los turistas se pasearon por Guadalajara. ¿Adónde fueron?

MODELO Lorenzo Martínez (9)
Lorenzo Martínez fue a la Plaza de la Liberación.

1. los señores Rivera (3)
2. Margarita Valdez (6)
3. el señor Álvarez (2)
4. Guadalupe Silva y yo (8)

5. tú (4)
6. todos (7)
7. la familia Torres (5)
8. el guía (1)

PLAZA TAPATÍA
CENTRO HISTÓRICO

1. Catedral
2. Museo Regional del Estado
3. Palacio Legislativo
4. Palacio del Gobernador
5. Plaza de la Liberación
6. Teatro Degollado
7. Plaza de los Mariachis
8. Iglesia de San Juan de Dios
9. Mercado Libertad

CHARLEMOS UN POCO MÁS

A. ¿Estudiaste ayer? Write eight things that you did yesterday. Tell your partner what you did and ask if he or she did the same things. Note what you both did. Be prepared to report to the class.

 EJEMPLO
Tú: **Yo estudié español y vi la tele. ¿Y tú?**
Compañero(a): **Yo vi la tele y limpié mi cuarto.**
Tú: **Los dos vimos la tele.**

LECCIÓN 1

Purpose The *Charlemos un poco más* activities are designed to allow students to create with language needed to talk about what they did during the day.

B. El sábado pasado. Call on individual students to describe each picture. Ask class if they agree with the description.

C. ¿Viajó Ud.? Allow 4–5 min for students to decide on questions. Then allow students to ask you their questions. Personalize by asking students about their travels.

CH. ¡A escribir! Allow one week for students to complete this assignment. Tell students to keep their stories simple enough for elementary school students to be able to read. Tell them to write only one or two sentences per illustrated page. Illustrations may be students' own drawings or cutouts from magazines. You may want to ask students to turn in their complete story for correcting before they write it on their illustrated pages. Have volunteers read their stories to class. Then display them on the bulletin board and/or publish them for entire class to read. You may want to give the illustrated stories to a local elementary bilingual class.

B. El sábado pasado.   Paco and Luis had a very busy day last Saturday. With your partner, recount their day by looking at the drawing below.

EJEMPLO   **Por la mañana Paco limpió la casa y Luis . . .**

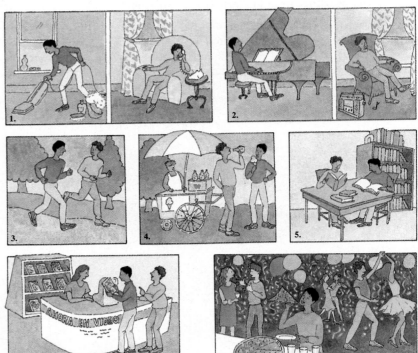

C. ¿Viajó Ud.?   What did your teacher do last summer? With a partner, prepare six to eight questions to ask your teacher about last summer. These should all be yes/no questions.

EJEMPLO   **¿Fue usted a México?**

CH. ¡A escribir!   With a partner, create a children's storybook titled **La historia de Bombón.** Describe one of his many adventures as a puppy. Illustrate your story. Begin by saying: **Un día, Bombón fue a . . .**

Dramatizaciones

A and B. Assign role play **A** to half the class and role play **B** to the other half. Allow 4–5 min for preparation. Then have students present their role plays to class. Do not allow students to use notes while they present.

A. Mi telenovela favorita . . . You missed your favorite soap opera yesterday and want to know what happened. Your partner saw it, so you have lots of questions to ask. Role-play the situation.

Tú

- Ask if Carolina spoke with her boyfriend.

- Ask what they talked about.

- Ask what happened at the party.

- Find out what happened then.

Compañero(a)

- Say they spoke at her house, then they walked to school together.

- Say they talked about Víctor Mario's party.

- Say that first, Víctor Mario danced with the brunette. Then he played the guitar and sang several very romantic songs to her.

- Say you don't know because Carmen called and you talked on the phone for an hour.

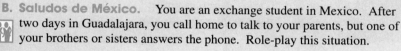

B. Saludos de México. You are an exchange student in Mexico. After two days in Guadalajara, you call home to talk to your parents, but one of your brothers or sisters answers the phone. Role-play this situation.

Tú

- Say hello and ask if your parents are at home.

- Say that you are fine but that you miss the family. Ask how they are.

- Tell three or four things that you did on your first day.

- Respond that you went out. Tell where you went.

- Say that you have to leave to go somewhere. Say where.

- Promise to write. Say good-bye.

Tu hermano(a)

- Say hello. Say that your parents aren't home. Ask how your partner is.

- Respond. Ask if he or she likes Guadalajara.

- Ask if he or she went out last night.

- React.

- Tell him or her to write about everything.

- Say good-bye.

C. Entrevista. You are writing an article for the school paper, and you need to find out what the principal and his or her family did during the weekend. Role-play this situation with your partner.

C. Entrevista. After allowing students 4–5 min to prepare their role plays, ask half the class to present theirs. Then have each pair write a short article based on what the "principal" said. This should be a cooperative writing effort. In pairs where a stronger and weaker student are working together, discreetly ask the weaker student to do the writing, and have the stronger student direct and edit what is being written. Ask the students who did not present their role plays to read their articles to the class.

Purpose These role plays are designed to recycle the structures and vocabulary needed to talk about what students did during the day. Encourage students to work without their books when preparing and performing their role plays.

¡No metas la pata!

IMPACTO CULTURAL

¡No metas la pata!

Te invito al ballet. Paul está visitando a su amigo Óscar en Guadalajara. Javier los invita al ballet folklórico el sábado.

Javier:	**Óscar, Paul, fíjense. Tengo tres boletos para el ballet folklórico el sábado.**
Óscar:	**¡Fantástico! Lo vi el año pasado.**
Paul:	**Uhhh. Lo siento pero . . . uh . . . uh no puedo ir.**
Óscar:	**¿Por qué? ¿Qué vas a hacer?**
Paul:	**Pues, la verdad es que prefiero quedarme en casa.**
Javier:	**Pero hombre, no puedes visitar Guadalajara sin ver el ballet folklórico. Es famosísimo.**
Paul:	**Tal vez, pero no me gusta el ballet. No me interesan ni las bailarinas ni la música clásica.**
Javier:	**Pero, Pablo, nuestro ballet sí te va a gustar.**

Why does Javier insist that Paul will enjoy the **ballet folklórico**?

1. Because he knows that the **ballet folklórico** is famous.
2. He assumes that Paul has never seen a good ballet company.
3. He realizes that Paul has a mistaken idea of what the **ballet folklórico** is.

❏ Check your answer on page 419.

Y ahora, ¡a leer!

Antes de empezar

Mira las fotos de los mariachis e indica si estos comentarios parecen ciertos **(C)** o falsos **(F)**. Lee la lectura y cambia, si es necesario, tus respuestos.

C	F		
C	F	**1.**	Los mariachis son músicos.
C	F	**2.**	Los mariachis tocan y cantan música religiosa.
C	F	**3.**	Los mariachis siempre son muy jóvenes.
C	F	**4.**	El traje tradicional de los mariachis es más formal que el traje de los músicos de una orquesta sinfónica.
C	F	**5.**	Con frecuencia los mariachis tocan en fiestas, bodas y bautismos.
C	F	**6.**	La música de los mariachis es alegre y ruidosa.
C	F	**7.**	El mariachi casi siempre lleva sombrero.

270 *doscientos setenta*

¡Viva el mariachi!

La música de los mariachis es, sin duda, la música nacional de México. Como los trovadores del pasado, los mariachis suelen aparecer en cualquier momento, dispuestos a serenar al público por unos cuantos pesos o, si les sonríe una chica hermosa, tocar y cantar toda la noche. Los vemos en todas partes: en fiestas, serenatas, bodas y bautismos. Su presencia basta para convertir una ocasión no especial en una fiesta improvisada.

Su música es ruidosa, rica, alegre y alborotada. Siempre crea un ambiente de fiesta y de carnaval. Las canciones de los mariachis son expresivas y están llenas de una emoción única e inolvidable.

El mariachi tradicional tiene su origen en el estado de Jalisco. Como el charro (el *cowboy* mexicano), lleva pantalones apretados, saco estilo bolero, corbata suelta y un sombrero ancho. Un cinturón, botas de cuero meticulosamente labradas y, a veces, espuelas de plata completan su traje típico.

Es interesante saber que la palabra "mariachi" no es ni de origen español ni de origen indio. ¡Es de origen francés! Según una explicación, durante la ocupación francesa, en el siglo XIX, un francés fue desesperadamente a la plaza a buscar músicos para la boda de su hija. Como no sabía español, decía *"mariage, mariage"* al llamar a los músicos mexicanos. La palabra francesa para "boda" es *mariage*. De allí, por extensión, estos músicos llegaron a llamarse "mariachis".

Verifiquemos

1. Nombra cuatro lugares donde los mariachis tocan y cantan normalmente.
2. Describe la música de los mariachis.
3. Describe el traje de los mariachis.
4. Describe las canciones de los mariachis.
5. Explica el origen de la palabra "mariachi".

LECCIÓN 1

doscientos setenta y uno **271**

¡Viva el mariachi!

Point out The term **trovadores** is a cognate of the English *troubadours,* referring to the European poet-musicians of the Middle Ages. Other descendants of the troubadours include the **tunas** of Spain and the **estudiantinas** of Mexico.

The unit has been set in Guadalajara, capital of the state of Jalisco. Tlaquepaque, in the same state, claims to be the home of the **mariachi** and the **charro.**

Verifiquemos

Suggestions First have students answer these questions in groups Then go over answers with class.

Answers

1 Tocan y cantan en fiestas, serenatas, bodas y bautizos.
2 Es rica, alegre, ruidosa y alborotada. Crea un ambiente de carnaval.
3 Los mariachis llevan pantalones apretados, saco estilo bolero, corbata suelta y un sombrero ancho. También llevan cinturón y botas de cuero y espuelas.
4 Sus canciones son expresivas, llenas de emoción.
5 Viene de la palabra francesa para boda, *mariage.* Resultó por falta de comunicación entre los franceses y los mexicanos.

Point out Some scholars believe that the term **mariachi** may have its origins in *nahuatl,* the language of the Aztecs. This theory is based on the fact that many *nahuatl* words end in **-chi** and **-che.**

OBJECTIVES

Communicative Goals

- Extending an invitation
- Accepting and declining an invitation
- Describing a trip

Culture and Reading

- *¡No me digas!*
  ¡Huy, qué caro!
  Shopping in a traditional Mexican market
- *Y ahora, ¡a leer!*
  El muralista José Clemente Orozco:
  A Mexican artist

Structure

- 6.3 Preterite of **hacer, ser, dar,** and **ver**

ACTIVE VOCABULARY

Diversiones

banda   ópera
muralista

Cuentos de hadas

La Cenicienta   hada madrina
cuento   príncipe
  … de hadas

Verbos

aceptar   regresar
aprender   ser *(pret.)*
dar *(pret.)*   ver *(pret.)*
entrar
hacer *(pret.)* ¡Me encantaría!
                 ¿Te gustaría?

Palabras y expresiones

agradable   ¡Cómo no!
conmigo   esta noche
contigo   ¡Huy!
demasiado(a)
invitado
plan
precio

¿ Qué compraste ?

Tlaquepaque, Tierra de Artesanos

GUÍA TURÍSTI

ANTICIPEMOS

¿Qué piensas tú?

1. ¿Qué tipo de información hay en la guía turística?

2. ¿Qué crees que compraron los jóvenes en la foto? En tu opinión, ¿para quiénes compraron estas cosas? ¿Por qué crees eso?

3. ¿Qué artesanías son típicas de esta región de México? ¿Por qué compran los turistas estas artesanías?

4. ¿De qué están hablando los dos jóvenes en esta página? ¿Qué crees que están diciendo? ¿Por qué crees eso?

5. ¿Para qué son los anuncios? ¿Cuáles te interesan más? ¿Por qué?

6. Un(a) amigo(a) te invita a uno de los lugares mencionados. ¿Quieres ir? ¿Por qué sí o por qué no? ¿Cómo le respondes a tu amigo(a)?

7. De qué vas a poder hablar al final de la lección?

Answers

Students should be allowed to answer in Spanish or English. Whenever they answer in English, repeat their answer in Spanish and have class repeat after you so they will start familiarizing themselves with the new vocabulary.

1 Es propaganda para excursiones a Tlaquepaque donde hay mucha artesanía. En la ciudad: museos, iglesias, mercados, restaurantes, murales, mariachis. En los alrededores: pueblos pintorescos, artesanos y sus artesanías, lago de Chapala, mercados al aire libre, etc.

2 Las respuestas varían.

3 Artesanías típicas de la región incluyen artículos de papel maché, faldas, blusas o vestidos típicos de Jalisco, chaquetas o cinturones de cuero, artículos de vidrio soplado, etc. Compran cosas porque necesitan regalos para amigos o familiares.

4 Él está invitando a la chica a salir. Ella quiere salir con él pero no puede. **Nuevo vocabulario:** Would you like to go . . .; I'm sorry, I can't; I have to . . .

5 Los anuncios son para conciertos, un parque de diversiones, un cine y un museo. Las respuestas varían.

6 Las respuestas varían.

7 **Van a tener nuevas oportunidades para hablar de lo que hicieron. También van a aprender a hacer, aceptar o rechazar una invitación.**

Purpose   To focus students on the language necessary to talk about what they did in the past and to extend, accept or refuse an invitation, and to encourage the development and use of critical thinking skills while observing and analyzing cultural differences and similarities related to tourist activities without forming judgments.

Point out   Juan Luis Guerra y 4.40 originated in the Dominican Republic in 1984. "Bachata Rosa" took the 1992 Grammy for Tropical Latin Album.

31:20–
34:01

Side 6, 20156 to 24988

Comprehension Checks

A complete set of the **Comprehension Checks** is available on cards in the Teacher's Resource Package.

1   31:27

Suggestion Contrast **hoy** and **ayer.**
1 ¿Quién es?
2 ¿Fue al cine ayer?
3 ¿Adónde fue ayer?
4 ¿Vio a su novia Mónica?
5 ¿A quién vio?
6 ¿Fue al cine Mónica con otro chico?

Side 6, 20354 to 20953

2   31:48

1 ¿Quién es? *(Point to each.)*
2 ¿Con quiénes está hablando Óscar ahora?
3 ¿Vieron Marisa y Javier a Mónica ayer?
4 ¿Vieron a Mónica con el otro chico?
5 ¿Cuándo vieron a Mónica?

Side 6, 20973 to 21245

3   31:57

Suggestions Identify the **figuritas de vidrio.** Mime buying and giving the figurine.
1 ¿Vio Marisa a Mónica?
2 ¿La vio en el cine? ¿en el mercado de artesanías?
3 ¿Vio Marisa a Mónica con el chico?
4` ¿Compró el chico una figurita de vidrio (una falda, una blusa)?
5 ¿Qué compró el chico?
6 ¿Le dio la figurita a Mónica? *(other names)*
7 ¿A quién le dio la figurita?
8 ¿Fue un gesto romántico?

Side 6, 21265 to 21858

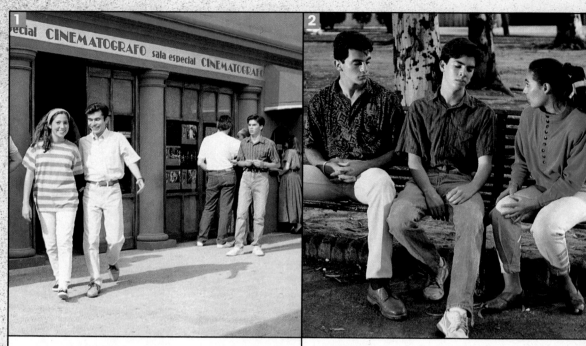

¡Pobre Óscar!
Ayer fue al cine, ¿y sabes a quién vio?
¡Vio a su novia Mónica con otro chico!

Ahora Óscar está hablando con Marisa y Javier.
Ellos también vieron a Mónica con el otro chico.

Óscar: ¿Quién fue ese chico?
Marisa: No sé. Yo también vi a Mónica con él. Pero no fue en el cine, fue en el mercado. Él compró una figurita de vidrio y le dio la figurita a Mónica. Fue un gesto romántico, ¿no crees?

274 doscientos setenta y cuatro

Purpose This section develops listening and reading comprehension of active vocabulary. Students should not be expected to achieve productive mastery at this point.

Javier: *Yo también los vi en el mercado.*
Óscar: *¿En serio?*
Javier: *Sí. Mónica compró un plato de cerámica. También compró una cacatúa de papel maché. Y bueno, pues . . . ¡le dio la cacatúa al chico!*
Óscar: *¡Cómo es posible! ¡Ella nunca me dio nada a mí!*

Ay, pobre Óscar. Está tan triste. Javier y Marisa quieren ayudarlo pero no saben qué hacer.

Marisa: *¿Tienes planes para esta tarde, Óscar?*
Óscar: *No, no tengo nada que hacer. ¿Por qué?*
Marisa: *¿Quieres salir con nosotros?*
Óscar: *Lo siento, pero estoy demasiado triste. Prefiero estar solo.*
Javier: *¡Óscar, por favor! ¡Qué tonto eres! Mónica no es la única chica del mundo. Ven, vamos a tomar algo.*

Al llegar al café, Óscar, Marisa y Javier ven a Mónica y al chico.
Marisa: *Mira quién está aquí.*

Mónica: *¡Óscar! Mira, te quiero presentar a mi hermano, Toño. Acaba de llegar a Guadalajara.*
Óscar: *¿Tu hermano?*

doscientos setenta y cinco **275**

Suggestions Begin by having students close their books while you narrate one section at a time, using the transparencies to clarify meaning without translation. Then ask **Comprehension Checks**. Repeat this process with each section.

Using the video Play one section at a time after narrating it using the transparencies. Freeze the video and ask **Comprehension Checks**. Repeat this process with each section.

7 `33:25`
1 ¿Llegan Óscar y sus amigos al café?
2 ¿Ven a Mónica y al chico?
3 ¿A quiénes ven?
4 ¿Quiere Mónica presentar al chico?
5 ¿Quién es el chico?
6 ¿Adónde acaba de llegar Toño?

Side 6, 23893 to 24988

4 `32:18`
Suggestions Identify the **plato de cerámica** and **cacatúa de papel maché.** Describe or show things made of the various materials mentioned.

Point out Cacatúa = *cockatoo.* Other popular papier-mâché birds are the **tucán** *(toucan)* and the **guacamayo** *(parrot).*
1 ¿Vio Javier a Mónica también?
2 ¿Dónde la vio?
3 ¿Compró Mónica un plato de cerámica (de vidrio)?
4 ¿Compró una cacatúa de papel maché (de cerámica, de vidrio)?
5 ¿Qué compró Mónica?
6 ¿Le dio la cacatúa al chico?
7 ¿A quién le dio la cacatúa ?
8 ¿Le dio Mónica algo a Óscar?

Side 6, 21878 to 22913

5 `32:53`
1 ¿Está triste Óscar?
2 ¿Quieren sus amigos ayudarlo?
3 ¿Quién quiere ayudar a Óscar?
4 ¿Por qué quieren ayudarlo?
5 ¿Saben Marisa y Javier qué hacer?

Side 6, 22932 to 23200

6 `33:03`
Suggestions Draw two datebook pages: one with nothing on it, one with lots of activities scheduled. Contrast **tiene planes / no tiene planes / no tiene nada que hacer.** Show pairs, groups, and single stick figures. Contrast **sólo / con amigos.** Name **otras chicas—María, Kati,** etc.
1 ¿Tiene Óscar planes para la tarde?
2 ¿Quiere salir con Marisa y Javier?
3 ¿Está demasiado triste?
4 ¿Prefiere estar sólo?
5 ¿Es Mónica la única chica?
6 ¿Hay otras chicas?
7 ¿Van Marisa y Javier a un café?
8 ¿Adónde van Marisa y Javier?
9 ¿Van a tomar algo?

Side 6, 23219 to 23873

TAPE/DISC

34:02–37:16

Side 6, 25015 to 30820

Early Production Checks

A full set of the **Early Production Checks** is on cards in the TRP.

Note Accept brief phrases or one- and two-word answers to all **Early Production Checks**. It is not necessary for students to answer in complete sentences.

 1 `34:08`

¿Quieren venir con nosotros?

Point out Lake Chapala, the largest natural lake in Mexico, is located 5,200 feet above sea level. Its fine climate and picturesque fishing villages have made it one of the most popular retirement communities in North America. Ecologists are working with the government to protect the lake.

Tlaquepaque is located about five miles from downtown Guadalajara. Mexico's largest arts and crafts center, it began as a site for glass factories, later joined by potters and other artisans of all types.

1 ¿Quién es? *(Point to Mónica, Lilia, Javier, Óscar.)*
2 ¿Conoce Mónica Tlaquepaque?
3 ¿Piensa llevarla Lilia?
4 ¿Piensa llevarla un día de éstos?
5 ¿Van Óscar y Javier a Tlaquepaque?
6 ¿Cuándo van a Tlaquepaque?
7 ¿Invitan los muchachos a Lilia y a Mónica?
8 ¿Aceptan las chicas?
9 ¿Tienen planes para el sábado Lilia y Mónica?
10 ¿Les gustaría ir con Óscar y Javier?
11 ¿Van a Chapala el sábado o el domingo?
12 ¿Tienen planes para el domingo Lilia y Mónica?
13 ¿Aceptan ir a Tlaquepaque el domingo?

Side 6, 25190 to 26121

¿ Q U É   D E C I M O S ...?

Al describir un viaje

1 ¿Quieren venir con nosotros?

2 ¿Recibiste mi última carta?

U N I D A D   6

---

2 `34:40`

¿Recibiste mi última carta?
1 ¿Quién es?
Continue asking questions, as above.

Side 6, 26134 to 27594

Purpose This section presents the lesson active vocabulary in real-life contexts as Mónica describes a trip to Tlaquepaque in detail.

3 ¡Compré un montón de cosas!

VI COSAS PRECIOSAS: FIGURITAS DE VIDRIO,

COSAS DE PAPEL MACHÉ,

Y ARTÍCULOS DE PIEL.

MÁS QUE NADA ME GUSTÓ LA CERÁMICA.

COMPRÉ UN MONTÓN DE COSAS A MUY BUEN PRECIO.

ENCONTRÉ REGALOS PARA TODA LA FAMILIA. Y, ¿SABES?, A TI TE COMPRÉ UN RECUERDO MUY BONITO.

¡SÉ QUE TE VA A GUSTAR!

4 Fue imposible subir.

FUE UN DÍA ESTUPENDO. LO PASAMOS MUY BIEN—HASTA LA HORA DE REGRESAR.

ÓSCAR, EL PRIMO GUAPÍSIMO DE LILIA, Y YO DECIDIMOS REGRESAR EN AUTOBÚS—O CAMIÓN, COMO LE DICEN AQUÍ. Y ESO SÍ QUE FUE UNA AVENTURA.

AL LLEGAR AL COCHE, TRATAMOS DE SUBIR LOS CUATRO, PERO FUE IMPOSIBLE. ES QUE COMPRÉ DEMASIADAS COSAS.

NO TE PUEDES IMAGINAR LO QUE PASÓ...

LECCIÓN 2

doscientos setenta y siete **277**

---

3   35:29

¡Compré un montón de cosas!

1. ¿Vio cosas preciosas o cosas feas Mónica?
2. ¿Vio figuritas de vidrio?
3. ¿Vio cosas de papel maché?
4. ¿Vio artículos de piel?
5. ¿Le gustó la cerámica a Mónica?
6. ¿Le gustó mucho o poco?
7. ¿Compró pocas cosas o un montón de cosas?
8. ¿Compró las cosas a buen precio o a mal precio?
9. ¿Encontró regalos para toda la familia?
10. ¿Compró un recuerdo para Isabel?
11. ¿Qué compró para Isabel?
12. ¿Le va a gustar a Isabel?
13. ¿Sabe Mónica qué le va a gustar a Isabel?

Side 6, 27606 to 29339

4   36:27

Fue imposible subir.

1. ¿Cómo fue el día en Tlaquepaque?
2. ¿Lo pasaron bien o mal?
3. ¿Trataron los cuatro de subir al coche?
4. ¿Fue posible?
5. ¿Fue imposible porque Mónica compró demasiadas cosas?
6. ¿Por qué fue imposible subir al coche?
7. ¿Quiénes decidieron regresar en autobús?
8. ¿Cómo llaman al autobús en México?
9. ¿Cómo es Óscar, según Mónica?
10. ¿Fue una aventura regresar en autobús?
11. ¿Puede imaginarse Isabel lo que pasó?
12. ¿Saben ustedes qué paso?
13. ¿Qué creen que pasó?

Side 6, 29353 to 30820

***S**uggestions*   Begin by having students close their books while you narrate one section at a time, using the transparencies to clarify meaning without translation. Then ask **Early Production Checks.** Repeat with each section.

Using the video   Play one section at a time after narrating it using the transparencies. Freeze the video and ask **Early Production Checks.** Repeat with each section.

A. ¡Me encantó Tlaquepaque!
Allow 2–3 min for students working individually to figure out correct order. Then, in groups of four or five, have students agree on correct sequence. Call on one group to read correct sequence: one student in group reads first sentence, another student reads second, etc. Have class confirm sequence.

1 Óscar y Javier invitaron a Mónica y Lilia a ir a Tlaquepaque. (7)
2 Mónica y Lilia aceptaron la invitación. (4)
3 El domingo los cuatro fueron a Tlaquepaque. (2)
4 Después de tanto caminar, tomaron un refresco al aire libre. (1)
5 Compraron tantas cosas que fue imposible subir al coche pequeño de Javier. (6)
6 Óscar y Mónica decidieron regresar en autobús. (3)

B. ¿Contigo?
Tell students to take turns inviting, accepting, and declining. Encourage them to use various formulas, not just one in model. Allow 3–4 min. Then call on pairs to do as role plays in front of class. Answers will vary.

C. ¿Vamos?
Allow 2–3 min to do in pairs. Then call on pairs to do for class. Answers will vary.

Conmigo / contigo

In order to express the idea of doing something *with* someone, use the following:

*conmigo
*contigo
  con usted / él / ella
  con nosotros(as)
  con ustedes / ellos / ellas

Ellos van **contigo**, ¿verdad?
No, van **con ustedes**.

*Note the special forms for **mí** and **ti**.

Extending, accepting, or declining an invitation

Extending an invitation:
  ¿Quieres ir conmigo?
  ¿Te gustaría ir a . . . ?

Accepting an invitation:
  ¡Claro que sí!
  ¡Me encantaría!
  ¡Cómo no!

Declining an invitation:
  Gracias, pero tengo otros planes.
  Gracias, pero no puedo.

A. ¡Me encantó Tlaquepaque! ¿En qué orden pasaron estas cosas?

1. Después de tanto caminar, tomaron un refresco al aire libre.
2. El domingo los cuatro fueron a Tlaquepaque.
3. Óscar y Mónica decidieron regresar en autobús.
4. Mónica y Lilia aceptaron la invitación.
5. Vieron todo tipo de artesanías allí.
6. Compraron tantas cosas que fue imposible subir al coche pequeño de Javier.
7. Óscar y Javier invitaron a Mónica y Lilia a ir a Tlaquepaque.

B. ¿Contigo? Invita a tu compañero(a) a estos lugares.

 MODELO   al cine
    Tú: **¿Quieres ir al cine conmigo?**
    Compañero(a): ¿Contigo? ¡Claro que sí! o
                Gracias, pero tengo otros planes.

1. a una fiesta
2. al baile
3. a la ópera
4. a un concierto de rock
5. a la biblioteca
6. a un restaurante
7. al zoológico
8. a un museo
9. a un café
10. a una discoteca

C. ¿Vamos? ¿Cómo responden estas personas a tu invitación?

 MODELO   Carlota y Pepe: jugar tenis
    Tú: **¿Les gustaría jugar tenis?**
    Compañero(a): ¡Cómo no! Nos encantaría. o
                Gracias, pero no podemos.

1. Samuel y Mateo: ver un video
2. Ramona: cantar con la banda
3. Toni: salir esta noche
4. Jesús y Héctor: ir al cine
5. Fito: tomar un helado
6. Andrés y Jacobo: correr en el parque
7. Lina y Yolanda: escuchar música en casa
8. Carla: ir de compras
9. Hugo y María: venir a casa a comer
10. Elsa: tomar una clase de gimnasia

Purpose These activities provide guided practice to students beginning to produce language needed to invite, to accept, or to decline an invitation, and to describe a series of past events.

CH. ¿Qué hicieron? No fuiste a la fiesta de tu clase de español anoche. Pregúntale a un(a) compañero(a) qué hicieron en la fiesta.

EJEMPLO tus amigos . . . y . . .

Tú:	**¿Qué hicieron . . . y . . .?**
Compañero(a):	**Comieron muchos tacos.**

VOCABULARIO ÚTIL:

hacer la comida	cantar mucho
comer muchos tacos	saludar a todos
aprender un baile	tomar mucha
nuevo	limonada
bailar con todos	no hacer nada
recibir a los invitados	¿ . . . ?

1. el (la) profesor(a)
2. tú y . . .
3. un(a) amigo(a)
4. . . . y . . .
5. tú
6. todos
7. el (la) director(a)
8. los padres

TEATRO DEGOLLADO
125 Aniversario
Opera

Filarmónica
DE JALISCO

CARMEN

Bizet

Director:
José Guadalupe Flores

11 y 13 abril   20:30 Hrs.

Abonos y boletos en Av. Juárez 638, Altos del Ex-convento del Carmen.
Informes en los Tels. 17-43-22, Ext. 51, 17-67-34 y 13-20-24.

LECCIÓN 2

Hacer

hice	hicimos
hiciste	
hizo	hicieron
hizo	hicieron

¿Qué **hicieron** ustedes?
No **hicimos** nada.

¿Qué **hiciste** tú?
Jugué tenis.

See **¿Por qué se dice así?**,
page G87, section 6.3.

D. ¿Y tú? Allow 2–3 min to do in pairs. Then ask several students what their partners did.

1 ¿Qué hicimos nosotros ayer? Bailamos.
2 ¿Qué hicieron Elena y Carmen ayer? Corrieron.
3 ¿Qué hiciste tú ayer? Miré (Vi) televisión.
4 ¿Qué hice yo ayer? Descansaste.
5 ¿Qué hicieron ustedes ayer? Hicimos la tarea (Estudiamos).

E. ¿Te gustó? Allow 2–3 min to do in pairs. Then ask individuals what their partner thought of each activity. Answers will vary.

Ser

fui	fuimos
fuiste	
fue	fueron
fue	fueron

La fiesta **fue** muy divertida.
Nosotros **fuimos** los primeros en llegar.

See **¿Por qué se dice así?**, *page G87, section 6.3.*

D. ¿Y tú ? Pregúntale a tu compañero(a) qué hicieron estas personas ayer.

 **MODELO** Sara
Tú: **¿Qué hizo Sara ayer?**
Compañero(a): **Fue al cine.**

1. nosotros **2.** Elena y Carmen

3. tú **4.** yo **5.** ustedes

E. ¿Te gustó ? Tú y tu compañero(a) están hablando de sus actividades. ¿Qué dicen?

EJEMPLO la exhibición de arte
Tú: **¿Te gustó la exhibición de arte?**
Compañero(a): **Fue interesante.**

la película anoche
las fiestas
el concierto de rock
la boda
los bailes del colegio
la exhibición de arte
la clase del profesor . . .
los exámenes

interesante
aburrido
fácil
difícil
divertido
emocionante
impresionante
agradable
cómico
romántico
bueno
malo

F. **¿Quién fue?** Tres compañeros de clase le mandaron rosas al (a la) profesor(a). ¿Quiénes fueron? Pregúntales a tus compañeros.

MODELO   Tú: **¿Fuiste tú?**
Compañero(a):   **No, no fui yo.** o
Sí, fui yo.

G. **¡Regalos!** Ayer fue el cumpleaños de Susana. ¿Qué le dieron sus amigos y su familia?

MODELO   Beto y Alicia
Beto y Alicia le dieron un libro.

1. su papá   **2.** sus abuelos   **3.** yo   **4.** Elena

5. tú   **6.** Guillermo   **7.** nosotros   **8.** sus hermanas

H. **Programas favoritos.** Pregúntales a cinco compañeros de la clase qué programas de televisión vieron anoche.

 MODELO   Tú: **¿Qué viste anoche?**
Compañero(a):   **Vi . . .** o
No vi televisión anoche.

LECCIÓN 2

Dar

di	dimos
diste	
dio	dieron
dio	dieron

Nosotros le **dimos** dos libros.
¿Qué le **diste** tú?

*See ¿**Por qué se dice así?**,
page G87, section 6. 3.*

Ver

vi	vimos
viste	
vio	vieron
vio	vieron

¿**Viste** la nueva película?
Sí, la **vi.**

*See ¿**Por qué se dice así?**,
page G87, section 6. 3.*

doscientos ochenta y uno **281**

F. **¿Quién fue?** At beginning of class, *secretly* designate three students to be the flower givers. Allow time for students to question each other until they discover the trio that sent the flowers. Insist they not reveal anything before they know all three names.

G. **¡Regalos!** Call on individual students. Have class confirm their answers.
1 Su papá le dio una bicicleta.
2 Sus abuelos le dieron un perro.
3 Yo le di una blusa.
4 Elena le dio un bolígrafo.
5 Tú le diste un disco compacto.
6 Guillermo le dio un video.
7 Nosotros le dimos una guitarra.
8 Sus hermanas le dieron unos pantalones.

H. **Programas favoritos.** Allow students to work in groups of five or six. Allow 2–3 min. Then call on individuals from each group to tell who saw what programs in their group.

CHARLEMOS UN POCO MÁS

A. El cine. Allow 2–3 min for students to identify the movie titles individually. Then call on individual students to give each title. Have class verify their answers. Allow another 3–4 min to ask group members which movies they saw. Check their answers by asking **¿Quién vio [película]? ¿Cuándo la viste?**

B. ¡Yo fui el príncipe! Tell students they have the opportunity to be casting directors. The idea is to select persons from the class that they consider best suited for each part. Allow 3–4 min to decide on cast. Then call on individuals to make their recommendations. Have them explain why they selected each person.

Point out Príncipe = prince, **la hada madrina** = the fairy godmother.

C. ¡Está furioso! Allow 2–3 min for pairs to come up with list of excuses. Then as each pair reads their list, ask class if it **is una excusa buena o una excusa débil**?

CHARLEMOS UN POCO MÁS

A. El cine. Below is a list of eight popular movies. Identify them. Then, in groups, ask your classmates if they saw these movies. Note the names of who saw which films.

 EJEMPLO   Tú: **¿Viste *Superhombre?***
                 Compañero(a):   **No, pero vi *Las tortugas ninja.***

Las tortugas ninja	Bailando con lobos	Superhombre
La guerra de las galaxias	La bella y la bestia	Los locos Addams
Lo que el viento se llevó	El mago de Oz	Solo en casa

B. ¡Yo fui el príncipe! Last night your Spanish class performed a version of **La Cenicienta** at your school's open house. You and your partner are trying to reconstruct the program. Tell who played each part. Two boys and five girls participated.

 EJEMPLO   **Eileen fue la hada madrina.**
                   Jackie fue una hermanastra.

C. ¡Está furioso! Your teacher is furious because last night no one did the homework assignment. With a partner, tell what excuses eight classmates (including the two of you) gave for not doing the work.

EJEMPLO   **Bob y Rick no hicieron la tarea porque fueron al cine.**

Purpose These activities are designed to allow students to describe past events in a variety of possible combinations.

CH. Le dio flores. Write a list of gifts that you gave to your family and friends last year. Then, in groups, compare lists and report to the class any gifts that more than two of you gave. Tell who received the gifts.

EJEMPLO   Tú: **¿A quiénes les diste regalos?**
            Compañero(a):   **Le di una foto a Lee y a mi tía le di . . .**

D. ¿Qué necesitamos hacer? Your parents were gone all day and left a list of chores for you and your brother or sister. Each of you has done some of the chores, but not all of them. Using the lists your instructor provides, ask your partner what he or she has done in order to find out what still needs to be done. Do not look at each other's lists.

EJEMPLO   Tú: **¿Alquilaste un video?**
            Compañero(a):   **No, no alquilé un video.**

> — limpiar tu cuarto
> — darle de comer al perro
> — prepararle la comida a tu hermano
> — ir a correos
> — limpiar el baño
> — comprar comida para el perro
> — hacer la tarea
> — alquilar un video
> — visitar a Abuelo
> — trabajar en el patio

E. ¿Qué hicieron? Your teacher will provide you and your partner with an activity chart. The drawings on the chart represent what five students, including yourself, did last Saturday. With your partner, figure out who did exactly the same things each of you did by asking each other questions.

EJEMPLO   Compañero(a):   **¿Quién bailó?**
            Tú: **Alberto y Ramona bailaron.**
            Compañero(a):   **¿Alguien más?**
            Tú: **Sí, Cruz también bailó.**

CH. Le dio flores. Allow students 2–3 min to write lists. Then allow them another 3–4 min to compare lists by asking each other **¿Le diste algo a [tu mamá]?**

D. ¿Qué necesitamos hacer? Allow 4–5 min for students to find out what remains to be done by questioning each other. Make sure they do not look at each other's lists. Have class verify correct answers.

E. ¿Qué hicieron? Allow 5–6 min for students to identify who did the same things they did. Have class verify their answers.

Extension Ask students to find out which of the remaining students on their list did the same things as the students on their partner's lists.

Dramatizaciones

A, B, C. Allow 5–10 min to prepare role plays. As each group finishes, have them practice doing it without notes. Then have students present their role plays in front of class. Ask comprehension check questions after each presentation.

A. ¿Qué pasa? You and your partner are talking about school and activities. Role-play this conversation.

Tú	Compañero(a)
■ Ask your partner if his or her math teacher gave an exam yesterday.	■ Answer yes. Say that it was easy.
■ Say that Greg says it was hard.	■ Say that Greg always says that exams are hard.
■ Ask if your partner went to the concert last night.	■ Answer yes. Say who went with you.
■ Ask if your partner enjoyed it.	■ Answer that you loved it.
■ Ask where he or she is going now.	■ Answer and ask your partner if he or she wants to go with you.

B. ¡Mira lo que compré! You and two friends run into each other in a café after each having been on a shopping spree. Two of you have lots of packages. Role-play the situation as you talk about . . .

- where you went.
- the things you bought.
- the price.
- the things you saw but didn't buy.

C. ¿Qué película viste? With your partner, discuss a movie that both of you saw recently. Find out . . .

- when your partner saw it.
- if he or she liked it.
- why he or she did or did not like it.
- where he or she saw it.
- with whom he or she saw it.

Purpose This section has students recycle, in student-centered role plays, all previously learned structures and vocabulary needed to describe what they did and to extend, accept, or decline an invitation.

Suggestions Do these role plays spontaneously, not from written scripts. Circulate among groups. Limit time allowed so that students do not get off task. Ask several pairs to recreate their exchange for whole class.

¡No me digas!

¡Huy, qué caro!   Al salir del Mercado San Juan de Dios, Paul se encuentra con su amigo Javier. Lee su conversación con Javier y luego contesta la pregunta.

Javier: **¡Hola, Pablo! Pero, hombre, parece que compraste todo el mercado.**

Paul: **Tienes razón, Javier. Pero no es todo para mí. Compré varios regalos para mi familia.**

Javier: **A ver, ¿qué compraste? Ahh, ¡qué bonitos! Me gusta el gato de papel maché. ¿Fue caro?**

Paul: **¡No, al contrario! Me costó solamente sesenta mil pesos.**

Javier: **¿Sesenta mil pesos? Es mucho, ¿no crees?**

Paul: **Pues, primero el vendedor me pidió noventa mil pesos. Yo le ofrecí sesenta mil y lo aceptó en seguida. Creo que es muy buen precio.**

Javier: **Hmmm. No estoy convencido. Alguien te dio gato por liebre aquí.**

Why does Javier react the way he does?

1. He obviously doesn't like the cat.
2. He thinks Paul paid too much for the cat.
3. Javier is offended that Paul didn't buy him a gift.

❏ Check your answer on page 419.

LECCIÓN 2   <u>doscientos ochenta y cinco</u>   **285**

IMPACTO CULTURAL

¡No me digas!

Purpose This section provides additional reading practice as students learn to avoid cross-cultural misunderstandings when shopping in a traditional Mexican market.

Suggestions Read the dialogue aloud for students so they may hear the proper intonation. Then have them read it. Ask comprehension check questions. Before turning to the explanations of answers on page 419, have students themselves try to explain why the wrong answers are wrong.

Point out The words **te dio gato por liebre** are derived from the expression **No dejes que te den gato por liebre** (or **No te dejes dar gato por liebre**) meaning "Don't take any wooden nickels," "Don't let them pull the wool over your eyes," "Don't let them put anything over on you" (literally, don't let them give you a cat for a hare).

Answers

1 It is possible that Javier didn't like the cat. But if he didn't, he did not express this at all. He actually says he likes it. Try another response.

② Paul feels that he got a bargain when he paid 30,000 pesos less than the vendor originally wanted. Javier, on the other hand, thinks that 60,000 pesos is too much to pay for a papier-mâché figurine. He obviously thinks Paul should have offered less than he did.

3 There is no indication that Javier even thought about Paul buying him a gift. This is not the correct answer.

Purpose

This section provides additional reading practice as students learn about one of Mexico's outstanding muralists, **el tapatío** (person from the state of Jalisco) José Clemente Orozco.

Suggestions

1 Give extra credit to students who research information on any of the three muralists mentioned and who write or give an oral report to class.

2 If art books with illustrations of murals are available in your library, you may bring some to class and interpret several murals for students, or let students interpret them.

3 Have students create a self-portrait mural by putting a picture or a symbol of themselves on the middle of a page (colored construction paper works very nicely) and then making a collage either of cutouts from magazines or drawings of their own. Each item on the "mural" should represent persons, places, events, qualities, or things significant to the individual. When the murals are finished, hang them around the class and every day have two or three students describe their mural to class.

Antes de empezar

These questions are an advance organizer for the reading that follows. First have students work in pairs. Then go over their answers with class.

Point out The adjective and noun **maya**, used in item 2 and in the reading, is invariable.

Answers

1 a
2 c
3 c
4 b

IMPACTO CULTURAL

Y ahora, ¡a leer!

Antes de empezar

Complete the statements that follow to find out how much you know about mural art. If you don't know the correct answer, make a reasoned guess. After you have read the selection, re-read your answers to see if you would change any of them.

1. Un mural es . . .
   a. una pintura hecha o aplicada sobre una pared.
   b. una pintura más grande que una pared.
   c. una pintura en una ventana.
   ch. una pintura en un almacén.

2. Los primeros muralistas probablemente fueron . . .
   a. franceses e italianos.
   b. ingleses.
   c. maya y aztecas.
   ch. artistas mexicanos del siglo XX.

3. Por lo general, los muralistas pintan . . .
   a. temas religiosos.
   b. temas clásicos.
   c. con colores brillantes.
   ch. sólo en blanco y negro.

4. En Estados Unidos . . .
   a. no hay muralistas.
   b. hay murales en muchos lugares.
   c. es ilegal pintar un mural en una pared.
   ch. todos los muralistas son mexicanos.

Verifiquemos

Después de leer el artículo sobre José Clemente Orozco, contesta las preguntas.

1. ¿Qué es un mural? ¿Cuál es el origen de los murales en México?
2. ¿Quiénes son los muralistas contemporáneos más conocidos?
3. Describe un elemento de los murales de José Clemente Orozco.
4. ¿Hay murales en tu comunidad? Si los hay, descríbelos y di dónde están.
5. Selecciona uno de los murales e interprétalo.

286 · doscientos ochenta y seis

Verifiquemos

Answers

1 Un mural es arte hecho en o aplicado a una pared o un muro. Los murales mexicanos originaron con los maya y los aztecas.

2 Los tres muralistas contemporáneos más conocidos son Rivera, Siqueiros y Orozco.

3 Las respuestas van a variar. Deben mencionar que Orozco fue un muralista con una pasión por lo sórdido de la historia. Fue un satirista sin igual en su arte.

4 Las respuestas van a variar.
5 Las respuestas van a variar.

El muralista José Clemente Orozco

El arte de los murales, es decir de las pinturas hechas o aplicadas sobre un muro o pared, es una de las contribuciones más importantes que ha hecho México al arte contemporáneo. El mural es un arte que tiene su origen en tiempos precolombinos, con los impresionantes murales de los maya y los aztecas, y que florece en este siglo durante la Revolución de 1910. Como la Revolución, el arte muralista es de carácter nacionalista, vigoroso y explosivo, con colores brillantes y temas sociopolíticos.

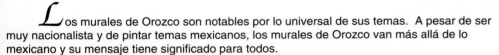

Los tres artistas sobresalientes del movimiento muralista son, sin duda, Diego Rivera (1886-1957), David Alfaro Siqueiros (1899-1974) y José Clemente Orozco (1883-1949). Frecuentemente considerado el mejor de los tres, Orozco fue un satirista sin igual, en particular cuando sus murales trataban temas sociopolíticos.

Los murales de Orozco son notables por lo universal de sus temas. A pesar de ser muy nacionalista y de pintar temas mexicanos, los murales de Orozco van más allá de lo mexicano y su mensaje tiene significado para todos.

Entre 1927 y 1934, Orozco vivió en Estados Unidos. Durante su estadía aquí, pintó murales en Pomona College en California, en la Universidad de Dartmouth en New Hampshire, y en la New York School for Social Research en Nueva York.

Probablemente uno de los mejores murales de Orozco es el que está en el Hospicio Cabañas, en Guadalajara. Allí se ve la verdadera fuerza de su arte: denuncia la manipulación política contrastando severamente los colores rojo y negro.

OBJECTIVES

Communicative Goals

- Describing a series of events in past time
- Discussing Indian cultures of Mexico

Reading

- *Leamos ahora*
  Tenochtitlán
  The origins of Mexico City
- Reading strategy: Identifying the main idea

Writing

- *Escribamos un poco*
  Writing a self-portrait
- Writing strategy: Writing a free-form poem

Structure

- 6.4 Preterite of **poder, tener, venir,** and **decir**

ACTIVE VOCABULARY

Una leyenda azteca

azteca	soldado
batalla	Tenochtitlán
dioses	trono
enemigo	valiente
guerra	volcán
héroe	atacar
indio	conquistar
leyenda	enamorarse (de)
palacio	morir (ue, u)
rey	proteger

Comidas

desayuno	cena
almuerzo	

Transportación

auto	chofer
avión	motocicleta
calandria	moto
camión	tren
carro	

¿Qué pasó?

GOLFO DE MÉXICO

YUCATÁN

Mérida ●

Uxmal

Chichén I

Kabah

MORELOS

VERACRUZ

CAMPECHE

QUINTANA ROO

★ México, D.F.
PUEBLA

TABASCO

OAXACA

Oaxaca

MÉXICO

B

Monte
Albán   Mitla

CHIAPAS

GUATEMALA

HOND

OCÉANO
PACÍFICO

0	300 Kilómetros

0	300 Millas

EL SALVADOR

Verbos

decir *(pret.)*	llegar
descubrir	pensar (ie)
gritar	poder *(pret.)*
hubo	tener *(pret.)*
lavar	venir *(pret.)*

Palabras y expresiones

antes de	problema
desafortunadamente	serio(a)
después de	
malo(a)	¡Cuéntame!
mismo(a)	¡Gracias a Dios!
moderno(a)	¡Qué barbaridad!
mundo	¿Qué pasó?

ANTICIPEMOS

Agencia de Viajes Amalia Portillo

Porfirio Díaz Nº. 858   México, D.F.

Nombre: Familia Gabriel Orozco   **Viaje:**   2 de julio al 17 de julio
Número de pasajeros: 4   **Hotel:**   ★★★★

Itinerario

12 de julio	17,20	Llegada a Oaxaca Alojamiento: Hotel Señorial	**16 de julio**	8,00 9,00	Desayuno Autobús a Uxmal y Kabah Almuerzo: Rancho Herrera
13 de julio	8,00 9,00 16,30	Desayuno Autobús a Monte Albán Almuerzo: sándwiches Regreso a Oaxaca Cena: libre		16,30 20,00	Regreso a Mérida Cena: Hotel Las Hamacas
			17 de julio	8,00 9,00	Desayuno Autobús a Chichén Itzá Almuerzo: sándwiches
14 de julio	8,00 9,00 16,30	Desayuno Autobús a Mitla Almuerzo: sándwiches Regreso a Oaxaca Cena: libre		16,30 20,00	Regreso a Mérida Cena: libre
			18 de julio	7,30 8,30 13,30	Desayuno Taxi al aeropuerto Llegada a México, D.F.
15 de julio	7,30 8,30 12,30	Desayuno Taxi al aeropuerto Llegada a Mérida Tarde: libre			

¿ Qué piensas tú ?

1. ¿Qué información hay en el itinerario?

2. ¿Qué hicieron los Orozco el segundo día? ¿El sexto día?

3. ¿Qué partes de México visitaron? ¿Puedes encontrar esos lugares en el mapa?

4. Estudia los nombres en el mapa. ¿Cuáles crees que son de origen español? ¿De qué origen son los otros?

5. ¿Crees que hubo una sola cultura indígena en México o hubo varias? ¿Por qué crees eso?

6. Dile a la clase todo lo que sabes de las antiguas culturas indígenas mexicanas. ¿Qué sabes de las culturas indígenas contemporáneas en México?

7. ¿De qué vas a poder hablar al final de la lección?

doscientos ochenta y nueve **289**

Purpose   To focus students on structures and vocabulary necessary to describe what they have done, and to encourage students to develop and use critical thinking skills as they learn to recognize and appreciate Mexican Indian cultures.

¿Qué piensas tú?

Answers

1 El nombre de los viajeros, número de viajeros, fechas del viaje, hora de llegadas, categoría de hoteles, tipo de tranportación, lugares que visitan.

2 **Segundo día** Desayunaron en el hotel. Fueron por autobús a las pirámides de Monte Albán. Comieron sándwiches en Monte Albán. Regresaron a las 4:30 de la tarde. Tuvieron la noche libre. **Sexto día** Desayunaron a las ocho. A las nueve tomaron un autobús a Chichén Itzá. Almorzaron sándwiches. Regresaron a Mérida a las cuatro y media. Tuvieron la noche libre.

3 Van a visitar Oaxaca y las ruinas de Monte Albán y Mitla. También van a Mérida en Yucatán. Allí van a Uxmal, Kabah y Chichén Itzá.

4 Origen español: Puebla, Hidalgo, Veracruz, Guerrero, Morelos. Origen indio: México, Tlaxcala, Oaxaca, Tabasco, Chiapas, Campeche, Yucatán, Quintana Roo, Chichén Itzá, Uxmal, Kabah, Mitla, Monte Albán. Los estudiantes deben deducir que algunos nombres son de culturas indias.

5 Los estudiantes deben sugerir varias culturas indígenas basándose en su conocimiento de culturas indígenas norteamericanas. También pueden mencionar culturas distintas basadas en condiciones distintas: la costa, el llano, las montañas, el tiempo, la agricultura. Todas son condiciones que pueden producir culturas distintas.

6 Es probable que sepan muy poco. Se les puede pedir que hagan alguna investigación en la biblioteca. Es posible que puedan mencionar a los aztecas pero que no sepan si son de México o de Sudamérica. Es de esperar que no sepan nada de las culturas indígenas contemporáneas. Se les puede mencionar que todavía existen unas cincuenta tribus indígenas en México. Entre ellas están los Tlaxcaltecanas,

Tarascanas, Tarahumaras, Maya, Yaquis, Tzotzis Tzeltals, Huastecas, Nahuas, Otomí, Mazahua, Huicholes, Coras, Totonacas, Seris y Lacandones. Por lo general los indios de México pertenecen a la clase baja y llevan una vida bastante difícil hoy en día.

7 Van a aprender a hablar de lo que ellos y otras personas hicieron, y en particular, a describir un incidente en el pasado. También aprenderán algo de las culturas indígenas de México.

37:17–
40:57

Side 6, 30853 to 37439

Comprehension Checks

Refer to the cards in the TRP for the **Comrehension Checks** for this *Para empezar.*

1 37:25

Suggestions Point out Mexico City and approximate location of the two volcanos on the map on page 257.
Point out 1 kilómetro = .62 miles; 25 kilómetros = approx. 15.5 miles.

Side 6, 31099 to 31550

2 37:41

Suggestions For each illustration, begin by naming the characters and their relationships. Break the narration down into simple units. Build the elements back into the more complex sentences of the narration when you are sure students understand the smaller units. Emphasize the preterite forms and contrast finished actions with present tense.

Equate known birthdates (Lincoln, Washington) with **nació**. Play the role of the king talking to his daughter: **¡Qué preciosa! Eres la joya más preciosa del mundo.** Show a piece of jewelry or draw a diamond to explain **joya.**

Side 6, 31568 to 31981

3 37:55

Suggestions Point out that Iztaccíhuatl is now 18. Give names and dates of known wars: **guerra.** Act out being sick. Contrast the king well one day, sick the next = **se enfermó.** Show that a conductor leads an orchestra, a general leads an army, an Aztec king leads his soldiers: **dirigir.**

Side 6, 32001 to 32371

4 38:08

Suggestions Gesture for **fuerte**. Name fictional or real examples of **valiente**. Identify people who are **a cargo de** different things—yourself/ class, principal/school, general/army. Play the role of the king seeking and not finding, using students: **¿Eres fuerte y valiente? No . . .**

Side 6, 32391 to 32835

UNA LEYENDA AZTECA

1

A unos veinticinco kilómetros de la Ciudad de México, hay dos volcanes, Popocatépetl e Iztaccíhuatl. Una leyenda azteca explica su origen.

2

Cuando nació Iztaccíhuatl, su padre, el rey de los aztecas, dijo, "Mi hija es la joya más preciosa del mundo".

3

Dieciocho años más tarde, durante una guerra, el rey se enfermó y no pudo dirigir a sus soldados.

7

Popocatépetl se fue a la guerra, donde luchó valientemente. Por fin, conquistó a los enemigos del rey.

8

Pero ese día, un hombre malo vin al palacio del rey. Iztaccíhuatl le preguntó, "¿Qué pasó en la batall de hoy?" Él le dijo, "Popocatépetl murió hoy en manos del enemigo La princesa se puso tan triste que se enfermó . . . y murió.

290 *doscientos noventa*

Purpose This section develops reading and listening comprehension of a series of events narrated in past time. Students should not be expected to achieve productive mastery at this point. The goal is not to translate, but to read/listen for comprehension as students learn to recount a series of past events.

4

Entonces el rey tuvo que buscar un soldado fuerte y valiente para poner a cargo de sus soldados. Desafortunadamente, no pudo encontrarlo.

5

Entonces el rey declaró, "Al soldado que conquiste a mis enemigos le daré mi trono y mi hija".

6

Un joven soldado desconocido dijo, "Yo soy Popocatépetl, el soldado más fuerte y valiente de toda la tierra. Yo voy a conquistar a los enemigos de mi rey". Iztaccíhuatl se enamoró de Popocatépetl inmediatamente.

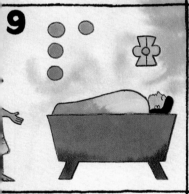

9

Cuando Popocatépetl regresó victorioso a la ciudad, le dijeron de la muerte de su querida Iztaccíhuatl.

10

El joven Popocatépetl construyó una pirámide donde puso a descansar a la princesa. Al lado construyó una segunda pirámide para proteger a Iztaccíhuatl.

11

Los dioses por compasión convirtieron las dos pirámides en volcanes. Desde entonces, Popocatépetl e Iztaccíhuatl duermen a poca distancia de la capital.

doscientos noventa y uno **291**

Suggestions Begin by having students close their books while you narrate one section at a time, using the transparencies to clarify meaning without translation. Then ask **Comprehension Checks**. Repeat this process with each section.

Using the video Play one section at a time after narrating it using the transparencies. Freeze the video and ask **Comprehension Checks**. Repeat this process with each section.

---

11   **40:33**

Suggestions Point out the gods: **dioses**. Gesture and use facial expression: **compasión**. Contrast the pyramid and the volcano—**Fue una pirámide, pero ahora es un volcán.**

|||||||||||||||||||||||||||||||||
Side 6, 36725 to 37439

---

5   **38:24**

Suggestions Name armies/individuals who have conquered others: **conquistar**. Identify enemies—football teams, boxers: **enemigos**. Use students as characters—identify one student as the soldier and one as the daughter; give your desk chair (**trono**) and your daughter to the soldier.

|||||||||||||||||||||||||||||||||
Side 6, 32854 to 33273

6   **38:39**

Suggestions Play the role of Popocatépetl. Act out fighting, conquering. Draw stick figures facing each other with hearts around them for **se enamoró.**

|||||||||||||||||||||||||||||||||
Side 6, 33293 to 33982

7   **39:02**

Suggestions Act out fighting: **luchar**. Make a "winner" gesture": **conquistar**.

|||||||||||||||||||||||||||||||||
Side 6, 34000 to 34434

8   **39:17**

Suggestions Use facial expression for **un hombre malo**. Act out. Elaborate: **Dijo que Popocatépetl murió, pero no es verdad.** Draw a stick figure lying on its back with cross/flowers/headstone. Contrast **No es verdad, Popocatépetl no murió / Es verdad, Iztaccíhuatl murió.**

|||||||||||||||||||||||||||||||||
Side 6, 34452 to 35412

9   **39:50**

Suggestion Play roles of various people telling Popocatépetl that Iztaccíhuatl died.

|||||||||||||||||||||||||||||||||
Side 6, 35433 to 35986

10   **40:09**

Suggestions Contrast the two pyramids—one being built versus one already built: **construyó una pirámide**. Act out carrying Iztaccíhuatl to the pyramid. Point out students who are **al lado de** other students. Act out protecting.

|||||||||||||||||||||||||||||||||
Side 6, 36005 to 36706

TAPE/DISC
40:58–
43:36

Side 6, 37474 to 42213

Early Production Checks

The **Early Production Checks** are available on cards in the TRP.

1 `41:03`

Tuvimos que regresar en camión.

1 ¿Quién es, la mamá de Mónica o de Lilia? *De Lilia.*
2 ¿Regresó Mónica, por fin? *Sí.*
3 ¿De dónde regresó, de Chapala o de Tlaquepaque? *De Tlaquepaque.*
4 ¿Tardó mucho en regresar Mónica? *Sí.*
5 ¿Tuvieron un problema Mónica y sus amigos? *Sí.*
6 ¿Pudieron subir en el coche? *No.*
7 ¿Por qué no pudieron subir, por los paquetes de Lilia o de Mónica? *De Mónica.*
8 ¿Quiénes tuvieron que regresar en camión? *Mónica y Óscar.*
9 ¿Hay algo de malo en regresar en camión? *No.*
10 ¿Tuvieron que esperar el camión un buen rato? *Sí.*
11 ¿Pensó Mónica en otro regalo? *Sí.*
12 ¿Para quién era el otro regalo, para su papá / mamá? *Para su mamá.*

Side 6, 37636 to 39060

2 `41:52`

No le dije nada a Óscar.
Accept brief phrases or one- and two-word answers, as shown in **1** above. It is not necessary for students to answer in complete sentences.

1 ¿Quiénes son? *(Point to Óscar, then Mónica.)*
2 ¿Quién entró a una tienda, Mónica o Óscar?
3 ¿Para qué entró a la tienda?
4 ¿Entró a la tienda por mucho tiempo?
5 ¿Le dijo a Óscar?
6 ¿Qué vio Mónica al salir de la tienda, a Óscar o el camión?

7 ¿Buscó Mónica a Óscar? ¿Lo encontró?
8 ¿Tuvo que subir Mónica al camión?
9 ¿Vio Óscar a Mónica subir al camión?
10 ¿Qué hizo Óscar, esperó otro camión o empezó a correr?
11 ¿Corrió hacia el camión?

Side 6, 39079 to 39983

¿QUÉ DECIMOS...?
Al describir una aventura

1 *Tuvimos que regresar en camión.*

2 *No le dije nada a Óscar.*

Purpose These dialogues are not intended for memorization. They show description of a series of past events in more natural contexts.

I. ¿Qué hubo? Tu amigo fue a otra ciudad la semana pasada. Dile lo que pasó en tu ciudad en su ausencia.

MODELO   una boda muy grande
Hubo una boda muy grande.

1. una fiesta en casa de . . .
2. un concierto de rock
3. un accidente de coches muy serio
4. una exhibición de arte moderno
5. un baile en la escuela
6. unos programas culturales en el centro de la ciudad
7. una exhibición de coches antiguos
8. un carnaval para los niños

Hubo: The preterite of *hay*

Hubo is both singular and plural. It means *there was* or *there were*.

Hubo un concierto excelente.
Hubo varios problemas.
No **hubo** buenas fiestas este verano.

I. ¿Qué hubo? Call on individual students. Have class repeat after you for pronunciation practice.
1 Hubo una fiesta en casa de . . .
2 Hubo un concierto de rock.
3 Hubo un accidente de coches muy serio.
4 Hubo una exhibición de arte moderno.
5 Hubo un baile en la escuela.
6 Hubo unos programas culturales en el centro de la ciudad.
7 Hubo una exhibición de coches antiguos.
8 Hubo un carnaval para los niños.

CHARLEMOS UN POCO MÁS

A. ¡Imposible!   In the pictures below, Mario and Estela are telling their friend Marta that they saw her boyfriend with another girl. With your partner, decide what they said.

LECCIÓN 3

doscientos noventa y siete **297**

CHARLEMOS UN POCO MÁS

A. ¡Imposible! Allow 5–10 min for pairs to write an appropriate commentary for each picture. Then ask each pair to read their commentary to class.

Purpose   These activities allow students to create with language recently learned as they describe a series of past events in a variety of possible combinations.

DRAMATIZACIONES

B. ¿Qué hicieron? Form groups of three or four. Your teacher will give you exactly four minutes to write down as many things as you can that members of your group did last week. Each activity that you list must include *who* did it and *what* they did.

EJEMPLO **Jack fue al cine con su familia.
Nancy y Clara jugaron fútbol.**

C. ¿Viniste . . . ? To find out more about your classmates, use the interview grids provided by your teacher. Find a classmate who fits each of the categories listed. When you find a person matching one of the catagories, have him or her sign your paper in the appropriate square. Remember that each classmate may only sign one of your squares.

CH. ¿Qué hiciste tú? In groups of four, discuss what each of you did last week. Find one thing that you did that the other three did not. Also try to discover one thing that the others did that you did not. Write down your findings.

Dramatizaciones

A. ¿Adónde fuiste? On your way to school, you run into somebody you haven't seen for a while. Role-play the situation.

Tú
- Greet each other; then ask what's new.
- Find out when the relative came to visit.

- Respond.

- Ask where your friend went shopping and what he or she bought.

Compañero(a)
- Say that a relative (specify who) is visiting your family.
- Say when, and add that your relative celebrated his or her birthday last week. Tell how old he or she is.
- Mention that you went shopping yesterday.
- Tell where you went shopping and what you bought.

B. ¿Qué pasó? A friend who has been ill has called you on the phone to find out what happened at school today. Role-play this conversation.

C. El "mall". You spent the whole day at the mall yesterday. You saw several interesting things that you are now dying to tell your best friend. Role-play the conversation with your partner.

298 doscientos noventa y ocho

UNIDAD 6

LEAMOS AHORA

Reading strategy:
Identifying the main idea

A. Anticipemos. Answer the questions to see how much you already know about the conquest of Mexico by the Spaniards. If you do not know the correct answers, make reasoned guesses.

1. Los españoles llegaron a Tenochtitlán, la capital de México . . .
   a. en 1492.
   b. antes de 1492.
   c. después de 1492.
   ch. No se sabe cuándo llegaron los españoles.

2. Cuando los españoles llegaron a Tenochtitlán por primera vez, París y Londres eran . . .
   a. más grandes que Tenochtitlán.
   b. más pequeños que Tenochtitlán.
   c. similares a Tenochtitlán.
   ch. grandes ciudades elegantes mientras Tenochtitlán era un pueblo pequeño, poco sofisticado.

3. Moctezuma, el rey de los aztecas, pensó que Hernán Cortés era . . .
   a. un amigo.
   b. un enemigo.
   c. un dios azteca.
   ch. el presidente de una nación.

4. Cuando los españoles llegaron a Tenochtitlán, . . .
   a. Moctezuma los recibió como invitados.
   b. Moctezuma los atacó como enemigos.
   c. decidieron destruir la ciudad inmediatamente.
   ch. Todas las respuestas son correctas.

5. Hernán Cortés y sus soldados . . .
   a. vivieron más de ocho meses en el palacio de Moctezuma como sus invitados.
   b. destruyeron completamente la ciudad de Tenochtitlán.
   c. asesinaron a Moctezuma y a cientos de aztecas.
   ch. Todas las respuestas son correctas.

LECCIÓN 3

doscientos noventa y nueve **299**

LEAMOS AHORA

A. Anticipemos.
Suggestions Have students answer these questions in small groups. Do not give them the correct answers at this time. After students have read the selection, have them come back to their answers and discover for themselves to what extent they had answered correctly.

Answers

1 c
2 b
3 c
4 a
5 ch

Leamos ahora is the principal reading of the unit. Its purpose is to provide students with additional practice in identifying the main idea in a paragraph. Students are not expected to understand every word. Rather they should focus on looking for the main idea of each paragraph as requested in Activity B.

B. La idea principal.

Suggestions Allow 2–3 min for students, working in pairs, to do the matching. Then go over answers with class.

Answers

1 Paragraph 3
2 Paragraph 6
3 Paragraph 4
4 Paragraph 1
5 Paragraph 2
6 Paragraph 5

C. Tenochtitlán.

Suggestions Have class count off from **uno** to **seis**, and ask students to remember their number. Then have all the *one's* work together in one group, all the *two's* in a another, *three's* in another, and so forth. Tell the *one's* to read the first paragraph and become experts on it. They may consult with each other if necessary. Have the *two's* become experts on the second paragraph, the *three's* on the third, and so forth. Next have the students form new groups so that each group has a *one*, a *two*, a *three*, etc. With books closed, have the expert on paragraph one relate the information to his or her group, then the expert on paragraph two, then three, and so forth. When finished, give class a short true/false or multiple-choice quiz. Students should take the quiz individually, not in groups.

Verifiquemos

Suggestions Call on individuals. Have them explain their answers.

B. La idea principal. In *Unidad 4* you learned that it is important to identify the main ideas expressed by the author, and that often the main idea expressed in a given paragraph is stated in the first sentences of the paragraph.

Before you begin to read, look at the main ideas listed below. Then scan the first sentence of each of the six paragraphs to find the main ideas. Match the main ideas listed below with the appropriate paragraphs. Work *very quickly*. Do not read every word at this point.

Número de párrafo

___ 1. Los aztecas invitaron a los españoles a su capital, como amigos, no enemigos.

___ 2. La Tenochtitlán moderna es ahora la ciudad más grande del mundo.

___ 3. En defensa de su rey, los aztecas atacaron a los españoles.

___ 4. Los españoles descubrieron la gran capital de los aztecas en el año 1519.

___ 5. Los aztecas pensaron que los españoles eran seres sobrenaturales.

___ 6. Cortés y unos indios enemigos de los aztecas conquistaron la capital de los aztecas.

C. Tenochtitlán. Now read the article and verify your responses.

Verifiquemos

Read the article. Then change any answers to **Anticipemos** (p. 299) that you think you answered incorrectly and be prepared to explain.

Tenochtitlán

En 1519, el conquistador Hernán Cortés llegó a Tenochtitlán, la capital del imperio azteca. Encontró allí una hermosa ciudad de más de 300.000 habitantes, más grande que las grandes ciudades europeas de la época.

Cuando los soldados aztecas vieron los barcos de Cortés por primera vez, pensaron que eran pirámides flotantes. Moctezuma, el rey de los aztecas, pensó que Cortés era Quetzalcóatl, un dios azteca que se fue en barco al este y prometió regresar algún día.

Pensando que era un dios, Moctezuma invitó a Cortés y a sus soldados a Tenochtitlán y los recibió con muchos regalos de oro y de piedras preciosas. Los españoles vivieron en el palacio de Moctezuma en Tenochtitlán por ocho meses. Pero cuando Cortés salió de la ciudad por unos días, sus soldados, temiendo una rebelión, tomaron prisionero a Moctezuma y asesinaron a cientos de indios.

Cuando los indios descubrieron que Moctezuma era prisionero, se rebelaron y atacaron a los españoles. Esa noche, llamada la Noche Triste, los españoles asesinaron a Moctezuma. Al tratar de salir de la ciudad, hubo una gran batalla en la que murieron cientos de indios y españoles.

En agosto de 1521, Cortés regresó a Tenochtitlán con los soldados españoles que sobrevivieron la Noche Triste y con cientos de indios tlaxcalanes, enemigos de los aztecas. Poco a poco, y destruyendo todo en su camino, Cortés conquistó Tenochtitlán. Sobre sus ruinas construyó una ciudad de estilo europeo, la ciudad que hoy llamamos la Ciudad de México.

Hoy, México, D.F. es la ciudad más grande del mundo, con 20 millones de habitantes. Recientemente, más de tres siglos después del descubrimiento de América, se empezaron a descubrir antiguos monumentos de la original Tenochtitlán.

LECCIÓN 3

trescientos uno **301**

A. Planeando. Students should notice that the writer used the letters of her first and last name vertically and around them created a series of statements about herself. She included some description, references to family and friends, likes, dislikes, and plans for the future. Her poem does not rhyme. She probably brainstormed ideas she might want to include and clustered them by topic.

ESCRIBAMOS UN POCO

Writing strategy:
Writing a free-form poem

A. Planeando. Sandra Alemán found a fun way to write a self-portrait in the form of a poem. Read her poem below and notice the form she used. Make a list of the elements she included. What do you think she did before she actually began to write her poem?

¿Quién soy?

Soy una chica única.
No soy ni **A**lta ni baja.
Mis amigos dice**N** que soy cómica.
Pero no creo que es ver**D**ad.
Tengo dos hermanos y una he**R**mana.
Tengo un gato y un perro t**A**mbién.

Me gust**A** leer, cantar y bailar.
No me gusta ni cocinar ni arreg**L**ar mi cuarto.
Quiero ser profesora de **E**spañol.
Estudio **M**ucho en mis clases.
Me encant**A** viajar.
Te**N**go dieciséis años.

¿Quién soy? ¡Soy **SANDRA ALEMÁN**!

Purpose In this section, students are asked to write a free-form poem using a letter of their first or last name in every statement.

Suggestion Briefly review strategies practiced in earlier units—brainstorming and clustering.

B. Empezando. Brainstorm all the things you might want to say about yourself. It might be helpful to make a cluster diagram of your list under topics such as: what I look like, my personality, my friends, my family, my likes and dislikes, what I want to do, etc.

C. Escribiendo. Now write a self-portrait poem about yourself. Begin and end your poem the way Sandra began and ended hers.

CH. Compartiendo. Share the first draft of your poem with two classmates. Ask them what they think of it. Is there anything they don't understand? Is there anything you have not mentioned that they would like to know? Do they think you should change something?

D. Revisando. Based on your classmates' comments, rewrite your poem, changing anything you want. You may add, subtract or modify what you had originally written. Before you turn it in for grading, share your composition with two other classmates. Ask them to focus on your grammar, spelling and punctuation. Correct any errors they notice before turning it in to your teacher.

E. Publicando. Prepare your poems for "publication" by writing them on large pieces of paper using your favorite colors. You may even want to mount them on cut-out silhouettes of yourself or something you mentioned in your poem.

B. Empezando. Allow 5–6 min for students to make their own clusters or outlines. Ask volunteers to tell what they have included and how they have grouped ideas. Encourage students to add to theirs as they hear ideas from others.

C. Escribiendo. Allow students time to write their first draft. Provide guidance where necessary. You may want to assign first draft as homework.

CH. Compartiendo. Have students gather in "response groups" of two or three. Allow them time to share their poems. Encourage them to comment on content, structure, and vocabulary. Remind group members to begin with at least one positive comment and then to make constructive suggestions.

D. Revisando. Tell students you will grade the poem holistically. Underline grammatical errors if you wish, but the grade should be affected only by errors that would confuse a native speaker accustomed to the writing of a nonnative. At this stage, students should develop a sense that they can write creatively in Spanish.

E. Publicando. Suggest that students create their own silhouettes by having a partner outline the shadow of their profile on a piece of white or black paper taped to the wall. Mount all the self-portrait poems on the wall without the final line and have class read the poems and try to identify the writer.

UNIT OBJECTIVES

Communicative Goals

When students have completed this unit, they will be able to use Spanish . . .
- to exchange information about sports
- to point out specific people and things
- to give information about people's physical condition
- to give and follow orders
- to describe what happened in the past
- to give the location of things

Culture

In this unit, students will study and compare . . .
- the popularity of U.S. sports in Latin America
- the achievements of leading Hispanic athletes
- a Hispanic All-Star baseball team

Reading and Writing Strategies

- Reading: Skimming
- Writing: Retelling an event

Structure

- Demonstratives
- Spelling changes in the preterite: $i \rightarrow y$, $c \rightarrow qu$, $g \rightarrow gu$, $z \rightarrow c$
- Direct object pronouns
- Stem-changing -ir verbs in the preterite: $e \rightarrow i$, $o \rightarrow u$
- Affirmative tú commands: Irregular forms
- Prepositions of location

¡Vamos al partido!

UNIT SETTING

Miami, in southeastern Florida, is the most southerly major city in the continental United States. Its location on the Atlantic coast and its subtropical climate have made it one of the great tourist centers of the world. With a population of 358,548, Miami is the 46th-largest U.S. city. People of Cuban origin account for over a quarter million residents in and around the city, most of them refugees from the period after Castro's rise to power in 1959 and during his release of Cubans seeking to leave the island in 1980. The Cuban influence is most strongly

Alabama
Georgia
★ Tallahassee
Océano Atlántico
Orlando
Golfo de México
FLORIDA
Miami

0   200 Kilómetros
0   200 Millas

Video Notes

To play the montage, use counter or bar code:

| 00:00 | – | 00:50 |

Side 7, 13 to 1523

To play the entire unit without stopping:

| 00:00 | – | 20:37 |

Side 7, 13 to 37100

Although practically every Spanish-speaking country is represented in Miami, Cuban Spanish predominates. As elsewhere in the Caribbean, **s** at the end of a syllable is pronounced like **h,** especially in casual speech. **¿Cómo estás?** is pronounced **¿Cómo etáh?** Some Cubans, Puerto Ricans, and Dominicans tend to pronounce inital **r** and medial **rr** as if they were a **jota: una pierna rota** becomes **una pierna jota.** The **ll** and the **y** are merged into one sound category but produced two ways: **calle** is pronounced **cáie** or **cádge** and **ayer** is pronounced **aiér** or **adgér.**

Photo

Pictured is the crowd at the school soccer game in Lesson 1. The game was videotaped at Killian Senior High School in Miami. Because of the large number of Hispanics in this part of Florida, soccer is a favorite sport in many schools. Killian High is well-known for its award-winning soccer team. You may wish to ask the students to comment on the ethnic diversity of the spectators.

felt in the neighborhood known as **la Pequeña Habana**, with its typical shops and restaurants. Besides its cultural diversity, the Miami area offers a variety of sports, both professional and amateur, including thoroughbred racing at Hialeah and Calder tracks, the Miami Dolphins of the National Football League, the Miami Heat of the National Basketball Association, and the Orange Bowl intercollegiate Classic, held annually on New Year's Day. Jai alai, a favorite sport with many Hispanics, is also popular.

¡Va a meter un gol!

OBJECTIVES

Communicative Goals

- Exchanging information about sports
- Pointing out specific people and things

Culture and Reading

- *¡No me digas!*
  ¿Béisbol en Latinoamérica? Popular sports with children and adults
- *Y ahora, ¡a leer!*
  Nuestras estrellas en el béisbol: A Hispanic All-Star baseball team

Structure

- **7.1** Demonstratives
- **7.2** Spelling changes in the preterite

ACTIVE VOCABULARY

Deportes

olimpíada	gimnasia
atletismo	golf
baloncesto	jai alai
béisbol	lucha libre
ciclismo	natación
esquí	salto de altura
fútbol	tenis
fútbol americano	volibol

En un partido

árbitro	ganar
aficionado/a	jugador/a
campo	… más
competencia	valioso(a)
entrenador/a	partido
equipo	perder
espectador/a	vencedores
estrella	lastimado(a)
falta	hospital
cobrar una …	

Partido de fútbol

cabezazo	gol
campo de fútbol	meter un …
defensor/a	patear

Partido de béisbol

bateador/a	jardinero/a
lanzador/a	… corto
receptor/a	base
guardabosques (m/f)	primera
	segunda
	tercera

Verbos

afectar	examinar
comunicar	meter
criticar	terminar

Demostrativos

esto, esta, estos, estas	aquel, aquella, aquellos, aquellas
ese, esa, esos, esas	

Palabras y expresiones

antepasado	¡Bien hecho!
durante	¡Dios mío!
lindo(a)	todo el día
mejor	¡Ya lo creo!
nota	
último(a)	

ANTICIPEMOS

El mundo de los deportes

sábado
HOY EN LA TELE

12:00 ATLETISMO
22 Campeonato Mundial

13:00 VOLIBOL
20 Campeonato Nacional de México
Cuartos de final, Mujeres

14:00 BÉISBOL DE LAS GRANDES LIGAS
18 Medias Blancas de Chicago
vs.
Yanquis de Nueva York

VÍA SATÉLITE

15:00 FÚTBOL AMERICANO COLEGIAL
8 Fuerza Aérea
vs.
Webster State

FÚTBOL AMERICANO PROFESIONAL
19:30 Delfines de Miami
24 vs.
Pieles Rojas de Washington

23:00 Vaqueros de Dallas
14 vs.
Osos de Chicago (*En directo*)

domingo
HOY EN LA TELE

10:00 AUTOMOVILISMO
8 Rally de Montecarlo

11:15 ESGRIMA
24 Torneo Internacional
Abierto Femenino

11:30 BOXEO
18 (*En directo*)

12:30 TORNEO DE SOFTBOL
16 15 equipos de la
Categoría de Tercera Fuerza

14:00 CLAVADOS
22 Trampolín: Exposición juvenil
Plataforma: Pruebas preolímpicas

VÍA SATÉLITE

15:00 PATINAJE ARTÍSTICO:
20 Juvenil femenino y masculino
PATINAJE DE VELOCIDAD

17:00 ESQUÍ ALPINO (*En directo*)
14 Descenso combinado masculino
Eslalom: Mujeres

¿Qué piensas tú ?

1. ¿Qué deportes representan los símbolos de estas páginas? ¿Hay algún símbolo que no reconoces? ¿Cuál?

2. ¿Para qué es este anuncio? ¿Cómo sabes? ¿Puedes combinar un símbolo con cada deporte en *El mundo de los deportes*?

3. ¿Qué deportes se practican en tu colegio? ¿En tu ciudad?

4. ¿Qué oportunidades tiene la gente joven para participar en los deportes? Explica tu opinión.

5. ¿Son muy importantes los deportes en Estados Unidos? ¿Por qué?

6. ¿Qué importancia tienen los deportes en tu escuela? En tu opinión, ¿deben tener más o menos importancia? ¿Por qué?

7. ¿Es importante estar en buen estado físico en Estados Unidos? ¿Por qué?

8. En tu opinión, ¿cuáles son las actitudes en los países hispanos hacia los deportes y hacia el estado físico? ¿Por qué crees eso?

9. ¿De qué vas a poder hablar al final de la lección?

Purpose To focus students on language related to sports and to use critical thinking skills by encouraging students to observe and compare differences and similarities between Latin Americans' attitudes towards sports and physical fitness and their own without forming judgments.

Suggestions Use the illustrations as an advance organizer. Have students explain their answers. Help them discover cross-cultural similarities in the love of sports.

ANTICIPEMOS

Note In Latin America, **clavados** is the term used for *diving*. In Spain, **salto (de trampolín, de plataforma)** is used.

¿Qué piensas tú?

Answers

1 La esgrima, los clavados, el patinaje, el boxeo, el esquí, el béisbol, el fútbol americano, el volibol, el automovilismo, el softbol.

2 Es un anuncio de programa de deportes en la televisión. Se sabe porque dice "Hoy en la tele" y da las horas y los canales.

3 Las respuestas varían. La mayoría de las escuelas norteamericanas tiene equipos de béisbol, fútbol americano y baloncesto. Algunas tienen otros deportes. Los equipos profesionales y semi-profesionales de estos deportes se encuentran en las grandes ciudades estadounidenses.

4 Los jóvenes pueden participar en las clases de educación física, en los equipos de las escuelas y de la ciudad y en clubes como la YMCA/YWCA.

5 Sí. Nuestra sociedad le da gran importancia y valor a la competencia. Los atletas profesionales ganan más que casi cualquier otra profesión.

6 Las respuestas van a variar.

7 Actualmente es sumamente importante el mantenerse en buen estado físico en EE.UU.: mantener el peso, comer comidas saludables, hacer ejercicio, etc.

8 Las respuestas van a variar. Es posible que los estudiantes no sepan nada de los países hispanos. En la mayoría de las ciudades grandes existe el mismo interés en el estado físico que en EE.UU. En el campo, la gente no tiene ni el tiempo ni el dinero para trotar, ir a un club o hacer gimnasia.

9 **Van a aprender a hablar de la participación en varios deportes y del estado físico.**

00:51–
04:22

Side 7, 1543 to 7868

Comprehension Checks

A full set of the **Comprehension Checks** is available on cards in the Teacher's Resource Package.

1   00:58

Suggestion Identify the two-page spread as a newspaper.
1 ¿Es un periódico?
2 ¿Se celebró en Miami la quinta Olimpíada de la división sur?
3 ¿Fue solamente atlética?
4 ¿Cuándo se celebró la Olimpíada?
5 ¿Hay fotos en el periódico?
6 ¿Son fotos de atletas y académicos?
7 ¿Son fotos de sus grandes triunfos?
8 ¿Hubo competencias atléticas? ¿académicas?

Side 7, 1749 to 2510

2   01:24

Suggestions Identify the **campo de fútbol,** the teams, the referee, the coach. Mime **cabezazo.**
Point out Another term for **campo de fútbol** is **cancha de fútbol.**
1 ¿Es el campo de fútbol?
2 ¿Son los equipos de Killian y de Palmetto?
3 ¿Hubo un gran partido entre los dos equipos? ¿Qué jugaron?
4 ¿Qué equipo ganó?
5 ¿Cuántos goles hubo?
6 ¿Quién metió el único gol?
7 ¿Metió el gol con un cabezazo?
8 ¿Quién es el jugador "estrella"?
9 ¿Cuales dos equipos son los mejores equipos del estado?
10 ¿Cuál es el mejor equipo de fútbol?

Side 7, 2528 to 3532

Deportes

BALONCESTO

Para los aficionados al baloncesto, hubo un formidable partido entre los equipos femeninos de South Miami y de Sunset. Aquí vemos al árbitro echar la pelota al comienzo del partido. South Miami defendió su título con habilidad, derrotando a Sunset 69 a 58.

1

OLIMPÍADA ATLÉTICA Y ACADÉMICA
24 de mayo

Ayer se celebró en Miami la quinta Olimpíada Atlética y Académica de la división sur. Aquí representamos algunos de los grandes triunfos atléticos y académicos de los jóvenes que participaron en las competencias.

FÚTBOL

En el campo de fútbol, hubo un gran partido entre los equipos de Killian y Palmetto. Los estudiantes de Killian ganaron 1 a 0. El único gol del partido lo metió el jugador "estrella", Juan Colón, con un brillante cabezazo. Después del partido, el entrenador de los vencedores dijo, "¡Sin duda, estos dos equipos son los mejores del estado!"

3   01:58

Suggestions Identify the game, the teams, the referee. Mime throwing the ball (**echar la pelota**).
1 ¿Son chicas o chicos?
Continue asking questions, as above.

Side 7, 3552 to 4342

Purpose This section is not meant for memorization or mastery; it sets the context for the language needed to talk about sports and provides comprehensible language without translation.

ATLETISMO

En el campo deportivo, Rafaela Delgado y Paula Wilson corrieron una carrera increíble. Delgado salió primero y mantuvo su posición hasta el último momento, cuando Wilson la pasó y ganó la carrera de 55 metros.

Samuel Rodríguez, un joven atleta de Coral Gables, saltó 6 pies con 9 pulgadas y ganó la competencia de salto de altura masculino.

JUEGOS ACADÉMICOS

Finalmente, en los juegos académicos, los chicos de segundo año de Killian High School sorprendieron a todo el mundo y ganaron la competencia de historia. ¡Bien hecho, chicos!

JAI ALAI

Este año, por primera vez, una exhibición de jai alai fue parte de nuestra Olimpíada. Jorge Campos, el número 37, jugó brillantemente para South Dade High School. Este joven de 17 años fue nombrado el jugador más valioso de la exhibición.

OTROS EVENTOS

8 Para otros resultados, véase **La Olimpíada** en la página 8.

ciclismo   natación   lucha libre   tenis   béisbol   gimnasia artística   golf

trescientos nueve **309**

4 – 5   02:25

Suggestions Identify the visible events. Mime jumping.
1 ¿Es el campo deportivo?
2 ¿Es la carrera de 55 metros?
3 ¿Quién salió primero?
4 ¿Ganó Rafaela Delgado?
5 ¿Mantuvo su posición hasta el último momento?
6 ¿Quién la pasó en el último momento, Rodríguez o Wilson?
7 ¿Quién ganó la carrera?
8 ¿De dónde es Samuel Rodríguez?
9 ¿Participó en la carrera?
10 ¿Participó en el salto de altura?
11 ¿Saltó 6 pies con 9 pulgadas?
12 ¿Cuánto saltó?
13 ¿Quién ganó el salto de altura?

Side 7, 4361 to 5526

6   03:05

Point out Jai alai is popular in Cuba, Mexico, and Spain. The game resembles handball except for the *cesta*, a basketlike container that is strapped to the player's arm, and may be played as singles or two or three to a team. It is a fast and dangerous game, with a ball the size of a baseball and harder than a golf ball being hurled at approximately 150 miles per hour.
1 ¿Qué deporte es?
2 ¿Es jai alai popular en Miami?
3 ¿Fue jai alai parte de la Olimpíada en Miami?
4 ¿Quién jugó brillantemente?
5 ¿Cuántos años tiene Jorge Campos, 17 o 18?
6 ¿Quién fue nombrado el jugador más valioso?

Side 7, 5547 to 6253

7   03:29

1 ¿Hubo juegos académicos en la Olimpíada de Miami?
2 ¿Son estos chicos de segundo o tercer año?
3 ¿En qué competencia ganaron los chicos de segundo año?
4 ¿Sorprendieron a todo el mundo?

Side 7, 6273 to 7076

Suggestions Begin by having students close their books while you narrate one section at a time, using the transparencies to clarify meaning without translation. Then ask **Comprehension Checks**. Repeat with each section.

Using the video Play one section at a time after narrating it using the transparencies. Freeze the video and ask **Comprehension Checks**. Repeat with each section.

8   03:57

1 ¿Dónde hay más resultados?
2 ¿Dónde están los resultados de ciclismo, aquí o en la página 8?
(other sports)

Side 7, 7097 to 7872

04:23–
07:32

Side 7, 7888 to 13542

Early Production Checks

A full set of the **Early Production Checks** is available on cards in the Teacher's Resource Package.

 1 **04:30**

¿Quién es ese señor?

1 ¿Quién es? *(Point to Alfredo, then José Luis.)* Alfredo / José Luis.

2 ¿Está listo Alfredo? *Sí.*

3 ¿Practicó el cabezazo? *Sí.*

4 ¿Qué practicó todo el día? *El cabezazo.*

5 ¿Quién está seguro que van a ganar? *Alfredo.*

6 ¿Contra qué equipo van a jugar? *Las Panteras.*

7 ¿Tienen las Panteras un buen equipo? *No.*

8 ¿Quiénes son mejores, las Panteras o el equipo de Alfredo y José Luis? *El equipo de Alfredo y José Luis.*

9 ¿Vinieron los padres de Alfredo al partido? *No.*

10 ¿Tuvieron que trabajar? *Sí.*

11 ¿Por qué no vinieron? *Tuvieron que trabajar.*

12 ¿Vinieron los padres de José Luis? *Sí.*

13 ¿Los ve José Luis (Alfredo)? *Sí/Sí.*

14 ¿Sabe José Luis quién es el señor de la camisa roja? *No.*

15 ¿Lo conoce José Luis (Alfredo)? *No/No.*

16 ¿Ya empieza el partido? *Sí.*

Side 7, 8078 to 9464

¿QUÉ DECIMOS...?

Al hablar de los deportes

1 ¿*Quién es ese señor?*

Purpose This section uses real language to talk about sports in a real-life situation.

2 ¡Dale, dale!

3 ¡Es un gran deportista!

¡Dale, dale!

Note Accept brief phrases or one- and two-word answers to all questions as shown in **1** on page 310. It is not necessary for students to answer in complete sentences.

1 ¿Ya comenzó el partido?
2 ¿Dónde está José Luis, junto al entrenador o con Alfredo?
3 ¿Lo ve su madre (su padre)?
4 ¿Cómo se llama el equipo de José Luis, los Cougars o las Panteras?
5 ¿Cómo juega José Luis, muy bien o muy mal?
6 ¿Cuántos goles metió en el último partido?
7 ¿Cuántos goles va a meter en este partido?
8 ¿Quién está seguro, el padre de José Luis o el señor de la camisa amarilla?
9 ¿Quién acaba de entrar en el partido?
10 ¿Ya comenzaron a jugar?
11 ¿Quién tiene la pelota?
12 ¿Quién dice "Dale, dale, dale"?
13 ¿Debe tener cuidado José Luis con el número 8 o el número 10?
14 ¿Dónde está el número 10, a su derecha o a su izquierda?

¡Es un gran deportista!

1 ¿Quién es un jugador de primera?
2 ¿Salió un artículo sobre José Luis en el periódico?
3 ¿Lo leyó el hombre?
4 ¿Es el hombre aficionado al fútbol o al béisbol?
5 ¿Qué deportes juega José Luis?
6 ¿Es un gran deportista José Luis?
7 ¿Va a meter un gol José Luis?
8 ¿Está muy entusiasmada la madre de José Luis?
9 ¿Le pasó algo a José Luis?
10 ¿Está tendido en el campo José Luis?
11 ¿A quién le dice "Haz algo" la madre de José Luis?

Suggestions Begin by having students close their books while you narrate one section at a time, using the transparencies to clarify meaning without translation. Then ask **Early Production Checks.** Repeat with each section.

Using the video Play one section at a time after narrating it using the transparencies. Freeze the video and ask **Early Production Checks.** Repeat with each section.

Point out English borrowings such as *baseball* and *football* are pronounced differently, depending on whether English or Spanish sound patterns predominate. One hears both **béisbol** and **beisból**, **fútbol** and **futból**, sometimes even from the same person.

4 ¿Estás lastimado?

4 ¿Estás lastimado?

1 ¿Quién es? *(Point to all.)*
2 ¿Empezó José Luis a patear un gol?
3 ¿Cómo dice José Luis que está?
4 ¿Está lastimado José Luis?
5 ¿Lastimaron dos defensores a José Luis?
6 ¿Les cobró una falta el árbitro a los defensores?
7 ¿Deben llevar a José Luis al hospital?
8 ¿Va un médico a examinar a José Luis?
9 ¿Qué le duele a José Luis, la pierna o el brazo?

06:48

Side 7, 12231 to 13542

CHARLEMOS UN POCO

A. ¡Gol! ¿Quién dijo estas cosas en el partido de ayer, un **jugador,** un **espectador** o **ambos**?

1. Ayer practiqué el cabezazo todo el día.
2. Soy más aficionado al béisbol.
3. Nosotros somos mejores.
4. Ya empieza el partido.
5. El árbitro les cobró una falta.
6. Metió tres goles en el último partido.
7. ¡Dale, dale!
8. ¡Dios mío, está tendido en el campo!
9. Está allí, junto al entrenador.
10. ¡Paco, haz algo!

B. ¿Cuánto cuesta? Tú estás en una librería. ¿Qué te dice el dependiente?

MODELO

Este diccionario de francés cuesta nueve dólares y noventa y cinco centavos.

1.

2.

3.

4.

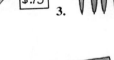
5.

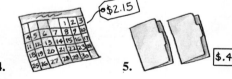
6.

7.

8.

9.

LECCIÓN 1

CHARLEMOS UN POCO

A. ¡Gol! As you read each item, have class respond.
1 un jugador
2 un espectador
3 un jugador
4 ambos
5 un jugador
6 un espectador
7 un espectador
8 un espectador
9 un espectador
10 un espectador

Expansion Call on individual students to read items and have class respond.

B. ¿Cuánto cuesta? Call on individual students.
1 Este cuaderno cuesta un dólar, cincuenta y nueve centavos.
2 Estos lápices cuestan setenta y cinco centavos.
3 Estos bolígrafos cuestan un dólar, diecinueve centavos.
4 Este calendario cuesta dos dólares, quince centavos.
5 Estas carpetas cuestan cuarenta y cinco centavos.
6 Este libro de literatura inglesa cuesta quince dólares, sesenta y nueve centavos.
7 Estos libros cuestan cuatro dólares, noventa y cinco centavos.
8 Este diccionario de español cuesta diez dólares, veintiocho centavos.
9 Esta mochila cuesta catorce dólares, setenta y nueve centavos.

Purpose These activities provide guided practice as students begin to produce new language necessary to exchange information about sports and to point out specific people and things.

C. ¿Quién es? Allow 2–3 min to do in pairs. Then call on different pairs to do for class.

1 ¿Conoces a esas señoras de los vestidos verdes? Sí. Son profesoras. Son las Sras. . . .

2 ¿Conoces a esos señores de los trajes elegantes? Sí. Son médicos. Son los Sres. . . .

3 ¿Conoces a esa mujer de la falda blanca? Sí. Es escritora. Es la Sra. . . .

4 ¿Conoces a esa señorita de la chaqueta morada? Sí. Es artista. Es la Srta. . . .

5 ¿Conoces a esa señora de la blusa con flores? Sí. Es locutora. Es la Sra. . . .

6 ¿Conoces a ese hombre de la camisa rosada? Sí. Es bombero. Es el Sr. . . .

7 ¿Conoces a esas señoritas de los sombreros rojos? Sí. Son abogadas. Son las Srtas. . . .

8 ¿Conoces a esos jóvenes de los trajes negros? Sí. Son camareros. Son los Sres. . . .

CH. ¿Ésa o aquélla? Allow 2–3 min to do in pairs. Then call on different pairs to do for class.

¡OJO! If students ask about the accents on **ésa** and **aquélla** in the title, tell them that written accents are always required when these words are used alone, without a noun.

1 ¿Te gusta ese suéter verde? No. Prefiero aquel suéter azul.

2 ¿Te gustan esas botas negras? No. Prefiero aquellas botas azules.

3 ¿Te gusta esa chaqueta morada? No. Prefiero aquella chaqueta azul.

4 ¿Te gustan esos pantalones blancos? No. Prefiero aquellos pantalones azules.

5 ¿Te gustan esos zapatos marrones? No. Prefiero aquellos zapatos azules.

6 ¿Te gusta ese vestido rojo? No. Prefiero aquel vestido azul.

7 ¿Te gusta esa camiseta rosada? No. Prefiero aquella camiseta azul.

8 ¿Te gusta esa sudadera gris? No. Prefiero aquella sudadera azul.

Demonstratives
Pointing out things far from you

ese	esos
esa	esas

Ese chico es mi primo.
¿Ves a **esas** señoras?

See **¿Por qué se dice así?**, *page G94, section 7.1.*

Demonstratives
Pointing out things farther away

aquel	aquellos
aquella	aquellas

Me gusta **aquella** chaqueta.
Aquellos chicos son del equipo de fútbol.

See **¿Por qué se dice así?**, *page G94, section 7.1.*

C. ¿Quién es? Estás en una boda y hay muchas personas que no conoces. Pregúntale a tu amigo(a) quiénes son.

MODELO señor / pantalones grises
Tú: **¿Conoces a ese señor de los pantalones grises?**
Compañero(a): **Sí. Es arquitecto. Es el Sr. . . .**

1. señoras / vestidos verdes   **2.** señores / trajes elegantes   **3.** mujer / falda blanca   **4.** señorita / chaqueta morada

5. señora / blusa con flores   **6.** hombre / camisa rosada   **7.** señoritas / sombreros rojos   **8.** jóvenes / trajes negros

CH. ¿Ésa o aquélla? A tu amiga le encanta el color azul. ¡Toda su ropa es azul! ¿Qué prendas prefiere?

MODELO Tú: **¿Te gusta esa blusa verde?**
Compañero(a): **No. Prefiero aquella blusa azul.**

   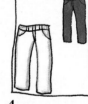

1. **2.** **3.** **4.**

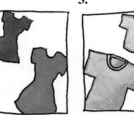  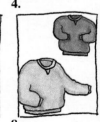

5. **6.** **7.** **8.**

D. ¡Es feo!   Tú y tu amigo(a) van de compras. ¿Qué comentarios hacen ustedes sobre las cosas que ven?

MODELO   blusa / feo
       Tú: **¿Qué piensas de esta blusa?**
       Compañero(a):   **¿Ésa? Es muy fea.**

1. vestido / elegante
2. falda / corto
3. zapatos / lindo
4. disco / aburrido
5. video / interesante
6. relojes / caro
7. camisa / grande
8. calcetines / feo

E. ¡Qué entusiasmo!   Acabas de conocer a un(a) joven. Pregúntale si es aficionado(a) a estos deportes.

MODELO   Tú: **¿Eres aficionado(a) al baloncesto?**
       Compañero(a):   **Sí, me encanta el baloncesto.** o
                            No, no me gusta el baloncesto.

 **1.**
 **2.**
 **3.**

 **4.**
 **5.**
 **6.**

 **7.**
 **8.**
 **9.**

LECCIÓN 1

Los deportes

atletismo

baloncesto / básquetbol

béisbol

lucha libre

ciclismo

esquí

fútbol

fútbol americano

gimnasia

golf

jai alai

natación

tenis

volibol

F. ¡No me digas! Call on individual students. After each response, have student go to board and write answer he or she gave.

1 Mi amigo . . . leyó el artículo pero no lo creyó.
2 Tú leíste el artículo pero no lo creíste.
3 Mis amigas . . . y . . . leyeron el artículo pero no lo creyeron.
4 Mis papás leyeron el artículo pero no lo creyeron.
5 El entrenador leyó el artículo pero no lo creyó.
6 Los jugadores leyeron el artículo pero no lo creyeron
7 Yo leí el artículo pero no lo creí.
8 Usted y yo leímos el artículo pero no lo creímos.
9 Los profesores de educación física leyeron el artículo pero no lo creyeron.

G. ¡Eres la estrella! In pairs, have one student interview the other. Tell students being interviewed to use their imagination as they make up their own sports history. Have students asking questions give a brief summary to class of their partner's responses.

H. Entrevista. Allow 3–4 min to work in groups. Then ask each group to report on the three most popular sports in their group. Answers will vary.

Spelling changes: *i → y*

leer

leí	leímos
leíste	
leyó	**leyeron**

An unaccented **i** becomes **y** when it occurs between two vowels.

¿Leyeron la novela?
Nosotros la leímos pero Anita no la **leyó.**
Ellas no me **creyeron.**

See **¿Por qué se dice así?,** *page G96, section 7.2.*

Spelling changes in verbs ending in *-car*

practicar

practiqué	practicamos
practicaste	
practicó	practicaron

The letter **c** changes to **qu** when it comes before **e** or **i.**

Practiqué el piano todo el día.
Yo **saqué** fotos en la boda de mi hermano.

See **¿Por qué se dice así?,** *page G96, section 7.2.*

Spelling changes in verbs ending in *-gar*

The letter **g** changes to **gu** when it comes before **e** or **i.**

Hoy no **jugué** golf.
Yo **llegué** a las tres, ¿y tú?

See **¿Por qué se dice así?,** *page G96, section 7.2.*

---

316 *trescientos dieciséis*

F. ¡No me digas! En una revista famosa salió un artículo extraordinario sobre la mala influencia de los deportes. ¿Cómo reaccionaron tú y tus amigos cuando lo leyeron?

MODELO Anita
Anita leyó el artículo pero no lo creyó.

1. mi amigo . . .
2. tú
3. mis amigas . . . y . . .
4. mis papás
5. el entrenador
6. los jugadores
7. yo
8. usted y yo
9. los profesores de educación física

G. ¡Eres la estrella! Eres el (la) mejor deportista de tu escuela. Tu compañero(a) es reportero del periódico estudiantil. Ahora está hablando contigo sobre tu participación en varios deportes. ¿Qué le dices?

 MODELO Compañero(a): **¿Qué deportes practicaste el año pasado?**
Tú: **Practiqué tenis, baloncesto y béisbol el año pasado.**

1. ¿Por qué no jugaste en el equipo de fútbol?
2. ¿Cuándo hiciste atletismo, el año pasado o el año antepasado?
3. ¿Practicaste otros deportes durante el verano?
4. ¿A qué deporte le dedicaste más tiempo?
5. ¿Qué deportes practicaste en el invierno?
6. ¿Qué deportes no te gustan, o te gustan todos?
7. ¿Cómo afectan los deportes a tus estudios? ¿Sacaste buenas notas el semestre pasado?
8. ¿En qué deportes piensas participar el año próximo?

H. Entrevista. Formen grupos de cuatro o cinco. Pregúntales a tus compañeros con qué frecuencia practicaron estos deportes el año pasado.

 MODELO béisbol
Tú: **¿Jugaste béisbol con frecuencia?**
Compañero(a): **Sí, jugué béisbol con frecuencia.** o
No, jugué béisbol raras veces. o
No, no jugué béisbol nunca.

con frecuencia	raras veces	nunca
●	●	●

1. volibol
2. golf
3. tenis
4. fútbol
5. ping pong
6. jai alai
7. fútbol americano
8. béisbol

I. ¿Lo terminaron? ¿Qué les preguntan sus padres a ti y a tus hermanos cuando piden permiso para salir? ¿Qué contestan ustedes?

MODELO tú: limpiar / cuarto
Compañero(a): **¿Limpiaste tu cuarto?**
Tú: **Empecé a limpiar mi cuarto pero no terminé.**

1. tú y tu hermana: estudiar / examen
2. hermana: lavar / coche
3. tú: leer / periódico
4. hermano: preparar / comida
5. todos nosotros: hacer / tarea
6. tú: lavar / ropa
7. tú y tu hermana: limpiar / baño
8. hermanos: trabajar en / patio

J. ¿Yo? ¿Qué dicen estas personas cuando les preguntas qué hicieron la semana pasada?

MODELO practicar el cabezazo
Practiqué el cabezazo.

1. pagar las cuentas   **2.** calificar exámenes   **3.** llegar a México

4. jugar fútbol   **5.** tocar la guitarra   **6.** sacar fotos

7. buscar un regalo para mi novia   **8.** comenzar unas clases de baile   **9.** empezar a estudiar computación

LECCIÓN 1

Spelling changes in verbs ending in *-zar*

The letter **z** changes to **c** when it comes before **e** or **i**.

Ya **empecé** mi clase de baile.
Me **especialicé** en biología.

See **¿Por qué se dice así?**, *page G96, section 7.2.*

I. ¿Lo terminaron? Allow 2–3 min to do in pairs. Then call on different pairs to do for class.
1 ¿Estudiaron para su examen? Empezamos a estudiar para nuestro examen pero no terminamos.
2 ¿Lavó su coche? Empezó a lavar su coche pero no terminó.
3 ¿Leíste el periódico? Empecé a leer el periódico pero no terminé.
4 ¿Preparó la comida? Empezó a preparar la comida pero no terminó.
5 ¿Hicimos la tarea? Empezamos a hacer la tarea pero no terminamos.
6 ¿Lavaste tu ropa? Empecé a lavar mi ropa pero no terminé.
7 ¿Limpiaron el baño? Empezamos a limpiar el baño pero no terminamos.
8 ¿Trabajaron en el patio? Empezaron a trabajar en el patio pero no terminaron.

J. ¿Yo? Call on individual students.
1 Pagué las cuentas.
2 Califiqué exámenes.
3 Llegué a México.
4 Jugué fútbol.
5 Toqué la guitarra.
6 Saqué fotos.
7 Busqué un regalo para mi novia.
8 Comencé unas clases de baile.
9 Empecé a estudiar computación.

A. ¡Éstos no son mis calcetines! Allow groups 3–4 min.

B. ¿Qué hizo Claudio?
After students have correct order (and there may be some variations), ask them to narrate what happened to Claudio.

CHARLEMOS UN POCO MÁS

A. ¡Éstos no son mis calcetines! While shopping, you accidentally bump into two other shoppers, and all of your purchases get mixed up. Based on the illustrations thhat your teacher gives you, decide to whom each item belongs.

EJEMPLO: Tú: **¡Éstos no son mis calcetines!**
Compañero(a) 1: **¿De quién son éstos?**
Compañero(a) 2: **Ésos son mis calcetines.**

B. ¿Qué hizo Claudio? The drawings below show what your friend Claudio did last Saturday. However, they are not in the correct sequence. With a partner, discuss what Claudio did and in what order.

Purpose The activities in this section are designed to allow students to create with language recently learned when talking about sports or pointing out specific people or things.

C. ¿Jugaste béisbol? Your teacher will give you an interview grid. Interview your classmates to find out who did each of the activities on the grid. When you find a classmate who has participated in an activity, write his or her name in that square. Then fill in the verb that describes what your classmate did. Your goal is to put a name in every square. Just remember, you can't put the same person's name in more than one square!

CH. ¡Qué ocupados! You and your partner didn't see each other all week. Now, when you finally meet, you have to tell each other every single detail about your week's activities. Consult the schedules provided by your teacher.

D. El partido de fútbol. You and a friend are looking at the photos taken for the school newspaper at last Saturday's soccer game. After discussing what happened, decide the order in which you want the pictures to appear in the paper. Then write captions for each picture describing the game.

C. ¿Jugaste béisbol? Allow 10–12 min. Circulate, checking to see that students are asking questions in the **tú** form and are correctly filling in the verbs in their grids. When one completes the grid, stop the activity and verify all answers by calling on students whose names appear on the grid.

CH. ¡Qué ocupados! Allow 10–12 min. Circulate to help students as necessary.

D. El partido de fútbol. This is a group writing activity. Have students work in groups of three to four. Tell students that they must agree on a correct order for the pictures. Then they must write a narrative that includes the entire sequence of events based on the photos. Collect the narratives and read several to class. Ask comprehension check questions.

DRAMATIZACIONES

A and B. Assign both role plays at the same time. Allow 8–10 min for students to prepare. Then have each group present their role plays to class. Ask comprehension check questions after each presentation.

C. ¿Qué pasó?
Encourage students to be creative in their explanations.

Dramatizaciones

A. ¿Qué nota sacaste? You and your friend are discussing grades. Role-play this situation.

Tú	**Compañero(a)**
■ Ask your partner if he or she heard that Julio got an A in English.	■ Answer yes and that you helped him. Tell what you did to help him.
■ Ask if Julio read *Huckleberry Finn*.	■ Answer no but that he saw the movie.
■ Say that he always plays soccer. Ask when he studied.	■ Say that he began to study Saturday morning and that he studied all day Saturday and Sunday.
■ Ask what grade your partner got.	■ Say that you got an A also. Ask what grade your partner got.
■ Say that you got a B because you played tennis all day Saturday and Sunday.	■ Say that's too bad.

B. El picnic. You and your partner are looking at pictures from your family's picnic last weekend. Your partner wants to know about some of the people and what they did. Role-play this situation.

Compañero(a)	**Tú**
■ Point to the picture of the two boys playing soccer and ask who they are.	■ Respond that they are your relatives. Specify the relationship.
■ Point to the picture of the woman in a red hat and ask who she is.	■ Tell who she is.
■ Ask why they had a picnic and what they did there all day.	■ Respond appropriately.
■ Ask who the man wearing the white shirt and pants is.	■ Say he is another relative and tell what he did at the picnic.
■ Tell your partner that he or she has a very interesting family.	■ Agree.

C. ¿Qué pasó? Imagine that you are one of the two teens in the drawing your teacher gives you. Both of you have just returned home from your school's football game, and your mother or father wants to know what happened. Role-play this situation with two classmates. One of them should play the part of a parent.

UNIDAD 7

Purpose These role plays are designed to recycle the structures and vocabulary needed to exchange information about sports and to point out specific people and things. Encourage students to work without their books when performing and preparing their role plays.

320 UNIDAD 7 Lección 1

¡No me digas!

¿Béisbol en Latinoamérica?   Cliff Curley, un maestro de primaria en Estados Unidos, está en Santo Domingo por dos días durante su viaje al Caribe. Está en un parque, hablando con un niño dominicano que acaba de conocer. Lee su conversación y luego contesta la pregunta que sigue.

Cliff: **Yo soy Cliff Curley. Y tú, ¿cómo te llamas?**

Niño: **Pepe Torres. ¿De dónde es usted?**

Cliff: **Soy de Estados Unidos. Estoy aquí de vacaciones. ¿Tú vienes al parque con frecuencia?**

Niño: **Todos los días. Mis amigos y yo venimos aquí a jugar.**

Cliff: **Ah. ¿Y qué juegan ustedes?**

Niño: **¡Béisbol! Yo soy el mejor bateador entre todos mis amigos.**

Cliff: **¡Ya lo creo! ¡Qué bien! Te felicito. Pero, ¿béisbol? Dime, ¿dónde aprendiste a jugar béisbol?**

Niño: **Mi papá me enseñó.**

Cliff: **¿Tu papá? ¡Qué interesante! Me sorprende que todo el mundo se interese tanto en el béisbol aquí.**

¿Por qué le sorprende a Cliff que a Pepe y a su padre les interese el béisbol?

1. Cliff, como maestro de primaria, no considera al béisbol un buen deporte para niños. Lo considera un deporte para adultos.
2. Cliff cree que los niños dominicanos no deben jugar deportes norteamericanos.
3. Cliff no sabe que el béisbol es un pasatiempo muy popular en Santo Domingo.

❏ Check your answer on page 419.

LECCIÓN 1

trescientos veintiuno **321**

Purpose This section provides additional reading practice as students learn to avoid cross-cultural misunderstandings by not assuming that certain sports are played only in the United States.

Suggestions Allow students to discuss possible explanations and try to arrive at consensus on correct answer before they check explanations on page 419.

Answers

1 Cliff may consider baseball unsafe for children, but nothing in the dialogue indicates this. On the contrary, he congratulates Pepe for being the best batter among his friends. Try another answer.

2 Cliff never says this nor does he give any indication that he thinks this. He actually seems quite pleased that Pepe plays so well. This is not the correct answer.

③ Cliff is clearly surprised to see that both parent and child are interested in baseball. He seems to be unaware that baseball is rivaling soccer in popularity in several Latin American countries, in particular, in the Dominican Republic, Cuba, and Puerto Rico.

IMPACTO CULTURAL

Y ahora, ¡a leer!

Antes de empezar

Answer these questions before reading the selection. If you do not know a particular answer, make a reasoned guess.

1. ¿Cuántos jugadores hay en un equipo de béisbol?
   a. nueve   **b.** diez   **c.** once   **ch.** doce

2. En tu opinión, ¿quiénes son los jugadores más importantes de un equipo de béisbol? ¿Por qué?
   a. el lanzador y el receptor
   b. los jugadores de primera, segunda y tercera base
   c. el jardinero corto y el jugador de primera base
   ch. los tres jardineros o guardabosques

3. ¿Por qué crees que el béisbol es tan popular en los países latinos?

Verifiquemos

The following selection, *Nuestras estrellas en el béisbol*, appeared in the magazine *Más*. Read it, then answer the following questions.

1. Según la lectura, ¿quiénes son los cuatro mejores bateadores entre estos jugadores?
2. Tres jugadores se comparan a otros jugadores legendarios. ¿Quiénes son? ¿A quiénes se comparan?
3. Según la lectura, dos de estos jugadores no tienen igual. ¿Quiénes son?
4. ¿De qué fecha a qué fecha es la temporada de béisbol?
5. ¿Por qué no se menciona el nombre de este equipo ni dónde juega?

NUESTRAS ESTRELLAS EN EL BÉISBOL

Más **ofrece el equipo ideal para esta próxima temporada con las figuras latinas más destacadas de la actualidad**

— Más DATOS —

INAUGURACIÓN DE LA TEMPORADA LUNES, 1 DE ABRIL	PARTIDO DE ESTRELLAS EN TORONTO MARTES, 9 DE JULIO	FIN DE LA TEMPORADA DOMINGO, 6 DE SEPTIEMBRE

JOSÉ CANSECO
Oakland A's
Jardinero: es el Babe Ruth del béisbol latino, corpulento y mítico, el único en sumar 40-40.

GEORGE BELL
Chicago Cubs
Jardinero: un año flojo no le resta mérito; es un bateador con potencia, distancia y frecuencia.

RUBÉN SIERRA
Texas Rangers
Jardinero: tan solo necesita consistencia para heredar el legado de Roberto Clemente.

JULIO FRANCO
Texas Rangers
Segunda base: el jugador más completo del béisbol. Sufre por vivir en la sombra de otros.

OZZIE GUILLÉN
Chicago White Sox
Jardinero corto: una chispa que inspira a cualquier equipo con su guante y bate.

EDGAR MARTÍNEZ
Seattle Mariners
Tercera base: necesita un mejor guante pero bateó .302 en 1990.

JOSÉ RIJO
Cincinnati Reds
Lanzador: un derecho con una recta y un mal genio que recuerda al gran Juan Marichal.

ANDRÉS GALARRAGA
Montreal Expos
Primera base: es grande con el guante. Por eso no tiene igual.

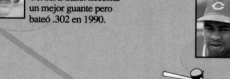

SUPER EQUIPO Nº 2
Receptor: Santos Alomar, Jr., *Cleveland Indians*
Lanzador abridor: Ramón Martínez, *L.A. Dodgers*
Relevista: Alejandro Peña, *New York Mets*
Primera base: Rafael Palmeiro, *Texas Rangers*
Segunda base: José Lind, *Pittsburgh Pirates*
Jardinero corto: Tony Fernández, *San Diego Padres*
Tercera base: Luis Salazar, *Chicago Cubs*
Guardabosque: Bobby Bonilla, *Pittsburgh Pirates*
Guardabosque: Sammy Sosa, *Chicago White Sox*
Guardabosque: Iván Calderón, *Montreal Expos*

BENITO SANTIAGO
San Diego Padres
Receptor: nadie, sea latino o americano, tiene mejor brazo.

CANDY MALDONADO
Cleveland Indians
Bateador designado: no perdona cualquier pelota mal lanzada.

JUAN AGOSTO
St. Louis Cardinals
Relevista: un zurdo muy valorado capaz de lanzar muchas entradas y perder pocos partidos.

OBJECTIVES

Communicative Goals

- Giving information about people's physical condition
- Giving and following orders
- Describing what happened in the past

Culture and Reading

- *¡No me digas!*
  ¿Cómo vamos?
  Understanding dialectal differences
- *Y ahora, ¡a leer!*
  ¡Cuidado con el volumen de tus audífonos!
  Rock music and hearing loss

Structure

- **7.3** Direct object pronouns
- **7.4** Stem-changing verbs in the preterite: **e → i** and **o → u**

2

¡Me duele muchísimo!

Deseándote una recuperación rápida

ACTIVE VOCABULARY

En la clínica del médico

aspirina	muletas
doler	paciente
dolor	pastilla
farmacia	recetar
fiebre	roto(a)
guardar cama	síntoma

El cuerpo humano

boca	nariz
brazo	oído
cabeza	ojo
cara	oreja
cuello	pecho
dientes	pelo
espalda	pie
estómago	pierna
garganta	rodilla
mano	tobillo

Complementos directos

me	nos
te	los
lo	las
la	

Verbos

abrir	extrañar
acompañar	invitar
bajar	levantar
cerrar (ie)	salvar
chocar	sufrir
experimentar	

Palabras y expresiones

apenas	al principio
audífonos	esta mañana
detalle	no se preocupe
sonido	
sólo	
vacaciones	
volumen	

Purpose   The purpose of this section is to focus students on the language necessary to identify body parts and to talk about their physical condition as well as to encourage the development and use of critical thinking skills while observing, analyzing, or comparing cultural differences and similarities without forming judgments.

ANTICIPEMOS

Chonchón

Quetzalcóatl

Lamia

Xochipilli

¿Qué piensas tú?

1. Mira las figuras en esta página. ¿Qué te parece raro o extraño de cada figura? ¿Por qué crees que tienen características físicas diferentes?

2. ¿Cuántas partes humanas puedes identificar en ellas? ¿Cuáles son?

3. ¿Conoces otros seres mitológicos con características físicas que son parte animal y parte humanas? ¿Quiénes son? Descríbelos.

4. En tu opinión, ¿qué representan estos personajes? ¿Por qué crees eso?

5. Mira la foto. ¿Qué le pasó al joven en la cama? ¿Qué le duele? ¿Qué crees que dice la tarjeta?

6. ¿Qué crees que está pensando o diciendo el joven?

7. ¿De qué vas a poder hablar al final de la lección?

¿Qué piensas tú?

Suggestions Explain the origins of the figures after students have responded to question 4. As students respond in English to questions 1, 2, and 5, repeat their descriptions in simple Spanish.

Answers

1 **Vocabulario nuevo:** Uno es una cabeza con orejas muy grandes. La mujer no tiene pies humanos; tiene patas de pato. La serpiente tiene la cabeza de un hombre. La otra figura tiene un cuerpo humano pero su cabeza es una calavera.

2 **Vocabulario nuevo:** Todo el cuerpo humano: cabeza, ojos, nariz, orejas, cuello, hombros, brazos, manos, torso, piernas, pies, etc.

3 Students may give examples from Greek and Roman mythology— Sphinx, Centaur, Minotaur, Medusa, Neptune, etc. If you have students from other cultures, encourage them to describe some of their culture's mythological figures.

4 Es probable que los estudiantes reconozcan que son figuras de la mitología o del folklore de los países hispanos. El de la cabeza con grandes orejas es un **chonchón**. El folklore chileno dice que el **chonchón** usa sus orejas grandes como alas para volar. Aparece en las noches sin luna y si la gente se burla de él, los castiga. En el folklore vasco, la mujer con patas de pato es una **lamia**. Como no era humana, por tener patas de pato, no se le permitía entrar en una iglesia. Una versión de la leyenda dice que se pasaba la vida cuidando a niños vagos. La serpiente es **Quetzalcóatl**, un dios de los aztecas. La leyenda dice que se había ido en barco por el Océano Atlántico hacia el este, prometiendo regresar algún día. El de la calavera es el dios azteca **Xochipilli**, dios del amor, la alegría, la belleza y la juventud.

5 Tuvo un accidente en el campo de fútbol. Le duele la pierna. La tarjeta probablemente expresa deseos de que se mejore pronto.

Suggestions Use the illustration as an advance organizer. Students should be allowed to discover the meaning of new vocabulary without translation, through the use of context clues and cognates.

6 **Vocabulario nuevo:** Me duele la pierna / brazo / cabeza / todo. No me siento bien. No quiero / puedo / tengo ganas de comer . . .

7 **Al final de la lección van a poder hablar del cuerpo humano y de cómo se sienten.**

UNIDAD 7   Lección 2   **325**

07:33–
10:25

Side 7, 13595 to 18743

Comprehension Checks

A full set of the **Comprehension Checks** is available on cards in the Teacher's Resource Package.

1 - **2**   `07:40`

Suggestions Identify the two pictures as two different days, emphasizing **ayer** and **hoy.** Describe 2: **Anoche María Teresa tuvo mucha tarea. No la hizo. Vio un programa en la tele,** etc. Then contrast 1: **Hoy no quiere ir a la escuela . . .**

1 ¿Quién es?
2 ¿Qué hora es?
4 ¿Quiere ir a la escuela?
5 ¿Tuvo tarea anoche?
6 ¿Hizo su tarea anoche?
7 ¿Qué hizo anoche?
8 ¿Cuándo terminó el programa de televisión?
9 ¿Durmió bien?
10 ¿Por qué no quiere ir a la escuela?

Side 7, 13798 to 14390

3 - **4**   `08:01`

1 ¿Está enferma María Teresa?
2 ¿Le duele la cabeza?
3 ¿Le duele el estómago?
4 ¿Tiene dolor de estómago?
5 ¿Tiene fiebre?
6 ¿Debe tomar unas aspirinas?
7 ¿Quiere tomar las aspirinas?
8 ¿Debe comer algo?
9 ¿Va a estar mejor después de desayunar?
10 ¿Si no está mejor, va a llamar al médico la madre?

Side 7, 14412 to 15348

326 *UNIDAD 7   Lección 2*

Son las siete de la mañana y María Teresa no quiere ir a la escuela. ¿Por qué?

Porque no hizo su tarea anoche. Vio un programa de televisión que terminó muy tarde y luego no durmió bien.

María Teresa: *Mami, creo que estoy enferma. Me duele mucho la cabeza. Y también tengo dolor de estómago.*
Mamá: *¡Ay, amor mío! ¿Qué te pasa?*

Mamá: *¿Tienes fiebre? ¿Por qué no tomas unas aspirinas?*
María Teresa: *No, mamá. No quiero tomar nada.*
Mamá: *Ay, hija. Entonces come algo. Si no te sientes mejor después del desayuno, llamamos al médico.*

Purpose This section develops listening and reading comprehension of active vocabulary needed to describe how one is feeling and what causes those feelings.

5

6

7

Después del desayuno . . .

María Teresa: ¡Ay, qué dolor! ¡Mamáaa! Mírame la pierna, por favor. Me duele tanto. Creo que la tengo rota. No puedo ni caminar. . . ¡ayyy!

Mamá: ¡Hija! Pero, ¿qué te pasa? ¿Qué te hiciste ayer?

María Teresa: Durante el partido de fútbol, choqué contra otra chica y cuando me caí, sentí un dolor tremendo en la pierna . . . y también en el pie.

Mamá: Pero, hija, ¿cómo no me dijiste nada anoche?

Mamá: Déjame ver . . . ¿puedes mover los dedos del pie?

María Teresa: Sí.

Mamá: Y el pie, ¿lo puedes mover también?

María Teresa: Sí, pero me duele, ¡ayyy!

Mamá: Ahora la pierna. Levántala un poco. Bien. Ahora bájala. Me parece que no tienes nada roto. Pero de todos modos, voy a llamar al médico.

8

Doctor: Hoy debes guardar cama todo el día.

María Teresa: ¡Ay, cuidado, doctor! También me duelen el brazo y la mano. Apenas la puedo abrir.

Mamá: Estoy furiosa contigo, María Teresa. ¿Cómo no me dijiste nada anoche? A ver, muéstrale al doctor, ¿puedes levantar el brazo?

María Teresa: Un poquito.

9

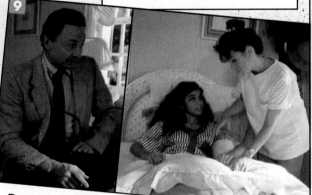

Doctor: Señora, no es nada. No fue golpe serio.

Mamá: Ay, hija. Pasa el día en cama hoy y, si mañana estás mejor, vamos a misa. Y después . . . ¿por qué no hacemos un picnic en el parque?

10

María Teresa: ¿A misa? ¿Al parque? Es que . . . ¡hoy es SÁBADO! ¡Ayyy, no!

trescientos veintisiete **327**

6 ¿Dónde van a hacer un picnic?
7 ¿Qué día es?
8 ¿Está María Teresa verdaderamente enferma?

Side 7, 17934 to 18743

5 – 6 `08:32`

Suggestions Act out colliding, falling, having great pain in your leg/foot.

1 ¿Le duele a María Teresa la pierna?
2 ¿Tiene mucho dolor?
3 ¿Puede estar rota la pierna?
4 ¿Puede María Teresa caminar?
5 ¿Qué jugó María Teresa ayer, fútbol o baloncesto?
6 ¿Chocó con otra chica?
7 ¿Se cayó?
8 ¿Sintió dolor en la pierna?
9 ¿Sintió dolor en el pie también?
10 ¿Dónde sintió un gran dolor?

Side 7, 15366 to 16418

7 – 8 `09:08`

Suggestion Demonstrate "hardly" moving arm/hand.

Point out In Hispanic countries and within some Hispanic communities in the U.S., doctors still make house calls.

1 ¿Puede María Teresa mover los dedos del pie?
2 ¿Puede mover el pie (la pierna)?
3 ¿Puede levantar (bajar) la pierna?
4 ¿Está rota la pierna (el pie, los dedos del pie)?
5 ¿Debe María Teresa guardar cama hoy?
6 ¿Debe tener cuidado el doctor?
7 ¿Le duele a María Teresa el brazo (la mano)?
8 ¿Puede abrir la mano?
9 ¿Está Mamá furiosa con María Teresa?
10 ¿Puede María Teresa levantar el brazo? ¿Puede leventarlo mucho o un poco?

Side 7, 16438 to 17914

9 – 10 `09:58`

Suggestions Some students may argue that she is really sick or injured, others that she is just pretending. Allow each group to present its case, and then have whole class vote to decide.

1 ¿Fue un golpe serio?
2 ¿Dónde va a pasar María Teresa el día?
3 ¿Adónde van a ir mañana, a misa o al parque?
4 Si está mejor mañana, ¿adónde van a ir todos?
5 ¿Van a hacer un picnic después de ir a misa?

TAPE/DISC

10:26–13:52

Side 7, 18771 to 24962

Early Production Checks

A full set of the **Early Production Checks** is available on cards in the Teacher's Resource Package.

1   10:33

Ya viene el doctor.

1 ¿Quién siente mucho dolor? *José Luis.*

2 ¿Está tranquilo José Luis (su mamá)? *No / no.*

3 ¿Quién viene, el doctor? *Sí.*

4 ¿Viene por el pasillo? *Sí.*

5 ¿Por dónde viene? *Por el pasillo.*

6 ¿Durmió mucho o muy poco José Luis anoche? *Muy poco.*

7 ¿Por qué durmió muy poco? ¿Tuvo que estudiar para un examen? *Sí.*

8 ¿Insistió José Luis en jugar hoy? *Sí.*

9 ¿Necesita saber el doctor todos los detalles? *No.*

10 ¿Está un poco agitada la mamá? *Sí.*

11 ¿Cómo está la mamá? *Un poco agitada.*

12 ¿Qué opina el padre de su hijo? ¿Cree que es un buen jugador de fútbol? *Sí.*

13 ¿Quién puede explicarle la situación al doctor? *José Luis.*

14 ¿Deben esperar afuera los padres? *Sí.*

15 ¿Dónde deben esperar los padres? *Afuera.*

16 ¿Quién tiene que examinar al paciente? *El doctor.*

Side 7, 18966 to 20723

¿QUÉ DECIMOS..?
Al hablar con el médico

1 **Ya viene el doctor.**

UNIDAD 7

Purpose This section presents language in real-life contexts designed to enable students to describe people's physical condition.

¡Una pierna rota!

Note Accept brief phrases or one- and two-word answers to all **Early Production Checks,** as shown in **1** on page 328. It is not necessary for students to answer in complete sentences.

1. ¿Quién sintió un dolor muy fuerte en la pierna?
2. ¿Sintió el dolor en la pierna derecha o izquierda?
3. ¿Le sigue doliendo?
4. ¿Puede levantar la pierna?
5. ¿No puede levantarla?
6. Y la pierna izquierda, ¿puede levantarla?
7. ¿Le duelen los brazos a José Luis?
8. ¿Puede levantarlos? ¿bajarlos?
9. ¿Le duele la cabeza?
10. ¿Puede moverla a la derecha? ¿a la izquierda?
11. ¿Parecen normales los ojos de José Luis?
12. ¿Tienen que observar a José Luis por una noche?
13. ¿Tuvo mucha suerte José Luis?
14. ¿Tiene una pierna rota o un brazo roto?

Side 7, 20746 to 22637

LECCIÓN 2

trescientos veintinueve **329**

Suggestions Begin by having students close their books while you narrate one section at a time, using the transparencies to clarify meaning without translation. Then ask **Early Production Checks.** Repeat with each section.

Using the video Play one section at a time after narrating it using the transparencies. Freeze the video and ask **Early Production Checks**. Repeat with each section.

3

No se preocupe, señora.

1 ¿Pueden estar tranquilos los padres de José Luis?
2 ¿Quién dice que pueden estar tranquilos?
3 ¿Tiene José Luis una pierna rota y un dolor de cabeza?
4 ¿Es muy serio lo de la pierna?
5 ¿Necesita pasar una noche en el hospital?
6 ¿Cuánto tiempo quieren tenerlo en observación?
7 ¿Comió José Luis antes del partido?
8 ¿Ya sirvieron la comida?
9 ¿Le pidió comida la enfermera?

Side 7, 22667 to 23830

4

Debe guardar cama.

1 ¿Cuándo pueden sus padres pasar a buscar a José Luis?
2 ¿Pueden pasar a buscarlo por la mañana o por la tarde?
3 ¿Le receta unas pastillas el doctor?
4 ¿Que le receta el doctor?
5 ¿Para qué son las pastillas?
6 ¿Debe tomarlas según las indicaciones del doctor?
7 ¿Va a poder andar al principio?
8 ¿Debe guardar cama al principio?
9 ¿Va a necesitar muletas para andar?
10 ¿Qué va a necesitar para andar?
11 ¿Se preocupa la mamá?
12 ¿Quién le dice que no se preocupe?
13 ¿Va a estar bien José Luis?

Side 7, 23851 to 24962

3 No se preocupe, señora.

4 Debe guardar cama.

CHARLEMOS UN POCO

A. Pues, primero . . .   ¿En qué orden ocurrieron estas cosas?

1. José Luis no pudo levantar la pierna derecha.
2. El doctor dijo, "Sólo tienes una pierna rota".
3. José Luis explicó lo que le pasó.
4. El doctor empezó a examinar al paciente.
5. José Luis pasó la noche en el hospital.
6. La enfermera pidió algo de comer para José Luis.
7. José Luis y sus papás fueron al hospital.
8. El doctor le recetó unas pastillas.
9. Los padres de José Luis salieron del cuarto.
10. Llegó el doctor.

B. ¡Ay, ay, ay!   ¿Qué información sobre los pacientes le da la enfermera al médico?

MODELO   Sra. Durango
A la Sra. Durango le duele el estómago.

1. Sr. Gómez   **2.** Srta. Ortiz   **3.** Lorenzo

4. Sarita   **5.** Juanita   **6.** Alfredo

LECCIÓN 2

El cuerpo humano

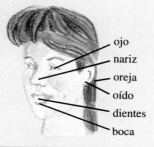

cabeza
pelo
cuello
garganta
brazo
pecho
estómago
espalda
mano (*f*)
pierna
rodilla
tobillo
pie

La cara

ojo
nariz
oreja
oído
dientes
boca

Doler (ue)
Used to talk about what hurts

Like the verbs **gustar** and **encantar**, the verb **doler** is always used with the indirect object pronoun and is usually in the third person singular or plural.

duele   duelen

¿**Te duele** la cabeza?
No, pero **me duelen** los ojos.

trescientos treinta y uno **331**

C. En el hospital.
Do first as a TPR activity with you giving commands to the whole class. Then have students repeat it in pairs with one giving the command, the other doing the activity.

1 Mueve la cabeza a la izquierda, a la derecha.
2 Toca el pie izquierdo, derecho.
3 Abre y cierra la mano izquierda, la mano derecha.
4 Levanta la pierna derecha, la izquierda.
5 Levanta y dobla la pierna derecha, la pierna izquierda.
6 Toca la nariz con la mano izquierda, derecha.
7 Levanta el brazo derecho, el brazo izquierdo.
8 Baja el brazo izquierdo, el derecho.
9 Mueve los dedos del pie derecho, del pie izquierdo.
10 Abre la boca.

CH. ¡Yo no!
Allow 2–3 min to do in pairs. Then call on several pairs to check their work.

1 Prepara la limonada. ¡No, yo no! Prepárala tú.
2 Alquila un video. ¡No, yo no! Alquílalo tú.
3 Pide unas pizzas. ¡No, yo no! Pídelas tú.
4 Ayuda a mamá y papá. ¡No, yo no! Ayúdalos tú.
5 Busca el correo. ¡No, yo no! Búscalo tú.
6 Compra la leche. ¡No, yo no! Cómprala tú.
7 Lava los platos. ¡No, yo no! Lávalos tú.
8 Sirve los tacos. ¡No, yo no! Sírvelos tú.

D. ¿Son responsables?
Allow 2–3 min for students to do it in groups of three. Then call on different groups to check their work.

1 ¿Cuándo van a limpiar su cuarto? Yo ya lo limpié. Yo voy a limpiarlo más tarde.
2 ¿Cuándo van a escribir la composición de inglés? Yo ya la escribí. Yo voy a escribirla más tarde.
3 ¿Cuándo van a estudiar español? Yo ya lo estudié. Yo voy a estudiarlo más tarde.
4 ¿Cuándo van a practicar el piano? Yo ya lo practiqué. Yo voy a practicarlo más tarde.
5 ¿Cuándo van a tomar las vitaminas? Yo ya las tomé. Yo voy a tomarlas más tarde.

6 ¿Cuándo van a leer la lección de historia? Yo ya la leí. Yo voy a leerla más tarde.
7 ¿Cuándo van a hacer los ejercicios? Yo ya los hice.]\Yo voy a hacerlos más tarde.
8 ¿Cuándo van a empezar el proyecto? Yo ya lo empecé. Yo voy a empezarlo más tarde.

Direct object pronouns

me	nos
te	
lo	los
la	las

Cómpra**la** en El Corte Inglés.
Lláma**nos** esta tarde.

Note that object pronouns always follow and are attached to affirmative commands.

*See ¿**Por qué se dice así?**, page G100, section 7.3.*

Placement of direct object pronouns

Object pronouns usually precede the verb. They may also follow and be attached to an infinitive or to the **-ndo** form of the verb.

Yo **la** conozco muy bien.
¿**Lo** vas a hacer esta tarde?
Tenemos que llevar**los**.
Estamos preparándo**la** ahora.

*See ¿**Por qué se dice así?**, page G100, section 7.3.*

C. En el hospital.
El (La) doctor(a) te está examinando. Haz lo que te dice.

MODELO levantar los brazos
Compañero(a): **Levanta los brazos.**
Tú:

1. mover la cabeza a la izquierda, a la derecha
2. tocar el pie izquierdo, derecho
3. abrir y cerrar la mano izquierda, la mano derecha
4. levantar la pierna derecha, la izquierda
5. levantar y doblar la pierna derecha, la pierna izquierda
6. tocar la nariz con la mano izquierda, derecha
7. levantar el brazo derecho, el brazo izquierdo
8. bajar el brazo izquierdo, el derecho
9. mover los dedos del pie derecho, del pie izquierdo
10. abrir la boca

CH. ¡Yo no!
Tu hermano(a) es muy irresponsable. ¿Qué dice cuando le das un mandato?

MODELO limpiar su cuarto
Tú: **Limpia tu cuarto.**
Compañero(a): **¡No, yo no! Límpialo tú.**

1. preparar la limonada
2. alquilar un video
3. pedir unas pizzas
4. ayudar a mamá y papá
5. buscar el correo
6. comprar la leche
7. lavar los platos
8. servir los tacos

D. ¿Son responsables?
En esta familia, un hijo es muy responsable y el otro es algo irresponsable. ¿Cómo contestan las preguntas de sus padres?

MODELO hacer tu tarea
Tú: **¿Cuándo van a hacer la tarea?**
Compañero(a) 1: **Yo ya la hice.**
Compañero(a) 2: **Yo voy a hacerla más tarde.**

1. limpiar su cuarto
2. escribir la composición de inglés
3. estudiar español
4. practicar el piano
5. tomar las vitaminas
6. leer la lección de historia
7. hacer los ejercicios
8. empezar el proyecto

Expansion Have students change roles and repeat exercise.

E. ¿Amigos? Tu mejor amigo(a) requiere mucha atención. ¿Qué le dices cuando insiste en que le prestes más atención?

MODELO   invitar a comer
               Compañero(a): **¡Nunca me invitas a comer!**
               Tú: **¡Te invité a comer la semana pasada!**

semana pasada	fin de semana	ayer	anoche	esta mañana
•	•	•	•	•

1. llamar por teléfono
2. visitar los fines de semana
3. ayudar con la tarea
4. llevar a un partido
5. saludar por la mañana
6. acompañar al cine
7. buscar antes de la clase
8. comprar un regalo

F. ¡Adiós! Tu familia va a mudarse a Alaska en septiembre y tus amigos quieren saber si los vas a recordar. ¿Qué te preguntan?

MODELO   visitarnos
               Compañero(a): **¿Vas a visitarnos?**
               Tú: **Sí, voy a visitarlos.** o
               No, no los voy a visitar.

1. extrañarnos
2. llamarnos por teléfono
3. invitarnos a visitar
4. acompañarnos a México
5. vernos durante las vacaciones
6. recordarnos
7. escribirnos con frecuencia
8. vernos a todos antes de irte

G. ¡Ganaron! Los Tigres tienen muchos aficionados pero no todos siguieron sus partidos el año pasado. ¿Los siguieron estas personas?

MODELO   María Luisa: no
               María Luisa no los siguió.

1. Norberto: sí
2. Miguel y Mariano: no
3. yo: sí
4. ustedes: sí
5. Alicia: sí
6. tú: no
7. Gonzalo y Martita: sí
8. nosotros: sí

LECCIÓN 2

Stem-changing -ir verbs in the preterite: e → i

Note that **e → i** stem-changing verbs change in the **usted/él/ella** and **ustedes/ellos/ellas** forms in the preterite.

Luisa **siguió** a Alberto y luego **seguí** yo.

Ellos **pidieron** un refresco; yo no **pedí** nada.

See ¿Por qué se dice así?, page G103, section 7.4.

trescientos treinta y tres **333**

Stem-changing -ir verbs in the preterite: o → u

Note that **o → u** stem-changing verbs change in the **usted/él/ella** and **ustedes/ellos/ellas** forms in the preterite.

Yo **dormí** muy bien.
¿Cómo **durmieron** ustedes?

See **¿Por qué se dice así?,** *page G103, section 7.4.*

H. ¡Qué rico! Después del partido, todos fueron a comer a un restaurante mexicano. ¿Qué hicieron allí?

EJEMPLO **Paco pidió enchiladas.**

Paco		la cuenta
yo		una mesa
los camareros	conseguir	más sillas
la familia López	pedir	tacos
tú	servir	bebidas
todos		enchiladas
la camarera		café
nosotros		bizcocho

I. Tengo sueño. Hubo una fiesta anoche en casa de Lupita. Hoy todos sus parientes están furiosos porque no pudieron dormir a causa del ruido. Según Lupita, ¿cuántas horas durmieron?

MODELO papá: 3
Papá durmió tres horas.

1. mi primo Fernando: 5
2. mamá: 2
3. mi tío Adolfo: 6
4. mis primas Isabel y Tina: 4
5. mis abuelos: 7
6. mi hermana Panchita: 3
7. yo: 1
8. el perro: toda la noche

J. Vacaciones. ¿Qué hicieron tú y tus amigos durante las vacaciones de primavera?

MODELO Mi amiga Berta _____ muchos videos.
Mi amiga Berta vio muchos videos.

VOCABULARIO ÚTIL:

tocar	preparar	leer	dormir
empezar	jugar	comprar	ver
trabajar	pedir	ir	tener

1. Inés y Amalia _____ diez horas cada noche.
2. Yo _____ fútbol todos los días.
3. Pedro _____ dos novelas históricas.
4. Teresa y Toño _____ pizza todos los días.
5. Yo _____ la guitarra en el parque.
6. Nosotros _____ de compras dos veces.
7. Leopoldo _____ que limpiar la casa.
8. Yo _____ a tomar clases de karate.

CHARLEMOS UN POCO MÁS

A. **¿Qué les duele?** After a strenuous week of hiking in the country, everyone has aches and pains. Your teacher will give you a list of the people you are to check on and the condition of people you have already seen. Ask your partner about the condition of the people on your list. Then answer your partner's questions about the people pictured on your list.

MODELO   Tú: **¿Qué le duele a Dolores?**
Compañero(a):   **Le duelen los pies.**

B. **¡Somos mejores amigos!**   Make a list of six things that you do for your best friend. Then read your list to your partner. Check the items on your lists that you both do for your best friends.

VOCABULARIO ÚTIL:

ver	escuchar	saludar	buscar	encontrar	llamar
esperar	ayudar	acompañar	invitar	visitar	extrañar

MODELO   Mi mejor amiga, Teresa
La invito a mi casa.
La ayudo con la tarea.

C. **¿Somos individualistas?**   Are your classmates individualistic, or do they all tend to do the same things? To find out, use the interview grid that your teacher provides. Find a classmate who fits each of the categories listed and have him or her sign your grid in the appropriate square. Remember that each classmate may only sign one square.

CH. **¿Son muy organizados?**   To find out which of your classmates are procrastinators, prepare a sheet of paper with three columns as shown below. In the **Preguntas** column, write five questions concerning weekly duties that you know your classmates should have done already. Then ask several classmates the questions. Record the names of your classmates in the appropriate column, according to their answers.

Preguntas	Sí	No
¿Empezaste el proyecto para la clase de historia?	Randy ya lo empezó.	Randy va a hacerlo más tarde.

CHARLEMOS
UN POCO MÁS

A. **¿Qué les duele?**
Allow 4–5 min. Then ask class to tell you what is hurting each of the hikers.

B. **¡Somos mejores amigos!** Allow 5–6 min. Then ask students to write on board those items that both of them do for their best friends.

C. **¿Somos individualistas?** Allow 8–10 min. When one student has signatures in all the squares, confirm by asking each student who signed if they did the activity in the block they signed.

CH. **¿Son muy organizados?** Allow 5–6 min. Then do a tally to find out how may procrastinators there are in the whole class.

Purpose These activities are designed to allow students to create with language recently learned as they describe people's physical condition and inquire about classmates' activities in a variety of possible combinations.

A and B. Assign both role plays at same time. Allow 4–5 min to prepare and then call on several pairs to perform their role plays for class. Check for comprehension by asking questions after each presentation.

C. Me duele . . . Allow 4–5 min for patients to describe their problem. Then call on several pairs to perform their role plays for the class. Check for comprehension by asking questions after each presentation.

Extension Have "patients" get a second and a third opinion from other doctors in the room.

CH. ¡Pobre Bombón! Ask class what body parts for animals have different names. Have them give the human equivalents.

Dramatizaciones

A. ¿Qué pasó? Your friend didn't meet you at the library last night. When you run into each other, you try to find out what happened. Role-play this situation with your partner.

Tú	Compañero(a)
■ Greet your partner and ask him or her what happened last night.	■ Answer that your cousins came to visit and you took them to Café de México.
■ Ask what they ate.	■ Say that your cousin Paco ordered five tacos and Sergio ordered an enchilada.
■ Ask who served them.	■ Say that your friend Lupe served you.
■ Ask if they liked the food.	■ Say they loved it. Explain that Paco ate too much and his stomach began to hurt at night.
■ Ask if Paco is all right now.	■ Say that he is fine and that he slept ten hours last night.

B. En el café. Yesterday afternoon you worked as a waiter or waitress in a café near school. Several of your classmates and three of your teachers came in for a snack. Today you are telling your best friend what happened at work. As your partner asks questions, tell who came by the café, what they ordered, and what you served them. Role-play this situation.

C. Me duele . . . You are a doctor, and your partner is your patient. The patient must describe a physical problem and explain what may have caused it. The doctor will interview the patient, giving him or her appropriate instructions depending on the ailment. Afterwards, the doctor will tell the patient what to do to get better.

CH. ¡Pobre Bombón! You are a veterinarian, and your partner, Bombón's owner, brings the dog in for his yearly checkup. Role-play Bombón's examination. Look at the drawing of Bombón that your teacher gives you. Note that, in Spanish, the names for some animal body parts are different from the names for human body parts.

UNIDAD

Purpose This section has students recycle, in student-centered role plays, all previously learned structures and vocabulary needed to describe the physical condition of several people and a dog.

Suggestions Do these role plays spontaneously, not from written scripts. Circulate among groups. Limit time allowed so that students do not get off task. Ask several pairs to recreate their exchange for the whole class.

¡No me digas!

¿Cómo vamos?   Gabriel, un mexicano que acaba de mudarse de México a Miami, habla con Pedro Báez, un amigo cubano que vive en Miami.

Gabriel: **¿Qué vamos a hacer esta noche, Pedro?**
Pedro: **No te preocupes. Ya lo tengo todo organizado.
           Primero vamos a Scratch, la mejor discoteca de
           Miami. Y después vamos al Versailles, en la Calle
           Ocho, a tomar un café. Todo el mundo va allí.**
Gabriel: **¡Fantástico! Pero, mi carro no funciona. ¿Podemos
           ir en el tuyo?**
Pedro: **¡Qué mala suerte! Mi hermana va a usarlo esta
           noche. Pero no importa. Podemos ir en guagua.**
Gabriel: **¿En guagua? ¡Hombre, habla español, por favor!**

¿Por qué cree Gabriel que Pedro no está hablando español?

1. Gabriel cree que la pronunciación y la gramática de Pedro no son buenas.
2. Pedro usa expresiones cubanas que Gabriel no entiende.
3. Gabriel cree que él habla español mejor que Pedro.

❏ Check your answer on page 420.

LECCIÓN 2

Purpose This section provides additional reading practice as students discover interesting cross-cultural information about dialect variance within the Cuban community.

Suggestions Allow 1–2 min to read dialogue. Ask students to discuss possible explanations and arrive at consensus on correct answer before checking response and explanations on page 420.

Answers

1 Gabriel may notice some differences between his own pronunciation and that of Pedro's, but he doesn't say anything about it in the dialogue. Pronunciation differences occur as much in Spanish as they do in English and are all equally valid. This is not the correct answer. Try another response.

2 Just as pronunciation will vary from country to country or region to region, so will certain vocabulary items. A **guagua** is a *bus* in Caribbean countries and a *baby* in some South American countries. Gabriel did not recognize the word because it is not commonly used in Mexico. This is the reason for his comment.

3 All of us tend to think that the way we speak is the norm, since that is what we have heard most often. Gabriel most certainly has noted differences between his Spanish and Pedro's, but he probably accepts them readily. There certainly is no indication in the dialogue that he feels that his Spanish is superior. Try another answer.

Y ahora, ¡a leer!

Purpose This section is intended to provide additional reading practice as students learn about the danger of damaging their hearing permanently if they listen to very loud music. Through use of cognates and context cues, students should be able to glean information without translation.

Antes de empezar

These questions are an advance organizer for the **¡Cuidado con el volumen de tus audífonos!** reading that follows.

Answers

Answers to all questions will vary depending on students' preferences.

Verifiquemos

Answers

1 No. Indicó que es mejor escuchar la música rock con el volumen lo suficiente bajo para fácilmente poder oír a otras personas hablar.

2 No. El estudio se hizo con dieciséis jóvenes.

3 Sí. Dieciséis personas escucharon música rock con audífonos a un volumen bastante alto por un período de tres horas.

4 No. Después de las tres horas, seis de las personas tuvieron dificultad en oír por un tiempo no especificado.

5 No. El resultado es que el escuchar música con audífonos diariamente por mucho tiempo puede afectar el oído permanentemente.

6 Sí. Noventa decibeles es considerado el nivel máximo de resistencia para el oído humano.

7 No. Los audífonos aumentan el volumen hasta ciento cincuenta decibeles.

8 Sí. Debes dejar de escuchar música si sientes dolor de oídos o ecos.

Y ahora, ¡a leer!

Antes de empezar

1. How often do you listen to rock music?
2. How do you like your music played: as soft background music or loud enough to drown out surrounding conversation?
3. Do you like to listen to music with earphones? Why?
4. When using earphones, how do you know if the music is too loud?

Verifiquemos

¿Sí o no?   Read the magazine article on the next page. Then, indicate if you agree or disagree with the following statements and explain why.

1. Un estudio que se hizo en el Hospital Universitario de la Universidad de Iowa indicó que es mejor escuchar la música rock con el volumen elevado para no poder oír a las otras personas hablar.
2. El estudio se hizo con dieciséis personas: ocho jóvenes y ocho adultos.
3. En el experimento, las dieciséis personas escucharon música rock con audífonos a un volumen bastante alto por un período de tres horas.
4. Después de las tres horas, todas las personas tuvieron dificultad en oír por un tiempo no especificado.
5. El resultado del experimento es que el escuchar música con audífonos diariamente por mucho tiempo no afecta el oído permanentemente.
6. Noventa decibeles es considerado el nivel máximo de resistencia para el oído humano.
7. Los audífonos, por ser pequeños, no pueden aumentar el volumen a más de noventa decibeles.
8. Si después de escuchar música con audífonos sientes dolor de oídos o ecos, debes dejar de escuchar música.

¡Cuidado con el volumen de tus audífonos!

En el Hospital Universitario de la Universidad de Iowa, Estados Unidos, se llevó a cabo un experimento con dieciséis jóvenes. ■ Todos estuvieron escuchando música rock con audífonos durante tres horas, a un volumen bastante alto. ■ Después de concluido este tiempo, seis de los jóvenes, ya sin audífonos, seguían oyendo un eco de los sonidos o experimentaron pérdida temporal de la audición. ■ De acuerdo a la investigación, esta pérdida temporal puede convertirse en un hecho permanente si nos dedicamos diariamente

— y por mucho tiempo — a escuchar música con audífonos a un volumen alto. ■ El doctor Phillip Lee, que dirigió el estudio, explicó: "Generalmente, noventa decibeles es considerado el nivel máximo de resistencia a que debe ser sometido el oído. ■ Sin embargo, los audífonos concentran más el volumen que un equipo de

sonido normal (sin audífonos), alcanzando sonidos de más de ciento cincuenta decibeles". ■ Para tu seguridad auditiva, ten muy presente estos consejos:

ᐱ Nunca mantengas el volumen de tus audífonos tan elevado que no puedas oír fácilmente a los otros hablar a tu alrededor.

ᐱ Deja de escuchar música con audífonos al primer síntoma de dolor de oídos, sordera temporal o ecos, después de apagado el equipo.

Tú Internacional,
Año 11, no. 9

LECCIÓN 2

OBJECTIVES

Communicative Goals

- Giving and understanding orders
- Giving the location of things

Reading

- **Leamos ahora**
  La maravilla de Miami:
  Tourism in Miami
- Reading strategy: Skimming

Writing

- **Escribamos un poco**
  Short news article
- Writing strategy:
  Retelling an event

Structure

- **7.5** Affirmative **tú** commands:
  Irregular forms
- **7.6** Prepositions of location

¡ Ponlo allí !

ACTIVE VOCABULARY

En el dormitorio

armario	mesita
cama	sillón
estante	televisor
lámpara	ventana

Un jugador lastimado

accidente	yeso
bata	zapatillas

Un partido de fútbol

arquero	empate
bloquear	trofeo
empatar	

Regalos

bombón	ramo de flores
revista	tarjeta

Colocación

a la derecha de	en
a la izquierda de	encima de
al lado de	enfrente de
cerca de	entre
debajo de	lejos de
delante de	sobre
detrás de	

Verbos

decidir	pedir (i, i)
escoger	tener cuidado
mover (ue)	

Palabras y expresiones

allí	a la vez
cosas	a propósito
persona	bienvenido
todo	como siempre
tráfico	por lo menos
	¡Qué amable eres!
	¡Qué vergüenza!

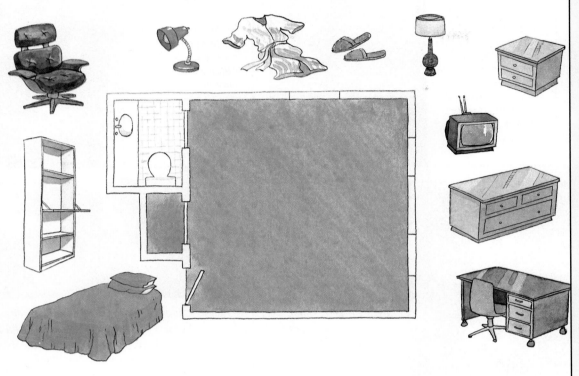

¿Qué piensas tú?

Answers

1 **Vocabulario nuevo:** Debajo de la cama, en el armario, encima de la cómoda, en un cajón, detrás de la puerta, etc.

2 **Vocabulario nuevo:** Deben poner el televisor enfrente de la cama o del sillón, al lado de la cama, etc.

3 **Vocabulario nuevo:** Hazme una limonada; traeme las zapatillas; ven acá, por favor; prepárame un bocadillo, etc.; Él va a tener que lavarse, bañarse, vestirse, caminar con muletas, etc.

4 Las respuestas van a variar. Es probable que digan que es necesario cuando el enfermo no puede levantarse, o cuándo está muy débil para hacerlo.

5 Las respuestas van a variar.

6 **Van a aprender a decir dónde están situadas ciertas cosas y a dar órdenes.**

¿Qué piensas tú?

1. José Luis necesita sus zapatillas pero no las encuentra. ¿Dónde en su cuarto debe buscarlas?

2. Éste es el cuarto de José Luis. Sus padres quieren arreglarlo para que José Luis esté lo más cómodo posible. ¿Cómo sugieres tú que lo arreglen? Di dónde crees que deben poner los muebles y otros artículos.

3. Dada su condición, ¿qué va a tener que pedirles a sus padres que hagan por él? ¿Qué debe hacer él mismo? ¿Por qué?

4. ¿Cuándo es necesario reorganizar los muebles en el cuarto de un enfermo? ¿Por qué?

5. ¿Tendrías que cambiar algo en tu cuarto si te rompieras la pierna como José Luis? ¿Qué cambiarías? ¿Por qué?

6. ¿De qué vas a poder hablar al final de la lección?

Purpose To focus students on vocabulary needed to give and understand orders and to point out specific people and things. This section also encourages students to develop and use critical thinking skills as they learn to recognize and appreciate Hispanic cultural influences on several major American cities.

13:53–
17:43

Comprehension Checks

A full set of the **Comprehension Checks** is available on cards in the Teacher's Resource Package.

 1   14:01

Suggestions Collect things from your desk. Explain that you have to decide where to put things. Talk through where you put each item: next to, on top of, to the right of, etc.
1 ¿Tiene José Luis la pierna rota?
2 ¿Por qué decimos "Pobre José Luis?"
3 ¿Vienen sus amigos a visitarlo?
4 ¿Quién viene a visitarlo?
5 ¿Le traen regalos?
6 ¿Qué le traen?
7 ¿Tiene José Luis que decidir dónde poner los regalos?
8 ¿Qué tiene José Luis que decidir?

2   14:16

Suggestions Point out José Luis's cast. Name a well-known brand of candies. Act out not knowing where to put the box. Contrast **cerca** and **lejos**. Act out opening the box.
1 ¿Quién es?
Continue asking questions, as above.

3   14:39

Suggestions Show a sports magazine. Draw a large and a small table and contrast the two.
1 ¿Quién es?
Continue asking questions.

4   14:56

Suggestions Point out the bouquet. Act out not being able to put something on your desk because it's too crowded with other things.
1 ¿Quién llega ahora?
Continue asking questions.

1

¡Pobre José Luis! Tiene la pierna rota. Por eso vienen a visitarlo sus amigos. Todos le traen regalos. Ahora él tiene que decidir dónde ponerlos.

2

Rita: ¿Te duele mucho la pierna?
José Luis: No tanto, Rita, pero el yeso es muy incómodo.
Rita: Pues, mira. Estos bombones son para ti. A ver, ¿dónde los pongo?
José Luis: Gracias, Rita. Ponlos aquí en la cama. Los quiero tener muy cerca. ¡Ábrelos, por favor!

3

Rubén le trae una revista de deportes. La va a poner sobre el escritorio.
José Luis: No, Rubén. Allí no. El escritorio está demasiado lejos. Ponla aquí en la mesita al lado de la cama.

4

Silvia llega con un ramo de flores.
José Luis: Gracias, Silvia. ¡Qué lindas! No puede ponerlas en el estante porque está cubierto de tarjetas.
José Luis: Ponlas en esta mesa. Sí, ahí a la derecha de la lámpara. Así puedo verlas mejor.

5

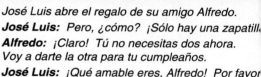

José Luis abre el regalo de su amigo Alfredo.
José Luis: Pero, ¿cómo? ¡Sólo hay una zapatilla!
Alfredo: ¡Claro! Tú no necesitas dos ahora. Voy a darte la otra para tu cumpleaños.
José Luis: ¡Qué amable eres, Alfredo! Por favor ponla debajo de la cama.

6

Su prima Carla le trae una bata.
José Luis: Gracias, Carla. ¡Me encanta! Necesito una bata nueva. Pero no en el armario, por favor. Ponla aquí, en la silla.

Purpose This section develops reading and listening comprehension of vocabulary used to give orders and talk about the location of things. Students should not be expected to achieve productive mastery at this point. The goal is not to translate, but to read/ listen for comprehension.

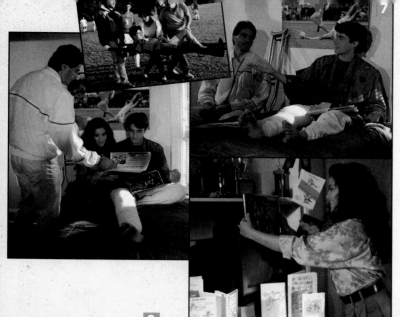

El entrenador llega con otro regalo para José Luis.

Entrenador: Ahora sí que eres famoso, José Luis. Mira esta foto. El fotógrafo del periódico estudiantil la sacó.

José Luis: ¡Ay, no! ¡Es terrible! ¡Me están llevando al hospital! No va a salir en el periódico, ¿verdad? ¡Qué vergüenza!

Entrenador: Al contrario, José Luis; ya salió. Eres un héroe ahora.

Carla: Es verdad, José Luis. Todo el mundo está hablando de ti.

José Luis: ¿Ah, sí? ¿De veras? Entonces ponla allá, Carla, encima del televisor. Así que, ¿no ganamos anoche?

Entrenador: No, pero tampoco perdimos. Empatamos: 1 a 1.

El regalo de Paco es en broma. Es un trofeo para el jugador más cómico del partido.

José Luis: Gracias, Paco. ¡Eres un verdadero amigo! Ponlo en el estante, detrás de los otros trofeos. ¡No quiero recordar lo que me pasó! Pero, muévete, hombre. Estás enfrente del televisor. Ya va a empezar el partido entre España y Argentina. Ven acá. Siéntate aquí. Podemos verlo juntos.

Papá: ¡Vaya, José Luis! Tienes amigos muy generosos, pero . . . ¡ya no hay espacio para más visitas!

trescientos cuarenta y tres **343**

5   15:19

Suggestions Point out that there's only one slipper, not two. Act out putting something under your chair, desk.
1 ¿Quién es?
Continue asking **Comprehension Checks.**

Side 7, 27559 to 28358

6   15:46

Suggestion Point out the robe, the closet, the chair.
1 ¿Quién es Carla?
Continue asking **Comprehension Checks.**

Side 7, 28377 to 28923

7   16:05

Suggestions Act out **vergüenza**. Contrast two scores—one where there is a winner and a loser, one which is a tie.
1 ¿Quién llega ahora?
2 ¿Trae un regalo para José Luis?
Continue asking **Comprehension Checks.**

Side 7, 28944 to 30130

8   16:45

Suggestions Give examples of joke gifts. Demonstrate putting something behind other things. Demonstrate standing in front of people, things.
1 ¿Quién es?
2 ¿Es el regalo de Paco una broma?
Continue asking **Comprehension Checks.**

Side 7, 30150 to 31143

9   17:19

Suggestion Point out that José Luis's room is now very crowded with gifts and cards.
1 ¿Tiene José Luis amigos muy generosos?
2 ¿Cómo son los amigos de José Luis?
Continue asking **Comprehension Checks.**

Side 7, 31164 to 31877

TAPE/DISC

17:44–
20:37

Side 7, 31904 to 37100

Early Production Checks

1   `17:51`

Pon el sillón más cerca.

1. ¿Está bien la cama allí?   *No.*
2. ¿Está demasiado lejos o cerca del baño?   *Lejos.*
3. ¿Pueden moverla?   *Sí.*
4. ¿Dónde la quiere la mamá, lejos o cerca de la puerta?   *Cerca.*
5. ¿Está mejor allí?   *Sí.*
6. ¿Dónde quiere la mesita, al lado de la cama o de la puerta?   *Al lado de la cama.*
7. ¿Dónde está la lámpara, encima de la mesa o de la mesita?   *Encima de la mesa.*
8. ¿Tiene paciencia la mamá?   *No.*
9. ¿Puede hacer todo a la vez el padre?   *No.*
10. ¿Lo siente la madre?   *Sí.*
11. ¿Está preocupada la madre?   *Sí.*
12. ¿Por quién está preocupada?   *Por José Luis.*
13. ¿Necesitan hacer otras cosas?   *Sí.*
14. ¿Dónde debe estar el televisor, en el estante o en la cama?   *En el estante.*
15. ¿Dónde necesitan poner el sillón?   *Más cerca de la cama.*
16. ¿Qué necesitan poner cerca de la cama?   *El sillón.*
17. ¿Para quién es el sillón, para las visitas o para los padres?   *Para las visitas.*

Side 7, 32085 to 34259

¿ Q U É   D E C I M O S ... ?
Al dar órdenes

1   *Pon el sillón más cerca.*

Purpose   These dialogues show the language of giving commands in more natural contexts. Unfamiliar structures are intended solely for comprehension, not for mastery or production by students.

2 Ven acá, mamá.

Note Accept brief phrases or one- and two-word answers to all **Early Production Checks**, as shown in **1** above. It is not necessary for students to answer in complete sentences.

1. ¿Vio los cambios José Luis?
2. ¿Quién hizo los cambios, la madre, el padre o ambos?
3. ¿Le gusta el cuarto así a José Luis?
4. ¿Abre la ventana el padre?
5. ¿Siente mucho calor o frío con el yeso?
6. ¿Quiere las zapatillas José Luis?
7. ¿Dónde están las zapatillas?
8. ¿Están allí generalmente?
9. ¿Dónde está la bata, sobre la cama o el sillón?
10. ¿Quiere una cosa más José Luis?
11. ¿A quién le pide un favor?
12. ¿Qué le pide a su madre?
13. ¿Va a prepararle una limonada la madre?

Side 7, 34280 to 35823

Fue un empate.

1. ¿Quién tiene la pierna rota, José Luis o Alfredo?
2. ¿Ganaron anoche?
3. ¿Les hizo mucha falta José Luis en el partido anoche?
4. ¿Quién ganó?
5. ¿Fue un empate?
6. ¿A quién le dice José Luis que empataron?
7. ¿Quién perdió un gol increíble?
8. ¿Qué perdio Alfredo?
9. ¿Bloqueó el arquero el cabezazo de Alfredo?
10. ¿Se cayó José Luis de la cama?

Side 7, 35845 to 37100

3   *Fue un empate.*

CHARLEMOS UN POCO

A. ¿Quién habla?   Estamos en la casa de José Luis después de su accidente. ¿Quién dice estas cosas: su mamá, su papá, Alfredo o José Luis?

MODELO   Ven acá, mamá.
          José Luis lo dice.

1. ¡No puedo hacerlo todo a la vez!
2. ¿Qué pasó en el partido anoche? ¿Perdimos?
3. Pues, podemos moverla. ¿Dónde la quieres?
4. Fue un empate.
5. La bata está sobre el sillón.
6. No ganó nadie.
7. Pon la mesita al lado de la cama.
8. Por favor, abre la ventana.
9. Ten paciencia, mi amor.
10. Tus zapatillas están debajo de la cama.
11. Ve a la cocina y prepárame una limonada.
12. El arquero me bloqueó el cabezazo.

B. Dime, mamá.   Pedro tiene que ayudar a su mamá hoy porque está enferma. ¿Qué le dice su mamá?

 MODELO   venir acá
          Ven acá.

1. salir por la puerta de atrás
2. ir a la tienda de don Gustavo
3. ser siempre cortés con él
4. decirle a don Gustavo que estoy enferma
5. hacer las compras en esta lista
6. poner las cosas en el carro
7. tener cuidado con el tráfico
8. venir directamente a casa

HAZ TU PARTE.
CONSERVA EL AMBIENTE.

LECCIÓN 3

Affirmative irregular *tú* commands

Infinitive	*Command*
decir	**di**
poner	**pon**
salir	**sal**
tener	**ten**
venir	**ven**
hacer	**haz**
ir	**ve**
ser	**sé**

See **¿Por qué se dice así?**, *page G105, section 7.5.*

CHARLEMOS UN POCO

A. ¿Quién habla? Ask whole class to respond as you read each item.

1 Su papá lo dice.
2 José Luis lo dice.
3 Su papá lo dice.
4 Alfredo lo dice.
5 Su mamá lo dice.
6 Alfredo lo dice.
7 Su mamá lo dice.
8 José Luis lo dice.
9 Su papá lo dice.
10 Su mamá lo dice.
11 José Luis lo dice.
12 Alfredo lo dice.

Extension Call on individual students to read each item and have class respond.

B. Dime, mamá. Allow 2–3 min to do in pairs. Have students alternate, each one doing every other item.

1 Sal por la puerta de atrás.
2 Ve a la tienda de don Gustavo.
3 Sé siempre cortés con él.
4 Dile a don Gustavo que estoy enferma.
5 Haz las compras en esta lista.
6 Pon las cosas en el carro.
7 Ten cuidado con el tráfico.
8 Ven directamente a casa.

Purpose These activities provide guided practice to students beginning to give orders and to give the location of people or things. The repetition built into the activities is intentional.

C. ¿Cómo? Allow 2–3 min
to do in pairs first. Then call on
individuals to give answers.

Point out The gesture for *come
here* in Hispanic countries is made
with the arm extended, the palm
of the hand down, and the fingers
moving quickly toward the palm of
the hand.

1 Ten cuidado.
2 Ven acá.
3 Ve a la tienda.
4 Pon el sillón allí.
5 Sé buena.
6 Haz la tarea.
7 Di "¡Hola!"
8 Sal de aquí.

C. ¿Cómo? Estamos en casa de los Fernández. ¿Qué están
diciendo los miembros de la familia? Usa estas frases para formar
un mandato apropiado para cada dibujo.

MODELO

venir acá	decir "¡Hola!"
poner el sillón allí	salir de aquí
ir a la tienda	hacer la tarea
ser buena	tener cuidado
hacer los sándwiches	

Haz los sándwiches.

1.

2.

3.

4.

5.

6.

7.

8.

CH. ¡Pobrecito!

Tu amigo(a) es muy desorganizado(a). Quiere hacer una fiesta en su casa el viernes por la noche. Dile cuándo debe hacer estas cosas.

MODELO **Haz la lista de los invitados el domingo por la mañana.**

pedir las pizzas
escoger la música para la fiesta
ir al mercado para comprar refrescos
llamar a los invitados
decirles "Bienvenidos" a los invitados
llevar las invitaciones al correo
poner los refrescos en el refrigerador
venir a mi casa por los discos

1. domingo por la tarde
2. lunes por la mañana
3. lunes por la tarde
4. martes por la tarde
5. miércoles por la tarde
6. jueves por la noche
7. viernes por la tarde
8. viernes por la noche

D. Me encanta mi cuarto.

¿Cómo describe tu amigo(a) su cuarto?

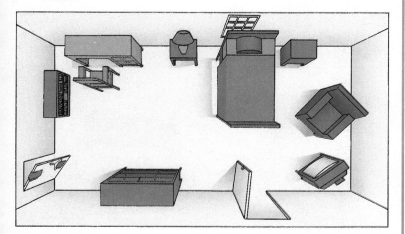

MODELO   **La lámpara** está en la mesita.

1. _____ está debajo de la ventana.
2. _____ está delante del escritorio.
3. _____ está detrás de la cama.
4. _____ están a la derecha y a la izquierda de la cama.
5. _____ está entre el armario y la puerta.
6. _____ está a la izquierda del armario.
7. _____ está al lado del televisor.
8. _____ está cerca de la puerta.

LECCIÓN 3

Prepositions of location
Used to tell where things or people are located

a la derecha de
a la izquierda de
al lado de
cerca de
lejos de
debajo de
encima de
sobre
delante de
enfrente de
detrás de
en
entre

Ponlo **encima de** la mesita.
Las zapatillas están **debajo de** la cama.

See ¿Por qué se dice así?, page G107, section 7.6.

trescientos cuarenta y nueve **349**

CH. ¡Pobrecito! Allow 2–3 min for students to work out answers individually. Then call on one student and have him or her give all eight commands. Have several other students give all the answers. The exact order will vary.
1 Llama a los invitados el domingo por la tarde.
2 Lleva las invitaciones al correo el lunes por la mañana.
3 Escoge la música para la fiesta el lunes por la tarde.
4 Ven a mi casa por los discos el martes por la tarde.
5 Ve al mercado para comprar refrescos el miércoles por la tarde.
6 Pon los refrescos en el refrigerador el jueves por la noche.
7 Pide las pizzas el viernes por la tarde.
8 Diles "Bienvenidos" a los invitados el viernes por la noche.

D. Me encanta mi cuarto.
Allow 2–3 min to do in pairs. Then call on individual students to give answers.
1 La cama está debajo de la ventana.
2 La silla está delante del escritorio.
3 La ventana está detrás de la cama.
4 Las mesitas están a la derecha y a la izquierda de la cama.
5 La cómoda está entre el armario y la puerta.
6 El estante está a la izquierda del armario.
7 El sillón está al lado del televisor.
8 El televisor está cerca de la puerta.

1 ¿Dónde ponemos el escritorio? Debemos ponerlo al lado de la puerta.

2 ¿Dónde ponemos la cama? Debemos ponerla entre las mesitas.

3 ¿Dónde ponemos el estante? Debemos ponerlo debajo de la ventana.

4 ¿Dónde ponemos el televisor? Debemos ponerlo cerca de la cómoda.

5 ¿Dónde ponemos la silla? Debemos ponerla enfrente del escritorio.

6 ¿Dónde ponemos la cómoda? Debemos ponerla al lado del televisor.

7 ¿Dónde ponemos las mesitas? Debemos ponerlas a la derecha y a la izquierda de la cama.

8 ¿Dónde ponemos la lámpara? Debemos ponerla sobre la mesita.

350 UNIDAD 7 *Lección 3*

E. ¿Qué decidió? Le pediste ayuda a un(a) amigo(a) a mover los muebles. ¿Qué dijo cuando le hiciste estas preguntas?

 MODELO

Tú: **¿Dónde ponemos el sillón?**

Compañero(a): **Debemos ponerlo enfrente del televisor.**

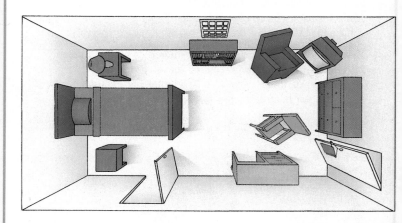

1.

2.

3.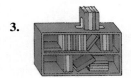

4.

5.

6.

7.

8.

F. Tengo mucha prisa. Tu amigo(a) tiene mucha prisa y no puede encontrar sus cosas. ¿Puedes ayudarlo(la)?

 MODELO   Compañero(a):   **No encuentro mi sombrero. ¿Lo ves por aquí?**

Tú: **Está en el piso.**

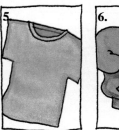 1.    2.    3.    4.

 5.    6.    7.    8.

LECCIÓN 3

F. Tengo mucha prisa.
Allow 2–3 min to do in pairs. Then call on individual students to give answers.

1 No encuentro mi suéter. ¿Lo ves por aquí? Está sobre la lámpara.
2 No encuentro mis pantalones. ¿Los ves por aquí? Están debajo de la cama.
3 No encuentro mi libro. ¿Lo ves por aquí? Está en el piso, entre la silla y el escritorio.
4 No encuentro mis zapatos. ¿Los ves por aquí? Están encima del escritorio.
5 No encuentro mi camiseta. ¿La ves por aquí? Está en la puerta.
6 No encuentro mi chaqueta. ¿La ves por aquí? Está en el piso al lado de la cama.
7 No encuentro mis calcetines. ¿Los ves por aquí? Están en la cama.
8 No encuentro mi mochila. ¿La ves por aquí? Está debajo de la silla.

Extension Have students repeat activity alternating roles.

G. ¿Dónde las pusiste?

Answers will vary.

1 ¿Dónde pusiste mis zapatillas?
Las puse . . .

2 ¿Dónde pusiste mis bolígrafos?
Los puse . . .

3 ¿Dónde pusiste mi reloj?
Lo puse . . .

4 ¿Dónde pusiste mis discos
compactos? Los puse . . .

5 ¿Dónde pusiste mi radio?
La puse . . .

6 ¿Dónde pusiste mi bata?
La puse . . .

7 ¿Dónde pusiste mis libros?
Los puse . . .

8 ¿Dónde pusiste mi mochila?
La puse . . .

H. ¡Trofeos! Call on individual
students.

1 Blanca puso su trofeo en la mesita.

2 Los hermanos Suárez pusieron su
trofeo entre las fotos.

3 Tú pusiste tu trofeo encima del
estante.

4 Sergio puso su trofeo debajo de la
lámpara.

5 Raquel y su hermano pusieron
sus trofeos al lado de una foto.

6 Yo puse mi trofeo a la izquierda
del televisor.

7 Joaquín puso su trofeo debajo de
la cama.

8 Carla puso su trofeo en el piso.

Poner

puse	pusimos
pusiste	
puso	pusieron
puso	pusieron

G. **¿Dónde las pusiste?** Para tu cumpleaños, tu hermano(a) limpió tu cuarto. El problema es que ahora no puedes encontrar varias cosas. Pregúntale dónde las puso.

 MODELO   cuaderno de biología

Tú: **¿Dónde pusiste mi cuaderno
de biología?**

Compañero(a): **Lo puse debajo de la cama.**

1. zapatillas   **4.** discos compactos   **7.** libros
2. bolígrafos   **5.** radio   **8.** mochila
3. reloj   **6.** bata

H. **¡Trofeos!** Todos los miembros del club atlético recibieron trofeos este año. ¿Dónde los pusieron?

MODELO

José y Anita
José y Anita pusieron sus trofeos en el escritorio.

1. Blanca

2. los hermanos Suárez

3. tú

4. Sergio

5. Raquel y su hermano

6. yo

7. Joaquín

8. Carla

CHARLEMOS UN POCO MÁS

A. La alcoba. Your teacher will give you and your partner drawings of a partially furnished bedroom. The rest of the furniture appears along the margin of the page. Ask your partner where to place the missing furniture and draw it where he or she tells you. Answer your partner's questions about the furniture that he or she needs to place in the bedroom. Don't look at each other's drawings!

EJEMPLO   Tú: **¿Dónde pongo la cama?**
          Compañero(a):   **Ponla entre las dos ventanas.**

B. ¿Dónde ponemos . . . ? During the summer break, your Spanish teacher is planning to rearrange the classroom. Describe where you think the furniture should be placed while your partner diagrams the new arrangement. **¡En español, por supuesto!**

C. ¿Qué es? Look around the classroom and select three specific items (e.g., a classmate's backpack, the teacher's pen, your jacket). Write down what they are. Do not let anyone see your list. In small groups, take turns giving the location of the items on your list without naming them. The other group members should try to identify them.

EJEMPLO   Tú: **Está detrás del escritorio de la profesora.**

CH. ¿Qué hiciste anoche? Write down everything you did between six and eight o'clock last night. Then, in groups of three or four, compare your lists of activities within the group. Make one list of the activities that all of you had in common. Then compare your group's list with those of other groups in the class. Now make a master list of all the activities everyone in the class had in common.

D. ¡Mandatos y más mandatos! Make a list in Spanish of all the commands your teachers have given you today. Compare your list with your partner's. On the chalkboard, write all the commands that both you and your partner listed.

CHARLEMOS UN POCO MÁS

A. La alcoba. Allow 10–15 min.

Extension Diagram your bedroom showing where all the furniture is placed and label it in Spanish. On another piece of paper diagram your bedroom again but draw only your bed. Give your partner the diagram with only your bed drawn in. Then, as you describe your bedroom, your partner will draw in the remaining furniture in the incomplete diagram. When you have finished, compare your partner's drawing to your own drawing of your bedroom.

B. ¿Dónde ponemos . . . ? Allow 8–10 min.

Extension After students have finished, have each pair exchange their drawings with another pair and repeat activity using the other pair's drawings.

Vocabulario opcional
proyector, grabadora, mapa, reloj de pared, cesto

C. ¿Qué es? Allow 10–12 min.

Expansion Have each group select the most difficult item presented among them. Then ask each group to present it for the rest of the class to guess.

CH. ¿Qué hiciste anoche? Allow 10–12 min. When groups start comparing with each other, have one student go to board and write the activities that all groups listed.

D. ¡Mandatos y más mandatos! To check for accuracy, go over quickly what students have written on board. Ask class to correct any errors.

Extension Tell students that since you are the one who usually tells them what to do, you are going to give them the opportunity to tell *you* what to do. Ask everyone to go to board and write a command telling you to do something. (They will have to use familiar commands.)

Purpose   These activities are designed to allow students to give commands and to give the location of people and things in a variety of possible combinations.

E. ¿Por qué no fuiste conmigo? Your friend wants to know why you didn't go with him or her last week to the places pictured under **Tú.** You want to know why your friend was not able to go with you to the places pictured under **Compañero(a).** Take turns giving excuses.

Tú

Compañero(a)

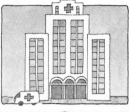

DRAMATIZACIONES

Dramatizaciones

A. ¡Ten cuidado! You are babysitting your little brother or sister. He or she has reached the questioning stage and is not very cooperative. Role-play this situation with a partner.

Tú	**Compañero(a)**
▪ Tell your partner to come here.	▪ Ask why.
▪ Say that you are both going to the store.	▪ Say that's okay.
▪ Tell him or her to wear a sweater.	▪ Ask why.
▪ Answer that it's cold.	▪ Ask when you are leaving.
▪ Tell him or her to be patient and to be careful.	▪ Ask why.
▪ Say that there is a lot of traffic.	▪ Ask why.
▪ Ask him or her to be good.	▪ Say okay.

B. ¡Pero, papá . . . ! Your parents have decided that you need to rearrange the furniture in your bedroom. As they suggest where to put certain items, you have conflicting ideas about where they should go. Role-play this situation with two classmates.

Purpose In *Dramatizaciones*, students recycle, in student-centered role plays, all previously learned structures and vocabulary needed to give commands. Encourage students to work without their books when preparing and performing their role plays.

LEAMOS AHORA

Reading strategy: Skimming

A. Anticipemos.   In this section, you will read about Miami. Before reading this selection, look at the photos and the title of the reading on the next two pages. Then answer the following questions.

1. What are two topics that you would expect to be developed in this reading?
2. What is one topic that you would like to have mentioned?
3. What do you expect will be the main message of this reading?

B. Hojeando.   Skimming means reading quickly in order to get the general idea of a passage. Skimming requires noting only information and clues that reveal the central theme or topic of a passage.

Now quickly skim through the first paragraph of **La maravilla de Miami.** Decide which phrase listed below with Párrafo 1 expresses the central theme of the first paragraph and which phrases are simply clues that provide an idea leading to the central theme. Then repeat the same process with the second and third paragraphs.

Párrafo 1
  a. El Hotel Intercontinental es latino.
  b. La joven de la recepción es latina.
  c. Miami es la ciudad más rica y moderna de Latinoamérica.
  ch. Los invitados van a beber champán, comer caviar y vestir los últimos diseños.
  d. "Estamos en la era del diseñador".

Párrafo 2
  a. El visitante latino queda sorprendido y agradado.
  b. El castellano se habla tanto en los círculos más humildes como en los más elegantes.
  c. El castellano es prácticamente el idioma oficial de Miami.
  ch. No es necesario hablar inglés.

Párrafo 3
  a. La Calle Ocho es la escena de una fabulosa fiesta en marzo.
  b. Los cubanos habitaron los barrios típicos como la Pequeña Habana.
  c. La transformación latina de Miami comenzó en los 60s.
  ch. Cubanos y otros latinoamericanos viven en todos los barrios de la ciudad.

C. Miami.   Read the selection on the next page and answer the questions that follow.

Leamos ahora is the principal reading of the unit. Its purpose is to teach students to skim paragraphs for their main ideas. Students are not expected to understand every word. Rather they should focus on looking for the central theme of each paragraph.

LEAMOS AHORA

A. Anticipemos.
Allow 2–3 min for students to write answers to these questions individually. Then in small groups have them compare answers to each question and come up with a group response to each question. After class reads the selection, come back and check if the group predictions were on target.

B. Hojeando.
Do as a class activity. Working in small groups, students should skim through the next two paragraphs in the reading and identify the central theme of each.

Answers

1 c
2 c
3 ch

La maravilla de Miami

La ciudad más rica y moderna de Latinoamérica está en Estados Unidos

El muchacho que recibe el coche a la entrada del Hotel Intercontinental es latino. Nada nuevo. La joven de la recepción también. Pero, eso no es todo. El ejecutivo que llegó en el Mercedes al baile de etiqueta de esta noche es latino, como lo son los demás invitados que van a beber champán, comer caviar y vestir los últimos diseños de Europa. "Estamos en la era del diseñador", como dice la canción humorística del famoso artista local Willy Chirino. Estamos en la ciudad más rica y moderna de Latinoamérica. Estamos en Miami.

El visitante latino en esta ciudad queda sorprendido—y agradado—por un detalle: no es necesario hablar inglés. El castellano es prácticamente el idioma oficial de Miami y se habla tanto en los círculos más humildes como en los más elegantes.

La transformación latina de Miami la comenzaron en los 60s los exiliados cubanos. Éstos habitaron los barrios típicos, como la Pequeña Habana, dominada por la famosa Calle Ocho *(S.W. Eighth Street)*. La Calle Ocho es la escena de una fabulosa fiesta en marzo. Hoy día, cubanos y otros latinoamericanos viven en todos los barrios de la ciudad.

En cualquier época es fabuloso visitar los restaurantes cubanos más auténticos de Miami. Éstos incluyen el Casablanca, donde predominan los temas políticos cubanos, el Versailles y La Carreta, donde todo el mundo va después del baile, o La Casa Juancho, donde se reúnen los políticos y economistas del Miami latino.

Pero para el visitante, Miami es la playa. Paseándose de norte a sur, se visita primero la playa de Bal Harbor, donde está uno de los centros comerciales más lujosos y contemporáneos de Miami. Luego se llega al fastuoso Hotel Fontainebleau, escena de tantas películas, y representativo del exceso y lujo de los 50s. Más al sur, en South Beach, se hallan las mejores discotecas, como Scratch, y los restaurantes de moda, como el Strand. De noche todo el mundo se viste de negro.

Pero aun aquí no hemos dejado el mundo latino. Estos muchachos con ropa tan *in* están conversando en español. ¿Por qué? ¡Porque son de la ciudad más rica y moderna de Latinoamérica—Miami!

Adapted from *Más* (invierno 1989)

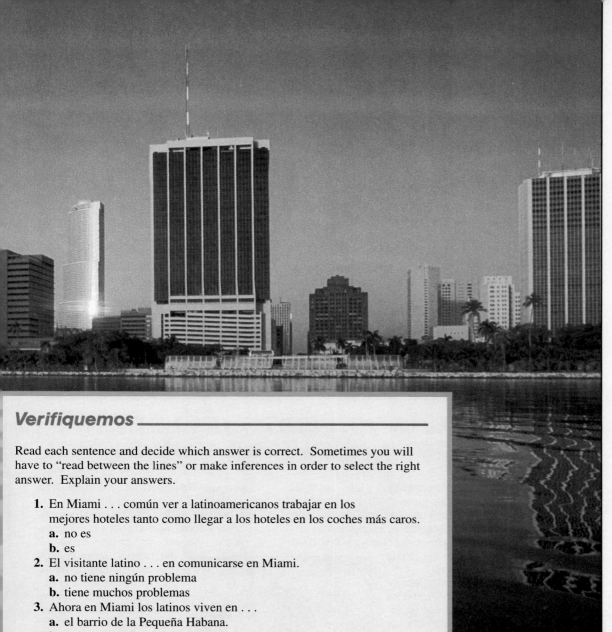

Verifiquemos

Read each sentence and decide which answer is correct. Sometimes you will have to "read between the lines" or make inferences in order to select the right answer. Explain your answers.

1. En Miami . . . común ver a latinoamericanos trabajar en los mejores hoteles tanto como llegar a los hoteles en los coches más caros.
   a. no es
   b. es
2. El visitante latino . . . en comunicarse en Miami.
   a. no tiene ningún problema
   b. tiene muchos problemas
3. Ahora en Miami los latinos viven en . . .
   a. el barrio de la Pequeña Habana.
   b. todas partes de la ciudad.
4. En Miami, después de ir a bailar un sábado por la noche, muchos latinos van a . . .
   a. discutir política en el Casablanca o en La Casa Juancho.
   b. comer algo en el Versailles o La Carreta.
5. En el Fontainebleau, Scratch y el Strand, todo el mundo se viste . . .
   a. de negro.
   b. de ropa *in*.

Verifiquemos

Answers

1 b
2 a
3 b
4 b
5 a and b

ESCRIBAMOS UN POCO

A. Empezando. Remind students that what they write will depend on for whom, why, and about what they are writing. Allow 3–4 min. Ask volunteers to answer the questions.

1 The dateline (**Bosque encantado**), name of the subject of the article (**Caperucita Roja**), day the events took place, the first of a sequence of events.

2 Paragraphs 2 and 3 continue the sequence of events, paragraph 4 gives a quote from **Caperucita**'s mother, paragraph 5 describes the consequences of the events.

3 Keep only the material that answers the questions *who? what? when? where? why?* For example, the mother's quote could be cut, as could the description of what **Caperucita** was bringing to her grandmother and why she was late in arriving at her grandmother's house.

4 The headline grabs the attention of the reader and summarizes the content of the article. The photo also gives the reader an idea of the events described in the article.

Writing strategy:
Retelling an event

A. Empezando. A newspaper reporter writes an article to retell an event. Read and discuss the newspaper article at the bottom of the page. Then answer the questions below.

1. What pieces of information are presented in the first paragraph?
2. What information is included in each of the next four paragraphs?
3. If the newspaper's editor had to shorten this article to fit a limited space, what would be the best way to cut the article without losing *essential* information?
4. What does the headline do? How does the "photo" add to the article?

¡LEÑADOR MATA UN LOBO Y RESCATA A ABUELA Y SU NIETA!

Bosque Encantado. La jovencita, Caperucita Roja, fue a visitar a su abuela el sábado. Le llevó una canastita de bizcocho y chocolate. Según ella, en camino se encontró con el lobo, pero esto no le preocupó porque el lobo le dijo que no tenía hambre.

La señorita Caperucita Roja tardó un poco más de lo normal en llegar a la casa de su abuela porque se detuvo a recoger flores en el bosque. Cuando llegó, vio que su abuela estaba en cama. Le pareció extraño porque su abuela tenía los ojos, las orejas y los dientes demasiado grandes. Pronto descubrió que no era su abuela sino el lobo en los pijamas de

su abuela. Gritó, pero el lobo no le hizo caso y empezó a comerse el bizcocho.

A este punto, Chucho Cortabosques la oyó gritar y corrió rápidamente a la casita de la abuela. Allí encontró al lobo comiendo bizcocho y tomando chocolate. Inmediatamente lo mató y rescató a la señorita Caperucita Roja y a su abuela, aterrorizadas, pero en buena salud.

"Yo siempre le digo a mi hija que no se detenga a hablar con desconocidos", dijo la madre de la jovencita. "¡Tal vez ahora va a creerme!"

El señor Cortabosques va a recibir una medalla de honor en una ceremonia especial en el ayuntamiento el martes próximo a las 8:00 de la noche.

Purpose In this section, students are asked to apply speaking and writing skills developed in the unit to a real-life writing task: here, a short news article. They will use strategies they began to develop in Unit 1: prewriting brainstorming and clustering, writing a first draft, peer feedback, and revision.

B. Planeando. Now you will write a short article reporting a recent event that you witnessed. If you'd rather, you may choose to be another kind of editor and write about a different topic. For example:

- A society editor (the wedding in Unit 4)
- A travel editor (Víctor and Manolo's trip to Madrid in Unit 5 or Mónica's trip to Guadalajara in Unit 6)
- A sports editor (the soccer game in this unit)

Think about the key pieces of information you must include about the event: **quién, qué, dónde, cuándo** y **por qué.** Think about description, details, and additional information that will make your article more interesting to your readers. Brainstorm a list of vocabulary you may need to write your article.

C. Organizando. Make a cluster diagram to help you organize before you write. Put the headline in the main circle, with the five vital pieces of information supporting it. Then cluster details and further explanations. Rank your supporting paragraph ideas from most to least important, and write your article in that order.

CH. Escribiendo. Use your cluster diagram to write the first draft of your article. Include as much information as possible, remembering that the least important information should come last, in case your editor in chief has to shorten your article.

D. Compartiendo. Share your draft with two or three classmates. Is there anything they don't understand? Is there information you should have included? Is there anything they think you should change?

E. Revisando. Revise and refine your article based on your classmates' suggestions. Before you publish your final version, share your article with two more classmates. This time ask them to edit for grammar, spelling, and punctuation.

B. Planeando. Remind students that they learned about brainstorming in Unit 1. You may want to brainstorm as a class activity, having volunteers list words and ideas on the board as they are called out. Ask students to make brainstorming suggestions in Spanish. Remind them that when brainstorming, all ideas are accepted—they will select those they want to use later.

C. Organizando. Allow 5–6 minutes for students to make their own clusters or outlines. Ask volunteers to tell what they have included and how they have grouped ideas. Encourage students to add to clusters as they hear ideas from others.

CH. Escribiendo. Allow students time to write their first draft. Provide guidance where necessary. You may want to assign the first draft as homework.

D. Compartiendo. Have students gather in "response groups" of two or three. Allow them time to share articles. Encourage them to comment on content, structure, and vocabulary. Remind group members to begin commentary with at least one positive comment, and then to make constructive suggestions.

E. Revisando. Tell students you will grade the composition holistically, based on overall effectiveness of communication. Underline grammatical errors if you wish, but the grade should be affected only by errors that would confuse a native speaker accustomed to the writing of a nonnative. At this stage, students should develop a sense that they can already write something a Spanish speaker would enjoy reading.

UNIT OBJECTIVES

Communicative Goals

When students have completed this unit, they will be able to use Spanish . . .
- to describe daily routines
- to describe how things are done
- to name foods
- to name and describe rooms in a house
- to express extremes
- to make comparisons
- to describe what is happening at the moment
- to tell what they usually do
- to describe what happened

Culture

In this unit, students will discover similarities and differences between the United States and Hispanic countries . . .
- in how the names of foods vary
- in mealtimes
- in the concept of punctuality
- while viewing the **Acueducto** and the **Alcázar** in Segovia
- in recipes for **gazpacho** and **tortilla española**

Reading and Writing Strategies

- Reading: Reading for detailed information
- Writing: Retelling a story

Structure

- Reflexive pronouns
- Adverbs
- Preterite of **estar**
- Absolute superlatives: **-ísimo**
- Comparatives
- Summary of present tense, present progressive, and preterite

¡En camino a Segovia!

UNIDAD 8

UNIT SETTING

Segovia lies on a hilltop surrounded by the Eresma and Clamores rivers in north central Spain. It was already over 700 years old when the Romans settled there around 80 B.C. Since then it has been home to many monarchs including Alfonso X el Sabio, Isabel la Católica, Carlos III, and Alfonso VI. From its glorious past, the famous **Acueducto**—Segovia's symbol—has survived the passage of time as a unique example of Roman engineering. Segovia's Gothic cathedral dates back to the middle of the sixteenth century. Built on the highest part

Video Notes

To play the montage:

| 20:43 | – | 21:25 |

‖‖‖‖‖‖‖‖‖‖‖‖‖‖‖‖‖‖‖

Side 8, 10 to 1265

To play the entire unit without stopping:

| 20:43 | – | 48:36 |

‖‖‖‖‖‖‖‖‖‖‖‖‖‖‖‖‖‖‖

Side 8, 10 to 50153

In the video, you will hear examples of the Spanish spoken in Madrid and in the north of Spain. Notice that the mother (but not the father) pronounces the **s** with an extreme retroflexing of the tongue tip, making the **s** sound rather "mushy." This pronunciation is a tendency in Madrid, but it becomes more consistent and generalized as you go northwest in the direction of Asturias. Notice too how the **ll** of **tortilla**, **cuchillo**, and **cochinillo** is consistently pronounced like the *dg* of *edge*, as is the **y**. In the northern two-thirds of Spain, the **z** and the soft **c** are given the *th*-like pronunciation of *thin*, which is kept distinct from the **s**.

Photo

The **Acueducto de Segovia,** which was built by the Romans, was still supplying water to Segovia during the first half of this century. The most impressive monument of its kind, the **Acueducto** is 728 meters long and consists of 167 archways reaching a height of 28.29 meters. Although the exact date of its construction is unknown, modern research places it during the reigns of the emperors Vespasian and Trajan, in the second half of the first century and the early part of the second century. This colossal piece of engineering stands as an eloquent testimonial to the architectural genius of Rome.

of the city, the "Lady of Spanish cathedrals," as it has come to be called, provides a panoramic view of the surrounding countryside. The **Alcázar**, perched on a rocky crag between the confluence of the Eresma and the Clamores, is a prime example of twelfth-century Castillian architecture. With its illustrious history, its cathedral, its Romanesque convents and monasteries, and its great wealth of monuments, Segovia ranks among Spain's most beautiful and interesting cities.

OBJECTIVES

Communicative Goals

- Describing daily routine
- Describing how things are done
- Naming foods

Culture and Reading

- *¡No me digas!*
  ¡Es una tortilla!
  Confusion caused by lexical differences
- *Y ahora, ¡a leer!*
  ¿Durazno o melocotón?
  Lexical variation in the names of foods

Structure

- **8.1** Reflexive pronouns
- **8.2** Adverbs

ACTIVE VOCABULARY

Rutina diaria

acostarse	lavarse
afeitarse	levantarse
arreglarse	peinarse
bañarse	pintarse
cepillarse	ponerse
despertarse (ie)	quitarse
divertirse (ie, i)	sentarse (ie)
dormirse (ue, u)	vestirse (i, i)
irse	

Comidas

bocadillo	mermelada
cebolla	mostaza
chorizo	pan
ensaladilla	pimienta
… rusa	puré de tomate
huevo	sal
lechuga	tomate
mantequilla	tortilla
mayonesa	

Cubiertos

copa	servilleta
cubiertos	taza
cuchara	tenedor
cuchillo	vaso
platillo	poner la mesa
plato	

Cocina

estufa   mesa   nevera

¡Es hora de levantarte!

Adverbios

alegremente	impacientemente
constantemente	lentamente
cuidadosamente	rápidamente
fácilmente	tristemente
formalmente	

Verbos

cancelar
desayunar
empacar
faltar

Complementos reflexivos

me	nos
te	se
se	

Palabras y expresiones

corto(a)	¿Algo más?
espejo	¡Cállate!
luego	¡Qué guapa
temprano	
todavía	

ANTICIPEMOS

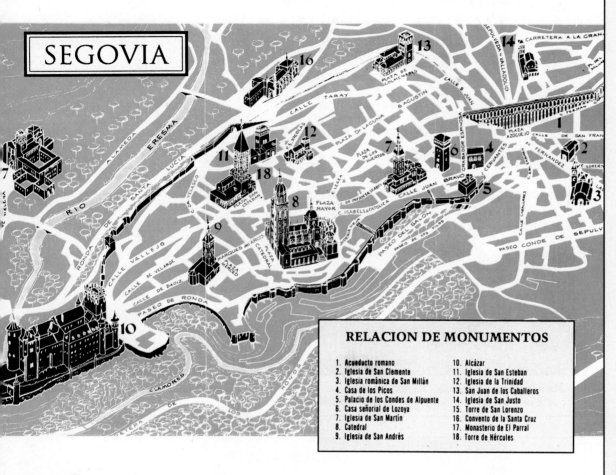

SEGOVIA

RELACION DE MONUMENTOS

1. Acueducto romano
2. Iglesia de San Clemente
3. Iglesia románica de San Millán
4. Casa de los Picos
5. Palacio de los Condes de Alpuente
6. Casa señorial de Lozoya
7. Iglesia de San Martín
8. Catedral
9. Iglesia de San Andrés
10. Alcázar
11. Iglesia de San Esteban
12. Iglesia de la Trinidad
13. San Juan de los Caballeros
14. Iglesia de San Justo
15. Torre de San Lorenzo
16. Convento de la Santa Cruz
17. Monasterio de El Parral
18. Torre de Hércules

¿Qué piensas tú?

1. ¿Qué tiene que hacer la chica en la foto para estar lista a las 8:30?

2. ¿Cómo tiene que hacer estas cosas?

3. ¿Qué tiene que hacer el chico en la foto para estar listo a las 8:30?

4. ¿Cómo va a tener que hacer estas cosas?

5. ¿Cuál es la ciudad en este mapa?

6. ¿Qué lugares en el mapa te gustaría visitar? ¿Por qué?

7. ¿De qué vas a poder hablar al final de la lección?

¿Qué piensas tú?

If students answer questions in English, paraphrase their answers in Spanish, providing them with the new vocabulary they will be learning.

Answers

1 Las respuestas van a variar.
Vocabulario nuevo: despertarse, levantarse, bañarse, pintarse, vestirse, peinarse, desayunar, cepillarse los dientes, etc.

2 Las respuestas van a variar.
Vocabulario nuevo: levantarse lentamente, pintarse cuidadosamente, vestirse y desayunar rápidamente, etc.

3 Las respuestas van a variar.
Vocabulario nuevo: ducharse, afeitarse, vestirse, desayunar, cepillarse los dientes, peinarse, etc.

4 Las respuestas van a variar.
Vocabulario nuevo: vestirse y desayunar rápidamente, etc.

5 Segovia.

6 Las respuestas van a variar. Es probable que seleccionen lugares como el Acueducto romano, el Alcázar, la catedral, etc.

7 **Podrán hablar de la rutina diaria, de cómo hacen varias cosas y de Segovia.**

Purpose To focus students on language related to describing daily routines and how things are done, and to encourage students to use critical thinking skills as they observe and compare differences and similarities in a map of a region of Spain.

Suggestions Use the illustrations as an advance organizer. Have students explain their answers. Help them discover cross-cultural similarities in reading the map of Spain.

21:26–
25:23

 Side 8, 1299 to 8427

Comprehension Checks

A full set of the **Comprehension Checks** is available on cards in the Teacher's Resource Package.

1   21:33

1 ¿Quién es?
2 ¿Dónde viven Marta y su familia?
3 ¿Va a una fiesta esta tarde?
4 ¿Dónde es la fiesta, en su casa o en casa de su amiga?
5 ¿Qué hora es?
6 ¿Está durmiendo la siesta Marta?
7 ¿Qué está haciendo Marta?

Side 8, 1512 to 2028

2   21:51

Suggestions Have a couple of students pretend to be sleeping. Then go up to each one and say **¡Despiértate!** Mime getting ready = **arreglarse** and getting up slowly = **lentamente.**

1 ¿Quién es? *(Point to Marta, her mother, and her sister.)*
2 ¿Quién dice "Despiértate, hija", su mamá o su hermana?
3 ¿Qué dice su mamá?
4 ¿Qué hora es?
5 ¿A qué hora es la fiesta, a las seis o a las siete?
6 ¿Todavía tiene que arreglarse Marta?
7 ¿Qué tiene que hacer Marta?
8 ¿Cómo se levanta Marta, rápida o lentamente?
9 ¿Va a su cuarto?
10 ¿Adónde va?

Side 8, 2040 to 2818

3   22:17

Suggestions Mime undressing = **quitarse la ropa** and bathing = **bañarse.** Gesture *Go away!* = **¡Quítate!**

1 ¿Se quita la ropa Marta?
2 ¿Qué se quita Marta?

364   UNIDAD 8   Lección 1

Marta Molina y su familia viven en Madrid.

1 Esta tarde, Marta va a una fiesta en casa de su amiga Inés, pero ya son las seis y Marta todavía está durmiendo la siesta.

Ven a mi casa. Hay una fiesta el viernes a las 19:00 Inés

2

Mamá: *Despiértate, hija. Ya son las seis. La fiesta es a las siete y todavía tienes que arreglarte.*

Marta se levanta lentamente y va a su cuarto.

3

Se quita la ropa para bañarse.

Marta: *Tere, ¡quítate! No tengo tiempo para hablar ahora. Tengo prisa.*

---

3 ¿Va a bañarse?
4 ¿Qué va a hacer?
5 ¿Es Marta / Tere?
6 ¿Quién dice "¡quítate!"?
7 ¿Qué dice Marta?
8 ¿Tiene Marta tiempo para hablar ahora?
9 ¿Tiene prisa?
10 ¿Por qué no tiene tiempo para hablar ahora?

Side 8, 2837 to 3535

Purpose This section sets the context for the language needed to talk about daily routines and provides comprehensible language without translation.

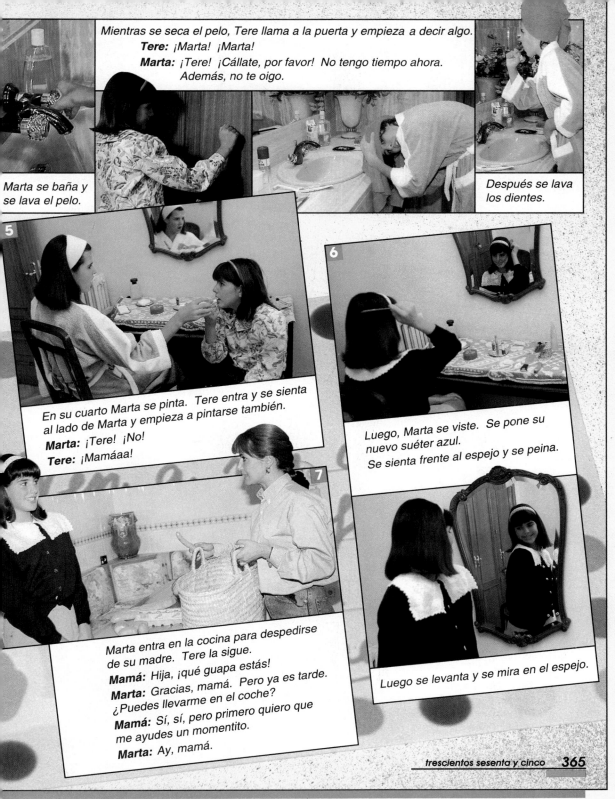

Mientras se seca el pelo, Tere llama a la puerta y empieza a decir algo.
Tere: ¡Marta! ¡Marta!
Marta: ¡Tere! ¡Cállate, por favor! No tengo tiempo ahora.
Además, no te oigo.

Marta se baña y se lava el pelo.

Después se lava los dientes.

5

En su cuarto Marta se pinta. Tere entra y se sienta al lado de Marta y empieza a pintarse también.
Marta: ¡Tere! ¡No!
Tere: ¡Mamáaa!

6

Luego, Marta se viste. Se pone su nuevo suéter azul.
Se sienta frente al espejo y se peina.

Luego se levanta y se mira en el espejo.

7

Marta entra en la cocina para despedirse de su madre. Tere la sigue.
Mamá: Hija, ¡qué guapa estás!
Marta: Gracias, mamá. Pero ya es tarde.
¿Puedes llevarme en el coche?
Mamá: Sí, sí, pero primero quiero que me ayudes un momentito.
Marta: Ay, mamá.

trescientos sesenta y cinco **365**

Suggestions Mime washing/drying hair = **lavarse/secarse el pelo.** Point out how you always have to tell [noisy student(s) in class] to be quiet = **¡Cállate!** Mime brushing teeth = **lavarse los dientes.**

1 ¿Se baña Marta? ¿Se lava el pelo?
2 ¿Qué hace Marta?
3 ¿Ahora, se seca el pelo Marta?
4 ¿Qué hace Marta?
5 ¿Llama Tere a la puerta?
6 ¿Empieza a decir algo Tere?
7 ¿Qué empieza a hacer Tere?
8 ¿Quién dice "Cállate"?
9 ¿Qué dice Marta?
10 ¿Tiene tiempo Marta para hablar con Tere?
11 ¿Oye Marta a Tere?
12 ¿Se lava los dientes Marta?
13 ¿Qué hace Marta?

Side 8, 3567 to 4815

5 | 23:24

Suggestion Mime putting on makeup = **pintarse.**

1 ¿Están Marta y Tere en el cuarto de Marta?
2 ¿Se pinta Marta? ¿Te pintas tú? *(Ask several students.)*
3 ¿Qué hace Marta?
4 ¿Se sienta Tere al lado de Marta?
5 ¿Dónde se sienta Tere?
6 ¿Empieza a pintarse Tere?
7 ¿Qué empieza a hacer Tere?
8 ¿Quién dice "¡No!"?
9 ¿Llama Tere a su mamá?

Side 8, 4842 to 5225

6 | 23:38

Suggestions Mime getting dressed = **vestirse.** Draw mirror on board and mime looking at self and combing hair = **peinarse.**

1 ¿Se viste Marta?
2 ¿Se pone su nuevo suéter azul?
3 ¿Qué se pone?
4 ¿Se sienta frente al espejo?
5 ¿Dónde se sienta?
6 ¿Se peina?
7 ¿Qué hace frente al espejo?
8 ¿Se levanta y se mira en el espejo?

Side 8, 5255 to 5823

Suggestions Begin by having students close their books while you narrate one section at a time, using the transparencies to clarify meaning without translation. Then ask **Comprehension Checks.** Repeat this process with each section.

Using the video Play one section at a time after narrating it using the transparencies. Freeze the video and ask **Comprehension Checks.** Repeat with each section.

7 | 23:58

Suggestion Mime waving goodbye = **despedirse.**

1 ¿Quién es? *(Point to each.)*
2 ¿Entra Marta en la cocina?
3 ¿Quiere despedirse de su mamá?
4 ¿Qué quiere hacer Marta?
5 ¿Entra Tere en la cocina también?
Continue asking questions, as above.

Side 8, 5843 to 6455

Suggestions
Point out **ensaladilla rusa**
= **ensalada de . . .** and **tortilla**
= **omelete de . . .** [point to each
ingredient as you name it]. Point to
other foods as they are named.
1 ¿Tiene todo para la excursión la
   mamá?
2 ¿Adónde van de excursión, a
   Madrid o a Segovia?
3 ¿Tiene la ensaladilla? ¿la tortilla?
   ¿el chorizo? ¿el pan?
4 ¿Qué dice Tere que faltan, los
   bocadillos o los cubiertos?
5 ¿Faltan las cucharas?
   ¿los tenedores? ¿los cuchillos?
   ¿las servilletas? ¿los vasos?
   ¿los platos?

Side 8, 6477 to 7335

9   24:48

Suggestions Point to and name
each food item. Say you eat breakfast at 7:00 A.M. = **desayuno.** Point
to what you eat for breakfast.
1 ¿Quién dice "Mira", Tere o su
   madre?
2 ¿Está listo el desayuno para
   mañana?
3 ¿Hay pan para el desayuno?
   ¿mantequilla? ¿mermelada?
4 ¿Tiene que irse Marta?

Side 8, 7363 to 7715

10   25:01

1 ¿Quiere decirle Tere algo a Marta?
2 ¿Tiene prisa Marta?
3 ¿Adónde va Marta?
4 ¿Dice Tere que no hay fiesta?
5 ¿Llamó la madre de la amiga de
   Marta?
6 ¿Está enferma la amiga de Marta?
7 ¿Hay fiesta esta tarde?

Side 8, 7739 to 8427

Mamá: Mira, aquí tengo todo para la excursión
a Segovia mañana: la ensaladilla rusa, la tortilla,
el chorizo y el pan para los bocadillos . . .
¿Falta algo más?

Tere: Sí, faltan los cubiertos: las cucharas, los
tenedores, los cuchillos y también las servilletas,
los vasos, y los platos . . .
Mamá: Ya, Tere.

Mamá: Mira, hasta el desayuno para mañana está
listo: el pan, la mantequilla, la mermelada . . .
Marta: ¡Mamá! ¡Tengo que irme!

Marta: ¡Tere! ¿Qué
quieres? ¡Tengo prisa!
Tere: Quiero decirte
que no hay fiesta.
Marta: ¿Cómo? ¿No
hay fiesta?
Tere: No. La madre
de Inés llamó y dijo que
Inés está enferma y que
no hay fiesta esta tarde.

¿QUÉ DECIMOS...?

Al describir la rutina diaria

1 *Un día muy especial.*

ESTA MAÑANA, COMO TODAS LAS MAÑANAS, ANDRÉS MOLINA SE DESPIERTA MUY TEMPRANO...

...Y SE LEVANTA INMEDIATAMENTE.

SE VISTE RÁPIDAMENTE.

SE LAVA LOS DIENTES...

...SE PONE EL RELOJ...

...Y SALE A CORRER.

PERO HOY NO ES UN DÍA TÍPICO. HOY LA FAMILIA MOLINA PIENSA HACER UNA EXCURSIÓN A SEGOVIA.

ENTONCES, ¿DÓNDE ESTÁN LOS OTROS? ¿TODAVÍA ESTÁN DURMIENDO?

trescientos sesenta y siete **367**

¿QUÉ DECIMOS...?

25:25–30:22

Side 8, 8459 to 17384

Early Production Checks

A full set of the the **Early Production Checks** is available on cards in the Teacher's Resource Package.

1 　　　　　　**25:30**

Un día muy especial.

1 ¿Es un día muy especial? *Sí.*
2 ¿Qué tipo de día es? *Muy especial.*
3 ¿Es por la mañana o por la tarde? *Por la mañana.*
4 ¿Es Andrés Molina? *Sí.*
5 ¿Se despierta muy temprano o muy tarde? *Muy temprano.*
6 Y tú, ¿te despiertas temprano o tarde? *(Ask several students.)*
7 ¿Se levanta inmediatamente? *Sí.*
8 ¿Cómo se viste, rápida o lentamente? *Rápidamente.*
9 ¿Se pone el reloj? *Sí.*
10 ¿Qué se pone? *El reloj.*
11 ¿Sale a correr? *Sí.*
12 ¿Qué hace Andrés? *Sale a correr.*
13 ¿Es un día típico hoy? ¿Es un día especial? *No. / Sí.*
14 ¿Piensa hacer la familia Molina una excursión a Segovia? *Sí.*
15 ¿Qué piensa hacer la familia Molina? *Una excursión.*
16 ¿Dónde está el resto de la familia, corriendo o durmiendo? *Durmiendo.*

Side 8, 8600 to 10655

Purpose This section describes daily routines in real-life situations. Students should not be overly concerned with understanding or translating every word. The **Early Production Checks** will help to identify the language they will need to describe how they go about doing their daily routines

Suggestions Begin by having students close their books while you narrate one section at a time, using the transparencies to clarify meaning without translation. Then ask the **Early Production Checks.** Repeat this process with each section.

Using the video Play one section at a time after narrating it using the transparencies. Freeze the video and ask the **Early Production Checks**. Repeat with each section.

2

26:39

Ya me levanto.

Accept brief phrases or one- and two-word answers to all Early Production Check questions, as shown in **1** on page 367. It is not necessary for students to answer in complete sentences.

1 ¿Quién es? *(Point to Marta, then to Tere.)*
2 ¿Quién dice "despiértate"?
3 ¿Qué dice Tere?
4 ¿Quién dice "¡Cállate! ¡Quítate!"?
5 ¿Qué dice Marta?
6 ¿Van de excursión hoy?
7 ¿Quién dice "¡Es hora de levantarte!", Tere o su mamá?
8 ¿Qué dice la mamá?
9 ¿Desayunan en quince o en diez minutos?
10 ¿Se levanta Marta? ¿Se levanta rápida o lentamente?
11 ¿Quién dice "arréglate"?
12 ¿Qué dice la madre?
13 ¿Tiene que lavarse el pelo Marta?
14 ¿Tiene que pintarse?
15 ¿Se lava el pelo Marta con frecuencia?
16 ¿Puede entrar en el baño Marta?
17 ¿Está su papá afeitándose?
18 ¿Qué está haciendo el papá de Marta?
19 ¿Quién vuelve a la casa, Andrés o Tere?
20 ¿Se quita la ropa? ¿Se baña?

Side 8, 10685 to 13177

3

28:03

Pásame el pan.

1 ¿Se sienta la familia a la mesa?
2 ¿Quién falta?
3 ¿Quién dice "¡Marta! ¡Ven!", la mamá o el papá?
4 ¿Tiene que secarse el pelo Marta?
5 ¿Qué tiene que hacer Marta?
6 ¿Quién tiene que darse prisa?
7 ¿Qué se va a enfriar, el café o el chocolate?
8 ¿Está muy guapa Marta?
9 ¿Quién dice que está muy guapa?
10 ¿Quién dice "Pásame el pan", Marta o Andrés?
11 ¿Qué dice Marta?
12 ¿Quiere mantequilla Marta? ¿y mermelada también?
13 ¿Quiere algo más el padre?
14 ¿Qué quiere el padre?

Side 8, 13211 to 14581

368 UNIDAD 8 Lección 1

2 Ya me levanto.

3 Pásame el pan.

Corta el chorizo.

Point out The word **refrigerador** is used as a synonym of **nevera**.

1 ¿Quién es? *(Point to Marta, then to mamá.)*
2 ¿Le ayuda Marta a su mamá?
3 ¿Es chorizo? ¿pan? ¿la ensaladilla rusa? *(Point to each.)*
4 ¿Quiere ayudar Tere?
5 ¿Qué va a traer Tere, la mayonesa o el pan?
6 ¿Dónde está la mayonesa, en la mesa o en la nevera?
7 ¿Qué está en la nevera?
8 ¿Va a traer los cubiertos Tere?
9 ¿Qué va a traer Tere?
10 ¿Cuántas cucharas necesitan? ¿tenedores? ¿cuchillos? ¿platos y vasos? ¿servilletas?
11 ¿Ya está la ensaladilla rusa?
12 ¿Quién la preparó, Marta o Tere?
13 ¿Quién dice "corta el chorizo"?
14 ¿Qué dice la madre?
15 ¿Para cuántas personas hay fruta?

Side 8, 14615 to 17384

LECCIÓN 1

A. ¿Qué hacen primero?
Allow 2 min. Then call on volunteer to give the correct order. Ask class to confirm his or her ordering.

1 Se despiertan temprano. (5)
2 Se levantan y se bañan. (8)
3 Se visten. (3)
4 Se sientan a la mesa para desayunar. (2)
5 Todos toman pan y chocolate o café. (7)
6 Se lavan los dientes después de comer. (1)
7 Preparan el almuerzo. (4)
8 Empacan los cubiertos. (6)

Variation Have students work in pairs while doing the ordering.

B. Primero me pongo . . .
Allow 2 min for individual work. Then call on individual students. Some answers may vary.

1 Qué te pones primero, el traje de baño o las sandalias? Primero, me pongo el traje de baño.
2 Qué te pones primero, los pantalones o los zapatos? Primero, me pongo los pantalones.
3 Qué te pones primero, la camiseta o los pantalones cortos? Primero, me pongo los pantalones cortos.
4 Qué te pones primero, la chaqueta o los calcetines? Primero, me pongo los calcetines.
5 Qué te pones primero, el suéter o la camisa? Primero, me pongo la camisa.
6 Qué te pones primero, el sombrero o las gafas de sol? Primero, me pongo el sombrero.

CHARLEMOS UN POCO

A. ¿Qué hacen primero? ¿Cómo se preparan los miembros de la familia Molina para hacer una excursión? Pon en orden cronológico esta lista de actividades.

1. Se lavan los dientes después de comer.
2. Se sientan a la mesa para desayunar.
3. Se visten.
4. Preparan el almuerzo.
5. Se despiertan temprano
6. Empacan los cubiertos.
7. Todos toman pan y chocolate o café.
8. Se levantan y se bañan.

B. Primero me pongo... Pregúntale a un(a) compañero(a) qué ropa se pone primero.

 MODELO   Tú: **¿Qué te pones primero, los zapatos o los calcetines?**
             Compañero(a): **Primero, me pongo los calcetines.**

1.   **2.**   **3.**

4.   **5.**   **6.**

Purpose These activities provide guided practice to students as they begin to produce to describe daily routine and how things are done.

C. ¿Qué me pongo? Según María, ¿qué se ponen ella y su familia para pasar la tarde en el parque?

MODELO hermano: ¿una camisa o una camiseta?
Mi hermano se pone una camiseta.

1. mamá: ¿un vestido elegante o pantalones?
2. papá: ¿un traje o unos jeans?
3. hermanos: ¿sandalias o zapatos elegantes?
4. yo: ¿pantalones cortos o un vestido?
5. mamá y papá: ¿gafas de leer o gafas de sol?
6. papá y yo: ¿pantalones cortos o pantalones largos?
7. hermana: ¿zapatos deportivos o sandalias?
8. todos: ¿suéteres o impermeables?

CH. ¡Buenos días! La familia de Carlos sigue la misma rutina todos los días. Según Carlos, ¿qué hacen todos?

MODELO papá / despertarse a las 6:00
Papá se despierta a las seis.

1. nosotros / levantarse temprano
2. yo / ponerse / pantalones cortos
3. tú / vestirse antes de comer
4. mi hermana / bañarse primero y / luego lavarse los dientes
5. papá / afeitarse primero y / luego lavarse el pelo
6. mamá y papá / sentarse a tomar el café
7. Roberto / acostarse temprano
8. por la noche, todos / dormirse inmediatamente

LECCIÓN 1

Reflexive Pronouns

me pongo	nos ponemos
te pones	
se pone	se ponen
se pone	se ponen

See **¿Por qué se dice así?,** *page G110, section 8.1.*

C. ¿Qué me pongo? Allow 2–3 min for pair work. Then call on several pairs to do each item. Answers may vary.

1 Mamá se pone pantalones.
2 Papá se pone jeans.
3 Mis hermanos se ponen sandalias.
4 Yo me pongo un vestido.
5 Mamá y papá se ponen gafas de sol.
6 Papá y yo nos ponemos pantalones largos.
7 Mi hermana se pone zapatos deportivos.
8 Todos nos ponemos suéteres.

CH. ¡Buenos días! First have students work in pairs. Allow 2 min. Then redo with whole class.
1 Nosotros nos levantamos temprano.
2 Yo me pongo pantalones cortos.
3 Tú te vistes antes de comer.
4 Mi hermana se baña primero y luego se lava los dientes.
5 Papá se afeita primero y luego se lava el pelo.
6 Mamá y papá se sientan a tomar el café.
7 Roberto se acuesta temprano.
8 Por la noche, todos se duermen inmediatamente.

Suggestions These activities may first be done in pairs and then repeated with the whole class, calling on individuals.

D. ¡Mando yo! Allow 2 min for students to do individually. Then call on individuals.

1 Levántate. Ya son las siete menos cuarto.
2 Vístete. Ya son las siete menos diez.
3 Siéntate a la mesa. Ya son las siete.
4 Lávate los dientes. Ya son las siete y cuarto.
5 Ponte el abrigo. Ya son las siete y veinticinco.
6 Haz la tarea. Ya son las cuatro.
7 Quítate la ropa y báñate. Ya son las nueve y cuarto.
8 Acuéstate y duérmete. Ya son las nueve y media.

E. ¿Y tú? Allow 2–3 min for pair work. Then ask individual students at what time their partner did any of the activities listed.

1 ¿A qué hora te levantaste ayer? Me levanté a . . .
2 ¿A qué hora te bañaste ayer? Me bañé a . . .
3 ¿A qué hora te peinaste ayer? Me peiné a . . .
4 ¿A qué hora te desayunaste ayer? Me desayuné a . . .
5 ¿A qué hora saliste para la escuela ayer? Salí para la escuela a . . .
6 ¿A qué hora te sentaste en tu primera clase ayer? Me senté en mi primera clase a . . .
7 ¿A qué hora regresaste a casa ayer? Regresé a casa a . . .
8 ¿A qué hora te acostaste ayer? Me acosté a . . .

F. Ve a la tienda. Allow 2 min for students to prepare individually. Then call on individuals to read one sentence at a time.

1 inmediatamente
2 directamente
3 Solamente
4 pacientemente
5 cortésmente
6 cuidadosamente
7 lentamente

Expansion After having gone through the paragraph one sentence at a time, ask a number of comprehension questions: **¿Cuándo sale Angelita? ¿Va a varias tiendas? ¿Necesita varias cosas la madre de Angelita? ¿Cómo espera Angelita?** etc.

Reflexive pronouns: Placement

Like object pronouns, reflexive pronouns may follow and be attached to an infinitive, an affirmative command, or the **-ndo** form of a verb.

¿Qué van a pone**rse** ustedes?
Acuésta**te** temprano.
Estamos durmiéndo**nos** aquí.

See **¿Por qué se dice así?,** *page G110, section 8.1.*

Adverbs

Adverbs answer the questions *how,* *when,* and *where* about the verb. Most adverbs that tell *how* an action is done are formed by adding **-mente** to the end of the feminine form of an adjective.

rápida + **-mente** rápidamente
alegre + **-mente** alegremente

See **¿Por qué se dice así?,** *page G113, section 8.2.*

D. ¡Mando yo! Tus papás no están en casa y por un día mandas tú. ¿Qué le dices a tú hermanito(a)?

MODELO 6:30 despertarse
Despiértate. Ya son las seis y media.

1. 6:45 levantarse
2. 6:50 vestirse
3. 7:00 sentarse a la mesa
4. 7:15 lavarse los dientes
5. 7:25 ponerse el abrigo
6. 4:00 hacer la tarea
7. 9:15 quitarse la ropa y bañarse
8. 9:30 acostarse y dormirse

E. ¿Y tú? Pregúntale a tu compañero(a) acerca de su rutina ayer.

MODELO despertarse
Tú: **¿A qué hora te despertaste ayer?**
Compañero(a): **Me desperté a . . .**

1. levantarse
2. bañarse
3. peinarse
4. desayunar
5. salir para la escuela
6. sentarse en su primera clase
7. regresar a casa
8. acostarse

F. Ve a la tienda. La mamá de Angelita quiere preparar una tortilla española pero no hay huevos. ¿Qué le dice a Angelita?

MODELO rápido
Ven acá **rápidamente.**

1. inmediato
2. directo
3. sólo
4. paciente
5. cortés
6. cuidadoso
7. lento

Sal de la casa __1__ y ve __2__ a la tienda. __3__ necesito media docena de huevos. Espera __4__ hasta que te puedan atender. Saluda __5__ al dependiente y despídete antes de salir. Ah, y por favor, cruza la calle __6__. No corras. Camina __7__.

G. Rutina diaria. Pregúntale a tu compañero(a) cómo hace estas actividades diarias?

EJEMPLO bañarse rápida o lentamente
Tú: **¿Te bañas rápida o lentamente?**
Compañero(a): **Me baño rápidamente.** o **Me baño lentamente.**

1. peinarse frecuente o infrecuentemente
2. despertarse fácil o difícilmente
3. arreglarse cuidadosa o rápidamente
4. peinarse rápida o lentamente
5. levantarse alegre o tristemente
6. vestirse informal o formalmente
7. hacer la tarea paciente o impacientemente

G. Rutina diaria. Allow 2–3 min for pair work. Then call on several pairs of students to repeat for class. Answers may vary.

1 ¿Te peinas frecuente o infrecuentemente? Me peino frecuentemente. o Me peino infrecuentemente.
2 ¿Te despiertas fácil o difícilmente? Me despierto fácilmente. o Me despierto difícilmente.
3 ¿Te arreglas cuidadosa o rápidamente? Me arreglo cuidadosamente. o Me arreglo rápidamente.
4 ¿Te peinas rápida o lentamente? Me peino rápidamente. o Me peino lentamente.
5 ¿Te levantas alegre o tristemente? Me levanto alegremente. o Me levanto tristemente.
6 ¿Te vistes informal o formalmente? Me visto informalmente. o Me visto formalmente.
7 ¿Haces la tarea paciente o impacientemente? Hago la tarea pacientemente. o Hago la tarea impacientemente.

H. Somos diferentes. Describe la rutina diaria de tu familia.

EJEMPLO hermana / arreglarse
Mi hermana se arregla lenta y cuidadosamente.

VOCABULARIO ÚTIL:

rápido	lento
frecuente	infrecuente
cuidadoso	descuidado
informal	formal
elegante	normal
alegre	triste
¿ . . . ?	

1. yo / despertarse
2. hermana / lavarse los dientes
3. mamá / levantarse
4. hermano / bañarse
5. hermana / vestirse
6. hermanito / acostarse
7. papá / afeitarse
8. hermanos / peinarse

I. Pon la mesa. Marta le está enseñando a Tere a poner la mesa. ¿Qué le dice?

MODELO a la derecha de la cuchara
Pon la taza a la derecha de la cuchara.

1. a la izquierda del plato
2. cerca del cuchillo
3. debajo del tenedor
4. a la derecha del plato

 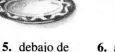

5. debajo de la taza
6. al lado del cuchillo
7. entre los cubiertos
8. encima del platillo

LECCIÓN 1

Adverbs in a series

When two or more adverbs are used together in a sentence, only the last one ends in **-mente**. The others end in the feminine form of the adjective.

Ella habla **cuidadosa, lenta** y **constantemente.**

*See ¿**Por qué se dice así?**, page G113, section 8.2.*

Al poner la mesa

tenedor   cuchillo

cuchara

servilleta   plato

taza y platillo

copa

vaso

trescientos setenta y tres **373**

H. Somos diferentes. Working in pairs, have students tell each other how they and their family members do their daily routine. Allow 2–3 min. Then ask individual students how they do these activities or how their partners do them. Answers will vary. Possibilities include:

1 Yo me despierto rápida y alegremente.
2 Mi hermana se lava los dientes cuidadosamente.
3 Mi mamá se levanta lentamente.
4 Mi hermano se baña infrecuente y descuidadamente.
5 Mi hermana se viste lenta y elegantemente.
6 Mi hermanito se acuesta triste y lentamente.
7 Mi papá se afeita frecuente y cuidadosamente.
8 Mis hermanos se peinan rapida e infrecuentemente.

Expansion Ask students which of these activities they do the same way their partner does them. Have them answer **Jack y yo nos levantamos lentamente.**

I. Pon la mesa. Allow 2–3 min for students to do in pairs. Then repeat activity by calling on individuals.

1 Pon el tenedor a la izquierda del plato.
2 Pon el vaso cerca del cuchillo.
3 Pon la servilleta debajo del tenedor.
4 Pon el cuchillo a la derecha del plato.
5 Pon el platillo debajo de la taza.
6 Pon la cuchara al lado del cuchillo.
7 Pon el plato entre los cubiertos.
8 Pon la taza encima del platillo.

Expansion Have students draw a "creative" place setting. Then have them describe their place setting as their partner draws it.

UNIDAD 8   Lección 1 **373**

CHARLEMOS UN POCO MÁS

 A. Mi rutina diaria. For your health class, you are supposed to keep a record of your daily activities from the time you get up in the morning until you go to school and then from the time school is over until bedtime. Write down everything you do and indicate the time. Then ask your partner about his or her daily routine. Put an asterisk on your schedule anytime both of you do the same thing at the same time.

B. El fin de semana. With a partner, take turns telling what is happening in each drawing of the International Club's camping trip.

MODELO **Andrea**
       Andrea se está lavando los dientes.

1. Pedro   **2. Ana**   **3. Alma y Berta**   **4. Jorge**   **5. tú**

6. Javier   **7. Sr. Ortega**   **8. Marta y yo**   **9. Julio y Paco**   **10. Srta. Montalvo**

C. Crucigrama. Your teacher will give to you and to your partner a cooperative crossword puzzle. You complete the vertical clues and then ask your partner for the horizontal clues. Your partner will ask you for the vertical clues. By cooperating, you will be able to solve the complete puzzle. Do not look at each other's puzzles. Ask each other definitions of the missing words.

EJEMPLO   Tú: **¿Cuál es el número cuatro horizontal?**
          Compañero(a): **Dijo "adiós" de una manera triste.**
          Answer: *tristemente*

CH. ¡Bocadillos! Allow 3–4
min for groups to decide. Then ask
each group to report to class what
they are going to prepare. Answers
will vary.

CH. ¡Bocadillos! Your Spanish class has decided to have a picnic. Your teacher has asked each group to select and prepare one Spanish bocadillo from the menu below. Find out what your group members would prefer from this menu. Decide if you will prepare it just as pictured or if you wish to doctor yours up with any of the following.

VOCABULARIO ÚTIL:

tomate	mantequilla	mayonesa
mostaza	cebolla	sal o pimienta
lechuga	salsa de tomate	

chorizo

tortilla de patatas

jamón

jamón y queso

anchoas

salchichas fritas

tortilla francesa

atún

queso

perrito

D. ¿Tú también? Find out how many things you and your partner do every day at the same time. Using the schedules your teacher provides, ask your partner questions until you know exactly what he or she does and answer all of your partner's questions. Don't look at each other's schedules until you have finished.

E. ¡Qué creatividad! Your mother has asked you to set the table, and you are feeling very creative. Decide how you would set the table using the items pictured below. Draw a sketch, but do not show it to anyone. As you describe your table setting to your partner, he or she will draw it. Then, you draw as your partner describes his or her place setting to you. When you have finished, compare each drawing to your originals.

LECCIÓN 1

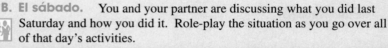

Dramatizaciones

A. ¡Ya es hora! You can't seem to get your brother or sister to move quickly this morning. Role-play this situation with your partner.

Tú	**Compañero(a)**
▪ Tell your partner to wake up, that it is already 7:00.	▪ Say that you are getting up.
▪ Tell your partner to get dressed.	▪ Tell what clothes you are putting on.
▪ Tell your partner to come to breakfast.	▪ Say that you are washing your face.
▪ Say that you are leaving in five minutes.	▪ Say that you are coming and that you are putting on your shoes. Ask what the weather is like.
▪ Say it's cool out and add that it is 7:45.	▪ Say that you are coming but that you are going to take off your sweater and wear your jacket.
	▪ Say that you are coming now.

B. El sábado. You and your partner are discussing what you did last Saturday and how you did it. Role-play the situation as you go over all of that day's activities.

¡No metas la pata!

¡Es una tortilla!   Luisa is an exchange student from Guadalajara, Mexico. On her second day in Madrid, she and a Spanish friend are having lunch out.

UNA TORTILLA, POR FAVOR.

CAFE IBERICA

Julia: (*Al camarero*) Una tortilla, por favor. (*A Luisa*) Está bien contigo, ¿no? Las tortillas son riquísimas aquí.

Luisa: Me gustan las tortillas, pero . . . ¿no vamos a pedir algo más? Yo tengo bastante hambre.

Julia: Sí, no te preocupes. Las tortillas son bien grandes aquí.

(*El camarero sirve la tortilla.*)

Julia: Aquí está. Buen provecho, Luisa.

Luisa: Pero, ¿qué es esto? ¡Nosotras no pedimos un omelete!

Why is Luisa surprised when the waiter brings the Spanish **tortilla?**

1. She's very hungry and just doesn't think one omelet will be enough for the two of them.
2. She doesn't like omelets.
3. She doesn't really know what a Spanish tortilla is like.

❏ Check your answer on page 420.

Purpose This section provides additional reading practice as students discover interesting cross-cultural information about lexical variations in the names of foods.

Suggestions Allow 1–2 min for students to read dialogue. Then ask them to discuss possible explanations and arrive at consensus on correct answer before checking response and explanations on page 420.

Answers

1 Luisa did say that she was very hungry, but she seemed to accept Julia's comment that the **tortillas** are nice and big. Her reaction does not seem to refer to the size of the omelet, but to the idea of the waiter's having brought an omelet. Try another response.

2 There is no indication that she doesn't like omelets. Try again.

③ She says that she likes **tortillas,** which indicates that she does know what they are. However, Luisa is from Mexico, where **tortillas** are pancake-thin corn flour or wheat flour breads. In Spain, a **tortilla** is an omelet. A **tortilla española** is made of eggs, sliced potatoes, and onions. This is the correct answer.

Y ahora, ¡a leer!

Purpose This section is intended to provide additional reading practice as students learn how the names of foods vary within the Spanish-speaking world.

Antes de empezar

In this section, students are made aware of how the names of foods vary within Great Britain and the United States before they read about variations in the names of foods in Hispanic countries.

Suggestions Use this activity as an advance organizer for the reading that follows. Allow 2–3 min for students to do individually or in pairs. Go over the correct answers with class.

Answers

1 **f** biscuits
2 **i** capsicum
3 **a** lift
4 **b** mince
5 **h** w. c. (water closet)
6 **g** treacle
7 **d** boot
8 **c** crisps
9 **e** bangers
10 **ch** gammon

Y ahora, ¡a leer!

Antes de empezar

In the United States, people in different regions have different names for the submarine sandwich—hoagy, grinder, garibaldi, etc. When people in different countries use the same language, such differences become even more noticeable. Look at the lists below and try matching each American English term with its British English equivalent.

American English	British English
1. cookies	a. lift
2. bell pepper	b. mince
3. elevator	c. crisps
4. ground round	ch. gammon
5. toilet	d. boot
6. molasses	e. bangers
7. trunk of a car	f. biscuits
8. (potato) chips	g. treacle
9. sausages	h. w. c. (water closet)
10. smoked ham	i. capsicum

Verifiquemos

After you have read the selection about food names, make a chart similar to the one below and give the appropriate name for each fruit or vegetable listed in the various Spanish-speaking regions.

Frutas y verduras			
EE.UU.	**México**	**Argentina**	**España**
avocado			aguacate
beans			
chili pepper			
corn on the cob			maíz en su mazorca
peach			
pineapple			
potato			

Verifiquemos

Frutas y verduras			
EE.UU.	**México**	**Argentina**	**España**
avocado	**aguacate**	**palta**	**aguacate**
beans	**frijoles**	**porotos**	**judías/habichuelas/frijoles**
chili pepper	**chile**	**ají**	**pimiento picante**
corn on the cob	**elote**	**choclo**	**maíz en su mazorca**
peach	**durazno**	**durazno**	**melocotón**
pineapple	**piña**	**ananá**	**piña americana**
potato	**papa**	**papa**	**patata**

¿Durazno o melocotón?

Los nombres de muchos comestibles varían de país a país y aun de región a región. Estas variaciones pueden causar gran confusión para el turista, ¡especialmente en restaurantes! Es interesante observar estas diferencias en los nombres de varias comidas en los países de habla española.

En algunos casos, la misma palabra se refiere a diferentes cosas, como en el caso de la tortilla en México y la tortilla en España. Otro ejemplo es el taco. Para el mexicano un taco es un tipo de

tiene diferentes nombres en diferentes países. El español dice patata cuando el mexicano y el argentino dicen papa. Lo que el español conoce como melocotón, el

¿Durazno o melocotón?

mexicano y el argentino conocen como durazno. La palta del argentino es el aguacate del mexicano.

Hay muchos ejemplos más de este tipo de variación. En México sirven frijoles, en Argentina porotos y en España frijoles (con el acento en la

primera sílaba), habichuelas y judías. Si quiere darle un sabor picante a una comída, el mexicano le añade chile, mientras el argentino le añade ají y el español, pimiento picante. Si quiere comer maíz tiemo en su mazorca, el argentino pido choclo y el mexicano pide elote. La fruta que llaman piña en México, en Argentina es ananá. Y en España, le dicen piña americana.

¿Aguacate o palta?

¿Cómo sabemos qué nos van a servir cuando viajamos a distintos países? No hay una respuesta fácil a esta pregunta. Uno simplemente tiene que ser un poco aventurero y reconocer que viajamos a otros países, no porque son idénticos al nuestro, sino precisamente porque son diferentes.

¿Elote o choclo?

bocadillo hecho de una tortilla mexicana Para et sudamericano, un taco es ¡el tacón de un zapato! Y un español dice ¡pero qué tacos! cuando oye a alguien decir malas palabras.

En otros casos, la misma fruta o verdura

¿Piña o ananá?

LECCIÓN 1

¿Durazno o melocotón?

Point out The title refers to the Mexican and Spanish words, respectively, for *peach*. In the illustrations, *corn on the cob* is **elote** in Mexico and **choclo** in Argentina; *avocado* and *pineapple* are **palta** and **ananá** in Argentina, **aguacate** and **piña** in Mexico.

OBJECTIVES

Communicative Goals

- Naming and describing rooms in a house
- Expressing extremes
- Making comparisons

Culture and Reading

- **¡No me digas!**
  Una invitación a cenar:
  Mealtimes in Hispanic countries
- **Y ahora, ¡a leer!**
  ¿Hora latina u hora americana?
  Cross-cultural variations in the concept of time

Structure

- **8.3** Preterite of **estar**
- **8.4** Absolute superlatives: **-ísimo**
- **8.5** Comparatives

¡La vista es bellísima!

ACTIVE VOCABULARY

La casa

alcoba	habitación
alfombra	muebles
baño	pasillo
cocina	sala
comedor	... de familia
garaje	servicios

Comida

apetito	fruta
cochinillo asado	postre
ensalada	sabroso(a)
fresas	

Descripciones

activo(a)	feliz
bello(a)	útil
cómodo(a)	viejo(a)
duro(a)	

Comparaciones

más	mejor(es) que
más ... que	peor(es) que
menos	tan ... como
menos ... que	

Verbos

estar *(pret.)*	quedarse
explorar	tocar
olvidar	

Palabras y expresiones

alcázar	río
ciudad	torre
enfermo(a)	viaje
escalón	
maleta	de repente
reina	otra vez
rey	

A N T I C I P E M O S

¿**Q**ué piensas tú ?

1. ¿Qué diferencias hay entre las casas en las fotos de esta página?

2. ¿Qué diferencias crees que hay en el interior de estas casas?

3. ¿Qué tipo de casa se ve en la página anterior? Se llama el Alcázar. ¿Quién crees que vive allí? ¿Cuándo crees que se construyó el Alcázar? ¿Por qué?

4. ¿Hay algo similar al Alcázar en tu estado? Si hay, descríbelo.

5. ¿Cómo crees que son las salas en el Alcázar—normales, grandes o grandísimas? ¿Y los muebles? ¿Los patios?

6. ¿De qué vas a poder hablar al final de la lección?

trescientos ochenta y uno **381**

Answers

1 Las respuestas varían.
Vocabulario nuevo: más grande / más pequeña; más vieja / más nueva; color; localidad, etc.

2 Las respuestas varían.
Vocabulario nuevo: más / menos cuartos, más / menos grandes, más / menos muebles, tamaño, cómodo, elegancia, etc.

3 Lo más probable es que los estudiantes piensen que es un castillo donde vivieron unos reyes y que nadie vive allí ahora. En realidad, tienen razón. El Alcázar es un castillo que se construyó en el siglo XII y en el cual vivieron varios reyes:
Alfonso VI (1072–1109)
Alfonso X el Sabio (1252–84)
Sancho IV (1284–95)
Fernando IV (1295–1312)
Alfonso XI (1312–50)
Pedro I el Cruel (1350–69)
Juan II (1406–54)
Enrique IV (1454–74)
Fernando (1479–1516) e
  Isabel (1474–1504) la Católica
Carlos I (1516–66)
Felipe II (1556–98)
Felipe III (1598–1621) y
Carlos III (1759–88)
Carlos III convirtió el Alcázar en el Real Colegio de Artillería. Actualmente es un Archivo General Militar.

4 Es posible que sugieran alguna mansión local o es posible que no se les ocurra ningún lugar. Si no sugieren nada, pregúnteles por qué no hay lugares similares.

5 Las respuestas varían.
Vocabulario nuevo: Trate de conseguir que sean específicos y digan algo como *The rooms are huge* para llevarlos a superlativos como **grandísimo, comodísimo,** etc.

6 **Van a poder comparar cualidades físicas, describir una casa y exagerar un poco al describir.**

Purpose   To focus students on the language necessary to describe the rooms of a house, to compare physical qualities, and to express extremes, and to encourage students to develop and use critical thinking skills while observing, analyzing, or comparing housing in the U.S. and in Hispanic countries.

Suggestions   Use photos as an advance organizer. Students should be allowed to discover meaning of new vocabulary without translation, through the use of context clues and cognates. Accuracy of pronunciation is not vital here. Allow students to guess at meaning without being distracted by constant correction of pronunciation errors.

30:24–
34:22

Side 8, 17413 to 24575

Comprehension Checks

A full set of the **Comprehension Checks** is available on cards in the Teacher's Resource Package.

 1 | 30:30

Suggestions Explain how when you go to a city where you don't know anyone, staying in a hotel = **quedarse**. Mime registering.

1 ¿Es la familia Molina?
2 ¿Están en el Hotel Infanta Isabel?
3 ¿Están en un hotel en Segovia o en Madrid?
4 ¿Es la primera vez que los hermanos se quedan en un hotel?
5 ¿Están registrándose los padres?
6 ¿Qué están haciendo los padres?
7 ¿Es muy curiosa Tere? ¿Es curiosísima?
8 ¿Cómo es Tere?
9 ¿Empieza a explorar?
10 ¿Qué empieza a hacer?
11 ¿Piensa que es interesante el hotel?

Side 8, 17609 to 18655

2 | 31:06

Suggestions Draw floor plan of house with entry hall = **salón de entrada.** Point to each piece of furniture.

1 ¿Es Tere o Marta?
2 ¿Está en el salón de entrada del hotel?
3 ¿Hay sillas en el salón de entrada? ¿un sofá? ¿un espejo? ¿mesas? ¿lámparas?
4 ¿Cómo es el espejo, grandísimo o pequeñísimo?
5 ¿Qué hay en la sala?
6 ¿Está impresionada Tere?
7 ¿Cómo está Tere?
8 ¿Se sienta en una silla Tere?
9 ¿Es elegante la silla?
10 ¿Cómo es la silla?
11 ¿Le gusta la silla a Tere?

12 ¿Es demasiado dura la silla? ¿Es demasiado dura tu silla?
13 ¿Es más blando el sofá?
14 ¿Cómo es el sofá, duro o blando?
15 ¿Son elegantísimos todos los muebles?
16 ¿Cómo son los muebles del hotel?
Continue asking questions, as above.

Side 8, 18680 to 20020

Esta noche la familia Molina va a quedarse en el Hotel Infanta Isabel en Segovia.

1

Es la primera vez que Tere y sus hermanos se quedan en un hotel. Mientras sus padres se registran,

Tere, curiosísima, empieza a explorar. "Hmmm . . . ¡qué interesante!" piensa Tere.

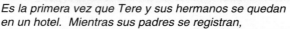

2 *En el salón de entrada hay sillas, un sofá, un espejo grandísimo, mesas y lámparas. Tere está impresionada.*

Se sienta en una silla elegante. Pero decide que no le gusta porque es demasiado dura.

El sofá es más blando. Todos los muebles son elegantísimos. Unos parecen más cómodos, otros menos cómodos, pero todos son impresionantes. No puede resistir tocar los otros muebles. "¡Qué bonitos!"

382 *trescientos ochenta y dos*

Purpose This section develops listening and reading comprehension of vocabulary needed to name and describe rooms in a house, make comparisons, and exaggerate while describing. Students should not be expected to achieve productive mastery at this point.

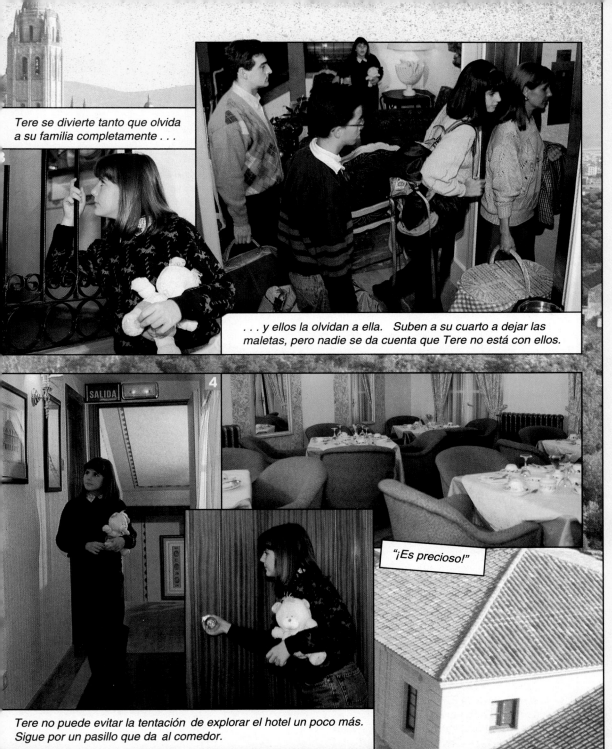

Tere se divierte tanto que olvida a su familia completamente . . .

. . . y ellos la olvidan a ella. Suben a su cuarto a dejar las maletas, pero nadie se da cuenta que Tere no está con ellos.

"¡Es precioso!"

Tere no puede evitar la tentación de explorar el hotel un poco más. Sigue por un pasillo que da al comedor.

3 | 31:52

Suggestions Name things you do **para divertirse.** Pretend to forget where you put something = **olvidarse.** Mime sudden realization = **darse cuenta.**

1 ¿Se divierte Tere?
2 ¿Se divierte mucho o poco?
3 ¿Olvida Tere a su familia?
4 ¿Olvida a su familia completamente?
5 ¿Olvida la familia a Tere?
6 ¿Suben al cuarto?
7 ¿Suben a dejar las maletas?
8 ¿Se dan cuenta que Tere no está con ellos?
9 ¿Quién se da cuenta que Tere no está con ellos?

Side 8, 20043 to 21135

4 | 32:29

Suggestion Point in photo to **pasillo,** then to **comedor.**

1 ¿Explora Tere el hotel un poco más?
2 ¿Sigue por un pasillo?
3 ¿Por dónde sigue?
4 ¿Da el pasillo al comedor?
5 ¿Adónde da el pasillo?
6 ¿Cómo es el comedor, bonito o precioso?

Side 8, 21153 to 22547

Suggestions Begin by having students close their books while you narrate one section at a time, using the transparencies to clarify meaning without translation. Then ask **Comprehension Checks.** Repeat this process with each section.

Using the video Play one section at a time after narrating it using the transparencies. Freeze the video and ask **Comprehension Checks.** Repeat with each section.

5 `33:16`

Suggestions Name things that impress you = **estar impresionado(a).** Also draw table with rug under it = **alfombra.**

1 ¿Quién es? *(Point to Marta, then Andrés.)*
2 ¿Están en su habitación?
3 ¿Están impresionados con la vista?
4 ¿Están muy impresionados o poco impresionados?
5 ¿Es grandísima la habitación?
6 ¿Cómo es la habitación?
7 ¿Es más grande o más pequeña que la sala de casa?
8 ¿Hay una alfombra?
9 ¿Es bonita o fea?
10 ¿Qué es bonita?

Side 8, 22568 to 23257

6 `33:40`

Suggestions Pretend being curious about what students have in their backpacks / purses / books = **curiosear.**

1 ¿Es Marta / Tere / la Sra. Molina? *(Point to Sra. Molina.)*
2 ¿Se da cuenta que no está Tere con ellos?
3 ¿Quién se da cuenta que no está Tere?
4 ¿Se da cuenta de repente?
5 ¿Estuvo curioseando por el hotel?
6 ¿Qué estuvo haciendo Tere?
7 ¿Debe andar una niña sola por un hotel?
8 ¿Andas tú solo(a) por un hotel? *(Ask several students.)*

Side 8, 23277 to 20430

7 `34:05`

1 ¿Quiénes son? *(Point to each.)*
2 ¿Quién dice "Olvídalo, cariño", Andrés o su papá?
3 ¿Ya están todos juntos?
4 ¿Van a comer ahora?
5 ¿Van a comer en un restaurante o en el río?
6 ¿Tiene Tere que darle la mano a su hermana?
7 ¿A quién tiene que darle la mano?

Side 8, 24050 to 24575

Marta y Andrés están muy impresionados con la vista desde su habitación.

Marta: ¡La habitación es grandísima! ¡Es más grande que la sala de casa!
Mamá: Y mira la alfombra. Es bonita, ¿no?

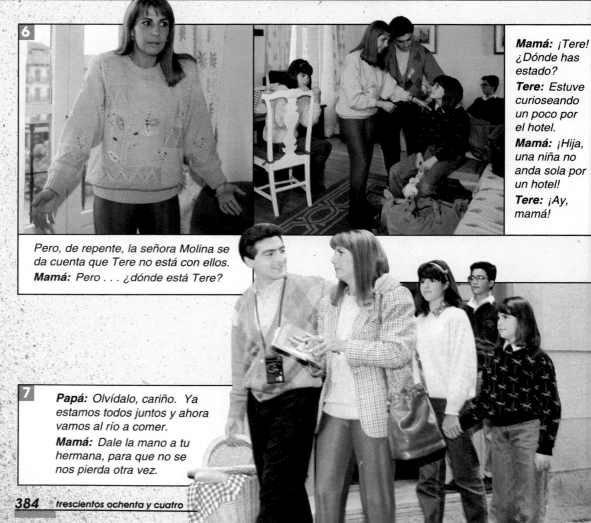

Pero, de repente, la señora Molina se da cuenta que Tere no está con ellos.
Mamá: Pero . . . ¿dónde está Tere?

Mamá: ¡Tere! ¿Dónde has estado?
Tere: Estuve curioseando un poco por el hotel.
Mamá: ¡Hija, una niña no anda sola por un hotel!
Tere: ¡Ay, mamá!

Papá: Olvídalo, cariño. Ya estamos todos juntos y ahora vamos al río a comer.
Mamá: Dale la mano a tu hermana, para que no se nos pierda otra vez.

384 trescientos ochenta y cuatro

¿QUÉ DECIMOS...?

Al hacer una excursión

1 ¡Estuvo riquísima!

Purpose This section presents the language students need to name and describe rooms in a house as well as to make comparisons and exaggerations in real-life contexts. Students should not be asked to memorize dialogues word for word.

Suggestions Begin by having students close their books while you narrate one section at a time, using the transparencies to clarify meaning without translation. Then ask **Early Production Checks**. Repeat this process with each section.

Using the video Play one section at a time after narrating it using the transparencies. Freeze the video and ask **Early Production Checks**. Repeat with each section.

¿QUÉ DECIMOS...?

34:23–
38:25

Side 8, 24592 to 31847

Early Production Checks

A full set of the **Early Production Checks** is available on cards in the Teacher's Resource Package.

1   **34:29**

¡Estuvo riquísima!

1. ¿Quiénes son? *(Point to each.) Marta, Andrés, Tere, Carlota y Francisco.*
2. ¿Cómo estuvieron los bocadillos, sabrosos o muy sabrosos? *Muy sabrosos.*
3. ¿Qué salió mejor que nunca, la tortilla o la ensaladilla? *La tortilla.*
4. ¿Cómo salió la tortilla? *Mejor que nunca.*
5. ¿Le gustó la ensaladilla rusa al papá? *Sí.*
6. ¿Estuvo riquísima? *Sí.*
7. ¿Cómo estuvo la ensaladilla? *Riquísima.*
8. ¿Quién la hizo, Marta o su mamá? *Marta.*
9. ¿Estuvo tan buena como la de su mamá? *Sí.*
10. ¿Encontró Andrés la ensaladilla tan buena como la de su mamá? *No.*
11. ¿La encontró buenísima o malísima? *Malísima.*
12. ¿Cree Andrés que va a ponerse enfermo? *Sí.*
13. ¿De veras va a ponerse enfermo o es una broma? *Es una broma.*
14. ¿Quién dice "¡Sé más amable con tu hermana!", Francisco o Carlota? *Carlota.*
15. ¿Qué dice Carlota? *Sé más amable con tu hermana.*
16. ¿Qué hay de postre? *Fruta.*
17. ¿Qué quiere el papá, fruta o bizcocho? *Fruta.*
18. ¿Quién quiere bizcocho? *Tere.*
19. ¿Va a comer bizcocho ahora o más tarde? *Más tarde.*
20. ¿Adónde van ahora, al Alcázar o al restaurante? *Al Alcázar.*

Side 8, 24743 to 26068

¡Son viejísimos!

Accept brief phrases or one- and two-word answers to all Early Production Check questions, as shown in **1** on page 385. It is not necessary for students to answer in complete sentences.

1 ¿Están en la Sala de Galera?
2 ¿Cómo es, grandísima o larguísima?
3 ¿Hay muebles en la Sala de Galera?
4 ¿Vive alguien allí?
5 ¿Quién dice "No seas tonta", Marta o Andrés?
6 ¿Qué dice Andrés?
7 ¿Son estos los tronos que usaron los Reyes Católicos?
8 ¿Quiénes usaron estos tronos, Fernando e Isabel o Francisco y Carlota?
9 ¿Son increíbles los tronos? ¿bonitos?
10 ¿Parecen muy cómodos?
11 ¿Son duros y viejísimos?
12 ¿Cómo son los tronos?

Side 8, 26083 to 28732

2 ¡Son viejísimos!

3 A ver si es más blanda que la mía.

4 ¡Qué vista!

LECCIÓN 2

A ver si es más blanda que la mía.

¡OjO! Because the Molinas are Spaniards, they use **vosotros** forms like the indirect object pronoun **os** in this dialogue. Students are not responsible for learning this or other **vosotros** forms used in this unit.

1 ¿Es el dormitorio del rey?
2 ¿Qué les parece el dormitorio del rey? ¿Es elegante? (Ask class's opinion.)
3 ¿Durmieron reyes en esa cama?
4 ¿Durmieron reinas allí también?
5 ¿Quiere saber Tere si la cama del rey es más blanda que su cama?
6 ¿Qué quiere saber Tere, si la cama es más blanda o más dura?
7 ¿Se permite tocar los muebles?
8 ¿Qué no se permite?
9 ¿Quién dice "Ven hija", Francisco o Carlota?
10 ¿Qué dice Carlota?
11 ¿Van a subir a la torre ahora?
12 ¿Qué van a hacer ahora?

Side 8, 28747 to 30082

4 37:27

¡Qué vista!

1 ¿Están en la torre?
2 ¿Es bellísima la vista desde la torre?
3 ¿Cómo es la vista?
4 ¿Se puede ver la catedral? ¿toda la ciudad? ¿las montañas? ¿el campo?
5 ¿Está de acuerdo el padre de Andrés?
6 ¿Es Segovia una ciudad interesante?
7 ¿Es una de las ciudades más interesantes que conoce Francisco?
8 ¿Cómo es Segovia?
9 ¿Cuántos escalones subieron, ciento treinta o ciento cuarenta?
10 ¿Los contó Tere?
11 ¿Cómo sabe Tere el número de escalones?
12 ¿Tienen que bajar los escalones ahora?
13 ¿Qué es mejor para el apetito, bajar los escalones o mirar la vista?
14 ¿Van a cenar esta noche en Cándido?
15 ¿Qué van a hacer esta noche?

Side 8, 30100 to 31847

CHARLEMOS UN POCO

A. De viaje. Have individuals read each item and call on a classmate to indicate where it was said. Have class confirm each answer.

1 visitando el Alcázar
2 comiendo al aire libre
3 comiendo al aire libre
4 visitando el Alcázar
5 visitando el Alcázar
6 comiendo al aire libre
7 visitando el Alcázar
8 visitando el Alcázar
9 comiendo al aire libre
10 visitando el Alcázar
11 comiendo al aire libre
12 visitando el Alcázar

B. En camino. Call on individuals. Have class confirm each answer.

1 Andrés estuvo veinte minutos corriendo por la mañana.
2 Marta estuvo cuarenta y cinco minutos peinándose y arreglándose.
3 Yo estuve una hora y media viajando en coche a Segovia.
4 Tere estuvo diez minutos subiendo a la torre del Alcázar.
5 Nosotros estuvimos dos horas y media comiendo al aire libre.
6 Mamá y Marta estuvieron quince minutos mirando el dormitorio del rey.
7 Todos estuvieron treinta minutos observando los tronos.

C. ¿Dónde? Have students work in pairs. Allow 2–3 min. Then ask individuals to tell you where they and their partners do specific things. Answers may vary.

1 Me baño en el baño.
2 Me pongo los zapatos en la alcoba.
3 Recibo a los invitados en la sala (de familia).
4 Veo televisión en la sala (de familia).
5 Desayuno en la cocina. *o* Desayuno en el comedor.
6 Hago la tarea en la alcoba.
7 Almuerzo en el comedor.
8 Me acuesto en la alcoba.
9 Me peino en el baño.
10 Ponemos el coche en el garaje.
11 Duermo en la alcoba.
12 Me lavo los dientes en el baño.
13 Arreglo la bicicleta en el garaje.
14 Hago gimnasia en la alcoba.
15 Preparo la comida en la cocina.

Estar

estuve	estuvimos
estuviste	
estuvo	estuvieron
estuvo	estuvieron

See **¿Por qué se dice así?**, *page G114, section 8.3.*

La casa

A. De viaje. Los Molina están en Segovia. Según su conversación, qué están haciendo: ¿visitando el Alcázar o comiendo al aire libre?

1. ¿Dónde están los muebles?
2. ¿Prefieres una manzana o una naranja?
3. ¿Qué hay de postre?
4. Nadie vive aquí ahora.
5. A ver si son tan cómodos como nuestros sillones.
6. Creo que voy a ponerme enfermo.
7. ¡Subimos muchos escalones!
8. Ésta se llama la Sala de la Galera.
9. ¿Te gustó la ensaladilla?
10. Esta cama es más blanda que la mía.
11. Los bocadillos estuvieron excelentes.
12. Se puede ver la catedral y toda la ciudad.

B. En camino. ¿Cuántas horas estuvieron los miembros de la familia Molina haciendo estas actividades?

MODELO   mamá: preparándose para el viaje (3 horas)
Mamá estuvo tres horas preparándose para el viaje.

1. Andrés: corriendo por la mañana (20 minutos)
2. Marta: peinándose y arreglándose (45 minutos)
3. yo: viajando en coche a Segovia (1 hora y media)
4. Tere: subiendo a la torre del Alcázar (10 minutos)
5. nosotros: comiendo al aire libre (2 horas y media)
6. mamá y Marta: mirando el dormitorio del rey (15 minutos)
7. todos: observando los tronos (30 minutos)

C. ¿Dónde? ¿En qué cuarto haces las siguientes actividades?

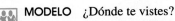

MODELO   ¿Dónde te vistes?
Me visto en la alcoba. o
Me visto en el baño.

1. ¿Dónde te bañas?
2. ¿Dónde te pones los zapatos?
3. ¿Dónde recibes a los invitados?
4. ¿Dónde ves televisión?
5. ¿Dónde desayunas?
6. ¿Dónde haces la tarea?
7. ¿Dónde almuerzas?
8. ¿Dónde te acuestas?
9. ¿Dónde te peinas?
10. ¿Dónde ponen el coche?
11. ¿Dónde duermes?
12. ¿Dónde te lavas los dientes?
13. ¿Dónde arreglas la bicicleta?
14. ¿Dónde haces gimnasia?
15. ¿Dónde preparas la comida?

Purpose   These activities provide guided practice to students beginning to produce structures and vocabulary necessary to describe a house, to make comparisons, and to exaggerate while describing.

CH. ¡Qué exagerado! ¿Qué dicen tus amigos cuando vienen a visitarte a tu nueva casa?

MODELO sala / cómodo
La sala es comodísima.

1. cocina / moderno
2. alcoba / lindo
3. comedor / pequeño
4. pasillo / largo
5. baño / feo
6. sala / elegante
7. garaje / grande
8. patio / cómodo

D. ¡Estuvo rico! Tú y tus amigos fueron a comer a un restaurante anoche. ¿Cómo describen la comida?

MODELO ensalada (bueno)
La ensalada estuvo buenísima.

1. fresas (rico)
2. pan (bueno)
3. tortilla (malo)
4. chorizo (sabroso)
5. jamón (bueno)
6. papas (malo)
7. café (rico)
8. quesos (sabroso)

E. ¡Es feísimo! Tú y tu amigo(a) van con tus padres a comprar muebles. ¿Qué comentarios hacen ustedes?

MODELO Tú: **¿Qué piensas de este sofá?**
Compañero(a): **¿Ése? Es feísimo.**

VOCABULARIO ÚTIL:

| elegante | feo | bello | lindo | moderno |
| caro | pequeño | largo | grande | precioso |

MODELO

1.

2.

3.

4.

5.

6.

7.

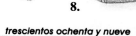
8.

Exaggerating physical qualities: *-ísimo* superlatives

Remove the **-o** ending of an adjective and add **-ísimo (-a, -os, -as)**.

bueno	buenísimo (-a, -os, -as)
alto	altísimo (-a, -os, -as)
largo	*larguísimo (-a, -os, -as)
rico	*riquísimo (-a, -os, -as)

Note the **g → gu** and **c → qu** spelling changes.

See ¿Por qué se dice así?, page G115, section 8.4.

F. ¡Qué feos! Allow 2–3 min. Then repeat activity with class by calling on several pairs.

1 ¿Quién tiene los pies más grandes? Igor tiene los pies más grandes.
2 ¿Quién tiene la cara menos simpática? El monstruo tiene la cara menos simpática.
3 ¿Quién tiene los dedos más largos? El monstruo tiene los dedos más largos.
4 ¿Quién tiene la cabeza más pequeña? Igor tiene la cabeza más pequeña.
5 ¿Quién tiene las piernas menos flacas? El monstruo tiene las piernas menos flacas.
6 ¿Quién tiene los ojos más grandes? Igor tiene los ojos más grandes.
7 ¿Quién tiene el pelo menos corto? Igor tiene el pelo menos corto.
8 ¿Quién tiene la nariz menos larga? El monstruo tiene la nariz menos larga.

G. ¡Se vende! Have students work in pairs. Allow 2 min. Then repeat activity with class by calling on individuals.

1 El comedor
2 La alcoba del hijo
3 La sala
4 El garaje
5 La alcoba de la hija
6 La oficina
7 El comedor
8 La sala de familia

Making unequal comparisons: *más* and *menos*

Spanish expresses *more* with **más** and *less* with **menos**.

Yo soy **más** alto.
Este video es **menos** interesante.

See **¿Por qué se dice así?**, *page G116, section 8.5.*

Making unequal comparisons: *más . . . que* and *menos . . . que*

más . . . que	*more . . . than*
menos . . . que	*less . . . than*

Ellas tienen **más dinero que** yo.
Tú tienes **menos tiempo que** él.

See **¿Por qué se dice así?**, *page G116, section 8.5.*

Making equal comparisons: *tan . . . como*

tan . . . como	*as . . . as*

Nosotros estamos **tan contentos como** ustedes.

See **¿Por qué se dice así?**, *page G116, section 8.5.*

F. ¡Qué feos! Pregúntale a tu compañero(a) cómo se comparan el monstruo e Igor.

MODELO manos más grandes
Tú: **¿Quién tiene las manos más grandes?**
Compañero(a): **El monstruo tiene las manos más grandes.**

1. pies más grandes
2. cara menos simpática
3. dedos más largos
4. cabeza más pequeña
5. piernas menos flacas
6. ojos más grandes
7. pelo menos corto
8. nariz menos larga

G. ¡Se vende! Héctor está hablando por teléfono con una persona interesada en comprar su casa. ¿Qué cuarto está describiendo?

MODELO Héctor (Tú): **Es más pequeño que el otro baño, pero es útil.**
Compañero(a): **El baño de los padres**

1. Está cerca de la cocina y es tan grande como la sala de familia.
2. Es tan grande como la alcoba de la hija.
3. Es más grande que la sala de familia y es perfecto para recibir a las visitas.

4. Es casi tan largo como la casa y hay espacio para dos coches.
5. Es menos grande que la alcoba de los padres y tan grande como la alcoba del hijo.
6. Es casi tan grande como la cocina y es perfecta para la computadora.
7. Es más grande que la cocina y es donde servimos comidas especiales.
8. Es menos grande y menos formal que la sala y es ideal para el televisor.

H. ¡Es mucho mejor! ¿Cómo se compara tu escuela con la escuela de estos estudiantes?

MODELO   Mi escuela tiene oficinas lujosas.

Tú: **Mi escuela tiene oficinas lujosas.**
Compañero(a):   **Es mejor que nuestra escuela.** o
Es peor que nuestra escuela. o
Es tan buena como nuestra escuela.

1. En mi escuela, la cafetería sirve comida buenísima.
2. Mi escuela no tiene gimnasio.
3. En mi escuela, hay un teatro enorme.
4. Mi escuela no tiene clases de computación.
5. En mi escuela, todos los estudiantes sacan "A".
6. En mi escuela, no hay tarea.
7. Mi escuela tiene un equipo muy bueno de fútbol.
8. En mi escuela, no hay recreo.

I. ¡Marcianos! Dos familias de extraterrestres acaban de llegar a tu patio. ¿Cómo los comparas?

MODELO   activo
Los Rotunis son más activos que los Vertundos. o
Los Vertundos son menos activos que los Rotunis.

Los Vertundos

1. feliz	3. alto
2. tímido	4. atlético

Los Rotunis

5. grande	7. serio
6. organizado	8. divertido

LECCIÓN 2

Making unequal comparisons:
mejor que and *peor que*

mejor que   *better than*
peor que   *worse than*

Este sillón es **mejor que** esa silla pero es **peor que** el sofá.
Esas blusas son **mejores que** éstas.

*See ¿**Por qué se dice así?**,*
page G116, section 8.5.

H. ¡Es mucho mejor! Allow 2–3 min. Then repeat activity with class by calling on several pairs. Answers will vary.

I. ¡Marcianos! Have students work in pairs. Allow 2 min. Then repeat activity with class by calling on individuals. Answers may vary.

1 Los Rotunis son más felices que los Vertundos. *o* Los Vertundos son menos felices que los Rotunis.
2 Los Vertundos son más tímidos que los Rotunis. *o* Los Rotunis son menos tímidos que los Vertundos.
3 Los Rotunis son más altos que los Vertundos. *o* Los Vertundos son menos altos que los Rotunis.
4 Los Rotunis son más atléticos que los Vertundos. *o* Los Vertundos son menos atléticos que los Rotunis.
5 Los Rotunis son más grandes que los Vertundos. *o* Los Vertundos son menos grandes que los Rotunis.
6 Los Vertundos son más organizados que los Rotunis. *o* Los Rotunis son menos organizados que los Vertundos.
7 Los Vertundos son más serios que los Rotunis. *o* Los Rotunis son menos serios que los Vertundos.
8 Los Rotunis son más divertidos que los Vertundos. *o* Los Vertundos son menos divertidos que los Rotunis.

Expansion Have students draw their own family of extraterrestrials. In pairs, have them compare their families, commenting on as many physical aspects as they can.

CHARLEMOS UN POCO MÁS

A. ¿Dónde estuviste?
Have students circulate and talk with several classmates. Allow 3–4 min. Ask who has a name in each square. Check by asking students whose names appear on the form if the information is true.

B. ¡Casas imaginativas!
You may want to have students draw their fairy tale houses at home the day before. After students have done the activity, put all the house drawings on your bulletin board so that everyone may see them. Use them for review during the rest of the week.

C. ¡Es comodísima! Allow 2–3 min for pair work. Then ask individuals what their partners thought about each item. Ask class if they agree. Answers will vary. Sample answers include:
¿Qué opinas de la blusa?
 ¡Parece feísima!
¿Qué opinas del trono?
 ¡Parece viejísimo!
¿Qué opinas de las naranjas?
 ¡Parecen buenísimas!
¿Qué opinas del gato?
 ¡Parece lindísimo!
¿Qué opinas del perro?
 ¡Parece grandísimo!
¿Qué opinas del vestido?
 ¡Parece elegantísimo!
¿Qué opinas de los jeans?
 ¡Parecen viejísimos!
¿Qué opinas de la lámpara?
 ¡Parece interesantísima!

A. ¿Dónde estuviste? Find classmates who match the description in each square on the grid that your teacher will provide. When you find a classmate who matches a description, write his or her name in the box. The goal is to have a name in every square. But remember, the same name may not appear more than once on your grid.

B. ¡Casas imaginativas! Draw a diagram of the house where your favorite fairy tale or cartoon characters might live. Then draw the same diagram but show only where the kitchen is located. Give it to your partner. Describe the rest of the house to your partner so that he or she will be able to diagram it. Compare your diagrams when you finish.

C. ¡Es comodísima! Look at the sketches below. With your partner share your opinions of each item.

MODELO Tú: **¿Qué opinas del sillón?**
Compañero(a): **¡Parece comodísimo!**

UNIDAD 8

Purpose These activities are designed to allow students to create with language necessary to describe a house, to make comparisons, and to exaggerate while describing.

CH. Un palacio real. Below is a diagram of a royal palace. With your partner, decide in what rooms the furniture around the diagram should be placed and how it should be arranged.

CH. Un palacio real. Allow 3–4 min for students to agree where each piece of furniture goes. Then call on individuals to tell class where they decided to place the specific pieces.

D. ¡Ay, la memoria! Your teacher will provide you and your partner with drawings of eight people you met at a party last weekend. You are both having difficulty remembering the names of all these people. Help each other identify each person by describing and comparing him or her with the others. You may ask each other questions, but do not look at each other's drawings until all eight persons have been identified.

EJEMPLO **Alicia no es muy alta pero es más alta que . . .**

D. ¡Ay, la memoria! Allow 10–15 min. Confirm each person's identity when finished.

Dramatizaciones

A. Mansiones y palacios. You are telling your partner about the governor's house that you saw yesterday. Role-play this situation.

Tú	**Compañero(a)**
■ Tell your partner that the house is huge.	■ Ask if it is also elegant.
■ Answer the question. Add that the piano in the living room is very ugly.	■ Ask how many TV sets there are in the house.
■ Answer that there are only two and that the TV set in the bedroom is bigger than the one in the living room.	■ Ask if the furniture is modern or old.
■ Answer and then say what you liked most.	■ Say that it's obviously a very interesting house.

Purpose This section has students recycle, in student-centered role plays, all previously learned structures and vocabulary needed to describe a house, to make comparisons, and to exaggerate while describing.

Suggestions Do these role plays spontaneously, not from written scripts. Circulate among groups. Limit time allowed so that students do not get off task. Ask one or two pairs to recreate their exchange for the whole class.

IMPACTO CULTURAL

¡No me digas!

Una invitación a cenar. Claudia arrived this morning in Barcelona from the United States. Her Spanish friend Silvia just picked her up at her hotel and is expaining what she has planned for the day. Read their conversation and then answer the question that follows.

Silvia:	**¡Te va a encantar Barcelona! Esta mañana vamos a visitar el Museo de Picasso. ¡Es increíble! De allí vamos a las Ramblas a caminar un rato. Es hermoso caminar allí. Allí también podemos almorzar, si quieres.**
Claudia:	**Bien. ¿Por qué no? ¿Y por la tarde? ¿Qué vamos a hacer?**
Silvia:	**Bueno, debemos regresar a tu hotel a descansar un rato. Pero a eso de las cinco y media vamos a visitar a mi amiga Pilar. Sé que te va a gustar. Es muy simpática. Ella va a acompañarnos al Pueblo Español. Es un barrio muy especial con casas representativas de toda España. Podemos pasar horas y horas allí.**
Claudia:	**¡Qué bien! Podemos cenar allí.**
Silvia:	**No, porque mamá insiste en que regresemos a casa a las diez. Va a prepararte una zarzuela de mariscos riquísima.**
Claudia:	**Ay, ya la puedo saborear. Pero, ¿a las diez de la noche?**

Why does Claudia seem dismayed by the dinner hour?

1. She thinks that Silvia is deliberately planning a late dinner to see how late she can stay up.

2. She thinks that Silvia's family is strange because they eat so late.

3. She thinks that Silvia made so many plans for the day that they won't be able to eat earlier.

❏ Check your answer on page 420.

Purpose This section provides additional reading practice as students learn to avoid cross-cultural misunderstandings when talking about mealtimes.

Suggestions Read the dialogue aloud for students so they may hear the proper intonation. Then have them read it. Ask comprehension check questions. Before turning to explanations of answers on page 420, have students themselves try to explain why the wrong answers are wrong.

Answers

1 Claudia may think this, particularly if she is tired, but she doesn't say so. Try again.

②Claudia is evidently unfamiliar with Spanish mealtimes. It is not unusual for a family to dine at 10:00 or 11:00 o'clock at night. Lunch is the main meal of the day and is usually eaten about 1:30 or 2:00. Although customs are changing in the larger cities, many businesses and schools still close for two or three hours for lunch and reopen about 5:00 for three or four more hours. Consequently, dinner is eaten late. The evening meal is usually lighter than the midday meal. This is the correct answer.

3 Claudia gives no evidence that she thinks this. Try another answer.

IMPACTO CULTURAL

Y ahora, ¡a leer!

Antes de empezar

1. When someone is invited to dinnner at 6:00 P.M., how late may he or she arrive and still be "on time"?
2. What do you think of a person who agrees to meet you for lunch at noon and then shows up at 12:45 P.M.?
3. What would you do if you had agreed to babysit your next-door neighbor's child and then received an invitation to a good friend's birthday party on the same evening?

¿Hora latina u hora americana?

La hora para levantarse, desayunar, almorzar, cenar, salir del trabajo, ir al teatro o llegar a una fiesta depende totalmente de la cultura. Tal vez por eso los alemanes al hablar de la hora dicen que el reloj vuela, los norteamericanos dicen que las reloj corre y los españoles que el reloj anda.

Desde el punto de vista de un hispano, en Estados Unidos almorzamos y cenamos demasiado temprano. ¿Por qué? Porque en la cultura hispana, el almuerzo simplemente no se sirve antes de la 1:30 o las 2:00 de la tarde, y la cena puede ser tan tarde como las 9:00 o 10:00 de la noche. Con frecuencia, al viajar en países hispanos, los norteamericanos se sorprenden al entrar en un restaurante al mediodía o a las seis de la tarde y encontrarlo casi vacío. Lo que no saben es que los camareros probablemente están pensando que los norteamericanos son un poco raros por querer almorzar o cenar tan temprano.

A propósito, el concepto de **mediodía** es también distinto. Generalmente en Estados Unidos cuando decimos "Te veo al mediodía" quiere decir que las dos personas

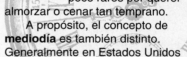

Verifiquemos

¿Sí o no?   After you read the article below, indicate whether or not the following behavior would be appropriate if you were living in a Spanish-speaking country or Hispanic community. Explain your answer.

1. llegar media hora tarde a una cena
2. aceptar una invitación a una fiesta y luego llegar dos horas tarde
3. hacer una cita al mediodía para estudiar para un examen
4. invitar a un amigo a almorzar contigo a las 12:30
5. hacer una reservación para cenar a las 10:00 de la noche
6. llegar una hora tarde a almorzar con un(a) amigo(a)
7. no aceptar una invitación a una fiesta porque vas a tener que llegar dos horas tarde
8. llegar tres minutos temprano a una cena

Verifiquemos

1 Sí. Es apropiado llegar de media a una hora tarde.
2 Sí. Es mejor llegar tarde que no llegar del todo.
3 No. Es mejor especificar la hora porque *mediodía* es muy vago.
4 No. Es muy temprano. El almuerzo no debe ser antes de la 1:30 o 2:00.
5 Sí. Es común cenar entre las 9:00 y las 10:00 y aun más tarde.
6 Sí. Es apropiado llegar entre media a una hora tarde a almorzar.
7 No. Es mejor llegar tarde que no llegar del todo.
8 No. No es apropiado llegar temprano a una cena. Es preferible llegar de media a una hora tarde.

se van a ver a las doce en punto. Cuando dos hispanos dicen esto, es que piensan verse entre las 12:00 y las 2:00 de la tarde. Para el hispano el mediodía consiste en un par de horas y no en las doce en punto.

El norteamericano es muy puntual desde el punto de vista de un hispano—quizás demasiado puntual. ¿Por qué? Porque el norteamericano casi siempre se presenta a la hora indicada cuando recibe una invitación a cenar o a una fiesta. Para el hispano es natural y hasta apropiada llegar media hora o hasta una hora tarde a una función social.

El llegar a la hora exacta es para el hispano llegar a la "hora americana". Si se llega a la hora indicada, lo más probable es que las personas que lo invitaron todavía no estén listos.

Cuando un hispano recibe una invitación a una fiesta, lo más importante es presentarse celebrar con los amigos que lo invitaron. Por eso, si uno tiene otro compromiso, es preferible llegar tarde a la fiesta después de cumplir con el otro compromiso, que rechazar la invitación y no presentarse.

OBJECTIVES

Communicative Goals

- Describing what is happening at the moment
- Telling what you usually do
- Describing something that happened

Reading

- **Leamos ahora**
  Gazpacho andaluz / Tortilla española
- Reading strategy: Reading for detailed information

Writing

- **Escribamos un poco**
  Short composition
- Writing strategy: Retelling a story

Structure

- **8.6** Present tense: A summary
- **8.7** Present progressive: A summary
- **8.8** Preterite: A summary

ACTIVE VOCABULARY

Comidas

albóndigas	legumbres
ajo	pescado
cochinillo	sopa de ajo
entremeses	tapas
gazpacho	verduras

Preparación

al gusto	receta
freír	sartén (f.)
probar (ue)	

Verbos

construir	soñar (ue) con
recomendar (ie)	volver (ue)

¡El cochinillo asado, por favor!

Palabras y expresiones

acueducto	¡Con calma!
castillo	¡Con cuidado!
fascinante	en seguida
mesón	¿Es todo?
recuerdo	hacer un tour
reservación	por aquí
siglo	
sonriendo	
variado	

A N T I C I P E M O S

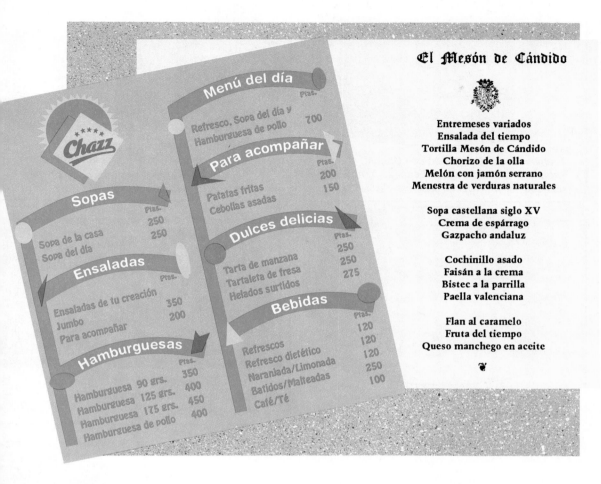

El Mesón de Cándido

Entremeses variados
Ensalada del tiempo
Tortilla Mesón de Cándido
Chorizo de la olla
Melón con jamón serrano
Menestra de verduras naturales

Sopa castellana siglo XV
Crema de espárrago
Gazpacho andaluz

Cochinillo asado
Faisán a la crema
Bistec a la parrilla
Paella valenciana

Flan al caramelo
Fruta del tiempo
Queso manchego en aceite

Menú del día

	Ptas.
Refresco, Sopa del día y Hamburguesa de pollo	700

Para acompañar

	Ptas.
Patatas fritas	200
Cebollas asadas	150

Sopas

	Ptas.
Sopa de la casa	250
Sopa del día	250

Ensaladas

	Ptas.
Ensaladas de tu creación	350
Jumbo	200
Para acompañar	

Dulces delicias

	Ptas.
Tarta de manzana	250
Tartaleta de fresa	250
Helados surtidos	275

Bebidas

	Ptas.
Refrescos	120
Refresco dietético	120
Naranjada/Limonada	120
Batidos/Malteadas	250
Café/Té	100

Hamburguesas

	Ptas.
Hamburguesa 90 grs.	350
Hamburguesa 125 grs.	400
Hamburguesa 175 grs.	450
Hamburguesa de pollo	400

¿Qué piensas tú?

1. ¿Qué tipo de comida ofrecen los dos menús? ¿Cómo son diferentes los dos restaurantes que tienen estos menús? ¿Cómo lo sabes tú?

2. ¿Has comido cochinillo asado alguna vez? Si no, ¿crees que te gustaría? ¿Por qué?

3. ¿Qué tipo de comida crees que sirven en el restaurante en la foto? ¿Por qué crees eso?

4. En tu opinión, ¿cómo es la comida típica de España? ¿Por qué crees eso?

5. ¿De qué vas a poder hablar al final de la lección?

ANTICIPEMOS

¿Qué piensas tú?

Answers

1 En **Chazz** sirven sopas, ensaladas, hamburguesas, postres y bebidas. También sirven papas fritas y cebollas asadas. En **El Mesón de Cándido** sirven entremeses, ensaladas, tortilla, chorizo, melón con jamón serrano, sopas y varios platos principales y postres. Los alumnos deben reconocer que en **Chazz** sirven comida chatarra mientras que en **El Mesón de Cándido** tienen un menú más extenso y sirven comidas más completas.

2 Lo más probable es que no hayan comido cochinillo asado. También es probable que expresen cierto miedo de probar algo "diferente" que no acostumbran comer.

3 Es obvio que no sirven comida chatarra aquí. Es posible que sus alumnos digan que sirven platos regionales o platos típicos de restaurantes que ellos conocen. Las fotos son del **Mesón de Cándido,** cuyo menú aparece aquí.

4 Lo más probable es que los alumnos no tengan idea de cómo es la comida española o que la confundan con comida mexicana. Tal vez piensen que no es diferente de su propia comida. Anímelos a considerar dónde está situada España, el clima, la costa, influencia europea, etc.

5 **Van a poder hablar más de comida. También harán un repaso del presente, presente progresivo y pretérito.**

Purpose To focus students on structures and vocabulary that allow them to describe what is happening at the moment, to tell what they usually do, and to describe something that happened in the past, as well as to encourage students to develop and use critical thinking skills as they learn to recognize and appreciate cultural differences in the foods we eat.

TAPE/
DISC

38:26–
44:02

Side 8, 31877 to 41950

Comprehension Checks

1 38:33

Suggestions Gesture *come here* = **ven**. Name two funny people and Carlos and compare them = **el más cómico**.

1 ¿Es un programa de televisión?
2 ¿Es "Cocinando con Carlos"?
3 ¿Es un programa muy popular o poco popular?
4 ¿Es Carlos Sartén un cocinero?
5 ¿Es muy famoso? ¿Es famosísimo?
6 ¿Quién dice "Ven, mamá. Mira", Marta o Tere?
7 ¿Ya empezó el programa?
8 ¿Es muy cómico Carlos?
9 ¿Es el cocinero más cómico del mundo?
10 ¿Cómo es Carlos?

Side 8, 32073 to 33100

2 39:09

Suggestions Have students turn to page 413 = **recetas**. Gesture *shhhh!* = **¡Cállate!**

1 ¿Van a preparar tapas hoy?
2 ¿Cuántas tapas van a preparar hoy?
3 ¿Son aperitivos las tapas?
4 ¿Son típicamente españolas las tapas?
5 ¿Quién es algo desorganizado, Carlos Sartén o el Sr. Molina?
6 ¿Son buenas las recetas de Carlos?
7 ¿Son realmente buenas o realmente fabulosas?
8 ¿Quién dice "cállate", Tere o su mamá?
9 ¿Van a ver lo que hace Carlos ahora?

Side 8, 33149 to 33640

3 39:26

Suggestions Contrast food cooking with raw ingredients = **en marcha / no en marcha**. Point to two things at same time = **mientras tanto**. Point to raw potatoes, then to frying potatoes = **freír**.

1 ¿Quién es?
Continue asking questions, as above.

Side 8, 33659 to 35700

400 *UNIDAD 8 Lección 3*

Bienvenidos a "Cocinando con Carlos", el programa favorito de toda España. Y ahora con ustedes, el famosísimo cocinero Carlos Sartén.

Tere: *Ven, mamá. Mira, ya empezó "Cocinando con Carlos". ¡Es tan cómico! Tiene que ser el cocinero más cómico del mundo. ¿No crees, mamá?*

Hoy vamos a preparar dos tapas, esos aperitivos tan típicamente españoles.

Mamá: *Es algo desorganizado, pero sus recetas son realmente fabulosas. Ahora cállate, hija. Vamos a ver lo que hace.*

Freí tres patatas cortadas así, una cebolla picada, seis huevos. Luego lo mezclo todo con los huevos, sal . . . al gusto. ¡Y nada de pimienta!

Tengo ya en marcha una riquísima tortilla española.

Luego se deja freír lentamente . . . y mientras tanto, preparamos la otra tapa.

Purpose This section develops listening and reading comprehension of vocabulary needed to describe what is happening at the moment, to tell what usually happens, and to describe something that happened in the past. The goal here is not to translate but to listen/read for comprehension.

¿Ya están listos? Bueno. ¡Sigamos con las albondiguitas! | *Primero se corta la carne. Con cuidado, por favor.* | *¡No se corten!* | *Luego se pica la carne.*

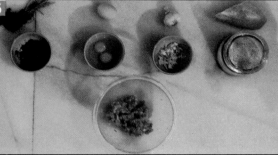
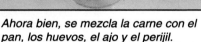

Ahora bien, se mezcla la carne con el pan, los huevos, el ajo y el perijil. | *Todo bien mezclado, ¿eh?*

Ahora se hacen bolitas con la mezcla. | *Veinte a treinta bolitas. ¡Bolita!* | *Todas del mismo tamaño, ¿eh?*

Ahora en una sartén se fríen lentamente las albóndigas con aceite de oliva. | *Pero, ¡con cuidado! ¡Que no se queme la cocina!*

cuatrocientos uno **401**

Suggestions Begin by having students close their books while you narrate one section at a time, using the transparencies to clarify meaning without translation. Then ask **Comprehension Checks**. Repeat this process with each section.

Using the video Play one section at a time after narrating it using the transparencies. Freeze the video and ask **Comprehension Checks**. Repeat with each section.

7 ¿Con qué se fríen?
8 ¿Se fríen con cuidado?
9 ¿Debe quemarse la cocina?
10 ¿Se queman las albóndigas que prepara Carlos?

Side 8, 38239 to 38930

4 | 40:36

Suggestions Gesture **cortar** and **picar**. Point to **albondiguitas**.
Point out Carlos's kitchen accidents are for comic effect. Students should be reminded to exercise caution when cooking.

1 ¿Pregunta si ya están listos?
2 ¿Qué pregunta?
3 ¿Quién dice "Sigamos", Carlos o la señora Molina?
4 ¿Sigue Carlos con las albondiguitas?
5 ¿Con qué sigue Carlos?
6 ¿Se corta la carne primero?
7 ¿Qué se hace primero?
8 ¿Se corta con cuidado?
9 ¿Quién dice "¡No se corten!"?
10 ¿Se corta Carlos?
11 ¿Luego se pica la carne?

Side 8, 35772 to 36755

5 | 41:10

Suggestion Act out **mezclar**.
1 ¿Es pan / un huevo / ajo / perijil? *(Point to each item.)*
2 ¿Se mezcla la carne con el pan, los huevos, el ajo y el perijil?
3 ¿Con que se mezcla la carne?
4 ¿Debe estar todo bien mezclado?

Side 8, 36799 to 37530

6 | 41:36

Suggestion Draw **bolitas** of varying sizes on board and compare = **del mismo tamaño**.
1 ¿Se hacen bolitas con la mezcla?
2 ¿Qué se hace con la mezcla?
3 ¿Cuántas bolitas se hacen, veinte a treinta o treinta a cuarenta?
4 ¿Se hacen todas las bolitas del mismo tamaño?
5 ¿Son del mismo tamaño todas las bolitas que hace Carlos?

Side 8, 37549 to 38170

7 | 41:59

Suggestions Point to **sartén** and **aceite de oliva**. Mention other brand names of **aceite**.
1 ¿Se fríen las albóndigas?
2 ¿Se fríen en una sartén?
3 ¿En qué se fríen las albóndigas?
4 ¿Qué se fríe en una sartén?
5 ¿Cómo se fríen, rápida o lentamente?
6 ¿Se fríen con aceite de oliva?

Suggestions Gesture calmly with hand = **con calma**. Gesture flipping an omelet onto a plate = **dar la vuelta**. Draw flames on board = **fuego**.

1 ¿Prepara Carlos la comida con calma?
2 ¿Es importante no dejar freír la tortilla demasiado?
3 ¿Dejó Carlos freír la tortilla demasiado?
4 ¿Se quita la tortilla del fuego cuando ya está hecha?
5 ¿Hay que darle la vuelta a la tortilla?
6 ¿Hay que pasarla a la sartén otra vez?
7 ¿Hay que ponerla al fuego unos minutos más?

Side 8, 38931 to 39800

1 ¿Quién dice "¡Tengan cuidado de no quemar las albóndigas!"?
2 ¿Tiene cuidado de no quemar las albóndigas Carlos?
3 ¿Hay que añadir salsa a las albóndigas?
4 ¿Añade salsa Carlos a las albóndigas que preparó?
5 ¿Es fácil?

Side 8, 39821 to 40790

1 ¿Es un plato de albóndigas? *(Point to tortilla, then to meatballs.)*
2 ¿Es una tortilla española? *(Point to tortilla, then to meatballs.)*
3 ¿Es una maravilla?
4 ¿Están preparadas con cuidado estas dos tapas?
5 ¿Es una tortilla exquisita?
6 ¿Cómo es la tortilla?
7 ¿Son unas albondiguitas fenomenales?
8 ¿Cómo son las albondiguitas?

Side 8, 40829 to 41367

1 ¿Nos desea Carlos "¡Buen apetito!"?
2 ¿Cuándo es el próximo programa de Carlos, la próxima semana o el próximo mes?
3 ¿Es muy cómico Carlos Sartén?

4 ¿Es un desastre también?
5 ¿Cómo es Carlos Sartén?
6 ¿Le salió todo bien o mal hoy?

Side 8, 41385 to 41950

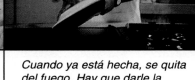

¡Con calma, con calma! ¡Ay, la tortilla! Es importante no dejar freír la tortilla demasiado.

Cuando ya está hecha, se quita del fuego. Hay que darle la vuelta.

Finalmente, hay que pasarla a la sartén y luego al fuego unos minutos más.

¡Caramba! ¡Tengan cuidado de no quemar las albóndigas!

Y ahora la salsa, ¡y ya está!

Qué fácil es, ¿verdad?

Miren este plato y esta tortilla. ¡Qué maravilla! Claro, preparados con cuidado, tendrán una tortilla exquisita y unas albondiguitas fenomenales.

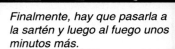

Bueno, hasta la próxima semana, Carlos Sartén les desea "¡Buen apetito!"

Tere: ¡Qué cómico! ¿verdad, mamá?

Mamá: Sí, es muy cómico, hija, pero qué desastre. Hoy todo le salió mal.

402   cuatrocientos dos

¿QUÉ DECIMOS...?

Al pedir la comida

1 Así trajeron el agua.

2 ¿Tienen una mesa reservada?

LECCIÓN 3

cuatrocientos tres **403**

44:03–
48:36

Side 8, 41972 to 50153

Early Production Checks

A full set of the **Early Production Checks** is available on cards in the Teacher's Resource Package.

1   `44:09`

Así trajeron el agua.
Suggestion Ask students if they know how tall 28 meters is in feet. If not, have them guess. (It is 96 feet.)
Point out This colossal piece of engineering is an eloquent testimonial to the architectural genius of Roman architects.

1 ¿Es la familia Molina? *Sí.*
2 ¿Es el acueducto de Segovia? *Sí.*
3 ¿Qué es? *(Point to aqueduct.) El acueducto de Segovia.*
4 ¿Cuánto mide en la parte más alta, 28 o 30 metros? *28 metros.*
5 ¿Quién lo construyó, el gobierno federal o los romanos? *Los romanos.*
6 ¿Cuándo lo construyeron, en el siglo primero o segundo antes de Jesucristo o después de Jesucristo? *Después de Jesucristo.*

Continue asking questions, as above.

Side 8, 42145 to 44047

2   `45:13`

¿Tienen una mesa reservada?
Accept brief answers to all questions, as in **1** above. Students need not answer in complete sentences.

1 ¿Es la familia Molina?

Continue asking questions, as above.

Side 8, 44065 to 45639

Purpose   These dialogues are not intended for memorization. Rather they show the language needed to describe what is happening at the moment, to tell what usually happens, and to describe something that happened in the past, in more natural contexts. Unfamiliar structures are intended solely for comprehension, not for mastery or production by students.

Suggestions   Begin by having students close their books while you narrate one section at a time, using the transparencies to clarify meaning without translation. Then ask **Early Production Checks**. Repeat this process with each section.

Using the video   Play one section at a time after narrating it using the transparancies. Freeze the video and ask **Early Production Checks**. Repeat with each section.

Cochinillo asado para todos.

1 ¿Quieren cochinillo asado?
2 ¿Ha probado Tere el cochinillo asado?
3 ¿Sabe que le gusta?
4 ¿Quiénes le dijeron que le va a gustar?
5 ¿Quieren algunos entremeses?
6 ¿Qué quieren?
7 ¿Quién quiere jamón serrano, Andrés o su padre?
8 ¿Qué quiere Marta, jamón serrano o tortilla?
9 ¿A quién le gustan las albóndigas, a Marta o a Andrés?
10 ¿Es su plato favorito?
11 ¿Quién pregunta si están listos para pedir?
12 ¿Qué pregunta el camarero?
13 ¿Piden los entremeses variados para empezar?
14 ¿Qué piden para empezar?
15 ¿Piden ensalada también?
16 ¿Qué piden de segundo plato, ensalada o cochinillo asado?

Side 8, 45655 to 47723

3 *Cochinillo asado para todos.*

4 *Me está sonriendo.*

Me está sonriendo.

1 ¿Quiénes son? *(Point to Carlota, then Tere.)*
2 ¿Le gustó el acueducto a Tere?
3 ¿Fue muy interesante el acueducto?
4 ¿Qué le gustó más a Tere, el acueducto o el castillo?
5 ¿Le gustaría vivir allí?
6 Y a ti, ¿te gustaría vivir en un castillo? *(Ask several students.)*
7 ¿Quién dice "No seas tonta", Andrés o Marta?
8 ¿Qué dice Andrés?
9 ¿Qué le gustó a Andrés, el pueblo, el castillo o el acueducto?
10 ¿Le encantaría salir a correr todas las mañanas?
11 ¿Qué le encantaría a Andrés?
12 ¿Qué le gustó más a Francisco, las tapas o el pueblo?
13 ¿Quién las preparó?
14 ¿Ya viene el cochinillo?
15 ¿Puede comer el cochinillo Tere?
16 ¿Le está sonriendo el cochinillo?

Side 8, 47750 to 50153

CHARLEMOS UN POCO

A. En Segovia. Call on individuals. If false, ask student to tell what the truth would be. Ask the class to confirm each answer.

1 falso. Es muy grande.
2 cierto
3 falso. Funcionó hasta mediados del siglo XX.
4 falso. Pudieron comer allí.
5 falso. Encontraron una mesa perfecta.
6 cierto
7 falso. A Francisco le encanta el jamón serrano.
8 cierto
9 cierto
10 falso. No lo quiere comer porque le está sonriendo.

B. ¿Te gusta? Allow 2–3 min for pair work. Then ask individuals if their partners like each item. Ask partners to confirm. Answers will vary. Some sample answers are:

1 ¿Te gusta el chorizo?
Sí, me gusta.
2 ¿Te gusta la tortilla española?
Me encanta.
3 ¿Te gustan los huevos (fritos)?
No, no los como nunca.
4 ¿Te gusta el queso?
Sí, me gusta.
5 ¿Te gustan las hamburguesas?
Me encantan.
6 ¿Te gusta el cochinillo asado?
No, no lo como nunca.
7 ¿Te gustan las manzanas?
Sí, me gustan.
8 ¿Te gusta la mayonesa?
No, no la como nunca.
9 ¿Te gusta el gazpacho?
Me encanta.

CHARLEMOS UN POCO

A. En Segovia. Di si son ciertos o falsos estos comentarios sobre la excursión de la familia Molina a Segovia. Si son falsos, corrígelos.

1. El acueducto de Segovia es muy pequeño.
2. Los romanos construyeron el acueducto.
3. El acueducto sigue funcionando ahora.
4. La familia Molina no pudo comer en el Mesón de Cándido.
5. La familia no encontró mesa en el mesón.
6. La familia Molina pidió el cochinillo asado.
7. A Tere le encanta el jamón serrano.
8. Papá pidió los entremeses variados.
9. A papá le gustó más que nada el almuerzo.
10. Tere quiere comer el cochinillo porque le está sonriendo.

B. ¿Te gusta? Pregúntale a tu compañero(a) si le gustan comer estas cosas.

MODELO   Tú: **¿Te gustan los bocadillos?**
Compañero(a): **Me encantan.** o
Sí, me gustan. o
No, no los como nunca.

1.

2.

3.

4.

5.

6.

7.

8.

9.

UNIDAD 8

Purpose These activities provide guided practice to students beginning to learn how to order a meal in a restaurant as well as to talk about what is happening at the moment, what happens regularly, and what happened in the past.

C. Mesón.

Acabas de entrar en el Mesón de Cándido. Completa la conversación con el camarero usando las siguientes frases.

Gracias, es perfecta la mesa.
Mélon y queso, por favor.
Sí, por favor. No conozco la comida aquí.
Sí, a nombre de . . .
Me trae la carne con patatas fritas, por favor.
¿Qué hay de postre?
Agua mineral, por favor.
Sí. La cuenta, por favor.
Sí, para empezar, el gazpacho y una ensalada mixta.
Buenas tardes.

Camarero: Buenas tardes, señor (señora, señorita).
Tú: . . .
Camarero: ¿Tiene una mesa reservada?
Tú: . . .
Camarero: Por aquí, por favor.
Tú: . . .
Camarero: ¿Desea ver la carta?
Tú: . . .
Camarero: ¿Está listo(a) para pedir?
Tú: . . .
Camarero: ¿Y de segundo plato?
Tú: . . .
Camarero: ¿Y para beber?
Tú: . . .
Camarero: ¿Quiere algo más?
Tú: . . .
Camarero: Fruta y queso o bizcocho.
Tú: . . .
Camarero: (*Más tarde.*) ¿Es todo?
Tú: . . .

CH. En el restaurante.

Cuando tú y tu familia van a un restaurante elegante, ¿qué pasa?

EJEMPLO **Papá pide la sopa de ajo.**

papá	comer	restaurante
la camarera	pedir	comida
mis hermanos	servir	entremeses
yo	beber	mesa
el cocinero	entrar	ensalada
todos	traer	café
los camareros	buscar	postre
mamá	preparar	frutas
	recomendar	refrescos
		sopa de ajo

En un restaurante

Requesting a table:
Una mesa para tres personas, por favor.
Tenemos una reservación a nombre de . . . .

Taking an order:
¿Desean ver la carta?
¿Está listo(a) para pedir?

Ordering a meal:
Para ella, la paella.
Quiero el gazpacho, por favor.
¿Tienen queso manchego?

C. Mesón. Allow 2–3 min for pair work. Then call on different pairs to act out each minidialogue.

C: Buenas tardes, señor(ita).
Tú: **Buenas tardes.**
C: ¿Tiene una mesa reservada?
Tú: **Sí, a nombre de . . .**
C: Por aquí, por favor.
Tú: **Gracias, es perfecta la mesa.**
C: ¿Desea ver la carta?
Tú: **Sí, por favor. No conozco la comida aquí.**
C: ¿Está listo(a) para pedir?
Tú: **Sí, para empezar, el gazpacho y una ensalada mixta.**
C: ¿Y de segundo plato?
Tú: **Me trae la carne con patatas fritas, por favor.**
C: ¿Y para beber?
Tú: **Agua mineral, por favor.**
C: ¿Quiere algo más?
Tú: **¿Qué hay de postre?**
C: Fruta fresca y queso o bizcocho.
Tú: **Melón y queso, por favor.**
C: ¿Es todo?
Tú: **Sí. La cuenta, por favor.**

CH. En el restaurante. Call on individuals. Ask class to confirm each answer. Answers will vary. Some sample answers are:
Papá pide la comida.
La camarera recomienda los entremeses.
Mis hermanos beben refrescos.
Yo como ensalada.
El cocinero prepara la comida.
Todos pedimos fruta.
Los camareros sirven la comida.
Mamá recomienda la sopa de ajo.

Present tense
A summary

There are three types of regular verbs: **-ar, -er, -ir.**

Some verbs undergo a change in the stem vowel:

e → ie	empezar	Ya **empieza** el partido.
o → ue	poder	Roberto no **puede** ir.
e → i	pedir	Papá **pide** un postre.

Some verbs have irregular **yo**-forms:

Salgo de casa a las siete. *(salir)*
Voy a levantarme tarde mañana. *(ir)*

*See ¿***Por qué se dice así?**, page G119, section 8.6.*

Present progressive
A summary

Estar + -ndo form of the verb:

Carla **está estudiando** ahora.
No **estamos comiendo** en este momento.

Some verbs undergo a vowel spelling change in the **-ndo** form.

dormir: **durmiendo**
leer: **leyendo**

*See ¿***Por qué se dice así?**, page G122, section 8.7.*

MODELO   levantarse: 7:00 A.M.
   Tú: **¿A qué hora te levantas?**
   Compañero(a): **Me levanto a las siete de la mañana.**

1. desayunar: 7:30 A.M.
2. irse a la escuela: 7:45 A.M.
3. tener el recreo: 11:00 A.M.
4. volver a casa: 1:30 P.M.
5. comer: 2:00 P.M.
6. descansar: 3:00 P.M.
7. salir con amigos: 4:15 P.M.
8. tomar un café: 5:30 P.M.
9. hacer la tarea: 6:30 P.M.
10. cenar: 9:00 P.M.
11. ver televisión: 10:00 P.M.
12. acostarse: 11:00 P.M.

E. Ocupados.   La familia Soler está muy ocupada esta tarde. ¿Qué están haciendo en cada cuarto?

MODELO   **La hija está viendo televisión en la sala.**

F. El verano pasado. ¿Con qué frecuencia hicieron ustedes estas actividades durante las vacaciones de verano? Pregúntale a tu compañero(a) y luego él o ella te lo va a preguntar a ti.

MODELO   ir de compras
Tú: **¿Con qué frecuencia fuiste de compras el verano pasado?**
Compañero(a):   **Fui de compras todos los días.** o **No fui de compras nunca.**

todos los días	mucho	pocas veces	nunca
•	•	•	•

1. jugar tenis
2. tocar la guitarra
3. almorzar en el parque
4. dormir hasta mediodía
5. leer novelas
6. hacer la tarea
7. ir al cine
8. practicar deportes
9. tener una fiesta en casa
10. comer pizza

G. ¿Qué hicieron?   Tú conoces bien a estas personas. ¿Qué hicieron durante el año?

MODELO   soñar con el cochinillo asado
Tere soñó con el cochinillo asado.

1. hacer una excursión a Tlaquepaque
2. casarse en la iglesia de San Antonio de Padua
3. no poder entender su horario
4. tomar muchos helados
5. romperse la pierna
6. correr detrás del autobús
7. decir "¡Tere, tengo mucha prisa!"
8. hacer un video de Montebello High
9. ponerse el reloj antes de ir a correr
10. tener que trabajar en el restaurante de su padre
11. pedir direcciones a la oficina de correos
12. ir de compras a Plaza Universidad
13. encantarle su profesor de historia
14. no poder bailar con Julio

Tere   **Pilar**   **Carlos**

Carmen   **Sara**   **Alicia y Kati**

Riqui   **Rafael y Betty**   **Leslie**

Manolo   **Mónica y Lilia**   **Óscar**   **José Luis**   **Marta**   **Andrés**

LECCIÓN 3

Preterite tense
A summary

There are two sets of endings for regular verbs, one for **-ar** verbs and one for **-er** and **-ir** verbs.

There are many irregular verbs in the preterite, such as **ir (fui), ser (fui)**, and **dar (di)**; and **tener (tuv-), poner (pus-)**, etc.

Some verbs undergo spelling changes in the preterite:

c → qu	buscar: **busqu-**
g → gu	llegar: **llegu-**
z → c	comenzar: **comenc-**

See **¿Por qué se dice así?,** *page G123, section 8.8.*

---

13 A Carmen le encantó su profesor de historia.
14 Leslie no pudo bailar con Julio.

Extension   Divide class into groups of three or four. Assign each group one or two of the photos. Ask each group to prepare a list of as many different things they can recall that the person(s) in the photo(s) did. Have each group read their list aloud so that class may verify what they wrote.

F. El verano pasado. Allow 2–3 min for pair work. Then ask individuals with what frecuency their partners did each activity. Ask the partners to confirm the answers given. Answers will vary. Some sample answers are:

1 ¿Con qué frecuencia jugaste tenis el verano pasado? Jugué tenis mucho.
2 ¿Con qué frecuencia tocaste la guitarra el verano pasado? No toqué la guitarra nunca.
3 ¿Con qué frecuencia almorzaste en el parque el verano pasado? No almorcé en el parque nunca.
4 ¿Con qué frecuencia dormiste hasta mediodía el verano pasado? Dormí hasta mediodía todos los días.
5 ¿Con qué frecuencia leíste novelas el verano pasado? Leé novelas todos los días.
6 ¿Con qué frecuencia hiciste la tarea el verano pasado? No hice la tarea nunca.
7 ¿Con qué frecuencia fuiste al cine el verano pasado? Fui al cine mucho.
8 ¿Con qué frecuencia practicaste deportes el verano pasado? Practiqué deportes todos los días.
9 ¿Con qué frecuencia tuviste una fiesta en casa el verano pasado? Tuve una fiesta en casa pocas veces.
10 ¿Con qué frecuencia comiste pizza? Comí pizza mucho.

G. ¿Qué hicieron? Allow 3–4 min for pairs to decide who did what. Then do activity with the whole class.

1 Mónica y Lilia hicieron una excursión a Tlaquepaque.
2 Rafael y Betty se casaron en la iglesia de San Antonio de Padua.
3 Carlos no pudo entender su horario.
4 Riqui tomó muchos helados.
5 José Luis se rompió la pierna.
6 Óscar corrió detrás del autobús.
7 Marta dijo "¡Tere, tengo mucha prisa!"
8 Pilar hizo un video de Montebello High.
9 Andrés se puso el reloj antes de ir a correr.
10 Sara tuvo que trabajar en el restaurante de su padre.
11 Manolo pidió direcciones a la oficina de correos.
12 Alicia y Kati fueron de compras a la Plaza Universidad.

A. ¿Te gusta . . .?
Have students circulate and talk with several classmates. Allow 4–5 min. Stop when someone has signatures in all the boxes. Check by asking the students who signed to confirm they like the specific food item.

B. ¿Los reconoces? Form eight groups. Assign each group one of the photos and allow 3–4 min to prepare lists. Then have each group read their list to the class, which will verify and add to the list if they can.

C. ¿Quién? ¿Qué?
Allow 5–8 min. Then ask individuals to read the captions they wrote for each of the persons. Have class confirm their answers.

Variation Have students write yearbook captions telling what three classmates did during the year. Then have them read one description at a time to see if the persons being described or class can identify the person.

CHARLEMOS UN POCO MÁS

A. ¿Te gusta . . .? Discover what your classmates' food tastes are like by finding someone who fits each description in the grid your instructor gives you. Have each person fitting a description sign the appropriate box. Remember that each person's signature may only appear once on the grid.

EJEMPLO **¿Te gusta la tortilla española?** o
¿Te gustan las hamburguesas?

B. ¿Los reconoces? Pictured below are places you will recognize in Spanish-speaking countries. With your partner, prepare a list of what these places are, where they are, and everything you can recall about them without going back to the units where they are presented.

C. ¿Quién? ¿Qué? You and your partner are editors of the school yearbook. Using the list your teacher provides, write captions telling which activity each person did, for each person whose name appears. Your partner will be able to describe the pictures missing on your page, and you should be able to describe the pictures missing on your partner's page. Ask each other questions but don't look at each other's yearbook pages until you have written all your captions.

Purpose These activities are designed to allow students to create with the language necessary to describe what is happening at the moment, to tell what they usually do, and to describe something that happened in the past.

CH. ¡Riesgo! In groups of three or four, prepare to play **Riesgo** (*Jeopardy*) by writing five questions and answers for each of the categories listed below. Then play **Riesgo** with another group. They will select a category and point value, and you will give them the answer to the question you had written for that slot. They, in turn, must respond with the correct question in order to receive the points. Then repeat the process by having your group select a category and point value from their gameboard. Keep alternating until your teacher calls time.

Ch. ¡Riesgo! This activity will take 20–30 min. Have students keep their questions and scoreboards to play again another day.

Deportes	Cultura	Profesores	Salud	Rutina diaria
20	20	20	20	20
40	40	40	40	40
60	60	60	60	60
80	80	80	80	80
100	100	100	100	100

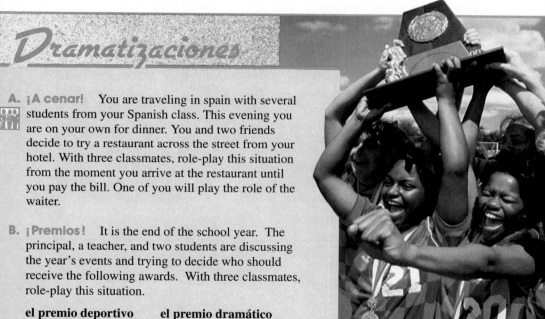

Dramatizaciones

A. ¡A cenar! You are traveling in spain with several students from your Spanish class. This evening you are on your own for dinner. You and two friends decide to try a restaurant across the street from your hotel. With three classmates, role-play this situation from the moment you arrive at the restaurant until you pay the bill. One of you will play the role of the waiter.

B. ¡Premios! It is the end of the school year. The principal, a teacher, and two students are discussing the year's events and trying to decide who should receive the following awards. With three classmates, role-play this situation.

el premio deportivo	**el premio dramático**
el premio escolástico	**el premio cómico**
el premio de español	**el premio de ciencias**

C. ¡No metas la pata! With three classmates, create a skit in Spanish that shows a cultural misunderstanding or resolves a problem.

LECCIÓN 3

DRAMATIZACIONES

A and B. Assign **A** and **B** at the same time. Allow 5–8 min to prepare role plays. Then have students present what they prepared to class. Ask comprehension check questions after each presentation.

In **Dramatizaciones,** students recycle, in student-centered role plays, all previously learned structures and vocabulary needed to describe what is happening at the moment, to tell what they usually do, and to describe something that happened. Encourage students to work without their books when performing their role plays.

LEAMOS AHORA

A. Anticipemos.

Suggestion Have students look at recipes on page 413 and follow these models when listing their ingredients. Answers will vary.

B. Detalles importantes.
First allow 2–3 min for students to answer these questions in pairs. Then call on individuals and have class confirm their answers.

Answers

1 Answers will vary.
2 Gazpacho: 3 pasos: Hacer un puré en la licuadora. Combinar y añadir las especies. Poner en la nevera. Tortilla: 4 pasos: Pelar y freír las papas y añadir cebolla. Batir huevos y agregar las papas, sal y pimienta. Freír lentamente. Darle la vuelta y pasar a la sartén de nuevo.

C. ¡Vamos a cocinar!

These two typical Spanish dishes would make excellent end-of-the-year party food. You may want to have class prepare them in the school kitchen (the **gazpacho** should be prepared the day before) or ask for student volunteers to prepare the recipes at home with parent supervision. Then have a Spanish fiesta.

Verifiquemos

1 a una sopa
2 c el tomate
3 ch Todas estas respuestas
4 ch huevos, papas y cebollas
5 a todos los ingredientes

LEAMOS AHORA

Reading strategy: Reading for detailed information

A. Anticipemos. ¿Qué comen ustedes en sus fiestas?

1. Haz una lista de los ingredientes que necesitas para preparar tu entremés favorito.
2. ¿Crees que ese entremés es popular en España también? ¿Por qué?

B. Detalles importantes. Certain types of readings require the reader to focus on the details. When reading for detailed information, you will need to read the selection more than once and pay close attention to the procedure being described, and perhaps make notes of details that you must remember. In the Spanish recipes that follow, for example, you cannot skim over the information. You must understand each step and follow it carefully to end up with a delicious dish instead of a disaster!

Look at the following recipes carefully and answer these questions.

1. ¿Qué ingredientes ya tienes en casa y qué necesitas comprar para el gazpacho? ¿Y para la tortilla española?
2. ¿Cuántos pasos requiere cada receta? Descríbelos.

C. ¡Vamos a cocinar! Read these authentic Spanish recipes; then answer the questions that follow. The **gazpacho,** which originated in southern Spain, is typically served during the summer months. The **tortilla** is usually served as a first course or an appetizer, throughout Spain.

Verifiquemos

1. El gazpacho es . . .
   a. una sopa.   **c.** una bebida.
   b. una ensalada.   **ch.** una caserola.

2. El ingrediente principal del gazpacho es . . .
   a. el aceite de oliva.   **c.** el tomate.
   b. el vinagre.   **ch.** el ajo.

3. El gazpacho se sirve . . .
   a. frío.   **c.** con vegetales picados.
   b. con cebolla picada.   **ch.** Todas estas respuestas.

412 *cuatrocientos doce*

UNIDAD 8

Purpose This is the principal reading of the unit. Its purpose is to teach students to read for detailed information using appropriate strategies. Students are not expected to understand every word. Rather they should focus on looking for the specific pieces of information requested. This strategy should be applied when reading to locate specific information.

412 UNIDAD 8   Lección 3

Gazpacho andaluz

Ingredientes

12	tomates	1/2	taza de aceite de oliva
1	lata grande de jugo de tomate	6	cucharadas de vinagre
1	pimiento verde	4	cucharitas de sal
1	cebolla		pimienta al gusto
1	pepino		
4	dientes de ajo		

Preparación

En una licuadora se hace un puré con los tomates, el jugo, el pimiento, la cebolla, el pepino y los dientes de ajo.

Se combinan el aceite, el vinagre, la sal y la pimienta. Se agrega a la sopa y se pone en la nevera por 24 horas. Se sirve frío. Se acostumbra servirlo con cebolla, tomate, pimiento y pepino picados. Sirve a 20 personas, aproximadamente.

Tortilla española

Ingredientes

3-4	papas
5	huevos
1	cebolla

aceite de oliva
sal y pimienta al gusto

Preparación

Se pelan y se pican las papas y se fríen en aceite de oliva hasta quedar doradas. Se agrega la cebolla picada por un minuto. En otro recipiente se baten los huevos y, poco a poco, se agregan las papas doradas. Se agregan sal y pimienta al gusto. Se fríe, muy despacio, con un poquito de aceite de oliva en una sartén. Cuando está bien firme, se quita del fuego y se le da la vuelta. Luego se pasa a la sartén de nuevo y se dora unos minutos más. Se sirve en un plato grande con ensalada y pan francés. Sirve de 3 a 5 personas.

4. Los ingredientes principales de la tortilla española son . . .

   a. papas y cebolla.   **c.** cebolla y aceite de oliva.

   b. aceite de oliva y huevos.   **ch.** huevos, papas y cebollas.

5. La preparación de la tortilla española requiere freír . . .

   a. todos los ingredientes.   **c.** las papas solamente.

   b. los huevos solamente.   **ch.** la cebolla y las papas solamente.

A. Empezando. Read the story with students. Use techniques of comprehensible input to clarify unknown words or phrases. The language of the story is not meant for mastery.

The form of such stories is very simple since their origin is in oral narration. The situation is identified, the characters introduced, the event is related, and the story ends with a "surprise" result. There is considerable repetition, which makes readers (hearers) think they know what will come next, but which also leads them to wonder what the result will be. The drawing shows the relationship between the man, the dog, and the burro.

B. Planeando. You may wish to have students talk about similar stories they have heard and/or read and to discuss how such stories illustrate cultural values. Students may want to work in pairs on this project. They may also illustrate their stories with drawings and/or with collages. Finished stories can be bound in a "book" and shared with other classes or reproduced for the members of the class as a souvenir of their first year of Spanish.

C. Organizando y escribiendo. Have a couple of students draw their cluster diagram or outline on board so others may see how to organize themselves. Point out that individuals will have their own organization, as all stories will differ. Allow time to write first draft. Provide guidance where necessary. You may want to assign first draft as homework.

ESCRIBAMOS UN POCO

Writing strategy:
Retelling a story

A. Empezando.   On the next page is a story from the American Hispanic Southwest. Read it and then discuss it. Does it remind you of other stories you have read? What do you think is the purpose of such stories? Describe the "form" of this story. How does the drawing enhance it?

B. Planeando.   Now you will write a short story in the style of *El hombre, el burro, y el perro.* You can retell a story such as the fable of the ant and the grasshopper, why the elephant has a trunk or how humans learned about fire. Or you may invent your own explanation for one of nature's mysteries. Possible beginning statements are:
  "Cuando el mundo era muy joven . . ."
  "En el momento en que nació el sol . . ."
  "Cuándo Dios se sentó a inventar el mundo, pensó . . ."
Decide what characters your story needs and how you will "set up" your surprise ending. Consider using dialog between the characters and a "twist" such as the repeated lines about *"días buenos y días malos."* Your ending should summarize the central idea:
  "Y por eso, el sol sale todos los días".
  "Y por eso, los pájaros pueden volar y los humanos no".
  "Y por eso, los árboles son mucho más altos que el hombre."
  "Y por eso, el hombre camina recto."

C. Organizando y escribiendo.   Brainstorm vocabulary you may need to write your story. Then make a cluster diagram or an outline before you write. Identify the characters and their relationship to each other, and decide on the sequence of events or dialog exchanges. Now write your first draft!

CH. Compartiendo y revisando.   Share your draft with two or three classmates. Is there anything they don't understand? Is there anything you need to add or change? Based on their suggestions, revise your story. Then share it with two other classmates and ask them to edit for grammar, spelling, and punctuation.

D. La versión final.   Now write the final version. If you like, illustrate it with drawings or pictures cut out of magazines. Then turn it in for grading.

E. Publicación.   When your stories have been returned, share them at an authors' reading and reception. Can speak in Spanish the whole time?

Purpose In this section, students are asked to apply speaking and writing skills developed in the unit to writing their own short story. Students will use strategies they began to develop in Unit 1: prewriting brainstorming and clustering, writing a first draft, peer feedback, and revision.

El hombre, el burro y el perro

Cuando Dios creó la tierra, creó también al hombre, y le hizo dueño de la tierra. Luego Dios decidió darle unos compañeros al hombre, y creó un burro y un perro.

Dios le dijo al hombre: "Tú te llamas hombre. Eres dueño de la tierra y vas a vivir sesenta años. Vas a tener días buenos y días malos, pero vas a tener más días buenos que malos".

El hombre pensó: "Sesenta años no es mucho tiempo".

Luego Dios le dijo al burro: "Tú te llamas burro. El hombre es tu dueño. Tú vas a vivir treinta años. Vas a tener días buenos y días malos, pero vas a tener más días malos que buenos".

Y el burro le contestó a Dios: "Si mi vida va a ser tan difícil, no quiero vivir tantos años. No quiero vivir más de veinte años".

Entonces el hombre le dijo: "Dios, dame los diez años que el burro rechaza" y Dios le dio diez años más al hombre.

Al perro Dios le dijo: "Tú te llamas perro, y el hombre es tu dueño. Vas a vivir veinte años. Vas a tener días buenos y días malos, pero vas a tener más días malos que buenos".

El perro dijo: "Dios, si mi vida va a ser tan difícil, no quiero vivir tantos años. No quiero vivir más de diez años".

El hombre vio otra oportunidad para alargar su vida y dijo: "Dios, dame los diez años que el perro rechaza". Y Dios le dio diez años más.

Y por eso, los primeros sesenta años el hombre tiene una vida decente. De sesenta a setenta es vida de burro; y de setenta para arriba ya es vida de perro.

Adaptado de: *El hombre, el burro y el perro*
Anaya, Rodolfo A. and Maestas, José Gregoria
Museum of New Mexico Press, Santa Fe, 1980

CH. Compartiendo y revisando. Have students gather in "response groups" of two or three. Allow time to share articles. Encourage them to comment on content first. Remind group members to begin commentary with at least one positive comment, and then to make suggestions on content. After they have commented on content, tell students to comment on any structure or vocabulary error they find in their classmates' stories. Tell them to focus especially on subject/verb, noun/adjective agreement errors. You may want to illustrate this type of error on board or on an overhead transparency. Tell them that in grading the stories, you will deduct points for agreement errors only.

D. La versión final. Encourage students to prepare a final version that is neat and clean. If they have access to a typewriter or computer, have them type it. If not, have them rewrite it using their best penmanship, leaving every other line blank. Suggest that students include several drawings to illustrate their stories, as in children's books.

E. Publicación. Have a formal reception, with refreshments. Have students form small reading circles (groups of three) and read their stories to each other. You may want to ask each group to select its best story, then have three groups form a reading circle and listen to the top three stories. This large group may then select the best story. Provide prizes for the winners.

IMPACTO CULTURAL ANSWERS

Which number did you pick? Read the item that corresponds to that number. If you picked an incorrect answer, then go back to the correct page and try again.

Lección preliminar: ¡De Nuevo México a Nueva York!, página 11

1. We have no way of knowing if Yolanda's mother knows how to prepare tacos and enchiladas. Reread the conversation and try another answer.
2. This may be correct but there is no indication of this in the girls' conversation. You should not jump to conclusions. Try again.
3. Ellen doesn't say this, but she implies it. This is the correct answer. New Mexican food is heavily influenced by the foods of Mexico. Puerto Ricans don't eat many corn-based foods. Rather, their diet tends to consist of rice dishes, fried bananas, chicken, and pork.

UNIDAD 1: Lección 1   ¿Cómo estás?, página 27

1. Since Mr. Peña greeted both of the boys, it was not necessary for Fred to wait to be introduced. Try again.
2. Nothing in the dialogue reveals a negative attitude toward foreign students. Consider another answer.
3. Right! Fred should have used the more formal **usted** form to address a teacher. Can you think of an appropriate greeting?

UNIDAD 1: Lección 2   ¡Somos americanos!, página 40

1. Nothing is said to indicate that León's knowledge of geography is deficient. In fact, Latin American students are usually very knowledgeable about world geography. Try another answer.
2. Actually, North Americans, Central Americans, and South Americans are all Americans. When speaking Spanish, if you are trying to say that you are from the United States, refer to yourself as **norteamericano(a)** to avoid confusion. This is the correct answer.
3. There is no indication that León is trying to fool Jennifer about anything, especially since he just met her. Try another response.

416 *cuatrocientos dieciséis*

UNIDAD 2: Lección 1   *El horario de Andrea, página 71*

1. There is no real basis in the dialogue for this assumption. Try again.
2. Carla is unfamiliar with class schedules in Latin American schools. It is not unusual for Latin American high school students to study twelve to fifteen different subjects a year. Classes do not meet every day, and, many schools have late afternoon and Saturday sessions. This is the correct answer.
3. There is nothing in the dialogue that implies that Andrea was exaggerating. If Tom thought that, he would probably have said something like "She must be exaggerating" or "She's got to be kidding." Try another response.

UNIDAD 2: Lección 2   *¡Qué inteligente!, página 85*

1. You have selected the correct answer. **Colegio** refers to a secondary or even a primary school— *not* to a college.
2. That is not at all likely, since José Antonio is Sonia's younger brother. Bill actually says that José Antonio cannot be more than fifteen or sixteen years old. Try again.
3. There is no evidence that José Antonio is a whiz kid. Sonia even says that she and her brother attend the same high school. Try another response.

UNIDAD 3: Lección 1   *De compras, página 116*

1. There is no evidence in this dialogue that people don't work in the afternoon. Try another response.
2. In Spain, Mexico, and most Latin American countries, the principal meal of the day is lunch. Many businesses close between 2:00 and 4:00 so that employees may go home for their main meal. Currently, however, in the larger cities, major department stores and international businesses remain open throughout the afternoon. Most stores do close later in the evening to allow additional shopping time. This is the correct answer.
3. Shops in Mexico, as in most cities of the Western world, do close down on certain religious holidays, but no indication was given that Tom was shopping on a religious holiday. Try another response.

UNIDAD 3: Lección 2   *¡Hay tanta gente!, página 131*

1. There is no indication that Tom knew what day it was. In fact, he kept asking Rosa what the special occasion might be. Try another response.
2. It is not unusual to see whole families—including aunts, uncles, and grandparents—enjoying themselves in the parks on any Saturday or Sunday. The parks are generally well-kept and provide very inexpensive entertainment for the whole family. This is the correct answer.
3. There is no indication that Tom believed Rosa was trying to fool him. He was simply surprised to see so many people in the park.

UNIDAD 4: Lección 1   ¡Toda la familia!, página 164

1. Mary Ann did not know that most Hispanics include not only parents and children in their family, but also aunts, uncles, and grandparents, and sometimes even cousins. This is the correct answer.
2. Nothing in the dialogue indicates that Mary Ann thought about this. This is not the correct answer.
3. This is a possible answer. However, Mary Ann did not mention anything about the grandmother living alone. Try another response.

UNIDAD 4: Lección 2   ¡No está en la guía!, página 181

1. There is no evidence that Larry didn't spell **Chacón** correctly. Try again.
2. Larry says that the number is not listed, but Claudio says that he is certain it is. There must be another reason.
3. Larry is looking for the number of Jorge Salinas Chacón under **Chacón** and not under **Salinas.** He has forgotten that names are alphabetized by the father's last name, not the mother's maiden name. This is the correct answer.

UNIDAD 5: Lección 1   Madrid de noche, página 219

1. Tom doesn't realize that an evening stroll (**un paseo**) is customary in many Hispanic cities. Entire families can be seen on the streets, even late into the evening. This is the correct answer.
2. Nothing in the dialogue indicates that Tom is unaware that large families live in that part of town. Consider another answer.
3. Tom may consider the streets unsafe, but the dialogue gives no indication that this is why he is surprised. Try again.

UNIDAD 5: Lección 2   La planta baja, página 236

1. Rick may well think that Betty is trying to distract him, since he is confused about what floor he is on. Actually, Betty knows that they are on the wrong floor. Try another answer.
2. In Spain, as in all Spanish-speaking countries, the ground floor of multistory buildings is the **planta baja.** On elevators, the button for the ground floor is marked **PB. La primera planta** is the first floor above the ground floor. This is why Betty suggests they have to go up one floor.
3. The shoes are on sale according to the advertisement in the window. This is not the cause for the confusion.

UNIDAD 6: Lección 1 Te invito al ballet, página 270

1. It is true that Javier knows that the **ballet folklórico** is famous; he says so himself. However, this does not guarantee that Paul will like it. Reread the conversation.
2. There is no indication that Paul has never seen a good ballet company, only that he hasn't enjoyed the ballet performances that he has seen. This is incorrect.
3. Javier understands that Paul doesn't like classical ballet. However, the **ballet folklórico** presents colorful and lively folk dances from all regions of Mexico and Javier feels quite certain that Paul will enjoy it. This is the correct answer.

UNIDAD 6: Lección 2 ¡Huy, qué caro!, página 285

1. It is possible that Javier didn't like the cat. But if he didn't, he did not express this at all. He actually says he likes it. Try another response.
2. Paul feels that he got a bargain when he paid 30,000 pesos less than the vendor originally wanted. Javier, on the other hand, thinks that 60,000 pesos is too much to pay for a papier-mâché figurine. He obviously thinks Paul should have offered less than he did.
3. There is no indication that Javier even thought about Paul buying him a gift. This is not the correct answer.

UNIDAD 7: Lección 1 ¿Béisbol en Latinoamérica?, página 321

1. Cliff may consider baseball unsafe for children, but nothing in the dialogue indicates this. On the contrary, he congratulates Pepe for being the best batter among his friends. Try another answer.
2. Cliff never says this nor does he give any indication that he thinks this. He actually seems quite pleased that Pepe plays so well. This is not the correct answer.
3. Cliff is clearly surprised to see that both parent and child are interested in baseball. He seems to be unaware that baseball is rivaling soccer in popularity in several Latin American countries, in particular, in the Dominican Republic, Cuba, and Puerto Rico.

UNIDAD 7: Lección 2 ¿Cómo vamos?, página 337

1. Gabriel may notice some differences between his own pronunciation and that of Pedro's, but he doesn't say anything about it in the dialogue. Pronunciation differences occur as much in Spanish as they do in English and are all equally valid. This is not the correct answer. Try another response.

2. Just as pronunciation will vary from country to country or region to region, so will certain vocabulary items. A **guagua** is a *bus* in Caribbean countries and a *baby* in some South American countries. Gabriel did not recognize the word because it is not commonly used in Mexico. This is the reason for his comment.

3. All of us tend to think that the way we speak is the norm, since that is what we have heard most often. Gabriel most certainly has noted differences between his Spanish and Pedro's, but he probably accepts them readily. There certainly is no indication in the dialogue that he feels that his Spanish is superior. Try another answer.

UNIDAD 8: Lección 1 ¡Es una tortilla!, página 377

1. Luisa did say that she was very hungry, but she seemed to accept Julia's comment that the **tortillas** are nice and big. Her reaction does not seem to refer to the size of the omelet, but to the idea of the waiter's having brought an omelet. Try another response.

2. There is no indication that she doesn't like omelets. Try again.

3. She says that she likes **tortillas** which indicates that she does know what they are. However, Luisa is from Mexico, where **tortillas** are pancake-thin corn flour or wheat flour breads. In Spain, a **tortilla** is an omelet. A **tortilla española** is made of eggs, sliced potatoes, and onions. This is the correct answer.

UNIDAD 8: Lección 2 Una invitación a cenar, página 395

1. Claudia may think this, particularly if she is tired, but she doesn't say so. Try again.

2. Claudia is evidently unfamiliar with Spanish mealtimes. It is not unusual for a family to dine at 10:00 or 11:00 o'clock at night. Lunch is the main meal of the day and is usually eaten about 1:30 or 2:00. Although customs are changing in the larger cities, many businesses and schools still close for two or three hours for lunch and reopen about 5:00 for three or four more hours. Consequently, dinner is eaten late. The evening meal is usually lighter than the midday meal. This is the correct answer.

3. Claudia gives no evidence that she thinks this. Try another answer.

¿POR QUÉ SE DICE ASÍ?

Manual de gramática

L E C C I Ó N

P R E L I M I N A R

LP. 1 Margin box: page 8

LP.1 GENDER OF NOUNS: INTRODUCTION
Naming Objects

Nouns name people, places, things, or concepts. In Spanish, nouns are either masculine or feminine. You must learn the gender of nouns as you learn their meaning, but there are some general rules. Most nouns that end in **-o** are masculine, and most nouns that end in **-a** are feminine.

Masculine Nouns		Feminine Nouns	
libro	*book*	mochila	*backpack*
cuaderno	*notebook*	carpeta	*folder*
lápiz	*pencil*	clase	*class*
papel	*paper*	pizarra	*chalkboard*
escritorio	*desk*	mesa	*table, desk*
borrador	*eraser*	silla	*chair*

LP.2 Margin boxes: pages 8, 9

LP.2 INDEFINITE AND DEFINITE ARTICLES
Talking about Nonspecific and Specific Things

■ The indefinite article, *a* or *an* in English, is used to refer to nonspecific things. The Spanish equivalent depends on whether the noun it refers to is masculine or feminine. Masculine nouns use the form **un;** feminine nouns use **una.**

Masculine Nouns		Feminine Nouns	
un libro	*a book*	una mochila	*a backpack*
un cuaderno	*a notebook*	una carpeta	*a folder*
un lápiz	*a pencil*	una clase	*a class*
un papel	*a paper*	una pizarra	*a chalkboard*
un escritorio	*a desk*	una mesa	*a table, desk*
un borrador	*an eraser*	una silla	*a chair*

¿POR QUÉ SE DICE ASÍ?

Preliminar

- The definite article, *the* in English, is used to talk about specific things. The Spanish equivalent depends on the gender of the noun it refers to. Masculine nouns use **el**; feminine nouns use **la.**

Masculine Nouns		Feminine Nouns	
el libro	*the book*	la mochila	*the backpack*
el cuaderno	*the notebook*	la carpeta	*the folder*
el lápiz	*the pencil*	la clase	*the class*
el papel	*the paper*	la pizarra	*the chalkboard*
el escritorio	*the desk*	la mesa	*the table, desk*
el borrador	*the eraser*	la silla	*the chair*

Vamos a practicar

a. ¡Caramba! A puppy was left alone in this room for 15 minutes, and now everything is a mess. Which items listed below do *not* appear in the room? On a separate piece of paper, write down the items you could not find.

cuaderno	mochila	carpeta
lápiz	mesa	papel
bolígrafo	libro	escritorio

b. ¿Qué hay? List as many school items as you can find in the puppy's messy room above. Make sure to include **un** or **una** before each item.

c. ¿Qué hay aquí? A substitute teacher doesn't know where things are in your classroom, so she asks you. Complete her questions.

MODELO ¿Dónde está **el** libro de español del profesor?

1. ¿Dónde está _____ cuaderno del profesor?
2. ¿Dónde está _____ silla del profesor?
3. ¿Dónde está _____ bolígrafo del profesor?
4. ¿Dónde está _____ papel del profesor?
5. ¿Dónde está _____ carpeta del profesor?

¿POR QUÉ SE DICE ASÍ?   **G3**

LECCIÓN 1

1.1 Margin box: page 25

Suggestion You may need to review the meanings of *singular* and *subject pronoun*. Verify that students understand these grammatical concepts.

Point out Both **tú** and **él** have written accents. Contrast **él** *(he)* with **el** *(the)* and **tú** *(you)* with **tu** *(your)*.

1.1 SUBJECT PRONOUNS: SINGULAR FORMS
Referring to People

Subject pronouns are used to talk to and about other people. In Spanish, the subject pronouns have the following forms:

Singular Subject Pronouns	
yo	*I*
tú	*you (informal)*
usted	*you (formal)*
él	*he*
ella	*she*
—	*it*

Yo (*I*) refers to the person speaking, **tú** or **usted** (*you*) to the person spoken to, and **él** or **ella** (*he, she*) to the person spoken about. The subject pronoun *it* in English is NEVER expressed in Spanish.

Yo soy Miguel.	*I am Miguel.*
Ella no es la profesora.	*She is not the teacher.*
¿Quién eres **tú**?	*Who are you?*
¿Es **usted** el Sr. Ramos?	*Are you Mr. Ramos?*
¿Quién es **él**?	*Who is he?*
¿Qué es? Es un perro.	*What is it? It is a dog.*

■ **Yo** is not capitalized unless it comes at the beginning of a sentence.

■ **Tú** and **usted** both mean *you*. **Tú** is the familiar form of address usually used with children, family, and friends. **Usted** is used to show respect or to indicate a more formal relationship with the person addressed. Customarily, **usted** is used to address teachers and elderly people, as well as adults you don't know well.

■ **Usted** is always used with anyone referred to by title:

Sr. (señor)	Prof. (profesor[a])
Sra. (señora)	Dr. (doctor)
Srta. (señorita)	Dra. (doctora)

Buenas tardes, Sra. Ramos. ¿Cómo está **usted**?
Muy bien, gracias, Dr. Sánchez. ¿Y **usted**?

■ When addressing someone directly, the definite article is not used with the title.

Buenos días, Sr. Castillo.
¿Cómo está usted, Sra. Ramírez?

However, when talking *about* someone, the definite article **el / la / los / las** is always used in front of the title.

¿Cómo está **la** Sra. Castillo?
El Sr. Romero es mi profesor de matemáticas.

Vamos a practicar

a. ¿Quién es?   Indicate which pronoun—**yo, tú, usted, ella, él**—you would use with the following people. Each pronoun may be used more than once.

1. your mother, when you are talking to her
2. your father, when you are talking about him
3. a male friend you are talking about
4. a close friend you are talking to
5. a female friend you are talking about
6. you, talking about yourself
7. a teacher you are talking to
8. your aunt, when you are talking about her

b. ¿Tú o usted?   Would you use **tú** or **usted** to address the following people?

1. your sister
2. the principal of your school
3. your Spanish teacher
4. your teenage cousin
5. the classmate who sits behind you
6. a clerk at the store
7. your best friend
8. the guidance counselor

c. Amigos y profesores.   Which pronoun would you use to refer to the following people?

MODELO   *Pablo* es mi amigo.
         ***Él* es mi amigo.**

1. *Diana* es mi amiga.
2. *La Srta. Montero* es mi profesora.
3. *El Sr. Whitaker* es mi profesor de historia.
4. *Alicia* es mi amiga.
5. *Juan* es mi amigo.
6. *El Sr. Pérez* es el director de la escuela.
7. *La Sra. Ramos* es mi profesora de matemáticas.
8. *José* es mi amigo.

¿POR QUÉ SE DICE ASÍ?   **G5**

Vamos a practicar

These exercises may be done as oral or written work.

> **Additional Exercises**
> Textbook: pages 24–25
> Cuaderno: Unidad 1, Lección 1

a. ¿Quién es?
1 tú
2 él
3 él
4 tú
5 ella
6 yo
7 usted
8 ella

b. ¿Tú o usted?
1 tú
2 usted
3 usted
4 tú
5 tú
6 usted
7 tú
8 usted

c. Amigos y profesores.
1 Ella
2 Ella
3 Él
4 Ella
5 Él
6 Él
7 Ella
8 Él

ch. Fotos.
1 ¿Quién es ella?
2 ¿Quién es él?
3 ¿Quién es él?
4 ¿Quién es ella?
5 ¿Quién es él?
6 ¿Quién es él?
7 ¿Quién es ella?
8 ¿Quién es ella?

1.2 Margin box: page 25

Point out The verb **ser** links two nouns or a noun and its adjectives.

ch. Fotos. A Mexican friend, Pilar, is showing you some photos she took at school. You are curious to know who the people in the photographs are. What would you ask her?

MODELO   Tú: **¿Quién es él?**
          Pilar: Es mi amigo Pablo.

1. Tú: ¿ . . . ?
   Pilar: Es mi profesora de español.

2. Tú: ¿ . . . ?
   Pilar: Es el Sr. Morales.

3. Tú: ¿ . . . ?
   Pilar: Es mi amigo Rafael.

4. Tú: ¿ . . . ?
   Pilar: Es mi amiga Teresa.

5. Tú: ¿ . . . ?
   Pilar: Es el profesor de matemátic

6. Tú: ¿ . . . ?
   Pilar: Es mi amigo Samuel.

7. Tú: ¿ . . . ?
   Pilar: Es Luisa, mi buena amiga.

8. Tú: ¿ . . . ?
   Pilar: ¡Caramba! ¡Soy yo!

1.2 THE VERB *SER*: SINGULAR FORMS

The singular forms of the verb **ser** (*to be*) are as follows:

Ser		
yo	**soy**	*I am*
tú	**eres**	*you are*
usted	**es**	
él	**es**	*he is*
ella	**es**	*she is*
—	**es**	*it is*

- **Ser** is used in the following ways:

  To describe physical characteristics and personality traits
Luis **es** alto y guapo.	*Luis is tall and good-looking.*
No **es** muy modesto.	*He is not very modest.*
Ana María **es** interesante.	*Ana María is interesting.*

  To tell where someone is from
Soy de California.	*I'm from California.*
Usted **es** de Miami, ¿no?	*You're from Miami, aren't you?*

  To identify someone or something
Silvia **es** la nueva chica.	*Silvia is the new girl.*
Es una escuela grande.	*It is a large school.*
¿**Eres** el amigo de Ricardo?	*Are you Ricardo's friend?*

Vamos a practicar

a. ¿Quién es? Identify these people at your school by combining items from each column. Be sure to use the verb form that corresponds to the subject. There are many possible answers.

MODELO **Tú eres mi amiga.**

la Srta./Sra. . . .
tú
él
usted   soy   el (la) profesor(a) de español
yo   eres   mi amiga
ella   es   un (una) estudiante muy bueno(a)
el Sr. . . .   mi amigo Andrés
el (la) Prof. . . .   un (una) profesor(a) excelente
¿ . . . ?   el (la) director(a) de la escuela
                        un(a) buen(a) amigo(a)

b. Una nueva estudiante. Carlos and Alicia meet at school for the first time. Complete their conversation with the appropriate forms of **ser.**

Carlos: Buenos días. _____ Carlos.
Alicia: Hola. Mi nombre _____ Alicia.
Carlos: Tú _____ la nueva chica, ¿verdad?
Alicia: Sí. _____ de Los Ángeles.
Carlos: Pues, ¡pobrecita! ¡El primer día de clases _____ terrible!
Alicia: ¿Terrible? ¡No! ¡_____ estupendo!

c. La primera semana. Use the appropriate form of **ser** to see what this student can say after the first week of Spanish classes.

Mi nombre _____ Alicia. _____ de California. La señora Pérez _____ mi profesora de español. _____ una profesora excelente. Ella _____ puertorriqueña.

1.3 SUBJECT PRONOUNS: USE

In Spanish, the subject pronoun is not usually used because the verb ending indicates the subject. For example, **eres** means *you are.*

■ All forms of **ser** are used without a subject pronoun when the subject is clearly understood from the context or when the English subject is *it.*

Soy el nuevo estudiante.   *I am the new student.*
Eres mi amigo.   *You are my friend.*
Es la profesora de español.   *She is the Spanish teacher.*
Es hora de clase.   *It is time for class.*

¿POR QUÉ SE DICE ASÍ?   **G7**

Vamos a practicar

These exercises may be done as oral or written work.

Additional Exercises
Textbook: pages 24–25
Cuaderno: Unidad 1, Lección 1

a. ¿Quién es? Answers will vary.

b. Una nueva estudiante.
Soy
es
eres
Soy
es
Es

c. La primera semana.
es/Soy/es
Es/es

1.3 Margin box: page 25

■ Subject pronouns are used in order to be very clear (that is, for clarification) or for emphasis.

Clarification:

¿Quién es **él**? ¿Beto o Toni?   *Who is he? Beto or Toni?*
Él es el señor Pérez y **ella** es   *He is Mr. Pérez and she is*
la señorita Montero.   *Miss Montero.*

Emphasis:

Yo soy de Bogotá; **él** es de   *I am from Bogota; he is from*
Caracas.   *Caracas.*

Vamos a practicar

a. No, ella es . . .   A new student is having difficulty identifying people in her Spanish class. How do her classmates respond to help her identify the right person?

MODELO ¿Es Beto? (Juan)
         No. Es Juan. Él es Beto.

1. ¿Es Sara? (Gloria)   5. ¿Es Luisa? (Ana)
2. ¿Eres Ana? (Lisa)   6. ¿Eres Alicia? (Elena)
3. ¿Es Carlos? (Roberto)   7. ¿Es Andrés? (Samuel)
4. ¿Eres Arturo? (Rudy)   8. ¿Es Susana? (Marta)

b. ¿De quién hablas?   Find out who María, Samuel, and Teresa are talking about by selecting the correct subject pronoun for each verb.

María: ___(1)___ soy María. ¿Quién eres ___(2)___?
Samuel: ___(3)___ soy Samuel.
María: ¿ ___(4)___ eres el nuevo estudiante?
Samuel: Sí. ¿Quién es tu amiga?
María: ___(5)___ es Teresa.
Samuel: Encantado. ___(6)___ soy Samuel Marín.
Teresa: Mucho gusto.

L E C C I Ó N 2

1.4 ¿DE DÓNDE . . . ? AND SER DE . . .

Used to Talk about Where Someone Is From

In order to ask where someone is from, Spanish uses **¿De dónde . . . ?** and a form of **ser.**

¿De dónde es usted?   *Where are you from?*

Vamos a practicar

These exercises may be done as oral or written work.

> **Additional Exercises**
> Textbook: pages 24–25
> Cuaderno: Unidad 1, Lección 1

a. No, ella es ...
1 No. Es Gloria. Ella es Sara.
2 No. Soy Lisa. Ella es Ana.
3 No. Es Roberto. Él es Carlos.
4 No. Soy Rudy. Él es Arturo.
5 No. Es Ana. Ella es Luisa.
6 No. Soy Elena. Ella es Alicia.
7 No. Es Samuel. Él es Andrés.
8 No. Es Marta. Ella es Susana.

b. ¿De quién hablas?
1 Yo
2 tú
3 Yo
4 Tú
5 Ella
6 Yo

1.4 Margin box: page 37

In order to say where someone is from, Spanish uses

> **ser + de + place**

Soy de San Francisco.　　*I am from San Francisco.*
¿María?　**Es de** México.　　*María?　She is from Mexico.*

- The names of countries in Spanish, as in English, are always capitalized.

- Sometimes the definite article is used with certain countries, although the tendency is to not use it. You should, however, recognize it if you hear or see it used with these countries.

  la Argentina　　　　el Paraguay
  el Brasil　　　　　　el Perú
  el Ecuador　　　　　el Uruguay
  los Estados Unidos

- The definite article is always used with El Salvador, because it is part of the country's name, and with la República Dominicana.

Vamos a practicar

a. ¡Sudamérica!　　Tell where the following people are from.

> MODELO　¿De dónde es Carmen? (5)
> 　　　　**Carmen es de Bolivia.**

1. ¿De dónde es Arturo? (4)
2. ¿De dónde es Enrique? (9)
3. ¿De dónde es Sara? (6)
4. ¿De dónde es Marta? (3)
5. ¿De dónde es Ana? (8)
6. ¿De dónde es Rafael? (1)
7. ¿De dónde es Mario? (5)
8. ¿De dónde es Lola? (10)
9. ¿De dónde es Samuel? (2)
10. ¿De dónde es Luisa? (7)

b. Capitales sudamericanas.　　Complete the following sentences.

> MODELO　Caracas es la capital de **Venezuela**.

1. Asunción es la capital de _____.
2. Bogotá es la capital de _____.
3. Lima es la capital de _____.
4. Buenos Aires es la capital de _____.
5. Quito es la capital de _____.
6. Montevideo es la capital de _____.
7. Brasilia es la capital de _____.
8. La Paz es la capital de _____.
9. Santiago es la capital de _____.
10. Caracas es la capital de _____.

¿POR QUÉ SE DICE ASÍ?　　　　　　　　　　　　　　　　　　　　　　**G9**

Vamos a practicar

These exercises may be done as oral or written work.

Additional Exercises
Textbook: page 37
Cuaderno: Unidad 1, Lección 2

a. ¡Sudamérica!
1　Arturo es de Perú.
2　Enrique es de Paraguay.
3　Sara es de Chile.
4　Marta es de Ecuador.
5　Ana es de Uruguay.
6　Rafael es de Venezuela.
7　Mario es de Bolivia.
8　Lola es de Brasil.
9　Samuel es de Colombia.
10　Luisa es de Argentina.

b. Capitales sudamericanas.
1　Paraguay
2　Colombia
3　Perú
4　Argentina
5　Ecuador
6　Uruguay
7　Brasil
8　Bolivia
9　Chile
10　Venezuela

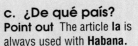

c. ¿De qué país?

Point out The article **la** is always used with **Habana.**

1 Es de El Salvador.
2 Es de Cuba.
3 Es de Nicaragua.
4 Es de Costa Rica.
5 Es de La República Dominicana.
6 Es de México.
7 Es de Honduras.
8 Es de Guatemala.
9 Es de Puerto Rico.
10 Es de Panamá.

ch. ¿De dónde eres?

1 Sí, soy de Santiago.
2 Sí, soy de San Salvador.
3 Sí, soy de San José.
4 Sí, soy de Caracas.
5 Sí, soy de La Habana.
6 Sí, soy de Montevideo.
7 Sí, soy de San Juan.
8 Sí, soy de Asunción.
9 Sí, soy de Managua.
10 Sí, soy de Santo Domingo.

1.5 Margin box: page 48

---

c. ¿De qué país? Tell which country these exchange students are from.

> MODELO Ana es de San Juan.
> **Es de Puerto Rico.**

1. Tina es de San Salvador.
2. Beto es de La Habana.
3. Tomás es de Managua.
4. Silvia es de San José.
5. Sara es de Santo Domingo.
6. Mario es de la Ciudad de México.
7. Luisa es de Tegucigalpa.
8. Eduardo es de la Ciudad de Guatemala.
9. Arturo es de San Juan.
10. María es de la Ciudad de Panamá.

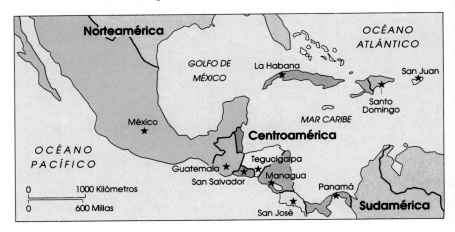

ch. ¿De dónde eres? What do these exchange students say when asked if they are from a particular country?

> MODELO Elena, ¿eres de Colombia?
> **Sí, soy de Bogotá.**

1. Bárbara, ¿eres de Chile?
2. Jorge, ¿eres de El Salvador?
3. Silvia, ¿eres de Costa Rica?
4. Carlos, ¿eres de Venezuela?
5. Marta, ¿eres de Cuba?
6. Víctor, ¿eres de Uruguay?
7. Beto, ¿eres de Puerto Rico?
8. Gloria, ¿eres de Paraguay?
9. Cristina, ¿eres de Nicaragua?
10. Ana, ¿eres de la República Dominicana?

L E C C I Ó N 3

1.5 GENDER OF NOUNS

In the **Lección preliminar,** you learned that a noun is a word that names a person, animal, place, thing, event, or concept. You also learned that in Spanish, all nouns have gender; they are either masculine or feminine. Most nouns that end in **-o** are masculine, and most nouns that end in **-a** are feminine.

- The gender of nouns that do not end in **-o** or **-a** must be learned as you learn their meaning.

Feminine Nouns	Masculine Nouns
la clase	el lápiz
la capital	el papel

- Nouns that refer to male people or animals are masculine; nouns that refer to female people or animals are feminine.

Feminine Nouns		Masculine Nouns	
amiga	*friend*	amigo	*friend*
chica	*girl*	chico	*boy*
directora	*principal*	director	*principal*
mamá	*mom*	papá	*dad*
profesora	*teacher*	profesor	*teacher*
señora	*Mrs.*	señor	*Mr.*
gata	*cat*	gato	*cat*

- Some nouns may be either masculine or feminine. When this is the case, only the definite article changes.

la estudiante	**el** estudiante
la turista	**el** turista
la artista	**el** artista

Vamos a practicar

a. ¿Masculino o femenino? Indicate if the following words are masculine or feminine.

MODELO   chico   doctora
          masculino: el chico   **femenino: la doctora**

1. papá
2. profesora
3. amigo
4. chica
5. mamá
6. director
7. señor
8. amiga
9. señora
10. profesor
11. directora
12. doctor

b. ¿Quién es? Answer the question according to the model.

MODELO   ¿Quién es? (director)
          Es el director.

1. profesor
2. profesora
3. padre
4. señorita Téllez
5. señora Roque
6. directora
7. señor López
8. mamá
9. amigo de papá

¿POR QUÉ SE DICE ASÍ?   **G11**

Vamos a practicar

These exercises may be done as oral or written work.

Additional Exercises
Textbook: pages 48–51
Cuaderno: Unidad 1, Lección 3

a. ¿Masculino o femenino?
1 masculino: el papá
2 femenino: la profesora
3 masculino: el amigo
4 femenino: la chica
5 femenino: la mamá
6 masculino: el director
7 masculino: el señor
8 femenino: la amiga
9 femenino: la señora
10 masculino: el profesor
11 femenino: la directora
12 masculino: el doctor

b. ¿Quién es?
1 Es el profesor.
2 Es la profesora.
3 Es el padre.
4 Es la señorita Tellez.
5 Es la señora Roque.
6 Es la directora.
7 Es el señor López.
8 Es la mamá.
9 Es el amigo de papá.

Ask what **estudioso** modifies.

Point out Even when subject pronouns are not stated, adjectives must agree in gender and number with the subject of the sentence.

Adjectives are words that describe nouns. For example, in the sentence **Anita es alta** (*Anita is tall*), **alta** is an adjective because it describes **Anita.** Other examples are:

Daniel es **delgado.**	*Daniel is thin.*
Tú eres **simpática.**	*You are nice.*
Soy **estudioso.**	*I am studious.*

In Spanish, an adjective that describes a masculine noun must also be masculine; one that describes a feminine noun must be feminine. In order to make adjectives masculine or feminine, you may have to change the ending.

■ Most adjectives in Spanish have a masculine ending **-o** and a feminine ending **-a.**

Adjective Endings		
Masculine	**-o**	estudios**o**
Feminine	**-a**	estudios**a**

Some adjectives with **-o/-a** endings are:

aburrido(a)	*boring*
alto(a)	*tall*
antipático(a)	*unpleasant*
atlético(a)	*athletic*
bajo(a)	*short*
bonito(a)	*pretty*
bueno(a)	*good*
cómico(a)	*funny*
delgado(a)	*slender, thin*
desorganizado(a)	*disorganized*
feo(a)	*ugly*
flaco(a)	*skinny*
generoso(a)	*generous*
gordo(a)	*fat, chubby*
guapo(a)	*good-looking, handsome*
mediano(a)	*average*
moreno(a)	*dark (hair, complexion)*
organizado(a)	*organized*
pelirrojo(a)	*red-haired, redheaded*
pequeño(a)	*small*
romántico(a)	*romantic*
rubio(a)	*blond*
serio(a)	*serious*
simpático(a)	*nice, pleasant*
tímido(a)	*timid*
tonto(a)	*silly, dumb*

¿POR QUÉ SE DICE ASÍ?

- Other adjectives have only one ending for both masculine and feminine nouns. These adjectives end in **-e** or in a consonant. Some of the adjectives that belong to this group are:

difícil	*difficult*
elegante	*elegant*
exigente	*demanding*
fuerte	*strong*
grande	*big, large*
inteligente	*intelligent*
interesante	*interesting*
joven	*young*
popular	*popular*

- When you use more than one adjective, the last one is connected by **y** (*and*).

Él es grande **y** fuerte.
Ella es alta, delgada **y** elegante.

- The word **y** becomes **e** whenever it is followed by a word beginning with **i** or **hi.**

Carlos **e** Isabel son guapos **e** inteligentes.

Vamos a practicar

a. ¡Ideales! Martín and Marta are going steady. Their friends say they are ideal for each other because they are so much alike. Describe them.

MODELO   Marta es alta y morena. (Martín)
Martín también es alto y moreno.

1. Marta es modesta y muy generosa. (Martín)
2. Martín es alto y simpático. (Marta)
3. Martín es inteligente y estudioso. (Marta)
4. Marta es delgada y muy guapa. (Martín)
5. Martín es interesante y muy romántico. (Marta)
6. Marta es organizada y seria. (Martín)
7. Martín es atlético y popular. (Marta)

b. ¡Qué diferentes! Julio and Gloria are also going steady, but no one expects their relationship to last because they are total opposites. Can you describe them?

MODELO   Julio es alto. (Gloria)
Gloria es baja.

1. Julio es rubio. (Gloria)
2. Gloria es interesante. (Julio)
3. Julio es gordo. (Gloria)
4. Gloria es organizada. (Julio)
5. Julio es simpático. (Gloria)
6. Julio es tonto. (Gloria)
7. Gloria es pequeña. (Julio)
8. Gloria es guapa. (Julio)

¿POR QUÉ SE DICE ASÍ?   **G13**

Vamos a practicar

These exercises may be done as oral or written work.

Additional Exercises
Textbook: pages 48–51
Cuaderno: Unidad 1, Lección 3

a. ¡Ideales!
1 Martín también es modesto y muy generoso.
2 Marta también es alta y muy simpática.
3 Marta también es inteligente y estudiosa.
4 Martín también es delgado y muy guapo.
5 Marta también es interesante y muy romántica.
6 Martín también es organizado y serio.
7 Marta también es atlética y popular.

b. ¡Qué diferentes!
1 Gloria es morena (pelirroja).
2 Julio es aburrido.
3 Gloria es delgada (flaca).
4 Julio es desorganizado.
5 Gloria es antipática.
6 Gloria es inteligente.
7 Julio es grande.
8 Julio es feo.

c. Mis amigos.

1 Pablo es organizado y muy generoso.
2 Lola es simpática y elegante.
3 Silvia es atlética y fuerte.
4 Arturo es alto y pelirrojo.
5 María es tímida y modesta.
6 Jaime es estudioso e interesante.
7 Luisa es gorda y bonita.
8 Carlos es guapo y cómico.
9 Lisa es popular e inteligente.
10 José es desorganizado y romántico.

ch. ¿Cómo eres tú?

Answers will vary.

c. Mis amigos.   How does Lisa describe her friends?

MODELO   Ana / alto / moreno
Ana es alta y morena.

1. Pablo / organizado / muy generoso
2. Lola / simpático / elegante
3. Silvia / atlético / fuerte
4. Arturo / alto / pelirrojo
5. María / tímido / modesto
6. Jaime / estudioso / interesante
7. Luisa / gordo / bonito
8. Carlos / guapo / cómico
9. Lisa / popular / inteligente
10. José / desorganizado / romántico

ch. ¿Cómo eres tú?   Choose five characteristics that describe you. Then do the same for your best male friend and your best female friend.

1. Yo soy . . .
2. Mi mejor amigo es . . .
3. Mi mejor amiga es . . .
4. Mi mejor amigo y yo somos similares porque él es . . . y yo soy . . .
5. Mi mejor amiga y yo somos diferentes porque ella es . . . y yo soy . . .

LECCIÓN 1

2.1 NUMBERS 0–30

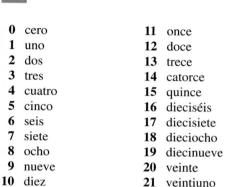

0 cero	**11** once	**22** veintidós
1 uno	**12** doce	**23** veintitrés
2 dos	**13** trece	**24** veinticuatro
3 tres	**14** catorce	**25** veinticinco
4 cuatro	**15** quince	**26** veintiséis
5 cinco	**16** dieciséis	**27** veintisiete
6 seis	**17** diecisiete	**28** veintiocho
7 siete	**18** dieciocho	**29** veintinueve
8 ocho	**19** diecinueve	**30** treinta
9 nueve	**20** veinte	
10 diez	**21** veintiuno	

- In addition to counting and giving numbers, these numbers can be used to tell how many things there are.

> **dos** clases
> **catorce** libros
> **veinte** estudiantes

- The number **uno** (including **veintiuno, treinta y uno,** etc.) becomes **un** before masculine nouns and **una** before feminine nouns.

Tengo **un** hermano y **una** hermana.	*I have one brother and one sister.*
El colegio tiene solamente veinti**una** computadoras.	*The school has only twenty-one computers.*
Hay veinti**ún** teléfonos.	*There are twenty-one telephones.*

Vamos a practicar

a. Seguro social.   Some new students want to enroll in Colegio San José, Puerto Rico. What are their Social Security numbers?

MODELO   314-25-0921
         tres, uno, cuatro, dos, cinco, cero, nueve, dos, uno

1. 119-28-2016
2. 015-23-1402
3. 516-09-2706
4. 327-10-2729
5. 925-17-1424
6. 021-21-1315
7. 525-19-2226
8. 319-11-3013
9. 517-12-2311

¿POR QUÉ SE DICE ASÍ?

G15

2.1 Margin box: page 66

Point out The numbers 16–19 and 21–29 are usually written as one word, though they can also be written as three words: **diez y seis, diez y nueve, veinte y uno.**

Point out When **veintiuno** is used before a masculine noun, it is shortened to **veintiún**, with a written accent.

Vamos a practicar

These activites may be done as oral or written work.

Additional Exercises
Textbook: page 66
Cuaderno: Unidad 2, Lección 1

a. Seguro social.
Expansion Tell students that long numbers, such as telephone and Social Security numbers, are often read in pairs, after the first digit. Then ask them to read these numbers that way: 314-25-0921 **tres, catorce, veinticinco, cero nueve, veintiuno.**

1 uno, uno, nueve, dos, ocho, dos, cero, uno, seis
2 cero, uno, cinco, dos, tres, uno, cuatro, cero, dos
3 cinco, uno, seis, cero, nueve, dos, siete, cero, seis
4 tres, dos, siete, uno, cero, dos, siete, dos, nueve
5 nueve, dos, cinco, uno, siete, uno, cuatro, dos, cuatro
6 cero, dos, uno, dos, uno, uno, tres, uno, cinco
7 cinco, dos, cinco, uno, nueve, dos, dos, dos, seis
8 tres, uno, nueve, uno, uno, tres, cero, uno, tres
9 cinco, uno, siete, uno, dos, dos, tres, uno, uno

b. Códigos postales.

Madison, WI   cinco, tres, siete, cero, seis

Ann Arbor, MI   cuatro, ocho, uno, cero, cuatro

Sacramento, CA   nueve, cinco, ocho, dos, siete

Las Cruces, NM   ocho, ocho, cero, cero, uno

Fort Worth, TX   siete, nueve, uno, uno, seis

Lexington, MA   cero, dos, uno, siete, tres

Atlanta, GA   tres, cero, tres, dos, siete

c. ¿Cuántos hay?

1 treinta libros de español
2 tres diccionarios
3 veintiún cuadernos
4 siete lápices
5 quince bolígrafos
6 nueve mochilas
7 veinte chicas
8 catorce chicos
9 una profesora
10 ocho carpetas

2.2   **Margin box: page 66**

---

b. Códigos postales.   Practice saying the following ZIP codes.

MODELO   Los Angeles, CA 90078
nueve, cero, cero, siete, ocho

Madison, WI	53706
Ann Arbor, MI	48104
Sacramento, CA	95827
Las Cruces, NM	88001
Fort Worth, TX	79116
Lexington, MA	02173
Atlanta, GA	30327

c. ¿Cuántos hay?   Tell how many of the following items Carolina can see in her Spanish classroom.

1. 30 libros de español
2. 3 diccionarios
3. 21 cuadernos
4. 7 lápices
5. 15 bolígrafos

6. 9 mochilas
7. 20 chicas
8. 14 chicos
9. 1 profesora
10. 8 carpetas

2.2   NOUNS AND ARTICLES: SINGULAR AND PLURAL FORMS

In the **Lección preliminar,** you learned that a noun is a word that names a person, animal, place, thing, event, or concept. You also learned that nouns are either masculine or feminine. Nouns may also be either singular or plural.

Formation of Plural Nouns	
Add -s to nouns that end in a vowel.	
SINGULAR	PLURAL
chico	chicos
estudiante	estudiantes
Add -es to nouns that end in a consonant.	
SINGULAR	PLURAL
profesor	profesores
capital	capitales

■ Nouns that end in **-z** change the **-z** to **-c** in the plural.

Hay un lápiz.   Hay cuatro lápices.

¿POR QUÉ SE DICE ASÍ?

In the **Lección preliminar,** you learned that the definite article **el** is used before singular masculine nouns and **la** before singular feminine nouns. Articles, like nouns, have singular and plural forms.

Point out Definite articles, equivalent to the English *the*, are used before nouns to designate particular persons or things.

Vamos a practicar

Additional Exercises
Textbook: pages 66–67
Cuaderno: Unidad 2, Lección 1

Definite Articles	
Singular	Plural
el	los
la	las

el libro   los libros
la carpeta   las carpetas

Vamos a practicar

a. ¡Muchos! Make the following expressions plural.

MODELO   la señora
las señoras

1. la escuela
2. la profesora
3. la amiga
4. el profesor
5. la clase
6. el estudiante
7. el lápiz
8. la estudiante
9. la carpeta
10. el papel

b. Yo tengo más. María always insists that she has more of anything than anyone else. How does she respond when her friends say they have these things?

MODELO   Tengo un cuaderno. (3)
Yo tengo tres cuadernos.

1. Tengo un bolígrafo. (5)
2. Tengo una carpeta. (2)
3. Tengo un diccionario. (2)
4. Tengo un libro. (4)
5. Tengo un borrador. (3)
6. Tengo un profesor muy guapo. (2)
7. Tengo un mapa. (2)
8. Tengo un lápiz. (7)
9. Tengo un amigo en España. (4)
10. Tengo una mochila. (2)

c. ¿Cuántos hay? Tell how many people there are in each of these categories at the assembly.

MODELO   señorita (6)
Hay seis señoritas.

1. amigo (22)
2. profesor (19)
3. director (2)
4. chica (11)
5. profesora (13)
6. señor (17)
7. chico (18)
8. estudiante (29)
9. señora (7)

¿POR QUÉ SE DICE ASÍ?   **G17**

a. ¡Muchos!
1 las escuelas
2 las profesoras
3 las amigas
4 los profesores
5 las clases
6 los estudiantes
7 los lápices
8 las estudiantes
9 las carpetas
10 los papeles

Expansion If students need more practice, add these items:
el colegio, la chica, el horario, la hora, la sala, la casa, la semana, el restaurante, el teléfono.

b. Yo tengo más.
1 Yo tengo cinco bolígrafos.
2 Yo tengo dos carpetas.
3 Yo tengo dos diccionarios.
4 Yo tengo cuatro libros.
5 Yo tengo tres borradores.
6 Yo tengo dos profesores muy guapos.
7 Yo tengo dos mapas.
8 Yo tengo siete lápices.
9 Yo tengo cuatro amigos en España.
10 Yo tengo dos mochilas.

c. ¿Cuántos hay?
1 Hay veintidós amigos.
2 Hay diecinueve profesoras.
3 Hay dos directores.
4 Hay once chicas.
5 Hay trece profesoras.
6 Hay diecisiete señores.
7 Hay dieciocho chicos.
8 Hay veintinueve estudiantes.
9 Hay siete señoras.

ch. ¿Por favor?

1 la mochila
2 los cuadernos
3 los lápices
4 las carpetas
5 el bolígrafo
6 el video
7 el diccionario
8 los papeles

2.3 Margin box: page 67

Point out For emphasis, the exact hour may be given as **en punto**: Son las siete en punto.

Point out With use of digital clocks, it is becoming more common to read time as it appears: **las once cuarenta y tres.**

Point out 1:00 uses **es** because it is singular; the other hours use **son** because they are plural.

Note In Spain, **la tarde** extends until after dark, sometimes even until after dinner (which may be 9:00 P.M. or later): **Son las ocho de la tarde.**

---

ch. ¿Por favor? Your younger brother always borrows your things. Tell what he wants to borrow now.

MODELO libro o libros
  el libro o **los libros**

1. mochila   3. lápices   5. bolígrafo   7. diccionario
2. cuadernos   4. carpetas   6. video   8. papeles

2.3 TELLING TIME

The hour, quarter hour, and half hour in Spanish are given as follows:

On the hour   Quarter hour   Half hour

Son las cinco.   **Son las nueve y cuarto.**   **Son las doce y media.**

The following expressions are used when telling time in Spanish:

Up to the half hour, add minutes to the hour using **y.**

Son las [*hour*] **y** [*minutes*].
3:20 Son las tres y veinte.
11:05 Son las once y cinco.

After the half hour, subtract minutes from the next hour using **menos.**

Son las [*next hour*] **menos** [*minutes*].
9:49 Son las diez menos once.
4:35 Son las cinco menos veinticinco.

- When talking about 1:00 (between 12:30 and 1:30), **es** is used instead of **son.**

  1:14 **Es** la una y catorce.
  12:35 **Es** la una menos veinticinco.

- *Noon* and *midnight* are expressed as **(el) mediodía** and **(la) medianoche.**

  La clase es **a mediodía.**   *The class is at 12:00 noon.*
  El programa es **a medianoche.**   *The program is at midnight.*

- In Spanish, A.M. = **de la mañana,** and P.M. = **de la tarde** (from 12:00 noon to dark) and **de la noche** (after dark).

  9:15 A.M. las nueve y cuarto **de la mañana**
  4:50 P.M. las cinco menos diez **de la tarde**
  11:00 P.M. las once **de la noche**

Point out Some speakers use **en la mañana / tarde / noche** to indicate time in a general sense.

- When no specific hour is mentioned, the expressions **por la mañana, por la tarde,** and **por la noche** are used.

> Tengo matemáticas **por la mañana,** historia **por la tarde** y computación **por la noche.**

> *I have math in the mxjorning, history in the afternoon, and computer class in the evening.*

- Be careful to distinguish between *what* time it is and *at* what time something occurs.

¿Qué hora es?	*What time is it?*
Son las dos y cuarto.	*It's two-fifteen.*

¿A qué hora es la clase?	*At what time is the class?*
A las dos y media.	*At two-thirty.*

- Many schedules—buses, trains, planes, theaters, museums—use a twenty-four-hour clock. In other words, after 12:00 noon, the hours are **13,00 h.** through **24,00 h.** (*1:00 P.M.–12:00 midnight*). Note: **h. = horas.**

> **15,00 h.** = **las tres de la tarde.**
> **20,30 h.** = **las ocho y media de la noche.**

In order to convert back to twelve-hour time, you must subtract twelve from the hour.

> **18,00 h.** (18 minus 12 =) *6:00 P.M.*
> **22,30 h.** (22,30 minus 12 =) *10:30 P.M.*

Vamos a practicar

a. ¿Qué hora es?   Give the time according to the following clocks.

MODELO   **Son las nueve y cuarto de la mañana.**

1. `9:50 PM`

2. `12:45 AM`

3. `4:25 PM`

4. `10:15 AM`

5. `7:30 AM`

6. `1:20 PM`

7. `10:55 AM`

8. `3:30 PM`

Vamos a practicar

Additional Exercises
Textbook: pages 67–68
Cuaderno: Unidad 2, Lección 1

a. ¿Qué hora es?
1 Son las diez menos diez de la noche.
2 Es la una menos cuarto de la mañana.
3 Son las cuatro y veinticinco de la tarde.
4 Son las diez y cuarto de la mañana.
5 Son las siete y media de la mañana.
6 Es la una y veinte de la tarde.
Note Since midday extends from noon until 2:00 P.M., a native speaker might say **Es la una y veinte del mediodía.**
7 Son las once menos cinco de la mañana.
8 Son las tres y media de la tarde.

b. ¿A qué hora? Answers will vary.

c. En punto.
1 A las nueve de la mañana.
2 A las once menos veinticinco de la mañana.
3 Al mediodía.
4 A la una y media de la tarde.
5 A las tres y cuarto de la tarde.
6 A las cinco y veinte de la tarde.
7 A las diez menos cuarto de la noche.
8 A las once de la noche.

ch. ¿Cuándo es?
1 A las ocho de la mañana. Por la mañana.
2 A las dos y cuarto de la tarde. Por la tarde.
3 A la una menos cuarto de la tarde. Por la tarde.
4 A las tres de la tarde. Por la tarde.
5 A las diez y cuarto de la mañana. Por la mañana.
6 A la una y diez de la tarde. Por la tarde.
7 A las cinco menos cuarto de la tarde. Por la tarde.
8 A las once de la mañana. Por la mañana.

2.4 Margin box: page 68

---

b. ¿A qué hora? At what time of day do you do the following things?

MODELO brush your teeth
A las siete y cuarto de la mañana.

1. get up in the morning
2. leave for school
3. eat lunch
4. go home from school
5. eat dinner
6. do your homework
7. watch TV
8. go to bed

c. En punto. At what times do planes leave San Juan bound for New York?

MODELO 7,30 h.
A las siete y media de la mañana.

1. 9,00 h.
2. 10,35 h.
3. 12,00 h.
4. 13,30 h.
5. 15,15 h.
6. 17,20 h.
7. 21,45 h.
8. 23,00 h.

ch. ¿Cuándo es? Julio is a very precise person. Pablo tends not to worry about details. How does each respond to the following questions?

MODELO ¿Cuándo es tu clase de matemáticas? (9,10 h.)
Julio: **A las nueve y diez de la mañana.**
Pablo: **Por la mañana.**

1. ¿Cuándo es tu clase de computación? (8,00 h.)
2. ¿Cuándo tienes educación física? (14,15 h.)
3. ¿Cuándo es tu clase de ciencias? (12,45 h.)
4. ¿Cuándo tienes español? (15,00 h.)
5. ¿Cuándo es tu clase de historia? (10,15 h.)
6. ¿Cuándo tienes música? (13,10 h.)
7. ¿Cuándo es tu clase de baile? (16,45 h.)
8. ¿Cuándo tienes inglés? (11,00 h.)

2.4 THE VERB TENER: SINGULAR FORMS

The verb **tener** (*to have*) is used to talk about things or activities that you have.

Tener	
yo	**tengo**
tú	**tienes**
usted	**tiene**
él, ella	**tiene**

Tienes español en la sala 22.	*You have Spanish in room 22.*
Eva **tiene** cinco clases hoy.	*Eva has five classes today.*
Tengo un problema.	*I have a problem.*

¿POR QUÉ SE DICE ASÍ?

a. Mi casillero.   Students always store a variety of things in their lockers. Following the cues, tell what you have in *your* locker.

> MODELO   cuaderno
> **Tengo (cinco) cuadernos.** o
> **No tengo cuadernos.**

1. lápiz
2. carpeta
3. bolígrafo
4. libro

5. mochila
6. foto
7. diccionario
8. mapa

b. Horarios.   José, Julia, and Elvira are discussing their class schedules. Find out how these compare by completing the conversation with the appropriate forms of the verb **tener.**

> MODELO   José **tiene** educación física a las tres.

Julia: Yo _____ matemáticas a las nueve.

Elvira: ¿Ah, sí? José también. José, ¿no _____ tú matemáticas a las nueve?

José: Sí. Y a las dos Julia _____ biología conmigo.

Elvira: Julia, ¿ _____ clase con la Srta. Gómez?

Julia: Sí, _____ inglés con ella. ¡Es mi profesora favorita!

c. ¿Cuál es tu horario?   Compare your schedule with the following students' schedules.

> MODELO   Miguel **tiene** educación física a la una.
> Yo **tengo** educación física a las _____.

1. Sara _____ matemáticas a las nueve menos cuarto.
   Yo _____ matemáticas a las _____.

2. Ramón _____ historia a las nueve y media.
   Yo _____ historia a las _____.

3. Gloria _____ ciencias a las diez y cuarto.
   Yo _____ ciencias a las _____.

4. Estela _____ inglés a las once.
   Yo _____ inglés a las _____.

5. Carlos _____ español a las dos menos cuarto.
   Yo _____ español a las _____.

6. Martín _____ educación física a las dos y media.
   Yo _____ educación física a las _____.

¿POR QUÉ SE DICE ASÍ? _____ **G21**

Additional Exercises
Textbook: pages 68–69
Cuaderno: Unidad 2, Lección 1

a. Mi casillero. Answers will vary.

b. Horarios.
tengo, tienes, tiene, tienes, tengo

c. ¿Cuál es tu horario?
Times in the second sentence will vary with students' own schedules.
1 tiene, tengo
2 tiene, tengo
3 tiene, tengo
4 tiene, tengo
5 tiene, tengo
6 tiene, tengo

UNIDAD

LECCIÓN 2

2.5 ADJECTIVES: SINGULAR AND PLURAL FORMS
Used to Describe People and Things

Adjectives, like nouns, have both singular and plural forms.

Formation of Plural Adjectives
If the singular form of an adjective ends in a vowel, add **-s.**

SINGULAR	PLURAL
buen**o**	buen**os**
perfeccionist**a**	perfeccionist**as**
excelent**e**	excelent**es**

If the singular form of an adjective ends in a consonant, add **-es.**

SINGULAR	PLURAL
popula**r**	popula**res**
fata**l**	fata**les**
difíci**l**	difíci**les**

- In Spanish, adjectives must agree in number (*singular / plural*) and in gender (*masculine / feminine*) with the noun they modify. Note that adjectives usually follow the noun.

  Él es mi profes**or** favorit**o.**   *He is my favorite teacher.*
  Las clas**es** son estupend**as.**   *The classes are fabulous.*

- When one adjective describes two or more nouns, one of which is masculine, the masculine form of the adjective is used.

  La profesora y el director son alt**os.**
  El patio y la cafetería son fantástic**os.**

- Words ending in **-ista** are either masculine or feminine.

  el artista
  la artista   *the artist*

  el pianista
  la pianista   *the pianist*

¿POR QUÉ SE DICE ASÍ?

UNIDAD

a. Descripciones. Choosing from the list of adjectives, tell how Sara describes her parents and her friends. There may be more than one correct answer in some instances.

Mi amiga Daniela es _____ . desorganizadas

Mi mamá y mi papá son _____ . simpáticas

Rafael es _____ . guapos

Susana y Victoria son _____ . tímida

Mi papá y yo somos _____ . inteligentes

Tú y Carlos son _____ . perfeccionistas

Mis amigas son _____ . alto

b. Me gusta mi nueva escuela. Help Elena complete this letter to her friend by providing the correct form of the adjective corresponding to each blank space.

1. excelente	**3.** bueno	**5.** fácil	**7.** divertido
2. exigente	**4.** interesante	**6.** simpático	**8.** aburrido

> Querida Carolina,
>
> ¡Hola! Mi nueva escuela es _1_ . Me gustan mucho los profesores. Son _2_ pero son _3_ también. Mis clases son _4_ pero no son _5_ . Los estudiantes son _6_ . Hay muchos chicos. Son _7_ . No son _8_ .
>
> ¿Cómo está todo en tu escuela? Escríbeme. Hasta pronto.
>
> Tu amiga
> Elena

c. ¿Cómo son? Combine the following into complete sentences to tell how some students describe your school.

MODELO Los profesores son _____ (bueno).
        Los profesores son **buenos.**

1. El colegio es _____ (estupendo).
2. La profesora de español es _____ (organizado).
3. Unos estudiantes son _____ (regular).
4. Otros estudiantes son _____ (estudioso).
5. Unas clases son _____ (fantástico).
6. Otras clases son _____ (aburrido).
7. Los profesores de matemáticas son _____ (exigente).
8. Las clases de educación física son _____ (bueno).

¿POR QUÉ SE DICE ASÍ?   G23

Additional Exercises
Textbook: pages 80–81
Cuaderno: Unidad 2, Lección 2

a. Descripciones.
Answers will vary. Possibilities are given below.
Mi amiga Daniela es tímida.
Mi mamá y mi papá son guapos, inteligentes, perfeccionistas.
Rafael es alto.
Susana y Victoria son desorganizadas, simpáticas, inteligentes, perfeccionistas.
Mi papá y yo somos guapos, inteligentes, perfeccionistas.
Tú y Carlos son guapos, inteligentes, perfeccionistas.
Mis amigas son desorganizadas, simpáticas, inteligentes, perfeccionistas.

b. Me gusta mi nueva escuela.
1 excelente
2 exigentes
3 buenos
4 interesantes
5 fáciles
6 simpáticos
7 divertidos
8 aburridos

c. ¿Cómo son?
1 estupendo
2 organizada
3 regulares
4 estudiosos
5 fantásticas
6 aburridas
7 exigentes
8 buenas

You know that **yo, tú, usted, él,** and **ella** are *singular subject pronouns* used to identify people without using or repeating their names. *Plural subject pronouns* are used when the subject of the sentence refers to two or more persons, places, or things.

Subject Pronouns			
	Singular	Plural	
I	**yo**	**nosotros** **nosotras**	*we* (masculine) *we* (feminine)
you (familiar) *you* (formal)	**tú** **usted**	**vosotros(as)** **ustedes**	*you*
he, it (masculine) *she, it* (feminine)	**él** **ella**	**ellos** **ellas**	*they* (masculine) *they* (feminine)

- **Yo** and **nosotros(as)** refer to the persons speaking, **tú, usted, vosotros(as),** and **ustedes** to the persons spoken to, and **él, ella,** and **ellos(as)** to the persons or things spoken about.

- **Nosotras** and **ellas** refer to groups of all females. **Nosotros** and **ellos** are used for mixed groups or groups of all males.

- As with singular pronouns, plural pronouns are used only for clarification or for emphasis.

    Clarification:
      No son **ellos,** son **ellas.**

    Emphasis:
      Nosotros somos inteligentes, **ellos** no.

- In Spain, **vosotros(as)** is used as the plural of **tú;** in Latin America, **ustedes** is used as the plural of both **tú** and **usted.**

Vamos a practicar

Vamos a practicar

a. **¿Quiénes?** What subject pronouns would you use to talk about the following people?

MODELO   Carlos y yo
         nosotros

a. ¿Quiénes?
1 ellas
2 nosotros (nosotras *if both are female*)
3 ellos
4 ustedes
5 ustedes
6 nosotros (nosotras *if both are female*)
7 ustedes
8 nosotros (nosotras *if both are female*)
9 ustedes

1. Carlota y María
2. mi amiga y yo
3. Manuel y Andrés
4. tú y tú
5. ustedes y el profesor
6. usted y yo
7. tú y Juan
8. tú y yo
9. tú y ella

¿POR QUÉ SE DICE ASÍ?

b. ¿Uno o más? Make the singular pronouns plural and the plural pronouns singular.

MODELO ustedes
usted

1. yo
2. nosotros
3. tú

4. él
5. usted
6. ellas

7. ustedes
8. ellos
9. nosotras

2.7 THE VERB SER

In **Unidad 1** (section 1.2), you learned the singular forms of the verb **ser** (*to be*). Here are both the singular and plural forms.

Ser			
yo	**soy**	nosotros(as)	**somos**
tú	**eres**	vosotros(as)	**sois***
usted	**es**	ustedes	**son**
él, ella	**es**	ellos, ellas	**son**

Somos muy simpáticos, ¿no?
Ustedes **son** norteamericanos, ¿verdad?
Mis clases no **son** fáciles.

Vamos a practicar

a. ¿Cómo son? Find out what Anita says about the people in her school by completing the blanks with the proper form of the verb **ser.**

MODELO Antonia y Andrea **son** rubias.

1. Carlota y yo _____ inteligentes.
2. Elena _____ muy bonita.
3. Roberto y Laura _____ antipáticos.
4. Tú _____ desorganizada.
5. La profesora Estrada _____ exigente.
6. Nosotras _____ delgadas.
7. Ustedes _____ altos.
8. Yo _____ guapa.
9. El Sr. Nogales _____ interesante.

*The **vosotros(as)** form is presented in the verb charts of the *Gramática* section for awareness and recognition. The form does not appear in the exercises, and therefore students will not be expected to produce it.

¿POR QUÉ SE DICE ASÍ?

_____ **G25**

b. ¿Uno o más?
1 nosotros(as)
2 yo
3 ustedes
4 ellos
5 ustedes
6 ella
7 usted
8 él
9 yo

2.7 Margin box: page 80

Vamos a practicar

Additional Exercises
Textbook: pages 80–81
Cuaderno: Unidad 2, Lección 2

a. ¿Cómo son?
1 somos
2 es
3 son
4 eres
5 es
6 somos
7 son
8 soy
9 es

Left margin column

b. Compañeros de clase. Answers will vary.
Possibilities include:
Ustedes son bonitas (if all are
  female), altos, desorganizados,
  interesantes, guapos.
Carlos es inteligente, tímido,
  fatal, simpático.
Yo soy inteligente, tímido, fatal,
  simpático.
Tú y tu amigo son altos, desorganizados, interesantes, guapos.
Nosotros somos altos, desorganizados, interesantes, guapos.
Tú eres inteligente, tímido, fatal,
  atlética, simpático, romántica.
María es inteligente, fatal,
  atlética, romántica.
Clara y Raúl son altos, desorganizados, interesantes, guapos.
Marta y yo somos altos, desorganizados, interesantes, guapos.
El Sr. Nogales es inteligente,
  tímido, fatal, simpático.

c. ¡Somos fantásticos!
1 Nosotros somos divertidos;
  ustedes son aburridos.
2 Nosotros somos simpáticos;
  ustedes son antipáticos.
3 Nosotros somos organizados;
  ustedes son desorganizados.
4 Nosotros somos guapos;
  ustedes son feos.
5 Nosotros somos inteligentes;
  ustedes son tontos.
6 Nosotros somos buenos;
  ustedes son malos.

ch. Mis amigos.
1 Alicia es simpática.
2 Raúl y Ernesto son altos.
3 Paco y yo somos delgados.
4 La Sra. Álvarez es gorda.
5 Yo soy morena.
6 Ustedes son guapos(as).
7 Tú eres pequeño(a).
8 Ellas son rubias.

2.8 Margin box: page 82

Main column

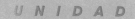

U N I D A D 2

b. Compañeros de clase. How does Mario describe the people in his Spanish class? There may be more than one correct answer in some instances.

> MODELO **María es atlética.** o **Ellos son altos.**

ustedes	inteligente
Carlos	bonitas
yo	altos
tú y tu amigo	tímido
nosotros	interesantes
tú	guapos
María	fatal
Clara y Raúl	atlética
Marta y yo	simpático
el Sr. Nogales	romántica

c. ¡Somos fantásticos! You are teasing a friend from a rival school. What do you say?

> MODELO fantástico / fatal
> **Nosotros somos fantásticos; ustedes son fatales.**

1. divertido / aburrido
2. simpático / antipático
3. organizado / desorganizado
4. guapo / feo
5. inteligente / tonto
6. bueno / malo

ch. Mis amigos. Carmen is describing people in her neighborhood. What does she say?

> MODELO el Sr. González / alto
> **El señor González es alto.**

1. Alicia / simpático
2. Raúl y Ernesto / alto
3. Paco y yo / delgado
4. la Sra. Álvarez / gordo
5. yo / moreno
6. ustedes / guapo
7. tú / pequeño
8. ellas / rubio

2.8 THE VERB *ESTAR*

The verb **estar** (*to be*) has the following forms:

Estar			
yo	**estoy**	nosotros(as)	**estamos**
tú	**estás**	vosotros(as)	**estáis**
usted	**está**	ustedes	**están**
él, ella	**está**	ellos, ellas	**están**

¿POR QUÉ SE DICE ASÍ?

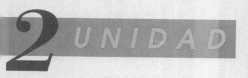

2 U N I D A D

Point out The location of an event is expressed with **ser**: **El concierto es en el auditorio.**

■ You already know that the verb **estar** is used in greetings and to talk about how people feel.

¿Cómo **está** usted? *How are you?*
¿**Estás** bien? *Are you OK?*
Sí, **estoy** bien. *Yes, I'm fine.*

■ **Estar** is also used to tell the location of people and things.

¿Dónde **está** Lima?
Pedro **está** en la biblioteca.
¿Por qué **están** ustedes aquí?
Ellas **están** en México.

Vamos a practicar

a. ¿Dónde están todos? Use the proper forms of the verb **estar** to help the school secretary locate the following people.

1. ¿Dónde _____ Marcos?
Marcos _____ en la clase de biología.

2. Y Alfredo, ¿dónde _____ él?
_____ en la clase de historia.

3. Y, ¿dónde _____ Tomás y Mario?
_____ en el gimnasio.

4. Y el otro profesor de educación física, ¿dónde _____?
_____ en la biblioteca.

5. Y, ¿dónde _____ tu amigo?
_____ en la clase de matemáticas.

b. ¿Dónde estamos? Susana and Clara are trying to find their way around their new high school. How would they ask someone where the following people and places are?

MODELO la cafetería
¿Dónde está la cafetería?

1. el gimnasio
2. los profesores de matemáticas
3. las computadoras
4. el teatro
5. la directora
6. nosotras
7. la oficina del director
8. las salas de música
9. la biblioteca
10. los baños

¿POR QUÉ SE DICE ASÍ? **G27**

Additional Exercises
Textbook: pages 82–83
Cuaderno: Unidad 2, Lección 2

a. ¿Dónde están todos?
1 está, está
2 está, Está
3 están, Están
4 está, Está
5 está, Está

b. ¿Dónde estamos?
1 ¿Dónde está el gimnasio?
2 ¿Dónde están los profesores de matemáticas?
3 ¿Dónde están las computadoras?
4 ¿Dónde está el teatro?
5 ¿Dónde está la directora?
6 ¿Dónde estamos nosotras?
7 ¿Dónde está la oficina del director?
8 ¿Dónde están las salas de música?
9 ¿Dónde está la biblioteca?
10 ¿Dónde están los baños?

c. ¿Dónde?

1 La señora Valdez está en la cafetería.
2 Alicia y Daniel están en la clase de álgebra.
3 El señor García está en el gimnasio.
4 María Hernández está en el teatro.
5 Las profesoras Gómez y Durán están en la oficina.
6 El profesor Fernández está en la clase de biología.
7 Guillermo y Margarita Lozano están en la sala veintiuno.
8 Los profesores de química están en el laboratorio.

ch. El Agente 006.

está, está, están, Están, está, estoy, estamos

2.9 Margin box: page 94

---

c. ¿Dónde? When the principal tries to locate various people over the PA system, the teachers respond. What do they tell him?

> MODELO el profesor Martínez / patio
> **El profesor Martínez está en el patio.**

1. la Sra. Valdez / cafetería
2. Alicia y Daniel / clase de álgebra
3. el Sr. García / gimnasio
4. María Hernández / teatro
5. las profesoras Gómez y Durán / oficina
6. el profesor Fernández / clase de biología
7. Guillermo y Margarita Lozano / sala 21
8. los profesores de química / laboratorio

ch. El Agente 006. Agent 006 is in a meeting with his division chief. Complete their conversation with the appropriate forms of **estar.**

> Jefe: ¿Dónde _____ el Agente 003?
> Agente 006: El 003 _____ en Bolivia.
> Jefe: ¿Dónde _____ los Agentes 014 y 002?
> Agente 006: _____ en Panamá.
> Jefe: ¿Dónde _____ el Agente 006?
> Agente 006: ¿El 006? Yo _____ aquí con usted.
> Jefe: ¿Y dónde _____ nosotros?
> Agente 006: Es un secreto.

LECCIÓN 3

2.9 INFINITIVES

The basic form of the verb used to name an action is called the *infinitive*. This is the form that appears in Spanish dictionaries. In English, infinitives begin with *to*: *to work, to run, to write*. In Spanish, the infinitive always ends in **-ar, -er,** or **-ir**: **trabaj*ar*, corr*er*, escrib*ir*.**

Some common infinitives are:

-ar verbs			
alquilar	*to rent*	mirar	*to look at*
calificar	*to grade*	participar	*to participat*
estar	*to be*	pasear	*to take a walk, ride*
estudiar	*to study*	practicar	*to practice*
hablar	*to talk, speak*	preparar	*to prepare*
jugar	*to play* (a game)	trabajar	*to work*
limpiar	*to clean*	viajar	*to travel*

G28

¿POR QUÉ SE DICE ASÍ?

-er verbs	
comer	*to eat*
correr	*to run*
hacer	*to do, make*
leer	*to read*
ser	*to be*
tener	*to have*
ver	*to see, watch*

-ir verbs	
escribir	*to write*
ir	*to go*
salir	*to go out, leave*
subir	*to go up, climb;*
	to get into (a vehicle)

▪ The infinitive is used to name activities. Notice that in English we often use the *-ing* form where Spanish uses the infinitive.

Mis pasatiempos favoritos son
   jugar fútbol, **ver** la tele y **leer.**
Siempre **estar** en casa es aburrido.

My favorite pastimes are playing
   soccer, watching TV, and reading.
Always being at home is boring.

Vamos a practicar

Vamos a practicar

Additional Exercises
Textbook: page 94
Cuaderno: Unidad 2, Lección 3

a. ¡Pasatiempos! What are your favorite pastimes? Select five from the list below.

MODELO   **Mis pasatiempos favoritos son . . .**

alquilar videos	comer	ver la tele
hacer la comida	jugar fútbol	hablar por teléfono
pasear en bicicleta	leer	limpiar la casa
estudiar	ir al teatro	escribir composiciones

b. Probablemente . . . List five things you will probably do today after school.

c. ¿Y usted? List five things you think your teacher will do today.

2.10   THE VERB IR AND IR A + INFINITIVE

2.10 Margin box: page 95

The verb **ir** (*to go*) is irregular. It has the following forms:

Ir			
yo	**voy**	nosotros(as)	**vamos**
tú	**vas**	vosotros(as)	**vais**
usted	**va**	ustedes	**van**
él, ella	**va**	ellos, ellas	**van**

¿POR QUÉ SE DICE ASÍ?

G29

Note
Ir a + *place* is taught in Unit 3, section 3.1.

Vamos a practicar

Additional Exercises
Textbook: pages 94–95
Cuaderno: Unidad 2, Lección 3

a. ¿Qué van a hacer?
Answers will vary. Possibilities include:
Carlos y yo vamos a trabajar en el restaurante, vamos a comer algo.
Arturo va a alquilar un video.
Ramón y Eva van a preparar la comida, van a salir con Mario y Ricardo, van a ver televisión.
Tú y Julio van a preparar la comida, van a salir con Mario y Ricardo, van a ver televisión.
Tú y yo vamos a trabajar en el restaurante, vamos a comer algo.
Natalia y Yolanda van a preparar la comida, van a salir con Mario y Ricardo, van a ver televisión.
Yo voy a estudiar para un examen.

b. Por la noche . . .
1 va
2 vamos
3 voy
4 van
5 va
6 van
7 vas
8 van

c. ¿Y los profesores?
1 La señorita Rivera va a limpiar la casa.
2 La señora Estrada va a hacer la comida.
3 Yo voy a leer un libro.
4 El señor Arenas y un amigo van a alquilar un video.
5 Mi secretaria y yo vamos a escribir una carta.
6 La señorita Rivera y la señora Estrada van a calificar exámenes.
7 Mi secretaria y yo vamos a jugar tenis.
8 El señor Arenas va a correr un rato.

■ To talk about what you are going to do, you can use:

$$\boxed{\textbf{ir} + \textbf{a} + \textit{infinitive}}$$

¿Qué **vas a hacer**? — *What are you going to do?*
Voy a limpiar la casa. — *I'm going to clean the house.*
Van a jugar fútbol. — *They're going to play soccer.*

Vamos a practicar

a. ¿Qué van a hacer? What are you and your friends planning to do after school today? Some may be planning to do more than one thing.

EJEMPLO **Ramón y Eva van a ver televisión.**

Carlos y yo	va a alquilar un video
Arturo	van a preparar la comida
Ramón y Eva	voy a estudiar para un examen
tú y Julio	vamos a trabajar en el restaurante
tú y yo	van a salir con Mario y Ricardo
Natalia y Yolanda	van a ver televisión
yo	vamos a comer algo

b. Por la noche . . . Complete the sentences with the correct form of **ir** to find out what this family is going to do this evening.

1. Mamá _____ a hacer la comida.
2. Nosotros _____ a comer.
3. Yo _____ a hacer la tarea.
4. Jaime y Marta _____ a alquilar una película.
5. Papá _____ a hablar con sus amigos.
6. Papá y mamá _____ a leer.
7. Tú _____ a jugar fútbol.
8. Ustedes _____ a hablar por teléfono.

c. ¿Y los profesores? Complete the sentences to see what the principal says she and her staff are going to do after school today.

MODELO la Sra. Estrada / ver televisión
     La señora Estrada va a ver televisión.

1. la Srta. Rivera / limpiar / casa
2. la Sra. Estrada / hacer / comida
3. yo / leer / libro
4. el Sr. Arenas y un amigo / alquilar / video
5. mi secretaria y yo / escribir / carta
6. la Srta. Rivera y la Sra. Estrada / calificar exámenes
7. mi secretaria y yo / jugar tenis
8. el Sr. Arenas / correr un rato

¿POR QUÉ SE DICE ASÍ?

2.11 *THE VERB TENER AND TENER QUE . . .*
Used to Talk about Possessions and Obligations

The verb **tener** (*to have*) has the following forms:

Tener			
yo	**tengo**	nosotros(as)	**tenemos**
tú	**tienes**	vosotros(as)	**tenéis**
usted	**tiene**	ustedes	**tienen**
él, ella	**tiene**	ellos, ellas	**tienen**

You already know that the verb **tener** is used to talk about things you have.

¿**Tienen** ustedes el video?	*Do you have the video?*
Tengo matemáticas a las 9:00.	*I have math at 9:00.*
No **tenemos** clase hoy.	*We do not have class today.*

■ To talk about what you are obligated to do, you can use:

tener que + *infinitive*

Tengo que limpiar mi cuarto.	*I have to clean my room.*
Tienes que trabajar.	*You have to work.*
Tenemos que estudiar.	*We have to study.*

Vamos a practicar

a. ¡Qué desorganizados! The Spanish teacher always finds that some students do not have the books or supplies they need. What did the following people forget today?

MODELO Alicia no **tiene** bolígrafo.

1. Delia no _____ papel.

2. Yo no _____ lápiz.

3. Beatriz y Magdalena no _____ cuaderno.

4. Nosotras no _____ el libro.

5. Alejandro no _____ borrador.

6. Ustedes no _____ carpeta.

7. Raimundo y yo no _____ mochila.

8. Tú no _____ bolígrafo.

¿POR QUÉ SE DICE ASÍ?

G31

Vamos a practicar

Additional Exercises
Textbook: page 96
Cuaderno: Unidad 2, Lección 3

a. ¡Qué desorganizados!
You may wish to point out that the indefinite article is usually omitted after **tener**, particularly in the negative.
1 tiene
2 tengo
3 tienen
4 tenemos
5 tiene
6 tienen
7 tenemos
8 tienes

b. ¡Qué noche!

1 Román tiene que estudiar para un examen de biología.
2 Francisca y Luisa tienen que escribir una composición.
3 Yo tengo que limpiar la casa.
4 Tú tienes que estudiar para la clase de historia.
5 Nosotros tenemos que trabajar mucho.
6 Tú y yo tenemos que hacer la comida.
7 Ellos tienen que ir a una clase.
8 Ustedes tienen que practicar el piano.

c. ¿Qué hacen el sábado?

1 Alicia tiene que limpiar la casa.
2 Mónica y yo tenemos que ir a la clase de baile.
3 Roberto y Antonio tienen que estudiar en la biblioteca.
4 Tú tienes que practicar el piano.
5 Yo tengo que estudiar para un examen.
6 Paula tiene que trabajar en el restaurante de su papá.
7 Ustedes tienen que hacer la tarea.
8 Tú y yo tenemos que hablar por teléfono.

ch. Tengo que . . .

1 Tengo que ir a trabajar a las cuatro de la tarde.
2 Tengo que practicar karate a las cinco y media de la tarde.
3 Tengo que estar en la escuela a las siete de la mañana.
4 Tengo que salir de la escuela a las tres menos cuarto de la tarde.
5 Tengo que hacer la tarea a las siete y media de la noche.
6 Tengo que hablar con el profesor a las once menos diez de la mañana.
7 Tengo que limpiar mi cuarto a las cuatro menos cuarto de la tarde.
8 Tengo que estudiar español a las ocho y cuarto de la noche.

b. ¡Qué noche! Tell what everyone has to do tonight by completing the sentences with the correct form of **tener.**

> MODELO   Estela / hablar con el director
> **Estela tiene que hablar con el director.**

1. Román / estudiar para un examen de biología
2. Francisca y Luisa / escribir una composición
3. yo / limpiar la casa
4. tú / estudiar para la clase de historia
5. nosotros / trabajar mucho
6. tú y yo / hacer la comida
7. ellos / ir a una clase
8. ustedes / practicar el piano

c. ¿Qué hacen el sábado? What do you and your friends have to do this Saturday?

> MODELO   Ana y Eva / hacer la comida
> **Ana y Eva tienen que hacer la comida.**

1. Alicia / limpiar la casa
2. Mónica y yo / ir a la clase de baile
3. Roberto y Antonio / estudiar en la biblioteca
4. tú / practicar el piano
5. yo / estudiar para un examen
6. Paula / trabajar en el restaurante de su papá
7. ustedes / hacer la tarea
8. tú y yo / hablar por teléfono

ch. Tengo que . . . At what time do you have to do the following?

> MODELO   comer: 6:00 P.M.
> **Tengo que comer a las seis de la tarde.**

1. ir a trabajar: 4:00 P.M.
2. practicar karate: 5:30 P.M.
3. estar en la escuela: 7:00 A.M.
4. salir de la escuela: 2:45 P.M.
5. hacer la tarea: 7:30 P.M.
6. hablar con el profesor: 10:50 A.M.
7. limpiar mi cuarto: 3:45 P.M.
8. estudiar español: 8:15 P.M.

L E C C I Ó N   1

3.1 IR A

Used to Talk about Destination

In **Unidad 2,** you learned that **ir a** is used with an infinitive to talk about what
you are going to do.

> **Vamos a correr** esta tarde.

Ir a is also used to talk about where you are going.

> **ir a** + *place*

> **Voy a** mi clase de baile.   *I am going to my dance lesson.*
> ¿**Vamos a** la biblioteca hoy?   *Are we going to the library today?*

- Note that when **a** is followed by **el,** the contraction **al** is formed.

> **a + el = al**

> Mi familia va **al** parque los   *My family goes to the park*
>   domingos.   *on Sundays.*
> ¿Qué tal si vamos **al** cine?   *How about if we go to the movies?*

- **Vamos,** the **nosotros** form, can also mean *let's.*

> **Vamos** a alquilar un video.   *Let's rent a video.*
> **Vamos** al cine.   *Let's go to the movies.*
> ¡**Vamos!**   *Let's go!*

Vamos a practicar

a. **¿Adónde van?**   Tell where the following people are going.

> MODELO Juanita **va** al Colegio San Martín.

1. María _____ al Colegio San Martín
   también.
2. Lisa y tú _____ al parque.
3. Felipe y yo _____ al gimnasio.
4. Yo _____ al cine.
5. Tú _____ a la clase de matemáticas.

6. Juanita _____ a la cafetería.
7. Hernán y Soledad _____ a la
   biblioteca.
8. Nosotros _____ al salón 21.
9. Enrique _____ al Lago Chapultepec.
10. Ustedes _____ al restaurante.

¿POR QUÉ SE DICE ASÍ?   **G33**

Point out The context makes
clear whether **vamos a** is
expressing the future or *let's.*

Vamos a practicar

These exercises may be done as
oral or written work.

Additional Exercises
Textbook: pages 110–111, 113
Cuaderno: Unidad 3, Lección 1

a. ¿Adónde van?
1 va
2 van
3 vamos
4 voy
5 vas
6 va
7 van
8 vamos
9 va
10 van

b. ¡Por fin, es viernes!

1 al
2 al
3 a la
4 al
5 a la
6 al
7 al
8 al
9 a la
10 a la

c. ¡Qué fin de semana!

1 Papá va al restaurante.
2 Tina y Luisa van a la biblioteca.
3 Mamá va a la clase de baile.
4 Tú vas al gimnasio.
5 Yo voy al cine.
6 Usted va al centro comercial.
7 Carlos y tú van al museo.
8 Usted y yo vamos al zoológico.
9 La profesora Pérez va al parque.
10 Ustedes van a la fiesta de un amigo.

ch. ¿Qué hacemos?

1 Sí, vamos a jugar fútbol.
2 Sí, vamos a leer libros.
3 Sí, vamos a ver televisión.
4 Sí, vamos a comprar ropa.
5 Sí, vamos a hacer ejercicio.
6 Sí, vamos a escuchar música.
7 Sí, vamos a comer pizza.
8 Sí, vamos a pasear.
9 Sí, vamos a hablar español.

3.2 **Margin box: page 111**

---

b. ¡Por fin, es viernes!   It's finally Friday, and you and some friends are discussing your plans for the weekend. Where is everyone going?

> MODELO   Pancho y Ricardo van **al** cine.

1. Lupe y María van _____ centro comercial.
2. Voy _____ Café Toluca.
3. Antonio y yo vamos _____ tienda.
4. Yolanda va _____ parque.
5. Vas _____ cafetería.
6. Vamos _____ zoológico.
7. Daniel va _____ gimnasio.
8. Voy _____ museo.
9. Tú y Carlos Javier van _____ fiesta.
10. Rosa María va _____ biblioteca municipal.

c. ¡Qué fin de semana!   Tell where these people are going on the weekend.

> MODELO   Carlos / clase de karate
> **Carlos va a la clase de karate.**

1. papá / restaurante
2. Tina y Luisa / biblioteca
3. mamá / clase de baile
4. tú / gimnasio
5. yo / cine
6. usted / centro comercial
7. Carlos y tú / museo
8. usted y yo / zoológico
9. la profesora Pérez / parque
10. ustedes / fiesta de un amigo

ch. ¿Qué hacemos?   Suggest that you and your friend do the following activities. Your friend will agree.

> MODELO   ¿Alquilamos un video?
> **Sí, vamos a alquilar un video.**

1. ¿Jugamos fútbol?
2. ¿Leemos libros?
3. ¿Vemos televisión?
4. ¿Compramos ropa?
5. ¿Hacemos ejercicio?
6. ¿Escuchamos música?
7. ¿Comemos pizza?
8. ¿Paseamos ahora?
9. ¿Hablamos español?

3.2 THE INDEFINITE ARTICLE AND HAY

The indefinite article has four forms in Spanish.

Indefinite Articles		
	Singular	Plural
Masculine	**un** (*a, an*)	**unos** (*some*)
Feminine	**una** (*a, an*)	**unas** (*some*)

Ella tiene **un** libro nuevo.   *She has a new book.*
Es **una** profesora muy exigente.   *She's a very demanding teacher.*
Hay **unas** tiendas interesantes allí. *There are some interesting stores there.*

¿POR QUÉ SE DICE ASÍ?

Hay, a form of the verb **haber,** means both *there is* and *there are*. In a question, **¿Hay?** means *Is there?* or *Are there?*

Hay un museo en el parque.	*There is a museum in the park.*
Hay unos refrescos aquí.	*There are some soft drinks here.*
¿Hay discos en oferta?	*Are there records on sale?*

■ The indefinite article is usually omitted when **hay** is used in the negative.

No hay cines en esta ciudad.	*There are no movie theaters in this city.*
¿No hay centros comerciales?	*Aren't there any shopping centers?*

Vamos a practicar

a. En mi ciudad.   Form sentences to indicate that the following are found in your town.

MODELO   restaurantes excelentes
 Hay unos restaurantes excelentes.

1. cines buenos
2. tiendas de computadoras
3. gimnasio grande
4. restaurante mexicano
5. biblioteca

6. cafetería
7. tiendas de discos para jóvenes
8. laboratorios de ciencia
9. clases de karate
10. tiendas elegantes

b. ¡Muchas cosas!   ¿Qué hay en tu mochila?

MODELO   3 libros
 Hay tres libros.

1. 1 diccionario
2. 1 calculadora

3. 3 lápices
4. 2 carpetas

5. 2 cuadernos
6. 1 examen

7. 4 bolígrafos
8. muchos papeles

c. ¿Quiénes son?   As you have lunch in the school cafeteria, your best friend is sitting with her back to the door and can't see who is walking into the cafeteria. What do you tell her?

MODELO   profesores   chica
 Son unos profesores.   Es una chica.

1. chicas
2. amigo

3. señor
4. señoras

5. chico
6. señores

7. profesor
8. profesoras

ch. Cerca de mi casa.   Tell if there are any of the following near your house.

MODELO   ¿Hay una tienda de discos?
 Sí, hay una tienda de discos. o No, no hay tiendas de discos.

1. ¿Hay una escuela?
2. ¿Hay un gimnasio?
3. ¿Hay un cine?

4. ¿Hay una biblioteca?
5. ¿Hay una cafetería?
6. ¿Hay un parque grande?

7. ¿Hay un café?
8. ¿Hay un museo?
9. ¿Hay un restaurante?

¿POR QUÉ SE DICE ASÍ?   **G35**

Point out When used without a noun, **no hay** means *there isn't / aren't any* and **¿no hay?** means *isn't / aren't there any?*

Vamos a practicar

> **Additional Exercises**
> Textbook: pages 111–112
> Cuaderno: Unidad 3, Lección 1

a. En mi ciudad.
1 Hay unos cines buenos.
2 Hay unas tiendas de computadoras.
3 Hay un gimnasio grande.
4 Hay un restaurante mexicano.
5 Hay una biblioteca.
6 Hay una cafetería.
7 Hay unas tiendas de discos para jóvenes.
8 Hay unos laboratorios de ciencia.
9 Hay unas clases de karate.
10 Hay unas tiendas elegantes.

b. ¡Muchas cosas!
1 Hay un diccionario.
2 Hay una calculadora.
3 Hay tres lápices.
4 Hay dos carpetas.
5 Hay dos cuadernos.
6 Hay un examen.
7 Hay cuatro bolígrafos.
8 Hay muchos papeles.

c. ¿Quiénes son?
1 Son unas chicas.
2 Es un amigo.
3 Es un señor.
4 Son unas señoras.
5 Es un chico.
6 Son unos señores.
7 Es un profesor.
8 Son unas profesoras.

ch. Cerca de mi casa.
Answers will vary.

U N I D A D **3**

3.3 THE VERBS GUSTAR AND ENCANTAR
Used to Express Likes and Dislikes

The verb **gustar** (*to like*) is used to express likes and dislikes. It is always preceded by **me, te,** or **le** to state that *I, you,* or *she* or *he* likes something.

Gustar		
I	(no) **me** gusta	(a mí)
you	(no) **te** gusta	(a ti)
	(no) **le** gusta	(a usted)
he *she*	(no) **le** gusta	(a él) (a ella)

¿**Te gusta** la profesora? — *Do you like the teacher?*
Me gusta mucho pero **no me** — *I like her a lot, but I don't like*
  gusta la tarea. — *the homework.*
A Carlos **le gusta** bailar. — *Carlos likes to dance.*

■ **A + mí / ti / usted / él / ella** is frequently used to emphasize or clarify who is doing the liking or disliking.

A ella no le gustan. — *She doesn't like them.*
A mí me encanta el chocolate. — *I love chocolate.*
¿Le gusta **a usted**? — *Do you like it?*

Encantar (*to really like, love*) is used to talk about things you really like or love. Like **gustar**, **encantar** is always preceded by **me, te,** or **le** when stating that *I, you,* or *she* or *he* really likes something.

Gustar		Encantar	
If one thing is liked:	*If one thing is disliked:*	*If one thing is really liked:*	
me gusta **te** gusta **le** gusta	no **me** gusta no **te** gusta no **le** gusta	**me** encanta **te** encanta **le** encanta	
If more than one thing is liked:	*If more than one thing is disliked:*	*If more than one thing is really liked:*	
me gust**an** **te** gust**an** **le** gust**an**	no **me** gust**an** no **te** gust**an** no **le** gust**an**	**me** encant**an** **te** encant**an** **le** encant**an**	

■ The verb ending for **gustar** and **encantar** always agrees with the thing or things that are liked. For this reason, these verbs are used mostly in the third-person singular and plural.

In this lesson, the prepositional phrase **a mí / ti / usted / él / ella** is presented for recognition, not for production. Students should not be expected to produce it at this time.

Note You may want to point out that, translated literally, **gustar** means *to be pleasing*.

Point out While you can express dislikes by using **gustar** in the negative, **encantar** is not used in the negative. Also point out that **gustar** and **encantar** are often used without an expressed subject: ¿Te gusta? ¡Me encanta!

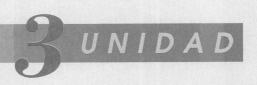

Profesor, ¿qué clase **le** gus**ta** más?	*Professor, which class do you like better?*
¿**Te** gus**tan** tus clases?	*Do you like your classes?*
Me encan**tan.**	*I love them.*
Me encan**ta** pasear en bicicleta.	*I love to go bike riding.*

■ If what is liked or disliked is expressed by an infinitive, then the third-person singular form of **gustar** or **encantar** is used:

¿Te gus**ta** correr?	*Do you like to run?*
No, pero me encan**ta** ir de compras.	*No, but I love to go shopping.*
Le gus**ta** leer y escribir cartas.	*She likes to read and to write letters.*

■ **Gustaría** and **encantaría** are used to soften a request or to respond to a request. Their English equivalents are *would like* and *would love.*

| ¿**Te** gusta**ría** ir conmigo? | *Would you like to go with me?* |
| No **me** gusta**ría** ir a La Cueva pero **me** encanta**ría** ir a La Posta. | *I wouldn't like to go to La Cueva, but I would love to go to La Posta.* |

Vamos a practicar

a. ¡Me gusta! Tell how you feel about each item listed below.

MODELO   recreo
Me gusta el recreo. o **No me gusta el recreo.**

1. fútbol
2. tarea
3. pizza
4. teatro
5. español
6. cafetería de la escuela
7. música rock
8. televisión
9. literatura

b. ¿Y a tu mamá? Tell if your mother (or another adult) likes the following.

MODELO   fiestas
Sí, le gustan las fiestas. o **No, no le gustan las fiestas.**

1. videos
2. películas
3. restaurantes
4. computadoras
5. parques
6. centros comerciales
7. tiendas de discos
8. casas grandes
9. novelas románticas

c. ¿Te gusta? Answer the questions to indicate if you like to do the following.

MODELO   ¿Te gusta ir al cine?
Sí, me gusta. o **No, no me gusta.**

1. ¿Te gusta ir de compras?
2. ¿Te gusta preparar la comida?
3. ¿Te gusta bailar?
4. ¿Te gusta estudiar en la biblioteca?
5. ¿Te gusta leer en casa?
6. ¿Te gusta hacer la tarea?
7. ¿Te gusta correr?
8. ¿Te gusta mirar videos?
9. ¿Te gusta escuchar música?
10. ¿Te gusta hablar por teléfono?

¿POR QUÉ SE DICE ASÍ?

G37

ch. ¡Le encanta!

1 Me encantan los animales.
2 Me encanta la escuela.
3 Me encantan los centros comerciales.
4 Me encanta escribir cartas.
5 Me encanta estudiar español.
6 Me encantan las tiendas.
7 Me encanta ir de compras.
8 Me encanta el cine.
9 Me encantan los bailes folklóricos.
10 Me encanta hablar por teléfono.

d. Preferencias. Students may answer in the affirmative or in the negative. Only afirmative answers are given here.

1 Me gustan los restaurantes buenos. *o* Me encantan los restaurantes buenos.
2 Me gusta hablar con mis amigos. *o* Me encanta hablar con mis amigos.
3 Me gustan las personas divertidas. *o* Me encantan las personas divertidas.
4 Me gusta hacer la comida. *o* Me encanta hacer la comida.
5 Me gusta alquilar videos. *o* Me encanta alquilar videos.
6 Me gusta comer pizza. *o* Me encanta comer pizza.
7 Me gusta ver la tele. *o* Me encanta ver la tele.
8 Me gusta leer. *o* Me encanta leer.
9 Me gusta pasear en bicicleta. *o* Me encanta pasear en bicicleta.
10 Me gustan las clases fáciles. *o* Me encantan las clases fáciles.

3.4 Margin box: page 125

ch. ¡Le encanta! Tina is a very cheerful person who loves everything. How does she describe her feelings about the following?

MODELO las clases   leer novelas
Me encantan las clases.   **Me encanta leer novelas.**

1. los animales
2. la escuela
3. los centros comerciales
4. escribir cartas
5. estudiar español
6. las tiendas
7. ir de compras
8. el cine
9. los bailes folklóricos
10. hablar por teléfono

d. Preferencias. Tell how much you like the following things.

MODELO los exámenes
No me gustan los exámenes. o
Me gustan los exámenes. o
Me encantan los exámenes.

1. los restaurantes buenos
2. hablar con mis amigos
3. las personas divertidas
4. hacer la comida
5. alquilar videos
6. comer pizza
7. ver la tele
8. leer
9. pasear en bicicleta
10. las clases fáciles

L E C C I Ó N   2

3.4 PRESENT TENSE: SINGULAR FORMS

In **Unidad 2,** you learned that infinitives in Spanish end in **-ar, -er,** or **-ir.** To tell who performs an action, you must conjugate the infinitive. This means you replace the infinitive ending with the ending corresponding to the subject. The following chart shows the singular endings.

Singular Present-Tense Endings		
Subject Pronoun	Verb Endings	
	-ar	-er/-ir
yo	-o	-o
tú	-as	-es
usted	-a	-e
él, ella	-a	-e

¿POR QUÉ SE DICE ASÍ?

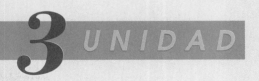

Below are sample singular conjugations for **-ar, -er,** and **-ir** verbs.

	-ar bail**ar**	**-er** comer	**-ir** escrib**ir**
yo	bail**o**	com**o**	escrib**o**
tú	bail**as**	com**es**	escrib**es**
usted	bail**a**	com**e**	escrib**e**
él, ella	bail**a**	com**e**	escrib**e**

Como a las siete. *I eat at seven o'clock.*
¿**Bailas** bien? *Do you dance well?*
Ana **escribe** muchas cartas. *Ana writes lots of letters.*

- The present tense of any Spanish verb has three possible English equivalents:

Corro en el parque.
{ *I run in the park.*
I am running in the park.
I do run in the park. }

Vamos a practicar _____

a. Después de clase. What do you do after class?

MODELO tomar un helado
Después de clase tomo un helado.

1. tomar un refresco 4. escribir cartas 7. leer un libro
2. correr veinte minutos 5. hablar por teléfono 8. tomar un helado
3. ver televisión 6. pasear en coche 9. comer un sándwich

b. ¿Qué haces? What questions was this person asked in a survey?

MODELO ¿ . . . ? No, no canto muy bien.
¿Cantas bien?

1. ¿ . . . ? Sí, bailo muy bien. 5. ¿ . . . ? No, no leo muchos libros.
2. ¿ . . . ? No, no veo mucha televisión. 6. ¿ . . . ? No, no preparo la comida.
3. ¿ . . . ? Sí, corro todos los días. 7. ¿ . . . ? Sí, tomo mucho helado.
4. ¿ . . . ? Sí, hablo español un poco. 8. ¿ . . . ? Sí, estudio por la noche.

c. Todos los días. Complete the following paragraph with the appropriate form of the verbs listed below to find out what José does every day after school.

1. salir 3. escuchar 5. hacer 7. estudiar
2. practicar 4. comer 6. escribir 8. ver

José __1__ de clase a las 3:00 de la tarde. Él __2__ karate dos horas hasta las 5:00.
Luego él va a casa y __3__ sus discos compactos por media hora. __4__ entre las
5:30 y las 6:00 de la tarde. Después de comer, __5__ su tarea, __6__ composiciones
o __7__ para exámenes. Por la noche, José __8__ televisión.

¿POR QUÉ SE DICE ASÍ? G39

Point out The English question forms are *Do I run?* and *Am I running?*

Vamos a practicar

Additional Exercises
Textbook: pages 125–127
Cuaderno: Unidad 3, Lección 2

a. Después de clase.
1 Después de clase tomo un refresco.
2 Después de clase corro veinte minutos.
3 Después de clase veo televisión.
4 Después de clase escribo cartas.
5 Después de clase hablo por teléfono.
6 Después de clase paseo en coche.
7 Después de clase leo un libro.
8 Después de clase tomo un helado.
9 Después de clase como un sándwich.

b. ¿Qué haces?
1 ¿Bailas muy bien?
2 ¿Ves mucha televisión?
3 ¿Corres todos los días?
4 ¿Hablas español?
5 ¿Lees muchos libros?
6 ¿Preparas la comida?
7 ¿Tomas mucho helado?
8 ¿Estudias por la noche?

c. Todos los días.
1 sale
2 practica
3 escucha
4 come
5 hace
6 escribe
7 estudia
8 ve

ch. ¿Qué hacen?
1 Usted escucha música.
2 Él trabaja en una tienda de ropa deportiva.
3 Yo leo una novela romántica.
4 María ve televisión.
5 Tú tomas refrescos.
6 Roberto escucha sus discos compactos.
7 Ella sale con sus amigos.
8 José corre en el parque.
9 Yo miro películas en la tele.
10 Tú comes mucho.

3.5 Margin boxes: pages 128–129

After **en**, the definite article may be used or omitted before the names of seasons: **en (el) verano.** The article is not used in this textbook.

UNIDAD

ch. ¿Qué hacen? What do the following people do in their free time?

MODELO Enrique / escribir cartas
Enrique escribe cartas.

1. usted / escuchar música
2. él / trabajar en una tienda de ropa deportiva
3. yo / leer una novela romántica
4. María / ver televisión
5. tú / tomar refrescos
6. Roberto / escuchar sus discos compactos
7. ella / salir con sus amigos
8. José / correr en el parque
9. yo / mirar películas en la tele
10. tú / comer mucho

3.5 THE SEASONS AND WEATHER EXPRESSIONS

The four seasons in Spanish are:

el verano	*summer*	**el invierno**	*winter*
el otoño	*fall*	**la primavera**	*spring*

Es **otoño** ahora.	*It is fall now.*
No vamos al parque en **invierno.**	*We don't go to the park in the winter.*
La **primavera** es mi estación favorita.	*Spring is my favorite season.*

When talking about the weather in Spanish, the third-person singular of the verb **hacer** is frequently used.

¿Qué tiempo **hace**?	*What's the weather like?*
Hace buen tiempo.	*The weather is good.*
Hace mal tiempo.	*The weather is bad.*
Hace (mucho) sol.	*It's (very) sunny.*
Hace (mucho) viento.	*It's (very) windy.*
Hace (mucho) calor.	*It's (very) hot.*
Hace (mucho) frío.	*It's (very) cold.*
Hace fresco.	*It's cool.*

To indicate that it's raining or snowing, say **Está lloviendo** or **Está nevando.**

¿**Está nevando** ahora?	*Is it snowing now?*
No, pero **está lloviendo.**	*No, but it's raining.*

To make a general statement, however, use the third-person singular of the verbs **llover** and **nevar.**

Llueve mucho por aquí.	*It rains a lot around here.*
Nieva muy poco.	*It snows very little.*

¿POR QUÉ SE DICE ASÍ?

Vamos a practicar

a. ¿Qué estación es?   The seasons in parts of South America are opposite those in the United States. What season is it in the cities followed by a question mark?

MODELO   Chicago, Illinois: verano .... Santiago, Chile: ?
   Es invierno en Santiago.

1. Miami, Florida: invierno .... Asunción, Paraguay: ?
2. Phoenix, Arizona: primavera .... La Paz, Bolivia: ?
3. Raleigh, North Carolina: otoño .... Lima, Perú: ?
4. Little Rock, Arkansas: verano .... Buenos Aires, Argentina: ?
5. Wichita, Kansas: ? .... Bogotá, Colombia: primavera
6. Norfolk, Virginia: ? .... Quito, Ecuador: otoño
7. Syracuse, New York: ? .... Montevideo, Uruguay: verano

b. ¿Qué tiempo hace?   Select the weather expression that most logically completes each sentence.

MODELO   En verano (hace calor / hace frío).
   En verano hace calor.

1. En primavera (hace buen tiempo / nieva).
2. En otoño (hace fresco / hace calor).
3. En verano (hace frío / hace mucho sol).
4. En invierno (nieva / hace fresco).
5. En verano (hace frío / hace buen tiempo).
6. En invierno (hace viento / hace mal tiempo).
7. En primavera (hace mucho frío / llueve).
8. En otoño (nieva / hace viento).

c. Las cuatro estaciones.   Pepe lives in Bolivia. How does he describe the weather during the various seasons?

MODELO   invierno / frío
   En invierno hace frío.

1. verano / calor
2. primavera / fresco
3. invierno / mal tiempo
4. verano / buen tiempo
5. primavera / buen tiempo
6. otoño / llueve
7. verano / sol
8. primavera / viento
9. invierno / nieva

ch. El inverso.   What season is it and what is the weather probably like in the following United States and South American cities on the same day?

MODELO   En Washington, D.C., es invierno. Nieva y hace mucho frío.
   ¿Y en Buenos Aires?
   En Buenos Aires es verano. Hace sol y hace mucho calor.

1. En El Paso, Texas, es verano. Hace mucho sol y hace mucho calor. ¿Y en Santiago de Chile?
2. En Boston, Massachusetts, es primavera y hace fresco. ¿Y en Lima?
3. En Des Moines, Iowa, es otoño. Hace viento y hace fresco. ¿Y en Montevideo?
4. En Portland, Oregon, es invierno. Llueve y hace frío. ¿Y en Quito?

¿POR QUÉ SE DICE ASÍ?   **G41**

Vamos a practicar

Additional Exercises
Textbook: pages 128–129
Cuaderno: Unidad 3, Lección 2

a. ¿Qué estación es?
1 Es verano en Asunción.
2 Es otoño en La Paz.
3 Es primavera en Lima.
4 Es invierno en Buenos Aires.
5 Es otoño en Wichita.
6 Es primavera en Norfolk.
7 Es invierno en Syracuse.

b. ¿Qué tiempo hace?
1 En primavera hace buen tiempo.
2 En otoño hace fresco.
3 En verano hace mucho sol.
4 En invierno nieva.
5 En verano hace buen tiempo.
6 En invierno hace mal tiempo.
7 En primavera llueve.
8 En otoño hace viento.

c. Las cuatro estaciones.
1 En verano hace calor.
2 En primavera hace fresco.
3 En invierno hace mal tiempo.
4 En verano hace buen tiempo.
5 En primavera hace buen tiempo.
6 En otoño llueve.
7 En verano hace sol.
8 En primavera hace viento.
9 En invierno nieva.

ch. El inverso. Answers may vary slightly.
1 En Santiago es invierno. Hace mucho frío y hace mal tiempo. (Nieva. Llueve.)
2 En Lima es otoño y hace frío. (Hace fresco. Hace viento.)
3 En Montevideo es primavera. Hace buen tiempo y hace calor.
4 En Quito es verano. Hace sol y hace calor.

U N I D A D

L E C C I Ó N 3

3.6 *PRESENT TENSE: PLURAL FORMS*

The plural endings for present-tense **-ar, -er,** and **-ir** verbs are shown in the chart below.

Plural Present-Tense Endings			
	Verb Endings		
Subject Pronouns	**-ar**	**-er**	**-ir**
nosotros(as)	**-amos**	**-emos**	**-imos**
vosotros(as)	**-áis**	**-éis**	**-ís**
ustedes	**-an**	**-en**	**-en**
ellas, ellos	**-an**	**-en**	**-en**

The following chart gives sample plural conjugations for **-ar, -er,** and **-ir** verbs.

	-ar bail**ar**	**-er** com**er**	**-ir** escrib**ir**
nosotros(as)	bail**amos**	com**emos**	escrib**imos**
vosotros(as)	bail**áis**	com**éis**	escrib**ís**
ustedes	bail**an**	com**en**	escrib**en**
ellas, ellos	bail**an**	com**en**	escrib**en**

Comemos en la cafetería de la escuela todos los días.
¿**Escriben** muchas cartas?
Bailamos en la discoteca los fines de semana.

We eat in the school cafeteria every day.
Do you write a lot of letters?
We dance at the discotheque on weekends.

Remember that present-tense verbs in Spanish have three English equivalents, as follows:

Escriben muchas cartas.

$\begin{cases} \textit{They write many letters.} \\ \textit{They are writing many letters.} \\ \textit{They do write many letters.} \end{cases}$

Vamos a practicar

a. ¿Y ustedes? Tell if you and your family usually do these activities together.

MODELO bailar
Bailamos juntos. o **No bailamos juntos.**

1. comer
2. leer
3. escuchar música
4. ver la tele
5. preparar la comida
6. pasear en bicicleta
7. salir a comer
8. alquilar videos
9. limpiar la casa

b. Profesionales. Use the expressions on the right to tell how these dedicated professionals usually spend their weekends.

MODELO **Los atletas practican horas y horas.**

pianistas	calificar exámenes
atletas	trabajar en su oficina
estudiantes	practicar horas y horas
profesores	tocar el piano
secretarias	escribir cartas
directores	estudiar

c. ¿Qué hacen todos? Tell what you and your friends do on weekends.

MODELO mi amiga y yo / tomar / refresco
Mi amiga y yo tomamos refrescos.

1. mis amigos y yo / practicar / karate
2. Elena y yo / mirar / película
3. mi amigo y yo / correr / parque
4. nosotros / comer / restaurante
5. mis amigos / ver / tele / noche
6. nosotros / leer / libro interesante
7. mamá y papá / alquilar / video
8. mis amigas / escuchar / discos

ch. Los sábados. You receive a letter from María, a pen pal in Guatemala, telling you a little about her weekends. To find out what she says, complete María's letter with the appropriate form of the verbs listed below.

1. trabajar
2. limpiar
3. practicar
4. estudiar
5. salir
6. ir
7. visitar
8. comer
9. ver
10. estudiar
11. hacer
12. esperar

Los sábados por la mañana mi papá _1_ en su oficina y mi mamá y yo _2_ la casa. Elena _3_ el piano y Roberto _4_ con un amigo. Por la tarde, toda la familia _5_ al parque. Todos nosotros _6_ al parque de diversiones y Roberto _7_ el zoológico. Por la noche, nosotros _8_ juntos y _9_ la tele. Los domingos Roberto y yo _10_ para las clases del lunes. ¿Qué _11_ tú los fines de semana? Yo _12_ tu carta.

Un abrazo muy fuerte de
María

¿POR QUÉ SE DICE ASÍ?

_____ **G43**

Vamos a practicar

Additional Exercises
Textbook: pages 140–143
Cuaderno: Unidad 3, Lección 3

a. ¿Y ustedes? Remind students that when referring to an all-female group, **juntos** becomes **juntas.** Students may answer in the affirmative or in the negative. Affirmative and negative answers are given alternately below.

1 Comemos juntos.
2 No leemos juntos.
3 Escuchamos música juntos.
4 No vemos la tele juntos.
5 Preparamos la comida juntos.
6 No paseamos en bicicleta juntos.
7 Salimos a comer juntos.
8 No alquilamos videos juntos.
9 Limpiamos la casa juntos.

b. Profesionales.
Los pianistas tocan el piano.
Los atletas practican horas y horas.
Los estudiantes estudian.
Los profesores califican exámenes.
Las secretarias escriben cartas.
Los directores trabajan en su oficina.

c. ¿Qué hacen todos?
1 Mis amigos y yo practicamos karate.
2 Elena y yo miramos una película.
3 Mi amigo y yo corremos en el parque.
4 Nosotros comemos en un restaurante al aire libre.
5 Mis amigos ven la tele de noche.
6 Nosotros leemos libros interesantes.
7 Mamá y papá alquilan un video.
8 Mis amigas escuchan discos.

ch. Los sábados.

1 trabaja	7 visita
2 limpiamos	8 comemos
3 practica	9 vemos
4 estudia	10 estudiamos
5 sale	11 haces
6 vamos	12 espero

In **Unidad 1,** you learned that the most common way to make a Spanish sentence negative is to put the word **no** before the verb.

No es verdad.	*It's not true.*
¿Por qué **no** vas con nosotros?	*Why don't you go with us?*
No es mi clase.	*It's not my class.*

Indefinite words are words that do not refer to anything or anyone specific. Certain indefinite words have contrasting negative forms.

Indefinite and Negative Words			
Affirmative Forms		Negative Forms	
algo	*something*	**nada**	*nothing, not anything*
alguien	*somebody*	**nadie**	*nobody, not anybody*
siempre	*always*	**nunca**	*never*
a veces	*sometimes*	**raras veces**	*seldom*

¿Van a comer **algo**?	*Are you going to eat something?*
Siempre como en casa.	*I always eat at home.*
Nunca estudio en la biblioteca.	*I never study at the library.*

■ In negative sentences, a negative word must always precede the verb. Note that when **no** precedes the verb, any other negative word follows it.

No hay **nadie** en el parque.	*There's nobody in the park.*
No vamos a comer **nada.**	*We're not going to eat anything.*
Nadie canta como ellos.	*Nobody sings like them.*
Nunca vamos a entrar.	*We're never going to get in.*

Vamos a practicar

a. **¡Qué ridículo!**   Eduardo likes to get on his sister's nerves by contradicting everything she says. What does Eduardo say when she makes these comments?

MODELO   Papá nunca ve la tele por la noche.
Papá siempre ve la tele por la noche.

1. Los señores Romano nunca están en casa.
2. Los profesores nunca califican exámenes.
3. Carmen no come nada.
4. Ramón no estudia nunca.
5. Nadie tiene computación los miércoles.
6. Tú y yo nunca caminamos juntos.
7. La profesora no habla con nadie.
8. Elena nunca escribe cartas.

Vamos a practicar

Additional Exercises
Textbook: pages 143–144
Cuaderno: Unidad 3, Lección 3

a. ¡Qué ridículo!
1 Los señores Romano siempre están en casa.
2 Los profesores siempre califican los exámenes.
3 Carmen come algo.
4 Ramón siempre estudia.
5 Alguien tiene computación los miércoles.
6 Tú y yo siempre caminamos juntos.
7 La profesora habla con alguien.
8 Elena siempre escribe cartas.

b. ¡Llueve! What do you do and what do you observe other people doing when it rains? Answer all the questions in the negative.

MODELO   ¿Escribes algo cuando llueve?
No, cuando llueve no escribo nada.

1. ¿Alguien escucha la radio cuando llueve?
2. ¿Hace algo para comer tu mamá cuando llueve?
3. ¿Siempre vas al zoológico cuando llueve?
4. ¿Lees algo en casa a veces cuando llueve?
5. ¿Alguien corre en el parque cuando llueve?
6. ¿Tomas helado a veces cuando llueve?
7. ¿Siempre subes a las lanchas cuando llueve?
8. ¿Juegas fútbol con alguien cuando llueve?

c. ¡Qué confusión! Enrique always gets everything backward. Help straighten him out by making his negative statements affirmative and vice versa.

MODELO   Nadie come en el restaurante.
Alguien come en el restaurante.

1. A veces escriben cartas en clase.
2. Alguien espera el autobús.
3. María y Carmen siempre caminan a casa.
4. Nunca compra nada.
5. Francisca no come nada.
6. Los profesores nunca califican exámenes.
7. Nunca paseamos por el parque.
8. Le gusta escuchar algo.
9. Nadie visita los museos.
10. Alguien lee un libro.

ch. Editor. As an editor for the school newspaper, you are always having to find ways to shorten the articles you are editing. How would you shorten these sentences?

MODELO   Elena no limpia la casa nunca.
Elena nunca limpia la casa.

1. No voy al parque nunca los viernes.
2. No estudia nadie los viernes.
3. No habla nadie como ella.
4. No me gusta nada.
5. No está nadie aquí.
6. Martín no sube a la montaña rusa nunca.
7. No come pizza nadie.
8. No pasa nada aquí.

b. ¡Llueve!
1 No, cuando llueve nadie escucha la radio.
2 No, cuando llueve mi mamá no hace nada para comer.
3 No, cuando llueve nunca voy al zoológico.
4 No, cuando llueve nunca leo nada en casa.
5 No, cuando llueve nadie corre en el parque.
6 No, cuando llueve nunca tomo helado.
7 No, cuando llueve nunca subo a las lanchas.
8 No, cuando llueve no juego fútbol con nadie.

c. ¡Qué confusión!
1 Nunca escriben cartas en clase.
2 Nadie espera el autobús.
3 María y Carmen nunca caminan a casa.
4 Siempre compra algo.
5 Francisca come algo.
6 Los profesores siempre califican exámenes.
7 Siempre paseamos por el parque.
8 No le gusta escuchar nada.
9 Alguien visita los museos.
10 Nadie lee un libro.

ch. Editor.
1 Nunca voy al parque los viernes.
2 Nadie estudia los viernes.
3 Nadie habla como ella.
4 Nada me gusta.
5 Nadie está aquí.
6 Martín nunca sube a la montaña rusa.
7 Nadie come pizza.
8 Nada pasa aquí.

LECCIÓN 1

4.1 POSSESSIVE ADJECTIVES

Possessive adjectives are used to indicate that something belongs to someone or to establish a relationship between people or things.

Éste es **mi** libro, ¿verdad?	*This is my book, isn't it?*
¿Gregorio es **tu** primo?	*Gregorio is your cousin?*

Possessive Adjectives					
	Singular	Plural	Singular	Plural	
my	**mi**	**mis**	**nuestro(a)**	**nuestros(as)**	*our*
your	**tu**	**tus**	**vuestro(a)**	**vuestros(as)**	*your*
	su	**sus**	**su**	**sus**	
his *her* *its*	**su**	**sus**	**su**	**sus**	*their*

■ Possessive adjectives are placed before the noun they modify.

Ustedes ya conocen a **su** novia.	*You already know his fiancée.*
Nuestra casa es muy grande.	*Our house is very large.*

■ Unlike English, Spanish possessive adjectives agree with what is possessed and not with the possessor. Like other adjectives, possessive adjectives agree in number and gender with the noun they modify.

Él trabaja con **sus** hijos.	*He works with **his** sons.*
Ella estudia con **tus** hijos.	*She studies with **your** children.*
Ellos salen con **su** hijo.	*They go out with **their** son.*

■ Another common way of expressing possession in the third person is with the preposition **de.** This construction is especially useful if the meaning of **su/sus** is not clear from the context.

Su libro está en la mesa.	*His book is on the table.*
El libro **de David** está en la mesa.	*David's book is on the table.*
Sus primos son simpáticos. Los primos **de ella** son simpáticos. }	*Her cousins are nice.*
Su boda es el sábado. La boda **de ellos** es el sábado. }	*Their wedding is on Saturday.*

Vamos a practicar

a. Álbum. Who are the people in the family album, according to Silvia?

MODELO prima Anita
Es mi prima Anita.

1. abuela Sara
2. tíos Miguel y Patricia
3. primo Enrique
4. primos Beto y Raúl
5. tíos Leopoldo y Nora
6. abuelos Pablo y Dolores
7. hermano Pablito
8. papás
9. hermanas Anita y Tina
10. tía Paula

b. ¿Dónde están? Where are the things these people misplaced?

MODELO los libros de Sara: gimnasio
Sus libros están en el gimnasio.

1. las carpetas de Fernando y Pilar: cafetería
2. el bolígrafo de Ramón: clase de inglés
3. los lápices de Felipe: salón 23
4. la mochila de Anita: laboratorio de química
5. el libro de inglés de Betina: salón de español
6. los cuadernos de Elena y Clara: teatro
7. el reloj de Paco: biblioteca
8. el disco de Jorge y Sara: clase de computación

c. Nuestra familia. You and your sister are describing your family to a friend. What do you say?

MODELO tía / rico / generoso
Nuestra tía es rica y generosa.

1. abuelo / exigente / antipático
2. primas / joven / bonito
3. mamá / inteligente / modesto
4. primos / atlético / fuerte
5. hermanos / alto / guapo
6. abuela / simpático / divertido
7. hermanas / rubio / delgado
8. padre / generoso / honesto

ch. ¡Incendio! During a fire drill at school, everyone dashes out into the hallway with what they have in their hands. What does Luisa say that she and her friends have with them?

MODELO yo
Yo tengo mis cuadernos.

1. David
2. Sara y Anita
3. tú
4. Raúl y yo

5. mis amigas
6. tú y Antonio
7. Alicia
8. yo

¿POR QUÉ SE DICE ASÍ? _____ **G47**

Vamos a practicar

These exercises may be done as oral or written work.

Additional Exercises
Textbook: pages 158–159
Cuaderno: Unidad 4, Lección 1

a. Álbum.
1 Es mi abuela Sara.
2 Son mis tíos Miguel y Patricia.
3 Es mi primo Enrique.
4 Son mis primos Beto y Raúl.
5 Son mis tíos Leopoldo y Nora.
6 Son mis abuelos Pablo y Dolores.
7 Es mi hermano Pablito.
8 Son mis papás.
9 Son mis hermanas Anita y Tina.
10 Es mi tía Paula.

b. ¿Dónde están?
1 Sus carpetas están en la cafetería.
2 Su bolígrafo está en la clase de inglés.
3 Sus lápices están en el salón 23.
4 Su mochila está en el laboratorio de química.
5 Su libro de inglés está en el salón de español.
6 Sus cuadernos están en el teatro.
7 Su reloj está en la biblioteca.
8 Su disco está en la clase de computación.

c. Nuestra familia.
1 Nuestro abuelo es exigente y antipático.
2 Nuestras primas son jóvenes y bonitas.
3 Nuestra mamá es inteligente y modesta.
4 Nuestros primos son atléticos y fuertes.
5 Nuestros hermanos son altos y guapos.
6 Nuestra abuela es simpática y divertida.
7 Nuestras hermanas son rubias y delgadas.
8 Nuestro padre es generoso y honesto.

ch. ¡Incendio!
1 David tiene sus libros.
2 Sara y Anita tienen sus lápices.
3 Tú tienes tu papel (tus papeles).
4 Raúl y yo tenemos nuestros cuadernos.
5 Mis amigas tienen sus cartas.
6 Tú y Antonio tienen sus carpetas.
7 Alicia tiene su periódico.
8 Yo tengo mi mochila.

d. ¡Todos hablan a la vez!

1 su
2 su
3 sus
4 nuestra
5 tu
6 sus
7 mi
8 nuestros

e. ¿Es verdad?

1 Sí, es la tía de Carlos.
2 Sí, es el padre de Ramón y Paloma.
3 Sí, es la hermana de Pepe y Teresa.
4 Sí, son los tíos de Enrique y Lupe.
5 Sí, son los primos de Norma.
6 Sí, es el esposo de Patricia.
7 Sí, son las tías de Lisa.
8 Sí, son los abuelos de Alberto.

4.2 Margin box: page 160

---

d. ¡Todos hablan a la vez! At a Fourth of July community picnic, everyone seems to be talking with a relative. Can you tell who is talking to whom?

MODELO   Lupe habla con __su__ prima Anita.

1. Enrique habla con _____ tío Joaquín.
2. Nora habla con _____ esposo Miguel.
3. Antonia habla con _____ sobrinos Beto y Raúl.
4. Lupe y yo hablamos con _____ tía Patricia.
5. Tú hablas con _____ prima Anita.
6. Julia habla con _____ tíos Leopoldo y Miguel.
7. Yo hablo con _____ abuela.
8. Nora y yo hablamos con _____ primos Paco y Angelita.

e. ¿Es verdad? At the same picnic, how does Julia confirm the following relationships?

MODELO   ¿Son sus padres? (David)
         Sí, son los padres de David.

1. ¿Es su tía? (Carlos)
2. ¿Es su padre? (Ramón y Paloma)
3. ¿Es su hermana? (Pepe y Teresa)
4. ¿Son sus tíos? (Enrique y Lupe)
5. ¿Son sus primos? (Norma)
6. ¿Es su esposo? (Patricia)
7. ¿Son sus tías? (Lisa)
8. ¿Son sus abuelos? (Alberto)

4.2   NUMBERS FROM 30 TO 100

30	treinta	60	sesenta
31	treinta y uno	66	sesenta y seis
32	treinta y dos	70	setenta
33	treinta y tres	77	setenta y siete
34	treinta y cuatro	80	ochenta
40	cuarenta	88	ochenta y ocho
44	cuarenta y cuatro	90	noventa
50	cincuenta	99	noventa y nueve
55	cincuenta y cinco	100	cien

Tengo **noventa** dólares en el banco.   *I have ninety dollars in the bank.*

Mi abuelo tiene **setenta y ocho** años.   *My grandfather is seventy-eight years old.*

- When a number ending in **uno** is followed by a masculine noun, **uno** becomes **un;** when it is followed by a feminine noun, **uno** becomes **una.**

Papá va a cumplir **cuarenta y un** años.   *Dad is going to be forty-one years old.*

Hay **sesenta y una** bicicletas.   *There are sixty-one bicycles.*

Vamos a practicar

a. ¿Cuántos cumplen hoy? A Hispanic radio announcer is wishing a happy birthday to anyone over thirty celebrating a birthday today. How old are the people who receive birthday greetings?

MODELO Lilia Sánchez / 55
Lilia Sánchez cumple cincuenta y cinco años.

1. Gloria Lara / 89
2. Francisco Granados / 45
3. Santiago Rojas / 72
4. Adela Guzmán / 38

5. Cristina Cordero / 57
6. Estela Espinosa / 66
7. Juan Gutiérrez / 93
8. Manuel Puentes / 100

b. ¿Cuál es su número? You are helping a friend phone the guests who are being invited to your teacher's surprise birthday party. Read the phone numbers to your friend.

MODELO Rafael Méndez / 922-7405
El número de Rafael Méndez es el nueve, veintidós, setenta y cuatro, cero cinco.

1. Eduardo Cordero / 757-9107
2. Linda Estévez / 444-7484
3. Humberto Ortiz / 235-7166
4. Amalia Montenegro / 941-5551

5. Samuel Caballero / 687-4690
6. María Inés Alarcón / 877-5775
7. Amanda Chávez / 278-6286
8. Ramón Lara / 898-0508

c. ¿Cuánto debemos? María González, treasurer of the Spanish Club, is writing out checks to pay for the last club party. What amount does she write on each check?

MODELO Florería Chávez: $38
treinta y ocho dólares

1. Heladería Montero: $67
2. Bebidas Quitased: $84
3. Mercado Véguez: $46
4. Pizzería Colón: $52

5. Banda Juventud: $95
6. Discos Fabia: $41
7. Papelería Lara: $39
8. Restaurante Tito: $53

ch. ¡Ganamos! The school basketball team is doing very well this season. What does Kevin say as he reports the scores for several games?

MODELO 46–40
Nuestro equipo, cuarenta y seis; su equipo, cuarenta.

1. 72–53
2. 48–37
3. 51–50
4. 43–38

5. 85–69
6. 94–56
7. 76–68
8. 97–89

¿POR QUÉ SE DICE ASÍ?

Additional Exercises
Textbook: pages 160–161
Cuaderno: Unidad 4, Lección 1

a. ¿Cuántos cumplen hoy?
1 Gloria cumple ochenta y nueve años.
2 Francisco cumple cuarenta y cinco años.
3 Santiago cumple setenta y dos años.
4 Adela cumple treinta y ocho años.
5 Cristina cumple cincuenta y siete años.
6 Estela cumple sesenta y seis años.
7 Juan cumple noventa y tres años.
8 Manuel cumple cien años.

b. ¿Cuál es su número?
Remind students that telephone numbers are commonly expressed in pairs, beginning with the second digit.
1 El número de Eduardo Cordero es el siete, cincuenta y siete, noventa y uno, cero siete.
2 El número de Linda Estévez es el cuatro, cuarenta y cuatro, setenta y cuatro, ochenta y cuatro.
3 El número de Humberto Ortiz es el dos, treinta y cinco, setenta y uno, sesenta y seis.
4 El número de Amalia Montenegro es el nueve, cuarenta y uno, cincuenta y cinco, cincuenta y uno.
5 El número de Samuel Caballero es el seis, ochenta y siete, cuarenta y seis, noventa.
6 El número de María Inés Alarcón es el ocho, setenta y siete, cincuenta y siete, setenta y cinco.
7 El número de Amanda Chávez es el dos, setenta y ocho, sesenta y dos, ochenta y seis.
8 El número de Ramón Lara es el ocho, noventa y ocho, cero cinco, cero ocho.

c. ¿Cuánto debemos?
1 sesenta y siete dólares
2 ochenta y cuatro dólares
3 cuarenta y seis dólares
4 cincuenta y dos dólares
5 noventa y cinco dólares
6 cuarenta y un dólares
7 treinta y nueve dólares
8 cincuenta y tres dólares

ch. ¡Ganamos!
1 Nuestro equipo, setenta y dos; su equipo, cincuenta y tres.
2 Nuestro equipo, cuarenta y ocho; su equipo, treinta y siete.
3 Nuestro equipo, cincuenta y uno; su equipo, cincuenta.
4 Nuestro equipo, cuarenta y tres; su equipo, treinta y ocho.
5 Nuestro equipo, ochenta y cinco; su equipo, sesenta y nueve.
6 Nuestro equipo, noventa y cuatro; su equipo, cincuenta y seis.
7 Nuestro equipo, setenta y seis; su equipo, sesenta y ocho.
8 Nuestro equipo, noventa y siete; su equipo, ochenta y nueve.
Extension Have students check sports scores from newspapers and report them to class.

Point out
- An accepted variation of **septiembre** is **setiembre**.
- Dates are also written this way with periods: **16.IX.94.**

Vamos a practicar

Additional Exercises
Textbook: pages 160–161
Cuaderno: Unidad 4, Lección 1

a. ¿En qué mes?
1 Celebramos la Independencia de Estados Unidos en julio.
2 Celebramos el Día de San Patricio en marzo.
3 Celebramos el Día de los Enamorados en febrero.
4 Celebramos el Día de los Inocentes en abril.
5 Celebramos el Día de Acción de Gracias en noviembre.
6 Celebramos la Navidad en diciembre.
7 Celebramos los cumpleaños de George Washington y Abraham Lincoln en febrero.
8 Celebramos el Día del Trabajador en septiembre.
9 Celebramos Año Nuevo en enero.
10 Celebramos la Noche Vieja en diciembre.

U N I D A D

4

4.3 THE MONTHS OF THE YEAR

enero	**abril**	**julio**	**octubre**
febrero	**mayo**	**agosto**	**noviembre**
marzo	**junio**	**septiembre**	**diciembre**

- The months of the year are not capitalized in Spanish.
- To ask for today's date, use one of these questions:

¿Cuál es la fecha de hoy?
¿Qué fecha es hoy? } *What is today's date?*

- To give dates in Spanish, follow this formula.

el + (*número*) + de + (*mes*)

Hoy es **el cuatro de diciembre.** *Today is December fourth.*
Mi cumpleaños es **el diecisiete de julio.** *My birthday is July seventeenth.*

- The first day of the month is always expressed as **el primero.**

Mi cumpleaños es **el primero** de mayo. *My birthday is the first of May.*

- In Spanish, when dates are written in numbers, the day comes before the month. The month may be written in Roman numerals.

el cinco de julio	**5-7**	o	**5-VII**
el veintitrés de mayo	**23-5**	o	**23-V**
el treinta de enero	**30-1**	o	**30-I**

Vamos a practicar

a. ¿En qué mes? In what month do we celebrate the following holidays in the United States?

MODELO el Día de la Raza (*Columbus Day*)
Celebramos el Día de la Raza en octubre.

1. la Independencia de Estados Unidos
2. el Día de San Patricio
3. el Día de los Enamorados / el Día de San Valentín
4. el Día de los Inocentes (*April Fools' Day*)
5. el Día de Acción de Gracias (*Thanksgiving*)
6. la Navidad (*Christmas*)
7. los cumpleaños de George Washington y Abraham Lincoln
8. el Día del Trabajador (*Labor Day*)
9. Año Nuevo
10. la Noche Vieja (*New Year's Eve*)

¿POR QUÉ SE DICE ASÍ?

U N I D A D

b. ¿Cuándo cumplen años?   When does Anita say her relatives celebrate their birthdays?

MODELO   tía Josefina: 4-V
   El cumpleaños de mi tía Josefina es el cuatro de mayo.

1. abuelita: 30-I
2. mamá: 26-XI
3. hermano Carlos: 28-II
4. tío Alfredo: 8-IV
5. papá: 12-VIII
6. tía Elena: 13-X
7. abuelito: 15-III
8. hermana Cristina: 23-VII

c. ¿Cuántos días?   Which months have 30, 31, and 28 days?

1. 30 días (4 meses)   2. 31 días (7 meses)   3. 28 días (1 mes)

ch. ¿Cuántos años cumples?   Elena is telling the ages and birthdays of her family members. What does she say?

MODELO   mamá: 63, 4-X
   Mi mamá cumple sesenta y tres años el cuatro de octubre.

1. hermano: 37, 5-VI
2. hija: 16, 23-IX
3. abuela: 81, 31-V
4. sobrino: 15, 20-XII
5. tía: 55, 15-II
6. papá: 61, 8-VIII
7. hermana: 39, 12-X
8. prima: 14, 1-VI

L E C C I Ó N 2

4.4 PERSONAL A

The direct object is the word that answers the questions *whom?* or *what?* after the verb.

Pepe is reading *the newspaper.*
What is Pepe reading?   *The newspaper* is the direct object.

I see *María.*
Who(m) do I see?   *María* is the direct object.

In Spanish, the direct object of a sentence determines whether the personal **a** is necessary. If the direct object is a person, an animal, or a group of people, it is preceded by the preposition **a,** commonly referred to as the personal **a.**

Saluda **a** tu tía.   *Greet your aunt.*
¿Por qué no llamas **a** Lupe?   *Why don't you call Lupe?*
¿Invitamos **al** profesor?   *Shall we invite the professor?*
Veo **a** María y **a** su perro.   *I see María and her dog.*

¿POR QUÉ SE DICE ASÍ?   G51

b. ¿Cuándo cumplen años?

1 El cumpleaños de mi abuelita es el treinta de enero.
2 El cumpleaños de mi mamá es el veintiséis de noviembre.
3 El cumpleaños de mi hermano Carlos es el veintiocho de febrero.
4 El cumpleaños de mi tío Alfredo es el ocho de abril.
5 El cumpleaños de mi papá es el doce de agosto.
6 El cumpleaños de mi tía Elena es el trece de octubre.
7 El cumpleaños de mi abuelito es el quince de marzo.
8 El cumpleaños de mi hermana Cristina es el veintitrés de julio.

c. ¿Cuántos días? You may want your students to memorize the following poem:

   Treinta días tiene septiembre,
   Treinta abril, junio y noviembre.
   Los demás, treinta y uno,
   Menos febrero mocho,
   Que sólo tiene veintiocho.

1 30 días: abril, junio, septiembre, noviembre
2 31 días: enero, marzo, mayo, julio, agosto, octubre, diciembre
3 28 días: febrero

ch. ¿Cuántos años cumples?
1 Mi hermano cumple treinta y siete años el cinco de junio.
2 Mi hija cumple dieciséis años el veintitrés de septiembre.
3 Mi abuela cumple ochenta y un años el treinta y uno de mayo.
4 Mi sobrino cumple quince años el veinte de diciembre.
5 Mi tía cumple cincuenta y cinco años el quince de febrero.
6 Mi papá cumple sesenta y un años el ocho de agosto.
7 Mi hermana cumple treinta y nueve años el doce de octubre.
8 Mi prima cumple catorce años el primero de junio.

4.4 Margin box: page 176

Point out The personal **a** may be used with pets, but not with other animals, to show humanlike affection. For example, the personal **a** is not used in **Ves el elefante.** Also remind students that **a + el = al.**

Vamos a practicar

Additional Exercises
Textbook: pages 176–177
Cuaderno: Unidad 4, Lección 2

a. ¡Celebramos!

1 Mamá invita a mis amigos.
2 María llama a sus abuelos.
3 Los niños rompen la piñata.
4 Todos comen helado.
5 Paco y Patricio sacan fotos.
6 Papá mira a los niños.
7 Todos escuchan la música.
8 Los jóvenes toman refrescos.

b. ¿Qué ves?

1 Veo a la novia.
2 Veo al fotógrafo.
3 Veo mucha comida.
4 Veo a los padres del novio.
5 Veo el piano.
6 Veo el pastel.
7 Veo a Kevin.
8 Veo a mi abuela.

4.5 Margin box: page 176

- If the direct object is not a person, a pet, or a group of people, the personal **a** is not used.

Veo la tele todos los días.   *I watch TV every day.*
Pepe está leyendo el periódico.   *Pepe is reading the newspaper.*

- When **alguien** and **nadie** are direct objects, they are preceded by the personal **a.**

¿Ves **a** alguien?   *Do you see anybody?*
No veo **a** nadie.   *I don't see anybody.*
Inés no invita **a** nadie.   *Inés is not inviting anybody.*

Vamos a practicar

a. ¡Celebramos! How does the Gómez family celebrate the children's birthdays? Use the personal **a** when necessary.

> MODELO   Los tíos visitan __a__ la familia Gómez.
>   Elena compra ____ invitaciones.

1. Mamá invita _____ mis amigos.   **5.** Paco y Patricio sacan _____ fotos.
2. María llama _____ sus abuelos.   **6.** Papá mira _____ los niños.
3. Los niños rompen _____ la piñata.   **7.** Todos escuchan _____ la música.
4. Todos comen _____ helado.   **8.** Los jóvenes toman _____ refrescos.

b. ¿Qué ves? Paquito, who is not very tall, is asking his friend Julio to tell him what he sees. How does Julio respond?

> MODELO   novio   coche de la novia
>   **Veo al novio.**   **Veo el coche de la novia.**

1. novia   **5.** piano
2. fotógrafo   **6.** pastel
3. mucha comida   **7.** Kevin
4. padres del novio   **8.** mi abuela

4.5   THE VERB **CONOCER**

The verb **conocer** (*to know, be familiar or acquainted with*) is a regular **-er** verb in all forms except the first person singular.

Conocer	
conozco	conocemos
conoces	conocéis
conoce	conocen
conoce	conocen

¿POR QUÉ SE DICE ASÍ?

Ustedes **conocen** a mi novia, ¿verdad?	*You know my fiancée, don't you?*
¿Conoces San Antonio?	*Do you know San Antonio?*
No **conozco** ese libro.	*I am not familiar with that book.*

- Note that you can be acquainted with a city or town, a book, a theory, someone's work, museums, and other sites, not just people. Remember, however, that the personal **a** is used *only* with people.

Vamos a practicar

a. ¿Conoces a mi tío José?   Tell what family members you know as you look at a friend's family album.

> MODELO   tío José (no)
> **No conozco a tu tío José.**

1. abuela (no)
2. tía Carmen (sí)
3. hermano Toño (sí)
4. perro Tulón (sí)
5. primas (no)
6. primo Carlos (sí)
7. hermanas (no)
8. padres (sí)

b. Es nueva.   Marta has just moved to town, and Rosalinda wants to help her get acquainted with the town. What does Rosalinda ask Marta?

> MODELO   el colegio
> **¿Conoces el colegio?**

1. la librería
2. el centro comercial
3. mi perro Yo-yo
4. el parque de diversiones
5. el profesor de español
6. la calle principal
7. la directora del colegio
8. el cine Cortez

c. En la escuela.   Your parents are visiting your school with you. What do they say when you ask them if they know the following people and places?

> MODELO   Francisco / Ana
> **Conocemos a Francisco pero no conocemos a Ana.**

1. Gerardo / Gloria
2. el profesor Díaz / su esposa
3. la biblioteca / la cafetería
4. Francisco / Rita
5. la directora / su esposo
6. la oficina de la directora / el laboratorio de ciencias
7. Paco / su prima
8. el teatro / la sala de computación
9. el gimnasio / el laboratorio de lenguas

¿POR QUÉ SE DICE ASÍ?

G53

Additional Exercises
Textbook: pages 176–177
Cuaderno: Unidad 4, Lección 2

a. ¿Conoces a mi tío José?
1 No, no conozco a tu abuela.
2 Sí, conozco a tu tía Carmen.
3 Sí, conozco a tu hermano Toño.
4 Sí, conozco a tu perro Tulón.
5 No, no conozco a tus primas.
6 Sí, conozco a tu primo Carlos.
7 No, no conozco a tus hermanas.
8 Sí, conozco a tus padres.

b. Es nueva.
1 ¿Conoces la librería?
2 ¿Conoces el centro comercial?
3 ¿Conoces a mi perro Yo-yo?
4 ¿Conoces el parque de diversiones?
5 ¿Conoces al profesor de español?
6 ¿Conoces la calle principal?
7 ¿Conoces a la directora del colegio?
8 ¿Conoces el cine Cortez?

c. En la escuela.
1 Conocemos a Gerardo pero no conocemos a Gloria.
2 Conocemos al profesor Díaz pero no conocemos a su esposa.
3 Conocemos la biblioteca pero no conocemos la cafetería.
4 Conocemos a Francisco pero no conocemos a Rita.
5 Conocemos a la directora pero no conocemos a su esposo.
6 Conocemos la oficina de la directora pero no conocemos el laboratorio de ciencias.
7 Conocemos a Paco pero no conocemos a su prima.
8 Conocemos el teatro pero no conocemos la sala de computación.
9 Conocemos el gimnasio pero no conocemos el laboratorio de lenguas.

ch. ¿Todos se conocen?
1 Estela conoce a la novia.
2 Yo conozco a los abuelos del novio.
3 Tía Angelita conoce a Gerardo.
4 Mis padres conocen a tío Gustavo.
5 Tú conoces a Mariluz.
6 Nosotros conocemos a todos.

4.6 Margin boxes: pages 177–178

Vamos a practicar

Additional Exercises
Textbook: pages 177–178
Cuaderno: Unidad 4, Lección 2

a. ¿Qué quieren?
1 Rafael quiere una radio.
2 Teresa y yo queremos unos discos.
3 Carlos quiere una computadora.
4 José y David quieren unos libros.
5 Yo quiero una bicicleta.
6 Ellos quieren una guitarra.
7 Ustedes quieren un coche.
8 Tú quieres un piano.
9 Juanito quiere un perro.

ch. ¿Todos se conocen?   While preparing the list of wedding guests, the bride's parents are trying to make sure each person knows at least one other guest. What do they say?

MODELO   Lourdes / Paco
Lourdes conoce a Paco.

1. Estela / novia
2. yo / abuelos del novio
3. tía Angelita / Gerardo
4. mis padres / tío Gustavo
5. tú / Mariluz
6. nosotros / todos

4.6   THE VERBS *QUERER* AND *VENIR*

Querer (*to want*) and **venir** (*to come*) belong to a group of verbs called stem-changing verbs (e → ie). In this group of verbs, the e in the stem becomes **ie** in all but the **nosotros** and **vosotros** forms in the present tense. Look at the charts below.

Querer	
quiero	queremos
quieres	queréis
quiere	quieren
quiere	quieren

Venir	
vengo	venimos
vienes	venís
viene	vienen
viene	vienen

Note that in the **yo** form, **venir** has an irregular **-go** ending and has no change in the stem vowel.

Ellos **quieren** un coche nuevo.   *They want a new car.*
Todos **queremos** helado.   *We all want ice cream.*
¿**Vienes** mucho al parque?   *Do you come to the park much?*
Vengo todos los domingos.   *I come every Sunday.*

■ The verb **querer** may be followed by an infinitive.

¿Quieres **ser** abogado?   *Do you want to be a lawyer?*
Ella no quiere **ir**.   *She does not want to go.*

Vamos a practicar

a. ¿Qué quieren?   What do the following people want for their birthdays?

MODELO   Paula: fiesta
Paula quiere una fiesta.

1. Rafael: radio
2. Teresa y yo: discos
3. Carlos: computadora
4. José y David: libros
5. yo: bicicleta
6. ellos: guitarra
7. ustedes: coche
8. tú: piano
9. Juanito: perro

¿POR QUÉ SE DICE ASÍ?

b. ¿Qué quieren hacer? What do the following people want to do on Sunday afternoon?

MODELO   mis papás / escribir una carta
Mis papás quieren escribir una carta.

1. Rosa / subir a las lanchas
2. tú / leer
3. Ana y yo / tocar la guitarra
4. Teresa y José / escuchar música
5. yo / ir al cine
6. ustedes / visitar a unos amigos
7. los novios / hablar por teléfono

c. ¿Qué quieres ser? What do the following students want to be?

MODELO   Clara **quiere ser** profesora.

1. Rafael y Teresa _____ cocineros.
2. Susana _____ abogada.
3. Julio y yo _____ mecánicos.
4. Claudia y Alicia _____ ingenieras.
5. Tomás _____ bombero.
6. Y tú, ¿qué _____?

ch. ¿Y ahora, qué? What do these people want to do at the wedding reception?

MODELO   Adela / ver / fotos
Adela quiere ver las fotos.

1. Luisa / preparar / comida
2. Jaime / sacar / fotos
3. tú / conocer a / novios
4. mis padres / saludar a / gente
5. Pedro y yo / escuchar / música
6. Paquito / comer / pastel
7. yo / bailar con / novio
8. Marta / beber / refresco

d. Todos los domingos. How often do the following people come to your house?

MODELO   **María viene todos los domingos.**

nunca	todos los días	domingos
verano	cuando hace sol	cuando hace buen tiempo
fines de semana	otoño	primavera

1. mi familia
2. David
3. mis primos
4. tú
5. tus hermanos
6. mis abuelos

e. Mi casa es tu casa. Why are the following people unable to come to your new neighbors' open house?

MODELO   Felipe / trabajar
Felipe no viene porque tiene que trabajar.

1. Alicia / limpiar la casa
2. ustedes / estudiar
3. yo / escribir una composición
4. Graciela y Roberto / correr
5. señora Ríos / calificar exámenes
6. tú / practicar el piano
7. José y yo / hacer ejercicios
8. Mamá y Marta / ir de compras

¿POR QUÉ SE DICE ASÍ?   **G55**

---

b. ¿Qué quieren hacer?
1 Rosa quiere subir a las lanchas.
2 Tú quieres leer.
3 Ana y yo queremos tocar la guitarra.
4 Teresa y José quieren escuchar música.
5 Yo quiero ir al cine.
6 Ustedes quieren visitar a unos amigos.
7 Los novios quieren hablar por teléfono.

c. ¿Qué quieres ser?
1 quieren ser
2 quiere ser
3 queremos ser
4 quieren ser
5 quiere ser
6 quieres ser

ch. ¿Y ahora, qué?
1 Luisa quiere preparar la comida.
2 Jaime quiere sacar fotos.
3 Tú quieres conocer a los novios.
4 Mis padres quieren saludar a la gente.
5 Pedro y yo queremos escuchar música.
6 Paquito quiere comer pastel.
7 Yo quiero bailar con el novio.
8 Marta quiere beber un refresco.

d. Todos los domingos.
Answers will vary.

e. Mi casa es tu casa.
1 Alicia no viene porque tiene que limpiar la casa.
2 Ustedes no vienen porque tienen que estudiar.
3 Yo no vengo porque tengo que escribir una composición.
4 Graciela y Roberto no vienen porque tienen que correr.
5 La señora Ríos no viene porque tiene que calificar exámenes.
6 Tú no vienes porque tienes que practicar el piano.
7 José y yo no venimos porque tenemos que hacer ejercicios.
8 Mamá y Marta no vienen porque tienen que ir de compras.

Spanish has three types of questions: tag questions, *yes/no* questions, and information questions.

- Tag questions ask the listener to agree or disagree with what the speaker is saying. They are formed by adding **¿no?** or **¿verdad?** to the end of a statement. When the sentence is negative, only **¿verdad?** may be used.

Eres de Ecuador, **¿no?**	*You're from Ecuador, aren't you?*
Este libro es muy interesante, **¿verdad?**	*This book is very interesting, isn't it?*
Él no es muy fuerte, **¿verdad?**	*He is not very strong, is he?*

- *Yes/no* questions can be answered with **sí** or **no.** These questions usually begin with a verb. The subject, if expressed, often comes at the end of the sentence.

¿Está bien usted?	*Are you all right?*
¿Te gusta la clase de inglés?	*Do you like English class?*
¿Conoce Julio a Paquito?	*Does Julio know Paquito?*
¿Ya están listos todos?	*Is everybody ready?*

- The third type are questions that request information. These questions begin with a question word.

Question Words			
¿Quién(es)?	*Who?*	**¿Cuánto(a)?**	*How much?*
¿Qué?	*What?*	**¿Cuántos(as)?**	*How many?*
¿Cuál(es)?	*Which? What?*	**¿Cuándo?**	*When?*
		¿Cómo?	*How? What?*
¿Dónde?	*Where?*	**¿Por qué?**	*Why?*

- Note that all question words have written accents.

- While most question words have only one form, **quién** and **cuál** have two: singular and plural.

¿Quién es tu tía favorita?	*Who is your favorite aunt?*
¿Quiénes son esas chicas?	*Who are those girls?*
¿Cuál es tu abuelo?	*Which (one) is your grandfather?*
¿Cuáles son tus clases favoritas?	*What are your favorite classes?*

- When **cuánto** modifies a noun, it must agree in number and gender with that noun. It has four forms: **cuánto, cuánta, cuántos,** and **cuántas.**

¿Cuánto helado quieres?	*How much ice cream do you want?*
¿Cuánta tarea tienes?	*How much homework do you have?*
¿Cuántos estudiantes hay?	*How many students are there?*
¿Cuántas horas practicas?	*How many hours do you practice?*

- When **cuánto** does not modify a noun, it has only one form.

  ¿**Cuánto** es?   *How much is it?*
  ¿**Cuánto** cuesta?   *How much does it cost?*

- Both **qué** and **cuál** correspond to the English word *what*. They are not always interchangeable, however.

  Qué asks for a definition or an explanation.
  ¿**Qué** es un "mariachi"?   *What is a **mariachi**?*
  ¿**Qué** está haciendo ahora?   *What is he doing now?*

  Cuál asks for a selection.
  ¿**Cuál** es la capital de   *What (which city) is the capital of*
     Venezuela?   *Venezuela?*
  ¿**Cuál** es tu primo?   *Which (one) is your cousin?*

- ¿**Cómo?** is used by itself to indicate disbelief or that the listener didn't hear what was said and wants it repeated. English usually uses *What?* in these instances.

  ¿**Cómo?** ¡Pero sólo tiene   *What? But he's only*
     catorce años!   *fourteen years old!*
  ¿**Cómo?** Perdón, pero la   *What? I'm sorry, but the*
     música está muy fuerte.   *music is too loud.*

Vamos a practicar

a. ¿No es verdad?   What can you say to get a friend to agree or disagree with you as you make the following statements?

MODELO   La fiesta es divertida.
         La fiesta es divertida, ¿verdad? o
         La fiesta es divertida, ¿no?

1. El profesor es muy inteligente.
2. Conchita es de la República Dominicana.
3. Hace calor.
4. Te gusta el helado.
5. Conoce a la señora Alba.
6. Tienes quince años.
7. Hace buen tiempo hoy.
8. Su cumpleaños es mañana.

b. La nueva escuela.   What does the new student in school want to know?

MODELO   La clase de álgebra es a las ocho.
         ¿Es a las ocho la clase de álgebra?

1. La señora Martínez es la profesora.
2. El gimnasio está cerca de la cafetería.
3. El almuerzo es al mediodía.
4. La clase de español es por la tarde.
5. La clase de computación es difícil.
6. Roberto está en la clase de español.
7. Sara trabaja después del colegio.
8. Los estudiantes escriben muchas composiciones.

¿POR QUÉ SE DICE ASÍ?   **G57**

Vamos a practicar

Additional Exercises
Textbook: page 179
Cuaderno: Unidad 4, Lección 2

a. ¿No es verdad?
Answers will vary. Check for correct use of tag questions.

b. La nueva escuela.
1 ¿Es la profesora la señora Martínez?
2 ¿Está cerca de la cafetería el gimnasio?
3 ¿Es al mediodía el almuerzo?
4 ¿Es por la tarde la clase de español?
5 ¿Es difícil la clase de computación?
6 ¿Está en la clase de español Roberto?
7 ¿Trabaja después del colegio Sara?
8 ¿Escriben muchas composiciones los estudiantes?

c. ¿Qué le pregunta?

1 Dónde
2 Cómo
3 Por qué
4 Quiénes
5 Cómo
6 Qué
7 Cuándo

ch. ¿Una boda?

1 Cuándo
2 Dónde
3 Cuál
4 Cómo
5 Quién
6 Cuántos
7 Qué
8 Quiénes
9 Cuándo (A qué hora)
10 Adónde

d. Un nuevo amigo.

1 Dónde
2 Cuántos
3 Cuántos
4 Cuántas
5 Cuándo
6 Quién
7 Qué
8 Dónde

c. ¿Qué le pregunta? You are at your friend's house and overhear only her part of a telephone conversation. Decide what she was asked by selecting the correct question word.

MODELO ¿*Qué/Cómo* estás? .... Bien, gracias, ¿y tú?

1. ¿*Dónde/Adónde* estás?.............................. Estoy en mi cuarto.
2. ¿*Cómo/Cuál* está tu mamá? .... ¿Mamá? Bien, muy bien. Pero no es posible hablar con ella ahora.
3. ¿*Qué/Por qué?* .... Porque ella y papá no están aquí.
4. ¿*Quién/Quiénes* están en casa?................. Mis hermanos, Julio, Manuel y yo.
5. ¿*Cómo/Cuáles* están todos?...................... Todos están bien pero Julio está un poco enfermo.
6. ¿*Qué/Cuál* tiene? .... Tiene indigestión. No es serio.
7. ¿*Cuánto/Cuándo* regresan tus padres?..... A las 9:30 o las 10:00 de la noche.

ch. ¿Una boda? Someone is trying to get more information about an upcoming wedding. Read the answers on the right, then complete that person's questions.

1. ¿ _____ es la boda?   Es el sábado por la tarde.
2. ¿ _____ es?   En casa de la novia.
3. ¿ _____ es la dirección?   Es 733 Camino del Rey.
4. ¿ _____ se llama la novia?   Cristina Salas.
5. ¿ _____ es el novio?   Gustavo Díaz Ortiz.
6. ¿ _____ invitados van a la boda?   Más de cien.
7. ¿ _____ van a servir?   Mucha comida y bebidas.
8. ¿ _____ van a la boda?   Todos los amigos de los novios.
9. ¿ _____ es el baile?   A las ocho y media.
10. ¿ _____ van los novios después de la boda?   Al Caribe.

d. Un nuevo amigo. You just met a new student. What do you ask him or her? Complete the questions.

MODELO ¿ **Cómo** te llamas?

1. ¿ _____ vives?
2. ¿ _____ años tienes?
3. ¿ _____ hermanos tienes?
4. ¿ _____ clases tienes, seis o siete?
5. ¿ _____ tienes inglés, por la mañana o por la tarde?
6. ¿ _____ es tu profesor de español, el señor Moreno o la señorita Fowler?
7. ¿ _____ vas a hacer después de las clases?
8. ¿ _____ vas a estudiar, en casa o en la biblioteca?

¿POR QUÉ SE DICE ASÍ?

e. ¿Qué escuchas? Riding the bus, you hear bits of conversation. Match the questions with the answers.

MODELO ¿Cuál es tu número de teléfono?
Es el 7-32-75-46.

1. ¿Dónde está Manuel?
2. ¿Cuántos hermanos tienes?
3. ¿Qué es eso?
4. ¿Quién es esa mujer?
5. ¿Cuándo quieres ir?
6. ¿Cómo se llama ese chico?
7. ¿Por qué no comes pizza?
8. ¿Cuánto cuesta ese libro?
9. ¿Cuál es tu número de teléfono?
10. ¿Adónde va José?
11. ¿Cuáles son los meses de invierno?
12. ¿Por qué estudias?

a. No me gusta.
b. Ernesto.
c. Tengo un examen mañana.
ch. Es el 7-32-75-46.
d. En la clase de historia.
e. Va a casa.
f. Catorce dólares.
g. Tengo tres hermanos.
h. Mañana a las ocho.
i. Un lápiz.
j. Es mi madrastra.
k. Son enero, febrero y marzo.

e. ¿Qué escuchas?
1 d
2 g
3 i
4 j
5 h
6 b
7 a
8 f
9 ch
10 e
11 k
12 c

L E C C I Ó N 3

4.8 *ESTAR* WITH ADJECTIVES

4.8 Margin box: page 191

You have been using the verb **estar** to tell where people and things are located.

Colombia **está** en Sudamérica.
Elena **está** en el gimnasio.

You have also used **estar** to talk about how someone is doing.

¿Cómo **está** usted?
Todos **estamos** bien.

- **Estar** is also used with adjectives to describe people's emotional and physical condition.

Paquito **está** muy contento. *Paquito is very happy.*
Estoy furiosa. *I am furious.*
¿**Estás** triste? *Are you sad?*

- **Estar** can also be used to describe tastes or appearances or to tell how something "seems" to the speaker.

La comida **está** rica. *The food is delicious.*
¡**Estás** muy elegante! *You look very elegant.*
El chocolate **está** delicioso. *The hot chocolate is delicious.*

¿POR QUÉ SE DICE ASÍ? **G59**

■ Some adjectives frequently used with **estar** are:

aburrido	*bored*
cansado	*tired*
contento	*happy*
delicioso	*delicious*
emocionado	*excited, moved*
furioso	*furious*
listo	*ready*
nervioso	*nervous*
ocupado	*busy*
preocupado	*worried*
rico	*delicious* (food)
tranquilo	*calm*
triste	*sad*

Vamos a practicar

a. ¿Cómo están?   Judging from these situations, how might the people feel?

MODELO   Luisa está en una boda. ¿Está tranquila o emocionada?
Está emocionada.

1. Ernesto tiene un examen en media hora y no está bien preparado. ¿Está tranquilo o nervioso?
2. Son las 11:00 de la noche y Julia todavía tiene que escribir una composición. ¿Está muy emocionada o muy cansada?
3. Antonio no tiene clases hoy. ¿Está contento o preocupado?
4. Tu mejor amiga vive en otra ciudad ahora. ¿Estás furiosa o triste?
5. No hay programas en la tele para tu hermanito. ¿Está tranquilo o aburrido?
6. Tenemos el examen final hoy. ¿Estamos tranquilos o preocupados?
7. Son las 5:00 y el campeonato de fútbol es a las 5:30. ¿Están todos emocionados o aburridos?
8. Estás en una boda. ¿Estás triste o aburrido?

b. Hoy hay examen.   Today there is a Spanish test. Tell how everyone feels.

MODELO   Juanita / nervioso
Juanita está nerviosa.

1. la profesora / tranquilo	5. yo / contento
2. Elena / aburrido	6. nosotros / cansado
3. Mario / furioso	7. tú / preparado
4. José y Manuel / triste	8. Pablo y Anita / preocupado

Vamos a practicar

Additional Exercises
Textbook: page 191
Cuaderno: Unidad 4, Lección 3

a. ¿Cómo están?
1 Está nervioso.
2 Está muy cansada.
3 Está contento.
4 Estoy triste.
5 Está aburrido.
6 Estamos preocupados.
7 Están emocionados.
8 Estoy triste. *o* Estoy aburrido. *o* Estoy...

b. Hoy hay examen.
1 La profesora está tranquila.
2 Elena está aburrida.
3 Mario está furioso.
4 José y Manuel están tristes.
5 Yo estoy contento(a).
6 Nosotros(as) estamos cansados(as).
7 Tú estás preparado(a).
8 Pablo y Anita están preocupados.

¿POR QUÉ SE DICE ASÍ?

c. ¿Cómo están todos?   Tell how these people feel at the wedding rehearsal.

MODELO   novia: nervioso y cansado
La novia está nerviosa y cansada.

1. los padres de la novia: tranquilo y contento
2. el fotógrafo: contento y ocupado
3. mi hermano y yo: aburrido y cansado
4. la hermana de la novia: emocionado y triste
5. el novio: nervioso y preocupado
6. las primas del novio: tranquilo y contento

ch. En el café.   After the game everyone goes for a bite to eat at their favorite hangout. What do various people say about the food?

MODELO   la comida / deliciosa
La comida está deliciosa.

1. tacos / bueno
2. pizza / fatal
3. café / terrible
4. pastel / sabroso
5. sándwiches / delicioso
6. chocolate / rico
7. helado / excelente
8. comida / malo

d. La boda.   Silvia is writing a note to her best friend describing her cousin's wedding reception. What does she say? Complete the note with the correct forms of **estar.**

Querida Ana,

   ¿Cómo (1) ? Yo (2) muy contenta. (3) en la boda de mi prima Sofía. Toda mi familia (4) aquí. Mi hermanito (5) aburrido, pero mis papás y yo (6) muy contentos. Mamá (7) muy emocionada. Los novios (8) nerviosos y también (9) cansados. ¡Ay! ¡Van a cortar el pastel! Te escribo más la semana próxima.

   Pero tú, ¿por qué no me escribes? ¿(10) muy ocupada? ¿(11) contenta?

Recibe un abrazo de tu amiga
Silvia

c. ¿Cómo están todos?
1 Los padres de la novia están tranquilos y contentos.
2 El fotógrafo está contento y ocupado.
3 Mi hermano y yo estamos aburridos y cansados.
4 La hermana de la novia está emocionada y triste.
5 El novio está nervioso y preocupado.
6 Las primas del novio están tranquilas y contentas.

ch. En el café.
1 Los tacos están buenos.
2 La pizza está fatal.
3 El café está terrible.
4 El pastel está sabroso.
5 Los sándwiches están deliciosos.
6 El chocolate está rico.
7 El helado está excelente.
8 La comida está mala.

d. La boda.
1 estás
2 estoy
3 Estoy
4 está
5 está
6 estamos
7 está
8 están
9 están
10 Estás
11 Estás

4.9 THE PRESENT PROGRESSIVE AND -NDO VERB FORMS
Describing Actions in Progress

In English, the present progressive is formed with the verb *to be* plus the *-ing* form of another verb.

> *I am watching TV.*
> *We are studying.*

In Spanish, the present progressive is formed with the verb **estar** plus the **-ndo** form of another verb.

Estoy pensando.	*I'm thinking.*
¿Qué **están haciendo**?	*What are you doing?*
Estamos bailando.	*We are dancing.*

-ndo Verb Forms
-ar verbs:
Drop the **-ar** ending and add **-ando** to the stem of the verb.
bail~~ar~~   bail**ando**   estudi~~ar~~   estudi**ando**
-er and **-ir** verbs:
Drop the **-er/-ir** ending and add **-iendo** to the stem of the verb.
com~~er~~   com**iendo**   escrib~~ir~~   escrib**iendo**   beb~~er~~   beb**iendo**   sal~~ir~~   sal**iendo**
When the stem of an **-er/-ir** verb ends in a vowel, **-iendo** changes to **-yendo**.
le~~er~~   le**yendo**   *reading*   cre~~er~~   cre**yendo**   *believing*

- In Spanish, the present progressive is used only to describe an action that is taking place *right at the moment*.

¿Qué **estás haciendo**?	*What are you doing?*
Estoy leyendo.	*I'm reading.*

An *-ing* expression in English does not automatically signal a progressive tense in Spanish. Consider the following examples:

Lola **sale** a las 8:00.	*Lola is leaving at 8:00.*
Vamos a estudiar juntos esta noche.	*We're going to study together tonight.*
Tienen una fiesta hoy.	*They're having a party today.*

- The verbs *come* and *go* are not ordinarily used in the progressive in Spanish.

Vamos a clase.	*We're going to class.*
Pablo **viene** a las cinco.	*Pablo is coming at 5:00.*

Some **-ir** verbs that undergo this change: **construir / construyendo**, **destruir / destruyendo**, and **huir / huyendo**.

Point out From a Spanish speaker's point of view, English overuses the present progressive. Unlike English, Spanish does not use the present progressive to express habitual, ongoing actions or future actions:
Viven en Miami.
They are living in Miami.
Voy a invitar a Carlos.
I am going to invite Carlos.

Note The **-ndo** forms of **ir** and **venir** are irregular: **yendo** and **viniendo**.

Vamos a practicar

a. ¿Cómo están pasando la tarde? How are these people spending their afternoon? What are they doing right now?

MODELO   Joaquín / jugar fútbol
Joaquín está jugando fútbol.

1. Gregorio / estudiar
2. tú / jugar con los niños
3. Marcos / practicar el piano
4. Dolores y yo / ver la tele
5. Paco y Rafael / escuchar música
6. Clara / escribir cartas
7. Papá / preparar la comida
8. mi primo / leer una novela
9. Inés / pasear en bicicleta
10. nosotros / correr en el parque

b. ¿Qué están haciendo todos? Your grandmother called and wants to know what everyone is doing. What do you tell her?

MODELO   Mi hermano **está escuchando** (escuchar) discos.

1. Mi hermano _____ (practicar) el piano.
2. Mi hermanita Elena _____ (escribir) una carta.
3. Mi hermana _____ (hacer) gimnasia.
4. Mi padrastro _____ (limpiar) la casa.
5. Mis primos, Javier y Jorge, _____ (ver) la tele.
6. Mi mamá _____ (leer) una novela.
7. Mi tía Isabel _____ (preparar) la comida.
8. Yo _____ (hablar) con usted.

c. ¿Qué están haciendo? You are watching people in the park. Describe what everyone is doing.

MODELO   Nora / cantar
Nora está cantando.

1. tú / sacar / fotos
2. un señor / hacer / gimnasia
3. dos muchachas / comer / sándwiches
4. una señorita / escribir / una carta
5. unos niños / correr
6. mis amigos / escuchar / la radio
7. una policía / caminar por el parque
8. mamá y yo / mirar / la gente
9. una señora / leer / un libro
10. un muchacho / jugar con / su perro

¿POR QUÉ SE DICE ASÍ?   **G63**

Vamos a practicar

Additional Exercises
Textbook: pages 192–194
Cuaderno: Unidad 4, Lección 3

a. ¿Cómo están pasando la tarde?

1 Gregorio está estudiando.
2 Tú estás jugando con los niños.
3 Marcos está practicando el piano.
4 Dolores y yo estamos viendo la tele.
5 Paco y Rafael están escuchando música.
6 Clara está escribiendo cartas.
7 Papá está preparando la comida.
8 Mi primo está leyendo una novela.
9 Inés está paseando en bicicleta.
10 Nosotros estamos corriendo en el parque.

b. ¿Qué están haciendo todos?

1 está practicando
2 está escribiendo
3 está haciendo
4 está limpiando
5 están viendo
6 está leyendo
7 está preparando
8 estoy hablando

c. ¿Qué están haciendo?

1 Tú estás sacando fotos.
2 Un señor está haciendo gimnasia.
3 Dos muchachas están comiendo sándwiches.
4 Una señorita está escribiendo una carta.
5 Unos niños están corriendo.
6 Mis amigos están escuchando la radio.
7 Una policía está caminando por el parque.
8 Mamá y yo estamos mirando a la gente.
9 Una señora está leyendo un libro.
10 Un muchacho está jugando con su perro.

ch. Todos están ocupados.

1 Su mamá está leyendo el periódico.
2 Sus hermanos están viendo (mirando) un video.
3 Su primo está tomando un refresco.
4 Su hermana y él están haciendo la tarea.
5 Sus abuelos están comiendo.
6 Su tío Paco está escribiendo una carta.
7 Su papá está tocando el piano.
8 Sus primos están hablando por teléfono.

d. En la escuela.

1 La profesora de matemáticas está explicando un problema.
2 La clase de español está mirando un video.
3 Los estudiantes de inglés están leyendo una lección.
4 La clase de educación física está haciendo ejercicio.
5 Los estudiantes de economía doméstica están preparando comida.
6 Los estudiantes de computación están trabajando mucho.
7 Los estudiantes de francés están aprendiendo mucho.
8 La secretaria está hablando por teléfono.

ch. Todos están ocupados.

Son las 7:00 de la tarde. ¿Qué está haciendo la familia de Raúl Romano?

EJEMPLO   sus hermanos
Sus hermanos están escuchando música.

1. su mamá   2. sus hermanos   3. su primo

4. su hermana y él   5. sus abuelos   6. su tío Paco

7. su papá   8. sus primos

d. En la escuela.

Mario is on his way to the principal's office. What does he see happening as he walks down the hall?

MODELO   profesor / biología / escribir / pizarra
El profesor de biología está escribiendo en la pizarra.

1. profesora / matemáticas / explicar / problema
2. clase / español / mirar / video
3. estudiantes / inglés / leer / lección
4. clase / educación física / hacer ejercicio
5. estudiantes / economía doméstica / preparar / comida
6. estudiantes / computación / trabajar / mucho
7. estudiantes / francés / aprender / mucho
8. secretaria / hablar por teléfono

¿POR QUÉ SE DICE ASÍ?

LECCIÓN 1

5.1 AFFIRMATIVE *TÚ* COMMANDS: REGULAR FORMS
Used When Giving Directions or Ordering People to Do Something

Note Irregular affirmative **tú** commands are presented in Unit 7. **Usted / ustedes** and negative **tú** commands are presented in ¡DIME! DOS.

To tell someone to do something, we use commands. Spanish uses special verb endings to give affirmative commands to anyone you would address as **tú**.

Affirmative *Tú* Commands		
estudi**ar**	**-a**	estudia
com**er**	**-e**	come
escrib**ir**	**-e**	escribe

Escribe la carta.	*Write the letter.*
Cruza la calle allí.	*Cross the street there.*
¡Corre!	*Run!*

- Note that the affirmative **tú** command form is the same as the present-tense form for **usted, él, ella.**

usted / él / ella form:	Ella **trabaja** muy poco.
affirmative **tú** command:	¡**Trabaja** más!

Vamos a practicar

Vamos a practicar

These exercises may de done as oral or written work.

> **Additional Exercises**
> Textbook: pages 213–214
> Cuaderno: Unidad 5, Lección 1

a. ¡Qué mandón! ¿Qué le dice Esteban a su hermanita?

MODELO (tomar) el metro
Toma el metro.

1. (escribir) una carta
2. (leer) el mapa
3. (limpiar) tu cuarto
4. (preguntar) dónde podemos comprar sellos
5. (regresar) antes de las cinco
6. (cambiar) un cheque de viajero
7. (escribir) "correo aéreo" en las cartas
8. (comprar) las tarjetas

b. ¡Atención, por favor! ¿Qué mandatos te dan tus profesores?

1. (abrir) el libro
2. (sacar) un lápiz
3. (escribir) con cuidado
4. (llegar) a clase temprano
5. (trabajar) más
6. (pasar) a la pizarra
7. (escuchar) por favor
8. (estudiar) para el examen

a. ¡Qué mandón!
1 Escribe una carta.
2 Lee el mapa.
3 Limpia tu cuarto.
4 Pregunta dónde podemos comprar sellos.
5 Regresa antes de las cinco.
6 Cambia un cheque de viajero.
7 Escribe "correo aéreo" en las cartas.
8 Compra las tarjetas.

b. ¡Atención, por favor!
1 Abre el libro.
2 Saca un lápiz.
3 Escribe con cuidado.
4 Llega a clase temprano.
5 Trabaja más.
6 Pasa a la pizarra.
7 Escucha por favor.
8 Estudia para el examen.

¿ POR QUÉ SE DICE ASÍ ? **G65**

5.2 Margin box: page 214

UNIDAD 5

c. ¿Adónde? Lorenzo quiere saber cómo llegar a la casa de Carlota. ¿Qué le dice Carlota?

1. cruzar	**3.** doblar	**5.** caminar	**7.** doblar	**9.** abrir
2. caminar	**4.** pasar	**6.** cruzar	**8.** caminar	

Primero _1_ la Avenida Méndez y _2_ una cuadra hasta llegar a la biblioteca. _3_ a la izquierda en la Avenida Ibarra. _4_ la iglesia y _5_ media cuadra más. _6_ la Calle Sotelo. _7_ a la derecha y _8_ media cuadra más. _9_ la puerta y ¡estás en mi casa!

5.2 NUMBERS: 100–1,000,000
Counting

Números: 100–1.000.000	
100	cien
101	ciento uno
102	ciento dos
200	doscientos
300	trescientos
400	cuatrocientos
500	quinientos
600	seiscientos
700	setecientos
800	ochocientos
900	novecientos
1.000	mil
2.001	dos mil uno
3.020	tres mil veinte
4.300	cuatro mil trescientos
5.400	cinco mil cuatrocientos
10.600	diez mil seiscientos
50.700	cincuenta mil setecientos
75.800	setenta y cinco mil ochocientos
100.999	cien mil novecientos noventa y nueve
1.000.000	un millón

- The use of the comma and the period in Spanish numbers is exactly the opposite of their use in English numbers. In Spanish, a period is used to separate hundreds, thousands, and millions. A comma divides whole numbers from decimals.

106	ciento seis
1.998	mil novecientos noventa y ocho
1.600.500	un millón seiscientos mil quinientos
510,25 ptas.	quinientas diez pesetas y veinticinco céntimos
6.320,80 ptas.	seis mil trescientas veinte pesetas y ochenta céntimos

■ The numbers between 200 and 900 agree in gender with the noun they modify.

205 mesas   doscient**as** cinco mes**as**
1.700 pesos   mil setecient**os** pes**os**

■ When speaking of 1,000, the article **un** is never used.

Gasté **mil doscientos** dólares.   *I spent one thousand two hundred dollars.*

■ When **millón** is used before a noun, **de** precedes the noun.

Un millón de personas.   *A million people.*
En la aduana, declaré **dos**   *In customs, I declared two*
millones de pesos.   *million pesos.*

Vamos a practicar

a. Orden cronológico.   Pon los exploradores en orden cronológico.

Hernán Cortés .... mil cuatrocientos ochenta y cinco
Vasco Núñez de Balboa .... mil cuatrocientos setenta y cinco
Juan Ponce de León .... mil cuatrocientos sesenta
Francisco Vásquez de Coronado........ mil quinientos diez
Hernando de Soto .... mil cuatrocientos noventa y seis
Francisco de Orellana .... mil cuatrocientos noventa
Francisco Pizarro .... mil cuatrocientos setenta y cinco

b. ¿Cuánto gastaron?   Las siguientes personas tienen que declarar sus gastos en la aduana. ¿Qué dicen?

MODELO   Manuel Ledesma 7.500 ptas.
       Yo gasté siete mil quinientas pesetas.

1. Amalia Acuña   29.645 ptas.   5. Isabel Valenzuela   17.415 ptas.
2. Santiago Gallegos   9.235 ptas.   6. Jorge Ledesma   64.525 ptas.
3. Dolores Pérez   44.815 ptas.   7. Evita Ramírez   15.110 ptas.
4. Cecilia Torres   31.975 ptas.   8. Mario Cabezas   52.700 ptas.

c. ¡Lotería!   ¿Cuánto ganaron estas personas en la lotería nacional de España?

MODELO   María Huerta 65.000 ptas.
       María Huerta ganó sesenta y cinco mil pesetas.

1. Pancho Gómez   7.500 ptas.
2. Lucila Rey   14.750 ptas.
3. Tomás Leñero   823.000 ptas.
4. Victoria Covarrubias   950.250 ptas.
5. Demetrio de la Arena   1.475.335 ptas.
6. Sara Pacheco   10.645.475 ptas.
7. Miguel Suárez   15.000 ptas.
8. Pilar Fuentes   250.000 ptas.

Vamos a practicar

Additional Exercises
Textbook: pages 214–215
Cuaderno: Unidad 5, Lección 1

a. Orden cronológico.
First have students list the names of the explorers and their birth-dates (in Arabic numerals) in chronological order. Then call on several students to read their lists. Send several students to board to write the dates as their classmates read their lists.
Juan Ponce de León (1460) explored Florida.
Vasco Núñez de Balboa (1475) explored the Pacific Ocean.
Francisco Pizarro (1475) explored Peru.
Hernán Cortés (1485) explored Mexico.
Francisco de Orellana (1490) explored the Amazon River.
Hernando de Soto (1496) explored the Mississippi River.
Francisco Vásquez de Coronado (1510) explored the southwestern U.S.

b. ¿Cuánto gastaron?
Point out The term **la aduana** means *customs*, where travelers must declare how much they have spent on purchases in a foreign country to determine whether they owe duty.
1 Yo gasté veintinueve mil seiscientas cuaranta y cinco pesetas.
2 Yo gasté nueve mil doscientas treinta y cinco pesetas.
3 Yo gasté cuarenta y cuatro mil ochocientas quince pesetas.
4 Yo gasté treinta y un mil novecientas setenta y cinco pesetas.
5 Yo gasté diecisiete mil cuatrocientas quince pesetas.
6 Yo gasté sesenta y cuatro mil quinientas veinticinco pesetas.
7 Yo gasté quince mil ciento diez pesetas.
8 Yo gasté cincuenta y dos mil setecientas pesetas.

c. ¡Lotería!
1 Pancho Gómez ganó siete mil quinientas pesetas.
2 Lucila Rey ganó catorce mil setecientas cincuenta pesetas.
3 Tomás Leñero ganó ochocientos veintitrés mil pesetas.
4 Victoria Covarrubias ganó novecientos cincuenta mil doscientas cincuenta pesetas.
5 Demetrio de la Arena ganó un millón cuatrocientos setenta y cinco mil trescientas treinta y cinco de pesetas.
6 Sara Pacheco ganó diez millones seiscientos cuarenta y cinco mil cuatrocientas setenta y cinco de pesetas.
7 Miguel Suárez ganó quince mil pesetas.
8 Pilar Fuentes ganó doscientos cincuenta mil pesetas.

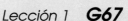

Ask students if they know any other verbs that have an irregular **yo** form. They should mention **conozco**, **tengo**, **vengo**, and **veo**.

Vamos a practicar

Additional Exercises
Textbook: pages 215–216
Cuaderno: Unidad 5, Lección 1

a. Sabemos mucho.
1 Roberto y Carlos saben que el inglés incorpora muchas palabras directamente del español.
2 Nosotros sabemos que los hispanos en Estados Unidos viven en California, Texas y Florida y muchos otros estados.
3 Yo sé que muchos hispanos vienen de México pero muchos vienen de otros países.
4 Beto sabe que hay siete estados que llevan nombres hispanos.
5 Mariela y yo sabemos que la mayoría de los hispanos en Estados Unidos viven en el suroeste del país.

Some Spanish verbs are regular in all but the **yo** form of the present tense. Three common verbs that fit this category are **saber** (*to know facts* or *to know how to do something*), **salir** (*to go out*), and **dar** (*to give*).

Saber		Salir		Dar	
sé	sabemos	**salgo**	salimos	**doy**	damos
sabes	sabéis	sales	salís	das	dais
sabe	saben	sale	salen	da	dan
sabe	saben	sale	salen	da	dan

No **sé** dónde está.	*I don't know where it is.*
¿**Salgo** por esta puerta?	*Do I go out this door?*
¿Cuánto le **doy**?	*How much do I give him?*

■ Other verbs with an irregular **yo** form include:

hacer	**hago**	*I do, make*
traer	**traigo**	*I bring*
poner	**pongo**	*I put*

■ **Saber** followed by an infinitive means *to know how to do something.*

¿**Sabes hablar** español?	*Do you know how to speak Spanish?*
José **sabe bailar** muy bien.	*José knows how to dance very well.*

Vamos a practicar

a. Sabemos mucho. ¿Qué saben estos estudiantes de los hispanos en Estados Unidos?

MODELO Elena: Hay mucha influencia hispana en todo el país.
Elena sabe que hay mucha influencia hispana en todo el país.

1. Roberto y Carlos: El inglés incorpora muchas palabras directamente del español.
2. nosotros: Los hispanos en Estados Unidos viven en California, Texas y Florida y muchos otros estados.
3. yo: Muchos hispanos vienen de México pero muchos vienen de otros países.
4. Beto: Hay siete estados que llevan nombres hispanos.
5. Mariela y yo: La mayoría de los hispanos en Estados Unidos viven en el suroeste del país.

b. ¡Qué talento!   La profesora quiere saber qué talento tienen sus estudiantes. ¿Qué dicen los estudiantes que saben hacer?

MODELO   Antonia / tocar / piano
Antonia sabe tocar el piano.

1. Ernesto y yo / hacer / tortillas españolas
2. tú y ella / bailar / tango
3. Román / dibujar / bien
4. Laura y su hermana / preparar / pastel
5. yo / tocar / guitarra
6. Enrique y Teresa / cantar / bien
7. tú / sacar / fotos
8. nosotros / leer / español
9. Conchita / hablar / francés
10. ustedes / jugar fútbol / bien

c. ¿Vamos a salir?   Hoy es el último día de clases para unos estudiantes de intercambio en Madrid.   ¿Cuándo salen para Estados Unidos?

MODELO   Norberto / viernes / 20:30
Norberto sale el viernes a las ocho y media de la noche.

1. yo / sábado / 15:00
2. Ricardo y Patricio / viernes / 7:00
3. Humberto / miércoles / 8:15
4. tú / martes / 5:30
5. Verónica y Hugo / jueves / 18:30
6. Rosa María / domingo / 2:00
7. nosotros / viernes / 7:45
8. ustedes / lunes / 14:15
9. ellos / sábado / 9:00
10. Bárbara / martes / 20:30

ch. El cumpleaños de Joaquín.   Hoy es el cumpleaños de Joaquín. ¿Qué le dan su familia y sus amigos?

1. Sus padres le __ dinero.
2. Yo le __ un video.
3. Nosotros le __ una fiesta.
4. Tú y Ramona le __ un pastel.
5. Su tío le __ un libro.
6. Anita le __ un reloj.
7. Sus abuelos le __ una guitarra.
8. Tú le __ un radio.
9. Pablo le __ una cámara.
10. Nosotras le __ un disco compacto.

¿POR QUÉ SE DICE ASÍ?

---

b. ¡Qué talento!
1 Ernesto y yo sabemos hacer tortillas españolas.
2 Tú y ella saben bailar el tango.
3 Román sabe dibujar bien.
4 Laura y su hermana saben preparar un pastel.
5 Yo sé tocar la guitarra.
6 Enrique y Teresa saben cantar bien.
7 Tú sabes sacar fotos.
8 Nosotros sabemos leer español.
9 Conchita sabe hablar francés.
10 Ustedes saben jugar futból bien.

c. ¿Vamos a salir?
1 Yo salgo el sábado a las tres de la tarde.
2 Ricardo y Patricio salen el viernes a las siete de la mañana.
3 Humberto sale el miércoles a las ocho y cuarto de la mañana.
4 Tú sales el martes a las cinco y media de la mañana.
5 Verónica y Hugo salen el jueves a las seis y media de la tarde (noche).
6 Rosa María sale el domingo a las dos de la mañana.
7 Nosotros salimos el viernes a las ocho menos cuarto de la mañana.
8 Ustedes salen el lunes a las dos y cuarto de la tarde.
9 Ellos salen el sábado a las nueve de la mañana.
10 Bárbara sale el martes a las ocho y media de la noche.

ch. El cumpleaños de Joaquín.
1 dan
2 doy
3 damos
4 dan
5 da
6 da
7 dan
8 das
9 da
10 damos

UNIDAD

LECCIÓN 2

You already know that the verb **gustar** is used to express likes and dislikes and that the verb **encantar** is used to talk about things you really like or love. Remember that both verbs are preceded by **me, te,** or **le** when stating that *I, you,* or *he or she* likes something.

Me gusta correr.
Me encanta el helado.
¿**Te gusta?**
Le gustan las camisetas.
¿**Le encanta** la ciudad?

When stating that *we, you* (plural), or *they* like something, **gustar** and **encantar** are preceded by **nos, os,** or **les.**

Gustar	Encantar
If one thing is liked:	*If one thing is really liked:*
me te le nos os les } gust**a**	me te le nos os les } encant**a**
If more than one thing is liked:	*If more than one thing is really liked:*
me te le nos os les } gust**an**	me te le nos os les } encant**an**

Nos encanta bailar.   *We love to dance.*
Les encanta el tenis.   *They love tennis.*
Les gustan estas camisetas.   *They like these T-shirts.*
No **nos** gustan los calcetines.   *We don't like the socks.*

¿POR QUÉ SE DICE ASÍ?

Vamos a practicar

a. ¡Qué exageradas! A Bárbara y a Susana siempre les encanta todo. ¿Cómo contestan estas preguntas?

> MODELO ¿Les gusta ver televisión?
> **¡Nos encanta ver televisión!**

1. ¿Les gusta comer pizza?
2. ¿Les gusta correr?
3. ¿Les gusta leer el periódico?
4. ¿Les gusta pasear en bicicleta?
5. ¿Les gusta bailar?
6. ¿Les gusta beber limonada?

b. Encuesta. Contestan estas preguntas sobre los gustos culinarios.

> MODELO ¿Les gusta el helado a tus padres?
> **No, no les gusta.** o **Les gusta mucho.** o **¡Les encanta!**

1. ¿Le gusta el pastel de chocolate a tu papá?
2. ¿Les gustan los refrescos a ti y a tus amigos?
3. ¿Te gusta la pizza?
4. ¿Le gusta el chocolate a tu madre?
5. ¿Les gusta el café a los profesores?
6. ¿Les gustan las hamburguesas a tus amigos?

5.5 STEM-CHANGING VERBS: E → IE AND O → UE

Some verbs in Spanish have an irregular stem. (The stem is the infinitive minus the **-ar, -er,** or **-ir** ending.) In these verbs, the final vowel of the stem changes from **e** to **ie** or from **o** to **ue** in all forms except **nosotros** and **vosotros.** You should learn which verbs are stem-changing verbs.

Stem-Changing Verbs			
e → ie **recomendar** (*to recommend*)		**o → ue** **poder** (*to be able, can*)	
recom**ie**ndo	recomendamos	p**ue**do	podemos
recom**ie**ndas	recomendáis	p**ue**des	podéis
recom**ie**nda	recom**ie**ndan	p**ue**de	p**ue**den
recom**ie**nda	recom**ie**ndan	p**ue**de	p**ue**den

¿Qué me recom**ie**nda usted?	*What do you recommend?*
¿Qué p**ie**nsas de él?	*What do you think of him?*
¿Cuánto c**ue**sta?	*How much does it cost?*
¿En qué p**ue**do servirles?	*How can I help you?*

¿POR QUÉ SE DICE ASÍ?   **G71**

Vamos a practicar

Additional Exercises
Textbook: pages 228–229
Cuaderno: Unidad 5, Lección 2

a. ¡Qué exageradas!
1 ¡Nos encanta comer pizza!
2 ¡Nos encanta correr!
3 ¡Nos encanta leer el periódico!
4 ¡Nos encanta pasear en bicicleta!
5 ¡Nos encanta bailar!
6 ¡Nos encanta beber limonada!

b. Encuesta. Answers will vary.

5.5 Margin boxes:
pages 230, 232

Note that in many dictionaries and in the Spanish-English glossary at the end of this book, stem-changing verbs are listed with their vowel change in parentheses: **recomendar (ie), poder (ue).**

■ The following is a list of some commonly used **e → ie** and **o → ue** stem-changing verbs.

e → ie	
comenzar (ie)	*to begin*
empezar (ie)	*to begin*
entender (ie)	*to understand*
pensar (ie)	*to think*
preferir (ie)	*to prefer*
querer (ie)	*to want*
recomendar (ie)	*to recommend*

o → ue	
contar (ue)	*to count*
costar (ue)	*to cost*
encontrar (ue)	*to find*
poder (ue)	*to be able, can*
recordar (ue)	*to remember*

u → ue	
jugar* (ue)	*to play*

■ The affirmative **tú** command form also undergoes this stem change.

Cuenta el dinero, por favor.   *Count the money, please.*
Rec**ue**rda la dirección.   *Remember the address.*

Vamos a practicar

a. ¿Qué quieres tú?   Tú y tus amigos van de compras hoy. ¿Qué quieren comprar?

MODELO   Gregorio **quiere** una camiseta.

1. Lisa __ unos lápices.
2. Mario y Hugo __ camisetas moradas.
3. Daniela y yo __ sudaderas anaranjadas.
4. Todos nosotros __ helado de chocolate.
5. Yo __ un teléfono negro.
6. Tú __ unos pantalones nuevos.
7. David __ zapatos.
8. Tú y Alejandra __ blusas bonitas.

b. ¿Qué prefieren?   Según Jorge, ¿cómo prefieren vestirse estas personas durante el fin de semana?

MODELO   mi hermano / camisa / rojo
   Mi hermano prefiere llevar una camisa roja.

1. mamá / pantalones / negro
2. mis hermanas / camisetas / amarillo
3. mi padre / camisa / blanco
4. tú / camiseta / rojo
5. yo / jeans / azul
6. tú y yo / sudaderas / anaranjado
7. mi abuelo / suéter / negro
8. mi tía Evita / vestido / verde

*Like the stem change **o → ue,** the stem vowel **u** of the verb **jugar** changes to **ue.**

¿POR QUÉ SE DICE ASÍ?

Vamos a practicar

Additional Exercises
Textbook: pages 230–232
Cuaderno: Unidad 5, Lección 2

a. ¿Qué quieres tú?
1 quiere
2 quieren
3 queremos
4 queremos
5 quiero
6 quieres
7 quiere
8 quieren

b. ¿Qué prefieren?
1 Mamá prefiere llevar pantalones negros.
2 Mis hermanas prefieren llevar camisetas amarillas.
3 Mi padre prefiere llevar una camisa blanca.
4 Tú prefieres llevar una camiseta roja.
5 Yo prefiero llevar jeans azules.
6 Tú y yo preferimos llevar sudaderas anaranjadas.
7 Mi abuelo prefiere llevar un suéter negro.
8 Mi tía Evita prefiere llevar un vestido verde.

c. ¡Qué familia!   La familia de Hugo tiene mucho talento. ¿Qué pueden hacer?

MODELO   escribir en italiano: abuela
Su abuela puede escribir en italiano.

1. bailar el tango: hermanas
2. preparar la comida: todos nosotros
3. correr tres millas: papá
4. usar la computadora: hermano
5. cantar en italiano: mamá
6. hacer pizza: mamá y papá
7. tocar el piano: yo
8. hablar italiano: abuelos y mamá

ch. ¿Qué juegas?   Di qué deportes juegan tú y tus amigos todos los domingos en el parque.

MODELO   Isabel / volibol
Isabel juega volibol.

1. yo / tenis
2. Arcelia / béisbol
3. Armando y Lucía / fútbol
4. tú / básquetbol
5. mis primos y yo / volibol

d. De compras.   Completa el diálogo con la forma correcta de los verbos indicados para descubrir qué están haciendo Andrea y Verónica.

1. encontrar	7. preferir (yo)	13. costar
2. querer	8. encontrar (nosotras)	14. contar
3. costar	9. querer	15. preferir
4. tener (tú)	10. probar	16. entender
5. tener	11. poder	17. poder
6. querer (tú)	12. poder	18. preferir

En una tienda

Andrea: Yo no _1_ nada, ¿y tú?
Verónica: Yo tampoco. _2_ comprar algo especial para Silvia
           pero todo _3_ demasiado.
Andrea: Sí, _4_ razón. Y nosotras no _5_ mucho dinero.
           ¿Dónde _6_ buscar ahora?
Verónica: _7_ ir a la sección de mujeres.
Andrea: ¡Qué buena idea! Probablemente _8_ algo allí.

Más tarde

Verónica: Ay, Andrea, mira. Yo _9_ esos pantalones verdes.
Andrea: ¿Por qué no te los _10_ ?
Dependiente: ¿En qué _11_ servirles, señoritas?
Verónica: ¿ _12_ decirme cuánto _13_ estos pantalones?
Dependiente: Cuestan 8.500 pesetas.
Verónica: Andrea, _14_ todo el dinero. Yo _15_ no comer.
Andrea: Ay , Verónica. Yo no _16_ cómo tú _17_ comprar
           pantalones y no comer. ¡Yo siempre _18_ comer!

¿POR QUÉ SE DICE ASÍ?   **G73**

---

c. ¡Qué familia!
1 Sus hermanas pueden bailar el tango.
2 Todos nosotros podemos preparar la comida.
3 Su papá puede correr tres millas.
4 Su hermano puede usar la computadora.
5 Su mamá puede cantar en italiano.
6 Su mamá y su papá pueden hacer pizza.
7 Yo puedo tocar el piano.
8 Sus abuelos y su mamá pueden hablar italiano.

ch. ¿Qué juegas?
1 Yo juego tenis.
2 Arcelia juega béisbol.
3 Armando y Lucía juegan fútbol.
4 Tú juegas básquetbol.
5 Mis primos y yo jugamos volibol.

d. De compras.
1 encuentro
2 Quiero
3 cuesta
4 tienes
5 tenemos
6 quieres
7 Prefiero
8 encontramos
9 quiero
10 pruebas
11 puedo
12 Puede
13 cuestan
14 cuenta
15 prefiero
16 entiendo
17 puedes
18 prefiero

Ordinal numbers specify the order of things in a series. In Spanish, the most frequently used ordinal numbers are those between one and ten.

Ordinal Numbers	
primero(a)	*first*
segundo(a)	*second*
tercero(a)	*third*
cuarto(a)	*fourth*
quinto(a)	*fifth*
sexto(a)	*sixth*
séptimo(a)	*seventh*
octavo(a)	*eighth*
noveno(a)	*ninth*
décimo(a)	*tenth*

Primero, deben ir a correos.   *First, you should go to the post office.*
Está en el **segundo** piso.   *It is on the second floor.*

■ Ordinal numbers agree in number and gender with the nouns they modify.

los **primeros** tres meses   *the first three months*
la **séptima** semana   *the seventh week*
el **cuarto** capítulo   *the fourth chapter*

■ **Primero** and **tercero** are shortened to **primer** and **tercer** before masculine singular nouns.

Está en el **tercer** piso   *It's on the third floor*
   del nuevo edificio.   *of the new building.*
Es el **primer** presidente   *He's the first Hispanic*
   hispano.   *president.*

Vamos a practicar

a. **¿Qué grado?**   ¿En qué grado están estos estudiantes?

MODELO   Federico (4)
   Federico está en el cuarto grado.

1. Gloria (6)
2. Lupe (10)
3. Timoteo (3)
4. Rolando (7)
5. Roberto (5)
6. Héctor (9)
7. Juanita (1)
8. Pepe (2)
9. Luisa (8)
10. Carlos (4)

Vamos a practicar

Additional Exercises
Textbook: page 231
Cuaderno: Unidad 5, Lección 2

a. ¿Qué grado?
1 Gloria está en el sexto grado.
2 Lupe está en el décimo grado.
3 Timoteo está en el tercer grado.
4 Rolando está en el séptimo grado.
5 Roberto está en el quinto grado.
6 Héctor está en el noveno grado.
7 Juanita está en el primer grado.
8 Pepe está en el segundo grado.
9 Luisa está en el octavo grado.
10 Carlos está en el cuarto grado.

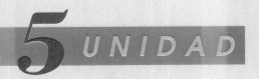

b. Familia numerosa. Tere es la hija más pequeña de una familia muy grande. ¿Cómo se llaman sus hermanos?

MODELO Tere (10)   Julio (5)
La décima hija se llama Tere.   **El quinto hijo se llama Julio.**

Paco	Benita	Daniela	Carmen	Julio	Pepe	Alicia	Beto	Nena	Tere
(1)	(2)	(3)	(4)	(5)	(6)	(7)	(8)	(9)	(10)

a. Daniela   **c.** Paco   **d.** Carmen   **f.** Benita   **h.** Alicia
b. Nena   **ch.** Tere   **e.** Julio   **g.** Pepe   **i.** Beto

L E C C I Ó N 3

5.7 STEM-CHANGING VERBS: E → I

Besides the stem-changing verbs you know, there is another group of stem-changing **-ir** verbs. In this group, the final vowel of the stem changes from **e** to **i** in all forms except **nosotros** and **vosotros**. Learn which **-ir** verbs have this stem change.

Stem-Changing Verbs: e → i			
pedir (*to order,* *ask for*)	**servir** (*to serve*)	**decir** (*to say,* *tell*)	**seguir** (*to follow,* *continue*)
pido	sirvo	digo	sigo
pides	sirves	dices	sigues
pide	sirve	dice	sigue
pedimos	servimos	decimos	seguimos
pedís	servís	decís	seguís
piden	sirven	dicen	siguen

¿Qué fruta fresca si**r**ven?   *What fresh fruit do you serve?*
Yo siempre p**i**do melón.   *I always order melon.*

- The verbs **decir** and **seguir** also have an irregular ending in the **yo** form: **digo** and **sigo.**

Siempre **digo** la verdad.   *I always tell the truth.*
Sigo derecho, ¿verdad?   *I continue straight ahead, right?*

¿POR QUÉ SE DICE ASÍ?   **G75**

b. Familia numerosa.

a La tercera hija se llama Daniela.
b La novena hija se llama Nena.
c El primer hijo se llama Paco.
ch La décima hija se llama Tere.
d La cuarta hija se llama Carmen.
e El quinto hijo se llama Julio.
f La segunda hija se llama Benita.
g El sexto hijo se llama Pepe.
h La séptima hija se llama Alicia.
i El octavo hijo se llama Beto.

5.7 Margin box: page 246

■ Here are some frequently used **e → i** stem-changing verbs. Note that they are listed with the vowel change in parentheses.

conseguir (i)	*to get, obtain*
decir (i)	*to say, tell*
pedir (i)	*to order, ask for*
repetir (i)	*to repeat*
seguir (i)	*to continue, follow*
servir (i)	*to serve*
vestir (i)	*to dress*

■ The affirmative **tú** command form and the present participle also undergo this stem change.

Pide algo para beber.	*Ask for something to drink.*
Sigue media cuadra más.	*Go another half block.*
Te estoy **diciendo** la verdad.	*I am telling you the truth.*
Ya están **sirviendo** el almuerzo.	*They are already serving lunch.*

Vamos a practicar

a. ¿Que sí o que no?   ¿Qué dicen los miembros de la familia Quiroga? ¿Quieren ir al cine o no?

MODELO   Mamá **dice** que no.

1. Yo ___ que sí.
2. Alicia y yo ___ que sí también.
3. Pues, yo ___ que no.
4. Y tú, mamá, ¿qué ___?
5. Los niños ___ que sí.
6. Papá ___ que sí.
7. Yo también ___ que sí.
8. ¿Tú también ___ que sí?

b. ¿Qué pedir?   Completa la conversación de Conchita y Lupita en el restaurante.

1. pedir	**3.** pedir	**5.** pedir	**7.** pedir
2. servir	**4.** pedir	**6.** pedir	**8.** pedir

Conchita: ¿Qué vas a _1_ ?
Lupita: No sé. ¿Qué me recomiendas?
Conchita: _2_ muy buenos sándwiches aquí. Yo siempre _3_ el de jamón y queso.
Lupita: ¿Cómo puedes decir que tú siempre _4_ jamón y queso? Cuando salimos, tú y yo siempre _5_ hamburguesas.
Conchita: No tienes razón. Tú y Ramón siempre _6_ hamburguesas. Yo _7_ papas fritas. Pero aquí yo siempre _8_ el sándwich de jamón y queso.

¿POR QUÉ SE DICE ASÍ?

a. ¿Que sí o que no?
1 digo
2 decimos
3 digo
4 dices
5 dicen
6 dice
7 digo
8 dices

b. ¿Qué pedir?
1 pedir
2 Sirven
3 pido
4 pides
5 pedimos
6 piden
7 pido
8 pido

c. ¡Al hacer cola!   ¿Quién sigue a quién al subir al autobús escolar?

MODELO   Mariela
Mariela sigue a José.

José   Carmen   tú   Esteban   yo   Inés   Silvia
Mariela   María   Mateo   Luis   Isabel   Rosario

1. tú   3. María y tú   5. Esteban   7. Rosario y Silvia
2. yo   4. Luis y yo   6. Isabel y yo   8. Carmen

c. ¡Al hacer cola!
1 Tú sigues a María.
2 Yo sigo a Luis.
3 María y tú siguen a Carmen.
4 Luis y yo seguimos a Esteban.
5 Esteban sigue a Mateo.
6 Isabel y yo seguimos a Luis.
7 Rosario y Silvia siguen a Inés.
8 Carmen sigue a Mariela.

ch. ¡Voy a cambiar!   Rubén López y su hermana Raquel están en un café.
Completa su conversación.

1. servir (ellos)   3. pedir   5. pedir   7. pedir   9. pedir
2. servir   4. decir   6. pedir   8. decir

Al entrar
Rubén: ¿Qué _1_ aquí, Raquel?
Raquel: _2_ unas papas fritas fantásticas. Yo siempre _3_ las papas
            y un refresco.
Rubén: Mamá _4_ que los sándwiches son muy ricos aquí.
Raquel: Pues, ¿por qué no _5_ tú por mí?
Rubén: Bueno. Si yo _6_ un sándwich y tú _7_ las papas fritas,
            puedo probar de todo.
Raquel: Sí, pero creo que hoy prefiero un bizcocho.
Rubén: Pero . . . ¿no _8_ que siempre _9_ las papas fritas?
Raquel: Sí, pero hoy voy a cambiar.

ch. ¡Voy a cambiar!
1 sirven
2 Sirven
3 pido
4 dice
5 pides
6 pido
7 pides
8 dices
9 pides

d. ¡Casa Botín!   Para descubrir algo de este famoso restaurante madrileño,
completa el párrafo con la forma correcta de los verbos indicados.

1. decir   3. pedir   5. pedir   7. servir   9. seguir
2. servir   4. decir   6. decir   8. seguir

Mis amigos _1_ que uno de los restaurantes más populares de Madrid es la Casa
Botín. Está en la calle de Cuchilleros. _2_ de todo allí pero la especialidad de la
casa es el cochinillo asado.° Ellos siempre lo _3_ cuando van allí. Mi amiga
Teresa _4_ que ella nunca _5_ el cochinillo. ¿Por qué no? Porque _6_ que allí
también _7_ un cordero° asado muy sabroso. Yo pienso comer en Casa Botín esta
tarde. Me dicen que es fácil llegar allí si yo _8_ por esta calle a la Plaza Mayor.
De la Plaza Mayor _9_ por el Arco de Cuchilleros, y ¡allí está!

cochinillo asado *roast suckling pig*   **cordero** *lamb*

d. ¡Casa Botín!
1 dicen
2 Sirven
3 piden
4 dice
5 pide
6 dice
7 sirven
8 sigo
9 sigue (sigo)

¿POR QUÉ SE DICE ASÍ?   **G77**

Vocabulario opcional
tener miedo *(to be afraid)*
tener sueño *(to be sleepy)*
tener ganas de *(to feel like)*

Vamos a practicar

Additional Exercises
Textbook: page 247
Cuaderno: Unidad 5, Lección 3

a. ¿Qué tienes?
1 hambre
2 razón
3 prisa
4 razón
5 calor
6 hambre
7 sed
8 prisa
9 razón
10 frío

An idiom is an expression that makes sense in one language but does not make sense when translated word for word into another language. The verb **tener** is used in several idiomatic expressions.

Tener Idioms	
tener hambre	*to be hungry*
tener sed	*to be thirsty*
tener calor	*to be hot*
tener frío	*to be cold*
tener prisa	*to be in a hurry*
tener razón	*to be right*

Tengo hambre pero no **tengo sed.**	*I am hungry but I am not thirsty.*
¿**Tienes frío?**	*Are you cold?*
Al contrario, **tengo calor.**	*On the contrary, I'm hot.*
Tienes razón, no **tenemos prisa.**	*You are right, we are not in a hurry.*

■ To express *very,* use **mucho(a).** Note that **hambre, sed, razón,** and **prisa** are all feminine. **Calor** and **frío** are masculine.

Tengo **mucha** hambre.	*I'm very hungry.*
Tenemos **mucha** prisa hoy.	*We are in a big hurry today.*
Dicen que tienen **mucho** frío.	*They say they are very cold.*

Vamos a practicar _____

a. ¿Qué tienes? Completa estas oraciones con una expresión idiomática.

MODELO Cuando tengo **prisa**, camino muy rápido.

1. Cuando tengo ___, voy a la cafetería.
2. Los profesores creen que siempre tienen ___.
3. Perdón, tengo ___. Mi clase empieza en dos minutos.
4. Tú no tienes ___; 4 + 44 no son 49.
5. En julio y agosto todos tenemos ___.
6. Voy a comer algo. Tengo mucha ___.
7. Cuando tengo ___, bebo agua.
8. Con permiso, tengo mucha ___. Mi autobús llega en dos minutos.
9. Tienes ___. No todos los hispanos en Estados Unidos son de México.
10. En invierno, tengo ___.

¿POR QUÉ SE DICE ASÍ?

b. ¿Qué les pasa?   ¿Por qué estas personas dicen esto?

MODELO   Elena: 10 + 11 son 22.
Porque no tiene razón.

1. Juanito: Quiero comer.
2. Norman: Quiero un refresco grande.
3. Anita: Son las nueve menos dos y mi clase es a las nueve.
4. Tomás: Quiero un sándwich de jamón y un sándwich de queso y patatas fritas.
5. Diana: Primero quiero dos vasos de agua y luego un café con leche.
6. Raúl: ¡Adiós! ¡Adiós! Ya viene mi autobús.
7. Joaquín: 5 + 6 son 11.
8. Amanda: Necesito mi chaqueta.
9. Carlos: No necesito toda esta ropa.
10. Bárbara: Granada es la capital de España.

b. ¿Qué les pasa?
1 Porque tiene hambre.
2 Porque tiene sed.
3 Porque tiene prisa.
4 Porque tiene hambre.
5 Porque tiene sed.
6 Porque tiene prisa.
7 Porque tiene razón.
8 Porque tiene frío.
9 Porque tiene calor.
10 Porque no tiene razón.

5.9 INDIRECT OBJECT PRONOUNS

5.9 Margin boxes: page 248

Indirect object nouns and pronouns answer the questions *to whom?* or *for whom?* something is done. Note in the following examples that *to* and *for* are often omitted in English.

What are you going to buy *David?*
Give *us* the money. We'll get it *for him.*
Don't forget to write *me.*

Object pronouns, like subject pronouns, are words that allow you to identify people without using or repeating their names. You are already familiar with the Spanish forms of indirect object pronouns from using the verbs **gustar** and **encantar.**

Indirect Object Pronouns			
a mí	**me**	**nos**	a nosotros(as)
a ti	**te**	**os**	a vosotros(as)
a usted	**le**	**les**	a ustedes
a él, a ella	**le**	**les**	a ellos, a ellas

Abuelita **nos** escribe mucho.	*Grandmother writes us a lot.*
¿**Te** sirvo más café?	*May I serve you more coffee?*
¿**Le** compro este disco?	*Shall I buy you this record?*
¿**Les** doy el dinero a ellos?	*Do I give them the money?*

■ Indirect object pronouns can be *clarified* or *emphasized* by using **a** + [a name or pronoun].

To clarify:

¿**Les** escribes **a Mónica** y **a Alicia** con frecuencia?	*Do you write Mónica and Alicia often?*
Yo voy a decir**les a ellos** la verdad.	*I am going to tell them the truth.*

To emphasize:

¡El problema es que **a mí** no **me** gustan las papas!	*The problem is that <u>I</u> don't like potatoes!*
Pues, ¡**a nosotros nos** encantan!	*Well, <u>we</u> love them!*

■ Usually the indirect object pronoun comes before the verb.

A ver si **le** encontramos una camiseta.	*Let's see if we can find him a T-shirt.*
¿**Te** traigo un café?	*Shall I bring you a cup of coffee?*
Me gustan mucho las películas de aventuras.	*I like adventure movies a lot.*

■ In sentences where there is an infinitive or **-ndo** form, the indirect object pronoun may be placed either before the conjugated verb *or* after and attached to the infinitive or **-ndo** verb form.

Te voy a traer el periódico. Voy a traer**te** el periódico.	*I'm going to bring you the newspaper.*
Le estoy escribiendo una carta. Estoy escribiéndo**le** una carta.	*I'm writing her a letter.*

■ With an affirmative command, the indirect object pronoun is always placed after and attached to the command form.

Sírve**me** el melón primero.	*Serve me the melon first.*
Carmen, tráe**me** el periódico, por favor.	*Carmen, bring me the newspaper, please.*
Silvia, cuénta**nos** de tu viaje por Europa.	*Silvia, tell us about your trip around Europe.*

■ In writing, when a pronoun is attached to the **-ndo** verb form or to command forms with two or more syllables, a written accent is always required.

Estamos **preparándole** una comida especial.	*We're preparing her a special meal.*
¡**Escríbeme** pronto!	*Write me soon!*
¡**Dímelo** ahora!	*Tell it to me now!*

Vamos a practicar

a. ¿Les gusta o no?   ¿Qué les gusta o no les gusta a estas personas?

MODELO   **Les encantan las papas fritas a mis hermanos.**

1. A ella ____ encantan los centros comerciales.
2. ¿A ti ____ gustan los almacenes grandes?
3. No ____ gusta ir de compras a mamá.
4. No ____ gusta a mí tampoco.
5. A mis hermanos ____ gusta escuchar la radio.
6. Las tiendas de discos ____ encantan a nosotros.
7. ¿Qué pasa? ¿No ____ gusta a usted la música?
8. A nadie ____ gusta.

b. ¿Qué les sirvo?   Dile al camarero qué debe servirles a estas personas.

MODELO   leche / a mí
         Sírveme leche, por favor.

1. un bizcocho / a él
2. unas hamburguesas / a ellos
3. un refresco / al Sr. Duarte
4. helado / a ellas y a mí
5. leche de chocolate / a los niños
6. un sándwich de queso / a la Sra. Duarte
7. papas fritas / a nosotros
8. un café / a mí

c. ¡Llegan pronto!   Los abuelos van a visitar a sus nietos en una semana. ¿Qué preguntas les hacen sus nietos cuando les hablan por teléfono?

MODELO   traer regalos
         ¿Van a traernos regalos? o
         ¿Nos van a traer regalos?

1. comprar ropa nueva
2. dar dinero
3. preparar comida especial
4. cantar algo todos los días
5. llevar al cine
6. traer fotos
7. leer un libro
8. llevar al zoológico
9. comprar videos
10. dar dulces

¿POR QUÉ SE DICE ASÍ?   **G81**

Vamos a practicar

Additional Exercises
Textbook: pages 248–249
Cuaderno: Unidad 5, Lección 3

a. ¿Les gusta o no?

1 le	**5** les
2 te	**6** nos
3 le	**7** le
4 me	**8** le

b. ¿Qué les sirvo?
1 Sírvele un bizcocho, por favor.
2 Sírveles unas hamburguesas, por favor.
3 Sírvele un refresco, por favor.
4 Sírvenos helado, por favor.
5 Sírveles leche de chocolate, por favor.
6 Sírvele un sándwich de queso, por favor.
7 Sírvenos papas fritas, por favor.
8 Sírveme un café, por favor.

c. ¡Llegan pronto!
1 ¿Van a comprarnos ropa nueva? *o* ¿Nos van a comprar ropa nueva?
2 ¿Van a darnos dinero? *o* ¿Nos van a dar dinero?
3 ¿Van a prepararnos comida especial? *o* ¿Nos van a preparar comida especial?
4 ¿Van a cantarnos algo todos los días? *o* ¿Nos van a cantar algo todos los días?
5 ¿Van a llevarnos al cine? *o* ¿Nos van a llevar al cine?
6 ¿Van a traernos fotos? *o* ¿Nos van a traer fotos?
7 ¿Van a leernos un libro? *o* ¿Nos van a leer un libro?
8 ¿Van a llevarnos al zoológico? *o* ¿Nos van a llevar al zoológico?
9 ¿Van a comprarnos videos? *o* ¿Nos van a comprar videos?
10 ¿Van a darnos dulces? *o* ¿Nos van a dar dulces?

Extension Have students give the grandparents' answer to each question.

ch. ¿Qué están haciendo?

1 Papá está leyéndole el periódico a Paquito. *o*
Papá le está leyendo el periódico a Paquito.

2 Yo estoy preparándoles la comida a todos. *o*
Yo les estoy preparando la comida a todos.

3 Anita está pidiéndome un disco (a mí). *o*
Anita me está pidiendo un disco (a mí).

4 Mis primos están sirviéndoles un refresco a los invitados. *o*
Mis primos les están sirviendo un refresco a los invitados.

5 Julio y Cruz están dándoles clases de baile a los niños. *o*
Julio y Cruz les están dando clases de baile a los niños.

6 Mamá está escribiéndoles cartas a sus amigos. *o*
Mamá les está escribiendo cartas a sus amigos.

7 Paquito está diciéndonos algo interesante (a nosotros). *o*
Paquito nos está diciendo algo interesante (a nosotros).

8 Mi tío está dándole dinero a mi prima. *o*
Mi tío le está dando dinero a mi prima.

d. ¡Qué familia!

1 me
2 le
3 les
4 les
5 nos
6 les
7 me
8 nos
9 Les
10 te

---

ch. ¿Qué están haciendo?   Es sábado por la tarde y todos están ocupados en la familia de Alberto. ¿Qué están haciendo?

MODELO   Juanita / servir / café / a sus abuelos
Juanita está sirviéndoles café a sus abuelos. o
Juanita les está sirviendo café a sus abuelos.

1. papá / leer / el periódico / a Paquito
2. yo / preparar / la comida / a todos
3. Anita / pedir / un disco / a mí
4. mis primos / servir / un refresco / a los invitados
5. Julio y Cruz / dar / clases de baile / a los niños
6. mamá / escribir / cartas / a sus amigos
7. Paquito / decir / algo interesante / a nosotros
8. mi tío / dar / dinero / a mi prima

d. ¡Qué familia!   ¿Qué hace esta familia durante la Navidad (*Christmas*)? Para saberlo, completa este párrafo con los complementos indirectos apropiados.

Mis padres siempre (1) dan un regalo interesante y especial para la Navidad. Generalmente, yo (2) compro una cosa a mi padre y otra a mi madre. Pero si no tengo mucho dinero, (3) doy algo a los dos. También (4) compro algo a mis abuelos. Ellos siempre (5) traen regalos a todos nosotros. Mis padres (6) dan dinero a mis abuelos. A mí (7) gusta eso mucho porque con frecuencia mis abuelos usan el dinero para comprar (8) más regalos a mí y a mis hermanos. ¿Y tú? ¿ (9) compras regalos a todos tus parientes? Y ellos, ¿ (10) dan muchos regalos a ti?

¿POR QUÉ SE DICE ASÍ?

LECCIÓN 1

UNIDAD

6

6.1 Margin boxes:
pages 264, 265

Point out The preterite form
leíste requires a written accent.

6.1 PRETERITE TENSE: REGULAR VERBS
Describing What You Did

Up until now, you have been talking in Spanish about events happening in the present. In this unit, you will learn to use the preterite tense to talk about events that happened in the past.

Preterite-Tense Verb Endings		
Subject	**-ar** verbs	**-er** and **-ir** verbs
yo	**-é**	**-í**
tú	**-aste**	**-iste**
usted	**-ó**	**-ió**
él / ella	**-ó**	**-ió**
nosotros(as)	**-amos**	**-imos**
vosotros(as)	**-asteis**	**-isteis**
ustedes	**-aron**	**-ieron**
ellos / ellas	**-aron**	**-ieron**

Below are examples of the three kinds of verbs in the preterite tense.

Bailar (-ar)	Correr (-er)	Salir (-ir)
bail**é**	corr**í**	sal**í**
bail**aste**	corr**iste**	sal**iste**
bail**ó**	corr**ió**	sal**ió**
bail**amos**	corr**imos**	sal**imos**
bail**asteis**	corr**isteis**	sal**isteis**
bail**aron**	corr**ieron**	sal**ieron**

Bailamos y **bailamos.**   *We danced and danced.*
Salí de la casa y **corrí**   *I left the house and ran*
   tras el autobús.   *after the bus.*

¿POR QUÉ SE DICE ASÍ ?   G83

■ Note that the preterite tense has two sets of endings: one for **-ar** verbs and the other for **-er** and **-ir** verbs.

■ Also notice that the **yo** form and the **usted / él / ella** forms require a written accent.

Adela **salió** primero.　　　*Adela left first.*
Yo no **estudié** anoche.　　　*I didn't study last night.*

■ The **nosotros** form of **-ar** and **-ir** verbs is the same in the present and preterite tenses. The context will help you decide which meaning is intended.

Cantamos todos los días.　　*We sing every day.*
Cantamos mucho ayer.　　　*We sang a lot yesterday.*

Vivimos en Texas ahora.　　*We live in Texas now.*
Vivimos allí tres años.　　　*We lived there three years.*

Vamos a practicar _____

a. **¡Qué horario!**　Leticia siempre está muy ocupada. Completa su carta a Amalia. ¿Qué le dice que hizo ayer?

1. preparar	**4.** recibir	**7.** ayudar	**10.** salir
2. comer	**5.** decidir	**8.** estudiar	**11.** correr
3. descansar	**6.** escribir	**9.** preparar	**12.** regresar

> Querida Amalia,
>
> ¡Qué día pasé ayer! A las doce le _1_ un sándwich a Pepita. Ella y yo _2_ en casa. Después yo _3_ por media hora. A las dos _4_ una carta de mi tía Julia. Después de leerla, _5_ contestar su carta inmediatamente. Le _6_ más de tres páginas. Después _7_ a mi mamá a limpiar la casa. Luego _8_ por dos horas. _9_ todas mis clases para el lunes. Entonces _10_ a correr. _11_ una milla. _12_ a casa a la hora de comer. ¡Uf! ¡Qué día!
>
> Un abrazo fuerte de
> Leticia

b. **¡Fuiste a México!**　Un(a) amigo(a) pasó sus vacaciones en México. ¿Qué le preguntas cuando regresa?

MODELO　　visitar muchos museos
　　　　　　¿Visitaste muchos museos?

1. cambiar mucho dinero	**6.** comprar regalos
2. mandar tarjetas postales	**7.** caminar mucho
3. escribir cartas	**8.** recibir muchos regalos
4. comer mucho	**9.** conocer a muchas personas
5. escuchar música	**10.** regresar ayer

¿POR QUÉ SE DICE ASÍ?

Vamos a practicar

These exercises may be done as oral or written work.

Additional Exercises
Textbook: pages 264–266
Cuaderno: Unidad 6, Lección 1

a. ¡Qué horario!
1 preparé
2 comimos
3 descansé
4 recibí
5 decidí
6 escribí
7 ayudé
8 estudié
9 Preparé
10 salí
11 Corrí
12 Regresé

b. ¡Fuiste a México!
1 ¿Cambiaste mucho dinero?
2 ¿Mandaste tarjetas postales?
3 ¿Escribiste cartas?
4 ¿Comiste mucho?
5 ¿Escuchaste música?
6 ¿Compraste regalos?
7 ¿Caminaste mucho?
8 ¿Recibiste muchos regalos?
9 ¿Conociste a muchas personas?
10 Regresaste ayer?

c. ¿Quién lo hizo?
Identifica a las personas que hicieron las cosas mencionadas. (Todas las personas están en tu libro de español.)

Manolo y Víctor	el papá de Manolo y Víctor
Carlos y Raúl	Víctor, Manolo y sus padres
Mónica	Lupe y su abuelo
Pedro Solís	Martín, Daniel y Riqui
Rafael y Betty	David, Martín, Kati y Alicia
Srta. Rivera	

MODELO   dejar una propina
El papá de Manolo y Víctor dejó una propina.

1. celebrar sus cumpleaños
2. cambiar un cheque de viajero
3. calificar exámenes
4. estudiar computación
5. pasar el verano en México
6. comer pizza en la Zona Rosa
7. hablar con la gente en Chapultepec
8. subir a los juegos en el parque de diversiones
9. comer en un restaurante en Madrid
10. bailar en su boda

ch. Línea ocupada.
Todos hablaron mucho por teléfono anoche. ¿Cuánto tiempo hablaron?

MODELO   Paquita **habló** media hora.

1. Juan y yo __ 45 minutos.
2. Mi mamá y mi tía __ 15 minutos.
3. Tú __ una hora.
4. Manuel __ 10 minutos.
5. Yo __ una hora y 15 minutos.
6. Tú y Anita __ 20 minutos.
7. Mi papá __ 50 minutos.
8. Mario y yo __ más de media hora.

d. Vivieron en México.
Esperanza y muchos de sus amigos vivieron en México por un tiempo. ¿Cuánto tiempo vivieron allí?

MODELO   Jorge: 2 años
Jorge vivió en México dos años.

1. Andrés y Matilde: 1 año
2. tú: 6 meses
3. Lidia: 5 años
4. yo: 3 años
5. mi prima: 2 años
6. ustedes: 7 años
7. Eduardo: 10 años
8. mi familia y yo: 3 años

e. Mucha hambre.
Ayer después de jugar fútbol, todos decidieron ir a comer algo. ¿Qué comieron y qué bebieron?

MODELO   Ángel: pizza   Tina y yo: leche
Ángel comió pizza.   **Tina y yo bebimos leche.**

1. Martina y yo: hamburguesas
2. Esteban y Roberto: mucha agua
3. tú: dos refrescos
4. Roberto y Tina: pastel
5. yo: limonada
6. Esteban: melón
7. tú y Tina: papas fritas
8. Martina y Tina: mucha leche

¿POR QUÉ SE DICE ASÍ?   **G85**

---

c. ¿Quién lo hizo?
1 Lupe y su abuelo celebraron sus cumpleaños.
2 Manolo y Víctor cambiaron un cheque de viajero.
3 La señorita Rivera calificó exámenes.
4 Carlos y Raúl estudiaron computación.
5 Mónica pasó el verano en México.
6 David, Martín, Kati y Alicia comieron pizza en la Zona Rosa.
7 Pedro Solís habló con la gente en Chapultepec.
8 Martín, Daniel y Riqui subieron a los juegos en el parque de diversiones.
9 Víctor, Manolo y sus padres comieron en un restaurante en Madrid.
10 Rafael y Betty bailaron en su boda.

ch. Línea ocupada.
1 hablamos
2 hablaron
3 hablaste
4 habló
5 hablé
6 hablaron
7 habló
8 hablamos

d. Vivieron en México.
1 Andrés y Matilde vivieron en México un año.
2 Tú viviste en México seis meses.
3 Lidia vivió en México cinco años.
4 Yo viví en México tres años.
5 Mi prima vivió en México dos años.
6 Ustedes vivieron en México siete años.
7 Eduardo vivió en México diez años.
8 Mi familia y yo vivimos tres años en México.

e. Mucha hambre.
1 Martina y yo comimos hamburguesas.
2 Esteban y Roberto bebieron mucha agua.
3 Tú bebiste dos refrescos.
4 Roberto y Tina comieron pastel.
5 Yo bebí limonada.
6 Esteban comió melón.
7 Tú y Tina comieron papas fritas.
8 Martina y Tina bebieron mucha leche.

f. ¡Noticias!

1 visitamos
2 Pasamos
3 nos preparó
4 comió
5 bebí
6 bebió
7 salimos
8 llevó
9 escuchamos
10 miramos
11 decidieron

6.2 Margin box: page 266

Point out The preterite forms of **ir** are the same as those of **ser**, to be presented in Lesson 2 (6.3).

---

f. ¡Noticias! Luisa está de vacaciones en Guadalajara. Ahora le escribe una carta a su amiga Natacha. ¿Qué le dice?

1. visitar	**7.** salir
2. pasar	**8.** llevar
3. prepararnos	**9.** escuchar
4. comer	**10.** mirar
5. beber	**11.** decidir
6. beber	

> ¡Hola, Natacha!
>
> ¿Cómo estás? Nosotros estamos muy contentos aquí. Ayer mamá y yo __1__ el Parque Agua Azul. ¡Es hermoso y tan tranquilo! __2__ toda la tarde allí. Para el almuerzo, el hotel __3__ unos sándwiches muy ricos. Pero mamá sólo __4__ fruta. Yo __5__ limonada, mamá no __6__ nada. Por la noche mi hermano Pascual y yo __7__ a pasear por el centro. Él me __8__ a la Plaza de los Mariachis donde __9__ la música alegre y __10__ a la gente pasar. Mis padres __11__ ir a un espectáculo de ballet folklórico. Todo fue muy divertido.
>
> Tu amiga
> Luisa

6.2 PRETERITE OF *IR*

Some verbs, like **ir**, have irregular preterite forms.

Ir	
fui	fuimos
fuiste	fuisteis
fue	fueron
fue	fueron

Fuimos al Patio Iglesias.	*We went to the Patio Iglesias.*
¿**Fuiste** al concierto?	*Did you go to the concert?*
Fueron a Madrid.	*They went to Madrid.*
No **fui** a la biblioteca.	*I didn't go to the library.*

G86

¿ POR QUÉ SE DICE ASÍ?

Vamos a practicar

a. ¡Vacaciones! Ayer empezaron las vacaciones y muchas personas ya salieron de la ciudad. ¿Adónde fueron?

EJEMPLO **Anita fue a San Antonio, Texas.**

Anita	fuiste a Los Ángeles
José y Pedro	fue a Las Vegas, Nevada
ustedes	fuimos a Miami, Florida
yo	fui a Chicago, Illinois
el profesor García	fueron a Boston, Massachusetts
tú	fueron a Nueva York, Nueva York
Martín y yo	fue a San Antonio, Texas

b. Un día típico. Ayer fue un día típico en el Colegio Dos Robles. ¿Adónde fueron estos estudiantes a las 11:10?

MODELO José: la biblioteca
José fue a la biblioteca.

1. Sara y Maité: cafetería
2. tú y tu hermana: gimnasio
3. yo: sala de música
4. mi amigo Pepe: clase de francés
5. Martín: laboratorio de química
6. Carmen y yo: patio
7. Marcos y Ana: sala de computación
8. ellas: clase de español

L E C C I Ó N   2

6.3 PRETERITE OF *HACER, SER, DAR, AND VER*

The verbs **hacer, ser, dar,** and **ver** are irregular in the preterite tense.

Hacer	Ser	Dar	Ver
hice	fui	di	vi
hiciste	fuiste	diste	viste
hizo	fue	dio	vio
hicimos	fuimos	dimos	vimos
hicisteis	fuisteis	disteis	visteis
hicieron	fueron	dieron	vieron

¿Qué **hiciste** ayer?	*What did you do yesterday?*
Fui el primero en llegar.	*I was the first to arrive.*
Me **dieron** un regalo muy caro.	*They gave me a very expensive gift.*
Isabel no **vio** a Marcos.	*Isabel didn't see Marcos.*

¿POR QUÉ SE DICE ASÍ?

Additional Exercises
Textbook: pages 266–267
Cuaderno: Unidad 6, Lección 1

a. ¡Vacaciones! Answers will vary.

b. Un día típico.
1 Sara y Maité fueron a la cafetería.
2 Tú y tu hermana fueron al gimnasio.
3 Yo fui a la sala de música.
4 Mi amigo Pepe fue a la clase de francés.
5 Martín fue al laboratorio de química.
6 Carmen y yo fuimos al patio.
7 Marcos y Ana fueron a la sala de computación.
8 Ellas fueron a la clase de español.

6.3 Margin boxes:
pages 279–281

Remind students that the preterite forms of **ser** are identical to those of **ir**.

Vamos a practicar

Additional Exercises
Textbook: pages 279–281
Cuaderno: Unidad 6, Lección 2

a. La tarea.

1 Los estudiantes buenos hicieron la tarea.
2 La profesora no hizo la tarea.
3 Nosotros hicimos la tarea.
4 Tú hiciste la tarea.
5 María y Timoteo no hicieron la tarea.
6 Yo hice la tarea.
7 El estudiante enfermo no hizo la tarea.
8 Los estudiantes malos no hicieron la tarea.

b. ¡Un pastel!

1 Estela y Norma no hicieron el pastel porque fueron a una fiesta.
2 Paco no hizo el pastel porque trabajó en el restaurante con su padre.
3 Nosotros no hicimos el pastel porque hablamos por teléfono toda la tarde.
4 Tú no hiciste el pastel porque limpiaste la casa.
5 Beatriz y Ernesto no hicieron el pastel porque escribieron una composición.
6 Ramiro y yo no hicimos el pastel porque salimos a comer.
7 Ustedes no hicieron el pastel porque escucharon música toda la noche.
8 Marta y Rolando hicieron el pastel.

c. ¿Quién fue?

1 ¿Fueron Cristina y Esteban?
2 ¿Fuiste tú?
3 ¿Fue Micaela?
4 ¿Fueron ustedes?
5 ¿Fue David?
6 ¿Fueron Elena y tú?

■ Note that unlike regular verbs, irregular verbs in the preterite do not have written accents.

Yo no **hice** nada anoche.	*I didn't do anything last night.*
¿Usted **fue** estudiante allí?	*You were a student there?*
¿Cuánto te **dio?**	*How much did he give you?*
Vi tres películas.	*I saw three movies.*

■ The preterite forms of the verb **ser** are identical to the preterite forms of the verb **ir.** The context will help you decide which verb is being used.

Él **fue** presidente por ocho años.	*He was president for eight years.*
No **fue** a la fiesta.	*He didn't go to the party.*

Vamos a practicar

a. La tarea. ¿Quiénes hicieron la tarea anoche?

MODELO Carlos y Ramona (sí)
Carlos y Ramona hicieron la tarea.

Carmen y Arturo (no)
Carmen y Arturo no hicieron la tarea.

1. los estudiantes buenos (sí)
2. la profesora (no)
3. nosotros (sí)
4. tú (sí)
5. María y Timoteo (no)
6. yo (sí)
7. el estudiante enfermo (no)
8. los estudiantes malos (no)

b. ¡Un pastel! Alguien hizo un pastel para la profesora. ¿Quién fue?

MODELO Elena: estudiar toda la noche
Elena no hizo el pastel porque estudió toda la noche.

1. Estela y Norma: ir a una fiesta
2. Paco: trabajar en el restaurante con su padre
3. nosotros: hablar por teléfono toda la tarde
4. tú: limpiar la casa
5. Beatriz y Ernesto: escribir una composición
6. Ramiro y yo: salir a comer
7. ustedes: escuchar música toda la noche
8. Marta y Rolando: hacer el pastel

c. ¿Quién fue? Unos estudiantes limpiaron la clase de español pero la profesora Alarcón no sabe quién lo hizo. ¿Qué le pregunta la profesora a la clase?

MODELO Margarita
¿Fue Margarita?

1. Cristina y Esteban
2. tú
3. Micaela
4. ustedes
5. David
6. Elena y tú

¿POR QUÉ SE DICE ASÍ?

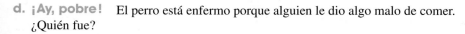

ch. ¡Mucho talento!   ¿Qué dice Laura del drama que su clase presentó anoche?

MODELO   Nicolás: fantástico
Nicolás fue fantástico.

1. Laura: estupendo
2. Julio y Tomasita: magnífico
3. tú: fenomenal
4. nosotros: muy bueno
5. Rebeca y Ada: especial
6. yo: excelente

d. ¡Ay, pobre!   El perro está enfermo porque alguien le dio algo malo de comer. ¿Quién fue?

MODELO   ¿Fue Enrique?
No, Enrique no le dio nada.

1. ¿Fue Sara?
2. ¿Fueron Hugo y Paco?
3. ¿Fueron tú y Tomás?
4. ¿Fuimos Víctor y yo?
5. ¿Fue Laura?
6. ¿Fueron ustedes?
7. ¿Fue Paquito?
8. ¿Fui yo?

e. Estampillas.   Carlitos tiene una colección de estampillas (*stamps*) de muchos países. ¿Qué tipo de estampillas le dieron estas personas?

MODELO   Su abuelo vive en Caracas.
Su abuelo le dio estampillas de Venezuela.

1. Yo vivo en Buenos Aires.
2. Bárbara vive en Asunción.
3. Sus primos viven en Lima.
4. Su mamá vive en Bogotá.
5. Tú vives en Madrid.
6. Luis y yo vivimos en Tegucigalpa.
7. Su amigo José vive en La Habana.
8. Tú y Luisa viven en La Paz.

f. Yo te vi.   Muchas personas fueron al concierto anoche. ¿A quiénes vieron allí?

MODELO   Nosotros **vimos** a los señores Ramírez.

1. Yo __ a tu prima.
2. Carlota __ a la profesora de inglés.
3. Ustedes __ a los músicos.
4. Josefina y yo __ a la familia Sánchez.
5. Tú __ al padrastro de Lilia.
6. Abel y Bernardo __ a mis abuelos.
7. Norberto __ a su amigo Rubén.
8. Ellos __ a los hermanos Gómez.

g. ¿Ya la viste?   ¿Cuándo vieron estas personas la mejor película del año?

MODELO   Román: anoche
Román la vio anoche.

1. Federico: la semana pasada
2. tú: en octubre
3. Amalia: anoche
4. Samuel y Gloria: en abril
5. Patricio y yo: en agosto
6. ustedes: en otoño
7. yo: el verano pasado
8. Doroteo y Emilio: ayer

¿POR QUÉ SE DICE ASÍ?
G89

h. ¿Héroe o asesino?

1 fue
2 fue
3 fue
4 hizo
5 recibió
6 dio
7 vieron
8 decidieron
9 fueron
10 mataron
11 volvieron
12 conquistaron
13 tomaron
14 Fueron

h. ¿Héroe o asesino? Completa estos párrafos con el pretérito de los verbos indicados y luego decide si, en tu opinión, Hernán Cortés fue un héroe o un asesino.

1. ser	**8.** decidir
2. ser	**9.** ser
3. ser	**10.** matar
4. hacer	**11.** volver
5. recibir	**12.** conquistar
6. dar	**13.** tomar
7. ver	**14.** ser

Mucha gente cree que Hernán Cortés _1_ un gran hombre. Otros dicen que él simplemente _2_ un conquistador en busca de oro. Él _3_ la persona responsable por la conquista de Tenochtitlán, la antigua capital de los aztecas.

Cortés _4_ dos viajes a la capital. En su primer viaje, Moctezuma, el rey de los aztecas, _5_ a Cortés y a sus soldados como sus invitados. Él les _6_ muchos regalos de oro. Cuando Cortés y sus soldados _7_ todo el oro de Moctezuma, ellos _8_ tomar prisionero a Moctezuma. Entonces los soldados aztecas

atacaron a los españoles y los españoles _9_ forzados a salir de Tenochtitlán. Pero antes de salir, los españoles _10_ a Moctezuma. Muchos soldados aztecas y españoles murieron en esa batalla.

Cortés y sus soldados _11_ una segunda vez a Tenochtitlán. Esta vez ellos _12_ a los aztecas y _13_ control de su capital. Miles de soldados aztecas murieron defendiendo su capital.

Ahora, ¿qué crees tú? ¿_14_ Cortés y sus soldados grandes hombres o simplemente conquistadores en busca de oro?

LECCIÓN 3

6.4 PRETERITE OF *PODER, TENER, VENIR, AND DECIR*

Four more irregular verbs in the preterite are **poder, tener, venir,** and **decir.** Note that these verbs share the same verb endings (except for **dijeron**) and that there are no written accents.

Poder	Tener	Venir	Decir
pude	tuve	vine	dije
pudiste	tuviste	viniste	dijiste
pudo	tuvo	vino	dijo
pudimos	tuvimos	vinimos	dijimos
pudisteis	tuvisteis	vinisteis	dijisteis
pudieron	tuvieron	vinieron	dijeron

No **pudimos** hacerlo.	*We couldn't do it.*
Tuve que subir al camión.	*I had to get on the bus.*
¿**Viniste** sola?	*Did you come alone?*
Sí, nos **dijo** la verdad.	*Yes, he told us the truth.*

▪ Note that the **ustedes / ellos / ellas** verb endings of **decir** are **-eron,** not **-ieron.**

No le **dijeron** nada a Javier.　　*They didn't say anything to Javier.*

Vamos a practicar

a. **¡Qué desastre!** La semana pasada fue el cumpleaños de mi abuelo pero no lo celebramos. ¿Por qué?

MODELO　primo Enrique: comprarle un regalo
　　　　Mi primo Enrique no pudo comprarle un regalo.

1. tío Rumaldo: venir de Guadalajara
2. tíos Javier y Josefa: prepararle una comida elegante
3. mamá y yo: hacerle un pastel
4. abuela: comprarle un traje nuevo
5. yo: darle nada
6. tú: traerle un libro interesante
7. tía Teresa: tomar el avión
8. primo Esteban: presentarle un regalo especial

¿POR QUÉ SE DICE ASÍ ? _____ **G91**

Vamos a practicar

Additional Exercises
Textbook: pages 294–296
Cuaderno: Unidad 6, Lección 3

a. ¡Qué desastre!
1 Mi tío Rumaldo no pudo venir de Guadalajara.
2 Mis tíos Javier y Josefa no pudieron prepararle una comida elegante.
3 Mamá y yo no pudimos hacerle un pastel.
4 Mi abuela no pudo comprarle un traje nuevo.
5 Yo no pude darle nada.
6 Tú no pudiste traerle un libro interesante.
7 Mi tía Teresa no pudo tomar el avión.
8 Mi primo Esteban no pudo presentarle un regalo especial.

b. ¿Qué pudiste hacer?

1 Mariano pudo limpiar su cuarto; no pudo limpiar la casa.
2 Sara y yo pudimos comprar platos; no pudimos comprar ropa.
3 Sara y Mariano pudieron estudiar español; no pudieron estudiar inglés.
4 Mariano pudo ir al cine; no pudo ir a cenar.
5 Mariano y yo pudimos practicar el piano; no pudimos practicar fútbol.
6 Mariano pudo hacer una comida; no pudo hacer un pastel.
7 Yo pude ver un programa en la tele; no pude ver una película.
8 Sara pudo salir con Cristina; no pudo salir con Toni.

c. Obligaciones.

1 Papá y yo tuvimos que preparar la comida.
2 Yo tuve que hacer la tarea para mañana.
3 Papá tuvo que lavar el perro.
4 Mamá tuvo que ir al banco.
5 Mi hermano y yo tuvimos que limpiar la casa.
6 Mis hermanas tuvieron que hacer un pastel.
7 Mamá tuvo que escribir cartas.
8 Mamá y papá tuvieron que trabajar el sábado.

ch. No sonó el teléfono.

1 Su mamá dijo que no pudo llamar porque tuvo que trabajar.
2 Yo dije que no pude llamar porque tuve que escribir muchas cartas.
3 Sus abuelos dijeron que no pudieron llamar porque tuvieron que ir al teatro.
4 Verónica dijo que no pudo llamar porque tuvo que dormir.
5 Tú y Paco dijeron que no pudieron llamar porque tuvieron que practicar con la banda.

b. ¿Qué pudiste hacer?
Antonio y sus hermanos pasaron el fin de semana con sus primos. ¿Qué dice Antonio cuando sus padres le preguntan qué hicieron él y sus hermanos?

MODELO   Sara: escribir tarjeta postal, no carta
Sara pudo escribir una tarjeta postal; no pudo escribir una carta.

1. Mariano: limpiar cuarto, no casa
2. Sara y yo: comprar platos, no ropa
3. Sara y Mariano: estudiar español, no inglés
4. Mariano: ir al cine, no a cenar
5. Mariano y yo: practicar piano, no fútbol
6. Mariano: hacer comida, no pastel
7. yo: ver programa en la tele, no película
8. Sara: salir con Cristina, no con Toni

c. Obligaciones.
¿Quiénes en tu familia tuvieron que hacer estas cosas la semana pasada?

MODELO   papá y yo: ir al supermercado
Papá y yo tuvimos que ir al supermercado.

1. papá y yo: preparar la comida
2. yo: hacer la tarea para mañana
3. papá: lavar el perro
4. mamá: ir al banco
5. hermano y yo: limpiar la casa
6. hermanas: hacer un pastel
7. mamá: escribir cartas
8. mamá y papá: trabajar el sábado

ch. No sonó el teléfono.
A Carlota le encanta hablar por teléfono. Pero no le llamó nadie a Carlota anoche. ¿Por qué?

MODELO   Mónica: estudiar
Mónica dijo que no pudo llamar porque tuvo que estudiar.

1. su mamá: trabajar
2. yo: escribir muchas cartas
3. sus abuelos: ir al teatro
4. Verónica: dormir
5. tú y Paco: practicar con la banda
6. Hugo: descansar
7. sus primos: estudiar para un examen
8. su amigo Pablo: leer un libro
9. ustedes: ver un programa en la tele
10. todos nosotros: hacer otras cosas

d. ¡Fama internacional!
En los conciertos de música latina en Miami, siempre hay personas de todas partes del mundo. ¿De dónde vinieron estas personas?

MODELO   el señor Valdez: Cuba
El señor Valdez vino de La Habana.

1. Gabriel: Perú
2. la familia Romero: Honduras
3. tú: Uruguay
4. Ramón y Lidia: Ecuador
5. Memo: Argentina
6. Lourdes y sus padres: El Salvador
7. yo: Estados Unidos
8. el pianista: Bolivia

¿POR QUÉ SE DICE ASÍ?

6 Hugo dijo que no pudo llamar porque tuvo que descansar.
7 Sus primos dijeron que no pudieron llamar porque tuvieron que estudiar para un examen.
8 Su amigo Pablo dijo que no pudo llamar porque tuvo que leer un libro.
9 Ustedes dijeron que no pudieron llamar porque tuvieron que ver un programa en la tele.
10 Todos nosotros dijimos que no pudimos llamar porque tuvimos que hacer otras cosas.

d. ¡Fama internacional!

1 Gabriel vino de Lima.
2 La familia Romero vino de Tegucigalpa.
3 Tú viniste de Montevideo.
4 Ramón y Lidia vinieron de Quito.
5 Memo vino de Buenos Aires.
6 Lourdes y sus padres vinieron de San Salvador.
7 Yo vine de Washington D.C.
8 El pianista vino de La Paz.

e. ¡Es hora de salir!   Al final de un día en Guadalajara, todos los turistas regresaron tarde al autobús. ¿De dónde vinieron?

MODELO   Raúl y Lola: Teatro Degollado
Raúl y Lola vinieron del Teatro Degollado.

1. Alejandra y sus padres: Mercado Libertad
2. Daniel: Parque Agua Azul
3. yo: centro
4. nosotros: Palacio Municipal
5. Delia: Casa de Artesanías
6. los señores Bermúdez: Plaza de los Mariachis
7. mis hermanos y yo: Tlaquepaque
8. la familia Angulo: Museo de Orozco

f. ¡Por fin!   Todos regresaron muy tarde al hotel anoche. ¿A qué hora regresaron?

MODELO   Mario: 11:00
Mario dijo que regresó a las once de la noche.

1. Hortensia: 12:45
2. Benjamín y Rosa: 11:35
3. el director de la escuela: 1:10
4. tú: 1:45
5. Laura y yo: 12:15
6. yo: 11:15
7. tú y Andrés: 2:05
8. la profesora de francés: 2:50

g. ¡Hasta pronto!   ¿Qué le dijo Ramona a su amiga Virginia? Para contestar, completa la carta con las formas correctas de **decir** en el pretérito.

Querida Virginia,

¿Qué tal? Espero que todo esté bien en Guadalajara.

¡No sabes lo que pasó en la clase de español ayer! La profesora nos (1) que, si queremos, podemos hacer un viaje a Guadalajara al final del año. Todos nosotros (2) que sí excepto Tomás. Cuando la profesora le preguntó por qué, Tomás le (3) que a él no le gusta los viajes.

Entonces, Rodolfo y Susana le (4), "Tomás, estás loco" y yo le (5) lo mismo. La profesora se enojó con nosotros y nos (6), "Ustedes no deben hablar así. Tomás no tiene que ir si no quiere". Yo (7), "Usted tiene razón, profesora. Perdón".

Todos los otros estudiantes (8) que sí, quieren ir. La profesora (9), "Tomás, tú no tienes que ir con nosotros si no quieres".

Pero ¡lo importante es que voy a verte muy pronto!

Un abrazo,
Ramona

e. ¡Es hora de salir!
1 Alejandra y sus padres vinieron del Mercado Libertad.
2 Daniel vino del Parque Agua Azul.
3 Yo vine del centro.
4 Nosotros vinimos del Palacio Municipal.
5 Delia vino de la Casa de Artesanías.
6 Los señores Bermúdez vinieron de la Plaza de los Mariachis.
7 Mis hermanos y yo vinimos de Tlaquepaque.
8 La familia Angulo vino del Museo de Orozco.

f. ¡Por fin!
1 Hortensia dijo que regresó a la una menos cuarto de la mañana.
2 Bejamín y Rosa dijeron que regresaron a las doce menos veinticinco de la noche.
3 El director de la escuela dijo que regresó a la una y diez de la mañana.
4 Tú dijiste que regresaste a las dos menos cuarto de la mañana.
5 Laura y yo dijimos que regresamos a las doce y cuarto de la mañana.
6 Yo dije que regresé a las once y cuarto de la noche.
7 Tú y Andrés dijeron que regresaron a las dos y cinco de la mañana.
8 La profesora de francés dijo que regresó a las tres menos diez de la mañana.

g. ¡Hasta pronto!
¡OjO! The subjunctive form **esté** in the second sentence of the letter is intended for comprehension only.
1 dijo
2 dijimos
3 dijo
4 dijeron
5 dije
6 dijo
7 dije
8 dijeron
9 dijo

UNIDAD

LECCIÓN 1

7.1 DEMONSTRATIVES
Used to Point Out Things and People

Demonstratives tell where objects or people are in relation to the person speaking:
*This book is mine. Do you want **that** blouse or **that one over there**?*

Spanish has three sets of demonstratives: one to point out someone or something
near the speaker, another to point out someone or something *farther away*, and a
third one used to refer to someone or something *a considerable distance* from both
the speaker and the listener.

Demonstratives						
	CERCA		LEJOS		MÁS LEJOS	
	m.	f.	m.	f.	m.	f.
singular	este	esta	ese	esa	aquel	aquella
plural	estos	estas	esos	esas	aquellos	aquellas

- Demonstratives may be used as adjectives or as pronouns. As adjectives, they agree
  in number and gender with the noun they modify and always go before the noun.

Esta semana no hay clases.	*This week there are no classes.*
¿Quién es **ese** señor?	*Who is that man?*
¡**Aquellas** chicas son gran deportistas!	*Those girls* (over there) *are very athletic.*

- When demonstratives are used as pronouns, they reflect the number and gender of
  the noun they replace and require a written accent.

No me gustan esos pantalones. Prefiero **éstos.**	*I don't like those pants. I prefer these.*
Estas blusas son bonitas, pero creo que **ésas** son más bonitas.	*These blouses are pretty, but I believe those are prettier.*
Tienes razón, pero **aquéllas** no son tan caras.	*You're right, but those over there are not as expensive.*

- **Esto** and **eso** are used to refer to concepts, ideas, and situations and to things
  unknown to the speaker. They never require a written accent.

Esto es imposible.	*This* (situation) *is impossible.*
¿Qué es **eso**?	*What is that?*

¿POR QUÉ SE DICE ASÍ?

UNIDAD

Vamos a practicar _____

a. ¡Ropa nueva! Para su cumpleaños, la mamá de Alma la lleva a comprar ropa nueva. ¿Qué le pregunta la madre a su hija cada vez que ve algo interesante?

MODELO   blusa
               ¿Te gusta esta blusa?

1. pantalones	**3.** zapatos	**5.** camisetas	**7.** sombrero
2. falda	**4.** suéter	**6.** chaqueta	**8.** botas

b. ¿De quién son estos lápices? Tú y un amigo fueron de compras. La dependiente puso todas sus compras en una bolsa. Ahora están decidiendo quién compró qué. ¿Qué dices al separar las cosas?

MODELO   **Éstos** son mis lápices.

1. _____ son mis carpetas.
2. _____ son tus cuadernos.
3. _____ es mi borrador.
4. _____ son mis libros.
5. _____ es tu regla.
6. _____ son tus bolígrafos.
7. _____ es mi diccionario.
8. _____ es mi mochila.

c. Mi familia. Invitaste a un amigo a una reunión familiar. ¿Qué le dices al identificar a los miembros de la familia?

MODELO   mis tíos
               Esos señores son mis tíos.

1. mi tío	**5.** mis tías
2. mi mamá	**6.** mi tía de Nueva York
3. mis abuelos paternos	**7.** mi papá
4. mi primo cubano	**8.** mi abuela materna

ch. ¡Al agua! Diana invitó a algunos amigos a nadar en la piscina de su casa. Mientras todos nadaban, Pepito, el hermano menor de Diana, puso toda la ropa en un cuarto. Ahora Diana y su mamá les ayudan a todos a encontrar su ropa. ¿Qué dicen?

MODELO   camisa / Mario
        Tú: **¿De quién es esta camisa?**
        Compañero(a): **Ésa es de Mario.**

1. zapatos / Manuel	**5.** calcetines / Lorenzo
2. sombrero / Óscar	**6.** falda / Josefina
3. sudadera / Susana	**7.** camiseta / Gregorio
4. chaqueta / Enriqueta	**8.** pantalones / Patricio

¿POR QUÉ SE DICE ASÍ? _____ **G95**

Vamos a practicar

These exercises may be done as oral or written work.

Additional Exercises
Textbook: pages 313–315
Cuaderno: Unidad 7, Lección 1

a. ¡Ropa nueva!
1 ¿Te gustan estos pantalones?
2 ¿Te gusta esta falda?
3 ¿Te gustan estos zapatos?
4 ¿Te gusta este suéter?
5 ¿Te gustan estas camisetas?
6 ¿Te gusta esta chaqueta?
7 ¿Te gusta este sombrero?
8 ¿Te gustan estas botas?

b. ¿De quién son estos lápices?

1 Éstas	5 Ésta
2 Éstos	6 Éstos
3 Éste	7 Éste
4 Éstos	8 Ésta

c. Mi familia.
1 Ese señor es mi tío.
2 Esa señora es mi mamá.
3 Esos señores son mis abuelos paternos.
4 Ese señor es mi primo cubano.
5 Esas señoras son mis tías.
6 Esa señora es mi tía de Nueva York.
7 Ese señor es mi papá.
8 Esa señora es mi abuela materna.

ch. ¡Al agua!
1 ¿De quién son estos zapatos? Ésos son de Manuel.
2 ¿De quién es este sombrero? Ése es de Óscar.
3 ¿De quién es esta sudadera? Ésa es de Susana.
4 ¿De quién es esta chaqueta? Ésa es de Enriqueta.
5 ¿De quién son estos calcetines? Ésos son de Lorenzo.
6 ¿De quién es esta falda? Ésa es de Josefina.
7 ¿De quién es esta camiseta? Ésa es de Gregorio.
8 ¿De quién son estos pantalones? Ésos son de Patricio.

d. ¡Me encantan!

d. ¡Me encantan! ¿Qué opinas de estas cosas?

MODELO **Me gustan esos zapatos negros pero me encantan aquéllos marrones.**

1.

2.

3.

4.

5.

6.

1 Me gusta esa blusa rosada pero me encanta aquélla blanca.
2 Me gustan esas camisetas verdes pero me encantan aquéllas rojas.
3 Me gusta ese vestido azul pero me encanta aquél amarillo.
4 Me gusta esa mochila verde pero me encanta aquélla azul.
5 Me gustan esos pantalones azules pero me encantan aquéllos grises.
6 Me gusta esa chaqueta anaranjada pero me encanta aquélla verde.

7.2 Margin boxes: pages 316, 317

7.2 SPELLING CHANGES IN THE PRETERITE

Some verbs require a spelling change in the preterite. These verbs are *not* irregular. Spelling changes occur only to maintain pronunciation.

Spelling changes that occur in preterite tense verbs follow some very specific rules. The spelling change rules listed below apply at all times.

■ An unaccented **i** between two vowels changes to **y.**

Leer	Oír	Creer
leí	oí	creí
leíste	oíste	creíste
leyó	**oyó**	**creyó**
leímos	oímos	creímos
leísteis	oísteis	creísteis
leyeron	**oyeron**	**creyeron**
leyendo	**oyendo**	**creyendo**

Note that this rule affects the **usted / él / ella** and **ustedes / ellos / ellas** forms of the preterite as well as the **-ndo** form of the verb.

The following three rules affect the **yo** form of the preterite in certain verbs to preserve the consonant sound of their infinitive ending: **-car, -gar,** and **-zar.**

■ The letter **c** changes to **qu** before **e** or **i.**

bus**car:** bus**qué,** buscaste, buscó, buscamos . . .
to**car:** to**qué,** tocaste, tocó, tocamos . . .

Other verbs of this type are:

calificar	criticar	dedicar	practicar
comunicar	chocar (*to collide*)	explicar	sacar

¿POR QUÉ SE DICE ASÍ?

- The letter **g** changes to **gu** before **e** or **i.**

    pa**gar:** pa**gué,** pagaste, pagó, pagamos . . .
    ju**gar:** ju**gué,** jugaste, jugó, jugamos . . .

    Other verbs of this type are:

    entregar (*to hand over, deliver*)
    llegar
    obligar
    pegar (*to beat, hit*)

- The letter **z** changes to **c** before **e** or **i.**

    empe**zar:** empe**cé,** empezaste, empezó, empezamos . . .
    comen**zar:** comen**cé,** comenzaste, comenzó, comenzamos . . .

    Other verbs of this type are:

    almorzar   especializar
    cruzar   utilizar

Other verbs that change **z** to **c** before **e** or **i** are:

caracterizar	individualizar
dramatizar	modernizar
familiarizar	personalizar
garantizar	popularizar
generalizar	tranquilizar
hospitalizar	

Vamos a practicar

a. ¡A leer!   En la familia de Alfonso, una noche por semana todos leen algo. ¿Qué leyeron anoche?

MODELO   Mamá **leyó** un artículo.

1. Mis hermanos _____ un libro nuevo.
2. Tú _____ el periódico.
3. Papá _____ una novela histórica.
4. Yo _____ una novela de horror.
5. Mi hermana _____ un artículo de deportes.
6. Todos nosotros _____ algo interesante.

b. ¿Cómo es?   Hay un nuevo estudiante en la escuela y la profesora de matemáticas quiere saber algo de él. ¿Qué le dice una muchacha de la clase?

MODELO   Rosa / canta bien
         Rosa oyó que canta bien.

1. Florencio / toma álgebra
2. Vicente y Rubén / es inteligente
3. yo / es deportista
4. ustedes / juega fútbol
5. Nena / es guapo
6. usted / le gusta la música
7. Alicia / no conoce a nadie
8. todos nosotros / es de Venezuela

¿POR QUÉ SE DICE ASÍ?   G97

Vamos a practicar

Additional Exercises
Textbook: pages 316–317
Cuaderno: Unidad 7, Lección 1

a. ¡A leer!
1 leyeron
2 leíste
3 leyó
4 leí
5 leyó
6 leímos

b. ¿Cómo es?
1 Florencio oyó que toma álgebra.
2 Vicente y Rubén oyeron que es inteligente.
3 Yo oí que es deportista.
4 Ustedes oyeron que juega fútbol.
5 Nena oyó que es guapo.
6 Usted oyó que le gusta la música.
7 Alicia oyó que no conoce a nadie.
8 Todos nosotros oímos que es de Venezuela.

c. ¿Cómo los ayudaste?

1 Elena le explicó las lecciones de historia todo el año.
2 Yo le expliqué las lecciones de drama todo el año.
3 Elena y yo le explicamos las lecciones de matemáticas todo el año.
4 Yo le expliqué las lecciones de física todo el año.
5 Elena y yo le explicamos las lecciones de computación todo el año.
6 Elena le explicó las lecciones de español todo el año.
7 Yo le expliqué las lecciones de inglés todo el año.
8 Elena y yo le explicamos las lecciones de biología todo el año.

ch. Instrumentos musicales.

1 tocó
2 toqué
3 tocaron
4 tocamos
5 tocó
6 tocaste
7 tocó
8 tocaron

d. Ayudé a todo el mundo.

1 tocaron, toqué
2 calificó, califiqué
3 buscaron, busqué
4 practicaste, practiqué
5 sacaron, saqué
6 comunicó, comuniqué
7 criticó, critiqué
8 explicó, expliqué

c. ¿Cómo los ayudaste?
Tú y Elena son muy buenos(as) estudiantes y también son muy generosos(as). ¿Cómo ayudaron a sus amigos a sacar buenas notas?

MODELO Antonio sacó una A– (A menos) en álgebra.   yo
Yo le expliqué las lecciones de álgebra todo el año.

1. Diana sacó una B+ (B más) en historia.   Elena
2. Hugo sacó una A– en drama.   yo
3. Carlota sacó una B+ en matemáticas.   Elena y yo
4. Paco sacó una C+ en física.   yo
5. Bárbara sacó una A en computación.   Elena y yo
6. Manuel sacó una A en español.   Elena
7. Mariela saco una B– en inglés.   yo
8. José sacó una A en biología.   Elena y yo

ch. Instrumentos musicales.
Muchas personas participaron en un programa musical la semana pasada. ¿Qué hicieron?

MODELO Antonio **tocó** el violín.

1. Inés _____ la trompeta.
2. Yo _____ el saxófono.
3. Hugo y Rodrigo _____ la guitarra.
4. Tú y yo _____ el clarinete.
5. Verónica _____ el oboe.
6. Tú _____ la flauta.
7. Roberta _____ el piano.
8. Federico y Clara _____ el violín.

d. Ayudé a todo el mundo.
¿Qué hicieron estas personas y qué hiciste tú?

MODELO Olga me **explicó** la lección de matemáticas y yo le **expliqué** la lección de español.

VOCABULARIO ÚTIL:

| buscar | comunicar | explicar | sacar |
| calificar | criticar | practicar | tocar |

1. Pedro y Alberta _____ el piano y yo _____ la guitarra.
2. La profesora _____ las partes difíciles de los exámenes y yo _____ las partes fáciles.
3. Mamá y papá _____ un regalo caro para ti y yo _____ un regalo barato.
4. Tú _____ el cabezazo ayer por la mañana y yo lo _____ ayer por la tarde.
5. Mis papás _____ fotos de los novios y yo _____ fotos de mis amigos.
6. Carla me _____ la información a mí y yo le _____ la información al director.
7. El profesor me _____ a mí y yo _____ a mi compañero.
8. Olga me _____ la lección de matemáticas y yo le _____ la lección de español.

¿POR QUÉ SE DICE ASÍ?

e. ¡Qué deportista!   Rosa y su hermana Margarita son muy deportistas. Según Rosa, ¿qué hicieron la semana pasada?

MODELO   lunes / mañana / yo / tenis
El lunes por la mañana jugué tenis.

1. lunes / tarde / Margarita y yo / volibol
2. martes / tarde / yo / golf
3. miércoles / mañana / yo / baloncesto
4. jueves / tarde / Margarita / tenis
5. viernes / tarde / Margarita / fútbol americano
6. sábado / mañana / yo / béisbol

f. Aeropuerto internacional.   Al aeropuerto de Miami llegan vuelos internacionales todo el día. ¿A qué hora llegaron estas personas?

MODELO   El señor Juan Uribe vino de Santo Domingo.
Él llegó de la República Dominicana a las siete y cinco de la tarde.

1. Horacio Tovares vino de Santiago.
2. Las hermanas Romano vinieron de la Ciudad de México.
3. Yo vine de Buenos Aires.
4. La familia Quiroga vino de San José.
5. Tú viniste de Bogotá.
6. El profesor Claudio Arabal vino de Madrid.
7. Julio Gómez vino de Tegucigalpa.
8. La doctora Josefina Clemente vino de Caracas.

LLEGADAS	
ORIGEN	HORA
San José	07,15
Bogotá	08,50
Madrid	10,10
Caracas	13,15
Tegucigalpa	14,45
México	15,45
Santo Domingo	19,05
Santiago	21,55
Buenos Aires	23,30

g. Algo nuevo.   Elisa y sus amigos practicaron deportes el domingo todo el día. ¿A qué hora empezaron?

MODELO   Armando (7:00 A.M.)
Armando empezó a jugar tenis a las siete de la mañana.

1. Arturo y yo (8:30 A.M.)   2. Tú (6:30 A.M.)   3. Juan (4:15 P.M.)

4. ustedes (2:00 P.M.)   5. yo (7:45 P.M.)

e. ¡Qué deportista!
1 El lunes por la tarde Margarita y yo jugamos volibol.
2 El martes por la tarde jugué golf.
3 El miércoles por la mañana jugué baloncesto.
4 El jueves por la tarde Margarita jugó tenis.
5 El viernes por la tarde Margarita jugó fútbol americano.
6 El sábado por la mañana jugué béisbol.

f. Aeropuerto internacional.
1 Él llegó de Chile a las diez menos cinco de la noche.
2 Ellas llegaron de México a las cuatro menos cuarto de la tarde.
3 Yo llegué de Argentina a las once y media de la noche.
4 Ellos llegaron de Costa Rica a las siete y cuarto de la mañana.
5 Tú llegaste de Colombia a las nueve menos diez de la mañana.
6 Él llegó de España a las diez y diez de la mañana.
7 Él llegó de Honduras a las tres menos cuarto de la tarde.
8 Ella llegó de Venezuela a la una y cuarto de la tarde.

g. Algo nuevo.
1 Arturo y yo empezamos a jugar fútbol a las ocho y media de la mañana.
2 Tú empezaste a jugar golf a las seis y media de la mañana.
3 Juan empezó a jugar baloncesto a las cuatro y cuarto de la tarde.
4 Ustedes empezaron a jugar béisbol a las dos de la tarde.
5 Yo empecé a jugar fútbol americano a las ocho menos cuarto de la noche.

h. La primera vez.
1 En esta foto comencé a llorar.
2 En esta foto mi hermano Germán comenzó a correr.
3 En esta foto comencé el colegio.
4 En esta foto mi hermano comenzó a conducir el coche.
5 En esta foto comencé a salir con mi novio Roberto.
6 En esta foto mi hermano comenzó a jugar fútbol.
7 En esta foto comencé la escuela secundaria.
8 En esta foto mi hermana comenzó la universidad.

i. De vacaciones.
1 sacó, saqué
2 empezaron, empecé
3 criticaron, critiqué
4 pagó, pagué
5 cruzaron, crucé
6 jugaron, jugué
7 practicaron, practiqué
8 empezaron, empecé

7.3 Margin box: page 332

U N I D A D

h. La primera vez.   Carolina está enseñándole un álbum de fotos a su mejor amiga. ¿Qué dice de cada foto?

MODELO: yo / andar
En esta foto comencé a andar.

1. yo / llorar
2. mi hermano Germán / correr
3. yo / el colegio
4. mi hermano / conducir el coche
5. yo / salir con mi novio Roberto
6. mi hermano / jugar fútbol
7. yo / la escuela secundaria
8. mi hermana / la universidad

i. De vacaciones.   Tú nunca haces lo que hacen las otras personas. ¿Qué hicieron tus amigos durante el verano y qué hiciste tú?

MODELO   Juan y Óscar **tocaron** la guitarra; yo no **toqué** nada. (tocar)

1. Rosana _____ muchas fotos; yo no _____ ninguna. (sacar)
2. Marcos y Luis Miguel _____ a estudiar baile; yo no _____ a estudiarlo porque no me gusta bailar. (empezar)
3. Los profesores _____ a los guías; yo no _____ a nadie. (criticar)
4. La directora _____ la cuenta del hotel; yo no _____ nada. (pagar)
5. Tú y Silvia _____ el océano Atlántico; yo no lo _____ porque no me gusta viajar en barco. (cruzar)
6. Eva y Alicia _____ fútbol todos los días; yo no _____ ni un solo día. (jugar)
7. Rosa y Lupe _____ karate; yo no _____ nada. (practicar)
8. Olivia y Fernando _____ una clase de arte; yo no _____ la clase porque ya tengo una clase de música. (empezar)

L E C C I Ó N 2

7.3 DIRECT OBJECT PRONOUNS

Direct objects answer the questions *what?* or *who(m)?* after the verb.

Ana María ve **la tele.**	*Ana María is watching TV.*
Escuchamos **música.**	*We listen to music.*
No conozco a **los profesores.**	*I don't know the teachers.*

Direct objects can be pronouns as well as nouns. Pronouns are used to avoid repetition of nouns.

Tocaron música clásica y **la** escuchamos en la radio.	*They played classical music, and we listened to it on the radio.*
¿Los Martín? No **los** conozco.	*The Martíns? I don't know them.*
Llamé a papá. **Lo** llamé ayer.	*I called Dad. I called him yesterday.*

The direct object pronouns in Spanish are given below.

Direct Object Pronouns			
me	**me**	**nos**	*us*
you (familiar)	**te**	**os**	*you* (familiar)
you (m. formal)	**lo**	**los**	*you* (m. formal)
you (f. formal)	**la**	**las**	*you* (f. formal)
him, it (m.)	**lo**	**los**	*them* (m.)
her, it (f.)	**la**	**las**	*them* (f.)

¿No **me** viste en el partido?	*Didn't you see me at the game?*
Los llevo al cine por la tarde.	*I take them to the movies in the afternoon.*
Nos van a llamar esta noche.	*They are going to call us this evening.*

- Like indirect object pronouns, direct object pronouns are placed before conjugated verbs.

Me ayudaron muchísimo.	*They really helped me a lot.*
Lo llevaron al hospital.	*They took him to the hospital.*

- In sentences where there is an infinitive or an **-ndo** verb form, the direct object pronoun may either come before the conjugated verb or it may come after and be attached to the infinitive or the **-ndo** verb form.

Estoy pagándo**la.** **La** estoy pagando.	*I'm paying for it.*
Queremos observar**lo.** **Lo** queremos observar.	*We want to observe him.*

- When telling someone to do something using a command, the object pronoun is always placed after and attached to the command form.

Levánta**los.** Bája**los.**	*Raise them. Lower them.*
Lláma**me.**	*Call me.*

- Remember that in writing, when a pronoun is attached to the **-ndo** verb form or to command forms with two or more syllables, a written accent is always required.

Estamos **mirándolo.**	*We're looking at it.*
Cómpralo aquí.	*Buy it here.*

Additional Exercises
Textbook: pages 332–333
Cuaderno: Unidad 7, Lección 2

a. ¿Dónde?

1 ¿Dónde? No la veo.
2 ¿Dónde? No lo veo.
3 ¿Dónde? No lo veo.
4 ¿Dónde? No los veo.
5 ¿Dónde? No las veo.
6 ¿Dónde? No lo veo.
7 ¿Dónde? No lo veo.
8 ¿Dónde? No las veo.

b. Me duele todo.

1 No lo puedo doblar.
o No puedo doblarlo.
2 No la puedo levantar.
o No puedo levantarla.
3 No lo puedo bajar.
o No puedo bajarlo.
4 No los puedo mover.
o No puedo moverlos.
5 No los puedo abrir.
o No puedo abrirlos.
6 No los puedo levantar.
o No puedo levantarlos.
7 No la puedo bajar.
o No puedo bajarla.
8 No la puedo tocar.
o No puedo tocarla.
9 No las puedo mover.
o No puedo moverlas.

c. ¿Con qué frecuencia?

1 Me llaman cuatro veces
al mes.
2 Me saludan treinta veces
al mes.
3 Me invita al cine dos veces
al mes.
4 Me acompaña a estudiar seis
veces al mes.
5 Me ayudan cuatro veces
al mes.
6 Me busca antes de las clases
cuatro veces al mes.
7 Me visitan una vez al mes.
8 Me espera después de las
clases ocho veces al mes.

UNIDAD 7

Vamos a practicar

a. ¿Dónde? Perdiste un lente de contacto en el partido de fútbol y ahora no puedes ver nada. ¿Qué contestas cuando tus amigos te dicen lo que está pasando?

MODELO Allí están Pepe y Ana.
¿Dónde? No los veo.

1. Allí está Juanita.
2. Allí está nuestro equipo.
3. Allí está el árbitro.
4. Allí están los Jaguares.
5. Allí están María y Francisca.
6. Allí está Ricardo.
7. Allí está el entrenador.
8. Allí están tus primas.

b. Me duele todo. Ayer jugaste fútbol todo el día y hoy te duele todo. Decidiste ir al médico. ¿Cómo le respondes al médico durante la examinación?

MODELO Compañero(a): Levanta los brazos.
Tú: **No los puedo levantar.** o **No puedo levantarlos.**

1. Dobla el brazo izquierdo.
2. Levanta la pierna derecha.
3. Baja el brazo izquierdo.
4. Mueve los pies.
5. Abre los ojos.
6. Levanta los brazos.
7. Baja la cabeza.
8. Toca la nariz.
9. Mueve las piernas.

c. ¿Con qué frecuencia? Tu hermanito está aprendiendo a hacer una encuesta. Te hace preguntas acerca de las actividades mensuales de tu familia y de tus amigos. Contéstalas.

MODELO ¿Con qué frecuencia te visitan tus abuelos? (3)
Me visitan tres veces al mes.

1. ¿Con qué frecuencia te llaman tus tíos? (4)
2. ¿Con qué frecuencia te saludan tus amigos? (30)
3. ¿Con qué frecuencia te invita al cine un amigo? (2)
4. ¿Con qué frecuencia te acompaña una amiga a estudiar? (6)
5. ¿Con qué frecuencia te ayudan tus amigos? (4)
6. ¿Con qué frecuencia te busca una amiga antes de las clases? (4)
7. ¿Con qué frecuencia te visitan tus primos? (1)
8. ¿Con qué frecuencia te espera un amigo después de las clases? (8)

ch. Preguntas y más preguntas. Tienes un(a) amigo(a) muy curioso(a). ¿Qué le contestas cuando quiere saber qué hiciste anoche?

MODELO Compañero(a): ¿Leíste el periódico?
Tú: **Sí, lo leí.** o **No, no lo leí.**

1. ¿Viste la tele?
2. ¿Preparaste la comida?
3. ¿Escuchaste tus discos compactos?
4. ¿Escribiste una carta?
5. ¿Limpiaste tu cuarto?
6. ¿Visitaste a tus abuelos?
7. ¿Ayudaste a tu mamá?
8. ¿Hiciste la tarea?

¿POR QUÉ SE DICE ASÍ?

---

ch. Preguntas y más preguntas.

1 Sí, la vi. *o* No, no la vi.
2 Sí, la preparé. *o* No, no la preparé.
3 Sí, los escuché. *o* No, no los escuché.
4 Sí, la escribí. *o* No, no la escribí.
5 Sí, lo limpié. *o* No, no lo limpié.
6 Sí, los visité. *o* No, no los visité.
7 Sí, la ayudé. *o* No, no la ayudé.
8 Sí, la hice. *o* No, no la hice.

d. ¡Amor!   Anoche Diana llamó a su amiga Nora para hacerle preguntas sobre su nuevo novio. ¿Qué le preguntó Diana a Nora?

MODELO   ¿ . . . ?   Sí, me invitó al cine.
           Diana: **¿Te invitó al cine?**

1. ¿ . . . ? Sí, me saludó esta mañana.
2. ¿ . . . ? No, no me llamó por teléfono anoche.
3. ¿ . . . ? No, no me buscó después de las clases el viernes.
4. ¿ . . . ? No, no me visitó en casa ayer.
5. ¿ . . . ? Sí, me ayudó con la tarea el lunes.
6. ¿ . . . ? Sí, me invitó a salir el viernes por la noche.
7. ¿ . . . ? Sí, me acompañó a un concierto de rock.
8. ¿ . . . ? Sí, me llevó a cenar la semana pasada.
9. ¿ . . . ? No, no me preparó una comida especial.
10. ¿ . . . ? Sí, me habló de su familia.

e. Demasiado que hacer.   Después de las clases, unos estudiantes están hablando de lo que tienen que hacer esta noche. ¿Qué dicen?

MODELO   ¿Leíste el libro para la clase de geografía?
           No, voy a leerlo esta noche. o
           No, lo voy a leer esta noche.

1. ¿Escribiste la composición para la clase de inglés?
2. ¿Hiciste la tarea de español?
3. ¿Leíste los artículos para la clase de biología?
4. ¿Practicaste la música para la banda?
5. ¿Estudiaste la lección de francés?
6. ¿Practicaste el cabezazo?
7. ¿Hiciste los problemas de álgebra?
8. ¿Preparaste la tarea de física?
9. ¿Escribiste el artículo para la clase de historia?
10. ¿Estudiaste la lección de química?

7.4   STEM-CHANGING VERBS IN THE PRETERITE:
E → I AND O → U

In **Unidad 5,** you learned about stem-changing verbs in the present tense. In the preterite, only **-ir** verbs undergo stem changes. Verbs that end in **-ar** and **-er** are regular and do not undergo stem changes in the preterite.

Nani **contó** todo el dinero.	*Nani counted all the money.*
No lo **entendí.**	*I didn't understand it.*
No **pensaron** en eso.	*They didn't think about that.*

¿POR QUÉ SE DICE ASÍ?

d. ¡Amor!
1 ¿Te saludó esta mañana?
2 ¿Te llamó por teléfono anoche?
3 ¿Te buscó después de las clases el viernes?
4 ¿Te visitó en casa ayer?
5 ¿Te ayudó con la tarea el lunes?
6 ¿Te invitó a salir el viernes por la noche?
7 ¿Te acompañó a un concierto de rock?
8 ¿Te llevó a cenar la semana pasada?
9 ¿Te preparó una comida especial?
10 ¿Te habló de su familia?

e. Demasiado que hacer.
1 No, voy a escribirla esta noche. *o* No, la voy a escribir esta noche.
2 No, voy a hacerla esta noche. *o* No, la voy a hacer esta noche.
3 No, voy a leerlos esta noche. *o* No, los voy a leer esta noche.
4 No, voy a practicarla esta noche. *o* No, la voy a practicar esta noche.
5 No, voy a estudiarla esta noche. *o* No, la voy a estudiar esta noche.
6 No, voy a practicarlo esta noche. *o* No, lo voy a practicar esta noche.
7 No, voy a hacerlos esta noche. *o* No, los voy a hacer esta noche.
8 No, voy a prepararla esta noche. *o* No, la voy a preparar esta noche.
9 No, voy a escribirlo esta noche. *o* No, lo voy a escribir esta noche.
10 No, voy a estudiarla esta noche. *o* No, la voy a estudiar esta noche.

7.4 Margin boxes: pages 333, 334

- In **-ir** stem-changing verbs, **e** becomes **i** and **o** becomes **u** in the **usted / él / ella** and the **ustedes / ellos / ellas** forms.

Pedir (e → i)	
pedí	pedimos
pediste	pedisteis
pidió	**pidieron**
pidió	**pidieron**

Dormir (o → u)	
dormí	dormimos
dormiste	dormisteis
durmió	**durmieron**
durmió	**durmieron**

Durmió muy poco anoche. *He slept very little last night.*
Sintió un dolor en la pierna. *He felt a pain in his leg.*
Me **pidieron** un favor. *They asked me for a favor.*
Ya **sirvieron** la comida. *They already served dinner.*

The following is a list of common stem-changing **-ir** verbs. Note that the letters in parentheses indicate stem changes in the present tense and in the preterite.

e → i (present and preterite)

conseguir (i, i)	*to get, obtain*
pedir (i, i)	*to ask for*
repetir (i, i)	*to repeat*
seguir (i, i)	*to follow*
vestirse (i, i)	*to get dressed*

e → ie (present) / e → i (preterite)

divertirse (ie, i)	*to have a good time*
preferir (ie, i)	*to prefer*
sentir (ie, i)	*to feel*

o → ue (present) / o → u (preterite)

dormir (ue, u)	*to sleep*
morir (ue, u)	*to die*

Vamos a practicar

a. ¡Ay, ay! Ayer, después del partido más importante del año, todos los miembros del equipo de volibol empezaron a sentirse adoloridos. ¿Dónde sintieron el dolor?

MODELO Mauricio
Mauricio sintió dolor en la pierna.

1. Arturo e Irene **2.** yo **3.** Horacio **4.** Elena y Roberto

5. tú **6.** Guillermo **7.** Alma y yo **8.** los hermanos Rey

¿POR QUÉ SE DICE ASÍ?

Vamos a practicar

Additional Exercises
Textbook: pages 333–334
Cuaderno: Unidad 7, Lección 2

a. ¡Ay, ay!
1 Arturo e Irene sintieron dolor en el cuello.
2 Yo sentí dolor en los brazos.
3 Horacio sintió dolor en los pies.
4 Elena y Roberto sintieron dolor de cabeza.
5 Tú sentiste dolor en todo el cuerpo.
6 Guillermo sintió dolor en la nariz.
7 Alma y yo sentimos dolor en las manos.
8 Los hermanos Rey sintieron dolor en las rodillas.

b. ¡Qué confusión! Ayer tú y unos amigos fueron a un restaurante. El servicio fue terrible. ¿Por qué?

MODELO   Marta: hamburguesa / pizza
Marta pidió una hamburguesa pero el camarero le sirvió pizza.

1. yo: bizcocho / sándwich
2. Paco y Luz: café con leche / leche
3. ustedes: pizza / hamburguesas
4. ellos: agua mineral / refrescos
5. Leonardo: melón / manzana
6. Armando y yo: leche / limonada
7. tú: sándwich mixto / sándwich de jamón
8. Ana María: fruta / bizcocho

c. Investigación. En tu opinión, ¿hay una relación entre las notas que recibes y el número de horas que duermes? Antes de contestar, di cuántas horas durmieron estas personas y qué notas sacaron en el último examen.

MODELO   **Joaquín durmió ocho horas y sacó una B.**

Estudiante	Horas	Nota
Joaquín	8	B
María	3	B
Alfredo y Tomás	7	A
Yo	5	C
Federico y Alicia	6	B
Hugo	9	A
tú	8	A
Elena	4	C
los jugadores de fútbol	8	C

1. María
2. Alfredo y Tomás
3. yo
4. Federico y Alicia
5. Hugo
6. tú
7. Elena
8. los jugadores de fútbol

L E C C I Ó N 3

7.5 AFFIRMATIVE TÚ COMMANDS: IRREGULAR FORMS

In **Unidad 5,** you learned how to use regular affirmative **tú** commands.

Limpia tu cuarto.   *Clean your room.*
Bebe la leche.   *Drink the milk.*
Escríbeme pronto.   *Write to me soon.*

¿POR QUÉ SE DICE ASÍ?   G105

b. ¡Qué confusión!
1 Yo pedí un bizcocho pero el camarero me sirvió un sándwich.
2 Paco y Luz pidieron café con leche pero el camarero les sirvió leche.
3 Ustedes pidieron pizza pero el camarero les sirvió hamburguesas.
4 Ellos pidieron agua mineral pero el camarero les sirvió refrescos.
5 Leonardo pidió melón pero el camarero le sirvió una manzana.
6 Armando y yo pedimos leche pero el camarero nos sirvió limonada.
7 Tú pediste un sándwich mixto pero el camarero te sirvió un sándwich de jamón.
8 Ana María pidió fruta pero el camarero le sirvió un bizcocho.

c. Investigación.
1 María durmió tres horas y sacó una B.
2 Alfredo y Tomás durmieron siete horas y sacaron una A.
3 Yo dormí cinco horas y saqué una C.
4 Federico y Alicia durmieron seis horas y sacaron una B.
5 Hugo durmió nueve horas y sacó una A.
6 Tú dormiste ocho horas y sacaste una A.
7 Elena durmió cuatro horas y sacó una C.
8 Los jugadores de fútbol durmieron ocho horas y sacaron una C.

7.5 Margin box: page 347

Point out There are only two instances in which the **tú** form has no final **s**: the familiar command and the preterite.

There are, in addition, eight irregular affirmative **tú** commands. Note how almost all are derived from the **yo** form of the present tense.

Affirmative Irregular *tú* Commands		
Infinitive	Present Tense **yo** Form	Command
decir	**di**go	**di**
poner	**pon**go	**pon**
salir	**sal**go	**sal**
tener	**ten**go	**ten**
venir	**ven**go	**ven**
hacer	**hag**o	**haz**
ir	**voy**	**ve**
ser	**soy**	**sé**

Ten paciencia.   *Be patient.*
Ven acá, mamá.   *Come here, Mom.*

■ Object pronouns always follow and are attached to affirmative commands. When one pronoun is attached, no written accent is required.

Hazlo tú.   *Do it yourself.*
Ponla en la mesa.   *Put it on the table.*

Vamos a practicar

a. **¡Mando yo!** Los padres de Mariana están de vacaciones. ¿Qué mandatos le da Mariana a su hermano menor?

MODELO   hacer lo que te digo
              Haz lo que te digo.

1. poner tus cosas en su lugar
2. salir a tiempo para la escuela
3. tener cuidado al cruzar la calle
4. venir directamente a casa después de las clases
5. decirme todo lo que te pasó en la escuela
6. ir al patio a jugar
7. hacer la tarea
8. ser bueno siempre

b. **¿Aquí?**   Tu amigo(a) te ayuda a arreglar tu cuarto. Contesta sus preguntas.

MODELO   ¿Dónde pongo la mesita? (al lado de la cama)
              Ponla al lado de la cama.

1. ¿Dónde pongo las lámparas? (en las mesitas)
2. ¿Dónde pongo el televisor? (en el estante)
3. ¿Dónde pongo la cama? (debajo de la ventana)
4. ¿Dónde pongo el escritorio? (a la derecha del estante)
5. ¿Dónde pongo las sillas? (a la derecha y a la izquierda del escritorio)
6. ¿Dónde pongo el sillón? (enfrente del televisor)

¿POR QUÉ SE DICE ASÍ?

Vamos a practicar

Additional Exercises
Textbook: pages 347–349
Cuaderno: Unidad 7, Lección 3

a. ¡Mando yo!
1 Pon tus cosas en su lugar.
2 Sal a tiempo para la escuela.
3 Ten cuidado al cruzar la calle.
4 Ven directamente a casa después de las clases.
5 Dime todo lo que te pasó en la escuela.
6 Ve al patio a jugar.
7 Haz la tarea.
8 Sé bueno siempre.

b. ¿Aquí?
1 Ponlas en las mesitas.
2 Ponlo en el estante.
3 Ponla debajo de la ventana.
4 Ponlo a la derecha del estante.
5 Ponlas a la derecha y a la izquierda del escritorio.
6 Ponlo enfrente del televisor.

c. Sí, mamá. Hoy es sábado y los padres de Susana tienen que ir a la oficina a trabajar. ¿Qué le dice su madre antes de salir?

MODELO: **Escucha** lo que te digo.

VOCABULARIO ÚTIL:

ser	tener	volver	poner	decir	salir
jugar	ir	pedir	escuchar	limpiar	hacer

1. _____ tu cuarto antes de salir.
2. _____ tu ropa en el armario.
3. _____ cuidado con las fotos en la mesita.
4. _____ de la casa antes de las 10:00.
5. _____ al correo para enviar las cartas.
6. _____ "buenos días" y "adiós" a todos en el correo.
7. _____ a casa antes de las 11:00.
8. _____ buena con tu hermanita.
9. _____ con ella por una hora por la tarde.
10. _____ tu tarea antes de ver la tele.

7.6 PREPOSITIONS OF LOCATION

Prepositions show the relationship between things. Prepositions of location tell where things or people are located.

Prepositions of Location	
a la derecha de	*to the right of*
a la izquierda de	*to the left of*
al lado de	*beside, next to*
cerca de	*near (to)*
lejos de	*far from*
debajo de	*under*
encima de	*on top of, over*
sobre	*on, over*
delante de	*in front of*
enfrente de	*facing, in front of*
detrás de	*behind*
en	*on, in*
entre	*between, among*

Está demasiado **lejos de**l baño.	*It's too far from the bathroom.*
¿Lo pusiste **cerca de** la puerta?	*Did you put it near the door?*
Está **al lado de** la cama.	*It is beside the bed.*
Pon la lámpara **encima de** la mesa.	*Put the lamp on top of the table.*

¿POR QUÉ SE DICE ASÍ?   **G107**

c. Sí, mamá.
1 Limpia
2 Pon
3 Ten
4 Sal
5 Ve
6 Di
7 Vuelve
8 Sé
9 Juega
10 Haz

7.6 Margin box: page 349

Additional Exercises
Textbook: pages 349–352
Cuaderno: Unidad 7, Lección 3

a. Vecinos.

1 El apartamento de los Pérez está debajo del apartamento de los Romero.
2 El apartamento de los Madrigal está a la izquierda del apartamento de los Ledesma.
3 El apartamento de los Gómez está a la derecha del apartamento de los Camúñez.
4 El apartamento de los Cameno está encima del apartamento de los Madrigal.
5 El apartamento de los Sarmiento está a la derecha del apartamento de los Cameno.
6 El apartamento de los Serrano está debajo del apartamento de los Bravo.
7 El apartamento de los Rodríguez está cinco pisos encima del apartamento de los Valdez.

b. ¿Dónde está el gato?

1 El gato está debajo de la cama.
2 El gato está entre las mesas (mesitas).
3 El gato está a la izquierda del escritorio.
4 El gato está lejos de la chica.
5 El gato está enfrente del televisor.
6 El gato está detrás de la silla.
7 El gato está en la ventana.
8 El gato está al lado del sillón.

UNIDAD 7

Vamos a practicar

a. Vecinos. ¿Dónde están los apartamentos de estas personas?

EJEMPLO Camúñez / Rodríguez
El apartamento de los Camúñez está debajo del apartamento de los Rodríguez.

1. Pérez / Romero
2. Madrigal / Ledesma
3. Gómez / Camúñez
4. Cameno / Madrigal
5. Sarmiento / Cameno
6. Serrano / Bravo
7. Rodríguez / Valdez

b. ¿Dónde está el gato? El gato no quiere salir de la casa y corre por todas partes para escaparse. Di dónde está.

MODELO **El gato está encima de la mesa.**

VOCABULARIO ÚTIL:

| al lado de | cerca de | debajo de | delante de | detrás de |
| en | encima de | entre | lejos de | enfrente de |

¿POR QUÉ SE DICE ASÍ?

7 UNIDAD

c. **¿Dónde lo pongo?** Alma está ayudándote a arreglar tu cuarto. ¿Qué le dices?

> MODELO lámpara (en / debajo de) mesa
> **Ponla en esa mesa.**

1. silla (al lado de / arriba de) escritorio
2. televisor (detrás de / enfrente de) cama
3. suéteres (en / encima de) armario
4. cómoda (al lado de / debajo de) puerta
5. estante (encima de / al lado de) mesita
6. fotos (detrás de / encima de) estante
7. lámpara (en / al lado de) sillón
8. escritorio (encima de / debajo de) ventana

ch. **¡Identifícalos!** Éstos son Lilia y sus mejores amigos. Están sentados en la clase de español. ¿Puedes identificarlos?

> MODELO Lilia está en el centro del grupo.
> **Lilia es el número cinco.**

1.   **2.**   **3.**

4.   **5.**   **6.**

7.   **8.**   **9.**

  a. Alfredo está a la derecha de Lilia.
  b. Rosa está detrás de Alfredo.
  c. Mariana está a la izquierda de Rosa.
ch. Esteban está a la izquierda de Mariana.
  d. Martín está delante de Lilia.
  e. Felipe está a la izquierda de Martín.
  f. Julia está detrás de Felipe.
  g. Rubén está delante de Alfredo.

c. **¿Dónde lo pongo?**
1 Ponla al lado de ese escritorio.
2 Ponlo enfrente de esa cama.
3 Ponlos en ese armario.
4 Ponla al lado de esa puerta.
5 Ponlo al lado de esa mesita.
6 Ponlas encima de ese estante.
7 Ponla al lado de ese sillón.
8 Ponlo debajo de esa ventana.

d. **¡Identifícalos!**
a Alfredo es el número seis.
b Rosa es el número tres.
c Mariana es el número dos.
ch Esteban es el número uno.
d Martín es el número ocho.
e Felipe es el número siete.
f Julia es el número cuatro.
g Rubén es el número nueve.

LECCIÓN 1

8.1 REFLEXIVE PRONOUNS
Used in Talking about Daily Routine

Reflexive pronouns are used when the object and the subject are identical. In these instances, the subject is doing something to itself. The forms of the reflexive pronouns are given in the chart below.

Reflexive Pronouns		
yo	**me** levanto	*I get up*
tú usted	**te** levantas **se** levanta }	*you get up*
él / ella	**se** levanta	*he/she/it gets up*
nosotros(as)	**nos** levantamos	*we get up*
vosotros(as) ustedes	**os** levantáis **se** levantan }	*you get up*
ellos / ellas	**se** levantan	*they get up*

Note the difference between these verbs when they are used with and without reflexive pronouns.

Se levanta inmediatamente.　　　　*He gets up immediately.*
Levanta a los niños temprano.　　　*He gets the children up early.*

Papá **se afeita** en el baño.　　　　　*Dad shaves in the bathroom.*
Hoy el barbero **afeita** a papá.　　　　*Today the barber shaves Dad.*

La mamá **se viste** rápidamente.　　　*The mother dresses quickly.*
La mamá **viste** a la niña.　　　　　　*The mother dresses the little girl.*

Gloria **se despierta** a las siete.　　　*Gloria wakes up at seven.*
Despierta también a su hermanito.　*She also wakes up (wakens) her little brother.*

■ Like direct and indirect object pronouns, reflexive pronouns precede conjugated verbs and follow affirmative commands, infinitives, and the **-ndo** form of the verb.

¿Dónde **me siento**?　　　　　　　　*Where shall I sit down?*
Marta, **levántate**.　　　　　　　　　*Marta, get up.*
Papá **está afeitándose**.　　　　　　*Dad is shaving.*
Tengo que **lavarme** el pelo ahora.　*I have to wash my hair now.*

¿POR QUÉ SE DICE ASÍ?

■ The following is a list of common reflexive verbs.

acostarse	*to go to bed*
afeitarse	*to shave*
arreglarse	*to get ready*
bañarse	*to bathe*
cepillarse (el pelo)	*to brush* (one's hair)
despertarse (ie)	*to wake up*
divertirse (ie, i)	*to have a good time*
dormirse (ue, u)	*to go to sleep, fall asleep*
irse	*to leave, go*
lavarse (los dientes)	*to wash up, brush* (one's teeth)
levantarse	*to get up*
peinarse	*to comb one's hair*
ponerse	*to put on* (clothes, makeup)
quitarse	*to take off* (clothes)
sentarse (ie)	*to sit down*
vestirse (i, i)	*to get dressed*

Most of the verbs have nonreflexive uses. Note, however, that some verbs change their meaning when the reflexive pronoun is added.

dormir	*to sleep*		**ir**	*to go*
dormirse	*to go to sleep, fall asleep*		**irse**	*to leave, go away*

Vamos a practicar

a. Primero me despierto. Horacio es un estudiante de intercambio en España. ¿Qué dice de su horario cuando le escribe una carta a su amigo Ramón?

despertarse	lavarse	sentarse	levantarse	ponerse
dormirse	bañarse	peinarse	irse	afeitarse

> Querido Ramón,
>
> ¿Cómo estás? Aquí todo va muy bien, pero mi día comienza muy temprano. Primero (1) a las cinco y media de la mañana. (¡Sí, hombre!) (2) a las seis menos cuarto y (3) , (4) y (5) . Luego, a las seis, (6) la ropa. A las seis y media, (7) a la mesa a desayunar y a estudiar un poco para las clases. Después del desayuno, (8) los dientes y a las siete menos cuarto (9) a la escuela. ¡Imagínate! Yo. . . ¡esa hora! ¡Y nunca (10) en clase! Te escribo más tarde.
>
> Tu amigo
> Horacio

Vamos a practicar

These exercises may be done as oral or written work.

Additional Exercises
Textbook: pages 371–372
Cuaderno: Unidad 8, Lección 1

a. Primero me despierto.
1 me despierto
2 me levanto
3 me afeito
4 me baño
5 me peino
6 me pongo
7 me siento
8 me lavo
9 me voy
10 me duermo

¿POR QUÉ SE DICE ASÍ?

b. Mamá se levantó primero.

Tú te lavas los dientes a las diez y media.

Todos nosotros nos despertamos a las seis menos cuarto.

Yo me levanto a las siete. / Me acuesto a las diez.

Mamá se levanta a las seis y cuarto y pone el café.

Mis hermanos se afeitan a las seis. / Se quitan la ropa para acostarse a las nueve y media.

Mamá y papá se sientan a la mesa a las seis y media y toman café.

c. ¡Que lo pases bien!

1 Báñate todos los días.
2 Despiértate temprano.
3 Lávate el pelo frecuentemente.
4 Lávate los dientes después de comer.
5 Lávate las manos antes de comer.
6 Duérmete temprano.
7 Péinate cada día.
8 Diviértete mucho.

ch. Tan temprano.

1 Pablo está afeitándose.
 o Pablo se está afeitando.
2 Gregorio está bañándose.
 o Gregorio se está bañando.
3 Mi madre y yo estamos sentándonos a la mesa.
 o Mi madre y yo nos estamos sentando a la mesa.
4 Enrique está lavándose el pelo.
 o Enrique se está lavando el pelo.
5 Tú estas lavándote los dientes.
 o Tú te estás lavando los dientes.
6 Leticia está poniéndose la ropa. o Leticia se está poniendo la ropa.
7 Yolanda y Raquel están levantándose. o Yolanda y Raquel se están levantando.
8 Ustedes están arreglándose.
 o Ustedes se están arreglando.

d. Todos los días.

1 Mamá y papá se levantan a las seis y veinticinco.
2 Papá se afeita a las seis y media.

---

b. Mamá se levantó primero. Berta describe el horario diario de su familia. ¿Qué dice? Forma oraciones usando palabras y frases de las dos columnas.

EJEMPLO **Mamá se levanta a las seis menos cuarto de la mañana.**

tú todos nosotros yo mamá mis hermanos mamá y papá	me acuesto a las 10:00 se afeitan a las 6:00 se levanta a las 6:15 y pone el café se sientan a la mesa a las 6:30 y toman café me levanto a las 7:00 se quitan la ropa para acostarse a las 9:30 te lavas los dientes a las 10:30 nos despertamos a las 5:45

c. ¡Que lo pases bien! Hoy Isabel se va para pasar el verano con sus abuelos. ¿Qué le dice su mamá?

MODELO acostarse temprano
Acuéstate temprano.

1. bañarse todos los días
2. despertarse temprano
3. lavarse el pelo frecuentemente
4. lavarse los dientes después de comer
5. lavarse las manos antes de comer
6. dormirse temprano
7. peinarse cada día
8. divertirse mucho

ch. Tan temprano. Son las seis de la mañana. ¿Qué están haciendo todos?

MODELO Elena / vestirse
Elena está vistiéndose. o **Elena se está vistiendo.**

1. Pablo / afeitarse
2. Gregorio / bañarse
3. mi madre y yo / sentarse a la mesa
4. Enrique / lavarse el pelo
5. tú / lavarse los dientes
6. Leticia / ponerse la ropa
7. Yolanda y Raquel / levantarse
8. ustedes / arreglarse

d. Todos los días. ¿Qué dice Julia de la rutina diaria de su familia?

MODELO Jorge
Jorge se despierta a las seis.

1. mamá y papá
2. papá
3. Jorge y Alberto
4. yo
5. Alberto
6. todos nosotros
7. mis hermanos y yo
8. Mariela
9. mamá

¿POR QUÉ SE DICE ASÍ?

---

3 Jorge y Alberto se visten (se ponen la ropa) a las siete menos cuarto.
4 Yo me baño a las siete y cinco.
5 Alberto se peina a las siete y cuarto.
6 Todos nosotros desayunamos (nos sentamos a desayunar) a las siete y veinticinco.
7 Mis hermanos y yo nos vamos al colegio a las ocho menos cuarto.
8 Mariela se lava los dientes a las ocho y media.
9 Mamá se acuesta a las diez y media.

Used in Talking about How Things Are Done

Adverbs answer the questions *how, when,* and *where* about the verb. You already know many adverbs that answer the questions *When?* and *Where?*

When? **ahora, en seguida, pronto, tarde, temprano; antes, después; a veces, nunca, siempre; ayer, hoy, mañana**

Where? **a la derecha, a la izquierda, al lado, debajo, delante, detrás, enfrente; allí, aquí; cerca, lejos**

Most adverbs that tell *how* an action is done are formed by adding **-mente** to the end of the feminine form of an adjective.

rápida + **-mente**   **rápidamente**
alegre + **-mente**   **alegremente**

Marta se levanta **rápidamente.**   *Marta gets up quickly.*
Se arregla **cuidadosamente.**   *She gets ready carefully.*
Generalmente, Andrés se despierta   *Generally Andrés wakes up early.*
   temprano.

- When two or more of these adverbs are used together in a sentence, only the last one ends in **-mente.** The others end in the feminine form of the adjective.

Se arregla **lenta y cuidadosamente.**   *She gets ready slowly and carefully.*
Habla **modesta y tímidamente.**   *He talks modestly and shyly.*

- An adjective that has a written accent keeps it when **-mente** is added.

Andrés corre **rápidamente.**   *Andrés runs quickly.*
Marta corta el chorizo **fácilmente.**   *Marta cuts the sausage easily.*

Vamos a practicar

a. Fantásticamente.   No fuiste a clase ayer. ¿Cómo describe tu amiga Luisa lo que pasó?

MODELO   señor García / cantar / estupendo
El señor García cantó estupendamente.

1. Tomasina y su hermana / bailar / fabuloso
2. el director / trabajar / alegre
3. Enriqueta / escribir una composición / tranquilo
4. Alonso y yo / contestar / correcto
5. la profesora / explicar la lección / fácil
6. Vicente y Victoria / hablar / inteligente
7. yo / correr / rápido
8. Hugo y Anita / estudiar / paciente

¿POR QUÉ SE DICE ASÍ?   **G113**

Vamos a practicar

Additional Exercises
Textbook: pages 372–373
Cuaderno: Unidad 8, Lección 1

a. Fantásticamente.
1 Tomasina y su hermana bailaron fabulosamente.
2 El director trabajó alegremente.
3 Enriqueta escribió una composición tranquilamente.
4 Alonso y yo contestamos correctamente.
5 La profesora explicó la lección fácilmente.
6 Vicente y Victoria hablaron inteligentemente.
7 Yo corrí rápidamente.
8 Hugo y Anita estudiaron pacientemente.

b. ¡Qué romántico!

1 Sí, y cantó profesional y fuertemente.
2 Sí, y leyó romántica y tristemente.
3 Sí, y habló calmada y claramente.
4 Sí, y contestó emocionada y contentamente.
5 Sí, y escucharon cortés y pacientemente.
6 Sí, y lloraron fácil y frecuentemente.
7 Sí, y bailó nerviosa y alegremente.
8 Sí, y salieron rápida y cuidadosamente.

c. Emociones. Answers
will vary. Some sample answers are given here.
Me despierto lentamente.
Me baño rápidamente.
Me lavo los dientes furiosamente.
Me pongo la ropa tranquilamente.
Me lavo el pelo alegremente.
Me siento en clase nerviosamente.

8.3 **Margin box: page 388**

---

b. ¡Qué romántico! Samuel y Sara se casaron. Tu amiga no pudo ir a la boda. ¿Cómo contestas sus preguntas?

MODELO ¿Tocó un organista? (fabuloso y fuerte)
Sí, y tocó fabulosa y fuertemente.

1. ¿Cantó un cantante? (profesional y fuerte)
2. ¿Leyó Ernesto? (romántico y triste)
3. ¿Habló la novia? (calmo y claro)
4. ¿Contestó el novio? (emocionado y contento)
5. ¿Escucharon los invitados? (cortés y paciente)
6. ¿Lloraron las madres? (fácil y frecuente)
7. ¿Bailó Rebeca? (nervioso y alegre)
8. ¿Salieron los novios? (rápido y cuidadoso)

c. Emociones. Generalmente, ¿cómo te sientes al hacer tu rutina diaria?

EJEMPLO **Me levanto alegremente.**

despertarse
bañarse
lavarse los dientes
ponerse la ropa
lavarse el pelo
sentarse en clase

{ nervioso
rápido
triste
alegre
tranquilo
cuidadoso
contento
tímido
furioso
lento }

L E C C I Ó N   2

8.3 *PRETERITE OF* **ESTAR**

■ The verb **estar** is irregular in the preterite. Its forms are like those of **tener.**

Estar	
estuv**e**	estuv**imos**
estuv**iste**	estuv**isteis**
estuv**o**	estuv**ieron**
estuv**o**	estuv**ieron**

Los bocadillos **estuvieron** excelentes.   *The sandwiches were excellent.*
La ensalada **estuvo** riquísima.   *The salad was delicious.*

¿POR QUÉ SE DICE ASÍ?

Vamos a practicar

a. ¿Dónde?   Nadie se encontró en casa de Ana ayer. ¿Dónde estuvieron todos?

MODELO   mamá / estar / 2 horas / mercado
Mi mamá estuvo dos horas en el mercado.

1. hermana / estar / 1 hora / café
2. papá / estar / 10 horas / oficina
3. hermano / estar / 8 horas / colegio
4. padres / estar / 2 horas / biblioteca
5. yo / estar / 3 horas / partido de fútbol
6. prima y yo / estar / 2 horas / cine
7. hermanita / estar / 6 horas / escuela
8. todos / estar / poco tiempo / casa

b. Delicioso.   Joaquín y su familia tuvieron un picnic ayer. ¿Cómo describe Joaquín la comida?

MODELO   bocadillos (rico)
Los bocadillos estuvieron ricos.

1. ensaladas (delicioso)
2. queso (bueno)
3. pan (fresco)
4. manzanas (malo)
5. tortillas españolas (frío)
6. chorizo (sabroso)
7. bizcochos (excelente)
8. chocolate (rico)

8.4 ABSOLUTE SUPERLATIVES: -ÍSIMO
Used to Express Extremes

The **-ísimo (-a, -os, -as)** ending may be attached to an adjective to express an extremely high degree of the quality of the adjective. Note how English uses such expressions as *exceedingly, extremely,* or *really* to express the same idea.

Los chicos son **guapísimos.**   *The guys are really cute.*
La casa es **feísima.**   *The house is extremely ugly.*

- These adjectives are formed by removing the **-o** from the masculine singular form of the adjective and adding **-ísimo (-a, -os, -as).** Note that the **-ísimo** ending always has a written accent.

Adjective	-ísimo form
alto	altísimo (-a, -os, -as)
bueno	buenísimo (-a, -os, -as)
difícil	dificilísimo (-a, -os, -as)
fácil	facilísimo (-a, -os, -as)
fuerte	fuertísimo (-a, -os, -as)
grande	grandísimo (-a, -os, -as)
malo	malísimo (-a, -os, -as)

- Some spelling rules may affect these adjectives.

c → qu	z → c	g → gu
rico ri**qu**ísimo	feliz feli**c**ísimo	largo lar**gu**ísimo

¿POR QUÉ SE DICE ASÍ?   *G115*

Vamos a practicar

Additional Exercises
Textbook: pages 388–389
Cuaderno: Unidad 8, Lección 2

a. ¿Dónde?
1 Mi hermana estuvo una hora en el café.
2 Mi papá estuvo diez horas en la oficina.
3 Mi hermano estuvo ocho horas en el colegio.
4 Mis padres estuvieron dos horas en la biblioteca.
5 Yo estuve tres horas en el partido de fútbol.
6 Mi prima y yo estuvimos dos horas en el cine.
7 Mi hermanita estuvo seis horas en la escuela.
8 Todos estuvimos poco tiempo en casa.

b. Delicioso.
1 Las ensaladas estuvieron deliciosas.
2 El queso estuvo bueno.
3 El pan estuvo fresco.
4 Las manzanas estuvieron malas.
5 Las tortillas españolas estuvieron frías.
6 El chorizo estuvo sabroso.
7 Los bizcochos estuvieron excelentes.
8 El chocolate estuvo rico.

8.4   **Margin box: page 389**

Vamos a practicar

Additional Exercises
Textbook: page 389
Cuaderno: Unidad 8, Lección 2

a. ¡Una nueva vida!

1 Mi casa es grandísima.
2 Mi escuela es modernísima.
3 Mis profesores son guapísimos.
4 Mis profesoras son elegantísimas.
5 Mi horario es buenísimo.
6 Mis amigas son inteligentísimas.
7 Mis amigos son simpatiquísimos.
8 Mi familia está contentísima.
9 Mi ciudad es hermosísima.

b. ¿Cómo son? Answers may vary slightly.

1 Su mamá es hermosísima.
2 Sus hermanos son gordísimos.
3 Elvira es inteligentísima.
4 Su hermana es flaquísima.
5 Sus abuelos son bajísimos.
6 Su tío Roberto es guapísimo.
7 Sus primos son fuertísimos.
8 Todos nosotros estamos felicísimos.

8.5 **Margin boxes: pages 390–391**

---

a. ¡Una nueva vida! La familia de Gloria acaba de mudarse a otra ciudad. ¿Cómo describe Gloria su nueva vida?

> MODELO   clases / fácil
> **Mis clases son facilísimas.**

1. casa / grande
2. escuela / moderno
3. profesores / guapo
4. profesoras / elegante
5. horario / bueno
6. amigas / inteligente
7. amigos / simpático
8. familia / contento
9. ciudad / hermoso

b. ¿Cómo son? ¿Cómo es la familia de Elvira?

> MODELO   papá
> **Su papá es altísimo.**

hermoso   alto   bajo   guapo   flaco
fuerte   inteligente feliz   gordo   grande

1. mamá
2. hermanos
3. Elvira
4. hermana

5. abuelos
6. tío Roberto
7. primos
8. todos nosotros

8.5   COMPARATIVES

When two qualities or quantities are compared, Spanish uses **más** and **menos**.

Este libro es **más** interesante.	*This book is more interesting.*
Me gusta éste **menos.**	*I like this one less.*
Está **más** cerca de la escuela.	*It's closer to the school.*
Ella es **menos** alta.	*She's shorter.*

- When both things being compared are expressed, Spanish uses **más . . . que** to express *more . . . than.*

Es **más** alto **que** su padre.	*He's taller than his father.*

- *Less . . . than* is expressed in Spanish by **menos . . . que.**

Esta cama es **menos** dura **que** la de abuelita.	*This bed is softer (less hard) than grandmother's.*

- When the things being compared are equal, Spanish uses the expression **tan . . . como.**

> Son **tan** cómodos **como** nuestros sillones.
> *They are as comfortable as our chairs.*
>
> Hablas **tan** bien **como** la profesora.
> *You talk as well as the teacher.*

- Like other adjectives, adjectives that are compared agree in number and gender with the nouns they modify.

> Teres**a** es más alt**a** que Arturo.
> **Los** profesor**es** están tan ocupad**os** como los estudiantes.

- The adjectives **bueno** and **malo** have special comparative forms: **mejor** and **peor.** Like other adjectives that end in consonants, the plural forms end in **-es: mejores, peores.**

> Salió **mejor** que nunca la tortilla.
> *The tortilla turned out better than ever.*
>
> Este restaurante es **peor** que el otro.
> *This restaurant is worse than the other one.*
>
> Estos jugadores son **peores.**
> *These players are worse.*
>
> Estas alfombras son **mejores.**
> *These carpets are better.*

Vamos a practicar

a. ¿Quién es más . . . ? Di cómo se comparan estos individuos.

MODELO ¿Quién es más alto?
La señora Delgado es más alta que Tomasito.

Señora Delgado   Tomasito

1. ¿Quién es más gordo?

Canela   Lobo

2. ¿Quién es más rubio?

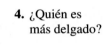

Germán   Ana

3. ¿Quién es más alto?

Marta   Esteban

4. ¿Quién es más delgado?

Gonzalo   Teodoro

5. ¿Quién es más bajo?

Golfo   Princesa

6. ¿Quién es más guapo?

Arturo   Frankenstein

Vamos a practicar

Additional Exercises
Textbook: pages 390–391
Cuaderno: Unidad 8, Lección 2

a. ¿Quién es más . . . ?
1 Canela es más gordo que Lobo.
2 Germán es más rubio que Ana.
3 Marta es más alta que Esteban.
4 Teodoro es más delgado que Gonzalo.
5 Princesa es más baja que Golfo.
6 Arturo es más guapo que Frankenstein.

b. No son buenos.

1 Su arquero es menos rápido que nuestro arquero.
2 Sus defensas son menos grandes que nuestros defensas.
3 Sus jugadores son menos fuertes que nuestros jugadores.
4 Sus aficionados son menos alegres que nuestros aficionados.
5 Sus uniformes son menos atractivos que nuestros uniformes.
6 Su entreneador es menos inteligente que nuestro entrenador.
7 Sus partidos son menos interesantes que nuestros partidos.
8 Su escuela es menos entusiasta que nuestra escuela.

c. ¿Qué prefieres?

Answers may vary slightly.
1 Me gustan más las papas fritas. o Me gusta menos la fruta.
2 Me gusta más el jamón. o Me gusta menos el chorizo.
3 Me gustan más las manzanas. o Me gustan menos las naranjas.
4 Me gusta más la ensalada. o Me gusta menos el postre.
5 Me gusta más el café. o Me gusta menos la leche.
6 Me gustan más las fresas. o Me gustan menos las cerezas.
7 Me gusta más el almuerzo. o Me gusta menos el desayuno.
8 Me gusta más la pizza. o Me gusta menos el cochinillo asado.

ch. Al contrario.

1 Al contrario, tu papá no es tan fuerte como mi papá.
2 Al contrario, tu papá no es tan guapo como mi papá.
3 Al contrario, tu papá no es tan inteligente como mi papá.
4 Al contrario, tu papá no es tan simpático como mi papá.

---

b. No son buenos. Los estudiantes de la escuela de Ricardo están hablando del equipo de fútbol de su escuela rival. ¿Qué dicen?

MODELO equipo: organizado
Su equipo es menos organizado que nuestro equipo.

1. arquero: rápido
2. defensas: grande
3. jugadores: fuerte
4. aficionados: alegre
5. uniformes: atractivo
6. entrenador: inteligente
7. partidos: interesante
8. escuela: entusiasta

c. ¿Qué prefieres? Di cuál te gusta más o cuál te gusta menos.

MODELO ¿Los bocadillos o las hamburguesas?
Me gustan más los bocadillos. o
Me gustan menos las hamburguesas.

1. ¿Las papas fritas o la fruta?
2. ¿El jamón o el chorizo?
3. ¿Las manzanas o las naranjas?
4. ¿La ensalada o el postre?
5. ¿El café o la leche?
6. ¿Las fresas o las cerezas?
7. ¿El almuerzo o el desayuno?
8. ¿La pizza o el cochinillo asado?

ch. Al contrario. Luci y Carlitos están hablando de sus papás. ¿Cómo le contesta Carlitos a Luci?

MODELO Luci: Mi papá es más alto que tu papá.
Carlitos: **Al contrario, tu papá no es tan alto como mi papá.**

1. Mi papá es más fuerte que tu papá.
2. Mi papá es más guapo que tu papá.
3. Mi papá es más inteligente que tu papá.
4. Mi papá es más simpático que tu papá.
5. Mi papá es más valiente que tu papá.
6. Mi papá es más rico que tu papá.
7. Mi papá es más famoso que tu papá.
8. Mi papá es más popular que tu papá.

d. ¿Mejor o peor? ¿Cómo te comparas tú?

EJEMPLO ¿Quién canta mejor que tú?
Mi mamá canta mejor que yo. o
Nadie canta mejor que yo. o
Todos cantan mejor que yo.

1. ¿Quién juega tenis mejor que tú?
2. ¿Quién nada peor que tú?
3. ¿Quién prepara la comida mejor que tú?
4. ¿Quién escribe peor que tú?
5. ¿Quién sabe geografía mejor que tú?
6. ¿Quién baila peor que tú?
7. ¿Quién pasea en bicicleta mejor que tú?
8. ¿Quién juega béisbol peor que tú?
9. ¿Quién habla español peor que tú?
10. ¿Quién toca la guitarra mejor que tú?

¿POR QUÉ SE DICE ASÍ?

---

5 Al contrario, tu papá no es tan valiente como mi papá.
6 Al contrario, tu papá no es tan rico como mi papá.
7 Al contrario, tu papá no es tan famoso como mi papá.
8 Al contrario, tu papá no es tan popular como mi papá.

d. ¿Mejor o peor? Answers will vary.

e. La mejor mueblería. Los muebles de la Tienda Plus son muy buenos, mientras que los muebles de la Tienda Cero son terribles. ¿Cómo se comparan estos muebles?

MODELO lámparas de la Tienda Plus
Las lámparas de la Tienda Plus son mejores que las lámparas de la Tienda Cero.

mesitas de la Tienda Cero
Las mesitas de la Tienda Cero son peores que las mesitas de la Tienda Plus.

1. sofás de la Tienda Cero
2. sillas de la Tienda Plus
3. muebles de la Tienda Cero
4. mesas de la Tienda Plus
5. televisores de la Tienda Cero
6. sillones de la Tienda Cero
7. neveras de la Tienda Plus
8. camas de la Tienda Plus

LECCIÓN 3

8.6 PRESENT TENSE: SUMMARY

The present tense is used to talk about what generally happens, what is happening now, or what does happen. There are three sets of endings for the three types of verbs.

Present Tense Verb Endings		
-ar	**-er**	**-ir**
-o	**-o**	**-o**
-as	**-es**	**-es**
-a	**-e**	**-e**
-amos	**-emos**	**-imos**
-áis	**-éis**	**-ís**
-an	**-en**	**-en**

Three sample regular verbs are:

Cantar	**Aprender**	**Subir**
canto	aprendo	subo
cantas	aprendes	subes
canta	aprende	sube
cantamos	aprendemos	subimos
cantáis	aprendéis	subís
cantan	aprenden	suben

¿POR QUÉ SE DICE ASÍ?

_____ **G119**

e. La mejor mueblería.
1 Los sofás de la Tienda Cero son peores que los sofás de la Tienda Plus.
2 Las sillas de la Tienda Plus son mejores que las sillas de la Tienda Cero.
3 Los muebles de la Tienda Cero son peores que los muebles de la Tienda Plus.
4 Las mesas de la Tienda Plus son mejores que las mesas de la Tienda Cero.
5 Los televisores de la Tienda Cero son peores que los televisores de la Tienda Plus.
6 Los sillones de la Tienda Cero son peores que los sillones de la Tienda Plus.
7 Las neveras de la Tienda Plus son mejores que las neveras de la Tienda Cero.
8 Las camas de la Tienda Plus son mejores que las camas de la Tienda Cero.

8.6 **Margin box: page 408**

- Some verbs in the present tense undergo a change in the stem vowel of all persons except the **nosotros(as)** and **vosotros(as)** forms.

Pensar	Poder	Pedir
e → ie	o → ue	e → i
pienso	puedo	pido
piensas	puedes	pides
piensa	puede	pide
pensamos	podemos	pedimos
pensáis	podéis	pedís
piensan	pueden	piden

- Some verbs in the present tense have irregular **yo** forms.

conocer:	**conozco**	traer:	**traigo**
dar:	**doy**	ver:	**veo**
hacer:	**hago**	decir:	**digo**
poner:	**pongo**	oír:	**oigo**
saber:	**sé**	tener:	**tengo**
salir:	**salgo**	venir:	**vengo**

- There are also verbs in the present tense that have irregular endings.

Estar	Ser	Ir
estoy	soy	voy
estás	eres	vas
está	es	va
estamos	somos	vamos
estáis	sois	vais
están	son	van

Vamos a practicar

Additional Exercises
Textbook: page 408
Cuaderno: Unidad 8, Lección 3

Vamos a practicar

a. **¡Dos semanas!** Celia está pasando dos semanas en un campamento. Para saber qué le escribe a su amiga, completa su carta con la forma apropiada de los verbos indicados.

1. estar	6. comer	11. ser	16. practicar	21. tener
2. estar	7. tener	12. almorzar	17. ser	22. querer
3. levantarse	8. hacer	13. dar	18. cantar	23. escribir
4. ir	9. ir	14. dormir	19. acostarse	24. poder
5. servir	10. nadar	15. preferir	20. encantar	25. decir

¿POR QUÉ SE DICE ASÍ?

Querida Sonia,

¿Cómo __1__ ? Yo __2__ muy contenta aquí. Todos los días nosotros __3__ muy temprano. Luego __4__ al comedor donde nos __5__ el desayuno. Yo generalmente __6__ mucho.

Después del desayuno, __7__ una clase de artesanías. Nosotros __8__ cosas muy bonitas en esa clase. A las 10:30 yo __9__ a la clase de natación. Todos __10__ en un río muy grande. ¡ __11__ muy divertido!

Nosotros __12__ al mediodía y luego nos __13__ tiempo para una siesta. Yo normalmente no __14__ porque __15__ escribir cartas o leer. Por la tarde nosotros __16__ varios deportes—tenis, volibol, béisbol. El entrenador __17__ muy simpático.

Por la noche __18__ y __19__ temprano. ¡Nos __20__ el campamento a todos! ¡Tú __21__ que venir el año que viene!

Escríbeme pronto. Yo __22__ recibir muchas cartas de ti. Si no me __23__ , yo no __24__ saber lo que está pasando contigo y con todos nuestros amigos. Mis padres no me __25__ nada. ¡Escribe!

Recibe un abrazo de tu amiga
Celia

b. ¿Cuándo?   Di cuándo haces estas cosas.

MODELO   estudiar mucho
Estudio mucho durante el año académico.

salir todas las noches
Salgo todas las noches durante las vacaciones.

siempre	durante las vacaciones	durante el año académico	nunca
●	●	●	●

1. hacer la tarea
2. levantarse tarde
3. leer muchas revistas
4. ver televisión
5. ir al campo
6. jugar fútbol
7. oír muchos discos y casetes
8. hablar por teléfono por horas
9. pasear en bicicleta
10. acostarse temprano
11. practicar deportes
12. dormir muchas horas
13. salir mucho con los amigos
14. llevar ropa muy informal

¿POR QUÉ SE DICE ASÍ?

G121

a. ¡Dos semanas!
1 estás
2 estoy
3 nos levantamos
4 vamos
5 sirven
6 como
7 tengo
8 hacemos
9 voy
10 nadamos
11 Es
12 almorzamos
13 dan
14 duermo
15 prefiero
16 practicamos
17 es
18 cantamos
19 nos acostamos
20 encanta
21 tienes
22 quiero
23 escribes
24 puedo
25 dicen

b. ¿Cuándo? For additional practice, have students tell when these things are done by others such as the class, their best friend, the teacher. Answers will vary. Some sample answers:
1 Hago la tarea durante el año académico.
2 Me levanto tarde durante las vacaciones.
3 Siempre leo muchas revistas.
4 Siempre veo televisión.
5 Nunca voy al campo.
6 Siempre juego fútbol.
7 Siempre oigo muchos discos y casetes.
8 Nunca hablo por teléfono por horas.
9 Paseo en bicicleta durante las vacaciones.
10 Me acuesto temprano durante el año académico.
11 Siempre practico deportes.
12 Duermo muchas horas durante las vacaciones.
13 Salgo mucho con los amigos durante las vacaciones.
14 Siempre llevo ropa muy informal.

8.7 *PRESENT PROGRESSIVE: SUMMARY*

The present progressive is used to tell what is happening at the moment of speaking. It is formed with the verb **estar** and the **-ndo** form of the verb.

> No puedo ayudarte ahora porque **estoy** estudi**ando** español.
> **Estamos** com**iendo** una tortilla española.
> ¿Qué **están** beb**iendo** los niños?

■ Stem-changing **-ir** verbs undergo a vowel change in the **-ndo** form.

dormir	**durmiendo**
seguir	**siguiendo**
pedir	**pidiendo**
repetir	**repitiendo**
decir	**diciendo**

■ When an unstressed **i** occurs between two vowels, the **-iendo** form becomes **-yendo**.

leer	**leyendo**
traer	**trayendo**
construir	**construyendo**

Vamos a practicar

a. **¿Tienen sueño?**   Son las diez de la noche. Según Silvia, ¿qué están haciendo todos?

MODELO Marta / escuchar / radio / dormitorio
Marta está escuchando la radio en el dormitorio.

1. mamá / leer / periódico / sala
2. Carlos y Elena / estudiar / dormitorio
3. yo / comer / sándwich / cocina
4. papá / ver / televisión / sala de familia
5. abuelita / escribir / carta / comedor
6. abuelita y yo / tomar / refresco / cocina
7. los bebés / dormir / habitación
8. Toni / lavarse / dientes / baño

b. **¡Vacaciones, por fin!**   Es el primer día de las vacaciones de verano. ¿Qué están haciendo todos?

MODELO Ángela

Ángela está visitando a sus abuelos.

¿POR QUÉ SE DICE ASÍ?

Additional Exercises
Textbook: page 408
Cuaderno: Unidad 8, Lección 3

a. ¿Tienen sueño?
1 Mamá está leyendo el periódico en la sala.
2 Carlos y Elena están estudiando en el dormitorio.
3 Yo estoy comiendo un sándwich en la cocina.
4 Papá está viendo televisión en la sala de familia.
5 Abuelita está escribiendo una carta en el comedor.
6 Abuelita y yo estamos tomando refrescos en la cocina.
7 Los bebés están durmiendo en la habitación.
8 Toni está lavándose los dientes en el baño.

1. Lisa y Rafael

2. Miguel

3. Los Tigres

4. David

5. la familia Garza

6. Marisela

7. Diana y Ofelia

8. Vicente y Leona

9. todos

8.8 PRETERITE: SUMMARY

The preterite is used to talk about what happened in the past. It has two sets of endings, one for **-ar** verbs and the other for **-er** and **-ir** verbs.

Preterite Regular Verb Endings	
-ar	**-er / -ir**
-é	-í
-aste	-iste
-ó	-ió
-amos	-imos
-asteis	-isteis
-aron	-ieron

Three sample verbs are:

Comprar	Romper	Salir
compré	rompí	salí
compraste	rompiste	saliste
compró	rompió	salió
compramos	rompimos	salimos
comprasteis	rompisteis	salisteis
compraron	rompieron	salieron

¿POR QUÉ SE DICE ASÍ?

G123

Many irregular verbs in the preterite have an irregular stem and use one set of endings for **-ar, -er** and **-ir** verbs.

Preterite Irregular Verb Endings
-ar /-er / -ir
-e -iste -o
-imos -isteis -ieron

Note that the **yo** and the **ustedes / él / ella** endings do not have a written accent.

The following are verbs in this category that you have studied.

estar:	**estuv-**	estuve, estuviste, estuvo, estuvimos, . . .
tener:	**tuv-**	tuve, tuviste, tuvo, tuvimos, . . .
poder:	**pud-**	pude, pudiste, pudo, pudimos, . . .
poner:	**pus-**	puse, pusiste, puso, pusimos, . . .
hacer:	**hic-**	hice, hiciste, **hizo**, hicimos, . . .
decir:	**dij-**	dije, dijiste, dijo, dijimos, dijisteis, **dijeron**
traer:	**traj-**	traje, trajiste, trajo, trajimos, trajisteis, **trajeron**

Note that there is a **c → z** spelling change in **hacer.** Also note that verbs with stems ending in **j** drop the **i** in the **ustedes / ellos / ellas** form: **dijeron, trajeron.**

■ The following three irregular verbs follow a different pattern.

ir: fui, fuiste, fue, fuimos, fuisteis, fueron
ser: fui, fuiste, fue, fuimos, fuisteis, fueron
dar: di, diste, dio, dimos, disteis, dieron

■ Some verbs undergo spelling changes in the **yo** form of the preterite.

c changes to **qu** before **e** or **i:** buscar → **busqué**
g changes to **gu** before **e** or **i:** llegar → **llegué**
z changes to **c** before **e** or **i:** comenzar → **comencé**

■ In **-er** and **-ir** verbs whose stems end in a vowel, the unaccented **i** changes to **y** in the third person singular and plural forms.

Leer	
leí	leímos
leíste	leísteis
leyó	**leyeron**

Oír	
oí	oímos
oíste	oísteis
oyó	**oyeron**

Vamos a practicar _____

a. Fuimos a España.   Laura y Rubén están hablando de las vacaciones de su familia en España el verano pasado. ¿Qué dicen que hicieron?

EJEMPLO   **Tú y yo nos divertimos en Valencia.**

	subimos a la torre en Segovia
tú	durmieron muy poco en Toledo
Tina y Marlena	bailamos en una discoteca
yo	estuvo muy contento en Bilbao
papá	fuiste de compras en Barcelona
tú y yo	se compraron unas camisas rojas en Madrid
todos	comió muy bien en Granada
mamá	cambié dinero en Burgos
	vieron una película en Valencia

b. ¡Una fiesta!   Ayer hubo una gran fiesta en casa de los Esparza. ¿Cómo ayudaron todos a hacer las preparaciones?

MODELO   papá / comprar / helado
          Papá compró el helado.

1. Alicia y Diana / escribir / invitaciones
2. padres / pedir / pastel
3. Martín / ir por / pastel
4. tú / enviar / invitaciones
5. todos nosotros / tener que / limpiar la casa
6. Julieta / conseguir / música
7. Carlitos / traer / refrescos
8. yo / buscar / música
9. Manuel y José / poner / mesa
10. mamá / hacer / comida

Vamos a practicar

Additional Exercises
Textbook: page 409
Cuaderno: Unidad 8, Lección 3

a. Fuimos a España.
Answers will vary. Some sample answers:
1 Tú fuiste de compras en Barcelona.
2 Tina y Marlena durmieron muy poco en Toledo.
3 Yo cambié dinero en Burgos.
4 Papá estuvo muy contento en Bilbao.
5 Tú y yo subimos a la torre en Segovia.
6 Todos bailamos en una discoteca.
7 Mamá comió muy bien en Granada.

b. ¡Una fiesta!
1 Alicia y Diana escribieron invitaciones.
2 Los padres pidieron el pastel.
3 Martín fue por el pastel.
4 Tú enviaste las invitaciones.
5 Todos nosotros tuvimos que limpiar la casa.
6 Julieta consiguió la música.
7 Carlitos trajo los refrescos.
8 Yo busqué la música.
9 Manuel y José pusieron la mesa.
10 Mamá hizo la comida.

MATERIAS DE CONSULTA

C1

APÉNDICE

EL ABECEDARIO

Note that the Spanish alphabet has four additional letters: **ch, ll, ñ,** and **rr.** When alphabetizing in Spanish, or when looking up words in a dictionary or names in a telephone directory, items beginning with **ch** or **ll** are listed separately after those beginning with **c** or **l,** respectively. Within a word, **ch** follows **c, ll** follows **l,**, **ñ** follows **n,** and **rr** follows **r.**

a	*a*	n	*ene*
b	*be* (*be* grande, *be* larga, *be* de burro)	ñ	*eñe*
		o	*o*
c	*ce*	p	*pe*
ch	*che*	q	*cu*
d	*de*	r	*ere*
e	*e*	rr	*erre*
f	*efe*	s	*ese*
g	*ge*	t	*te*
h	*hache*	u	*u*
i	*i*	v	*ve, uve* (*ve* chica, *ve* corta, *ve* de vaca)
j	*jota*		
k	*ka*	w	*doble ve, doble uve*
l	*ele*	x	*equis*
ll	*elle*	y	*i griega, ye*
m	*eme*	z	*zeta*

PRONUNCIACIÓN

■ Las vocales

Spanish has five vowel sounds: **a, e, i, o,** and **u.** The pronunciation of these vowels is short, clear, and tense and does not vary. When speaking Spanish, avoid the tendency to lengthen the vowels or to vary their pronunciation, as in English. For pronunciation practice of the vowel sounds in Spanish, see the section titled **Pronunciación y ortografía** in the *Cuaderno de actividades,* Unidad 1, Lección 1.

■ Las consonantes

For pronunciation practice of the consonant sounds in Spanish, see **Pronunciación y ortografía,** *Cuaderno de actividades,* Unidad 1, Lección 1.

■ Acentuación

All Spanish words have one stressed syllable, which may or may not have a written accent.

A. Spanish words that end in a vowel, in **-n,** or in **-s** are regularly stressed on the next-to-the-last syllable.

    arte   profe**so**ra   **lla**man   panta**lo**nes

B. Spanish words that end in a consonant other than **-n** or **-s** are regularly stressed on the last syllable.

    us**ted**   varie**dad**   capi**tal**   direc**tor**

C. Words that do not follow the preceding rules require a written accent.

    fan**tás**tico   **lás**tima   invita**ción**   in**glés**

VOCABULARIO
ESPAÑOL - INGLÉS

VOCABULARIO
español-inglés

This **Vocabulario** includes all active and most passive words and expressions in **¡DIME!** (Exact cognates, conjugated verb forms, and proper nouns used as passive vocabulary are generally omitted.) A number in parentheses follows all entries. This number refers to the unit and lesson in which the word or phrase is introduced (and, when there is more than one number, reentered). The number **(3.1)**, for example, refers to **Unidad 3**, **Lección 1.** The unit and lesson number of active vocabulary—words and expressions students are expected to remember and use—is given in boldface type: **(3.1)**. The unit and lesson number of passive vocabulary—words and expressions students are expected to recognize and understand—is given in lightface type: (3.1). The abbreviation **LP** stands for **Lección Preliminar.**

The gender of nouns is indicated as *m.* (masculine) or *f.* (feminine). When a noun designates a person or an animal, both the masculine and feminine form is given. Irregular plural forms of active nouns are indicated. Adjectives ending in **-o** are given in the masculine singular with the feminine ending (**a**) in parentheses. Verbs are listed in the infinitive form, except for a few irregular verb forms presented early in the text. Stem-changing verbs appear with the change in parentheses after the infinitive.

All items are alphabetized in Spanish: **ch** follows **c, ll** follows **l, ñ** follows **n,** and **rr** follows **r.**

The following abbreviations are used:

adj.	adjective	*m.*	masculine
adv.	adverb	*pl.*	plural
art.	article	*poss.*	possessive
conj.	conjunction	*pres.*	present
dir. obj.	direct object	*pret.*	preterite
f.	feminine	*pron.*	pronoun
fam.	familiar	*refl.*	reflexive
form.	formal	*sing.*	singular
imper.	imperative	*subj.*	subject
indir. obj.	*in*direct object		
inf.	infinitive		

A

a to (3.1)

  a *(personal)* **(4.2)**

  a continuación following, what follows

  a eso de around *(time)* (8.2)

  a la/las . . . at . . .*(time)* **(2.1)**

  a la parrilla grilled (8.3)

  a mí/ti/usted/él/ella to me/you *(fam. sing.)* / you *(form. sing.)*/ him/her **(3.1)**

  a pie walking, on foot **(3.3)**

  a propósito by the way **(7.3)**

  a veces sometimes **(3.3)**

abogado *m.,* **abogada** *f.* lawyer **(4.2)**

abril *m.* April **(4.1)**

abrir to open **(7.2)**

abuela *f.* grandmother **(4.1)**

abuelo *m.* grandfather **(4.1)**

  abuelos *m. pl.* grandparents **(4.1)**

aburrido(a) bored **(2.2)**

acá here, around here (7.3)

acabar de to have just (4.2)

académico(a) academic (7.1)

accidente *m.* accident **(7.3)**

aceite *m.* **de oliva** olive oil (8.3)

aceptar to accept **(6.2)**

acompañar to accompany **(7.2)**

acostarse (ue) to go to bed **(8.1)**

acostumbrarse a to become accustomed to (8.3)

actitud *f.* attitude (7.1)

actividad *f.* activity (3.1)

activo(a) active **(8.2)**

actor *m.* actor **(4.2)**

actriz *f.* actress **(4.2)**

acueducto *m.* aqueduct **(8.3)**

además besides, in addition (4.1)

adiós good-bye **(1.1)**

¿adónde? (to) where? **(3.1) (4.2)**

adorno *m.* decoration (8.3)

adulto *m.,* **adulta** *f.* adult (5.1)

afectar to affect **(7.1)**

afeitarse to shave **(8.1)**

aficionado *m.,* **aficionada** *f.* fan **(7.1)**

afiche *m.* poster (2.3)

agitado(a) agitated, upset (7.2)

agosto *m.* August **(4.1)**

agradable agreeable, nice **(6.2)**

agradado(a) pleased (7.3)

agregar to add (8.3)

agricultor *m.,* **agricultora** *f.* farmer **(4.2)**

agua *f.* water **(5.3)**

  agua mineral mineral water **(5.3)**

  agua mineral con gas carbonated mineral water (5.3)

  agua mineral sin gas noncarbonated mineral water (5.3)

¡ah! oh! (LP)

ahora now **(1.3)**

ahorro *m.* saving (LP)

¡ajá! aha! **(LP)**

ajo *m.* garlic **(8.3)**

al *conj.* **(a + el)** to the + *m. sing.* noun **(3.1)**

  al aire libre outdoors **(3.1)**

  al contrario on the contrary **(1.3)**

  al cruzar upon crossing **(5.1)**

  al final at the end (5.1)

  al gusto to one's liking, to taste *(cooking)* **(8.3)**

  al lado de beside, next to **(5.1) (7.3)**

  al principio at first **(7.2)**

alameda *f.* tree-lined walk, park (3.1)

albóndiga *f.* meatball **(8.3)**

  albondiguitas *f. pl.* little meatballs (8.3)

alborotado(a) exciting, lively (6.1)

alcanzar to catch up, reach (6.3)

alcázar *m.* fortress, royal palace **(8.2)**

alcoba *f.* bedroom **(8.2)**

alegre happy, joyful (6.1)

alegremente gladly, joyfully **(8.1)**

alemán *m.* German *(language)* (3.1)

alfombra *f.* rug, carpet **(8.2)**

álgebra *m.* algebra **(2.1)**

algo something **(2.3) (3.3)**

  ¿algo más? anything else? **(8.1)**

alguien someone **(3.3)**

almacén (*pl.* **almacenes**) *m.* department store **(5.1)**

almorzar (ue) to eat lunch **(5.3)**

almuerzo *m.* lunch **(2.1) (5.3) (6.3)**

alojamiento *m.* lodging, housing (6.3)

alquilar to rent **(2.3)**

alrededor (de) around (7.2)

¡alto! stop! (6.3)

alto(a) tall (1.3); high *(volume)* (7.2)

allá there, over there (6.1)

allí there, over there **(7.3)**

amarillo(a) yellow **(5.2)**

ambiente *m.* ambience (6.1)

americano(a) American **(1.2)**

amigo *m.*, **amiga** *f.* friend **(1.1)**

amistad *f.* friendship (2.3)

amor *m.* love (4.1)

anaranjado(a) orange **(5.2)**

ancho(a) wide (6.1)

andar to walk (7.2)

animal *m.* animal **(4.3)**

anoche last night **(6.1)**

antepasado(a) previous, before last **(7.1)**

anterior previous (7.2)

antes de before **(6.3)**

anticipemos let's anticipate (LP)

antiguo(a) ancient, old (3.2)

antipático(a) disagreeable **(2.2)**

antropología *f.* anthropology (3.2)

anuncio *m.* announcement, advertisement (4.1)

año *m.* year **(4.1)**

apagado(a) turned off *(equipment)* (7.2)

aparcamiento *m.* parking (5.2)

apariencia *f.* **física** physical appearance (5.1)

apellido *m.* last name, surname **(4.1)**

apenas scarcely, hardly **(7.2)**

aperitivo *m.* appetizer, hors d'oeuvres (8.3)

apetito *m.* appetite **(8.2)**

aplicado(a) applied (6.2)

aprender to learn **(6.2)**

apretado(a) tight (6.1)

aquel, aquella, aquellos, aquellas that, those *(over there)* **(7.1)**

aquí here **(3.1)**

árbitro *m. f.* umpire, referee **(7.1)**

Argentina *f.* Argentina **(1.2)**

argentino(a) Argentine, Argentinian (1.2)

armario *m.* closet **(7.3)**

arquero *m.*, **arquera** *f.* goalie, goalkeeper *(soccer)* **(7.3)**

arreglar to fix (7.3)

arreglarse to get ready **(8.1)**

arreglo *m.* arrangement (4.2)

arte *m. f.* art **(2.1)**

  bellas artes fine arts (3.1)

artesanía *f.* handicrafts (6.1)

artículo *m.* article **(4.3)**

artista *m. f.* artist, entertainer **(4.2)**

artístico (a) artistic

  gimnasia artística gymnastics (7.1)

  patinaje artístico figure skating (7.1)

ascensor *m.* elevator (5.2)

asesinar to assassinate (6.3)

asesinato *m.* assassination (3.3)

así so, thus (6.1)

aspirina *f.* aspirin (7.2)

Asunción Asunción *(capital of Paraguay)* **(1.2)**

atacar to attack **(6.3)**

atención *f.* attention (4.1)

aterrorizado(a) terrified (7.3)

atlético(a) athletic **(1.3)**

atletismo *m.* track and field **(7.1)**

atracción *f.* attraction (6.3)

audición *f.* audition (1.3); hearing (7.2)

audífonos *m. pl.* headphones **(7.2)**

auditivo(a) auditory (7.2)

auditorio *m.* auditorium (1.3)

aun even (7.3)

aún still, yet (7.3)

auto *m.* auto, car **(6.3)**

autobús *m.* (*pl.* **autobuses**) bus **(3.2)**

automovilismo *m.* sports car racing **(7.1)**

autor *m.* **autora** *f.* author **(4.2)**

aventura *f.* adventure (6.2)

aventurero *m.,* **aventurera** *f.* adventurer (8.1)

avión *m.* plane **(6.3)**

¡ay! oh!; oh, no! **(LP) (1.1)** ouch! (7.1)

ayer yesterday **(6.1)**

ayudar to help **(6.2)**

ayuntamiento *m.* city hall (7.3)

azteca *m. f.* Aztec **(6.3)**

azul blue **(5.2)**

B

bailar to dance **(3.1)**

baile *m.* dance **(2.3)**

bajar lower **(7.2)**

bajarse to get off, get down **(5.1)**

bajo(a) short **(1.3)**

baloncesto *m.* basketball **(7.1)**

ballet *m.* **folklórico** ballet folklórico *(Mexican folk dance troupe)* **(6.1)**

banco *m.* bank **(5.1)**

banda *f.* band **(6.2)**

bañarse to take a bath **(8.1)**

baño *m.* bathroom **(2.2) (8.2)**

barco *m.* boat (6.3)

barrio *m.* neighborhood (7.3)

base *f.* base **(7.1)**

bastante enough (3.2)

bata *f.* bathrobe **(7.3)**

bastar to be enough (6.1)

batalla *f.* battle **(6.3)**

bateador *m.,* **bateadora** *f.* batter *(baseball)* **(7.1)**

batido *m.* milkshake (8.3)

batir to beat (8.3)

bautizo *m.* baptism (6.1)

beber to drink **(2.3)**

béisbol *m.* baseball **(7.1)**

bello(a) beautiful **(8.2)**

    bellas artes fine arts **(3.1)**

biblioteca *f.* library **(2.2)**

bicicleta *f.* bicycle **(2.3)**

bien well, okay, fine **(1.1)**

  bien, gracias fine, thank you **(1.1)**

  ¡bien hecho! well done! **(7.1)**

  bien, ¿y tú? fine, and you? *(fam. sing.)* **(1.1)**

bienvenido(a) welcome **(7.3)**

bilingüe bilingual (1.3)

billete *m.* bill *(money)* (5.1)

biología biology (2.2)

bizcocho *m.* sponge cake **(5.3)**

blanco(a) white **(5.2)**

bloquear to block **(7.3)**

blusa *f.* blouse **(5.2)**

boca *f.* mouth **(7.2)**

bocadillo *m.* sandwich **(8.1)**

boda *f.* wedding **(4.2)**

Bogotá Bogotá *(capital of Colombia)* **(1.2)**

boleta *f.* report card **(2.1)**

boleto *m.* ticket **(6.2)**

bolígrafo *m.* ballpoint pen **(LP)**

bolita *f.* little ball **(8.3)**

Bolivia *f.* Bolivia **(1.2)**

boliviano(a) Bolivian (1.2)

bombero *m.,* **bombera** *f.* fire fighter **(4.2)**

bombón *m.* chocolate covered candy, bonbon **(7.3)**

bonito(a) pretty **(1.3)**

borrador *m.* eraser **(LP)**

bosque *m.* forest **(3.2)**

botas *f. pl.* boots **(5.2)**

boxeo *m.* boxing **(7.1)**

Brasil *m.* Brazil **(2.1)**

Brasilia Brasilia *(capital of Brazil)* **(2.1)**

¡bravo! bravo!, hooray! **(4.1)**

brazo *m.* arm **(7.2)**

brillante brilliant (4.2)

broma *f.* joke **(7.3)**

bruto *m.* brute **(7.1)**

buen good **(3.2)**

  ¡buen provecho! enjoy your meal! (8.1)

bueno(a) good **(2.2)**

buenas noches   good evening, good night **(1.1)**

buenas tardes   good afternoon **(1.1)**

buenos días   good morning, good day **(1.1)**

Buenos Aires   Buenos Aires *Ècapital of Argentina)* **(1.2)**

buscar   to look for **(5.3)**

~~~~C~~~~

caballeros *m. pl.*   gentlemen (5.2)

caballo *m.*   horse (6.1)

cabeza *f.*   head **(7.2)**

cabezazo *m.*   header *(soccer shot)* **(7.1)**

cacatúa   cockatoo *(tropical bird)* (6.2)

cada   every, each (4.1)

caerse   to fall, fall down (7.2)

café *m.*   café **(3.1)**   coffee **(5.3)**

cafetería *f.*   cafeteria **(2.2)**

caja *f.*   cash register, cashier's station (5.2)

calandria *f.*   horse-drawn carriage **(6.3)**

calcetines *m. pl.*   socks **(5.2)**
   par de calcetines   pair of socks **(5.2)**

calcomanía *f.*   decal, sticker (2.3)

calendario *m.*   calendar (4.1)

caliente   hot **(5.3)**

calificar   to grade **(2.3) (3.2)**

calor *m.*   heat **(3.2)**
   hacer calor   to be hot *(weather)* **(3.2)**
   tener calor   to be hot *(physical condition)* **(5.3)**

¡cállate!   be quiet! **(8.1)**

calle *f.*   street **(5.1)**

cama *f.*   bed **(7.3)**

camarera *f.*   waitress **(4.2)**

camarero *m.*   waiter **(4.2)**

cambiar   to change; to exchange *(money)* **(5.1)**

caminante *m. f.*   walker, traveler (5.1)

caminar   to walk **(3.2)**

camino *m.*   road, way (4.1)

camión *m.*   bus *(Mexico),* truck **(6.3)**

camisa *f.*   shirt **(5.2)**

camiseta *f.*   T-shirt **(5.2)**

campamento *m.*   camp (3.1)

campeonato   championship (7.1)

campo *m.*   field **(7.1)**; countryside (8.2)
   campo de fútbol   soccer (or football) field **(7.1)**

canadiense   Canadian (1.2)

canastita *f.*   little basket (7.3)

cancelar   to cancel, call off **(8.1)**

canción *f.*   song **(6.1)**

cansado(a)   tired **(4.3)**

cantante *m. f.*   singer **(4.2)**

capaz   capable (6.1)

capital *f.*   capital **(1.2)**

cara *f.*   face **(7.2)**

Caracas   Caracas *(capital of Venezuela)* **(1.2)**

característica *f.*   characteristic (7.2)

¡caramba!   wow! hey! what! **(LP)**

cariño   dear (8.2)

carne *f.*   meat (8.3)

caro(a)   expensive **(5.2)**

carpeta *f.*   folder **(LP)**

carpintero *m.,* **carpintera** *f.*   carpenter (4.2)

carta *f.*   letter **(2.3),** menu **(5.3)**

carusel *m.*   merry-go-round **(3.2)**

carro *m.*   car **(6.3)**
   carros chocones *m.pl.*   bumper cars (3.2)

casa *f.*   house **(2.3)**

casado(a)   married **(4.2)**

casarse   to get married (4.2)

caserola *f.*   casserole (8.3)

casete *m.*   cassette (3.3)

casi   almost (2.3)

caso *m.*   case (8.1)

castellano *m.*   Spanish *(language)* (2.1)

castillo *m.*   castle **(8.3)**

catedral *f.*   cathedral (8.2)

causar   to cause (8.1)

cebolla *f.*   onion **(8.1)**

celebrar to celebrate **(4.1)**
cemento *m.* cement (8.3)
cena *f.* dinner **(6.3)**
cenar to eat dinner, supper **(8.2)**
Cenicienta: La Cenicienta Cinderella **(6.2)**
centro *m.* downtown, center **(3.1)**
  centro comercial shopping center **(3.1)**
cerámica *f.* ceramics (6.2)
cerca de near **(5.1) (7.3)**
cerrado(a) closed (3.1)
cerrar(ie) to close **(7.2)**
ciclismo *m.* cycling **(7.1)**
ciencias *f. pl.* science **(2.1)**
  ciencias naturales natural sciences **(2.1)**
cine *m.* movie theater **(3.1)**
  ir al cine to go to the movies **(3.1)**
cinturón *m.* belt (6.1)
circo circus (3.1)
círculo *m.* circle, club, group (7.3)
circunstancia *f.* circumstance (6.3)
cita *f.* date, appointment (8.2)
ciudad *f.* city **(8.2)**
claro of course (2.1)
  ¡claro que sí! of course! **(2.2)**
  sí, claro yes, of course **(5.3)**
clase *f.* class **(LP)** type (3.1)
clavados diving (7.1)
cocina *f.* kitchen **(8.2)**
cocinero *m.,* **cocinera** *f.* cook **(4.2)**
coche *m.* car **(3.3)**
  en coche by car **(3.3)**
cochinillo *m.* suckling pig **(8.3)**
  cochinillo asado roast suckling pig **(8.2)**
cognado *m.* cognate (5.1)
coleccionador *m.,* **coleccionadora** *f.* collector (3.1)
colegio *m.* school **(2.2)**
Colombia *f.* Colombia **(1.2)**
colombiano(a) Colombian (1.2)
combinar: no combina bien it doesn't match *(clothes)* **(5.3)**
comedia *f.* play *(theater)* **(6.1)**
comedor *m.* dining room **(8.2)**
comentar to comment (5.1)

comenzar(ie) to begin **(7.1)**
comer to eat **(2.3) (3.2)**
comestible *m.* food (8.1)
cómico(a) funny **(1.3)**
comida *f.* food, meal **(2.3)**
  hacer una comida to make dinner (2.3)
  comida chatarra fast food (3.1)
comienzo *m.* beginning (7.1)
como: como siempre as usual **(7.3)**
¿cómo? how? what? **(4.2)**
  ¿cómo está usted? how are you *(form. sing.)* ? **(1.1)**
  ¿cómo estás? how are you *(fam. sing.)*? **(1.1)**
  ¿cómo no? why not ? **(6.2)**
  ¿cómo se llama? what's your *(form. sing.)* name? **(1.2)**
  ¿cómo te llamas? what's your *(fam. sing.)* name? **(1.2)**
cómodo(a) comfortable **(8.2)**
competencia *f.* competition **(7.1)**
composición *f.* composition **(5.1)**
comprar to buy **(3.2)**
compromiso *m.* commitment (8.2)
computación (clase de) *f.* computer *(class)* **(2.1)**
computadora *f.* computer **(2.1)**
comunicarse to communicate **(7.3)**
comunidad *f.* community (3.2)
común common (4.1)
con with **(2.3)**
  con calma calmly **(8.3)**
  con cuidado carefully **(8.3)**
  con énfasis with emphasis **(5.3)**
  con permiso excuse me, with your permission **(4.2)**
concentrar to concentrate (7.2)
concierto *m.* **de rock** rock concert **(3.3)**
concluido(a) concluded (7.2)
condición *f.* condition (7.3)
confección *f.* ready-to-wear clothing (5.2)
conmigo with me **(6.2)**
conocer to know, be acquainted with **(4.2)**
conocimiento *m.* knowledge (1.3)

conquistar to conquer **(6.3)**
conseguir (i, i) to get, obtain **(5.3)**
consejo *m.* advice (7.2)
considerado(a) considered (6.2)
considerar to consider (7.1)
consistir to consist (8.2)
constantemente constantly **(8.1)**
construir to construct **(8.3)**
contacto *m.* contact (2.3)
  ponerse en contacto to contact
    (2.3)
contar (ue) to count **(5.2)**
contemporáneo(a) contemporary
  (6.2)
contento(a) happy **(4.3)**
contigo with you **(6.2)**
contra against (3.2)
contrastando contrasting (6.2)
conversación *f.* conversation (5.1)
conversar to converse (4.3)
convertir (ie, i) to convert (7.2)
copa *f.* tournament cup, trophy
  (3.1); goblet, wine glass **(8.1)**
corazón *m.* heart (7.1)
corbata *f.* necktie (6.1)
correos *m. pl.* post office **(5.1)**
  oficina *f.* **de correos** post office
    (5.1)
correr to run, to jog **(2.3) (3.2)**
corresponder to correspond (4.1)
cortado(a) cut (8.3)
cortar to cut **(4.3)**
corto(a) short **(8.1)**
cosa *f.* thing **(7.3)**
costar (ue) to cost **(5.2)**
costarricense Costa Rican (1.2)
crecimiento *m.* growth (4.3)
creer to believe (4.3) *pret.* **(7.1)**
criticar to criticize **(7.1)**
cruzar to cross **(5.1)**
cuaderno *m.* notebook **(LP)**
cuadra *f.* city block **(5.1)**
¿cuál(es)? what? which? which
  one(s)? **(1.2)** **(4.2)**
  ¿cuál es la fecha de hoy? what's
    today's date? **(4.1)**
cualquier(a) anyone, anything,
  whichever (6.1)

¿cuándo? when? **(2.1) (3.2) (4.2)**
¿cuánto(a)? ¿cuántos(as)? how
  much? how many? **(4.1) (4.2)**
cuarto *m.* room, bedroom **(2.3)**
cuarto(a) fourth **(5.2)**
  . . . menos cuarto quarter to/of . . .
    (time) **(2.1)**
  . . . y cuarto quarter past . . .
    (time) **(2.1)**
cuartos de final quarter finals (7.1)
cubano(a) Cuban (1.2)
cubierto(a) covered (7.3)
cubiertos *m. pl.* place settings **(8.1)**
cuchara *f.* spoon **(5.3) (8.1)**
cucharita *f.* teaspoon (8.3)
cuchillo *m.* knife **(8.1)**
cuello *m.* neck **(7.2)**
cuenta *f.* bill, check **(5.3)**
¡cuéntame! tell me! **(6.3)**
cuento *m.* story **(6.2)**
  cuento de hadas fairy tale
cuero *m.* leather (6.1)
¡cuidado con . . . ! look out for . . . !,
  beware of . . . ! **(1.2)**
cuidadosamente carefully **(8.1)**
cuidar to take care of (2.3)
cumpleaños *m.* birthday **(4.1)**
cumplir ___ años to be ___ years
  old **(4.1)**
curiosear to look around, snoop
  (8.2)
curioso(a) curious (8.2)

~~~~CH~~~~

champán *m.* champagne (7.3)
chaqueta *f.* jacket **(5.2)**
charlar to chat **(4.3)**
charro *m.* Mexican cowboy (6.1)
chatarra: comida chatarra fast
  food (3.1)
cheque *m.* check **(5.1)**
  cheque de viajero traveler's
    check **(5.1)**
chica *f.* girl **(1.1)**
chico *m.* boy **(1.1)**
Chile *m.* Chile **(1.2)**
chileno(a) Chilean (1.2)

chocar   to collide, run into **(7.2)**
chofer *m. f.*   driver **(6.3)**
chorizo *m.*   sausage **(8.1)**

∼∼∼D∼∼∼

¡dale!   hit it! (4.1); kick it! (7.1)
dama *f.*   lady (3.3)
dar   to give **(5.1)**   *pret.* **(6.2)**
  dar un paseo   to take a walk (5.1)
  darse cuenta   to realize (8.2)
  darse prisa   to hurry up (8.1)
    ¡date prisa!   hurry up! (8.1)
dato *m.*   fact (2.3)
de   from **(1.2)**
  de acuerdo   agreed (7.2)
  de acuerdo a   according to (7.2)
  de compras   shopping **(3.1)**
  ¿de dónde?   from where? **(1.2)**
    (4.2)
  de etiqueta   full dress, formal (7.3)
  de la mañana/tarde/noche   in the
    morning/afternoon/evening
    (specific time) **(2.1)**
  de moda   stylish (5.2)
  de primera   first-class, first-rate
    (7.1)
  de repente   suddenly **(8.2)**
  de todos modos   anyway (7.2)
  de vacaciones   on vacation (7.1)
  ¿de veras?   really? **(3.1)**
debajo de   under **(7.3)**
deber   to be obliged, should, must
  (5.1)
decidir   to decide **(7.3)**
décimo(a)   tenth **(5.2)**
decir (i)   to say, tell **(5.3)**
  pret. **(6.3)**
decoración *f.*   decoration (4.2)
dedo *m.*   finger **(7.2)**
  dedo del pie *m.*   toe (7.2)
defender(ie)   to defend (3.2)
defensor *m.*, **defensora** *f.*   guard
  (soccer) **(7.1)**
dejar   to leave (behind) (5.3)
del *conj.* **(de + el)**   from the + *m.*
  sing. noun **(4.2)**

delante de   in front of **(7.3)**
delgado(a)   thin **(1.3)**
delicioso(a)   delicious **(4.3)**
demasiado(a)   too, too much **(6.2)**
denunciar   to denounce (6.2)
departamentos *m. pl.*   departments
  (in a department store, etc.) **(5.2)**
  departamento de caballeros
    men's **(5.2)**
  departamento de deportes
    sports **(5.2)**
  departamento de electrónica
    electronics **(5.2)**
  departamento del hogar
    housewares **(5.2)**
  departamento de jóvenes   teens',
    young people's **(5.2)**
  departamento de niños
    children's **(5.2)**
  departamento de señoras/mujeres
    women's **(5.2)**
dependiente *m. f.*   salesclerk **(5.2)**
deporte *m.*   sport **(3.3)**
deportista *m. f.*   sportsman, sports-
  woman (3.1)
deportivo(a)   athletic, sport,
  pertaining to sports (5.2)
derecha *f.*   right, right side **(5.1)**
  a la derecha   to/on the right **(5.1)**
    (7.3)
derecho   straight ahead **(5.1)**
derivar   to derive (4.1)
derrotar   to defeat (7.1)
desafortunadamente
  unfortunately **(6.3)**
desastre *m.*   disaster (8.3)
desayunar   to have breakfast **(8.1)**
desayuno *m.*   breakfast **(6.3)**
descansar   to rest **(3.2)**
desconocido(a)   unknown (6.2)
descubrimiento *m.*   discovery (6.3)
descubrir   to discover **(6.3)**
desear   to desire, wish **(5.3)**
desesperadamente   desperately
  (6.1)
desorganizado(a)   disorganized
  (1.3)
despacio   slow, slowly (8.3)

despedida *f.* farewell, good-bye, leave-taking **(1.1)**

despedirse (i, i) to say good-bye, take leave **(8.1)**

despertarse (ie) to wake up **(8.1)**

después afterwards
  después de after **(6.3)**

destruir to destroy (6.3)

detalle *m.* detail **(7.2)**

detective *m. f.* detective (LP)

detenerse to stop (7.3)

detrás de behind **(7.3)**

di *imper.* tell, say **(7.3)**

día *m.* day (2.2)
  día del padre Father's Day (5.2)
  día del santo saint's day (4.1)
  día festivo holiday (5.1)

diariamente daily (5.1)

dibujo *m.* drawing **(4.3)**
  clase de dibujo art class **(2.1)**
  hacer dibujos to draw **(4.3)**

diccionario *m.* dictionary (2.1)

diciembre *m.* December **(4.1)**

diente *m.* tooth **(7.2)**
  diente de ajo clove of garlic (8.3)
  lavarse los dientes to brush one's teeth **(8.1)**

diferencia *f.* difference (5.1)

diferente different (5.3)

difícil difficult **(2.2)**

¡dígame! *form.* tell me! **(3.2)**

¡dime! *fam.* tell me! (1.1)

dinero *m.* money **(5.1)**

Dios *m.* *(pl.* **dioses***)* God **(6.3)**
  ¡Dios mío! my gosh! my God! **(7.1)**

dirección *f.* address (2.3)

directo: en directo live *(radio or TV broadcast)* (7.1)

director *m.,* **directora** *f.* principal *(of a school),* director, **(1.1)**

directorio *m.* directory (5.2)

dirigir to direct (6.3)

disco *m.* record **(3.1)**
  disco compacto compact disc (3.3)

discoteca *f.* discotheque **(3.3)**

diseñador *m.,* **diseñadora** *f.* designer (7.3)

diseño *m.* design (7.3)

dispuesto(a) willing (6.1)

distinto(a) distinct, different (3.1)

diversión *f.* diversion, entertainment (3.2)
  parque de diversiones amusement park **(3.2)**

divertido(a) amusing, funny **(2.2)**

divertirse (ie, i) to have a good time **(8.1)**

divorciado(a) divorced **(4.2)**

doblar to turn **(5.1)**

docena *f.* dozen **(6.1)**

doctor (Dr.) *m.,* **doctora (Dra.)** *f.* doctor (1.1) **(4.2)**

dólar *m.* dollar **(5.1)**

doler (ue, o) to hurt **(7.2)**

dolor *m.* pain **(7.2)**
  dolor de cabeza headache **(7.2)**
  dolor de estómago stomachache **(7.2)**

dominado(a) dominated (7.3)

domingo *m.* Sunday **(2.1)**

dominicano(a) Dominican (1.2)

¿dónde? where? **(1.2) (4.2)**
  ¿de dónde? from where? **(1.2) (4.2)**
  ¿dónde está...? where is...? **(1.2)**

dondequiera wherever (6.1)

doña *f.* doña *(title of respect used before first names of married or older women)* (4.2)

dorado golden (8.3)

dormir (ue, u) to sleep **(7.2)** *pret.* **(7.3)**

dormirse (ue, u) to go to sleep **(8.1)**

dormitorio *m.* bedroom **(8.2)**

Dr., Dra. (abbreviation of **doctor, doctora**) doctor (1.1) **(4.2)**

dramatizaciones *f. pl.* dramatizations, role plays (LP)

dueño *m.,* **dueña** *f.* owner (5.3)

durante during **(7.1)**

duro(a) hard **(8.2)**

e (*before words beginning with* **i** *or* **hi**) and **(2.2)**
eco *m.* echo (7.2)
economista *m. f.* economist (7.3)
Ecuador *m.* Ecuador **(1.2)**
ecuatoriano(a) Ecuadoran (1.2)
edad *f.* age **(4.1)**
edificio *m.* building (6.2)
educación familiar home economics (2.1)
educación *f.* **física** physical education **(2.1)**
ejecutivo(a) executive (7.3)
el *art.* the **(LP)**
él *pron.* he **(1.1)**
elegante elegant **(1.3)**
elevado(a) elevated, raised *(volume)* (7.2)
ella she **(1.1)**
ellas *f.* they **(2.2)**
ellos *m.* they **(2.2)**
emocionado(a) moved, touched *(emotions)* **(4.3)**
emocionante moving, touching (3.2)
empacar to pack **(8.1)**
empate *m.* tie *(in sports)* **(7.3)**
empezar (ie) to begin *pret.* **(7.1)**
en in, on **(LP) (7.3)**
  en coche by car **(3.3)**
  en común in common (3.2)
  en directo live *(radio or TV broadcast)* (7.1)
  en general generally (4.1)
  en oferta on sale **(3.1)**
  en punto on the dot (8.2)
  en seguida right away **(8.3)**
  en serio seriously, really (6.2)
enamorarse(de) to fall in lovewith **(6.3)**
encantado(a) delighted **(1.2)**
encantar to really like, love **(3.1) (5.2)**
  le encanta(n) he/she/it, you *(form. sing.)* really like(s), love(s) **(3.1)**

me encanta(n) I really like, love **(3.1)**
me (te, le) encantaría I (you *fam. sing.,* he/she/you *form. sing.*) would really like, love to **(3.1) (6.2)**
  te encanta(n) you *(fam. sing.)* really like, love **(3.1)**
encima de on top of, over **(7.3)**
encoger to shrink (5.3)
encontrar (ue) to find, to meet **(5.2)**
enchilada *f.* enchilada *(corn tortilla dipped in hot sauce and filled with meat or cheese)* (LP)
enemigo *m.,* **enemiga** *f.* enemy **(6.3)**
enero *m.* January **(4.1)**
enfadado(a) angry (5.3)
énfasis *m.* emphasis (5.3)
enfermarse to become ill (6.3)
enfermero *m.,* **enfermera** *f.* nurse **(4.2)**
enfermo(a) sick **(8.2)**
enfrente de facing, in front of **(7.3)**
enfriarse to cool, get cold *(food)* (8.1)
enorme huge, enormous **(6.1)**
enriquecer to enrich (1.3)
ensalada *f.* salad **(8.2)**
  ensaladilla rusa potato salad *(Spain)* **(8.1)**
entender (ie) to understand **(5.2)**
entero(a) entire, whole (3.2)
entonces then (5.1)
entrada *f.* entrance, ticket (6.1)
entrar to enter **(6.2)**
entre between **(5.1) (7.3)**
entremeses *m. pl.* appetizers, hors d'oeuvres **(8.3)**
entrenador *m.,* **entrenadora** *f.* coach **(7.1)**
entrevista *f.* interview **(3.2)**
enviar to send (2.3)
época *f.* epoch (6.3)
equipo *m.* team **(7.1)**; stereo equipment (7.2)

eres you *(fam. sing.)* are **(1.1)**

es he/she/it is, you *(form. sing.)* are **(1.1)**

  ¿es todo? is that all? **(8.3)**

  es un placer (I'm) pleased to meet you **(1.2)**

esa(s) *see* **ese**

escalón *m.* stair, step **(8.2)**

escapar to escape (4.3)

escaparate *m.* display window (5.1)

escena *f.* scene (7.3)

escoger to select **(7.3)**

escribir to write **(2.3) (3.2)**

escritor *m.*, **escritora** *f.* writer **(4.2)**

escritorio *m.* desk **(LP)**

escuela *f.* school **(1.1)**

  escuela secundaria high school **(2.2)**

escuchar to listen to **(3.1) (3.2)**

ese, esa, esos, esas that, those **(7.1)**

esgrima fencing (7.1)

eslalom slalom (7.1)

eso that (6.2)

esos *see* **ese**

espacio *m.* space (7.3)

espalda *f.* back **(7.2)**

español *m.* Spanish **(LP)**

español *m.*, **española** *f.* Spaniard (2.1)

especial special **(3.3)**

especialmente especially (2.2)

especificado(a) specified (8.2)

espectador *m.*, **espectadora** *f.* spectator **(7.1)**

espejo *m.* mirror **(8.1)**

esperar to wait for **(2.3)**, to hope (6.2)

espía *m. f.* spy (5.2)

esposa *f.* wife **(4.1)**

esposo *m.* husband **(4.1)**

  esposos *m. pl.* husband and wife, spouses **(4.1)**

espuela *f.* spur (6.1)

esquí *m.* skiing **(7.1)**

  esquí alpino downhill skiing **(7.1)**

esquina *f.* corner **(5.1)**

esta, estas *see* **este**

está he/she/it is, you *(form. sing.)* are **(2.2)**

estación *f. (pl.* **estaciones**), season *(of the year)* **(3.2)** station **(5.1)**

estadía *f.* stay (6.2)

estado *m.* state (4.3) (7.1)

  estado físico physical condition (7.1)

Estados Unidos *m. pl.* United States **(1.2)**

estadounidense *m. f.* United States citizen (1.2)

estamos we are **(2.2)**

están they, you *(pl.)* are **(2.2)**

estante bookshelf **(7.3)**

estar to be **(2.2)** *pret.* **(8.2)**

  estar a mano to be readily available (4.2)

  estar listo(a) to be ready (4.2)

estás you *(fam. sing.)* are **(2.2)**

este *m.* east (1.2)

este, esta, estos, estas this, these **(7.1)**

estilo *m.* style (6.3)

esto *pron.* this (8.2)

estómago *m.* stomach **(7.2)**

estos *see* **este**

estoy I am **(2.2)**

estrella *f.* star (1.3) **(7.1)**

estudiante *m. f.* student **(LP)**

estudiantil student *(adj.)*, pertaining to students (7.3)

estudiar to study **(2.3) (3.2)**

estudioso(a) studious **(1.3)**

¡estupendo! great! wonderful! **(1.1)**

europeo(a) European (6.3)

examen *m.* exam **(2.3)**

examinar to examine **(7.1)**

excelente excellent **(2.2)**

exceso *m.* excess (7.3)

excursión *f.* excursion, short trip **(6.1)**

exhibición *f.* exhibition **(6.1)**

exigente demanding **(1.3)**

existir to exist (6.3)

experimentar to experiment **(7.2)**

experimento *m.* experiment (2.2)
explicación *f.* explanation (6.1)
explicar to explain **(5.3)**
explorar to explore **(8.2)**
explosivo(a) explosive (6.2)
exquisito(a) exquisite (8.3)
extrañar to miss **(7.2)**
extraño(a) strange (7.2)
extrovertido(a) extroverted **(1.3)**

fabuloso(a) fabulous **(6.1)**
fácil easy **(2.2)**
fácilmente easily **(8.1)**
falda *f.* skirt **(5.2)**
falta *f.* foul *(soccer)* **(7.1)**
  cobrar una falta to call a foul
  (7.1)
faltar to be lacking, missing **(8.1)**
  ¡no faltes! don't miss it! (4.1)
familia *f.* family **(4.1)**
familiar pertaining to the family,
  familial (6.1)
famoso(a) famous (4.2)
fantástico(a) fantastic **(2.2)**
farmacia *f.* pharmacy **(7.2)**
fascinante fascinating **(8.3)**
¡fatal! terrible! awful! **(1.1)**
favor *m.* favor
  por favor please **(1.1)**
favorito(a) favorite (3.2)
febrero *m.* February **(4.1)**
fecha *f.* date *(on the calendar)* **(4.1)**
¡felicidades! congratulations! **(4.1)**
feliz *(pl.* **felices)** happy **(8.2)**
feo(a) ugly **(1.3)**
fiebre *f.* fever **(7.2)**
fiesta *f.* fiesta, party **(5.3)**
figura *f.* figure (7.2)
figurita *f.* figurine (6.2)
  figurita de cristal crystal figurine
  (6.2)
fila *f.* row (4.2)
fin *m.* end **(3.3)**

fin de semana weekend **(3.1)**
  (3.3)
  ¡por fin! at last! **(2.1) (4.3)**
fingir to pretend (5.3)
firme firm (8.3)
flaco(a) skinny **(1.3)**
flor *f.* flower (4.2)
florecer to flower (6.2)
flotante floating (6.3)
formalmente formally **(8.1)**
foto *f.* photo **(2.1)**
fotógrafo *m.,* **fotógrafa** *f.*
  photographer **(4.2)**
francés *m.* French **(2.1)**
franco *m.* franc *(French monetary*
  unit) (5.1)
frecuentemente frequently **(3.3)**
freír to fry **(8.3)**
fresa *f.* strawberry **(8.2)**
fresco(a) cool **(3.2)**
  hacer fresco it's cool out **(3.2)**
frijoles *m. pl.* beans (LP) (8.1)
frío *m.* cold **(3.2)**
  hace frío it's cold **(3.2)**
  tener frío to be *(feel)* cold **(5.3)**
frito(a) fried **(5.3)**
  papas/patatas fritas french fries
  (5.3)
fruta *f.* fruit **(8.2)**
fuego *m.* fire (8.3)
fuente *f.* fountain **(5.1)**
fuerte strong **(1.3)**
fuerza *f.* force (4.3)
fuimos we went **(5.3)**
funcionar to function, work (8.3)
furioso(a) furious **(4.3)**
fútbol *m.* soccer **(2.3)**
  fútbol americano football **(7.1)**
futbolista *m. f.* soccer (or football)
  player **(4.2)**

ganar to win **(7.1)**
garaje *m.* · garage **(8.2)**
garganta *f.* throat **(7.2)**

gato *m.*, **gata** *f.* cat (6.2)

gazpacho *m.* gazpacho (*cold pureed vegetable soup from Spain*) **(8.3)**

generalmente generally (3.1)

generoso(a) generous **(1.3)**

gente *f.* people **(3.2)**

geografía *f.* geography **(2.1)**

gigante *m.* giant (4.1)

gimnasia *f.* gym class, gymnastics **(2.1)**

  gimnasia artística gymnastics **(7.1)**

gimnasio gymnasium **(2.2)**

girar to turn (5.3)

gol *m.* goal (*soccer*) **(7.1)**

  meter un gol to make a goal **(7.1)**

golf *m.* golf **(7.1)**

golpe *m.* blow, hit (7.2)

golpear to hit, bang on (6.3)

gordo(a) fat **(1.3)**

gracias thank you **(LP)**

  gracias a Dios thank goodness, thank God **(6.3)**

gran great (1.3)

grande big, large **(1.3)**

gratis free (4.2)

gris gray **(5.2)**

gritar to yell (6.3)

grupo *m.* group (3.1)

guagua *f.* bus (*Cuba, Puerto Rico*) (7.2)

guante *m.* glove (*baseball*) (7.1)

guapo(a) good-looking, handsome, pretty **(1.3)**

guardabosques *m. f.* fielder (*baseball*) **(7.1)**

guardar cama to stay in bed **(7.2)**

guardería *f.* day care (2.2)

guatemalteco(a) Guatemalan (1.2)

guerra *f.* war **(6.3)**

guía *f.* **telefónica** telephone directory **(4.2)**

guitarra *f.* guitar **(5.1)**

gustar to like **(3.1) (5.2)**

  le gusta(n) he/she/it/you (*form. sing.*) like(s) **(3.1)**

  me gusta(n) I like **(3.1)**

me (te, le) gustaría I (you *fam. sing.*, he/she/you *form. sing.*) would like **(3.1)**

te gusta(n) you (*fam. sing.*) like **(3.1)**

gusto: el gusto es mío the pleasure is mine **(1.2)**

  al gusto to one's liking, to taste (*cooking*) (8.3)

H

habilidad *f.* skill, ability (7.1)

habitación *f.* room, bedroom **(8.2)**

habitante *m. f.* inhabitant (6.3)

hablante *m. f.* speaker (8.1)

hablar to talk, speak **(2.3) (3.2)**

  hablar por teléfono to talk on the phone **(2.3)**

hacer to make, do **(2.3)** *pres.* **(5.1)** *pret.* **(6.2)**

  hace buen tiempo it's nice out, the weather is good **(3.2)**

  hace calor it's hot **(3.2)**

  hace fresco it's cool **(3.2)**

  hace frío it's cold **(3.2)**

  hace mal tiempo it's awful outside, the weather is bad **(3.2)**

  hace sol it's sunny **(3.2)**

  hace viento it's windy **(3.2)**

  hacer caso to pay attention (7.3)

  hacer dibujos to draw **(4.3)**

  hacer ejercicio to exercise **(4.3)**

  hacer la comida to fix dinner, to prepare a meal **(3.3)**

  hacer la tarea to do homework **(2.3)**

  hacer un informe to give a report **(6.1)**

  hacer un tour to take a tour (3.1) **(6.1)**

  hacer una reverencia to take a bow (5.3)

hacia toward (4.3)

hada madrina *f.* fairy godmother **(6.2)**

hallar   to find (7.3)
hamburguesa *f.*   hamburger **(5.3)**
hasta   until **(5.1)**
  hasta luego   good-bye, see you later **(1.1)**
  hasta mañana   see you tomorrow **(1.1)**
hay   there is, there are **(LP) (3.1)**
haz *imper.*   do, make **(7.3)**
hecho *m.*   fact (7.1)
hecho(a)   made, done (6.2)
  bien hecho   well done (7.1)
helado *m.*   ice cream **(3.2)**
hermana *f.*   sister **(4.1)**
hermanastra *f.*   stepsister **(4.2)**
hermanastro *m.*   stepbrother **(4.2)**
hermano *m.*   brother **(4.1)**
  hermanos *m. pl.*   brother(s) and sister(s) **(4.1)**
hermoso(a)   beautiful **(6.1)**
héroe *m.,* **heroína** *f.*   hero, heroine **(6.3)**
¿hicieron?   did you *(pl.)*? did they? **(5.3)**
hija *f.*   daughter **(4.1)**
hijo *m.*   son **(4.1)**
  hijos *m. pl.*   children, son(s) and daughter(s) **(4.1)**
hispano(a)   Hispanic **(4.3)**
historia *f.*   history **(2.1)**
histórico(a)   historic(al), of historical importance (3.2)
hogar *m.*   home (5.2)
¡hola!   hello! **(1.1)**
hombre *m.*   man (5.2)
hondureño(a)   Honduran (1.2)
hora *f.*   hour, time **(2.1)**
  ¿a qué hora es . . . ?   at what time is . . . ? **(2.1)**
  hora de estudio   study hall **(2.1)**
  ¿qué hora es?   what time is it? **(2.1)**
horario *m.*   schedule **(2.1)**
hospicio *m.*   hospice, children's home, orphanage (6.2)
hospital *m.*   hospital **(7.1)**
hotel *m.*   hotel **(5.1)**

hoy   today **(2.1)**
  hoy día   nowdays (4.3)
hubo   there was, there were **(6.3)**
huevo *m.*   egg **(8.1)**
humano(a)   human (7.2)
humilde   humble (7.3)
humorístico(a)   humorous (7.3)

∿∿I∿∿

idéntico(a)   identical (8.1)
identificar   to identify (7.2)
iglesia *f.*   church **(5.1)**
igualmente   likewise **(1.2)**
imaginar   to imagine (6.2)
imagínate   imagine (4.1)
impacientemente   impatiently **(8.1)**
imperio *m.*   empire (6.3)
impermeable *m.*   raincoat (5.2)
importante   important (4.1)
impresionado(a)   impressed (8.2)
impresionante   impressive **(4.3)**
improvisado(a)   improvised (6.1)
incluido(a)   included (4.2)
incluir   to include (4.2)
incómodo(a)   uncomfortable (7.3)
increíble   incredible (7.1)
indicaciones *f. pl.*   instructions (7.2)
indicado(a)   indicated (8.2)
indicios *m. pl.*   clues (LP)
indígeno(a)   indigenous, native (6.1)
indio(a)   Indian **(6.3)**
influencia *f.*   influence (4.3)
información *f.*   information (5.2)
informática *f.*   computer science (2.2)
inglés *m.*   English **(2.1)**
ingrediente *m.*   ingredient (8.3)
inmediatamente   immediately (5.1)
inolvidable   unforgettable (6.1)
instalar   to install (4.2)
inteligente   intelligent **(1.3)**
interesante   interesting **(1.3)**
interesar   to interest (5.1)
invierno *m.*   winter **(3.2)**

invitación *f.* (*pl.* **invitaciones**) invitation **(5.2)**

invitado *m.*, **invitada** *f.* guest **(6.2)**

invitar to invite **(7.2)**

ir to go **(2.3)** *pret.* **(6.2)**

  ir de compras to go shopping **(3.1)**

irse to leave, go, go away **(8.1)**

itinerario *m.* itinerary (6.3)

izquierda *f.* left, left side **(5.1)**

  a la izquierda to/on the left **(5.1)** **(7.3)**

<hr>

J

jai alai *m.* jai alai **(7.1)**

jamón (*pl.* **jamones**) *m.* ham **(5.3)**

  jamón serrano smoked ham *(Spain)* (5.3)

jardín *m.* (*pl.* **jardines**) garden (3.2)

  jardín zoológico zoo **(3.3)**

jardinero *m.*, **jardinera** *f.* fielder *(baseball)* **(7.1)**

  jardinero corto shortstop **(7.1)**

jeans *m. pl.* (blue) jeans **(5.2)**

jersey *m.* sweater (5.2)

Jesucristo Jesus Christ (8.3)

joven (*pl.* **jóvenes**) *m. f.* young person **(5.2)**

joya *f.* jewel (6.3)

joyería *f.* jewelry; jewelry department or store **(5.2)**

juego *m.* game, ride **(3.3)**

  juegos infantiles *m. pl.* children's rides **(3.2)**

  juegos mecánicos rides **(3.3)**

  juegos olímpicos Olympics (7.1)

jueves *m.* Thursday **(2.1)**

jugador *m.*, **jugadora** *f.* player **(7.1)**

jugar (**ue**) to play *(a game)* *infin.* **(2.3)** *pres.* **(5.2)** *pret.* **(7.1)**

jugo *m.* juice (8.3)

julio *m.* July **(4.1)**

junio *m.* June **(4.1)**

juntarse to get together (5.1)

juntos(as) *pl.* together **(2.3)**

justo(a) just, exact (6.3)

juvenil *adj.* youthful, junior *(sports)* (7.1)

juventud *f.* youth (3.3)

<hr>

K

karate *m.* karate **(2.3)**

kilo kilo *(weight)* **(6.1)**

kilómetro kilometer (.62 mile) (1.1)

<hr>

L

la *art.* the **(LP)**

la *dir. obj. pron.* her, it **(7.2)**

La Cenicienta Cinderella **(6.2)**

La Paz La Paz *(administrative capital of Bolivia)* **(1.2)**

laboratorio *m.* laboratory **(2.2)**

labrado(a) patterned *(leather)* (6.1)

lado *m.* side (4.3)

lago *m.* lake **(3.2)**

lámpara *f.* lamp **(7.3)**

lancha *f.* small boat, rowboat **(3.2)**

lanzador *m.*, **lanzadora** *f.* pitcher *(baseball)* **(7.1)**

lápiz *m.* (*pl.* **lápices**) pencil **(LP)**

largo(a) long **(5.2)**

las *art.* the **(2.1)**

las *dir. obj. pron.* them **(7.2)**

lástima: ¡qué lástima! what a shame! **(2.3) (4.2)**

lastimado(a) hurt **(7.1)**

lata *f.* tin can (8.3)

lavarse to wash up **(8.1)**

  lavarse los dientes to brush one's teeth **(8.1)**

  lavarse el pelo to wash one's hair **(8.1)**

le *indir. obj. pron.* to/for him, her, you *(form. sing.)* **(3.1)**

lección *f.* (*pl.* **lecciones**) lesson **(LP)**

leche *f.* milk **(5.3)**

lechuga *f.* lettuce **(8.1)**

leer to read *infin.* **(2.3)** *pres.* **(3.2)** *pret.* **(7.1)**

legumbres *m. pl.* vegetables, legumes **(8.3)**

lejos far **(5.1)**
  lejos de far from **(5.1) (7.3)**

lengua *f.* language (4.3)

lentamente slowly **(8.1)**

leñador *m.* woodsman (7.3)

les *indir. obj. pron.* to/for them, you *(pl.)* **(5.2)**

levantar to raise, pick up **(7.2)**

levantarse to get up **(8.1)**

leyenda *f.* legend **(6.3)**

libre free **(5.3)**

libro *m.* book **(LP)**

licuadora *f.* blender (8.3)

liga *f.* league **(7.1)**
  grandes ligas major leagues **(7.1)**
  ligas menores minor leagues **(7.1)**

ligero(a) light (7.2)

Lima Lima *(capital of Peru)* **(1.2)**

limonada *f.* lemonade **(5.3)**

limpiar to clean **(2.3)**

lindo(a) pretty, lovely **(7.1)**

línea *f.* line (4.2)

lista *f.* list **(LP)**

listo(a) ready (4.3)
  estar listo to be ready (4.2)

literatura *f.* literature **(2.1)**

lo *dir. obj. pron.* him, it **(7.2)**
  lo siento I'm sorry **(5.3)**

lobo *m.* wolf (7.3)

locura *f.* madness, insanity (6.3)

locutor(a) announcer (8.3)

los *art.* the **(2.1)**
  los fines de semana (on) weekends **(3.3)**

los *dir. obj. pron.* them **(2.2) (7.2)**

lucha libre *f.* wrestling (7.1)

luchar to fight, struggle (6.3)

luego then **(8.1)**
  hasta luego good-bye, see you later **(1.1)**

lugar *m.* place (3.1)

lujo *m.* luxury (7.3)

lujoso(a) luxurious (7.3)

lunes *m.* Monday **(2.1)**

~~~~ **LL** ~~~~

llamar to call **(5.2)**

llamarse to be named **(1.2)**
  me llamo my name is **(1.2)**
  se llama his, her, your *(form. sing.)* name is **(1.2)**
  te llamas your *(fam. sing.)* name is **(1.2)**

llegada *f.* arrival (6.3)

llegar to arrive **(6.3)**

lleno(a) full (6.1)

llevar to wear, carry **(5.2)**
  llevar a cabo to carry out (7.2)

llorar to cry (4.3)

llover(ue) to rain **(3.2)**

lloviendo *(inf.* **llover***):*
  está lloviendo it's raining **(3.2)**
  llueve it's raining **(3.2)**

~~~~ **M** ~~~~

madrastra *f.* stepmother **(4.2)**

madre *f.* mother **(4.1)**

maestro *m.,* **maestra** *f.* teacher **(4.2)**

magnífico(a) magnificent (3.1)

maíz *m.* corn (8.1)

mal bad **(3.2)**

maleta *f.* suitcase **(8.2)**

malo(a) bad **(6.3)**

mamá *f.* mom **(4.1)**

manera *f.* manner, way (5.1)

mano *f.* hand (6.3) **(7.2)**

mantener to maintain (7.1)

mantequilla *f.* butter **(8.1)**

manzana *f.* city block **(5.1)**; apple **(5.3)**

mañana *adv.* tomorrow **(2.3)**

mañana *f.* morning **(2.1)**
  esta mañana this morning **(7.2)**

mapa *m.* map **(2.1)**

maravilla *f.* marvel (7.3)

marco *m.* mark *(German monetary unit)* (5.1)

marcha: tener en marcha to have (be) underway (8.3)

mariachi *m.* mariachi *(Mexican band of strolling musicians playing string and brass instruments)* (6.1)

marrón *(pl.* **marrones)** brown (5.2)

martes *m.* Tuesday (2.1)

marzo *m.* March (4.1)

matar to kill (3.3)

matemáticas *f. pl.* mathematics (2.1)

materno(a) maternal (4.1)

maya *m. f.* Maya (6.2)

mayo *m.* May (4.1)

mayonesa *f.* mayonnaise (8.1)

mayoría *f.* majority (4.3)

más more (2.1) (8.2)

más . . . que more . . . than (8.2)

me *dir. obj. pron.* me (7.2)

me *indir. obj. pron.* to/for me (3.1)

me encantaría I would love to (6.2)

me *refl. obj. pron.* myself (8.1)

me llamo my name is (1.2)

medalla *m.* medal (7.3)

mediano(a) average (1.3)

medianoche *f.* midnight (2.1)

médico *m.,* **médica** *f.* doctor (4.2)

medio(a) half (5.1)

. . . y media half past . . . *(time)* (2.1)

mediodía *m.* noon, midday (2.1)

medir (i, i) to measure (4.1)

mejor better (7.1)

mejor(es) que better than (8.2)

melón *(pl.* **melones)** *m.* melon (5.3)

mencionado(a) mentioned (6.2)

menos less, minus (2.1) (8.2)

menos . . . que less . . . than (8.2)

. . . menos cuarto quarter to *(time)* (2.1)

mensaje *m.* message (6.2)

menú *m.* menu (5.3)

mercado *m.* market (6.1)

merienda *f.* snack, light meal (5.3)

mermelada *f.* marmalade, jam (8.1)

mes *m.* month (4.1)

mesa *f.* table **(LP)** (8.1)

mesita *f.* nightstand, small table (7.3)

mesón *m.* restaurant, *(originally an inn, tavern)* (8.3)

meter: meter un gol to score a goal (7.1)

metro *m.* subway (5.1) meter *(distance)* (7.1)

mexicano(a) Mexican (1.2)

mezcla *f.* mixture (8.3)

mezclar to mix (8.3)

mi, mis my (1.1) (4.1)

mientras while (3.3)

mientras tanto in the meantime, meanwhile (3.2)

miércoles *m.* Wednesday (2.1)

militar *m.* military (3.2)

milla *f.* mile (1.1)

ministerio *m.* government department (2.2)

mío(a) mine (1.2)

mirar to look at (2.3)

mirar a la gente to people-watch (3.2)

misa *f.* mass *(religious service)* (7.2)

mismo(a) same (6.3)

misterio *m.* mystery (LP)

mitológico(a) mythological (7.2)

mochila *f.* backpack **(LP)**

moda *f.* style (5.2)

estar de moda to be stylish (5.2)

moderno(a) modern (6.3)

modesto(a) modest (1.3)

moneda *f.* coin (5.1)

montaña *f.* mountain (4.3)

montaña rusa roller coaster (3.2)

Montevideo Montevideo *(capital of Uruguay)* (1.2)

montón *m.* pile, heap (6.2)

monumento *m.* monument (3.1)

morado purple (5.2)

moreno(a) ·dark-haired, dark-complexioned, black (1.3)

morir (ue, u) to die (6.3)

mortero *m.* mortar (8.3)

mostaza *f.* mustard **(8.1)**

mostrar (ue) to show (7.2)

moto, motocicleta *f.* motorcycle **(6.3)**

mover (ue) to move **(7.3)**

  ¡muévete! move! (7.3)

muchacha *f.* girl **(4.2)**

muchacho *m.* boy **(4.2)**

mucho a lot, much **(3.1)**

  mucho gusto pleased to meet you **(1.2)**

mudarse to move (7.2)

muebles *m.pl.* furniture **(8.2)**

muerto(a) dead (4.2)

  muerto de hambre starving (8.3)

mujer *f.* woman (5.2)

muletas *f.pl.* crutches **(7.2)**

mundo *m.* world **(6.3)**

mural *m.* mural **(6.1)**

muralista *m. f.* muralist **(6.2)**

muro *m.* wall (6.2)

museo *m.* museum **(3.1)**

música *f.* music **(2.1)**

  música clásica classical music (6.1)

músico *m.,* **música** *f.* musician **(4.2)**

muy very **(4.2)**

  muy bien, gracias, ¿y usted? fine, thank you, and you? (1.1)

～～～ N ～～～

nacer to be born (6.3)

nacionalista(a) nationalistic (6.2)

nada nothing **(3.3)**

nadie no one, nobody **(3.3)**

naranja *f.* orange **(5.3)**

nariz *f.* nose **(7.2)**

natación *f.* swimming **(7.1)**

negro(a) black **(5.2)**

nervioso(a) nervous **(1.3)**

nevar(ie) to snow **(3.2)**

  está nevando it's snowing **(3.2)**

  nieva it's snowing **(3.2)**

nevera *f.* refrigerator **(8.1)**

ni . . . ni neither . . . nor **(1.3)**

nicaragüense Nicaraguan (1.2)

nieta *f.* granddaughter **(4.1)**

nieto *m.* grandson **(4.1)**

  nietos *m. pl.* grandchildren **(4.1)**

nieva *(inf.* **nevar***)* it snows **(3.2)**

niña *f.* child **(3.2)**

niño *m.,* **niña** *f.* child **(3.2)**

nivel *m.* level (7.2)

no no **(LP)**

  no se preocupe don't worry **(7.2)**

  ¿no? isn't that so? **(1.3)**

noche *f.* night **(3.2)**

  buenas noches good night, good evening **(1.1)**

  esta noche tonight **(6.2)**

nombrado(a) named **(7.1)**

nombre *m.* name **(4.1)**

  nombre de pila first name, Christian name **(4.1)**

  mi nombre es my name is **(1.2)**

norte *m.* north (1.2)

nos *dir. obj. pron.* us **(5.2)**

nos *indir. obj. pron.* to/for us **(5.2) (7.2)**

nos *refl. obj. pron.* ourselves **(8.1)**

nosotros, nosotras we **(2.2)**

nota *f.* grade **(7.1)**

noticias *f. pl.* news (5.1)

novela *f.* novel **(3.1)**

noveno(a) ninth **(5.2)**

novia *f.* fiancée **(4.1);** bride **(4.2);** girlfriend **(5.1)**

noviembre *m.* November **(4.1)**

novillada *f.* bullfight with young bulls and novice bullfighters (3.1)

novio *m.* groom **(4.2);** boyfriend, fiancé **(5.1)**

nuestro(a), nuestros(as) our **(4.1)**

nuevo(a) new **(4.2)**

nunca never, not ever **(3.3)**

número *m.* number **(2.1)**

O

observación *f.* observation **(7.2)**
occidental *m.* western (3.2)
octavo(a) eighth **(5.2)**
octubre *m.* October **(4.1)**
ocupación *f.* occupation, job (6.1)
ocupado(a) busy **(4.3)**
oeste *m.* west (1.2)
ofensivo(a) offensive (6.2)
oferta *f.* offer, bargain **(3.1)**
  en oferta on sale (3.1) (5.2)
oficina *f.* office **(2.2)**
  Oficina del Censo Census
    Bureau (4.3)
oído *m.* (inner) ear **(7.2)**
oír to hear *pret.* **(7.1)**
ojo *m. pl.* eye **(7.2)**
Olimpíadas *f. pl.* Olympics **(7.1)**
olvidar to forget **(8.2)**
omelete *m.* omelet (8.1)
ópera *f.* opera **(6.2)**
oportunidad *f.* opportunity, chance
  (1.3)
oreja *f. pl.* ear **(7.2)**
organizado(a) organized **(1.3)**
origen *m.* origin (6.1)
oro *m.* gold (6.3)
orquesta *f.* **sinfónica** symphony
  orchestra (6.1)
otoño *m.* autumn **(3.2)**
otro(a) other, another **(5.3)**
  otra vez again **(8.2)**
¡oye! hey! say! listen! **(2.1)**

P

paciente *m. f.* patient **(7.2)**
padrastro *m.* stepfather **(4.2)**
padre *m.* father **(4.1)**
  padres *m. pl.* parents, mother and
    father **(4.1)**
paella *f.* paella *(Spanish rice dish
  seasoned with saffron)* (8.3)
pagar to pay for **(5.2)** *pret.* **(7.1)**

página *f.* page **(4.2)**
país *m.* country, nation (1.3)
palabra *f.* word (4.3)
palacio *m.* palace **(6.3)**
pan *m.* bread **(8.1)**
panameño(a) Panamanian (1.2)
panqueque *m.* pancake (8.1)
pantalones *m. pl.* pants, slacks **(5.2)**
papá *m.* dad **(4.1)**
papas *f. pl.* potatoes **(5.3)**
  papas fritas french fries **(5.3)**
papel *m.* paper **(LP)**
  hoja de papel sheet of paper **(LP)**
  papel maché papier mâché (6.3)
par *m.* pair **(5.2)**
  par de calcetines pair of socks
    (5.2)
para for, intended for **(2.3) (3.1)**
  (5.3)
Paraguay *m.* Paraguay **(1.2)**
paraguayo(a) Paraguayan (1.2)
parar to stop (7.2)
pararse to stand up (5.3)
pared *f.* wall (6.2)
pareja *f.* couple, pair (3.1)
pariente *m. f.* relative **(4.2)**
parque *m.* park **(3.1)**
  parque de diversiones amusement
    park **(3.2)**
parte *f.* part (2.3)
participar to participate **(2.3)**
particular private, particular (3.1)
partido *m.* match, game *(sports)*
  (7.1)
pasar to go past, spend time **(3.3)**
  (5.1)
pasatiempo *m.* pastime (2.3)
pasear to take a walk, ride **(2.3)**
  (3.2)
paseo *m.* walk, stroll, promenade
  (5.1)
pasillo *m.* hall **(2.2) (8.2)**
pasión *f.* passion (6.2)
paso *m.* step **(5.1)**
  paso a paso step by step **(LP)**
pastel *m.* cake **(4.3)**
pastilla *f.* pill *(medication)* **(7.2)**
patata *f.* potato *(Spain)* **(5.3)**

patatas fritas   french fries **(5.3)**
patear   to kick **(7.1)**
paterno(a)   paternal **(4.1)**
patinaje   skating (7.1)
  patinaje artístico   figure skating
    (7.1)
  patinaje de velocidad   speed
    skating (7.1)
patio *m.*   patio **(2.2)**
pecho *m.*   chest **(7.2)**
pedir (i, i)   to order, ask for **(5.3)**
    pret. **(7.3)**
peinarse   to comb one's hair **(8.1)**
pelar   to peel (8.3)
película *f.*   movie, film **(2.3)**
pelirrojo(a)   red-haired, redheaded
    (1.3)
pelo *m.*   hair **(7.2)**
pensar (ie)   to think **(5.2) (6.3)**
peor(es) que   worse than **(8.2)**
pepino *m.*   cucumber (8.3)
pequeño(a)   small, little **(4.1)**
perder(ie)   to lose **(7.1)**
pérdida *f.*   loss (7.2)
perdido(a)   lost (7.3)
perdón   excuse me, forgive me **(1.1)**
perejil *m.*   parsley (8.3)
perfeccionista *m. f.*   perfectionist
    (2.2)
perfumería *f.*   perfume and
    cosmetics department **(5.2)**
periódico *m.*   newspaper **(3.2)**
permiso *m.*   permission (3.1)
  con permiso   excuse me, with
    your permission **(4.2)**
permitir   to permit (8.2)
pero   but **(3.1)**
perro *m.*   dog **(1.1)**
  perrito *m.*   hot dog (5.3); puppy,
    little dog
persona *f.*   person **(7.3)**
personaje *m.*   character, person
    (4.1)
Perú *m.*   Peru **(1.2)**
peruano(a)   Peruvian (1.2)
pescado *m.*   fish *(as food)* **(8.3)**
peseta *f.*   peseta *(Spanish monetary
    unit)* **(5.1)**

peso *m.*   peso *(Mexican monetary
    unit)* (5.1)
piano *m.*   piano **(2.3)**
picado(a)   chopped, minced (8.3)
  carne picada   ground meat
    (8.3)
pie *m.*   foot **(7.2)**
  a pie   walking, on foot **(3.3)**
piedra *f.* **preciosa**   precious stone
    (6.3)
piel *f.*   skin (6.2)
pierna *f.*   leg **(7.2)**
pimienta *f.*   pepper **(8.1)**
pimiento *m.*   bell pepper (8.3)
pintar   to paint (6.2)
pintarse   to put on makeup (8.1)
pintoresco(a)   picturesque (6.2)
piñata *f.*   piñata **(4.1)**
pirámide *f.*   pyramid (6.3)
pisar   to step (5.3)
piso *m.*   floor *(of a building)* **(5.2)**;
    floor *(of a room)* (7.3)
pizarra *f.*   chalkboard **(LP)**
placer: es un placer   pleased to meet
    you **(1.2)**
planes *m. pl.*   plans **(2.3)**
planta *f.*   floor *(of a building)* **(5.2)**
  planta baja   ground floor **(5.2)**
plata *f.*   silver (6.1)
platillo *m.*   saucer **(8.1)**
plato *m.*   plate **(8.1)**
  plato principal, segundo plato
    main dish **(8.3)**
plaza *f.*   plaza, town square **(5.1)**
plomero *m.*, **plomera** *f.*   plumber
    (4.2)
¡pobrecito(a)!   poor thing! poor boy
    (girl)! **(1.1)**
poco: un poco   a little **(2.3)**
poder (ue, u)   to be able, can
    (5.2) *pret.* **(6.3)**
poema *m.*   poem (2.3)
policía *f.*   police force;
    m. f. policeman, policewoman (5.1)
político *m.*, **política** *f.*   politician
    (4.2)
pollo *m.*   chicken **(8.3)**
  pollo frito   fried chicken **(8.3)**

pon *imper.* put **(7.3)**
ponche *m.* punch (4.3)
poner to put **(5.1)** *pret.* **(7.3)**
  poner a cargo to put in charge (6.3)
  poner la mesa to set the table **(8.1)**
ponerse to put on *(clothes)* **(8.1)**; to become (8.2)
popular popular **(1.3)**
por for **(1.2)**
  por aquí around here **(8.3)**
  por ejemplo for example **(5.2)**
  por eso for that reason, therefore (3.2)
  por favor please **(1.1)**
  ¡por fin! at last! **(2.1) (4.3)**
  por la mañana/tarde/noche in the morning/afternoon/ evening *(general time)* **(2.1)**
  por lo menos at least **(7.3)**
  ¿por qué? why? **(1.1) (4.2)**
  ¡por supuesto! of course! **(4.1)**
  por todos lados all over the place (5.1)
posible possible (7.3)
posición *f.* position (7.1)
postre *m.* dessert **(8.2)**
práctica *f.* practice **(2.3)**
practicar to practice **(2.3)** *pret.* **(7.1)**
precio *m.* price **(6.2)**
precioso(a) precious (1.3) (6.3) (8.2)
precisamente precisely (8.1)
precolombino(a) pre-Columbian (6.2)
predominar to predominate (7.3)
preferir (ie, i) to prefer **(5.2)**
preguntar to ask *(for information)* (5.1)
preliminar preliminary (LP)
preocupado(a) worried **(4.3)**
preocuparse to worry (7.2)
preparación *f.* preparation (8.3)
preparar to prepare **(2.3) (3.2)**
presencia *f.* presence (6.1)
primavera *f.* spring **(3.2)**

primero(a), primer first **(5.2)**
primo *m.* **prima,** *f.* cousin **(4.1)**
  primos *m. pl.* cousins **(4.1)**
princesa *f.* princess **(6.3)**
principal principle, main (5.3)
príncipe *m.* prince (6.2)
principio *m.* beginning (8.3)
prisionero *m.*, **prisionera** *f.* prisoner (6.3)
probar (ue) to taste **(8.3)**
probarse (ue) to try on (5.2)
problema *m.* problem **(6.3)**
Prof. *see* **profesor**
profesión *f.* profession (4.2)
profesor *m.*, **profesora** *f.* **(Prof.)** teacher, professor **(LP)**
profesorado *m.* faculty (2.2)
programa *m.* program **(6.1)**
prometer to promise (6.3)
promoción *f.* marketing, promotion, sale (5.2)
pronto soon **(6.1)**
propina *f.* tip **(5.3)**
propio(a) own (4.2)
proteger to protect **(6.3)**
próximo(a) next, near (7.3)
proyección *f.* projection (4.3)
prueba *f.* trial, test (7.1)
pueblo *m.* town, village (6.2)
puerta *f.* door **(LP)**
puertorriqueño(a) Puerto Rican (1.2)
pues well, then **(1.2)**
pulgada *f.* inch (7.1)
puntual punctual (8.2)
pupitre *m.* student desk **(LP)**
puré *m.* puree (8.3)

¿qué? what? **(LP) (4.2)**
  ¿qué fecha es hoy? what's the date today? **(4.1)**
  ¿qué pasa? what's the matter?, what's going on? **(3.1)**
  ¿qué pasó? what happened? **(6.3)**
  ¿qué tal? how's it going? **(1.1)**

¡qué! how! **(4.2)**

  ¡qué amable eres! you're so kind! **(7.3)**

  ¡qué barbaridad! what nonsense! what an outrage! **(6.3)**

  ¡qué bien! good! wonderful! **(3.2)**

  ¡qué guapa! how beautiful! **(8.1)**

  ¡qué lástima! what a shame! **(2.3) (4.2)**

  ¡qué mala suerte! what bad luck! **(4.3)**

  ¡qué raro! how strange! **(4.1)**

  ¡qué ridículo! how silly! how ridiculous! **(4.3)**

  ¡qué sorpresa! what a surprise! **(6.1)**

  ¡qué vergüenza! how embarrassing! **(7.3)**

quedar to be left, remain **(5.1)**

quedarse to stay, remain **(8.2)**

quejarse to complain (5.3)

quemar to burn (8.3)

querer (ie) to want **(4.2) (5.2)**

  quiero presentarle *(form.)* / **quiero presentarte** *(fam.)* **a . . .** I want to introduce you to . . . **(1.2)**

querido(a) dear, beloved (6.3)

queso *m.* cheese **(5.3)**

¿quién? ¿quiénes? who? **(1.1) (3.1) (4.2)**

quiero *see* **querer**

química *f.* chemistry **(2.1)**

quinto(a) fifth **(5.2)**

quitar to remove, take away (8.3)

quitarse to take off *(clothes)* **(8.1)**

  ¡quítate! go away! (8.1)

Quito Quito *(capital of Ecuador)* **(1.2)**

quizá(s) perhaps (4.3) (8.2)

radio *f.* radio **(3.2)**

ramo *m.* **de flores** bouquet of flowers **(7.3)**

rápidamente rapidly **(8.1)**

raro(a) strange (4.1)

raras veces rarely **(3.3)**

rato *m.* a short time period, a while (2.3)

  un buen rato quite a while (6.3)

realidad *f.* reality (4.3)

rebelar to rebel (6.3)

rebelión *f.* rebellion (6.3)

recepción *f.* reception (desk) **(5.1)**

receptor *m.,* **receptora** *f.* catcher *(baseball)* **(7.1)**

receta *f.* recipe **(8.3)**

recetar to prescribe *(a medication)* **(7.2)**

recibir to receive **(5.1)**

recientemente recently (4.3)

recipiente *m.* container (8.3)

recoger to gather (7.3)

recomendar (ie) to recommend **(5.2) (8.3)**

reconocer to recognize (2.2)

recordar (ue) to remember **(5.2)**

recreo *m.* recess **(2.2)**

recuerdo *m.* souvenir **(6.2)**

rechazar to reject (8.2)

refresco *m.* soft drink **(2.3)**

regalo *m.* gift **(5.1)**

región *f.* region (6.2)

regla *f.* ruler *(for measuring)* **(LP)**

regresar to return, go back (3.1) **(6.2)**

regreso *m.* return (6.3)

regular okay, so-so, not bad **(2.2)**

reina *f.* queen **(8.2)**

relacionado(a) related (8.2)

religioso(a) religious (6.1)

reloj *m.* clock, watch **(2.1)**

reorganizar to reorganize (7.3)

repetir (i, i) to repeat **(5.3)**

reportar to report (6.3)

reportero *m.,* **reportera** *f.* reporter **(4.2)**

representar to represent (7.1)

rescatar to rescue (7.3)

reservación (*pl.* **reservaciones**) *f.* reservation **(8.3)**

reservado(a) reserved (8.3)

resistir to resist **(6.1)**

responder to respond, answer (6.2)

respuesta *f.* answer (5.2)
restaurante *m.* restaurant **(2.3)**
resto *m.* rest (8.1)
reunirse to get together, meet (7.3)
revista *f.* magazine **(7.3)**
revolución *f.* revolution (6.2)
rey *m.* king **(6.3) (8.2)**
rico(a) delicious **(3.3) (5.3)**
ridículo(a) ridiculous (2.2)
  ¡qué ridículo! how silly! how
    ridiculous! **(4.3)**
río *m.* river **(8.2)**
riquísima delicious (6.1) (8.2)
rodilla *f.* knee **(7.2)**
rojo(a) red **(5.2)**
romántico(a) romantic **(1.3)**
romper to break **(4.1)**
ropa *f.* clothes **(5.2)**
  ropa interior underwear (5.2)
rosado(a) pink **(5.2)**
roto(a) broken **(7.2)**
rubio(a) blond **(1.3)**
rueda *f.* **de fortuna** Ferris wheel
  (3.2)
ruidoso(a) noisy, loud (6.1)
ruinas *f.* ruins (6.1)

〜〜〜 **S** 〜〜〜

sábado *m.* Saturday **(2.1)**
saber to know **(5.1)**
sabor *m.* flavor (3.2)
saborear to taste, savor (8.2)
sabroso(a) delicious **(8.2)**
sacar to take out **(4.2)** *pret.* **(7.1)**
  sacar fotos to take pictures **(4.2)**
sal *f.* salt **(8.1)**
sal *imper.* leave **(7.3)**
sala *f.* classroom **(2.2)** living
  room **(8.2)**
  sala de familia family room **(8.2)**
salado(a) salty **(5.3)**
salir to go out, leave **(2.3) (5.1)**
salón *m.* **de entrada** lobby (8.2)
salsa *f.* sauce (8.3)
  salsa de tomate ketchup (8.1)

saltar to jump **(7.1)**
salto *m.* **de altura** high jump **(7.1)**
saludo *m.* greeting **(1.1)**
salvadoreño(a) Salvadoran (1.2)
salvar to save **(7.2)**
sándwich *m.* sandwich **(5.2)**
  sándwich mixto grilled ham and
    cheese sandwich *(Spain)* **(5.3)**
Santiago Santiago *(capital of
  Chile)* **(1.2)**
santo *m.,* **santa** *f.* saint (4.1)
sartén *f.* frying pan **(8.3)**
sátira *f.* satire (6.2)
satirista *m. f.* satirist (6.2)
se *refl. pron.* himself, herself,
  yourself *(form. sing.),* themselves,
  yourselves **(8.1)**
sé *imper.* be **(7.3)**
secar to dry (8.1)
secretario *m.,* **secretaria** *f.*
  secretary **(4.2)**
seguir (i, i) to continue, follow **(5.3)**
según according (7.3)
segundo(a) second **(5.2)**
seguridad *f.* security, safety **(7.2)**
sello *m.* stamp **(5.1)**
semana *f.* week **(2.1)**
  fin(es) de semana weekend(s)
    (3.1) (3.3)
  la semana pasada last week **(6.1)**
semejanza *f.* similarity (5.1)
sentado(a) seated (8.2)
sentarse (ie) to sit down **(8.1)**
señor (Sr.) *m.* Mr. **(1.1)**
señora (Sra.) *f.* Mrs. **(1.1)**
señorita (Srta.) *f.* Miss **(1.1)**
septiembre *m.* September **(4.1)**
séptimo(a) seventh **(5.2)**
ser to be **(1.1)** *pret.* **(6.2)**
  ser de to be from **(1.2)**
serenar to serenade (6.1)
serenata *f.* serenade (6.1)
serio(a) serious **(2.2)**
servicios *m. pl.* restroom **(8.2)**
servilleta *f.* napkin **(8.1)**
servir (i, i) to serve **(5.3)**
severo(a) severe (6.2)

sexto(a)   sixth **(5.2)**

sí   yes **(LP)**

  sí, claro   yes, of course **(5.3)**

siempre   always **(3.3)**

¡siéntese!   sit down! (1.1)

siglo *m.*   century **(8.3)**

significado *f.*   significance, meaning (6.2)

siguiente   following, next (5.1) (6.3)

silencio *m.*   silence (4.1)

silla *f.*   chair **(LP)**

sillón *m.*   easy chair **(7.3)**

símbolo *m.*   symbol (7.1)

simpático(a)   nice, charming **(1.3)**

simplemente   simply (3.2)

sin   without (5.3)

  sin duda   without a doubt (4.3)

  sin embargo   nevertheless (7.2)

síntoma *m.*   symptom **(7.2)**

situación *f.*   situation (7.2)

sobre   on, over **(7.3)**

sobrenombre *m.*   nickname **(4.1)**

sobresaliente   outstanding (6.2)

sobrevivir   to survive (6.3)

sobrina *f.*   niece **(4.1)**

sobrino *m.*   nephew **(4.1)**

  sobrinos *m. pl.*   niece(s) and nephew(s) **(4.1)**

sol *m.*   sun **(3.2)**

soldado *m.*   soldier **(6.3)**

soler (ue)   to be accustomed to (6.1)

sólo   only (4.2) **(7.2)**

soltero(a)   single, unmarried **(4.2)**

sombrero *m.*   hat **(5.2)**

sometido(a)   submissive, docile (7.2)

somos   we are **(2.2)**

son   they, you *(pl).* are **(2.2)**

  son la/las . . .   it is . . .*(time)* **(2.1)**

sonido *m.*   sound **(7.2)**

sonriendo   smiling **(8.3)**

sonriente   smiling (8.3)

sonrisa *f.*   smile (4.2)

soñar(ue) (con)   to dream (about) **(8.3)**

sopa *f.*   soup **(5.3)**

  sopa de ajo   garlic soup **(8.3)**

sordera *f.*   deafness (7.2)

sórdido(a)   sordid (6.2)

sorprender   to surprise (7.1)

soy   I am **(1.1)**

Sr., Sra., Srta.   *see* **señor, señora, señorita**

su, sus   his, her, your *(form. sing., pl.),* their **(4.1)**

subir   to go up, climb, get into *(a vehicle)* **(3.2)**

sudadera *f.*   sweatshirt **(5.2)**

suelto(a)   loose (6.1)

suerte *f.*   luck (7.2)

  ¡qué mala suerte!   what bad luck! **(4.3)**

suéter *m.*   sweater **(5.2)**

suficiente   sufficient, enough (8.3)

sufrir   to suffer **(7.2)**

sugerir (ie, i)   to suggest (7.3)

sur *m.*   south (1.2)

suroeste *m.*   southwest (4.3)

~~~~ T ~~~~

taco *m.*   taco *(Mexico: corn tortilla with filling)* **(6.1)**   *(Spain: a bad word)* (8.1)

tacón *m.*   heel *(of shoe)* (8.1)

tal vez   perhaps, maybe (8.2)

talla *f.*   size *(clothing)* **(5.2)**

tamaño *m.*   size (8.3)

también   also **(1.3)**

tampoco   neither, not either (5.1)

tan   so (2.2) (4.3)

  tan . . . como   as . . . as **(8.2)**

tanto(a)   so much (2.3)

tapas *f. pl.*   appetizers, hors d'oeuvres *(Spain)* **(8.3)**

taquilla   ticket office, ticket window (6.2)

tarde *f.*   afternoon **(3.2)**; *adv.* late **(2.2)**

tarea *f.*   task, homework **(2.3)**

tarjeta *f.*   card **(7.3)**

  tarjeta de embarque   boarding pass (6.1)

  tarjeta postal   postcard (6.1)

taza *f.* cup **(8.1)**

te *dir. obj. pron.* you *(fam. sing.)* **(7.2)**

  ¿te gustaría? would you like to? **(6.2)**

te *indir. obj. pron.* to/for you *(fam. sing.)* **(3.1)**

te *refl. obj. pron.* yourself *(fam. sing.)* **(8.1)**

teatro *m.* theater, drama **(2.1)**; auditorium *(school)* **(2.2)**

tele (televisión) *f.* TV (television) **(2.3)**

telefónica: guía *f.* **telefónica** telephone directory **(4.2)**

teléfono *m.* telephone **(2.1)**

televisión (tele) *f.* TV (television) **(2.3)**

televisor *m.* TV set **(7.3)**

temer to fear **(6.3)**

templo *m.* temple **(3.2)**

temporada season *(weather)* **(3.1)**; season *(sports)* **(7.1)**

  temporada de novilladas bullfighting season with young bulls and novice bullfighters **(3.1)**

temprano early **(8.1)**

ten *imper.* have, be **(7.3)**

tendido(a) *adj.* lying down, flat **(7.1)**

tenedor *m.* fork **(8.1)**

tenemos we have **(2.3)**

tener to have *sing.* **(2.1)** *pl.* **(2.3)** *pret.* **(6.3)**

  tener ___ años to be ___ years old **(4.1)**

  tener calor to be hot **(5.3)**

  tener cuidado to be careful **(7.3)**

  tener frío to be cold **(5.3)**

  tener hambre to be hungry **(5.3)**

  tener lugar take place **(4.1)**

    tendrá lugar will take place **(4.1)**

  tener presente to keep in mind **(7.2)**

  tener prisa to be in a hurry **(5.3)**

tener que (+ inf.) to have to (+ inf.) **(2.3)**

  tener razón to be right **(5.3)**

  tener sed to be thirsty **(5.3)**

tengo I have **(2.1)**

tenis *m.* tennis **(7.1)**

Tenochtitlán Tenochtitlán *(ancient capital of the Aztecs)* **(6.3)**

tentación *f.* temptation **(8.2)**

tercero(a), tercer third **(5.2)**

terminar to finish, terminate **(7.1)**

¡terrible! terrible! **(1.1)**

tía *f.* aunt **(4.1)**

tiempo *m.* weather, time **(3.2)**

  del tiempo seasoned **(fruit)** **(5.3)**

tienda *f.* store, shop **(3.1)**

  tienda de discos record shop **(3.1)**

tiene he/she/it has, you *(form. sing.)* have **(2.1)**

tienen they/you *(pl.)* have **(2.3)**

tienes you *(fam sing.)* have **(2.1)**

tierra *f.* earth, land **(6.3)**

tímido(a) timid **(1.3)**

tino *m.* aim **(4.1)**

tío *m.* uncle **(4.1)**

  tíos *m. pl.* aunt(s) and uncle(s) **(4.1)**

típico(a) typical **(3.3)**

título *m.* title **(7.1)**

tiza *f.* chalk **(LP)**

tobillo *m.* ankle **(7.2)**

tocar to touch **(8.2)**

  tocar un instrumento to play a musical instrument **(4.3)**

todavía still **(8.1)**

todo *pron.* everything, all **(7.3)**

todo(a), todos(as) all **(7.3)**

  todo el día all day **(7.1)**

  todo el mundo everyone **(4.2)**

  todos los días every day **(3.3)**

todos *pron.* everyone, all **(2.3)**

tomar to eat, drink, take *infin.* **(3.1)** *pres.* **(3.2) (5.1)**

tomate *m.* tomato **(8.1)**

tonto(a) foolish, silly **(1.3)**

torneo *m.* tournament (7.1)

torre *f.* tower **(8.2)**

tortilla *f.* potato omelet *(Spain)*; cornmeal or flour pancake *(Mexico)* **(8.1)**

trabajar to work **(2.3)**

tradición *f.* tradition (5.1)

tradicional traditional (6.1)

traer to bring **(5.3)**

tráfico *m.* traffic **(7.3)**

traje *m.* suit **(5.2)**

  traje de baño bathing suit (5.2)

trampolín *m.* spring-board, diving board (7.1)

tranquilo(a) tranquil, calm (1.3)

tratar de to try to, attempt to (6.3)

tren *m.* train **(6.3)**

triste sad **(4.3)**

tristemente sadly **(8.1)**

trofeo *m.* trophy **(7.3)**

trono *m.* throne **(6.3)**

trovador *m.* troubadour (6.1)

tu, tus *poss. adj.* your *(fam. sing., pl.)* **(2.1) (4.1)**

tú *subj. pron.* you *(fam. sing.)* **(1.1)**

turista *m. f.* tourist (5.1)

tuyo(a) your *(fam. sing.)* (7.1)

¡uf! ugh! **(2.3)**

último(a) last **(7.1)**

un, una *art.* a, an **(LP) (3.1)**

  un poco a little **(2.3)**

único(a) only (7.1)

universidad *f.* university **(5.3)**

unos(as) some **(LP) (3.1)**

  unos cuantos a few (8.3)

Uruguay *m.* Uruguay **(1.2)**

uruguayo(a) Uruguayan (1.2)

usted you *(form. sing.)* **(1.1)**

ustedes you *(pl.)* **(2.2)**

utilizar to utilize, use (2.3) (8.3)

útil useful **(8.2)**

¡uy! oh!, ugh! **(2.1)**

V

va he/she/it goes **(2.3)**

vacaciones *f. pl.* vacation **(7.2)**

vacío empty (8.2)

vale okay *(Spain)* **(5.3)**

válido(a) valid (5.2)

valiente valiant, brave **(6.3)**

valioso(a) valuable (7.1)

vamos we go **(2.3)** let's **(3.1)**

van they go **(2.3)**

variación *f.* variation (8.1)

variado(a) varied **(8.3)**

variedad *f.* variety (3.1)

varios(as) several (3.1)

vas you *(fam. sing)* go **(2.3)**

vaso *m.* glass **(8.1)**

ve he/she/it sees, you *(form. sing.)* see **(3.2)**

ve *imper.* go; see **(7.3)**

vecindad *f.* neighborhood (4.3)

vencedor *m.,* **vencedora** *f.* victor, winner (7.1)

  vencedores *m. pl.* winners **(7.1)**

venezolano(a) Venezuelan (1.2)

Venezuela *f.* Venezuela **(1.2)**

venir(ie, i) to come **(4.2)** *pret.* **(6.3)**

ventana *f.* window **(7.3)**

veo I see **(3.2)**

ver to see, watch *infin.* **(2.3)** *pres.* **(3.2)** *pret.* **(6.2)**

  a ver let's see **(3.3)**

verano *m.* fall **(3.2)**

¿verdad? isn't that so? **(1.3)**

verdadero(a) true, real (6.2)

verde green **(5.2)**

verduras *f. pl.* green vegetables **(8.3)**

vergüenza *f.* shame, embarrassment (7.3)

verso *m.* verse **(2.3)**

ves you *(fam. sing.)* see **(3.2)**

vestido *m.* dress **(5.2)**

vestir (i, i) to dress **(5.3);** to wear (7.3)

vestirse (i, i)   to get dressed **(8.1)**
vez *f.*   time (5.2)
  a la vez   at the same time **(7.3)**
  a veces   sometimes **(3.3)**
viaje *m.*   trip **(8.2)**
victorioso(a)   victorious (6.3)
video *m.*   video **(2.1)**
viejo(a)   old **(8.2)**
viento *m.*   wind **(3.2)**
  hace viento   it's windy **(3.2)**
viernes *m.*   Friday **(2.1)**
vigoroso(a)   vigorous (6.2)
vinagre *m.*   vinegar (8.3)
visitante *m. f.*   visitor (7.3)
visitar   to visit **(3.2)**
vista *f.*   view (8.2)
viuda *f.*   widow (4.2)
viudo *m.*   widower (4.2)
volar (ue)   to fly **(6.1)**
volcán *m.*   volcano (6.3)
volibol *m.*   volleyball **(7.1)**
volumen *m.*   volume **(7.2)**
volver (ue)   to come back, return **(8.3)**
voy   I go **(2.3)**
vuelo *m.*   flight **(6.1)**

y   and **(1.1)**
  . . . y cuarto   quarter past . . . *(time)* **(2.1)**
  . . . y media   half past . . . *(time)* **(2.1)**
ya   already, now (1.1)
  ¡ya lo creo!   I believe it! **(7.1)**
yeso *m.*   cast *(for broken arm or leg)* **(7.3)**
yo   I **(1.1)**

zapatería *f.*   footwear (5.1); shoes *(shoe department)*, shoe store or **(5.2)**;
zapatillas *f. pl* .   slippers **(7.3)**
zapatos *m.pl.*   shoes **(5.2)**
  zapatos deportivos   athletic shoes **(5.2)**
zarzuela *f.*   seafood stew (8.2)
zona *f.*   zone, area (3.1)
zoológico *m.*   zoo **(3.2)**
zumo *m.*   juice (8.3)
  zumo de naranja   orange juice (5.3)
zurdo (a)   left-handed (7.1)

ÍNDICE
Gramática / Funciones / Estrategias

This index lists the grammatical structures, the communicative functions, and the reading and writing strategies in the text. Entries preceded by a ● indicate functions. Entries preceded by a ■ indicate strategies. The index also lists important thematic vocablary (such as days of the week, family members, sports). Page references beginning with *G* correspond to the *¿Por qué se dice así?* (Manual de gramática) section.

P

- paragraph writing *149*
participles, present *G62*
past tense (*see also* preterite)
  irregular verbs *294 – 295,*
    296 – 297, 388, G87 – G88, G91,
    G114
    regular verbs *264 – 265,*
      G83 – G84
pedir *246, G75 – G76*
pensar *230*
personal **a** *176, G51 – G52*
place
  at home *388*
  at school *82*
  in the community *110, 208 – 209,*
    262 – 263
plural
  adjectives *80, G22*
  articles *67, 68, G16 – G17,*
    G34 – G35
  nouns *66, G16 – G17*
  subject pronouns *G24*
poder
  present *230*
  preterite *294, G91*
- poem, writing a free-form *302 – 303*
● pointing out things: away from you,
  close to you, farther away *313 – 314*
poner
  present *G68*
  preterite *352*
¿por qué? *G56 – G57*
possession
  adjectives *158, 159, G46*
  with **de** *G46*
prepositions
  location *349, G107*
  prepositional phrases *211*
present participle *G62*
present progressive *192, G62*
present tense
  irregular verbs *G6 – G7, G20,*
    G25, G26 – G27, G29 – G30,
    G31, G52 – G53, G54, G68
  reflexive *371, G10 – G11*

regular plural forms *140, G42*
regular singular forms *125,*
  G38 – G39
stem-changing *G31, G54,*
  G70 – G71, G75 – G76
preterite tense
  irregular forms *279 – 281,*
    294 – 295, 296 – 297,
    G87 – G88, G91
  plural forms *265*
  regular forms *264 – 265,*
    G83 – G84
  singular forms *264*
  spelling changes *316, G96 – G97*
  stem changes *333 – 334,*
    G96 – G97
professions *176*
pronouns
  object
    a + [a name or pronoun]
      G79 – G80
    direct *332, G100 – G101*
    indirect *248, G79 – G80*
  placement *G79 – G80,*
    G100 – G101, G105 – G106
  reflexive *371 – 372, G10 – G11,*
    G105 – G106
  with **gustar** *G36 – G37,*
    G71 – G72
  subject
    equivalent of English *it G4 – G5*
      for clarification or emphasis
      G7 – G8
    nonuse *G7 – G8*
    plural *G24*
    singular *G4 – G5*
    tú vs. **usted** *G4 – G5*
    with titles *G4 – G5*

Q

¿qué? *G56 – G57*
querer *177, G54*
  querer ser *178, G54*
question words (*see* interrogative
  expressions)
¿quién(es)? *24, G56 – G57*

VIDEO CREDITS

For D.C. Heath and Company

Producers   Roger D. Coulombe

Marilyn Lindgren

For Videocraft Productions, Inc.
Boston, Massachusetts

Executive Producer   Judith Webb

Project Director   Bill McCaw

Directors   James Gardner

Lynn Hamrick

Producers   Diego Echeverría

David Vos

Associate Producer   Krista Thomas

Post Production Supervisor   Annemarie Griggs

Director of Photography   Jim Simeone

Sound Recordist   James Mase

Editors   Steve Bayes

Paul Kopchak

Graphic Designer   Alfred De Angelo

Music   Marc Bjorkland

Sound Mixers   Joe O'Connell

Kurt Selboe

Narrators   Lilliam Martínez

Nicolás Villamizar

Local Producers

Preliminary Lesson	Rica Groennou
Unit 1: Montebello, California	Nancy Garber
Unit 2: San Juan, Puerto Rico	Rica Groennou
Unit 3: Mexico City, Mexico	Emily Gamboa
Unit 4: San Antonio, Texas	Linda Tafolla
Unit 5: Madrid, Spain	Christina Lago
Unit 6: Guadalajara, Mexico	Emily Gamboa
Unit 7: Miami, Florida	Fabio Arbor
Unit 8: Segovia, Spain	Christina Lago

ILLUSTRATION CREDITS

Susan Banta (Colorist): 208-209, 226-227, 244

Ken Barr: 7, 20-22, 34-35, 46-47, 64-65, 78-79, 92-93, 156-157, 208-210, 226-227, 242-244

Meryl Brenner: 90, 91, 94, 268, 307, 315r, 331, 373, 375b, 379, 392, 406, 413

Penny Carter: 24, 37, 51, 82, 248, 268, 348, 354, 395

Carlos Castellanos: 11, 27, 28, 49, 50, 52, 71, 81, 85, 146, 162, 164, 181, 185, 219, 224, 225, 234, 236, 245, 273, 285, 297, 321, 324, 337, 358, 371, 377

Daniel Clifford (Colorist): 64, 65, 78, 79, 92, 93, 210, 242, 243

Leslie Evans: G75, G77, G96, G99, G104, G108, G109, G112, G116, G117, G123

Tim Jones: 344, 393, 408

Tim McGarvey: 5, 8, 10, 62, 63, 68b, 95, 212-214, 349, 350, 388, 390

Claude Martinot: 23, 25, 29, 38, 52t, 83, 239, 247, 263, 280, 294, 315l, 319, 331, 332, 354, 390t, 391

Cyndy Patrick: 136, 137, 151, 170, 171, 290, 291, 305

Brent Pearson: 186, 187, 194

Deb Perugi: 15, 30, 31, 41, 59, 151, 158, 167, 168, 175, 203, 257, 288, 361, G9, G10

Robert Roper: 206, 207

Christina Ventoso: 40, 318, 374

Steve Voita: 262, 263, 276, 277, 292, 293, 310-312, 328-330, 344-346, 367-369, 385-387, 403-405

Anna Vojtech: 301, 325, 415

Linda Wielblad: 142, 144, 145, 160, 167, 176, 177, 178, 179, 192, 193, 195, 196, 211, 228, 229, 231, 232, 233, 250, 281, 296, 313, 314, 351, 370, 375t, 389

PHOTO CREDITS

Cover: Mural by Xochitl Nevel Guerrero, with Zala Nevel, Consuelo Nevel, & Roberto C. Guerrero; Teens by Nancy Sheehan/©DCH.

Front Matter: i: Nancy Sheehan/©DCH; **v:** Laurie Platt Winfrey,Inc.; **xi:** *tl, ml, & br:* John Henebry/©DCH; *tr,* Jose Hernández-Claire/©DCH; *bl,* Tim Hunt/©DCH; **xii:** *t&b,* John Henebry/©DCH; **xiii:** *t&m,* John Henebry/©DCH; *b,* Videocraft/©DCH; **xiv:** *all,* John Henebry/©DCH; **xv:** *t&b,* Lourdes Grobet/©DCH; *m,* Cameramann Int'l.,Ltd.; **xvi:** *all,* Gary Hartman/©DCH; **xvii:** *t&b,* Tim Hunt/©DCH; **xviii:** *t&b,* Jose Hernández-Claire/©DCH; **xix:** *t&b,* John Henebry/©DCH; **xx:** *t&b,* Tim Hunt/©DCH.

Preliminary Lesson: All photos by John Henebry except: **10:** Tim Hunt/©DCH.

Unit One: All photos by John Henebry except: **18:** *#1 insets, #2, #3:* Videocraft/©DCH; **19:** *#4, #5, #6, #7,* Videocraft/©DCH; **30:** *tr,* Nancy Sheehan/©DCH; *br,* Robert Frerck/Odyssey; **31:** *tl,* D. Donne Bryant/DDB Stock Photo; *tc,* Chip & Rosa Maria Peterson; *tr,* Stuart Cohen/Comstock; *ml,* Robert Fried/DDB Stock Photo; *b,* Roy Morsch/The Stock Market; **33:** Videocraft/©DCH; **44-45:** Videocraft/©DCH.

Unit Two: All photos by John Henebry except: **62-63:** *background,* Doug Mindell/©DCH; **70:** *bl,* Beryl Goldberg; *br,* Tim Hunt/©DCH; **87:** Tim Hunt; **99:** *t,* Stuart Cohen/Comstock; *b,* Nancy Sheehan/©DCH; **101:** *tl,* Owen Franken/Stock Boston; *tc,* Nancy Sheehan/©DCH; *bl&br,* Peter Menzel.

Unit Three: All photos by Lourdes Grobet/©DCH except: **102-103:** Luis Villota/The Stock Market; **106:** *tm (#2) & br (#9 inset),* Cameramann Int'l.,Ltd.; **107:** *ml (#6),* David Ryan/DDB Stock Photo; *br (#7),* Mike Mazzachi/Stock Boston; *br (#7 inset),* Ulrike Welsch/PhotoEdit; **114:** *both,* Robert Frerck/Odyssey; **115:** *tl,* Robert Frerck/Odyssey; *ml,* Beryl Goldberg; *tr,* Chip & Rosa Maria Peterson; *mr,* Cameramann Int'l.,Ltd.; *b,* Herminia Dosal/Photo Researchers,Inc.; **117:** *l,* Stuart Cohen/Comstock; **119:** *br,* Cameramann Int'l.,Ltd.; **120:** *br (#3),* Dana Hyde/Photo Researchers,Inc.; **121:** *(#4 all),* Videocraft/©DCH; *r (#6),* Robert Frerck/Odyssey; **128:** *t,* Stuart Cohen/Comstock; *(#1),* Dave Forbert/Superstock; *(#2),* Daniel Komar/DDB Stock Photo; *(#3),* Tim Hunt/©DCH; *(#4),* Larry Mangino/The Image Works; *(#5),* Superstock; *(#6),* Larry Downing/

Woodfin Camp & Associates; *(#7),* Shostal/Superstock; *(#8),* Jim Howard/FPG International; *(#9),* Harvey Lloyd/The Stock Market; **130:** *t,* John Henebry/©DCH; *b,* Cameramann Int'l.,Ltd.; **133:** *t,* D. Donne Bryant/DDB Stock Photo; *b,* Joe Viesti/Viesti Associates; *br (t inset),* David Ryan/DDB Stock Photo; br (b inset), Ulrike Welsch; **136:** *all,* Videocraft/©DCH; **137:** *(#6 & 7),* Videocraft/©DCH.

Unit Four: All photos by Gary Hartman/©DCH except: **154:** Videocraft/©DCH; **155:** *tr,ml, bl:* Videocraft/©DCH; **163:** *both,*

Freda Leinwand; **165:** *t&b,* Tim Hunt/©DCH; *m,* Tim Hunt and Nancy Sheehan/©DCH; **177:** *tl,#3, #4,* John Henebry/©DCH; *tr,#2,#5, #8,* Jose Hernández-Claire/©DCH; *#6,#7,* Lourdes Grobet/©DCH; **180:** *t,* Bob Daemmrich/Stock Boston; *m,* P. Barry Levy/Profiles West; *b,* Owen Franken/Stock Boston; **186-187,191:** Videocraft/©DCH; **197:** *t,* Peter Menzel/Stock Boston; *m,* Andy Levin/Photo Researchers,Inc.; *b,* Bob Daemmrich/The Image Works; **200:** Francisco J. Rangel.

Unit Five: All photos by Tim Hunt/©DCH except: **205:** *tr,* Videocraft/©DCH; **218:** *t,* Marcelo Brodsky/DDB Stock Photo; *b,* David Wells/The Image Bank; **221:** *t&br,* Robert Frerck/Odyssey; *bl,* Robert Frerck/Woodfin Camp & Associates; **235:** *t,* Bob Daemmrich/Stock Boston; *m,* Robert Frerck/Odyssey; **251:** Robert Frerck/Odyssey; **255:** G. Anderson/The Stock Market.

Unit Six: All photos by Jose Hernández-Claire/©DCH except: **259:** *ml,* Videocraft/©DCH; **260-261:** *all,* Videocraft/©DCH; **269:** *t,* Francisco J. Rangel, *b,* Bob Daemmrich; **270:** Cameramann Int'l.,Ltd.; **271:** Harvey Lloyd/The Stock Market; **274-275:** *all, except #1 & #2,* Videocraft/©DCH; **284:** *t,* Francisco J. Rangel; *bl,* D. Donne Bryant/DDB Stock Photo; *br,* Beryl Goldberg; **287:** *t,* Robert Frerck/Woodfin Camp & Associates; *m,* C.J. Collins/Photo Researchers,Inc.; *b,* Kal Muller/Woodfin Camp & Associates; **288:** *l,* Carl Frank/Photo Researchers,Inc.; *cl,* David Ryan/DDB Stock Photo; *c,* Robert Frerck/Odyssey; *cr,* D. Donne Bryant/DDB Stock Photo; *r,* Robert Fried; **290-291:** David Hiser/Photographers/Aspen; **298:** Beryl Goldberg; **300:** *l&r,* Robert Frerck/Odyssey; *c,* Stephanie Maze/Woodfin Camp & Associates.

(Continued on following page)